the last closet

CASTALIA HOUSE

the last closet

THE DARK SIDE OF AVALON

MOIRA GREYLAND

CASTALIA HOUSE

The Last Closet: The Dark Side of Avalon

Moira Greyland

Published by Castalia House
Kouvola, Finland
www.castaliahouse.com

Editor: Vox Day
Cover: Steve Beaulieu

ISBN: 978-952-7065-20-4

Contents

Acknowledgements

I would like to thank all the people who helped me with this book. My husband, Michael, who brought me endless cups of coffee, read chapters, and listened to me talk and cry, even when I felt like a lunatic for doing so.

My best friend Elizabeth, who read chapters, listened, offered editorial advice with patience and clarity, and tolerated my transformation from a sex-positive Berkeley chick to something entirely different. Despite my rather unfashionable views, she has always accepted me as I am.

Thanks to Deirdre Saoirse Moen, who broke my story and gave me the courage to tell the rest of it. Thanks to Vox Day, my editor and publisher, who inspired me to be bold in my approach.

Thanks also to Gary Bryant, Deacon Jim Hunt, Chris Angus, and all the other men of God who listened to my story and encouraged me to tell it.

Thanks to the COGs, (Children of Gays) who let me know that I was not alone. Robert Oscar Lopez, Katy Faust, Denise Schick, Brandi Walton, Heather Barwick of *Heather Has Two Mommies*, Millie Foxx, Brittany Newmark, and all those who wisely do not use real names lest the bullying get any more dangerous.

Thanks to Pete Smith, who sent me many, many newspaper clippings to help me fill in the blanks about my father and his peculiar history; David Fanning, who constructed the annotated bibliography of my father's works; and Jack Sarfatti, who related some interesting facts about their friendship.

Thanks, much love, and hugs to Nick Bosson, who bravely told his own story of survival at my father's hands. Thanks also to Nick's late wife Kelly, a beautiful woman who stood by him and made it possible for him to tell his story., so you can see the real-life consequences.

To Kenny, Jean, Sterling, Sean, Rick, Smiley, Eric, Patrick, and the many others who suffered and could not tell their stories. It is for you that I write, both those of you who have died, and those who live through emotional death through being, as Tori Amos put it, *"silent all these years."*

Thanks, blessings, and strength to those of you who have written letters to me, so many of which began with the fateful words: *"I never told anyone about this before."*

Also, blessings and strength to all survivors who cannot talk about what happened, and to all of you who will, one day, gain the courage to share your own stories.

Your pace, your life, and your story: They all belong to you and you alone. Don't accept pressure either to keep silent or to share. You will know when you are ready. It is for you that I am writing, and it is for your freedom that I am praying.

You're lying awake with the sheet over your head…
The memory of heartbreak just crept in your bed
And no tears or pleading could stop what they did
Fight back now, take your life back, put the monsters to bed!

Put the monsters to bed, tuck them all into bed
And be the good Mother you wish that you had
Put the monsters to bed, ugly claws into bed
They can't hurt you when they're sleeping, put the monsters to bed!

Sometimes so much pain comes you feels like you're dead
And you know you'd fill an ocean with the tears that you've shed
But take back your time, and take back your bed
And just like little children, put the monsters to bed.

Put the monsters to bed, tuck them all into bed
And be the good Father you wish that you had
Put the monsters to bed, scaly wings into bed
They can't hurt you when they're sleeping, so put the monsters to bed!

And sometimes it feels like your mind's not your own
Or that you'll give in to the pain you've known
But hang on my love, because you're not alone
Hang on and you know we'll survive!

Put the monsters to bed, put your anguish to bed
And take back the future that you should have had
For your life's worth much more than the pain you ignore
Let your nightmares see the daytime…
Let them vanish in the sunshine…
Make a future instead,
Put the monsters to bed.

La la, la la, wake your dreams out of bed!
La la, la la, try hope instead!

—Moira Greyland, "The Monster's Lullaby"

Foreword

I read four or five of Marion Zimmer Bradley's books in high school. I started with *The Heritage of Hastur*, then read two or three more Darkover novels that caught my eye in the Arden Hills library. While I didn't find them sufficiently entertaining to continue with the series, they were just interesting enough to inspire me to pick up a trade paperback of *The Mists of Avalon* not long after it was published by Del Rey in 1984. As it happens, I still have that much-ballyhooed monstrosity, its long-untouched pages now yellowing on a dusty bookshelf in the attic.

The Mists of Avalon was a massive 876-page bestseller heavily marketed as a feminist take on Camelot and the legends of King Arthur, and was critically hailed for being very different than the usual retellings of the classic tale. It was different, and in some ways, with its grim darkness and overt sexuality, *The Mists of Avalon* might even be considered a predecessor of sorts to George R.R. Martin's *A Game of Thrones*. I found it to be too much of a soap opera myself, and certainly not a patch on Chrétien de Troyes, Thomas Malory, or even T.H. White, although there were a few salacious sections that did serve to liven up the book considerably.

But even as a red-blooded young man, some of those sections struck me as perhaps a little *too* salacious. While I can't say that I had any inkling of what the author's habits or home life were at the time, I can say that I detected a slight sense of what I can only describe as a *wrongness* from the book. Arthur didn't love Guinevere, but was pining away for his half-sister? Sir Lancelot was not only Galahad, but also Arthur's bisexual cousin? Instead of being a tragic love triangle, Arthur, Launcelot, and Guinevere were a swinging threesome? And Mordred was not only Arthur's son, but the product of incest knowingly orchestrated by Merlin for pagan purposes to boot?

Yeah, that's not hot. That's just weird and more than a little grotesque.

I don't recall if I ever actually finished the novel or not, but I know I didn't bother reading any of its many sequels. I felt that I had given this vaunted feminist author a fair shake and delved as deeply into Ms. Bradley's strange psyche as I wished to go, little knowing that what I dismissed as freakish feminist literary antics were merely scratching the surface on what was actually an intergenerational psychosexual horror show.

Three decades later, despite being a science fiction author and editor myself, I found myself increasingly at odds with the creepy little community known as SF fandom, which can best be described as the cantina crowd from *Star Wars*, only depressed, overweight, and sexually confused. At the same time, I was also becoming increasingly aware of a *wrongness* that emanated from that community like a faint, but unmistakably foul odor.

There were rumors about the real reason behind science fiction grandmaster Arthur C. Clarke's bizarre relocation from southern California to Sri Lanka. There was the arrest of David Asimov, son of science fiction legend Isaac Asimov, for the possession of the largest stash of child pornography the police had ever seen. There were the public defenses offered by many science fiction authors on behalf of the SFWA member and convicted child molester Ed Kramer. There was the naming of NAMBLA enthusiast and homo-horrorporn author Samuel Delaney as SFWA's 2013 Damon Knight Memorial Grand Master.

And then, of course, there was the historical Breendoggle, a fifty-year-old debate among science-fiction fandom concerning whether a child molester, Walter Breen, should have been permitted to attend the science-fiction convention known as Pacificon II or not. Believe it or not, the greater part of fandom at the time was outraged by the committee's sensible decision to deny Breen permission to attend the 1964 convention; science-fiction fandom continued to cover for the notorious pedophile even after his death in 1993. In "Conspiracy of silence: fandom and Marion Zimmer Bradley", Martin Wisse wrote:

> *Why indeed did it take until MZB was dead for her covering for convicted abuser Walter Breen to become public knowledge and not just whispered amongst in the know fans. Why in fact was Breen allowed to remain in fandom, being able to groom new victims? Breen after all was first convicted in 1954, yet could carry out his grooming almost unhindered at sf cons until the late nineties. And when the 1964 Worldcon did ban him, a large part of fandom got very upset at them for doing so.*

The fact that fandom had been covering for pedophiles for decades was deeply troubling. And yet, we would soon learn that this *wrongness* in science fiction ran even deeper than the most cynical critics suspected.

On June 3, 2014, a writer named Deirdre Saorse Moen put up a post protesting the decision of Tor Books to posthumously honor Tor author and World

Fantasy Award-winner Marion Zimmer Bradley, on the basis of Bradley's 1998 testimony given in a legal deposition about her late husband. When Moen was called out by Bradley fans for supposedly misrepresenting Bradley, she reached out to someone she correctly felt would know the truth about the feminist icon: Moira Greyland, the daughter of Marion Zimmer Bradley and Walter Breen.

Little did Moen know how dark the truth about the famous award-winning feminist was. For when Moira responded a few days later, she confirmed Moen's statement about Marion Zimmer Bradley knowing all about her pedophile husband's behavior. However, she also added that her famous mother had been a child molester as well, and that in fact, Bradley had been far more violently abusive to both her and her brother than Breen!

I will not say more about the harrowing subject of this book because it is the author's story to tell, not mine. But I will take this opportunity to say something about the author, whom I have come to admire for her courage, for her faith, and most of all, for her ability to survive an unthinkably brutal upbringing with both her sanity and her sense of humor intact.

Moira does not wallow in her victimhood. Nor does she paint her victimizers as soulless devils, indeed, her empathy for those who wronged her so deeply is more than astonishing, it is *humbling*. Her strength of character, her integrity, and her faith in a God she was raised to believe did not exist are almost inexplicable, particularly in an age where adult college students cannot face unintended microaggressions without the support of their university administrations, the campus police, and physician-prescribed pharmaceuticals.

Her story is more than a triumph of the human spirit, more than a tale of survival, and more than a devastating indictment of a seriously depraved community. It is an inspiration to everyone, particularly for anyone who has ever been subjected to abuse or ill-treatment as a child.

Moira's message is clear: they can hurt you, they can harm you, and they can leave you with scars that last a lifetime, *but they cannot touch your soul.* Their sins are not your sins and their shame is not your shame. And there is a light that is always waiting to heal those who summon the strength to walk out of the last closet and turn their back on the darkness inside it.

Vox Day
4 December 2017

Introduction

I am the child of three gay parents.

The first was my notorious father, Walter Breen. In 1989, I turned my father in to the police after witnessing him molest an underage boy. He died in jail after being sentenced to thirteen years in San Quentin.

The second was my famous mother. Marion Zimmer Bradley was an award-winning science-fiction author with a history of poverty and heinous abuse from her drunken father and a life she tried to fill with charity and love. During an unhappy marriage, she found her true love in my father, a paranoid, schizophrenic, polymath genius and lifelong pedophile. During her 27-year involvement with him, my mother both abetted and participated in his crimes.

The third was my mother's former lover, Elisabeth Waters, who I was taught to call my stepmother. These days, however, Lisa prefers to pretend she is nothing but my "cousin", which begs the question: what on Earth was my "cousin" doing in my mother's bed? More than that, why would she dishonor my mother's memory by denying the substance of their 20-year relationship? Elisabeth spent two decades at Marion's side and in her bed, and helped her cover up some of Walter's crimes. She has tried to whitewash my mother's history, pretending that my mother was a "church-going Episcopalian", when in fact Marion was a pagan priestess who was happiest when she was leading occult rituals.

My mother's story is ultimately a tragic one, even though some of the tragedy came in the form of the tragedies she inflicted on other people. Can my mother be blamed for acting as she did, given the horrors she herself lived through? I believe that regardless of the pain one endures, we are all responsible for our own actions, and she must be responsible. After all, one might expect that enduring abuse would lead any reasonable person to not want to subject anyone else to it.

The reality of gay relationships is nothing like what we are led to believe. As a child, I was expected to approve and champion them as gay parents, even though they were parents who rejected each other and rejected me. I was supposed to become a lesbian and even to cooperate with their efforts to make me become one, but I always knew that I was not supposed to talk about that reality, let alone oppose it. They made it clear that exposing others to the truth would be the worst thing I could ever do to them. It would be an unconscionable personal betrayal.

One wonders why simply telling the truth about my life and theirs would be considered a betrayal, unless there really was something wrong with what they were doing.

In our culture, closets go far beyond sexual choices or identity: They represent what we are not allowed to want. The difference between who we are and who we must pretend to be is contained in a closet. The closet to which I am referring involves the depths of my very soul.

Throughout my life, I have had to cope with living in a series of closets. I could not admit to my parents that I wanted to be a girl because they thought girls were disgusting. I had to hide my femininity away as though I had been born sexless. I could not tell my parents that I was interested in boys because they wanted a gay child. I had to hide my conventional dreams of a family and a white picket fence away and hope I would not be found out. I couldn't even ask them for something as simple as a doll, because a doll represented the traditional gender roles they hated and would make them think I wanted to be like one of those girls they found so disgusting.

I could never tell my parents that their revolving door of sexual insanity made me wish that I was dead. I could never, ever admit my opposition to the way they chose to live. My feelings, my anguish, and my pain all had to be locked safely away in a closet.

Throughout my childhood, I just wanted my mother and father to love each other, to love me, and to stop bringing other people home for sex. I wanted to live in a normal family where no one would hurt me and expect me to regard it as freedom.

What is The Last Closet? It is the last thing I am not supposed to be allowed to think or to feel, is the bundle of facts that lead me to oppose gay marriage and nontraditional relationships. I know from personal experience that these relationships are social constructs which only exist to create sexual anarchy and to confuse sex with love. Since sex is good, freedom is good, and love is good, sexual libertines believe we should provide sex, freedom, and love all to our children.

And then hope they don't kill themselves as a result.

There are many people who would like to believe that my mother was not aware of my father's crimes—especially the fans of her fiction—but this is not true. She wrote a book involving a man-boy love story when she was nineteen,

The Catch Trap, and she edited *Greek Love*, my father's treatise on pederasty and wrote a companion article for it. Her own court testimony clearly demonstrates her knowledge of his sexual relationships with young boys. Also in the public record is her defense of him during the 1963 "Breendoggle" scandal in the science-fiction world when they were newly involved, so it should be apparent to even her most staunch defenders that she was no victim, but rather my father's partner in crime.

And then, there is also the fact that she herself molested both my brothers and me.

Although my father was a child molester himself and I doubt he would have objected to any of the sexual acts my mother imposed upon us, I am convinced that he objected strongly to her brutality. I feared her and loved him. One might remark, flippantly, that he was only a serial rapist while she was a violent, icy monster whose voice caused my stomach to twist up with fear. How can I paint my father as a villain when he was the one who comforted me after my mother's assaults?

It is possible that my mother was never capable of controlling her temper or her sexual desires enough to prevent the violence she committed. I question the completeness of this view, however, because a person who commits crimes while enraged normally expresses some modicum of remorse for them afterward.

I never saw a shred of that from her.

I am not writing this book because I am looking for sympathy, nor do I need anyone to confirm or support what I have written in the pages that follow. My experience is my own, and I am primarily speaking to those unfortunates who have shared an experience that is similar to mine. You may see yourself in these pages, or you may not. My hope is to bring a measure of healing to all who need it and to give a voice to the voiceless.

Throughout this book, I have forced myself to occasionally call Walter Breen "my father" instead of "Walter", as had been my usual habit. My brother changed his name from Patrick Russell Donald Breen to Mark Greyland as an understandable way to distance himself from our father, whom he now more customarily calls "Beardo the Weirdo." They were once close, but I cannot blame my brother for now wanting to deny that they were even related.

In this book, I have only talked about my recollections that I have some way to independently corroborate. In a few cases, I have mentioned something that my mother or someone else told me they had seen or done. While I have omitted a number of events that I still clearly recall, the reason is that I cannot provide any material evidence to support those recollections.

Regardless, coming out of The Last Closet means I am finally free to tell the truth about my life.

If you are still trapped in a closet, I hope you will someday feel the same freedom to tell the truth about your own.

Moira Greyland

Chapter 1

The Closet is Built: My Mother's Early Life (1930–1949)

Something is rotten in the state of Denmark.

—Marcellus, *Hamlet*; Act 1 Scene 4

My mother was born Marion Eleanor Zimmer on June 3, 1930, on a farm in Albany, New York. Her mother, Evelyn Parkhurst Conklin Zimmer, ran the farm and was a noted Scottish historian. Her father, Leslie Zimmer Sr., worked the farm and also worked as a carpenter since the farm did not produce enough to support them and he was too proud to go on welfare.

The oldest of three, my mother had two natural brothers: Leslie Jr. and the late Paul Edwin Zimmer, the youngest, as well as one adopted brother, Paul's childhood friend Don Studebaker. From the time she was three years old Marion made up stories, which her mother would dutifully transcribe. Over time Marion, Paul, and Don all became writers, although my mother was the only one to achieve significant success. Leslie Jr. did not write, and he did not get along with any of the other three siblings, being more or less a chip off the old block.

Marion's family lived in terrible poverty during the Great Depression. She remembered owning only one dress and walking to school every morning after milking the cows and performing other farm chores. She spoke of the cows with great affection. She never got along with Leslie Jr., whom she regarded as violent, and she was often in the position of having to defend both Paul and Don from him.

Marion once quipped that her mother regarded a daughter as a "handy household gadget." Afflicted with allergies and a serious arthritic condition, pain was a constant feature of my mother's life. She hated housework of any sort. Once she became a mother herself, Marion tried hard to avoid all housework, preferring to be the family breadwinner instead by earning money with her writing.

Marion loved opera and had dreamed of becoming an opera singer herself one day. Every Saturday morning she would listen to the Metropolitan Opera on the radio while she did the ironing. She hated ironing, but listening to the opera made it tolerable for her. My mother had a beautiful singing voice, but had, as she put it, neither the health nor the money to pursue a singing career. Even so, she would often walk around the house singing operatic arias. Her love for the aria "Mi Chiamano Mimi" resulted in her brother Paul always calling her Mimi instead of Marion.

There was a cultural schism in her childhood household, where Leslie Sr. regarded women as being fit for little more than cooking and cleaning. Leslie Sr. was a typical man of his era, the sort of man Archie Bunker might have been modeled after. He was often judgmental and narrow minded. He objected to Marion's wish to attend college and wanted her to stay home and work on the family farm. My grandmother was in favor of my mother going to college, but she would not oppose my grandfather even to help Marion, and she was firmly in agreement with him concerning cooking and cleaning being female tasks. She left Marion to fight her own battle with her father alone.

Marion loved school, regarding it as a refuge from her home. She also loved reading, especially science fiction, history, and music. The only thing she hated about school was the policy of making all girls play basketball. In the opinion of the school, the girls needed the exercise, an attitude which infuriated my mother. Between her farm chores, the constant pain of her arthritis, and the five-mile walk from her home to the school, playing basketball added insult to injury. Once she was done with school, she refused to ever exercise again.

My grandfather must have had some good qualities in him to induce my grandmother to marry him, but those good qualities vanished once tragedy struck his life. He turned to alcohol to cope with his grief when his sister drowned, and he began to abuse his wife and his daughter. He once threw my grandmother down the stairs and savagely beat both her and my mother on occasion. He raped Marion repeatedly in her young teens, always in the front seat of the family truck. He would drive my mother far enough away to be out of the view of the house and swear her to silence. When she finally called the police about the abuse, he was arrested. However, my grandmother forced my mother to drop the charges against him because his incarceration would end their meager income and the family would starve.

After being released, my grandfather came home from jail, raped my mother once more, and told her, "Now we're even, we can be friends."

Marion never forgave her mother for making her drop the charges and forcing her to endure yet another rape, and yet I sometimes heard her speak with kindness toward her father although they did not remain in touch after she left home. My mother seemed to think her father had little control over himself because he was a drunk, and she blamed him less than he deserved. She often said, "People do drunk what they want to do sober." It was as though she held her father to a lower standard and accepted his crimes as natural failings, but she could not forgive her mother for failing to stop him.

Marion did remain in contact with her mother until the latter's death even though they did not get along.

Even as a child, my mother was emotionally strong. She was a fighter at every point, always absolutely intent on doing things her own way. She told me that the one thing she said which her mother hated most was "Me do it all myself." Her mother, naturally, wanted to help her, but Marion's need for independence was too great to accept it.

Marion always considered herself to be a "dwarf among giants." She was 5'2 ¾", and very defensive about the ¾ inch, as if it helped her feel taller. I have wondered if her pretense of great physical strength and power was a compensation for the helplessness she felt when she was brutalized by her father.

I find it almost unbearable to imagine my grandfather physically overpowering my mother. It fills me with a fury and an outrage I cannot describe. I think I can understand her need to proclaim strength and endless victory, no matter what was happening. In her own heart, Marion probably felt that she had to win somehow, even if she lost. She found victory in not allowing her will to be destroyed by her father. And yet, her need to win meant that someone else had to lose.

I can imagine my mother thinking "I can't let him win. He can't get away with this. It is not fair for him to be bigger and stronger if this is what he is going to do." Ironically, she ended up emulating him in many ways because to survive required strength, and he was the strongest thing in her home. Psychologists are familiar with this phenomenon; they call it "introjecting the abuser."

Mother told me that she gave up on God because He didn't save her from her father. The results of this decision were tragic, as over time, it encouraged tens of thousands of her readers to follow in her footsteps, away from Christianity and into a spirituality that pretended to offer more. But no matter what spiritual practice she wandered into, it amounted to the same thing: a way for her to control divinity as a substitute for her own inability to control her father.

As a result of her stubborn independence, Marion managed to get involved in a few things which upset her parents a lot. In her teens, Mother was fascinated with carnivals and dreamed of running away to the circus. She even worked in a local carnival as a target for a knife-thrower named Dino. She had a scar on her breast because Dino once accidentally struck her in the chest with a knife when a photographer's flash momentarily blinded him. But it was always the trapeze artists that she loved the most, even though she knew that her rheumatoid arthritis would prevent her from ever becoming one.

Marion's love for carnivals and the trapeze resulted in her early novel, *The Flyers*, later published as *The Catch Trap*. *The Flyers* was written in 1948 and published in 1979. It involved a love affair between a man and an underage boy. She would tell me much later that John Travolta wanted to make a movie of it, but only if he could replace the boy in the story with a girl. She was very proud of having refused Travolta and of having insisted that her story must remain exactly as she wrote it.

It seems curious that my mother's vision of sexuality was so twisted by the age of eighteen that she would write a pederastic love story. Did her father's rapes somehow persuade her that sexuality was invariably cross-generation and coercive? Did it seem less threatening to displace a sexual relationship onto a man and a boy than write about a coercive love interest between an older man and a less powerful and younger girl? Or was there a real-life inspiration for *The Catch Trap*?

I have heard but I cannot prove that my mother's brother Don's adoption came after he had a youthful sexual involvement with her much younger brother Paul. Since the rumors of their involvement are hearsay and I know no details, I can only speculate that Paul and Don were the inspiration for the lovers in *The Catch Trap*.

Where Don is an author who has been living as an openly gay man for many decades now, Paul became the kind of hyper-masculine man who refused to neuter his male cats and had children with three different women, despite only being married to one of them. He spoke with fury of anyone who tried to "neuter" men by getting in the way of their full sexual expression with anyone. If anyone had suggested Paul was gay to his face, I expect he would have angrily denied it.

Of course in many cases, same-sex liaisons between younger people do not invariably create gay adults, nor even necessarily indicate a tendency that will be reliably followed. It is entirely possible to have an experimenting child end up not only straight, but very straight indeed. There is no shortage of examples of people who have been gay for decades but eventually end up straight and married to partners of the opposite sex by choice.

Marion was involved in science-fiction fandom from the time of its inception in 1945. She was accustomed to spending hours in the school library reading everything she could find, sometimes even playing hooky from school to read at the library. Fortunately, she was well-liked by the librarians, who refused to turn her in. She especially liked the work of Henry Kuttner, Edmond Hamilton, C. L. Moore, and Leigh Brackett, often mentioning the latter in our home.

She wrote her first book in 1947, when she was seventeen: a rewrite of Bellini's opera *Norma*, which was published posthumously as *The Forest House*. *Norma* is about a powerful Druidic priestess who has a forbidden relationship with a Roman and bears two children by him. He is unfaithful to her with her best friend Adalgisa, a younger and much less powerful woman. After contemplating killing her two children, she reveals the identity of her Roman lover to her people, and he is sentenced to death. She climbs atop his funeral pyre and dies with him.

It might be informative to look through my mother's books to see if there are any positive relationships in them between older men and younger women or if all such relationships were unequal and rooted in force. There are parallels between *Norma* and my mother's relationship with my unfaithful father. Walter abandoned her again and again for very young, powerless boys.

Marion was writing for pulp magazines and publishing what we call fanzines today even before she was out of high school. She was involved with *Day*Star*, *Ad Astra*, and *Anything Box*, which may have been the inspiration for Zenna Henderson's 1965 short story of the same name. Her first professional sale was the short story "Outpost" from an amateur fiction contest in *Amazing Stories*. "Outpost" was first published in the fanzine *Spacewarp*, Vol. 4, no. 3 in December 1948, and then in *Amazing Stories* Vol. 23, No. 12 the following December.

Marion once said in an interview that she became a lesbian in her teens. Her father broke up one of her early lesbian relationships by calling the cops on her, but this only increased her determination to go her own way. It could be said that she had reclaimed her sexuality in a way her father was helpless to either control or to compete with. She was, in effect, conquering her rapist by repudiating his entire gender.

Marion had a number of liaisons with women, including one named Dorothy, who was the namesake for my middle name. My mother always spoke well of Dorothy. There was also a longer, very dramatic, and explosive relationship with a woman named Carrie. Marion seemed to have retained less friendship and fewer good feelings for Carrie than for Dorothy, though I do not know why. But I never knew my mother to accept any responsibility for the failure of a relationship.

She eventually met a lesbian named Barbara Grier, who introduced her to a lesbian group called *The Daughters of Bilitis*, founded by four lesbian couples in San Francisco in 1955. Its original purpose was to counteract the loneliness felt by lesbians and later to educate lesbians about rights and lobbying. My mother contributed to *The Ladder*, their newsletter which began in 1956. She also wrote for its gay counterpart: *The Mattachine Review*.

She wrote a succession of novels for Monarch Books (*I Am a Lesbian*, 1962, *The Strange Women*, 1962), and Corinth Books (*My Sister, My Love*, 1963, *Twilight Lovers*, 1964, and *No Adam For Eve*, 1966) under different pseudonyms, including "John Dexter", "Miriam Gardner", and "Lee Chapman". They were considered lesbian pornography at the time, although they were much tamer than anything we would regard as pornographic today. A complete list of her pseudonyms, the works she wrote under them, and their publication dates appears in the appendix containing her bibliography.

Marion's writing was one of several aspects of her life where she rejected femininity. In 1962, Damon Knight, whom she mentioned often at home, said that "her work is distinctively feminine in tone, but lacks the clichés, overemphasis and other kittenish tricks which often make female fiction unreadable by males."

My impression is that she was more focused on the story than on how she felt about it, and this is primarily what made her style seem so different from that of her female contemporaries.

I believe she identified femininity with vulnerability to men, which to her meant violent rape. Thus, she found it intolerable. In a 1988 interview, she spoke with annoyance and disdain about having to wear one's hair a certain way or going along with any feminine stereotype. She did not want her characters to have a pair-bond as their ultimate goal, especially not a conventional male-female one. There was never any "happily ever after" for her or for her female characters; they were required to forge their own future from something other than love, or at least something other than blissful matrimony.

Although Marion never affected the flannel shirt and khakis uniformly worn by the lesbians I grew up around in the Bay Area, it would have been difficult to imagine a less feminine woman than my mother. Her voice, her body language, her mannerisms, and her attitude all spoke of power and only power as *the* priority in dealing with other people. She was just as unfeminine in a dress as she was in pants. She never dressed to look nice, and she regarded doing so as a betrayal of feminism.

She refused to value appearances and regarded doing so as selling out to the patriarchy. Feminine body language and behavior was considered to be repulsive and out of the question because it might attract men, and permitting men to be attracted by those things was wrong because it will teach them the wrong thing. She believed women were supposed to educate men to appreciate us only for our minds, and therefore it was a woman's responsibility to absolutely reject any male appreciation which is the result of our appearance or femininity. Any man who dares to love our femininity is an evil oppressor and should not be provided with any sex, ever.

In my mother's imagination, for a woman to have sex with a masculine man was to risk her life as well as her sanity.

Despite her intelligence, my mother never anticipated that men would quickly reason their way around this preposterous attitude. All a man needs to do to obtain sex from a feminist is to pretend to go along with these ideas in every way and insist that he only loves her for her *mind*. And if he will be deemed trustworthy even more quickly if he is willing to assume a parasitic role and permit her to pay for everything. The most important thing is that a man cannot express *any* opinion about thin women being more attractive than fat women. The more a man can tolerate, or better yet, pretend to desire fat women, the quicker he will be provided sex, the more female partners he will have access to, and the more his feminist partners will accept him having multiple partners.

Apparently, we women are too dimwitted to figure out that rather than believing this feminist nonsense, men simply learned to tell us what we wanted to hear.

After Marion graduated from high school, she attended the New York State College for Teachers, now known as University at Albany, SUNY from 1946 to 1948. Her goal was to become a teacher, but she dropped out, mostly because her father believed that "education on a woman was like lips on a chicken", and he refused to support her. In response, she told him she would marry the first kind, decent, sober man who asked her, and that is exactly what she did.

Marion married the fifty-year-old Robert Alden Bradley on October 26, 1949, when she was only nineteen. They had corresponded for three years but never met. She always called him "Brad."

Brad was a fellow science-fiction fan, and he was very supportive of her writing. Marion felt that Brad was a marvelous conversationalist and told me that the reason she stayed with Brad as long as she did despite their many differences was this: "He knew he could trust me with his money, and we never ran out of things to talk about."

She was grateful to Brad for teaching her to drive and for sending her to college at Hardin-Simmons. Marion graduated with three majors, in English, Spanish, and psychology. Her Spanish was good enough to permit her to write a credible translation of *El Villano in su Rincon* by Lope de Vega that was printed privately in 1971. She was also interested in parapsychology, though not religion. The only religion she consistently claimed in my hearing was Spiritualism, and she took Rosicrucianism very seriously. She also took voice lessons in college. She loved Gilbert and Sullivan and continued to sing throughout her life.

Brad and Marion had one son, my late half-brother David Robert Bradley (1950–2008), but she desperately wanted more children, and Brad absolutely did not. When she became pregnant again after David was born, he obliged her to have an abortion. When Marion refused to have any more abortions, Brad simply declined to ever have sex with her again. She hated him for this and cited it as the primary reason she left him for my father after 16 years of marriage.

Toward the end of her life she told me that Brad was a very strange man who reminded her of a space alien, although she couldn't really explain any reason for it. She also told me that she never cried anymore and didn't like crying because she did nothing but cry for over a year after she had first married, and it had never done her a "damned bit of good." That being said, she did cry rather a lot while I was young. I can hardly blame her, between her absolutely appalling upbringing, the never-ending poverty she experienced, and the unhappy end of her first marriage.

She was not one to put up with anyone else crying either, regardless of age or reason. After all, crying was a sign of weakness, and proof that a woman was not strong enough to solve her own problems.

Not long after Marion left Brad, my grandmother unexpectedly left Leslie Sr. and moved to California with Paul and Don after catching Leslie Sr. in a compromising position with a cow. My mother told me this story with a combination of amusement and fury, upset that her mother had more concern for the morals and modesty of the cow than for her own daughter. The other factor contributing to my grandmother's departure was a series of violent altercations between Leslie Jr. and Don, in which Leslie Jr. was the instigator and Don got the worst of it.

I am told that when my grandmother left and they carried the old piano out of the house, the only thing Leslie said to her was, "Babe, would you turn on the TV?"

Armchair Psychology

Marion's mother is passive and does not protect her from her violent, sexually abusive father. Her father is the strongest personality in her house. In psychological theory, "introjecting the abuser" means we would take on traits of the strongest parent, instead of the weakest one, regardless of the parent's sex. Marion learned that love was not available from either men or women and that the only way to obtain freedom was to get married and, eventually, to make her own money. She also learned that violence was acceptable and tended to coincide with power.

Marion learned that although women were safer than men, they were not entirely safe either. She had relationships with women that were hysterical and highly dramatic. Her most stable love relationships were with men despite the drama she brought to them; Marion was married to Brad for sixteen years and to my father for thirty-four years. Even when she had been with Lisa for twenty years, Marion still described Walter as the love of her life.

Marion learned that sex was fundamentally coercive and that she would either be forced, or she would force. One sees this again and again in the unequal relationships and in the unsatisfactory substitutes for conventional male-female relationships she created in her writing. The Renunciates or Free Amazons in her *Darkover* books gave up the right to marry, based on her idea that simply shacking up instead of getting married would magically create a superior relationship.

It was Marion's vision that living together without marriage vows would somehow sidestep the coercive, unequal situation she equated with marriage. But while reversing the power dynamic and vesting it with women might seem an obvious way to right the perceived wrongs of the marriage structure, it did not work. Marion held all the power in her family, and yet she was not only cruel and punitive but irrational and would punish others savagely on a whim. The matriarchy she created was not just and good; it was oppressive and terrifying and left her children feeling like caged animals, wishing for escape or death and much too frightened to cry.

Marion appeared to have fused femininity with helplessness and vulnerability in her mind. She wrote characters into her books ranging from the most oppressed to the least and seemed to handle those still in their figurative or literal chains with sensitivity and kindness. Invariably, her characters who escaped oppression did so by rejecting their femininity and taking on a more masculine persona, in an obvious echo of her own life's path.

Marion was given a model of educated, intelligent, and oppressed womanhood in her mother, and while she rejected the oppression to which she was subjected, she also rejected her own womanhood, becoming instead a female caricature of her violent father.

Primarily due to her intelligence, Marion was able to attract two husbands although she was not happy with either of them. Her conflicted relationship with sex almost guaranteed she would end up pursuing relationships with men where sex was either problematic or nonexistent, as was the case in both of her marriages.

Marion was fundamentally unable to trust other people. As a child, she went to her mother for help but was betrayed and sent back to her father to endure more abuse. Psychologists describe the basis of the "borderline conflict" as an abused child going back and forth between father and mother, looking for love and safety but not finding it in either one of them. As a result of her borderline conflict, Marion became a violent, masculinized woman, hating and mistrusting men and only able to tolerate those who were neither conventionally masculine nor feminine. Ironically, she ended up internalizing her father's oppressive version of masculinity, and he lived on through her.

In the end, Marion became the very oppressor she hated.

Chapter 2

My Father's Early Life
(1928–1961)

Oh, what a noble mind is here o'erthrown!

—*Ophelia*, Hamlet Act 1, Scene 3

I will be telling my father Walter's story from his perspective since there is no way to verify or disprove any of his claims beyond his military service record. I have drawn from what Walter told me and from his own autobiography, as well as what his friends and my brothers have shared with me. I am not claiming that his account is true or untrue, only that it is what he believed. I cannot pretend to reconcile all the things he told me. All I can do is transmit what he said and leave it to you to figure out what happened.

My father, the noted numismatic author Walter Henry Breen, was born in San Antonio, Texas, on September 5, 1930. He was orphaned as an infant, a foundling abandoned on the running board of a truck. He told me he was originally named James Douglas Headrick, and thought he might have been the illegitimate child of a famous young Juilliard pianist.

He was adopted by Nellie Mehl Breen (Mary Helena Brown Mehl) and her husband Walter Breen, a traveling salesman. I never once heard my father say a single good word about his adoptive mother, although he dearly loved his mostly-absent father. Of his mother he had this to say: "She was about as fit to raise a kid like me as a chimpanzee would have been." He had many complaints about her, the mildest of which was that she force-fed him peanut butter sandwiches, which made him sick. Apparently, she was both overbearing and violent as well as religious in a terrifying way, and believed that everything not strictly Catholic was a source of immediate and eternal damnation.

My father had three birth certificates with different years and locations. He told me this was because his mother obtained the two fraudulent birth certificates, dated 1929 and 1928, respectively, because she wanted him to leave the house and start earning money with the Army Air Force. He also told me that his mother used the name "William Brown" on one of the birth certificates in an effort to hide him from his adoptive father after they divorced and she moved to West Virginia.

His arrest records and military records use the 1928 birthdate, but he always insisted to me that the 1930 birthdate was correct. I see no reason to dispute that a child knows exactly how old he is: When we are young, our age is the center of our identity.

One small anecdote about Walter's feelings regarding his age: Marion was born in June of 1930, whereas he was born in September of the same year. One day, she said, "Now that we're both fifty–" and he stopped her abruptly, saying, "Speak for yourself", as though it was offensive to him to be considered fifty when he would still be 49 for another few months. Walter always regarded Marion as being the older of the two of them and would not accept any claim to the contrary.

I am going to quote from Walter's autobiography here in order to permit him to describe his childhood in his own words:

1933: I learned to read and write on my own, well before I was 3 years old. When I was 4, I wanted to know more about how the human body worked, so I made friends with a neighbor who was a medical student, and I borrowed his copy of Gray's ANATOMY, managing to understand a fair amount of it with his help. I also remember reading a dictionary, which meant that the way I talked made me a green monkey among the pink monkeys in the orphanage in later years. The Walter Damrosch radio programs—which I heard infrequently, but loved — turned me on to classical music for which I was starved from then on.

In 1937, when Walter was six, his adoptive mother returned to Catholicism and divorced his adoptive father. She retained custody of Walter, then moved to West Virginia and changed his name to William Brown so that his adoptive father could not find him. Walter later expressed regret that he had not been able to see his adoptive father more often after the divorce. Since divorce is forbidden by the Catholic Church, it seems an extremely odd thing to do as the result of returning to it. Was there some kind of abuse of her or of my father? If so, my father was either completely unaware of it or did not speak about it at all.

After the divorce, my father and his adoptive mother moved to Wheeling, West Virginia, as the 1940 census reflects. She put him into a Catholic orphanage, where she got a job as a janitor. He later compared the orphanage to a concentration camp. He told me that he was expected to believe that God delighted in their sufferings, and he told me stories of the overwhelming brutality that took place in the orphanage, including beatings with coat hangers and electrical cords.

Walter's mother put clothespins on his member if she caught him touching it. He spoke with fury of being required to sleep with his hands outside the bed so that he would not touch himself. He claimed that the only "love" he ever experienced was with a priest at the orphanage but he gave no details, other than regarding it as a transformative experience. This is the point at which Walter began to confuse sex with love in his mind.

Despite these unusual circumstances, he completed grade school in only 22 months.

In 1941, his mother decided that Walter had a vocation for the priesthood and put him into the Trinitarians monastery in Hyattsville, Maryland. He had to obtain a special dispensation from the Apostolic Delegate because he was only eleven years old. He never gave any details beyond "It didn't work out" to explain what became of his supposed priestly vocation.

After that, Walter returned to the orphanage where his mother worked and went to high school. He graduated from Central Catholic High School in Wheeling, West Virginia, in 1943 a few months before he turned 14. He was the youngest and smallest kid in his class. He referred to his classmates as "walking Polish jokes" and thought they hated him because he was into books and music instead of sports, cars, and girl-chasing. Even then, he objected strenuously to the idea of having to prove his masculinity.

After completing high school at 13, my father had nothing to do but hang around at the rectory at the Catholic orphanage where his mother still worked. He must have been absolutely miserable there because despite his hatred of traditional masculinity, he decided to enlist in the military and get mixed up with the most traditionally masculine situation on the planet.

He enlisted in the Army Air Force at the age of sixteen on October 3, 1946, using the false birth certificate with the 1928 birthdate his mother had gotten him. He was sent to the San Antonio Aviation Cadet Center (subsequently renamed Lackland Air Force Base) for training. His military identification number was 18 324 478, and he listed his mother as a dependent. His other specifications included the following: Height: six feet, one inch; Eye color: hazel; Hair color: brown; IQ: 144; Vision: 20/20–20/15.

An IQ of 144 is very high, being 12 points more than is required to join Mensa, the high IQ association, and puts an individual in the top 0.02 percent of the population. Only one in 596 people has an IQ that high.

Nevertheless, Walter Breen had one of the shortest military careers in history. On December 3rd, 1946, he was beaten up and left for dead by his fellow soldiers. He later told me they attacked him because they found out he was homosexual.

The beating caused a severe head injury with memory loss. He was taken to the station hospital with total amnesia about his life. The hospital staff contacted his mother, and she immediately came out to see him. She was not helpful at all, but scared him half to death. He said in his autobiography that his mother *"...sent a priest to reinstruct me in the Catholic religion, complete with threats of hellfire for what I know now to have been relatively minor doubts and questionings."* Imagine being in the hospital, and all your mother will do is send a priest to make sure you are a good Catholic after scaring you to death!

My father remained in the hospital for some time after that, diagnosed not only with the head injury but with paranoid schizophrenia and homosexuality. This was, of course, decades prior to the 1987 decision of the American Psychiatric Association to stop classifying homosexuality as a mental disorder.

Many years later, Walter told his friends a story about having developed his photographic memory through a head injury received in a plane crash during World War II. The problem is that the war ended in 1945, more than a year before his hospitalization, so this story is obviously not true. Even if he had been in a plane crash of some sort, he never mentioned being in combat to me, and considering that only two months passed between his enlistment and his subsequent beating, he clearly never saw combat. He was barely out of boot camp! Also, Walter's superior memory had already manifested itself in his unusual scholastic history.

That being said, there was one detail related to the plane crash story that cannot be disputed. Regardless of its origins, his photographic memory was indisputable: He could recite entire passages from phone books his friends would hand him.

On an even less plausible note, both he and my mother were convinced that they had been abducted by aliens, though I have never seen a single little green man at any of our family homes, and I am not much of a believer in that sort of thing. Pardon me for being boring, but I find tales of alien abduction to be as dismal as stories about being stuck in line at the DMV. I cannot find anything useful to say about purported alien abductions, other than to hope the aliens they encountered were more interesting than the probing accounts of the Whitley Strieber set.

Seriously, must all space aliens be creepy gray New Agers? Why do they all look alike? Why do they invariably sexually abuse the abductees? If they want to create human/alien hybrids, why can't they do it via in vitro and birth the result in an alien female or a machine incubator? Why do they always speak in telepathy? And those outfits—sheesh! Shouldn't a visiting space alien at least be expected to be aware of the most basic sartorial advances we have made on Earth? If we can invent so many different cool outfits for science-fiction aliens, why would actual alien dress be so universally dreary?

If my parents were alien abductees, why did they not have better alien stories to tell? My mother never mentioned her purported abduction as being an inspiration for Darkover. If we are to believe abductees, all aliens ever do is to come to earth, abuse cows, and scare the proverbial pants off of people. How does one go from being abducted and abused by aliens to writing science fiction about aliens who never come to Earth or probe anyone?

For Walter, life in the hospital was more solitary, and more tragic than his imagined alien abductions or anachronistic plane crashes. My father was in a hospital bed, he was only sixteen years old, and his injuries and subsequent diagnoses had already ended his military service. His mother's visit provided no comfort and no emotional support, only terror and threats of hellfire. And worst of all, he had lost his connection with the only father he had ever known.

Walter's amnesia had resulted in a temporary loss of his ability to read and write, and he had to learn how to do so again. Afterward, he continued his autodidactic education, first from the hospital library and later in public libraries.

Back in those days, homosexual men were routinely discharged through Section 8, but it should be clear that my father's head trauma and schizophrenia went far beyond that. His autobiography said he was discharged as "Inadaptable" for military service in February of 1947. The usual definition of Section 8 is mental unfitness for military service.

He was sent home to his mother, who kept him locked up in his room, viewing him as potentially dangerous. He says that her mind was going at that time: a reasonable, even kind interpretation for much of their interactions up to that point. I have never heard my father say anything good about the military, despite his VA benefits providing him with a hospital bed for a very long time.

In September of 1947, my father began attending St. Edward's College in Austin, Texas. He became the organist and assistant choirmaster for the college choir and the local boy choir associated with the grade school at St. Edwards.

He had learned to play the organ. He had been given a few weeks of lessons by a colleague, presumably as a gift—there was certainly no money to pay for ongoing piano or organ lessons, certainly not to explain the years and years of daily practice which his level of ability would ordinarily have required. His ability to play was on the level of a savant. He could sight read any music placed before him from Puccini to Liszt.

I hope I can make clear that my father's ability to play the piano in such a short time could be compared to becoming a champion powerlifter after a few weeks of weightlifting, or winning a karate tournament after watching a few Bruce Lee movies. His accomplishment was staggering, but he took his ability as lightly as the rest of the things he did very well without study or training.

Walter's autobiography states that although he loved music and college, his health began breaking down at that time. He occasionally had epileptic seizures when he performed on the piano, which precluded a serious solo career as a pianist. On the day before Thanksgiving, two months into his time at St. Edwards, he was admitted into the VA hospital yet again, feeling run down and unable to sleep. The next day, his mother showed up at the hospital and disowned him so ferociously and loudly that the hospital staff and the police barred her from ever visiting him again. He was treated with sedatives and vitamins.

He was attending college and doing what he loved. From my knowledge of him, working as an organist and a choirmaster would have been the nearest thing to his fondest dream. Although he loved coins, classical music was dearer to his heart than anything else. I remember him telling me about sitting on an airplane reading the score of *Madama Butterfly* with the tears running down his cheeks.

It was sad to read in his autobiography about how his health broke down while he was doing something that he loved so much. It was a very difficult year and he had no family on whom to rely or friends to whom he could talk. His mother had kept him under house arrest in her home. Any woman who would disown her sick son in the hospital was not likely to be a good caretaker for anyone, let alone for a teenager coping with a massive head injury and severe mental illness.

Given his head injury and schizophrenia, it was a wonder he lasted as long as he did outside the hospital. Reading his autobiography, I ended up with the impression that the hospital became a form of surrogate family for him.

While in the hospital, Walter began to learn about coins, an interest which would become his prevailing passion for the rest of his life. Not only did he read everything he could find about coins, but he began to correspond with other numismatists, including Wayte Raymond, a numismatic publisher, and the coin dealer John J. Ford, Jr. who later claimed to have discovered him. He corresponded with William Guild about "patterns:" coin prototypes which are important to collectors.

Walter remained in the VA hospital from September of 1947 until May of 1948. He was released because the hospital needed his bed for a more acute case. The VA sent him to the Hayden Memorial Goodwill Inn in Boston, not knowing that it was a facility for juvenile delinquents. Walter did not object. He was interested in transferring to Hayden because Dr. Sheldon, whom he admired greatly, had done his research there.

He did not remain in the facility in Boston, but, in his own words, "bummed around" instead, mostly studying coins and going to concerts. But before long his health broke down again, and on October 8, 1948, he was admitted to the Cushing VA Hospital, where he remained until August 1950. While he was there, he corresponded with John J. Ford Jr. and arranged to meet Wayte Raymond in person after his discharge. On December 2, 1950, Wayte Raymond hired him to go to the National Archives in Washington to study American coins and to fill in the gaps of numismatic knowledge. He met Dr. Sheldon at that time, as well as other people he admired, and worked at the National Archives until March of 1951.

In 1951, my father had several jobs in numismatics. He spent time at the Smithsonian with his friend Stuart Mosher, the Curator of Numismatics and Editor of *The Numismatist*, which was the monthly journal for the ANA, or the American Numismatic Society.

While Stuart Mosher was unable to work for a time, my father served as Acting Editor for *The Numismatist* during the spring of 1951, doing everything from editing to layout. His first numismatic publication appeared in *The Numismatist* in 1951. Mosher was grooming my father to replace him, but Lew Reagan, the General Secretary of North American Numismatics, opposed this. My father did not state a reason for Lew Reagan's opposition, but I am certain a few might be guessed at. He also worked at the American Numismatic Society for a brief time. My father went through the Stepney Hoard of Connecticut Coppers at Stack's, but left, complaining of hearing too many shouting matches between his coworkers.

In between these very odd jobs, my father went back to college. On February 14, 1951, he read about the "New Plan" at Johns Hopkins University. The "New Plan" was a way to get through college more quickly by challenging courses and taking final exams instead of doing the entire course. My father took the SAT and claimed to have scored "a pair of 800s on them", although is almost certainly not true considering his Army-measured IQ of 144. Regardless, he did well enough on the SAT to be accepted to Johns Hopkins in June 1951 and began classes with a concentration on the German language. He already knew a lot of German due to mail-order classes he had taken while at Cushing Hospital, but the mail-order courses offered no credits. He had no credits from his one partial semester spent at St. Andrews, and his VA benefits would cover exactly one year of college. His participation in the New Plan was a way to complete his college degree within the time he could afford to be there.

The New Plan let him take exams to fulfill course requirements instead of attending classes. He described his year spent this way as "a dreadful grind", and he was at the point of dropping out twice. Still, he made it through with an 87 average and just enough credits to qualify for a degree in mathematics, which he received the following June, in 1952.

He was elected to the Maryland Alpha Chapter (JHU) of Phi Beta Kappa and showed his respect for that society by wearing his golden key on the zipper of his trousers. His other extracurricular activities included the Astronomy Club, the History of Ideas Club, and Phalanx, an early version of Mensa. He wrote for the *Numismatic Scrapbook* which, unlike *The Numismatist*, paid him for his articles.

While completing his rigorous school schedule, he worked for the coin dealer Tom Warfield from the Mason-Dixon Coin exchange, and he also assisted in writing coin catalogues for the American Numismatic Association, in 1952.

A few skeptics have questioned his singular feat of completing a four-year degree between June 1951 and June 1952, but the college confirmed it, as did photos in the Johns Hopkins yearbook. At that time, my father was tall and slim, broad-shouldered and clean-shaven. His hair was black, and it fell in soft finger-waves like a film star from the Forties. I never saw him looking even remotely like he did in his college yearbook picture.

Another event that my father felt worthy of noting in his autobiography took place in August of 1952. Apparently, the FBI tried to arrest him as a draft dodger despite his military service and discharge. He described the situation as a "hilarious mixup" and it was resolved without creating any more problems for him.

Within a few months my father began working full time for the New Netherlands coin company as an auction cataloguer and he remained there until 1960. He complained that he would have made better money as a ribbon clerk at Woolworth's and had to supplement his income by writing for any coin publication which would pay him. He also made money through what he called "cherry picking." His coin expertise, unrivaled by anyone in the business, enabled him to look at a pile of coins and figure out very quickly which ones would be worth anything at resale. Wayte Raymond's 1953, 1954, and 1957 editions of his Standard Catalogue included a lot of my father's writing as well as Raymond's Guidebook. Much of what he did was what he called "coin cataloguing", where he would describe the physical characteristics of individual coins so that collectors could decide what they wanted to buy.

During his life, my father received many literary awards. My father's first book, *Proof Coins Struck by the United States Mint, 1817–1901*, was published in 1953. Twice he received the ANA's Heath Literary Award, in 1953 and 1991. He reported regularly winning awards from the Numismatic Literary Guild, or NLG, including the Clemy Award in 1985 and the Book of the Year Award. He received the Fifth Award in Poet Laureateship of California in 1962, and he received the Silver Medallion of Honor from Roosevelt University in 1965. He received the Professional Numismatists Guild's Fobert Friedberg Award in 1988.

My father's interest in science was not limited to mathematics, geology, or medicine. He became a member of the Rittenhouse Astronomical Society and was made Honorary Vice President in 1958. Later, the Rittenhouse Society awarded him the title of "Numismatic Scholar of the Twentieth Century" in 1992, citing his "generous contribution to knowledge through [his] enormous number of books, catalogues and magazine and newspaper articles and columns…[and] amazing breadth and depth of extensive research on all phases of American numismatics" ("Rittenhouse," 1992, p.81).

I never heard him mention any award that he had received. Walter took no pride in his awards nor in anything that was status-related. The only things that impressed my father were intelligence, musical ability, and good writing.

I wish I could continue with a litany of my father's impressive accomplishments. Sadly, the next thing my father was involved with was directly connected to his eventual downfall.

Dr. William Herbert Sheldon was a controversial psychologist and numismatist, and long-time mentor of my father. I often heard his name mentioned in our home. Dr. Sheldon's theories included somatotype and constitutional psychology, which sought to correlate body type with temperament—an idea popular with eugenicists. Although his theories in their original form are no longer taken seriously in his field, elements of somatotype taxonomy, such as the words ectomorph, mesomorph, and endomorph, are still in use today.

Between 1953 and 1956, my father was working with Dr. Sheldon in the

Constitutional Laboratory at Columbia Medical School. He had become the coordinator of parapsychological research studies of New York's gifted children, also called the "Superkids." Among the Superkids were my father's long-time friends and colleagues, Jack Sarfatti and Robert Bashlow. An unfortunate part of my father's "research" on the Superkids was to bring them into the New York science-fiction fandom. Given my father's future tendency to use science-fiction conventions as a place to locate gifted boys to groom and later molest, I cannot overlook the possibility that my father was sexually exploiting at least some of the Superkids.

My father loved children, especially boys, in much the same way many of us love a rare steak. Every child he met, Superkid or not, would be encouraged to go to science-fiction conventions, which meant they would often be separated from their parents for hours at a time and available to talk with him.

When my father attended science-fiction conventions, he would usually sit in a high-traffic area playing with a spinning mirrored disc or other science-related toy, until a curious male child would approach him. This was his usual method of seduction during the Seventies and Eighties that I personally witnessed, and I conclude that he first developed it in the Fifties.

While these public interactions might at first seem harmless, when one adds to it the heady mix of adult attention lavished on the vulnerable boy, reassurance of the boy's remarkable intellect whether it was true or not, and intense, highly-focused conversations, the result frequently produced a victim who was willing to provide more or less anything that Walter wanted from him.

This slow, attention-driven means of obtaining influence over a child by an adult is called "grooming." During the grooming process, the child would become convinced that my father saw something in them that nobody else saw, and came to believe that under his tutelage they would be able to accomplish great things due to the amazing abilities he attributed to them. Naturally, the more completely my father could persuade them, the more vulnerable they became and the more they felt they needed him. The vampiric process transformed him from an interesting stranger into an emotionally-bonded surrogate parent with dark intentions none of them were capable of imagining.

Once he managed to separate the boy from other adults who might interfere with him, Walter would provide the groomed child with pot and often other hallucinogens. He would also keep the boy up much later than usual. Then, Walter would show him very tasteful pornography disguised as educational materials. Sooner or later, he would make some sort of sexual invitation to the stoned, very tired boy. Walter was patient, and often the overt sexual invitations would only occur later, during week-long parent-free visits to his home by the boys, whose parents foolishly believed their children were being given a wonderful opportunity to spend time with an influential, intelligent mentor.

In 1954, my father was arrested for exposing himself to a young man under a boardwalk in Atlantic City. Since he was tried as a first offender, he received only probation. What we may think of as a pervert—a flasher or a child molester—is more clearly described as a sexual addict. Where many sexual addicts do not reach the level of criminal behavior, some do, and among these some are very dangerous indeed. It makes the most sense to view my father and his conduct through the frame of sexual addiction.

Sexual addiction is described at length by Pat Carnes in his book *Contrary to Love*. The book describes the mental and emotional state of the sexual addict from the fantasies, to the planning and the eventual acting out. Where public exhibition might seem a very mild act compared to the ones my father was eventually convicted of, these acts occur on a spectrum. There is an escalation over time, since as with any drug, the acting out never produces a feeling quite as good as the fantasies promise. Each escalation represents an effort by the sexual addict to finally feel the way they think they should feel at the point of sexual release. Naturally, this works about as well as gambling in a casino does: the odds are always against you, and the only thing you can ever choose is how much you are willing to lose.

Animal studies show that chimpanzees, like humans, quickly become addicted to behaviors which have a varied schedule of rewards: card games are addicting, all types of gambling are addicting, and addicts will persist much longer in these kinds of activities than the rewards should excuse. The sex addict, like any addict, is gambling with their brain chemistry. But whereas a drug addict cannot injure his drug of choice, a sex addict will routinely destroy one hapless victim after another.

Exposing oneself in public is a symptom of sexual addiction and an act which is usually played out in fantasies for a long time before the sex offender summons the nerve to first act out his fantasy in public. It can be surmised that when Walter was first arrested, it was not the first time he had exposed himself. In fact, it may have not even been the first time he was reported for such a crime. To put this in perspective, while my father's first arrest for lewd conduct was in 1954, his first conviction and incarceration did not take place until 1989, *35 years later*. It should be noted that most people do not report sex crimes, and men are even less likely to report them than women, given the shame that is inherent in admitting such a thing happened to them.

It should be noted that one of my father's goals was to change the paradigm so that he would not be perceived as a rapist. Not only would this reduce the possibility of legal ramifications, but it would enable him to victimize a given victim many times, rather than only once. To this end, not only did he supply drugs to his chosen victims, but money, trips, restaurant meals, toys, even presents such as bicycles. This is what happens when a high-IQ predator has a long time to think about how he will commit his crimes.

My father continued to work in the numismatic field while he was carrying out research on the Superkids. He edited *MANA NEWS Quarterly*, 1956–60, and continued to catalogue coins. He became increasingly active in the science fiction community and edited *FANAC*, a long-running fanzine. He also wrote book reviews, analytics, and critical studies.

In January 1957, my father conducted the "Cent Collectors' Forum" as a regular feature in *The Numismatist*. He sold an article, "Numismatics USA" to Encyclopedia Britannica in 1958, which did not appear in print until their 1965 edition. He was credited with writing the index of Charles Hapgood's *Earth's Shifting Crust* but claimed that a lot of the ideas for the work were developed in discussions between himself and Charles Hapgood.

Earth's Shifting Crust, published in 1958, featured a foreword by Albert Einstein and denied the existence of continental drift, suggesting the pole shift hypothesis as an alternative. This is the idea that there have been geologically rapid shifts in the rotational axis of the Earth as well as in the geographic location of the poles and that these shifts create cataclysmic floods and earthquakes.

Walter knew he would not be able to make a living writing for coin publications, so under the direction of Dr. Sheldon, he completed a premedical course at Columbia University. He applied to literally every medical school in the USA but was rejected by all of them. It is possible that someone in a university admissions office got wind of his tendencies and spread the word around, or it might be that his grades were not the straight As which a medical school might have been expecting, given his remarkable test scores.

He applied to graduate school programs in other fields, eventually being accepted by UC Berkeley in September of 1960 to do graduate work in sociology. He felt that his double 800 scores in the GRE and his Miller Analogies score in the middle 90's were more a factor in his acceptance than his mediocre grades. His master's thesis was *The Changing Social Status of the Musician*.

Since my father never worked on only one thing, while he was at graduate school he edited the Metropolitan Numismatic Journal for the Metropolitan Coin Company from 1961 to 1965. By this time, not only was my father a renowned coin expert but a scholar of repute on many different subjects. He was fluent in seven languages: French, German, Italian, Spanish, and the three Biblical languages. He was a lightning calculator, which he would demonstrate as a party trick. He was an excellent pianist, organist, and accompanist, as well as an expert on medieval and baroque music.

Among his enormous written catalogue of works, one can find the slightly more embarrassing inclusions of monographs on dirty limericks as well as his favorite fortune cookies. He also wrote prolifically on the shameful subject of pederasty from the perspective that it was the natural form of homosexuality, arguing for its widespread acceptance. Later in life, his writings and passionate arguments on this subject would help the judge decide his fate.

On a more absurd note, Walter believed firmly in the notion of reincarnation and claimed knowledge of his past lives in ancient Greece and Atlantis. These traits made him very attractive to my mother, who found as close to a soulmate in him as it was possible for her to find in a man.

But the course of true love never did run smooth.

—Lysander, *A Midsummer Night's Dream*

Armchair Psychology

My father's story is a tragedy.

Walter Breen grew up without the father he loved, with a mother who continually hurt him. His mother had been completely rejected by his father, as had he, to his childish way of thinking, and this became the model for his life. Men and boys were sought after and desired, and any attention from men was a victory. He regarded women as being universally superfluous, vain, intellectually inferior, and cruel.

He suffered atrocious physical abuse as well as emotional abuse from women, from his mother and the nuns in the orphanage. This might explain how he tolerated Marion for so long. She created a familiar emotional atmosphere of power and control, but she did not actually hit him, so he was able to maintain a degree of autonomy. She also never rejected him in the way his own mother had. Nevertheless, he viewed himself as the victim of every woman who was in his social sphere in any way, including me.

Considering how terrible his hygiene, attire, diet, and smell were when I knew him, I am certain that those factors would have been a red flag to employers as well as to acquaintances who declined to socialize with him. Since my father had known so few men throughout his life, they were a mystery to him. He desperately needed male attention and was only able to acquire it as a child through inappropriate sexual contact with a priest, a male authority he should have been able to trust. Sex for him *was* love, and to him, it was something women could never understand because of their inexplicable and unreasonable need for commitment.

In stark contrast to his obvious emotional and personal deficits, his intelligence and other gifts set him apart. To vulnerable people isolated by their intelligence he appeared to be a gift from God, but he was actually their worst nightmare, a thing that went bump in the night.

Walter was a stupendously intelligent polymath with many specialties and areas of remarkable ability, yet he was brain-damaged and observably mentally impaired to anyone who knew him. His paranoid schizophrenia, coupled with his high intelligence, caused him to consider his own ideas to be gospel truth no matter how absurd, dangerous, or amoral they were.

My father was well aware of the laws against molesting children. He was also aware that sometimes the children he molested would cry out in terror, and he would silence us through threats of various kinds. He felt, like any animal trainer, that our responses could be changed over time and acclimatized to anything he desired. He was certain that the orgasms he intended to produce in us would change our minds about what he was doing, especially since he regarded all ob-jections to his sexual desires to be the result of puritanical anti-sex brainwashing. Having rationalized his actions, he did not hesitate to utilize drugs that lowered his victim's inhibitions and helped him realize his objectives.

By the time he had become involved with my mother, he had been molesting children and young teens for decades. He was settled in what he wanted to do and what he believed about it. He found a perfect partner in crime with my mother, who had no objection to having sex with children herself.

By the standards of his day, my father was mentally ill—sick enough to be committed involuntarily to a mental hospital. He was released not when he was cured, but when his military benefits ran out. All paranoid schizophrenia involves a fixed system of delusions, beliefs impervious to outside or contradictory information, and his delusions about his victims allowed him to continue committing sex crimes unimpeded by guilt or shame.

An extended quote from an article written by Walter's friend Jack Collins, "In Remembrance of Walter Breen", that was published in *The Rare Coin Review* of Bowers and Merena Galleries, Inc. in the summer of 1994 may be illuminating.

Even then, Breen was considered an anomaly, with a phenomenal memory that could digest an entire page of a Manhattan telephone directory in just a few minutes, and then moments later recite upon command any address and telephone number when prompted with the resident's name.

In 1960, I attended a California State Numismatic Association convention at the Ulysses S. Grant Hotel, in San Diego… Someone pointed out a tall, bushy-haired individual wearing a dirty white antique automobile car duster, carrying a small paper bag with a large grease stain on the side… I watched him as he turned and left the bourse room and walked to the center of the hotel lobby, where he sat down on a round tufted velvet banquette, opened his paper bag, extracted a large pork chop, and ate it in a flash, leaving a few scattered fragments in his beard.

Sometime about that same year, I heard from a mutual friend, Jon Hanson, that Walter had come into Beverly Hills to examine auction lots at the Coin Gallery, operated by Abner Kreisberg and Jerry Cohen, on Beverly Drive. They had just renovated the store, including the installation of an expensive new red carpet. Jon pulled up in front to let Walter out of the car while he looked for a parking space. It was during a pouring rainstorm, and Walter landed with both feet in a river of rainwater at the curb. He ran into the store, sat down on a small stool, took off both sandals and socks, and then proceeded to wring the wet socks out on the new red carpet.

Kreisberg, Cohen, and their secretary, Harriet, all watched aghast with their mouths and eyes open wide in complete disbelief. Walter, as many know who knew him well, was totally oblivious of the world around him. He had no concept of what he was doing, only that he had to get those wet socks off.

Chapter 3

My Parents Meet, and Make Some Odd Agreements (1962–1964)

WEDDING OF MINDS

Walter Breen, 27-year-old Columbia University bachelor, dangles his Phi Beta Kappa key importantly these days, and sounds off on genetics.

He has organized a "Lonely Genius Club" for the purpose of producing future generations of geniuses. Breen has 28 male intellectuals in his club. They are seeking 28 female geniuses. The ultimate aim is matrimony. Breen says that when two true geniuses marry they usually produce a little genius. Without this quality in both parents, he avers, the chances of getting a genius in the family are about one in a million. Breen himself is said to be one of about 200 persons in the United States with an IQ close to 200.

Breen's theory sounds okay. But he is a bachelor, and we fear he knows but little about the practical side of matrimony. How long would two geniuses last across the breakfast table? When we run across two geniuses at the same time, they are always at each other's throats. The male ego wouldn't fare very well in such an intellectual atmosphere. We suspect it wouldn't be very long before Reno had a genius club of its own.

The Times Record (Troy, New York) Nov. 26, 1957, Page 10

In 1957 my father came up with the notion of breeding little geniuses, which somehow justified an article published in *The Times Record*. This article makes an important point, one that I doubt my father ever thought all the way through: How well would two geniuses get along over time? Worse, how would they fare caring for children who might not live up to their grandiose expectations?

"And wait just one cotton-picking minute," the reasonable skeptics in the audience might say. "Walter Breen is gay, and he hates his mother. What on

Earth is he doing looking for a *wife*?" Well, there is only one way to reliably acquire children who can be relied upon to not go to the police when you molest them. Not only that, but if you manage to find a sufficiently intelligent woman, perhaps the children will be smart enough to be interesting the rest of the time.

My father was not a heartless Humbert Humbert like the protagonist in *Lolita*, interested in my mother only for her breeding potential. When he met my mother, he had four other girlfriends. In addition, unlike Humbert Humbert, my father made no secret whatsoever of his desires, even going so far as to write a book about them.

Although his primary sexual interest was children, my father would gladly accept sexual contact with anything with a pulse. He would have furiously denied the label "bisexual", as do many gays who sleep with opposite sex partners. In the gay community, "bisexual" either means gay and in denial, or it means indecisive and untrustworthy. Gay men, even those who sometimes still have sex with women, often talk about how disgusting women are. For a woman to remain sexually involved with a gay man takes a certain amount of masochism, even for the most vehement of feminists.

My mother was an established writer long before she met my father. She was best known for *Falcons of Narabedla* (1957), *The Door Through Space* (1961), *Seven from the Stars* (1961), and *The Colors of Space* (1963). *Sword of Aldones* was nominated for a Hugo in 1963.

In 1963, my father was writing for *Coin World*, including his famous coin column *Bristles and Barbs*. "Bristles" referred to his ubiquitous beard, and "Barbs" referred to the insults he slung at dishonest coin dealers. *Bristles and Barbs* was transferred over to *Coins* magazine in July of 1966, where it ran until March of 1985, with an eleven-month absence in 1981. Between 1963 and 1972, my father's friend and colleague Lester Merkin hired him part time to write his coin catalogues. With his colleague Don Taxay, he formed the *Institute of Numismatic Authenticators*, dormant since the founding of *ANACS* or the *American Numismatic Association Certification Service*. He also tried to set up a curriculum of numismatics at Roosevelt University, but he was not able to obtain the necessary funding.

My father initially met my mother through their mutual correspondence in a science-fiction fanzine, then personal correspondence for the next three years. They were attracted to each other's writing, which is normal for high-IQ types. It is often the easiest way for high-IQ types to come up with a useful assessment of another person's intelligence.

When Marion and Walter finally met in person at a science-fiction convention in early 1963, the first thing they did was to fall into bed together, promptly begetting my brother Patrick. If they had not met that way, it is almost certain they would have met through Mensa. They were among the first Mensa members in the USA, both appearing in the 1962 edition of *The Mensa Register* with entries on facing pages, almost as if they were destined to meet.

Here are their entries, edited lightly for clarity.

Mrs. Marion Z. Bradley, Box 158, Rochester, TX

Deist but not church member. Novelist/student (languages, education). Fantasy Amateur Press Association; Circus Fans of America; Fellowship of the Ring; IPSO (amateur press society.) The literature of homosexuality and variance; Spanish language. Opera; fantasy and science-fiction fandom; Tolkien fandom; circuses; amateur publishing; education of gifted children; legal reform of laws relating to censorship; occultism of the magical, cabalistic school.

Lowbrowed highbrow; pulp novelist desiring to write quality work some day; frustrated musician. Member number 182

Mr. Walter Henry Breen, 2404 Grove St. Berkeley California, USA Unaffiliated. Born in Texas 1930. Graduate student (sociology) (Univ. of Calif) /writer/numismatist. AB. M (President) Foundation for the Gifted Child Inc: Phi Beta Kappa; AAAS; Synthesists, Phalanx (Baltimore) Intl. Publishers Speculative Organization; Golden Gate Futurians; Fanoclasts; Elves', Gnomes', & Little Men's Science Fiction, Chowder and Marching Society.; Fellowship of the Ring, numerous SF clubs and amateur press associations. Classical music; other fine arts, science, especially relating to human behavior, sexology; SF; literature; numismatics (especially US) comparative religion, mathematics, especially number theory, aspects of medicine, psychiatry, gifted children, constitutional psychology, handwriting analysis, semantics, the "best" world, etc.

Busy bohemian with a Bushy Barbarian Beard. Will try almost anything once.

Member number 190

As I mentioned previously, my father's IQ was tested at 144. My mother never mentioned her IQ to me, but it obviously tested high enough for her to get into Mensa, which means that it was at least 132. My father did not remain in Mensa long after having met my mother because the politics and infighting drove him crazy. I never heard my mother say a good thing about Mensa. She was ferociously anti-elitist and objected to Mensa for its elitism despite her previous membership; an ironic objection for someone who sought a high-IQ husband there. After all, one cannot buy membership, inherit membership, or gain entry through who you know, as the only way to get into Mensa is to pass a qualifying test.

I suppose that once my mother and father had found each other in Mensa, neither of them needed it any more.

Why is there so much infighting in Mensa and in the high-IQ community? When you are looking for your tribe, their opinions matter to you. When people in the high-IQ community say stupid things, it is much more troublesome than it is when "normals" do so. Often, people in Mensa find so much stupidity there that they seek membership in the higher echelons of the high-intelligence community such as Triple 9, Prometheus, or Mega, hoping that more raw intellect will eliminate all the undesirable traits of the people you meet. Of course, this is not true. When it comes to intelligence, the higher you go, the worse the infighting and the weirder the people become, even if some of them are truly remarkable.

How can a high-IQ person be stupid? One reason is a cognitive bias common to high-IQ people: the notion that because one is intelligent, everything one says and thinks is intelligent despite one's ignorance on any topic one has not studied. My opinions on math or physics are totally meaningless because of my lack of knowledge about them. However, many high-IQ people cannot admit their ignorance even if it is glaringly obvious to others.

The other reason is that many disciplines require a great deal of, well, discipline. Where my father developed astonishing pianistic skills in very little time, and his photographic memory was phenomenal, abilities like this are more commonly found in an idiot savant than in the average high-IQ person. Developing a skillset or a knowledge base requires time, time, time, and a lot of study, and there are no shortcuts. Even if one has unusual sensitivity and perceptive skills, a tremendous amount of knowledge and practice goes into being an authority on any field. Simply having a high IQ guarantees nothing but itself.

Sometimes a high-IQ person who does one thing very well will assume that the other things they can do must be equally amazing. I know a person in Prometheus who translates novels between four languages, but his poetry is repulsive, and a person in Triple 9 who writes boring music. Of course, it is unusual to be able to write music at all, let alone good music, and ditto for poetry. After all, we can always improve if we do not need to view ourselves as perfect the first time out. My mother used to say that one's first million words are crap so one might as well get them out of the way.

I have met wonderful, brilliant people in all the high-IQ societies, as well as a few dangerous, scary individuals since high-IQ is not limited to those of good character. And yes, often the dangerous, scary ones *were* the wonderful, brilliant ones. I really doubt that my mother had any idea that she would be finding not only a polymath genius, but a dedicated sexual criminal who would systematically deceive and betray her even though she cooperated with every aspect of his life and his philosophy. I doubt my father thought the loving woman he found would be psychotic and violent, and would tyrannize him for their entire life together.

Some high-IQ types do not have any accomplishments at all, and some have many. There is far more to creativity and good conversation than intelligence, even if there is a much better chance in Mensa of meeting the kind of people you would not find in a supermarket. It makes sense both to seek a tribe in Mensa if you think you need it, and then to abandon it when it ceases to meet your needs. Depending on your abilities, Mensa can be fun, or it can be frustrating. Naturally, the things one finds in Mensa can be found in all counterculture societies since the one thing all counterculture societies have in common is their discomfort with normal life.

My mother and father made quite a spectacle together. My mother and father both took pains to look like stereotypical Berkeley hippies: my father would wear Birkenstock sandals, flower-printed shorts. and tie-dyed shirts. He also wore dashikis, or African-printed shirts. The "formality" of an event made no difference to him. He despised suits and ties. She wore baggy clothing to hide her weight and strove to look as though she was completely unaware of her appearance. She never wore makeup and would have been outraged if someone suggested it.

When my mother met my father, she was still married to her first husband Brad. To her great annoyance, he refused to give my mother a divorce. Back in those days, divorce required the consent of the husband. Like a proper feminist, my mother forced the issue. She told Brad she was pregnant, knowing that he absolutely refused to support another child. She said that if he denied her a divorce she would drag him into court, swear the child was his, and force him to support it. Brad gave in and gave her the divorce she wanted, and even had the decency to die just a few years later.

They were deeply in love and were so in tune with one another that they would buy each other the same books and musical recordings as presents as they followed their wealth of common interests together. They loved to play "Name That Tune" while listening to the classical music stations KKHI and KDFC, which were always on. He played the piano, and she sang. They talked for hours about absolutely everything. They had read many of the same books and loved many of the same authors. Both knew mythology, history, and the classics well. He wrote, and she wrote. He proofread her work and offered editorial suggestions. These wonderful aspects of their relationship continued for decades.

Chapter 4

The World's Weirdest Engagement
(1963)

Mother stands for comfort.
Mother will hide the murderer.
Mother hides the madman.
Mother will stay mum.

—Kate Bush, "Mother Stands for Comfort", *Hounds of Love* (1985)

When my mother and father were preparing to move in together and get married, there was a scandal in the science fiction community about my father's sexual abuse of approximately ten children. These were not idle rumors but overt, public acts with many witnesses. Some people were concerned that my mother would abandon him if she found out, and some hated him and wanted him gone while still others hoped she would civilize him.

My mother chose to defend him, both at the time and in her sworn testimony in 1999. She knew exactly what he was doing.

I have mentioned fanzines before: newsletters written and mailed within the science fiction community. Fanzines were the primary way that people in science fiction communicated with one another other back when there was no Internet. One of these included a long article about my father's conduct, written by Bill Donaho circa 1963.

I have included this article below, edited to remove in-jokes, repetition, and some things that would have only made sense to the people directly involved. Be warned that it is sexually graphic and more than a little upsetting to read; the original text appears in its entirety in Appendix A.

Should Walter Breen be banned from fandom and Worldcon (Pacificon II) because he is harming children? Author Bill Donaho asked a wide group of friends for advice. Controversy followed: some people dispute banning anyone, some people feared liability if Walter committed a crime, and at the end, he was banned from attending one Worldcon convention: Pacificon II.

From the first day Walter arrived in Berkeley, he was known to be a homosexual, even before his own words, chosen appearance, and conduct confirmed it. Nobody cared about that at all: consenting adults and all that. Because fandom is a culture of misfits, abnormal, even dangerous behavior is accepted.

Walter's conduct was so bad that it called the culture of sexual tolerance into question: many people thought "consenting adults" should not include toddlers. Many wanted something done about it, but nobody wanted to call the cops.

A few people hated Walter, even those who had many other homosexual friends. They thought Walter was different. A few refused to associate with him, even threatening violence if he came too close.

Walter's victims included a girl, age 3, a boy, age 13, another boy, [later referred to as Glenn] age 10, and a boy known as G2, age 7, as well as several other nameless teenagers, both male and female.

At a fan meeting, a mother found her 13 year old son in bed with Walter, who had his arm around him as they watched TV. After that, she instructed the children to barricade themselves behind furniture in their room if Walter ever came back. She wanted him banned from her house, but other people didn't want to ban anyone.

Walter molested the 3 year old girl in public, more than once. She had been trained to strip when she saw him. He would "rub her down." He also used a pencil, rubbing the eraser back and forth in the general area of the vagina, not quite masturbating her. People, including her parents, objected. Nobody thought she was hurt, because of her age.

Later, Walter acted surprised that people were upset about this, and said "But why didn't somebody say something! I wouldn't have dreamed of doing it if I'd thought someone objected." There were fears that Walter would continue this as the little girl got older. Eventually, her mother objected.

Walter gave a bicycle to a boy named Glenn that he was having an active sexual relationship with. He quipped "One gear for each position." Once he and Glenn had been sitting on a couch, and a fan walked in on them, surprising Walter into dashing into the bathroom, clutching his open fly. At least three other fans reported glowing descriptions of sex with Glenn given to them by Walter.

"Glenn and I began with mutual masturbation and worked up to 69. Then Glenn wanted to try buggering me, so I let him. Then I buggered him."

People found this more shocking than amusing. However, nobody liked Glenn, and thought "Who cares what happens to the little bastard?" Others felt that Glenn was not likable because he had a difficult home life and that Walter was not good for him.

Walter was also seeing a 7 year old boy: G2. His mother's boyfriend Danny warned Walter away, but the kid would sneak off to see Walter, to his delight. Walter said Danny had "betrayed" him, even though they had never been friends. Danny thought "If anyone who has a kid lets Walter even speak to it, he should have his head examined." Most people agreed with this.

Walter claims "I never even *seduce* a teen-ager. The kids *always* seduce me!" Maybe. But one teenaged boy, who left after the first day of a week-long visit with Walter said "Walter *may* always be the one who's seduced, but he makes it goddamn clear he's available."

Walter's recent behavior has been getting many Berkeley parents not just alarmed, but semi-hysterical. If Walter is in the same room with a boy, he never takes his eyes off him. If the kid goes to the bathroom, Walter gets up and follows him. He answered complaints with his same "If I had the least idea anyone objected" story. Knowing Walter, I can believe that he was oblivious to the signs of strong objections.

People hoped that his impending marriage to Marion Zimmer Bradley would change him, thinking: "Maybe she'll reform him. He may have had mistresses before, but he's never been fully committed to a woman. Besides, maybe she'll keep him so busy he won't have time for other outlets." Most of us think this is unrealistic: change comes only when it is wanted, and Walter is extremely satisfied with himself as he is. The other position is "It'll only be a short time until she comes to her senses. Obviously she knows about Walter and accepts him, but let's see what happens to tolerance-in-theory when he starts making passes at her 12-year-old son."

Many people think Walter is dangerous to children: he has stated himself that he has had sexual relations with children of both sexes and multiple ages. Others are not sure if Walter is actually hurting the kids. Also, while Walter can evidently be most tender and loving when he wants to, he has behaved brutally to some of his lovers after he has tired of them. He has stated that he has had sex with young teen-age girls without using contraceptives.

So, Walter is dangerous to children. Everyone should have a certain amount of social responsibility, and I would be a coward if I did not at least TRY to do something about the danger Walter represents. Some people want to have Walter committed. I want to surgically separate Walter from fandom.

How could a strong, independent woman like my mother, a woman who had been raped by her own father, ever tolerate being with a child molester like Walter Breen? Some people would like to believe that she did not know about her husband's behavior, but her sworn testimony makes it very clear that she did know about it. She simply didn't object. Here is a portion of my mother's deposition:

MR. DOLAN: Did you ever publicly defend Walter in terms of his not being a pedophile?

MZB. Yes, I did.

MR. DOLAN: And was that during the "Boondoggle"?

MZB. Yes.

MR. DOLAN: Can you tell me why you would publicly state that Walter was not a pedophile when you knew that he had been having sex with a minor child?

MZB. Because, as I said, [Glenn] did not impress me as a minor child. He was late in his teens, and I considered him—I think he would have been old enough to be married in this state legally, so I figured what he did sexually was his own business."

And

MR. DOLAN: (Attorney). Did you know that he had a relationship with [Glenn]?

MZB. I became aware of it, yes.

MR. DOLAN: When did you become aware of it?

MZB. Shortly after we were married. At that time I treated [Glenn] like one of my own children. He and my son David used to go swimming together and such.

MR. DOLAN: *And to your knowledge, how old was [Glenn] when your husband was having a sexual relationship with him?*

MZB. *I think he was about 14 or possibly 15. I'm not certain.*

MR. DOLAN: *And what did he tell you?*

MZB. *Well, he told me that he and [Glenn] were sleeping together. And I said that I had believed that was an intellectual position. He told me it was not. I was very upset.*

MR. DOLAN: *What else did Walter tell you on the subject of his relationship with [Glenn]?*

MZB. *I know that he gave him a bicycle.*

MR. DOLAN: *When did he give him the bicycle?*

MZB. *It was before I had come to live with him.*

MR. DOLAN: *Did you ever talk to the police about a sexual relationship between Walter and [Glenn]?*

MZB. *I don't remember. I know that I talked to a lawyer Walter had at the time.*

MR. DOLAN: *Can you tell me the context of your conversation, please?*

MZB. *Largely that I had heard that [mother of Glenn] had said that she had nothing to complain about in [Glenn]'s relationship with Walter. And I thought that, well, because [Glenn] would come—he had been accused of stealing milk out of refrigerators, and he would come to dinner with us, and he obviously hadn't eaten for a long time.*

MR. DOLAN: *How did you hear that [mother of Glenn] had no complaints about the sexual relationship between your husband and her minor child?*

MZB. *She told me.*

MR. DOLAN: *And when did you speak with her about this?*

MZB. *It was, as I say, shortly after we were married.*

MR. DOLAN: *And what was the nature of the conversation with [mother of Glenn] regarding your husband's sexual interactions with her son?*

MZB. *I don't remember that we spent any time on it. Mostly she was telling me that I was not a good writer, that I was a commercial hack, and that she was a great and artistic poet. I told her that at least I could feed my kids on what I did, and that if she had kids to feed, she'd probably do it too or—that is, write commercially.*

MR. DOLAN: What about the subject matter between the sex of your husband and her son did you discuss that led you to believe that she had no complaint about this sexual relationship?

MZB. I think what she said almost exactly was "I find nothing to complain about," but I can't remember exactly. That was, I think, about 25 or 30 years ago."

There you have it. She knew. She had always known.

While it might be admirable that Marion fed Glenn and allowed him to stay in their home, it was outrageous that she went along with my father sodomizing him. It was equally outrageous that the biggest concern she reveals in her testimony was the offense she took at being called a commercial hack, not the fact that Glenn's mother was not properly caring for her son or that her husband was molesting the young man.

Marion and Walter were married on Valentine's Day in 1964. Like good flower children, they bought my mother's ring at the dime store. I never saw either one of them ever wear a wedding ring. They both habitually mocked and derided marriage, and called it "an outdated screwing license." There was never any point in their relationship where Walter intended any form of sexual exclusivity for either of them, although I know Marion would have preferred it.

Chapter 5

My Father's Grand Vision
(1962–1964)

I have been assured by a very knowing American of my acquaintance in London, that a young healthy child well nursed, is, at a year old, a most delicious nourishing and wholesome food, whether stewed, roasted, baked, or boiled...

—Jonathan Swift, *A Modest Proposal*

My father's Grand Vision was only a little less soulless and bizarre than the ideas found in Swift's famous satire. The difference is that Walter was entirely serious. My father believed that the best, most intimate way to express love to children—to everyone—was to have sex with them. In his mind, sex was love, and any effort to separate love and sex was a consequence of limited thinking. Since love is best expressed by sex, everyone should have sex with all people all the time. He believed that the practice of unlimited sex would bring about a utopia that would end all the ills of human society.

But sex is not love, it is not parenting, and it is not nurturing. It is also not friendship, it often does not reflect any actual connection between two people, and it can be experienced in very different ways by the people involved.

Unlimited sex does not make society whole. It makes a home an empty place because the one thing sex *does* do is to catalyze a relationship into "consider pair-bond", "sex only" or "leave now." In the case of a child—who cannot choose—none of those three possibilities is workable, healthy, or safe; it means that the child is exposed to an adult situation which they can neither control nor avoid and where the adult might choose any of the top three the child can only choose from two: cope somehow or protest.

There are many reasons children elect to cope with abuse instead of protesting it. They may be escaping from something worse, or legitimately fear the punishment which will come if they defy an adult by protesting.

My father and mother both detested gender roles, and anything overtly masculine or feminine was ruthlessly mocked. No opening doors for women, no check-paying, no dating, and no gallantry. No masculine dress, no short hair, no sports, no fighting, no building things, no creating businesses, no military anything, and especially no competition or success. Anger was unacceptable in men. Men were expected to be cheerleaders for women. Male success was only tolerated if it did not involve competition.

Women could lead, achieve, and succeed. Women could pay bills, write books, run businesses, make things, build things, and even compete. Women could be angry and men had to absorb it without complaining. No dresses, heels, or makeup, no long hair, and no looking good for men. Neither women nor men were expected do anything to control their weight, and any man who objected to a fat woman was a soulless cretin.

Why do people object to fat in themselves and in their partners? Excess fat is indicative of age and ill health, which are not good things to choose in a potential partner. Excess fat in our culture is also very common for women who have been sexually abused and have chosen an easy way to keep men safely at a distance.

Theoretically, men and women would choose each other for their lofty thoughts. Instead, men would merely have to pretend to go along with all the dumb feminist ideas, put up with the fat and the unattractive clothes, and they could get laid as much as they want. There is no need for the honorable intentions and self-control that a traditional society might expect of them.

Heck, a man can have five or six women at once if he learns how to play the polyamory game. Psychologize the woman you want, and the extra women you also want, about how humans are not biologically intended for monogamy. Frame jealousy as "immaturity", and women will comply with multiple sexual partners rather than be abandoned or shamed. Many Berkeley women will even pay the bills in a situation like this.

I doubt my father anticipated the former situation, but if it led to more sex, it was still good.

Getting rid of gender roles amounts to getting rid of adulthood. The only state in which girls and boys are very similar is in utero, and the older they become, the more different they become. We cannot "socialize" these differences away, but as many of us know to our sorrow, we can be shamed out of being who and what we are.

In many cases, the idiotic behavior of adolescents is expected and tolerated. They can be persuaded to do stupid things by adults and forgiven afterward because their brains are not finished growing. How does one recognize an adolescent? A body which is maturing but which is not yet mature. We do not expect the same level of decision making and maturity from an adolescent as we do from an adult.

What is the real implication of being an adult man or woman? A potential or actual pair bond and a responsibility to others, especially to children. There is no room at all for promiscuous sex in an adult man or woman. It is irresponsible to the children who need their parents to not be idiots and to the grandchildren who need their parents to not be destroyed by their grandparents.

Denying gender roles denies adulthood and adult responsibilities. It creates an extended adolescence and encourages ongoing stupid decisions.

Of course when gender roles are rejected, they invariably get reversed. When women reject femininity, they usually become a bad caricature of a man. Men who reject masculinity end up as bad caricatures of women. Why is this? When a woman declines to dress like a woman, she still must wear clothing of some sort. Either she will end up looking like a poster child for Goodwill, or she will be dressing like a man.

The bottom line is that the women end up hyper-responsible, and the men end up useless.

What women do not understand is that where they make relationship decisions based on their oxytocin levels, men ordinarily think hard about relationships and make plans and decisions which are not emotionally based. Worst of all, men lie to women that they do not take seriously as long-term partners. Why? Because telling women the truth usually results in screaming fights and ends sexual access. Men know they can make women believe them. Men even know that they are often smarter than women, and they also know their sexual access depends on never letting a woman know anything about that. They know that women would not forgive them for making the choices they do.

Seriously, what would a man say? "I decided that I would sleep with you and those other five women because I wanted sex and you went along with it. None of you really strikes me as the one I really want. So while I'm waiting for Miss Right, you all can be Miss Right Now, and I will recite whatever psychobabble that will get you to let me keep having sex with all of you." Naturally, not every Berkeley guy is like that—not even most of them—but in a social milieu where a man does not get to be a man, his priorities are going to be different, and his feelings toward women may differ from the norm.

Personally, I think it is disgusting to rob men of masculinity or women of femininity. It would be equally pointless to try to train your cat to be a dog, or vice versa. Sure, men and women can be compelled to act in stupid ways to survive in that social setting, but nothing on earth will create happiness in doing so.

And this is something I have seen again and again: women who are "strong" or "dominant" are invariably angry that their men aren't stronger while they emotionally pound them into the ground every time they show a hint of a spine.

According to my father, all sexual limitations or "hangups" were solely the result of Christian indoctrination. The Church, my father explained, was conspiring to control sexual expression as a way of increasing its own power at the expense of humanity. Imposing sexual guilt and shame would keep Christians weak and helpless. He thought that having guilt and shame about sex was the most terrible thing which could possibly befall a human being. Naturally, unlimited sex would end all sex-based guilt and shame, thus saving humanity from this terrible evil.

Guilt and shame about sex exist for very good reasons. Sex can be literally life and death in many ways. Girls can get pregnant young, as we know from child marriages in other nations. Girls can die in childbirth, or if they are given abortions, they might understand that their child is now dead—a devastating load to carry. Girls and boys can both catch and transmit venereal disease if an adult inflicts such a thing on them; some venereal diseases are asymptomatic for years.

Humor me for a moment and entertain the notion that the much-derided notion of a virgin bride is valuable not because someone is shaking a finger at her but because a virgin will not be carrying a venereal disease which might create death, or a child which might belong to another man. Most importantly, a girl who is allowed to remain a virgin will not have the hideous emotional problems which come from being raped or sexualized too early. After all, since the best indicator of future behavior is past behavior, if a girl has been sexualized before she is married, she might even choose promiscuity, which means ongoing risk of disease, pregnancy, and even more emotional trouble.

My father regarded only his own conception of Christianity as correct. He thought Jesus was a gay pedophile sexually involved with a young, teenaged John, the Beloved Disciple. He spent a lifetime studying the Bible and Biblical languages trying to "prove" this unfortunate notion. Christianity as commonly taught was an obstacle to his goal of universal love, so he expected us all to both deny Christianity and ridicule it in others, and to help other people understand how wrong it was. If we could drive another person out of faith, it was a huge win for him because then he could step into the breach and present orgasms as an alternative to faith.

Anyone who opposed my father's Grand Vision was a Puritanical prude, motivated not by virtue but by a wish to have religion and bureaucracy dominating human existence. Prudishness, he felt, was the evil result of religion, standing in the way of universal love. To him, a prude was the lowest form of life.

My father disapproved of any kind of boundaries between people at all, regarding them as an impediment to universal love. He observed nudity at home and expected everyone else to do so too. When he answered the door, he would either be naked or wearing nothing but a towel.

My father regarded certain forms of clothing as oppressive. He refused to wear socks or underwear because they limited his body's freedom of motion and delayed the speed of dressing and undressing. He felt it was bad enough to have to wear pants, let alone having to wear underpants. His dream was a world where people would be nude at home, on the subway, and in the grocery store, and where they felt free to have sex anywhere at all.

Ordinary people learn to keep clothes on because it is safer to be very selective about our nakedness. We are the most vulnerable when naked.

Furthermore, my father was intent that all bodily functions should also be stripped of shame. He absolutely refused to close the bathroom door when he used the toilet, and if he was keeping company with a male human, he expected them to urinate together. If you were having a conversation with him, he would follow you to the bathroom or expect you to follow him. After all, going to the bathroom is natural, and he insisted that people should not have hangups about such a natural function.

He would laugh, kindly, if anyone expressed shame or unwillingness about his expectations. We could be around him in clothes if we could tolerate his air of amused, superior condescension. If people did not want to go naked, that was their hangup, and it was up to him to set them straight and help them learn the error of their ways. The message was clear: His way of doing things was right, and nothing else would be accepted.

My father regarded homosexuality as the natural state of men and something which could be enjoyed by anyone open minded enough to try it. He thought that the only reason anyone ever became straight was the pressures of religion and society. At no time did my father ever regard heterosexuality as being real: He believed all males who thought they were straight were merely "hung up" and "in denial." He thought that the moment they were exposed to sex with other men, they would "embrace their natural homosexuality" and never bother with women after that.

My father felt that enough exposure to his logic, early sex, and the "right" hallucinogens would "raise the consciousness" of the poor unfortunates who did not agree with him. He thought it was vital to rid people of their sexual hangups as young as possible since it was much easier to influence the thinking of a child than an adult.

My father believed that early sexual experience would create gay children by helping them get in touch with their "natural homosexuality." He was aware that people imprint on their earliest sexual experiences, and he took advantage of this. He often said that boys had to have experience with a man before they were old enough to be "ruined" by sexual attraction to a girl. He felt that having sex with boys early would help them embrace their natural homosexuality and give them strength to resist the societal pressure to become straight.

He had no concept whatsoever that molesting children hurt them. Having sex with a child, to him, was not a crime with terrible consequences including flashbacks, massive dysfunction in life, and suicide attempts. Instead, what everyone else called "child molesting" was his way of creating the wonderful life which would naturally result from the universal love created by having sex with everyone. If anyone dared to challenge this belief, he would furiously deny it. Much later, when his victims dared to oppose him, he decided that they were either mentally unfit or that they had been brainwashed by "The Establishment."

A child marriage does not suffer from the fear of impermanence because the child will never be able to leave her husband to seek a love match of her own. Still, the child will remain a child, always under the authority of her husband, always expected to submit and to obey. In our culture, it can be imagined how such a relationship would stunt the growth of a child, who will always remain a child. Is it fair to a child to keep them dependent on another adult and require not only filial obedience but sexual servitude? It is not love, but slavery. It is very good for the men who have slaves, but it is not good at all for the children.

Perhaps a closer parallel for our purposes is the practice of Bacha Bazi, or "Boy Play", a kind of child-slavery most commonly found in Afghanistan. These boys are dressed up as women and expected to perform as erotic dancers. They are also expected to be available for sexual services. Again, they are bought and sold. Should we conclude that because this has been done in Afghanistan since time immemorial, it is somehow acceptable? There was a case in 2015 of an

American military person who was disciplined for intervening when he heard a boy screaming in pain because he was being sodomized. At no point is sodomy ever going to feel "good" to a child. For some of us, it is something we can be forced to tolerate. But it exists for the "good" of the adult, never for the child. Somehow, the notion of "Greek Love" seems a little less romantic when it is put into its proper context of a screaming, crying boy with a bleeding backside.

KABUL, Afghanistan—In his last phone call home, Lance Cpl. Gregory Buckley Jr. told his father what was troubling him: From his bunk in southern Afghanistan, he could hear Afghan police officers sexually abusing boys they had brought to the base.

"At night we can hear them screaming, but we're not allowed to do anything about it," the Marine's father, Gregory Buckley Sr., recalled his son telling him before he was shot to death at the base in 2012. He urged his son to tell his superiors. "My son said that his officers told him to look the other way because it's their culture."

Rampant sexual abuse of children has long been a problem in Afghanistan, particularly among armed commanders who dominate much of the rural landscape and can bully the population. The practice is called bacha bazi, literally "boy play," and American soldiers and Marines have been instructed not to intervene—in some cases, not even when their Afghan allies have abused boys on military bases, according to interviews and court records.

The policy has endured as American forces have recruited and organized Afghan militias to help hold territory against the Taliban. But soldiers and Marines have been increasingly troubled that instead of weeding out pedophiles, the American military was arming them in some cases and placing them as the commanders of villages—and doing little when they began abusing children.

—*New York Times*, Joseph Goldstein, Sept. 20, 2015

Everyone in our family was expected to join with my father in the goal of "raising consciousness." We were not to interfere in his goals, nor were we permitted to question him in any way, or object to what he was doing. If we did so, it proved that we were "hung up" and needed him to "raise our consciousness" so that he could correct our errors. He did not have to tell us about his Grand Vision. He had talked about it so often we knew it like the back of our hands.

He did not acknowledge any sexual taboo as being legitimate. My father spoke derisively of the prohibition on sex with children as "ageism" and insisted "that children had the right to have sex." He thought there was no purpose whatsoever to having an incest taboo and considered it a way to "limit" love between parents and children.

At times, he expressed the belief that the government was spying on him and intended to destroy him because he alone had the secret to universal love, and he alone knew that this would result in freedom for mankind—a freedom he felt certain would be opposed by the government. He felt it was love itself the cops and the government was trying to shut down, as though love was the same thing as violating children.

My father blamed women for the imposition of conventional morality on males. Women were innately worthless and never to be trusted. Women frequently failed to understand his vision, and they undermined his important work with the males in our community. One woman could wreck a man by making him abandon sex with men and abandon universal sex. Females simply could not transcend the Judeo-Christian ethic or their need to "breed", and they were not capable of understanding his level of thought.

It was only female ideas about fidelity and sexual ownership which resulted in what he considered to be the atrocious cage called marriage. A woman's sexual appeal to men could make even the most carefully constructed argument fall to ruins. Therefore, men had to learn to resist them. He counseled all the young men he was working with to disdain, discount, and avoid women as much as possible.

Naturally, only smart people agreed with him. Anyone who opposed his ideas was mentally inferior despite their accomplishments in other areas.

He expected my mother to understand that at no point would he ever be faithful to her since that was not their shared goal. He had a much more exalted purpose, and she had to live with it. She was expected to agree with him, and fortunately for him, she did.

Why would such an intelligent man with such a keen interest in science hang his hopes on such unprovable nonsense? He made a cognitive error very common to high IQ-types: Where scientists are expected to question their own beliefs and to rigorously challenge them through research, he concluded that since he was smart, any thought which walked across his mind *had* to be true. My father was a good scientist in terms of his research on coins, but in the areas of where his delusional system was functioning his conclusions were damaging and absurd.

Here is a description of my father by Donald Mader from "Before Stonewall"; Mader is one of the founders of Paidika (Journal of Paedophilia):

He would then go to the spare bedroom to return with his stash and rolling papers. If it was at all a warm night, without a stitch of clothes on he would subsequently settle in on the couch and hold forth for another six hours or so on his research on Greek Love (he was constantly revising the book for a proposed second edition); or other things such as exploration of his former lives; or the occasion when he had to defend his family and friends by making "sigils of power" with his fingers and hurling "flaming pentacles" at Lovecraftian monsters which had attacked them while they were ensconced in a hot tub in Marin County; or the time he had been overcome by a mystic trance on a visit to Glastonbury and was granted a vision of purple flames towering above the ruins and visited by the Wise Old Man. (Another acquaintance, a New York University writing instructor who in the 1960s had penned a classic of pederastic pornography under the pseudonym Colin Murchison, had also heard this tale, and always insisted the Wise Old Man was probably Breen's confused recollection of a custodian trying to extract him from the flower bed into which he had toppled backward after ingesting too much of some mind-altering substance.) You never knew quite what to expect from Walter; but one can imagine the effects such vivid accounts must have had on thirteen-year-olds.

Chapter 6

Greek Love, His and Hers
(1962–1964)

It used to be the love that dare not speak its name and now it's the love that won't shut the f*** up.

—Bette Midler

My mother and father had begun a longstanding professional collaboration of the sort that many writers could only dream of: In 1964, my father published his book *Greek Love* under the pseudonym "J. Z. Eglinton" and dedicated it to "My beloved wife." In 1965, my mother published her companion article "Feminine Equivalents of Greek Love in Modern Fiction" in my father's short-lived *International Journal of Greek Love.* I am including full copies of a review of *Greek Love* by one of my father's contemporaries, my own thoughts on a brief excerpt from my mother's article, and excerpts from a few pro-pedophile writers so you can see the commonalities between them.

My mother's ideas are as repulsive as my father's. However, they shed light on her own conduct and her pervasive defense of my father. In case anyone doubts my mother's participation in my father's book, this is from her court testimony in 1999:

MZB: He wrote a book called "Greek Love" under the name of John Eglington.

MR. DOLAN: And you reviewed some of the manuscripts of that book before it was published?

MZB: Yes, I did.

MR. DOLAN: And did you contribute by doing proofreading?

MZB: I did proofreading, yes.

MR. DOLAN: Did you do some editorial work on that book?

MZB: I attempted to, but I found out afterward that everything I had done had been thrown out by the publisher, Robert Bashno [sic].

Robert Bashlow, not Bashno, is one of the Superkids referenced in Chapter 2.

Greek Love was a treatise on the history of homosexuality and pederasty. It strongly criticized the "adultification" of homosexuality and maintained that historically, homosexual relationships have always been between an adult and a much younger boy. It even asserted that sexual contact with children would somehow prevent juvenile delinquency.

Advocacy for pedophilia is not nearly as rare as it should be. There are a dismaying number of pro-pedophile gay and lesbian societies. Wikipedia lists about fifty, though many are defunct, and I hope many more will be defunct soon. The most famous of these in the USA is NAMBLA, which featured the infamous slogan: "Sex before eight, or it's too late."

Pedophilia is wrongly categorized by proponents as the "emancipation" of children. Many gay activists support pedophilia by claiming that the children have "rights" to have sex and that the "rights" of adults to have sex with them is simply a natural extension of sexual freedom. Put another way, as my mother said it, "Children have the right to have sex" and "Children are brainwashed into believing they do not want sex."

I have included this article about my father to illustrate that the issue of homosexuality is inextricably linked with pederasty and pedophilia according to its own supporters. It is an unpopular public topic in the gay community because its implications are more likely to result in routine denouncement of all homosexual activity than in widespread acceptance of sex with children. The requirement within the community is to keep the intergenerational aspects hidden from straights until the world is "ready" to accept this "freedom."

From: "Walter H. Breen (J. Z. Eglinton) (1928–1993)", by Donald Mader, *Before Stonewall: Activists for Gay and Lesbian Rights in Historical Context*, Vern Bullough, 2002.

Rev. Donald H. Mader (1948–) is a photographer, publisher and boylove activist, currently working as an assistant pastor. Mader is one of the founders of Paidika (Journal of Paedophilia.)

Recent scholarship has emphasized homosexualities rather than simply the term homosexual. It is startling to note that, although coming from a very specific point of view, one of the pioneering studies by an American, "Greek Love" anticipated this by at least thirty years. Walter Henry Breen (also known by his pseudonym J. Z. Eglinton) was the most important theorist of man-boy love….

Pederasty is presented as a legitimate form of homosexuality instead of a violent crime which results in physical injury and never-ending emotional consequences. Furthermore, my father is lauded as a scholar rather than called a criminal.

Breen independently affirmed, as they had, the distinction between what he termed "Greek love" (pederasty, or intergenerational homosexual relationships) and "androphile homosexuality" (eroticism between adult males). Although he himself argued that androphile homosexuality had usurped the "true" tradition of homosexuality which belonged to Greek love, viewed in a critical perspective this renewed insight opened the way in the United States for an understanding of homosexual behavior as a protean rather than a unitary phenomenon.

Pederasty is the most authentic form of homosexuality. Adult-adult homosexuality is a modern invention. This amounts to an attempt to sanitize criminal conduct.

It is one of his specialized books, Dies and Coinage, *published in 1962 by Robert Bashlow, which provides a link to our topic here. Breen and Bashlow shared more interests than numismatics: both had an erotic interest in younger males. A wealthy coin and bullion dealer who had already created one press for numismatic publications, Bashlow was persuaded to fund another press for issuing material on "sexual questions." Called the Oliver Layton Press, its first book was* Greek Love *(1964) by Breen, who for it adopted the pseudonym created for him by Bashlow, by which he was to be known in homosexual circles, J. Z. Eglinton.*

Robert Bashlow was one of my father's research subjects, or Superkids, at Columbia University. He became the publisher for *Greek Love*, no doubt introjecting his abuser and becoming the pedophile who initiated him.

It is not, however, his personal eccentricities, but his book Greek Love *for which Breen deserves notice. The 500 page volume is divided into two almost equal parts: the first is a theoretical discussion and justification for man-boy homosexual relationships; the second is a survey of the cultural history of such relationships.*

Crimes against children are the subject of rhapsodical admiration, and there is no concern for the victims whatsoever.

Breen is claiming for his Greek love, which he defines as the relation between an adult man and a younger boy (generally between ages twelve and seventeen) in which neither is exclusively homosexual—for only a man with heterosexual experience could guide the boy to a heterosexual outcome, which is the goal of Greek love. The man supplies a role model and the love (unconditional positive regard) which enables the boy's personality to develop healthily, performs a pedagogical function by teaching specific skills, and generally initiating the boy into the adult world and its complexities and responsibilities (including preparing him for eventual heterosexual relations), and within this framework shares sexual or erotic experiences with the boy, who will then apply this experience in heterosexual practice. In return, the man accepts the boy's love and admiration, and attains sexual satisfaction from their shared experience.

The utter hubris of deciding that sex is a suitable exchange for adult male mentoring is absurd. The willingness of the author to discuss it in such glowing terms makes one wonder what he has done and to whom. Place this firmly against the backdrop of one of my father's victims, screaming in agony, against this long-winded description of "love."

The major problem, he still maintains, is that these relationships are illegal; society should understand them, tolerate them, give them room to develop and flourish, and judge each relationship by its result.

The result, of course, is physical and emotional trauma. By all means, judge these "relationships" by the misery they produce.

FEMININE EQUIVALENTS OF GREEK LOVE IN MODERN FICTION

(International Journal of Greek Love, Vol. 1 No. 1, 1965, Page 48)

MARION ZIMMER BRADLEY San Francisco

ABSTRACT: Exact counterparts to male Greek love relationships are more frequently encountered in lesbian literature than in male homosexual literature from the Victorian epoch to date.... Tragic denouements in such fiction, when found at all, arise either when the older woman fears and rejects such attachments or when outsiders misunderstand them and forcibly break up the affairs, even as in actual case histories in both genders.

Mother argues that the reason that sexual relationships between girls and women are invariably disastrous is that they are interrupted and stigmatized by "society", and she believes that these relationships should be allowed to continue.

There are exceptions, but in general the pattern of Greek love between woman and girl is one of emotion rather than sensuality, involving heroine-worship, admiration, emulation.... They usually occur between a maturing girl— somewhere between nine and sixteen—and a woman of mature years. Mother- less girls, or those with inadequate maternal attention and support, appear to feel the greatest need for these attachments, usually from a lack of understanding or tenderness in their lives.

Tragedy results when a motherless child seeks love from an adult and becomes her sexual victim.

The relationship is usually as good—or as bad—as the women with whom the girl is lucky or unlucky enough to fall in love.... Tragedy, however, seems not to be inherent in such a relationship (unless ... the woman is herself corrupt), but occurs only when (1) the relationship is misunderstood and interrupted by outsiders, or (2) the older woman fears or rejects such an attachment.

I disagree wholeheartedly with my mother's conclusions. It is self-serving, vile, and corrupt in the extreme to use vulnerable children as sexual partners. It is criminal to misconstrue a child's tolerance or participation as anything other than the things children will tolerate for any semblance whatsoever of maternal love.

These "relationships" are neither motherhood, which is selfless and helps a child grow into independence, nor romantic love, which is meant to grow into a permanent bond. They twist the girl away from normal adulthood and into protracted emotional dependence.

Only in keeping the relationships non-sexual is there even a chance of creating the healing of the mother-wound which is so clearly illustrated in each of my mother's examples. Sexualizing even a substitute mother-child relationship puts intolerable adult emotional demands on a child, and sublimates all the needs of the child to the desires of the adult. Just ask the victims twenty to forty years later when they can talk about what happened.

In his book *Paedophilia: The Radical Case*, Tom O'Carroll discusses Beth Kelly's article in *Paidika* "Speaking Out on 'Women/Girl Love'—Or, Lesbians

Do 'Do It' ". This is an example of a former child-victim who introjected her abuser and became the pedophile who sexualized her. The article title alone is horrifying.

> *But what about Beth Kelly, now mature in years, and a radical lesbian feminist, who, as a "precocious" eight year old, developed a relationship with a grown woman? She writes:*

>> *The first woman I ever loved sexually was my great-aunt; our feelings for each other were deep, strong, and full. The fact that she was more than fifty years older than I did not affect the bond that grew between us. And, yes, I knew what I was doing—every step of the way—even though I had not, at the time, learned many of the words with which to speak of these things.*

An adult relative is willing to exploit her much younger niece, who needed the attention enough to tolerate, even welcome, the destruction of her sexual boundaries. Judging by my mother's essay, it is most likely another case of a motherless girl needing love from an older woman and being led to "pay for it" in a predictable way.

>> *Aunt Addie was a dynamic, intelligent, and creative woman who refused, all her life, to be cowed by convention. In an extended family where women played out "'traditional" housewifely roles to the hilt, she stood out a beacon of independence and strength. She was a nurse in France during the First World War, had traveled, read books, and lived for over twenty years in a monogamous relationship with another woman.*

How is it that the author's aunt did not find an age-appropriate partner to replace her former one? How could she seamlessly shift between a relationship with an adult and with her eight-year-old niece, who was more than *fifty years younger?* Are we meant to conclude that for lesbian women, incestuous intergenerational relationships are normal and desirable?

>> *Her lover's death pre-dated the start of our sexual relationship by about two years. But we had always been close and seen a great deal of each other. In the summers, which my mother, brother, and*

I always spent at her seashore home, we were together daily. In other seasons, she would drive to visit us wherever we were living and often stayed for a month or so at a time.

Aunt Addie used a small girl to replace the adult lover she had lost.

I adored her; that's all there was to it. I had never been taught at home that heterosexual acts or other body functions were dirty or forbidden, and I'd been isolated enough from other children to manage to miss a lot of the usual sexist socialisation learned in play.

The issue is not the "dirtiness" or "forbidden-ness" of such a liaison or the sexual acts associated with it. The issue is in the emotional results for the child. As noted elsewhere, early experience is the best way to predict later experiences. A girl who might have looked forward to a marriage and family is now locked into a system where her entire relational life will depend on seducing young girls, in invariably time-limited, temporary, and exploitative relationships. There will never be an adult relationship resulting from such a perversion of normal affections. As to the "sexist socialisation" she claimed is learned in play, are we to conclude that she thinks all hetero relationships are sexist?

It never occurred to me that it might be considered 'unnatural' or 'antisocial' to kiss or touch or hold the person I loved, and I don't think that Addie was terribly concerned by such things either. I do know that I never felt pressured or forced by any sexual aspects of the love I felt for her. I think I can safely say, some twenty years later, that I was never exploited physically emotionally, or intellectually - in the least.

Yes, the author has never felt exploited, and because of her "relationship", she sees nothing wrong with exploiting other children.

As so often happens, this joyous liaison eventually foundered on the rocks of parental disapproval, when Beth's mother chanced upon her and Addie in bed together. But disapproval of paedophilia or, rather, disapproval of child sexuality, has a significance far beyond its disastrous impact on the lives of the relatively limited numbers of children and adults in paedophilic relationships.

The disapproval is not the problem. The disapproval exists because of the predatory nature of these relationships, and because of the natural wish of parents to prevent their children from being sexualized, used, and heartbroken by preda-tory adults. After all, how can you sit down for Sunday dinner with your aunt if she has been teaching you unsavory practices after midnight and has broken up with you to sexually abuse your little sister? The way to make sure there are no unsavory practices and no breakups is to keep people, especially relatives, out of the beds of children.

The impact of the sex-negative outlook has to be seen in a wider societal context in order to appreciate its full significance.

Being sex-positive means approving of pedophilia?

These next excerpts are from "There Can Be No Emancipation of Women Without the Emancipation of Children: The Kanalratten Manifesto", by Kanal-ratten, an anarchist commune of women and children in Berlin. *Kanalratten* means canal rats, or sewer rats, in German slang.

We define female paedophilia as love between girls and adult women which is voluntary and includes sexual satisfaction; it is not a form of domination over other people since it is a form of life in which we have no need to dominate or possess children.

An ironic statement since sexual abuse of children invariably results from domination and possession. We, as children, are not free to refuse or to oppose adult wishes, even evil ones.

We wish to live without power over children and without the lifeless sexuality of adults. Adult sexuality means the destruction of life and the environment. The destruction of the environment precedes the destruction of child sexuality.

So adult-adult relationships are "lifeless", and anti-environmental.

Relationships with children other than those in the permitted categories of family, upbringing, home, and education are either not allowed or criminalized. Any attempt to break out of this machine of death is prevented.

Traditional relationships are a "machine of death", and sexualized, molesting adult-child relationships are not? The opposite is true. Children have always done best in families, protected by parents. It is pedophilia which brings misery, behavioral problems, drug abuse, and suicide.

We consider contacts which involve pressure, coercion, extortion, or prohibition to be incidences of violence rather than paedophilia. Those who claim that paedophilia consists of abuse, rape, and sadistic force are furthering the fascist discrimination of paedophile love. For us, however, it is fascist to imprison children in families so that no other kinds of relationships are possible.

Since children cannot oppose adult wishes, how on earth can pressure, coercion, and so forth ever be separated from pedophilia? Pedophilia *is* abuse and rape. Claiming that children are "imprisoned" rather than protected by families is insane. This is an extension of the mentality which denies that rape is rape unless one is thrown down in a gutter and raped by a stranger.

Paedophilia is our only means of preventing motherhood from being the only permitted form of living together with children. We attack the rapist father, but in no way allow ourselves to be forced into a motherly power relationship/dependency. We demand that children be given rights rather than protection, so that they can escape from families which they do not like or where they are mistreated.

Fathers are attacked, motherhood is assaulted, and the dependency of children on adults is vilified. This boils down to wanting children unprotected so they can be sexual targets. A child's discontent with his or her family is now an excuse for sexual abuse of the child, really?

The emancipation of women is not possible without the emancipation of children and childhood. A satisfying sexuality cannot be achieved without discussing the forbidden/suppressed topics of lesbian and child sexuality, without abolishing the divisions between body zones, sexuality and tenderness, sexual and non-sexual areas, age differences, and work. They try to separate every girl and woman from her sexuality so that they can later only function as sperm receptacles and mothers.

Sexuality can only be "satisfying" if it is between adults and children, resulting in the sexualization of all relationships? So much for all of human history.

Girls are destroyed by adults so that their resistance is broken and they let themselves be treated as victims and protected. They must put up with everything until they give in and are no longer able to resist the macho state. They then pass on this inability to other girls, rather than joining with them to offer resistance.

Girls are supposedly abused by men, but the author wants to paint female sexual abusers as emancipators. The author confuses freedom with her wish that female children would want to be sexually abused by adult women.

They know that children can become sexually excited, but they forbid sexual gratification. No opposition to families, schools, homes, and the whole moral world remains; rather their influence is becoming ever more widespread. Special courses for teachers, training programs to teach kindergarten children to say "no" and other such devices to protect children are contrivances to help and protect adults and the state, because they do not allow children to say "yes." They are the complement to or the substitute for male violence.

Children having the capacity for sexual arousal does not mean that they have the need for such arousal, especially from adults! Teaching children to say no to sexual abuse by adults is a way to protect them, even if it spoils the fun of would-be molesters.

We are the victims when ... other campaigners make no distinction between relationships based on mutual consent and relationships based on force. But they force us to live according to their ideas which they think are suitable for our modern times. We do not want to give any state money to the "wildwassers" nor do we want to help the pedagogues to control us, but we want to live with children.

The poor author paints herself as a *victim* because she confuses a child's inability to refuse a sexual overture from an adult with "consent." Children cannot consent to sexual relationships because there is no way for them to understand the consequences. The author says she wants to live with children. What she means is that she wants to separate children from their parents and have sexual encounters with them, imagining that this will somehow be beneficial. Lunacy.

There you have it. Pedophilia is the inevitable result of limitless sexual "freedom", and its defenders are hiding in plain sight in the gay community. My mother and father agreed about molesting children and agreed to live together with this shared outlook. In both my mother and my father's writings on pedophilia, their premise was the same as that given by the other pro-pedophile writers quoted in this chapter. They all want society to "understand" these "relationships" and judge them by their results.

Of course, judging these "relationships" by their results might not result in the conclusions my mother might want. In the examples from my mother's article the usual outcome of a pedophilic relationship is heartbreak or suicide, and in the examples presented by the other lesbian writers the result of being the victim of a lesbian pedophile is to become a lesbian pedophile.

Invariably, pedophilia is framed by pedophiles in terms of "children's rights." Not the rights of children to bodily autonomy and protection from predatory adults but the alleged right to have sex with adults. Those of us who lose parents to insanity, neglect, or death seek substitute parents, for love and nurturing, not for sex. Sex is something we are expected to endure, just as we are expected to endure beatings and whatever else our parents choose to put us through. It is facile and repulsive to hear anyone pretending that their wish to predate overrides our need for safety.

Talking to a broken adult thirty years after the offense is not the same as talking to a motherless child who is paying for companionship in a twisted and inescapable way. The adult victim might show her wounds, which do not heal. The child-victim is often too frightened to speak, let alone being able to get help. There is no good result, and the judgment on adults who commit these crimes should be swift.

Chapter 7

What Haunted the House of My Brother's Birth?
(1964–1972)

I was born in a house of cards
I can feel the wind blowing under my bed
A bad breeze, a cold breeze, hatred and danger
And no way out that isn't worse instead.

—Moira Greyland

My brother Patrick Russell Donald Breen, now called Mark Archer Greyland, was born on Halloween of 1964. In later years, he took exception that my mother had named him for Patrick Breen—a member of the infamous Donner Party. No, it was no accident. My mother would have sprouted wings and flown away before she would have missed a literary reference.

My father did not anticipate that in breeding pet children, one cannot choose their IQ or their interests or anticipate their level of sexual compliance. Where my father loved talking math, music, hallucinogens, and sex with high-IQ children, his interest in us beyond those dimensions was minimal. He wanted conversation and sex. Period. Dressing us, providing meals, doctor visits, or helping us with homework was not interesting to him. Although it is wrong to abdicate all parts of child rearing which do not further personal goals, my father only did what he wanted to do, and anyone who wanted his time and attention was stuck with his interests.

My brother David left home in 1964, shortly after my father arrived. Although my mother testified in court that at fourteen, he was a little older than the boys my father preferred and that David allegedly liked my father, he voted with his feet and left. Why? He told me that they both invited him to bed. Yes, you read that right.

Mother and Father lived with my brother Patrick at 1300 Arch Street in North Berkeley. I will relate the household lore about the Arch Street house, not because I believe it, but because they believed it and because my brother Patrick still believes it. It may give insight into the level of suspension of disbelief required in our family.

Mother lost a twin in both her first pregnancies and claimed that Patrick's twin haunted the house. She would tell us in later years that the twin would violently rock the cradle when Patrick was not in it, and she could sometimes see him lying next to Patrick when he was sleeping. She claimed that babysitters refused to stay when they discovered that they could not endure the sound of a baby crying when the only baby they could find was sleeping. Mother claimed that there was a room in the lower story that nobody could ever go into because of the "astral cold" and because it was haunted by a pair of floating eyes.

Why did it have to be floating eyes? Why not a floating nose or a few floating ears? It could be surmised that this could be an unsurprising consequence of when a fantasy author like my mother is stuck doing baby care instead of writing stories: Her stories leak over into her life. I know I am supposed to believe the stories, but they sound preposterous to me.

The question that really matters is this: what was haunting that house? Are we seriously to believe that a couple of rational adults think their house is haunted, or might something else be going on? Was the house haunted by pain and misery, and as usual, my mother turned her own feelings and desires into storytelling? Could it be that my father was already proving himself to be less than ideal as a husband and a father, or did we, perhaps, really have floating eyes in our basement? You'll have to make up your own mind. I find it hard to swallow this kind of lore, especially when the source is a noted author of fiction. Why would this not be simply another fiction, and perhaps the reality was much more boring? Perhaps the "ghosts" in our house amounted to my mother and my father sharing a house and populating it with all their old baggage and misery from their lives before.

My mother was deeply in love with my father, and by all appearances he was deeply in love with her. She mentioned him running after her in an airport, shrieking, "Beloved!" She felt that this was a mark of devotion rather than derangement. To be fair, she also mentioned a time that he tried to strangle her on the steps of the opera house. I did not witness either event, but Mother remembered them. It should be noted that this encompassed the range of conduct which my mother was willing to accept from my father.

In the context that my mother had married a man who was already sexually active with several teenaged and younger children and now had inadvertently driven off her oldest son, could it be that the chickens were coming home to roost in the form of a marriage vow that could not result in anything good for my mother?

After all, the one thing my mother could never be was a teenage boy.

Chapter 8

Science Experiment
(1966)

I was not born for love
I was not born for need
And no human reason would do,
But Mom thought her genes
Would go well with his genes
And my Daddy liked him a lot too.

Worse luck, Mom and Dad
Though it made you sad
You both ended up in the sack
And your eugenic plan
Raise a high-IQ clan
Was now something you couldn't get back.

—Moira Greyland, *Science Experiment*

My father wanted the high-IQ children he bred to have different fathers so that he could observe the level of IQ variance the different fathers would produce. He was not particular about the age of his intended fathers and chose the sixteen-year old boy genius Kevin Langdon to be my biological father. However, my mother became pregnant by my father before they could arrange for another breeding encounter with him. Kevin and I later became friends, and a DNA test confirmed that he is not my father.

He wrote this description of his relationship with my father at my request.

When I saw Moira's statement that she was writing about Walter's youth I had a strange reaction, because when I met Walter I was 16 and he was an "old man" of about 30.

When I was 15 and 16 I participated in a program, in my last semester in high school, at UC Berkeley. A few other students and I went to Berkeley for half of each day; the other half we were at San Rafael High. Then in the Fall, still 16, I began my Freshman year at Berkeley.

Partway through my first semester I met Walter Breen on campus. We immediately recognized that we had a lot of intellectual interests in common. Walter became a mentor to me, exposing me to many things that I hadn't known about before, including the ideas of thinkers in a wide variety of fields, classical music, and unusual cultural practices of various kinds, including science-fiction fandom, Mensa, and alternative sexuality.

Walter never approached me in a sexual manner, though he made no secret of his sexual inclinations. Perhaps I was outside his preferred age range. He did include me in a threesome with Marion for a short time but there was no sexual contact between Walter and me.

Walter also carefully avoided the subject of drugs. I knew nothing about his use of pot—and that created an unfortunate situation. One summer Walter was away for several months and he let me stay in his apartment while he was gone. One of Walter's and my friends, Dennis Crain, visited me at Walter's and raided his stash of drugs; I was completely unaware of what he was up to. When Walter returned he was furious.

Walter became one of my closest friends. We spent a lot of time together, one-to-one and in the context of the strange science-fiction fandom scene in the Bay Area in the 60s and the also-strange Mensa community. The cultural revolution was in full swing and all kinds of conventional ideas were put into question; it was hard to have a sense of which way was up in the midst of the chaos. Walter was a weirdo in the kingdom of the weird and for a time everything went well.

Walter was the editor of the fandom newsletter Fanac. That put him at the center of a lot of the action and he did a very good job of covering it. The scene in fandom in the 60s was very active and very weird, weird enough that Walter was only one of many strange characters who were a part of it.

However, when the news got out regarding Walter's sexual offenses many people were appalled and condemned him—but others defended him. It created a huge sensation.

Walter was barred from attending a Worldcon in the SF Bay Area in the early 1960s, but the organizers of the meeting relented and allowed him to attend the last day.

I stayed in touch with Walter for many years, but with considerably less contact after the early 1970s.

Here is a selection from my mother's testimony on the subject. Notice that she lied about his age as she did with the other young men who shared their bed, claiming he was "21 or 22" rather than 16.

MR. DOLAN: Who was Kevin?

MZB: He was a young man. At that time there were many multiple marriages, and at that time Walter and Kevin formed a triangle. It went on only for a short time.

MR. DOLAN: Okay. How old was Kevin?

MZB: I think he was 21 or 22.

I was born on January 10, 1966 in Alta Bates Hospital in Berkeley, CA. At the time, our family was living in my mother's dream house on Regent Street in Berkeley.

I was named Moira Evelyn Dorothy Breen for a few reasons. First for Moira Shearer, the prima ballerina from "The Red Shoes;" then Evelyn for my grandmother, and Dorothy was a woman my mother had been involved with. My initials were no accident: "MEDB", or Medhbh (Maeve) as it would be rendered in Gaelic, was the name of the evil queen in the most famous tale in Irish mythology, The Táin Bó Cúailnge or "Cattle Raid of Ulster."

If that isn't a preposterous intellectual affectation, I don't know what is.

My mother has related a lot of drama to me about my birth. Because she was diabetic, I was nearly ten pounds, and it was debilitating for her to have such a large baby. My shoulders were so broad that the doctor had to break my collarbone to deliver me; she told me that she literally died on the operating table.

She claimed to have had a near death experience, relating the story with her characteristic drama. While she was "dead", she met people from her past who told her she could come back and raise the girl she had always wanted or leave me with *him* to raise.

Where she was in a terrible situation during my birth, I also had to be revived, but that was much less important in her story. I was "born blue": not breathing, with the cord wrapped around my neck. I survived as you might have guessed, but what does that matter? Her story makes much better reading, with a death, mysterious words from beyond the grave... Perhaps I am simply a buzz-kill, with no aliens, and no otherworldly voices. I was just a child.

My mother's perspective on my birth might lend perspective to everything else in this book. She told me again and again that I "killed her." It was strange to reflect on the fact she felt it would be so dangerous for my father to raise me that she literally "came back from the dead" to save me from him.

No matter how many times I have heard this story, I have never been able to accept her contention that she had "always wanted a girl." After all, I caused her no end of trouble. She also told me that my father never got over the shock of being the father of a girl. She said this as though having a girl could be genuinely shocking to a man, even shocking enough to permanently injure any man forced to endure such a unexpected event. I can make no sense of it though. I have met many fathers who have never described the concept of having a daughter as being shocking in any way.

With her usual disregard for boundaries, my mother told me that my father never had sex with her again after I was born. It seemd as if she repeated this story to me almost a million times. Walter told me in later years that he had begun to find her to be physically repulsive due to the weight she gained during her pregnancy with me. Marion, on the other hand, believed from that her pregnancy—or perhaps the shock of his wife bearing him a daughter—had rendered him impotent, which was exactly what he wanted her to believe.

That way, she would not be overly distressed by his sexual liaisons with others.

Chapter 9

The SCA and the Cruel Mother (1966–1967)

Mother, dear mother, when we were thine, you never did dress us, coarse or fine.

—"The Cruel Mother", (Child 20)

In 1966, both my parents were going to school. Walter got his M.A. from the University of California, Berkeley, in June of 1966. He regarded it as being "as useful as a second hole in the head."

Marion was also working on a Master's at UC Berkeley between 1965 and 1967, but she stopped taking classes after my father failed his PhD orals; he accused the committee of homophobia. I do not know the details of why he failed, but if he presented any part of his research for *Greek Love*, it is completely understandable why they would not have wanted to approve a dissertation on such an unsavory and illegal topic. According to Marion, Walter had a nervous breakdown after he failed the oral examination.

However, as a consequence of her literary success, Marion was later awarded an honorary Master's degree as well as six honorary doctorates.

Marion met Diana Paxson in 1966, and that year they founded the SCA, or the Society for Creative Anachronism, together. Diana was a graduate student in medieval studies at Mills College, which meant that she and my mother shared many interests. During their lifelong friendship, they "divided up" all the major mythologies and legends they wanted to write about, with Mother doing the Arthurian legends and Diana writing about the Norse gods.

Later, Diana married my mother's adopted brother Don, in what was intended to be a sort of platonic "group marriage" with my mother's youngest brother Paul Edwin Zimmer and my aunt Tracy. Before they got married, Paul got Diana pregnant with her firstborn son: my cousin Ian. Nobody blinked an eye or would admit to having the slightest difficulty with the situation even though it did create problems.

A family tree is not something one can take an eraser to. In what passed for my family, everyone would try to claim that it doesn't matter who fathered a child. It is up to all of us to care for it. But parents still have parental feelings, even if our Berkeley ideology requires us to pretend that we do not: of course it left Ian in a difficult position, forever having to explain the bad behavior of his parents, and it meant Tracy had a daily reminder that her new husband had many other sexual and emotional interests. This was the first time that Paul fathered a child whose mother he had not married, but not the last.

Paul and Tracy and Don and Diana and my grandmother all lived together in a huge house in the Berkeley Hills. The house was called Greyhaven, and it was at Greyhaven that the first SCA event was held. My aunt Diana still lives there, with her son Ian and an assortment of other people. Where in *The Lord of the Rings*, The Grey Havens was a place for elves to retire and injured Hobbits like Frodo Baggins to recover, in Berkeley Greyhaven was simply a center of creative activity. It was a writer's colony of sorts and has provided a safe haven for many people. To this day, the walls are filled with proofs of book covers for the dozens and dozens of books that have been written there.

My mother loved The Society for Creative Anachronism. It is a fun place for the misfits of society to play. It is a wonderful, amazing organization where people can pretend to live as though they were living in the Middle Ages, with all the gallantry, pageantry, and beautiful costumes but none of the plagues, privies, or feudal atrocities which would have been involved in any actual reality.

The SCA is an openly idealized version of living history, never encouraging the factual aspects of the middle ages. Both men and women can achieve rank, even kingship, on the field of combat, and one is honored not for birth, pandering, or financial success, but for achievements of various kinds in the arts.

To become king, one first fights one's way into becoming a knight through a series of tournaments. The final victor of a Crown tournament becomes king. Mostly men have earned the title, though a few women have also done so. Imagine this in the modern day, and boxers and wrestlers will run the government: a throne won with a gaudy belt and with a thrown chair to the head!

One problem with all this speculative medieval history is that it has allowed and encouraged historical revision. Modern paganism is not historical in the slightest but comes from speculation, wishful thinking, and outright falsification of history. In the milieu of the SCA, usually imagined to be in the 11th century, the Irish were imagined to be pagans instead of the deeply Catholic nation they have been since before the 5th century.

So instead of sacrificing one other at Stonehenge, as the archaeology indicates was the case, the Druids were reimagined as happy, free feminists, skipping naked through the trees, practicing Western free love, open marriages, and magically avoiding all normal consequences. After all, what fun would it be if all the Sixties-style bed-hopping and pot-smoking was met with era-appropriate Christian horror as well as the traditional legal and physiological consequences?

The SCA is a deeply political organization, with a great deal of infighting, internal schisms, and endless interpersonal wars, but that is what happens when people make clubs of any sort. However, it is also a comfortable place for pedophiles to hide, and where they can find access to vulnerable children, for much the same reasons as we saw in science-fiction fandom's Breendoggle. Misfits are expected to be nice to other misfits, to be accepting of their idiosyncracies, and to give them the benefit of the doubt for even the most bizarre behavior. That being said, I am hopeful that some amount of housecleaning has taken place in the SCA since my experience with it, and that there is more safety for children now than there was then.

Where my mother excelled at writing books, inventing new planets, and creating mythological societies, she was neither capable nor interested when it came to taking care of her children. At the best of times our house was full of ants and cockroaches, and we had irregular and absent meals. I remember being cold and hungry. My brother remembers finishing everyone else's plates, even chewing the marrow from the chicken bones because he was so hungry. Mother obviously kept us alive, but not at a level which other people would have found acceptable.

Walter was financially irresponsible, and would hide the bills instead of paying them. He lost my mother's Regent Street house that way, and Marion never forgave him for it—although she inexplicably kept trusting him to pay the bills for many more years. He did not buy groceries, he would not do even a scrap of housework or baby care, and he did not cook. I remember once when I was older, my mother asked my father to help around the house, and he screamed at her that it was the "thin end of the wedge!" Walter believed that she really wanted him to do *all* of it. Doing anything would result in him doing everything, so he did nothing.

Since Marion was so famous, no one suspected her of being a neglectful mother, much less a dangerous one. My mother took pains to make sure that nobody knew the truth about her, although she was not especially vigilant about her public image in other ways. When we were very little, she simply discouraged anyone from visiting our house unless we were throwing a party. That meant nobody saw the day-to-day chaos. In later years, she gave up altogether on looking good, and the house was overrun.

Although she managed to hide our filthy, vermin-filled, food-challenged house from people most of the time, she got sick once, and my father was completely unable to step into her shoes. This left us with no parents, rather than the half-parent she usually managed to be.

Bjo Trimble, a science fiction writer and colleague of my parents, came to visit our family in 1967 before we left Berkeley. Many years later, she saw me at an SCA event and told me what she saw at my mother's house. The following passage is taken from a letter she wrote to me in response to my questions.

When did you first meet Marion and Walter, and under what circumstances?

I met Marion when she came to her first Worldcon: Denvention, 1959. She'd already been published, but she had no idea what to expect at the con. I was going to Denvention alone, and asked if anyone wanted to room with me. The con-com put us together. I helped Marion put on makeup for her costume. It was several years before John met Marion. We met Walter at a LASFS (Los Angeles Science Fantasy Society) meeting. Got to talking, found some similarities in interests.

How often did you see them?

They lived in the Bay Area, so we didn't see them very often. Sometimes Walter would come to LA on coin business, and he stayed with us.

Did anything about them strike you as odd?

Marion was a fantasy writer, and Walter was a science fiction fan. We knew a lot of people like that, so they didn't seem any odder than most fans.

Did you find anything about them to respect or to like?

We liked Marion's willingness to help new young and new writers. She had worked in isolation for so long, she understood how other writers felt. Many of them could not even admit to a liking for "that Buck Rogers stuff."

How did the people you know feel about them?

I don't think we ever discussed either Marion or Walter very much with others. For one thing, we didn't like the SCA people who clustered around Marion, and Walter didn't seem to make friends easily.

When did you first suspect something was wrong with their self-care and their parenting?

Marion was overweight, so she dressed to disguise that. This made it difficult to know how well she took care of herself. Walter always looked like an unmade bed, but that was so in keeping with a lot of fans, we never noticed anything about it. He never smelled bad.

We didn't know much about their parenting skills because we only met them at SCA events. The boy [David] was in his surly teens, so no one thought much about that. You were a cute, shy little girl. Again, nothing that aroused our suspicions. We only saw them and you kids very occasionally. The people who should know more is the local SCA people like Diana Paxton. I doubt you'll get much from her. Very few people went to their house. They would visit others.

The one and only time I noticed anything wrong about their parenting was when I was visiting the Bay Area, and Walter invited me over to talk a bit. He didn't mention that Marion was down with really bad flu and barfing all over the bedroom and bathroom. When I walked in the house, the smell was awful. Diapers had been just dumped in the middle of the kitchen floor, and the pile was about knee-high. Dirty dishes were cluttering the counter and the sink. There was sour milk in the refrigerator.

Walter seemed to be absolutely helpless to even wash dishes. I thought it was weird that a MENSA member had so little survival instinct. I mean, the mark of intelligence is to stay alive, right? One child was toddling around, the other one crying in its crib (sorry, I don't recall which child was which). Both had dirty diapers. Marion was throwing up. Walter was just walking around looking confused. He did not pick up or comfort either child.

What did you do to help?

I couldn't leave this situation. So I gathered the diapers in a couple of laundry baskets and sent Walter around the corner to a laundromat. I told him to just read the rules in large letters on the laundromat wall and he'd do fine. Just don't cram all the diapers in one washer, and use the amount of soap suggested. I cleaned up the children, fed them some cereal, changed their bedding and washed the dishes. I swept and mopped everywhere I could, because the house was very dirty. I didn't clean up the bathroom or their bedroom; I figured this was Walter's job to mop up Marion's vomit.

Walter didn't come back for a long time, and when he did, he had only half of the diapers. The rest were stuck in a washer that had overflowed the laundromat with soap. Leaving Marion with the kids, I walked Walter back to the laundromat where we untangled the diapers, apologized to the owner for the soapy mess, and washed all the diapers again. I left Walter to watch the diapers in the dryer, and walked back to the house. Marion was asleep and the kids were screaming their heads off. I can't blame Marion; she was exhausted from throwing up all day.

At this point, I was completely exhausted. Finally Walter came back with the clean diapers, after using up far more coins than needed. He asked about dinner, obviously expecting me to produce a hot dinner on the spot. I told him he could order in. We had Chinese food that night.

Were they grateful? Or worried about the law intervening?

Were they grateful? Not much. Walter got upset when I decided to leave. He seemed to think I'd accept his invitation to stay the night, but I wasn't putting myself in the position of being housekeeper any longer. I may not be smart enough to be in MENSA, but I danged well know when and how to get out of a bad situation! There was no question about the law, because it never occurred to me to call in the law. Back then, there were no agencies to call in, so it would have been a police matter.

How did your friendship with them survive over time?

I'd not call it a friendship at any time. After the diaper adventure, Marion acted as if I'd invaded their house just to make them look bad (who was I going to tell?). Her memory of that day was entirely different from mine; I had barged in, intimidating Walter and the kids. I'm not sure why I'd have done that! Walter didn't want to admit I'd done them a major favor. So I was done. John was not enthused about Walter, and he didn't know Marion. So we lost nothing by dropping this relationship.

Any other thoughts?

Only that I wish someone had known how dysfunctional your family was. Had anyone noticed and spoken up about their suspicions, you kids might have been spared a great deal of trauma and harm. This was something that local people should have done. We lived too far away to judge the situation. The diaper adventure was my only time in their house, so aside from Walter having no housekeeping skills, nothing spoke to me about a deeper problem. I'm sorry for that.

I note a few things about Bjo's letter. First, my mother was angry that someone had found out what was really happening in our house, because her reputation was more important to her than caring for three hungry children living in filth. She reacted with suspicion and resentment instead of relief and gratitude. Walter was virtually a non-entity, completely incapable of helping and unwilling to even try when Marion was sick. We children might as well have been pots and pans for all the concern either of our parents displayed.

Bjo's response to our plight was both normal and humane; she went above and beyond the call of duty to help us, and in return was met with nothing but obliviousness and resentment from our parents.

Chapter 10

The Nurse and the Lunatic
(1967–1972)

Not want Mommy, want Marie.

—Moira, age 2

We moved to New York in late 1967 because Lester Merkin had promised my father a job. We drove cross-country in the snow, and I got sick. I remember only one thing from that trip: I remember my father going out in the snow when we were in a motel to buy me orange juice. That is my earliest memory. I remember the cold coming in the door of our ground-floor motel room when he opened it. I remember he was wearing dark clothing, and he was all wet and snowy carrying me my orange juice.

The job from Lester Merkin did not materialize, and we lived on unemployment for a while as a result. Nevertheless, my mother lost no time in founding the East Kingdom of the SCA, which spread all over the East Coast and Canada.

Over time my father's fame in coin circles grew. He was hailed as the foremost expert on coins in his day. As he modestly told me, he was "God to a quarter of a million coin collectors." He was often called upon to be an expert witness in legal cases regarding the authentication of rare coins.

In 1968 when I was two, we lived in a house which seemed enormous to me at the time: 2 Swaim Avenue in Staten Island. For that matter my bed was gigantic, but I was very small. My brother Patrick and I shared a room. We had two tall beds next to each other and would sit between them and play. Our room had large square windows in four panes, and the roof in our room wasn't flat but steepled or gabled. The house was beautiful, though my mother later described it as "grubby."

Outside, there were a lot of trees and some construction. It snowed in the winter. Our street was rocks and dirt with some asphalt, and my mother drove a huge station wagon. I liked to sit on the back deck—except once, when I got sick to my stomach and Mother yelled at me a lot for wanting to sit in one of the seats.

I had a babysitter named Marie. She was black and large and comforting. I loved her very much. Eventually, my mother became jealous and made her leave. She told me with great anger that I used to cling to Marie and push her away. and say, "Not want Mommy, want Marie." My mother seemed to think that I should apologize to her for this and that I should be embarrassed for my past disloyalty to her.

I remember Marie as a warm presence, and it is probable that she is the main reason I did not become psychotic. I could not bond with my mother any more than I could have bonded with a block of ice. I bonded very quickly to Marie, however, and the house was a much sadder place once she left. When Lisa told me that she had died, many years later, I cried as if my heart was going to break even though I could barely remember anything about her. I just knew she held me and loved me and didn't make loud, scary noises or leave me cold and hungry like my own mother did.

It may well have been that my mother was unable to regulate her emotions; she was incapable of restraining herself when she got angry or upset and became brutal. It was during this period that I began to understand that my mother was not safe and that I was afraid of her.

In 1969, I was three years old. My father had very dark hair back then, and he always seemed to be in the other room. He was not around very much, and I didn't know whether it was because he didn't like me or if he was just busy. When I saw him, it was mostly when he was sick with what I was told was epilepsy. My mother told me that I would stand on a chair and pat his head and say, "Poor Daddy, you're so sick." When he was not having seizures, he seemed angry. Still, I loved him, and I wanted him to love me.

My mother wanted to teach my brother to read when he was about four: He was fourteen months older than I was. I don't know how she went about it, but her methods didn't work and she gave up. I wanted her to teach me to read, but she absolutely refused because she didn't want my brother to feel bad. I didn't think he would care. So, I taught myself to read when I was three, and my mother regarded this as a sign that I was stubborn and disobedient. She never let me forget it. She resented me for it and seemed to believe that in learning how to read, I had somehow injured my brother.

My father was working in Manhattan and they had to cross the Verrazano Bridge to get to his workplace. My father didn't drive very much, so Mother drove him. Once he took us to work with him for a little while. At his work, there was a smiling man and a lot of carpet and counters like one might see in a jewelry store that had coins in them. Best of all, there were candies that were neither gum nor just candy but halfway between. I liked the candies a lot.

My mother held meetings for the SCA at our house back then, and she roasted something called a "suckling pig" which she said like "sucking pig" for dinner on Twelfth Night, or January 6. It smelled good. Everyone wore costumes, which back then already seemed fairly normal. It was nice to have so much food on the table, and it was fun. The light was warm, and people were smiling and happy. I smelled a hot spicy drink that was probably mead or mulled wine. There was a chair I liked which had dark woven straw on the back.

Even though my mother was very busy and happy when people were around, when there were no visitors it was a different story. My mother was often angry and frustrated, and it seemed I never got finished finding ways to upset her. She felt everything was my fault. Even her private frustration with my father's distance and disinterest was my fault. I just knew he wasn't around a lot and they certainly didn't kiss. They fought, but my mother would only say that Daddy was sick.

Walter was obviously miserable, moody to the point of frequent tears, overtly suicidal, and he talked about his life and his feelings as though he was caught in the middle of a grand tragedy. When I was little, I couldn't identify it as mental illness, but I was aware something was very wrong. He blamed my mother for his misery, which my brother and I understood. He felt completely powerless to rescue either himself or us from her evil clutches, and this also meant that although I could come to him and cry on his shoulders about the horrible stuff she did and said to me, he could never actually stop her from doing a thing. He was the tallest victim in a house of very small victims.

Their relationship was a mass of contradictions. They loved each other, but they often fought noisily. Marion would cry, drink excessively, scream insults at my father—calling him "Oathbreaker" in particular—and threaten suicide. Walter would yell and storm and threaten suicide. He seemed to feel that she was a monster who had imprisoned us all. I was afraid of her—much more than I was ever afraid of him with his epilepsy and screaming. I never thought he wanted to hurt me.

Sometimes her anger and frustration showed up in awful ways. It was as though there was three of her: Mommy 1, Mommy 2, and Mommy 3. Mommy 1 was friendly, Mommy 2 cried a lot and wanted something that didn't make any sense to me, and Mommy 3 was utterly vicious. The only way to deal with Mommy 3 was to hide and hope she didn't find you. I remember closets. I remember the conflicting feelings of hiding inside them.

Darkness. Relief at being out of her way. Fear of what would happen when the light came back on.

What I remember, more than almost anything else, was her constant talk about how sexually frustrated she was. I have always been aware that in her universe, her frustration was *my* fault. She thought that she didn't look the same after I came along and that was my fault, that my daddy didn't love her anymore and that was my fault, and that meant she was really agitated about something that didn't make sense to me.

This all finally came to a head when she was giving me a bath. I don't want to think about what she wanted me to do to her. Or the hot water, which got too hot when she got mad. Or her hands around my neck. Or the water, which went around the top of my head in a circle that got smaller, finally disappearing. I can still feel it. All I knew is what I had to do if I wanted to stay out of the water.

There are smells I absolutely hate to this day. I still smell them in my dreams and in my waking nightmares.

All I could think about was the smell. The horrid folds of flesh with stuff growing in them, and the sitting on you, the crushing, the flesh, the smell, the burning water, the water in my face, me pleading and her stuff in my mouth. I hated the taste. Bitter and sour at the same time, and nasty white stuff. Dark red pinky little bits of flesh. Trying to get away. Scared beyond scared. No way to escape. I am a toy to her. She doesn't get enough sex. I have to give it to her. I can't breathe. I hate the smell. I hate the taste. And all the time is her, she's so sexy, she's so sexy, she's so beautiful. Sexy and beautiful like a slug, like a sea cucumber, like a crushed snail. I hate her and her greasy brown hair, her huge fat belly, and her too-warm flesh crushing my face. I hate her thighs, her legs, the smell of that powder on her thighs. I hate her for making me do that to her.

A mother is supposed to be a comforting person who bakes cookies for you and comforts you when you are hurt, not a terrifying, screaming monster.

I imagine this is difficult to read. Writing about this is almost impossible.

Chapter 11

My Father Begins My Education: Sex, Pot, and Kindergarten (1970–1971)

Incest is Nicest spelled sideways.

—Walter Breen

In 1970 I was four years old. My brother had just started school at Public School 5. I was still too little to go, and I was jealous because I was stuck at home all day. Mostly what I did at home was read books like Frederick Phleger's *You Will Live Under the Sea*. I was so enthralled by the idea of scuba diving to an underwater house that I would make masks and paper flippers and oxygen tanks out of red and green construction paper. I also read all the Dr. Seuss I could get my hands on and anything else I could find.

We had a Siamese cat named Solange. I was terrified of big dogs, so Mother got me a German Shepherd puppy, and we named her Gretel. She told me a story about her being stolen because she was purebred, and then she escaped before being hit by a car on her way back home. From an adult perspective, I have no idea how my mother came up with a story like that. Why not just tell me she got loose and was hit by a car? I cannot say for certain because I have no way of knowing, but it does not seem likely that anyone would come to Staten Island to steal the kind of dog which would be owned by people of our means. She was obviously not bought from a breeder.

Our family added another dog, named Griff, short for Griffin. He was half Lab and half Newfoundland, huge and strong. He used to take me for walks. It was impossible for me to control him, and in retrospect I don't understand why she sent me out alone with him. Walking down our snow-covered rocky street by myself did not worry me. It was no problem, as far as I was concerned. Being dragged around by our huge dog was more frightening to me.

Once when it was snowing, I had gone down the street to visit a little girl who lived there. I was wearing a little snow jacket, and my friend and I had fun. When I got home, my mother was furious: She said she had been looking all over for me. Somehow, walking the dog alone was not a cause for concern, but going to visit a friend alone was. I still remember her standing on the porch screaming at me.

My mother wrote all the time: books she called "pot boilers": anything she could write for money, even if they ended up being used as kindling. I did not know what she was writing, of course. I only knew that she was writing and that we were not to disturb her; God help us if we interrupted her while she was writing!

I know from my father's autobiography that he was writing for Sybil Leek's *Astrology Journal* and was the editor from 1970–1971. He did professional horoscopes for people and wrote liner notes for Parnassus Records. He took any paid writing assignment he could find: his version of writing pot boilers. I remember that there were astrology magazines all over our house: silver-grey and dark blue covers, with astrological charts like my father was so fond of making.

My mother took me to get my picture taken one day, and it was a very strange and awful experience. Because I was always cold, I wore tights day and night, and on picture day my mother was intent that I would wear not only a dress but little ankle socks that folded down with frilly underpants. Cold, thought I. Cold, cold, cold, cold, *cold!*

I lost that battle. It took both Mother and Father to hold me down by main force and rip me out of my tights. It might be imagined that I already had plenty of reasons to be frightened of being even slightly undressed, aside from the cold. Mother took me, dressed up like a very miserable little doll, down a long, cold sidewalk with the wind making my legs cold. On the way to the photographer, a little old lady stopped us and asked me, "Are you a nice little girl?" I responded, apparently rather dryly, "No, I'm a live banana."

Marion repeated that story many times, claiming, in her words, that I was "a master of irony" before I was six years old. Naturally, Mother was not concerned about WHY I would not want to be undressed. She was completely oblivious to the fact that being out of my tights prompted a fear reaction much like a severe phobia or a panic attack. Yet to me, I had been ripped once more out of my only security. The only thing I cared about when I got back home was getting back into my white tights, my only layer of protection from them. My safety was now partially ruined because the pair of them could rip me out of my tights whenever they chose.

My brother made friends at school and began to bring them around, notably two brothers named Kenny and John. Kenny was six like my brother, and John was twelve. My parents let me go to their house with my brother, and that was fun. They had a screeching pet monkey, which was strange. I had never seen a monkey that close before, and I hoped it would never get out of its cage. I was afraid of it. The upstairs, where the monkey lived, was dimly lit, cramped, and crowded. My father was glad to have Kenny and John around, and he had them come over to our house whenever he could.

One day, John did something painful to me that I did not understand. My father understood, though. In later years he would gleefully recount to me, with an awful look in his eyes and almost cartoonishly villainous hand-rubbing delight, how John kept trying to have sex with me, or, as he put it to my disgust, "get into me."

Walter talked and talked about sex all the time, using heaps of anatomically correct language which I will not repeat here. I felt so ashamed when my father would talk about my private parts as though they belonged to him. His words made me feel embarrassed and afraid, almost as if he'd smeared his icky words all over me. I knew I was not supposed to hate his anatomically correct language and I was not supposed to feel embarrassed by it; I was supposed to love it, to enjoy what John did to me, and to want to experience it again and again. That way, I would not be "hung up" about sex, which was what my father seemed to care about more than anything.

I could never understand why my father was so happy about what John had done to me. He thought it was something wonderful, as though now I would be okay with experiencing more of the same, and I would stop being such a *prude*.

I hate that word so much.

A "prude" is anyone who runs away when they see Daddy getting *that look* in his eyes. "Prude" means I don't want to have sex. "Prude" means I don't want to have sex with my father. But I didn't. I could not see what was wrong with wanting my father to love me like a daughter and not like *that*?

Walter was a big fan of all sex, and I mean *all* sex. He simply could not see sex as damaging, frightening, or harmful to anyone of any age, and he thought that fear of sex, or prudishness, was a problem to overcome instead of a reaction to potential danger. He seemed to believe that one episode of sex would lead to more and more sex, that everyone's willingness to have sex would increase, and soon everyone would be having sex with everyone—his Grand Vision for the world. He believed that the more sex everyone had, the better the world would be, no matter what pain it caused.

The next year, my father tried a new solution to solve my prudishness: drugs. Walter loved pot and smoked it constantly. He did not love all drugs, only hallucinogens like LSD, MDMA, or ADAM, and psilocybin mushrooms. Strangely enough, he despised alcohol and coffee, and mocked them as "America's popular diuretics." Marion loved alcohol and LSD but hated pot, and was as judgmental about people smoking pot as he was about drinking alcohol. This meant that Walter had to be careful about what she saw him doing.

Walter was eager to introduce my brother and me to pot-smoking, but he did not want my mother to know about it. So one day, he sent my brother and me down the rocky, snow-covered street to stay with two of their friends: Don and Donna. I believe he told Marion that they could babysit us. Back then, "babysit" meant more than one thing, although I doubt that Marion knew that he meant the other kind of babysitting, where we would be supervised through a drug experience.

Don and Donna were a young married couple. They were nice, friendly, very kind, and they gave us something good to eat. I think it was chocolate hash brownies that were not too chocolaty. They also got my brother and me stoned by blowing smoke in our faces. This made me cough, but I only cried a little. Afterward I curled up on a heap of pink, fluffy fiberglass insulation and fell asleep.

After this indoctrination into drug use, Walter smoked pot around me whenever he had a chance, invariably when my mother was writing or asleep. He thought it would be good for me to get a contact high even if he couldn't get me to toke the joints. My brother was willing to smoke pot whenever my father wanted him to, but I hated it. It made me sleepy, which I think was what my father intended. Mostly it made me cough.

I was always asthmatic, and I had to sleep on two pillows because lying flat on my back made it hard for me to breathe. Anything that interfered with my breathing was very frightening to me. I was afraid I would die. And no, there was no medical care available for my asthma. They would have me use my father's Primatene Mist, an old-fashioned over-the-counter asthma inhaler, whenever my coughing got too bad. My father coughed all the time: your run-of-the-mill smoker's cough, and he used Primatene Mist many times a day.

I hated the dull, sleepy way that pot made me feel. Even then my nature was to prefer to be very sharp, very alert. Even when I was little, I was afraid that all kinds of bad things could happen if I didn't watch out for them. I could not have articulated this then, but somehow I knew I needed to keep my eyes out for trouble.

I do not know what drugs my father gave me other than pot back then. My brother Patrick believes he was given LSD repeatedly, and remembered this happening in a medical setting, as though my father's Columbia University experiments from ten years before had continued. Patrick developed global synesthesia including visual hallucinations: more or less constant pineapples, fish and repetitive patterns floating across his visual field. His visual hallucinations have never stopped, although my brother is able to do artwork around them.

Walter always told me that pot would lower my inhibitions, but when he talked like that, it made me want to run away from him. Of course, sometimes running away was not possible, as I learned on the day my father raped me.

I do not know how Walter managed to catch me that day, whether he put something into my orange juice, or whether he just grabbed me when I was drawing or doing something else.

We were alone in the house. My brother was not at home and my mother had gone to a science-fiction convention. Walter was acting very strangely. He was not speaking in his usual detached, intellectual tone, but was yelling and grinning and rubbing his hands together. He was shouting that it was his birthday and that I was his birthday present. I had no idea why he was yelling, and the only birthday present I had ever heard about was when he used to read *The Hobbit* to us.

I was scared, and more than scared, I was *terrified*, because he did not sound like himself.

After he caught me, he took me into the bathroom. He held me up in his arms in front of him facing the mirror after getting my clothes off. He impaled me, holding me up so he could watch himself. I broke the towel bar trying to get away, but there was no getting away on the cold bathroom floor. It hurt a lot and there was blood. He was heavy and I hated him. I don't remember a lot about the actual rape except that the bathroom floor was cold, and it hurt a lot, and there was blood. I believe that my screams were more than just upsetting to my father, they were extremely *disappointing*. I think he imagined that I would like what he was doing and he was angry to discover that I didn't.

It might surprise you to know that this was one of the very few times he raped me. Perhaps it was because I was a girl and he strongly preferred boys. Or perhaps he realized on some level that I would never be a suitable participant in his Grand Vision. He did not entirely give up, though. Instead, he went on trying to find ways to persuade me to be willing. The pressure to not be a "prude" never stopped, not the entire time I lived around him.

But that day was one of his very rare lapses into brutality. He even said to me afterward, "Don't talk or I'll kill you."

After it was all over, I kept trying to find a corner of my bed that felt safe after that, but no corner was safe and everything was cold. Even when I put all the pillows on top of me, I still felt cold. I couldn't sleep enough to make it all go away. I thought Walter had gone crazy, and I was afraid he was going to go crazy again. There was no sleep which would drive the nightmare away.

When my mother came home she was angry at me because my underwear had been ruined by my blood; I had put them back on afterward. She informed me that I must have hurt myself with a toy car.

To this day, I still have flashbacks when I see anyone behind me in the mirror.

Walter was never held accountable for raping me. Not by Marion and not by anyone else. In our family, no one ever dared to get angry with Walter for his actions. Marion would scream at him, of course, but she screamed at everyone, so she was not holding him responsible for any particular thing. It would have been out of the question for her to say anything about what he did because he was sick, therefore he was not responsible for his actions.

Walter portrayed himself as being weak and helpless and a victim of many different things. Anyone who was angry with him was just another victimizer, and I certainly could not act like one of those evil people, especially because he already saw me that way. I could never permit myself to be angry with him because it's not nice to be angry with poor sick people.

Even now.

Chapter 12

I Start School, and Reap the Whirlwind
(1971–1972)

Mama's gonna make all of your nightmares come true
Mama's gonna put all of her fears into you
Mama's gonna keep you right here under her wing
She won't let you fly but she might let you sing
Mama's gonna keep baby cozy and warm

…Of course Mama's gonna help build the wall

—Pink Floyd, "Mother", *The Wall* (1979)

When I was 22, I read an essay that my mother had written when I was five years old. She wrote about how tragic it was that I was so different and how she was certain that the public schools would destroy a "green monkey" like me: the normal monkeys would tear me apart. My mother painted herself as a tragic heroine who was powerless to prevent the utter and inevitable destruction of her allegedly extraordinary daughter.

I was furious about the essay in the light of her conduct. She knew exactly what would happen to me before she put me into public school, and she put me there anyway. My mother was firmly sold on the value of public schools and felt that they needed to be supported, even if the collateral damage included me.

Before I started school, my mother had my IQ tested as a matter of course. Never mind the results—She declined to tell me anything about my IQ for many years, at which point she told me the range I was in and continued to conceal the actual results until I was 18. Suffice to say that my IQ test confirmed all her worst fears and fondest wishes. I was as bizarre as my parents had always hoped I would be; like them both, I am a member of Mensa.

Another mother might have made sure that I was put into a gifted school or made sure that there would be adequate intervention if things did not go well for me. After all, if you own a cat you must buy cat food, and horses eat hay. She and my father had deliberately bred me to be gifted, and once she had her confirmation that their experiment had succeeded, it would only have made sense to make sure that I could become what she seemed to want me to be by putting me in a school where I would have an appropriate education.

I could speculate unkindly that doing anything to make certain I stayed out of the hell she anticipated would have avoided the hand-wringing tragedy of it all or simply conclude that she did not feel she could afford a gifted school for me. The fact of the matter is that she did not approve of gifted schools or any kind of private schools for any reason.

Where I would have benefited mightily from a school where there were other children like me, she could not stand the idea of sending me to one. For her, any kind of private school was a place where rich, snobby kids were dropped off in gold-plated limousines by their personal valets and spent their weekends flying about in diamond-encrusted private jets, snacking on foie gras, and flinging hundred-dollar bills out the windows of their sports cars.

My mother was never going to let me turn into a snob, whether an intellectual snob or an upwardly mobile one, even if that meant I would undergo the harm she knew I faced in a normal school. She was not only anti-elitist but ambivalent about the concept of giftedness even though she had gone along with my father's eugenics experiments and even belonged to Mensa before she met him. I do not think she questioned her own intelligence, but resented other intellectuals who were not her or my father.

I believe my mother objected most to the idea of an IQ-based meritocracy, understandably preferring to value actual accomplishment over mere capability. Mother had also been different in school, but for her school had been a dream, an escape from farm chores and hunger and her abusive father. Her school was small and rural, and she didn't tell me about having been teased anywhere nearly as much as she did about other children's complaints about how she had messed up the grading curve for them. School, for her, had been a resounding success.

One thing Mother knew: a proper heroine fulfills her objective no matter what. Now it was up to me to live up to her proud example. Would I succeed?

Not like she did. Not on a tintype.

When I started kindergarten at P.S. 5 in Staten Island, I was so excited to finally be allowed to go to school. I already knew how to read, and I had been bored silly at home. In my naivete, I thought all the other children would be like me. As you might expect, the other kids detested me. I was different and I caused problems for them. I was outspoken and brash. I asked and answered too many questions. I talked funny, more like an adult, with way too many words in my vocabulary. Even back then I remember discussing with my brother how we could talk more like the other kids.

The school had no idea what to do with me. There was nothing for me to learn in kindergarten. So I sat in class drawing dolphins and otters while the other kids wrestled with more age-appropriate Dick and Jane: "See Spot Run. Run, Spot, Run." When we had show-and-tell, I brought a carriage I had made out of a five-gallon ice-cream container and two green wine bottles, and I wore crepe paper dresses I had made; this also did nothing to improve my popularity.

I got teased for my speech, my name, and my grades. "Einstein" was a popular epithet, though I only had a vague idea who that was, and I didn't understand why they called me that. When the teasing escalated to violence, I became frightened. I began searching for anything I could do to reduce my visibility. Still, a lot of the blame for the disaster of school was my fault, although at the time I had no idea how to stop it, how to prevent it, or how to fit in.

I did everything I could to minimize my strangeness, but it was never enough. My mother actively opposed any effort I made to fit in. Dressing like the other kids was impossible, since my mother dressed me out of a second-hand store, and there was no money for new clothes. But more importantly, Mother despised the very idea of my trying to fit in, even to save myself from violence. If I had dared to mention such a thing, she probably would have feigned a heart attack from the shock. After all, I was Different, and That Was What Mattered. And since I was there to live out *her* fantasies, my difference was to be maintained at all costs.

I changed my name very shortly after beginning school. It was obvious no teacher or student was ever going to be able to pronounce Moira and that it was going to continue to make me visible in a bad way. So, I went by Dorothy until I was 18, at which time I decided I didn't care whether other people could pronounce my name or not.

The school figured out that something was wrong and moved me to second grade. After all, most kids do not get harassed by other kids to such an extent that they change their names in order to try to reduce their difference. They would have allowed me to skip me more grades, but they were worried about the social consequences. They thought my being several years younger than my classmates would not be good for my social development.

Eventually, I came to terms with being different and realized that the people who hated me and hurt me were actually trying to help me in their own fashion—to shame me into conformity, a very human, if misguided, instinct. I am not claiming that what they did was right, only that it was understandable.

Chapter 13

Greenwalls, Greyhaven, and the Basement (1972–75)

The little blue-painted girl who had borne the fertilizing blood was drawn down into the arms of a sinewy old hunter, and Morgaine saw her briefly struggle and cry out, go down under his body, her legs opening to the irresistible force of nature in them.

—Marion Zimmer Bradley, *The Mists of Avalon*

On Columbus Day, 1972, I was sitting in class when I was called into the office and taken out of school from P.S. 5, thankfully forever. My mother and father put my brother and me on a plane to California: they were going to drive the moving truck themselves, and we would stay with my grandmother at her house called Greyhaven. My brother and I were escorted to the gate and onto the plane, and everybody was very nice to us. We landed in San Francisco, and then we got onto a helicopter to go to the Oakland Airport.

My grandmother was there to meet my brother and me, along with her friend, a lady named Mrs. Hodgehead. I do not think my grandmother drove. My grandmother was a gentle, kind woman who kept her book-filled attic spotless. It was a comfortable landing place for generations of children. I would see her after school every day when I was small, and I can still remember the smell of her homemade banana bread.

We stayed at Greyhaven for the next few weeks while my parents drove cross-country from Staten Island to Berkeley. It is an enormous, dilapidated mansion of sorts in the Berkeley Hills, a block from the Claremont Hotel. It is five small stories, built on a steep slope. The bottom two stories are, or were, unfinished basement, while the third story is the main floor with the kitchen, a living room, a dining room, a bathroom, a bedroom and an underground pantry room. The fourth story has a bathroom, several bedrooms, and an outdoor terrace looking onto the garden and the entire Bay Area. The fifth story is actually two levels, and it amounts to its own apartment: a lower room and an upstairs with a kitchen, a small bedroom, and a balcony surrounding the entire apartment with bookshelves nearly all the way around.

When my parents arrived, we moved into a house on Hamilton Place, up a steep flight of stairs in a really dismal part of Oakland. There was nothing much I remember about the house except that it was small and narrow, and under the story we lived on there was a huge, vacant, completely unfinished basement. The neighborhood was not good, and my mother wanted to live closer to my grandmother.

So rather than enrolling us in an Oakland school, my brother and I were enrolled in John Muir School, a few blocks directly downhill of Greyhaven. Mother would drop me off there in the morning, and I would walk to school. After school, I would walk back to sit upstairs to do my homework with my grandmother. Mother would pick me up and take me home later in the day.

When my brother and I were at Greyhaven, we would play with my cousins Ian and Fiona. Ian was a year younger than me and Fiona two. As noted, my brother was fourteen months older than I was. Ian was the son of Diana and Paul, who were not married, and Fiona was the daughter of Paul and Tracy, who were. At that time there was one other cousin, the baby Robin. He was the son of Don and Diana, who were married, and he was later discovered to be autistic. He was disabled to the point of never developing speech, although once when he was small, my uncle Paul thought he heard him say, "I want some of that." He ended up institutionalized because as he got older, he became harder and harder to handle. We could not really play with him, even when he was young.

I was at John Muir to finish second grade, and my brother was in third grade. I was smaller than the other people in my classroom, as before; I still talked funny, and I had developed an awful temper. I was brought into a theater class, and since it was after the beginning of the term, the school play had been cast already. I wanted to be the lead, and I threw a gigantic tantrum when they told me I could not be. I think I ended up with a part despite my dreadful conduct.

Not everyone was as forgiving of my strangeness and bad temper as the drama teacher was though. One day, off in the trees on the downhill side of the school, a kid threw a big block of wood at my head, hitting me in the forehead. I still have the scar. I was unconscious until after the end of school that day. Three girls found me, and I woke up with them standing over me. They took me to the office, where the principal, Mr. Baugh, mopped the blood off my forehead.

My head wound had bled. It was less than an inch long and did not need stitches, but it was deep. I remember him telling me I needed to have some gauze to put on it. At the time, I had no idea what "gauze" was, and even more confusing, it sounded like he was saying "gaws." I recovered well, although the scar offends my vanity.

When I was at Greyhaven, I had some unfortunate run-ins with an individual from the Pagan community named Isaac Bonewits. Some people called him the "Pagan Pope." He was a frequent visitor to Greyhaven and a friend of my parents. I hated Isaac and refused to be in the same room with him, even if the only way I could articulate my objections to him was to say "He tickled me!"

One day Isaac came to my mother when I was six years old and told her he wanted to have sex with me. He told her that there was a girl just my age at the commune he lived in, and she had had sex with all the men there, and she was so "free" and so "uninhibited" that it would be "good for me" to do the same thing with him. Her response was one I have heard her repeat so very many times in front of a variety of audiences:

"She won't have to do anything. She won't have to be anything. All she'll have to do to get attention is to open her legs." She seemed to think that saying this to a man who wanted to rape her six-year-old daughter would somehow educate him and show the world that she was a Great Feminist Thinker.

I have heard her repeat that story again and again. It was so humiliating to me, and it showed me just how little she cared what happened to me. Yes, she's a great feminist thinker. Yes, I must never allow myself to think I can get male attention by getting raped, and instead I must Create because Creating is my only purpose in being alive.

And she does not care what he does to me. I am dead. Why am I still alive?

I do not like talking about what happened with Isaac, and so I am going to say as little as I possibly can. In fact, rather than spending a lot of ink describing a long list of this and that which will turn me into a gooey weeping mess, I am going to give only the barest outline of one event:

The upper-level basement floor was cold and concrete. My mouth bled. I smelled things I did not want to smell and tasted things I did not want to taste. The bare wall frames with no sheetrock had cloudy, clear plastic wrap across them that had been partly shredded with age. There was a lot of dirt on the floor, which was not really level. I couldn't breathe. And I hate him with every fiber of my being.

By the time I was six years old, I was absolutely convinced that my parents were both unreliable and dangerous. I felt my mother was deliberately cruel and dangerous and that my father was oblivious. Even if he loved me, his idea of what "love" was left very little room for my bodily integrity. I knew I needed to look to other people for help, sanity, and a better example.

I knew my uncle Don was an artist, so I used to collect snail shells for him because I was certain he could find something artistic to do with them. To his credit, he never laughed at me or showed disdain for what I had brought him.

Sometimes on Sundays when Greyhaven had afternoon tea, I used to walk to a bakery called The Bread Garden across from the Claremont Hotel on Domingo. I befriended the bakers, and I would tell them about what was happening at home. I remember hearing Ann Murray's "Snowbird" playing in the bakery while they made these huge chocolate cookies with gooey white frosting inside.

My mother asked me why I was hanging out at the bakery. I told her, bluntly, that I needed someone to tell my troubles to, and she was absolutely incensed. You might think I had told her I had robbed a bank. She seemed to think that I didn't have any troubles, and if I did, I had no right to tell them to anyone.

When I was seven, a man named Serpent came to live at Greyhaven. He was cooking for the family in exchange for a place to stay. He had jokingly called himself the "Humble Servant", but perhaps because he was very tall and quite thin, this had gotten changed into the "Humble Serpent." His real name was Robert Cook. He was highly artistic, and he had a much better mind than most of the people I knew.

Serpent and I became fast friends, and he became my first informal foster father. He used to give me "page lessons" where he taught me to cook and to make things, with the objective of having me play a page at the Renaissance Faire and the Society for Creative Anachronism. I don't know if I mentioned that the SCA and the Faire always involved the study of real-life skills.

Eventually, Serpent got a girlfriend, Catherine. She was beautiful: She had blonde curly hair and a smile that lit up the room. She was strong and capable and kind, and I adored her. I still do! She took one look at me and said, "You've got to make her a girl. She can't be a page."

So he made me a Henry VIII-era Tudor dress that was spectacularly beautiful, with a black velvet bodice trimmed with gold and red stitching, a gold underskirt, and let me be a girl. Catherine and Robert Cook married and were a gigantic blessing in my life. Catherine became the mother-figure who essentially showed me that I could be a girl of another sort than my own mother was.

Chapter 14

All Summer in a Day
(1972–74)

I think the sun is a flower,
That blooms for just one hour.

—Ray Bradbury, "All Summer in a Day"

"All Summer in a Day" is a science fiction story by Ray Bradbury about children living on a planet which rains every day of the year but one. The protagonist of the story spends that one beautiful day locked in a closet by the other kids. My situation was slightly different: in a school career spanning years of bullying and violence, I had all summer in a day at a gifted school before I got to go back to Hell.

When I was six or seven, my aunt Diana and her friend Rusty Sporer taught me to ride. Rusty was a big, tall man, and he had two daughters. He was a member of the OTO, or Ordis Templi Orientis—one of many occultists who were friends of my mother and father. He owned horses and was friends with an old girlfriend of my father's named Anya. Anya lived on a beautiful ranch in Los Altos with trees everywhere, and it felt safer than anywhere I had ever been.

Rusty taught me to ride bareback first and then progressed to a bareback pad and finally to a saddle. He told me that once I had fallen off a horse ten times, I would be a horsewoman. Naturally, I wasted no time falling off ten times. I was unafraid, and so happy. Learning to ride was absolutely the most fun I had ever had, and I felt completely at ease with the horses.

Anya was very taken with me. She was a teacher at a gifted school. I was sent to Anya's gifted school in Los Altos for one glorious day when I was eight. It was a dream come true. For one day, I was not a freak; for one day, the other kids were like me. I thought that if I lived with Anya, I would get a decent education with no fear of violence, and I would not have to BART everywhere or hide in my bedroom in terror of my mother's rages.

Anya offered to adopt me and get me a spectacular education, as she could easily do at her school. This became the source of one of the bloodiest fights that I ever had the misfortune to overhear between my mother and my father.

My father was all for it and thought that for me to be in a gifted school would be a dream come true. He understood far better than Mother did what it was like for me since he had been through the same sort of thing. Not only had he heard from me day in and day out about what had happened to me in school, he had been a victim of violence in school as well. I was not in the habit of confiding in Mother. She was rarely interested, let alone sympathetic unless she had an audience to impress. At the time I knew she was not helpful, so I didn't reach out to her, but she saw me coming home bruised and bloody often enough that she should reasonably have known how much trouble and danger I lived in at my school.

Mother had been mildly teased at school, but mostly her intellect brought admiration from her classmates and excellent grades from her teachers. To her, school was her escape. She was nowhere near as bizarre as either my father or I had been in school. She either didn't understand what school was like for me, or she simply did not think what was happening to me was important. Maybe she thought I would have something to "learn" from being in a public school. Perhaps she was responding from her emotions, and like a child latching onto a forgotten toy, she was not going to let me out of her sight.

I wanted to go to live with Anya, more than I had ever wanted anything else in my life. I knew she wouldn't hit me, and if I went to a real school, I wouldn't get teased or beaten up anymore, and I would get a real education instead of being bored all day, every day.

My mother dug in her heels. She didn't want to "lose" me and noisily threatened suicide if my father let me live with Anya. She got her way.

John Muir only went through third grade, and we were expected to attend fourth grade at a school below Martin Luther King Junior Way on Ashby called Malcolm X. I was bused there for a school visit, and I was beaten up in class for being the wrong color. I refused to go back. My brother was already enrolled in Malcolm X, but he got in a fight that was rather worse. A classmate stabbed him in the hand with a pencil, and my brother saw red and pounded the kid's face in. He "woke up" sitting on the kid's chest. Rather than risk any more of this, our parents put both of us into an alternative school.

Mother drove us since there was no realistic way to bus or BART there. That school was an interesting place, albeit useless in terms of education. The students did whatever they wanted to. There was a boy who cooked all day long, and his only mistake was that he typically baked things with way too much baking powder, and I can still taste it whenever I remember that school. I wanted to learn more than they were willing to teach. Mostly, I did crafts, and I read a lot, which is what I would have done at home. I dressed horse dolls by making them little hand-stitched saddles out of leather and wire.

There was a Christmas play. Yes, in the Berkeley of the Seventies Christmas was still allowed! I was an angel, and my father played Santa Claus—truly a dream come true for him. I made angel wings for my costume, about three feet long. The base was heavy cardboard, and I had made feathers for them out of rows and rows and rows of crepe paper, so they looked as much like actual wings as possible. My white dress was a long white nightgown of some sort.

The thing I remember most, though, is that I was a holy terror, and I used to throw chairs at people when I got upset. I believe they were too socially conscious to discipline me much though.

At the same time, my brother and I were taking swimming and trampoline classes at the YMCA. The swimming classes were sequential and progressive, beginning with "Minnows and Guppies" and ending up with "Sharks and Killer Whales", which included elementary lifesaving techniques.

My concern about the lifesaving techniques is that while it might be informative to teach a class of children how to be amateur lifeguards, actual lifesaving involves far more physical strength and endurance than one might come to expect if you are practicing on willing volunteers in a swimming pool rather than practicing on frightened victims in open water. As we will see later, the only real-world application I ended up with involved me remembering that it was absolutely forbidden to try to save a life when we were wearing heavy or restrictive clothing lest we turn one victim into two.

My brother took the same classes as I did, and he loved the trampoline. I believe Mother took us both to school and to swimming class after school because they were close together in time. We were expected to take BART home together afterward since the YMCA was only two blocks from the BART station.

During that time, my brother had piano lessons. I don't know what happened, but he quit, and I was not allowed to have piano lessons, though I asked for them. Every time my brother couldn't do something, I was barred from doing it lest I "make him feel bad." This made me very angry; why should I be punished for being able to do things that he could not? Why did my future have to be sacrificed to make sure he didn't feel inadequate?

It went beyond merely denying me lessons. I taught myself how to play a little from the John Thompson book on the piano. I could make my hands work together, but I'm sure it was not amazing. I remember learning to play one piece which had the lyrics "Stately as princes the swans part the lilies and glide under the willows." It was a pretty song, and I'm sure that my halting playing was offensive, at least to my mother. She told me I had "no touch" for the piano and made sure I understood I was not even to try to play. I stopped rather than risk any more of her ire.

I started taking ballet classes when I was almost seven. Mother would drive me to the Oakland Ballet and wait with the other mothers, although I knew she did not want to be doing this. Later on, she enrolled me in the professional school at the San Francisco Ballet, which I did not understand at the time. I had thought I was simply taking normal ballet classes. My mother only drove me a few times to my twice-weekly classes, and then she had her friend Jaida accompany me on BART to downtown, and then we took the bus from there to way out in the Sunset. After class, I always wanted to go to the amazing bakery nearby and eat some carb-laden pastry: ballet could make anyone hungry, and we worked very hard.

When I was about eight, I had to get myself to ballet class, and I made the BART trip alone. This was only dicey when I got home after dark. We lived on Fulton St. at that point: three blocks east of Ashby BART, and it was a walk I made hundreds of times alone. I was always frightened. Always. But I knew better than to tell that to my mother: She would scoff at me. I can't tell you how often she told me I "carried myself like a victim." She would demonstrate how tough she was and how straight she stood, and show me how strong she was when she walked. I believe I was meant to conclude that if only I could be like her, I would not have to be afraid of walking alone. After all, an eight-year-old child should be perfectly safe wandering around downtown San Francisco and Berkeley alone, right?

There were times when public transit did not go well at all. One day, I was in downtown Berkeley, and I was walking into a BART station, and a man brushed up against me and put his hand on my privates, saying "Why don't you slip me up your box?" or something like that. I got away, and I was very shaken up. When I got home and told my mother, she told me that I carried myself like a victim, and if I was tough like her, it would never happen.

Another time, when I was about ten, I wanted to go riding, and I knew there was a stable at Golden Gate Park, so I took BART and a bus out there, and I set off from the bus stop on foot to find the stable. I did not find them, but I found a place where someone was keeping a horse, and she let me have a short bareback ride, which was tremendous fun. Unfortunately, as I was walking back to the bus stop, there was a man in the bushes, probably a homeless man, and he called out to me. I don't remember what he said, but I was terrified, and I ran all the way to the police substation close to the edge of the park. I told them what happened, and I had an asthma attack. I don't remember whether my mother came and got me or whether I took public transportation home. She probably came and got me because of the asthma attack. It would have taken rather too long for me to recover.

My mother claimed that the only reason I was targeted by the guy in the park and the guy at the BART station was that I "carry myself like a victim." She then put on an embarrassing demonstration about how tough she was and told me a story about walking through Harlem at midnight. She said that when she did, a gentleman stopped her and asked her what she was doing there, and he did not assault her after she told him that she was not afraid. My interpretation of the story is that the gentleman felt it was dirty pool to mess with crazy women who are out alone in the wrong part of town. I did not think for a microsecond that my hugely fat mother would impress anyone as being "tough" when she was rather less physically fit than a microwave oven.

Now to be fair, it is completely possible—even likely—that I *do* carry myself like a victim. At twelve, and even much older than that, I did not have anything resembling "situational awareness" as the martial arts or military types would say, and I was certainly not able to defend myself with any guaranteed method, no matter how many knives I carried.

After some time with the school, we were coming up on the *Nutcracker* and I was slated to be cast as something or other. Our classes had gone from two to three times a week, and I was beginning to struggle with my asthma and with severe exhaustion. I was born with a mitral valve prolapse, which has tended to limit how hard I could exercise without chest pain and weakness.

When I was almost nine, I began to get a lot taller, and the head of the school informed my mother that I was going to be too tall to be a ballerina: height/weight requirements were absolute. At our full growth, we were allowed to be 100 pounds and granted one extra pound per inch. They told my mother that if I was 5'8 or above as they expected, I would simply never be able to make the weight. Not with my shoulders.

Eventually, I decided to quit ballet, and to become an actress instead.

During my time in ballet, my mother made a judgment about me which she mentioned years later. She told me I was neither the best nor the worst dancer in the class, but I was the only one who was always on the beat, and she knew that I was destined to become a musician and not a dancer. I did not resent this judgment, and I still feel it was probably the most insightful observation she ever made about me.

I loved to dance, though, and have continued to dance throughout my life. Ballet has made more of a difference for me in all physical endeavors than any other discipline, bar none. It has made every form of dance easily understandable because the core of the movement made sense, and everything was a variation on the basic building blocks I learned in ballet.

I had been attending yet another alternative school way up in the Berkeley Hills. It was called "Kilimanjaro", though my brother and I called the place "Kill-a-kid-jaro." My mother had gotten me into the school because of my Tuscarora (Iroquois Nation) ancestry. She had not thought this out especially well: the basic philosophy of this school was that color was what mattered, and I was the wrong color. Despite my Indian cheekbones, which are obvious to anyone of Native American ancestry, I was as pale as any Celt or German from the rest of my family tree, and once again I did not fit in.

I remember learning to hide from the other kids when things got ugly. One day, after I had been badly beaten by a couple of kids up there, I had hidden in a locked restroom until after the end of recess. After the bell, I ran as fast as I could down to the bus stop, terrified that the kids who had hit me would have seen me leave. I was bloody when I got to the bus stop and hid near it until I heard the bus at a distance. I can still remember how relieved I felt when I got on the bus and it pulled away from the bus stop, when I realized that they had not found me and I was going to get home safely.

It seemed my mother was willing to put me into any kind of an alternative school at all provided that it was not a gifted school. This meant I remained a freak. I have come to believe that her issue with private or alternative schools was less about money and more about giftedness, which is a strange attitude for a former Mensa member to take. It is almost as though she was willing to solve any problem except the real one. At Kilimanjaro, I went from merely sounding like a freak to looking and sounding like a freak. Seriously, sending an assertive, scrawny, gifted, overly verbal, pale-faced child to a school which prioritizes non-white ethnicity above all? To claim a category of difference for me which I was obviously not entitled to? What did she think was going to happen? She might as well have painted a target on my back!

Chapter 15

The Lonely House with the Lemon Tree
(1973–1976)

There was no believing she was getting better as you could not tell which one of her would wake up at any moment. It is so much easier to bear being hurt yourself than being blamed for someone hurting someone else. The shame from that alone is this boulder I have hanging around my neck.

—Mark Greyland, "Secret Keeper No More"

My mother had moved us to the first of three houses on Fulton St. in Berkeley from Hamilton Place in Oakland. Our house was behind another house, and it was small and dingy. My parents had their bedroom in a carpeted garage, and my brother and I had a bedroom. The house was on the block between Ashby and Prince St., about a mile west of Greyhaven. Mother no longer needed to pick us up from Greyhaven after school because we could walk home ourselves.

My relationships with my mother and father were no better in California than they had been in New York. My mother was a frustrated, unhappy woman, and my big mouth made me a frequent target of her wrath. My father did not spend time with me voluntarily, although I loved him and regarded him, overall, as far safer than she was.

My father now had a full-time job, unfortunately in New York as the Vice President of FCI, or First Coinvestors Inc., under Stanley Apfelbaum. He cataloged parts of the Pine Tree sales, some of which were named for him. Despite his expertise, he never collected coins himself beyond a very few kept in a small box. He invariably claimed that collecting coins was for rich people.

My father's fame and influence were growing. In 1975, he gave a lecture at Princeton University, "Tolkien and the Occult Revival", which was sponsored jointly by the English Department, the Infinity Club, a student science-fiction group, and the Society of Middle-Earth Readers. He also gave a seminar at the

Esalen Institute in Big Sur for scientists and physicists, sponsored by his friend and colleague, Jack Sarfatti. The topic was "Some Effects of Music on Consciousness: Overview and Preliminary Explorations." My father's fame, coupled with his commute to New York, made for increasing distance between him and our family. Maybe he felt he didn't need my mother or me any longer.

His employment with First Coinvestors was a boon to him for many years because, apparently unbeknownst to him, he and his room would be watched so that he could never sleep with any underage people while at coin conventions. Once First Coinvestors went out of business many years later, they could no longer protect him.

My father would commute to New York two weeks per month, though there were times when he was gone for a lot longer than that. Once he was gone for a few months. I missed him terribly when he was gone, and my mother was worse in his absence. When he was home and she did what she did, I could go to him, and he would dry my tears and hold me. When he was gone, there was nowhere to run.

Here is a quote from Donald Mader's essay describing Walter's conduct as a house guest in New York at that time:

Although based in Berkeley, California, Breen was frequently in New York for business in the 1970s and 1980s. … He'd arrive around 7:00 p.m., and somewhere around 9:30 p.m. he would take out his Y Ching and throw his changes. This would inevitably produce something to the effect that it was "dangerous to cross the great water" which he would interpret as a warning that it was inadvisable to take the subway back under the East River, and ask to stay the night.…

On another of his visits, with malice aforethought, I arranged for another Atlantean, Rick Nielsen, photographer and owner of a gay cardshop-annex-gallery on lower Seventh Avenue in the Village, to come around so they could compare their past lives. They could agree on nothing; one insisted Atlanteans wore yellow robes; the other insisted on white and so forth. By 4:00 a.m. when they decided they must have lived on the lost continent in different eras, I had long since ceased to find the confrontation amusing.

This set of recollections describes my father accurately. He was happiest holding forth for hours on end with his friends while smoking pot and wearing nothing. In comparison, my mother and brother and I must have seemed so dull to him. Nobody was admiring him or listening to hours and hours of his rambling, scholarly discourse.

While we were living in that Fulton St. house, my father's relationship with my mother began to deteriorate. My mother wanted my father's love, but he no longer desired her sexually and he made no secret of the fact. Her fury and anguish at this development was painful to watch, but it was dangerous too, because she often took her feelings out on anyone who crossed her path.

One night when I was eight years old, I knocked on their bedroom door. I don't remember what I was asking for, it might have been a glass of milk or something like that. She screamed at me and said through noisy tears, "Do you want me to give you my heart bleeding?" I was stunned and didn't know what to do. Later, I asked my father why she had been so upset, and he said in a very stiff, formal, grim kind of voice, "Your mother and I were making love." He made it sound as though he might have been saying, "Your mother and I were amputating each other's limbs."

I felt no maternal bond with my mother. None. I was terrified of her, even though I really did not want to be. I felt so alone in her presence. Her menace never stopped, even if she wore the happy face. One wrong word from me, or even the wrong facial expression, and the world would end.

I also knew her well enough to know that any weakness on my part would make her worse. Even then I felt that she was more dangerous when she thought she had the upper hand. I learned to oppose her at an early age, like the puffer fish that is unpleasant to take a bite out of. It didn't save me from everything, but it did save me from subjugation, which I saw in my brother and my father, and which terrified me in a way that I can barely describe. It was bad enough to live with her. To silence my protests and to allow myself to be enslaved was unthinkable.

My tactics horrified my brother. He thought that opposing her would cause her to become violent. He was right, of course, but I thought that I would go through far less hell if I endured the occasional beating but I would not allow myself to be forced to think what she wanted, and I would not be forced to accept her version of events and say what she wanted me to say. I am afraid that sounds like an awfully weird mindset for a little girl, but that was what I thought and felt.

My mother was so miserable and frustrated that she often beat me severely, for no reason I could see except her temper. She told me when I was an adult that I was such a bad child that she had to stop herself from beating me to death on at least two occasions. She seemed to think that I should sympathize with her for having to raise such a monster as I was.

My mother was violent with me on many different occasions when we lived in that house. Once she threw the dog's water dish at me. I remember walking along College Avenue with her one day, and I had been holding her hand, like a daughter might do at that age. Without warning, she twisted the skin on the back of my hand with her fingernails until she drew blood. I have no idea what I did. I must have said something wrong, but my impression was that her "discipline" of me was random and had nothing to do with my disobedience. My sense of honor told me she was unjust: I knew when I deserved to be punished, and most of the things she did to me made no sense at all.

To this day, I am not clear on what I did that made me such a failure at being a daughter. I have no doubt that I was a bratty child, but many children are brats and do not deserve to die. It might have been that she saw my rebellion and my refusal to surrender as a line in the sand she thought she could beat out of me.

I am speculating here. Maybe since Patrick had surrendered and she did not fight with him, she thought beating me to the point of surrender would get us to stop fighting. Does that make any sense? There was never a point at which I accepted her "discipline" and then was hugged and forgiven. I did not see what she was doing as just, nor did I see myself as misbehaving. To me, what she did was only about her temper, not my behavior. I knew I was naughty, but I was not punished for naughtiness. I was punished randomly, for how she felt.

It was in that house that I had reason to dread the shower, and not the bathtub.

I didn't want my mother in the shower with me. If I could BART to ballet class by myself, why on earth would I need my mother to help me in the shower? She was not there to help me get clean. In fact, I felt a lot less clean after the shower. I don't want to talk about what she did. I can't talk about what she did. I can't think about what she did.

To this day, I have trouble with the shower. Sometimes I have so much trouble with the flashbacks from this incident that I pile towels or clothing across my chest. Sometimes I have to force myself into the shower, because being naked is unbearable, feeling the water on my skin reminds me of her hands on my skin and her voice whispering threats in my ear. Even now, sometimes I have to count backwards from one hundred to keep myself from stumbling out of the shower with a head full of soap and a heart full of pain.

Here is an excerpt from Elisabeth Waters' deposition when she was being asked about my mother molesting me in the shower:

MR. DOLAN: Let's go on to another topic here. Do you have any information that would pertain to Marion Zimmer Bradley having any sexual interaction with Moira Stern?

ELISABETH WATERS: No.

MR. DOLAN: Have you ever heard that issue discussed at any time?

ELISABETH WATERS: I have heard Moira say some things about it.

MR. DOLAN: What have you heard Moira say about it?

ELISABETH WATERS: She said that one time her mother fondled her breasts while she was in the shower.

MR. DOLAN: Anything else?

ELISABETH WATERS: That Moira said to me, no.

MR. DOLAN: Okay. Did you ever ask Marion if any of that was true?

ELISABETH WATERS: Yes.

MR. DOLAN: What did Marion say?

ELISABETH WATERS: She said that children before the age of puberty didn't have erogenous zones.

MR. DOLAN: Anything else she said to you?

ELISABETH WATERS: No.

MR. DOLAN: When did she tell you that?

ELISABETH WATERS: When I asked her if—when I said that Moira was—when I said that I had been visiting Moira in the hospital, and that Moira had said that Marion fondled her breasts in the shower.

MR. DOLAN: How old was—strike that. What year was this that you had this discussion with Marion Zimmer Bradley?

ELISABETH WATERS: I guess it would have been around 1990.

MR. DOLAN: Did you ever ask Marion if she actually did fondle Moira?

ELISABETH WATERS: No.

MR. DOLAN: Did you ever inquire of Marion whether there was any truth about Moira's statement that Marion had been touching her breasts when she was in the shower?

ELISABETH WATERS: No, I just told her Moira had said that, and she said that children that age didn't have erogenous zones.

This is what she said to the lawyers in 1999 before making an agreement that she would only continue to testify if they did not ask her any more questions about me:

> MR. DOLAN: *Did you ever tell Elisabeth Waters that children didn't have erogenous zones?*
>
> MZB: *I may well have.*
>
> MR. DOLAN: *Do you have the belief that children don't have erogenous zones?*
>
> MZB: *At the time I believed it.*
>
> MR. DOLAN: *And what time was that?*
>
> MZB *I think it was probably when my own kids were young."*

One day Mother tied me to a chair at the kitchen table and threatened to pull out my teeth with a pair of pliers. She thought she was teaching me to not bite my brother. It makes me feel very strange when I talk about things like this. Worse, Patrick was there and saw and heard the whole thing because it was being done for his "benefit."

Here is what Lisa told the attorney about it in her deposition:

> MR. DOLAN: *What did Marion tell you about that episode?*
>
> ELISABETH WATERS: *That Moira kept biting Patrick, and she couldn't think of any way to stop her, so she tied her to a chair and threatened to pull out all of her teeth with pliers, and Moira became hysterical, and Marion untied her and let her go, and Moira never bit her brother again.*

I never forgot this incident, but it would not have mattered if I had. My mother bragged and bragged about how she had "cured" me of biting my brother. However, I continued to bite him until we lived in the next house, and we quit fighting. Naturally, my mother never had the slightest curiosity about *why* I was biting him rather than trying to train me out of it with yellow plastic rope and pliers. It was my reflexive defense, which began because Patrick was bigger than I was, and we fought like cats and dogs. For comparison's sake, declawed cats and beaten dogs routinely become "fear-biters." I believe that was the case with me.

My mother petted and coddled my brother Patrick, which made me furiously jealous. I cannot remember a single time that she ever hit him or yelled at him.

That does not mean it did not happen, only that she did not do it in front of me. He told me that her methods with him took a very different form. He remembers to this day hiding under a table listening to me scream while she beat me. When asked about physical abuse, this is what Patrick said:

Physical. Absolutely. But that is so much easier to bear than head games. Screaming is bad, but little whispers and threats work so much better to chill your blood and recreate being cold and naked hiding under tables hearing the shouting.

—Mark Greyland, "Secret Keeper No More"

In a way, I believe he got the worse end of the deal, being coddled while his baby sister was beaten; how does one's young manhood survive being treated as too weak to endure what your baby sister must endure? Patrick ended up thinking that if only he could do something differently, he could save me or stop her from hurting me.

Mother was entirely aware of what she did because she and my father both wanted to do away with conventional gender roles. My father disdained masculinity and anything which went along with it and spoke as if traditional masculinity was the source of all the evils in the world. For this reason, I had to be trained to not be girlish, and any signs of masculinity in Patrick had to be forcibly eradicated. It did not surprise me in the least that she would coddle him while roughing me up. Only years later did I understand that Patrick let himself be destroyed by her because he thought he could protect me by doing so.

I trance out and visions fill me at the drop of a hat, then the cold spot from everything you agreed to being a joke and the sound of screams rise and I'm balling up and "too late, too late could I have done more" wars with "she never listened anyway you are nothing and the pain for her rises and ....

—Mark Greyland, "Secret Keeper No More"

Patrick has told me that what we call survivor's guilt has long been a fixture of his life. I shudder to think of what it did to him. I was the firebrand, the noisy brat, the focus of her rage. I cannot imagine being in the position of trying to behave well enough to keep another human being from committing violence against a smaller person.

Patrick used to tell me that Mother was like the hamster that ate her babies.

One story my mother told me when we were living in the house with the lemon tree has always stuck with me. She told me she had bashed a cat's brains in with a rock for refusing to nurse its young. She felt that what she had done was good and right, and I was expected to honor her for being so concerned about the health of kittens that she would kill their neglectful mother.

It seems to me that this view was shortsighted. I also felt a bit like the kittens.

Chapter 16

The Sad Waltz
(1976)

agony shrieks hollowly from what is left of my soul
I too can be crumpled up and thrown away
Dying, I feel I might just disappear
wordless

—Moira Greyland, "Ghosts"

The Sad Waltz (*Valse Triste*) was a short film made in '76 by Bruno Bozzetto, which I saw with my father. Set to music by Sibelius of the same name, it was about a little grey kitten whose home had been bombed into ruins. She would see mirages of the things that had been there before: a bright kitchen with a grandmother and a rocking chair, a bird in a cage, a saucer of milk; all things a kitten would love... but each time she tries to leap onto Grandmother's lap or catch the bird, she discovers she is hanging from rubble by her claws.

My home was also a mirage, and I cannot watch that film without disproportionate tears. I had famous parents, loved by everyone, and a home people loved to visit: it was a place people felt they could be themselves, but it only felt like that to the visitors. Real love? Real acceptance? Mirages. I, too, ran from one thing to another, looking for love, since I could not run to my mother and father. I have found my share of mirages, but in the final analysis, I am the mirage: the child prodigy who is supposed to "save the world", destined in my father's imagination to bring his Grand Vision to the world.

In reality, I am not a child prodigy destined to save the world. I was a little girl who wanted her mommy and daddy to love her, but they were too busy achieving their own goals to bother with me. The reality of who I was did not agree with what they wanted me to be. I could not be the adoring sycophant my mother wanted. I would not participate in my father's Grand Vision. Yet my refusal of them put me on the outside of my own family. I was not loved,

I was nothing. I was part "prodigy" and part monster: a living, breathing, irreconcilable difference.

The last thing in Valse Triste which winks out of sight is the grey kitten herself.

Did I disappear too? I tried. Sometimes interacting with my parents was unavoidable. I never stopped hoping that they would love me since I was as naive as the grey kitten in the film. Nearly every interaction reminded me that our family was a mirage. My mother and father did not love me: to the contrary, and not only was I not safe, I was in danger much more of the time than I care to think about, even now.

It was beyond them not loving me. I was not supposed to notice that where they said they loved me, my interactions with my mother nearly always involved her rage and frightening physical outbursts, and my father openly disliked and mistrusted me because there were things he wanted to do that I simply could not do. He told me plainly that he had no more interest in me than if I had been a stranger… and yet I am supposed to act happy and believe that I am loved by this wonderful, creative family which is so accepting of difference. Well, perhaps some difference.

Not mine.

When I was ten, I tried to commit suicide; I took a lot of aspirin in front of my mother. She ignored my suicide attempt. I don't know why she was so indifferent. It's possible that she was too absorbed with her own pain to worry about me. Maybe she thought I was trying to upstage her. After all, both she and my father routinely threatened suicide, though I do not think either of them ever made a serious attempt.

I wanted to die. I didn't see any way that my pain would ever get better, and I didn't think I wanted to spend what life I had left being a punching bag for my mother. I handled my symptoms alone, downstairs, but I realized that if I was to remain alive I might as well find something to do. Even if my life didn't matter to her, it was going to matter to me.

Why was I so miserable that I decided that dying was the only way out of my pain? Several things happened when I was ten, a few good, but many bad.

First the good: my mother sent me to a wonderful summer camp that year and the year before. I would routinely wake up at 4 a.m. and go down to the barn to catch the horses and throw feed. Then, an hour later we would saddle everyone up, hanging bridles on the saddle horns and leaving everyone scheduled to be ridden in their halters until the ride. I was a constant presence and a good rider. I ended up being a kind of teacher's aide on trail rides, and I was even allowed to teach a riding class. I warmed to leadership and to teaching and knew I had found an important part of my life.

I also got a bicycle just prior to this, and I was practiced enough to ride it all over town. I hated to take public transit anywhere, although I did constantly from the time I was about seven. There was simply no alternative. My father could not be relied upon to drive because it upset him so badly and because he was working, albeit working at home. Mother was also working, writing to put food on the table.

My best friend back then was named Rohana, and she was a few years younger than I was. She lived six blocks north on Fulton from Prince St. to Derby, and I would walk to her house all the time. Her father Elliot Kenin was a banjo player of some note, and he sang funny and wonderful songs. Sometimes Rohana and I would sit on Shattuck Avenue near the BART station to sell the jewelry we made.

I was very interested in fishing, and Elliot took the bunch of us fishing. I caught a little perch, and he sliced its head off and cooked it. I was horrified by the fact that it had to be killed, but we ate it, and it was delicious. I was also disappointed in myself that I ate it but lacked the courage to kill it.

I wanted to make some money, so I worked for our neighbor Ted on Fulton Street. He gave me a quarter an hour to pick strawberries for him, and later he would give me a dollar an hour when I asked for a raise. Then, I got a paper route for the Oakland Tribune, and I had to bike through the part of Oakland every morning early which was between Adeline and Shattuck, from the farthest edge of West Berkeley to several blocks into Oakland. Nothing too fearsome happened except that people routinely stiffed me for their newspapers, which infuriated my father when he came with me to try to help me collect. I believe I only kept the paper route for three months or so. I felt at the time that it was a scary part of town, and it was ridiculous for me to be out there. Although nothing untoward happened other than the loss of money, it was more good luck than good management.

There was a fellow in Berkeley who would give me five dollars a month to have advertisements for him on my bicycle spokes, and so once a month, my brother and I would head over to his house on Martin Luther King Junior Way to put his paper circles into our wheels. Rohana and I also used to make jewelry together and go to craft fairs with her mother Millea.

I learned to sew. Sewing was both good and bad. Mother did me a great kindness by showing me how to operate her sewing machine. My friend from the Faire, Sally Schneider, taught me how to sew things together. The first thing

I made with my mother's sewing machine was a shirt: I had come up with the design myself from things I had seen. It was to be a typical Renaissance Faire peasant shirt with a yoke back and a collar. I did not do a good job, and I ruined three yards of lavender cotton fabric.

My mother was incensed. You would think I had blown up a city by her level of rage. To her I had *wasted* fabric, and we could not afford it. Worse than that, it was my fault because I had refused to use a pattern. It didn't matter to her that no patterns existed for what I wanted to make. It was the principle of the thing: If I had used a pattern, I would not have wasted the three yards of fabric.

But I did not change my evil ways.

When I was in kindergarten and second grade with nothing to do, I had done a lot of drawing—as in a *lot*. All that drawing never made me an artist though. To this day, my drawings have only been workmanlike visual shorthand. I could give a general idea of what I intended to make, but my drawings were nothing that anyone would put on their wall.

Fortunately, I was better at sewing than I was at drawing. I learned very quickly how to draft patterns with a ruler and a piece of tailor's chalk, and I could soon make nearly any kind of costume. At the Renaissance Faire, I had to sew my own costumes or pay someone else to if I could not borrow something. One of the first things I learned to make was skirts, both pleated and gored, then shifts, or chemises and then bodices. A corset was like a bodice but with a stronger lining and more boning, and it could often be cut in one piece provided the center front was right on the grain and the laced back was not too diagonal. Of course, the boning obscured any stretch that could have even tried to come in.

Shapes for corsets and bodices, and even shifts, bum rolls, ruffs and hoopskirts, were all easy to remember. I have the kind of memory for shapes that lets me know what a good curve looks like. It is the same aspect of memory which enables me to spell: I remember what things look like, no matter what language they are in. I would be lost if I tried to spell with rules or phonics.

The first time I had to make something which really needed a premade pattern was a Victorian corset. I had already made several on a straightforward pattern I could easily alter according to the measurements of the girl needing it, recut it— even make a new pattern with my usual ruler and tailoring chalk—but this style of corset used a new pattern which was a nightmare of small curved pieces and gussets. I borrowed the pattern from one of the ladies at Court. It took a few tries, that one, between figuring out how to get the satin to not fray to shreds while putting it together (Fray-check!) and even having to clip a few seam allowances before sewing the pieces together so that the curves would lie flat. Once I got an overlock machine, which we would call a "serger" today, fraying edges were no longer an issue.

Sewing was very good for me, but it made a lot of friction with my mother. Not just for the fabric I ruined but because once I started making things, I had heaps of new ways to upset her. Let us not imagine for a moment that she was angry because I was a better seamstress than she had ever been within a few weeks of learning to operate a sewing machine. It could not possibly have been that.

No, it was because I was an evil hammer-thief.

One day, she decided I had stolen her hammer, and she went nuts over it. It was a reasonable suspicion: I routinely used a hammer with the two-piece tool we used to install grommets, or extra-large eyelets. It was not likely that anybody but I would ever use a hammer in our house. My father didn't use tools, nor did my brother.

I had not stolen her hammer. My denial did no good, and she told me again and again that I was lying. Defending myself was pointless: Mother was positive that everything I said was a lie. I was compulsively truthful. I insisted on telling the truth no matter how damning to me because I didn't want to get hit any more.

This was not the first or the only time she had accused me of stealing from her. She routinely accused me of stealing her clothes—a much less reasonable suspicion. Where I was a scrawny child of ten, she was around 250 pounds at just under 5'3". I could not have worn her clothing even if I had wanted to. The accusation itself made me uncomfortable, not just for the punishment which would come with neither evidence nor proof but for the fact that her clothing smelled like her, and I didn't want to think about that.

I did lie to her once, that I can remember.

I took a bath one day, and I wanted to shave my legs like a big girl. I knew my mother would not want me to do so: after all, we did not do anything for men. Or at least I was not supposed to: she shaved her legs all the time. I used her razor, not knowing how to do it properly, and I cut a strip off the front of my shin, about four inches by half an inch. It was superficial, but bled like mad. When my mother heard my screams, she burst into the bathroom, like a responsible parent. She asked me what I had done, and I told her that I had been splashing around and the razor fell on me.

Marion's drinking was another matter. Alcohol was always around: my mother believed that if my brother and I were allowed to drink alcohol, it would prevent drinking from being a big mystery. Also, alcohol could be relied upon to do to me what pot was supposed to do: make me stupid and encourage me to lower my guard. They were always trying to find something that would get me to stop being such a prude! Marion kept sweet alcoholic drinks called "Hereford Cows"— rather like Bailey's Irish Cream—which my brother and I were encouraged to drink. But for whatever reason, I am not especially interested in drinking—I somehow picked up my father's horror of alcohol.

I was oblivious to a lot of my mother's drinking and never attributed her mood swings to alcohol. My brothers described her as a drunk though. I knew that often when she got upset, she would pour herself a drink, so I thought the moods caused the drunkenness. I also believed, in my childish fashion, that if she drank alcohol when she was upset, she would suddenly turn into an alcoholic, and that prospect terrified me since she had spoken so much about the awful things her father had done when he was drunk. Once she got very upset and poured herself a large Bloody Mary. I drank the gin from the top of her tomato juice to keep her from becoming an alcoholic. It tasted horrible.

My father took me to two movies at the University Theater near UC Berkeley when I was ten. One was *Tommy*, which terrified me. I did not know what a flashback was at the time, but that was the reason I got so violently upset that I had to leave the theater during the show: I was having flashbacks, and I was a mess emotionally. He was not happy with me about this. The other movie was *Rocky Horror Picture Show*, which I liked. He loved it and was very happy and excited when he saw it. He seemed to think that the people in the movie really understood what he was trying to do.

Sometimes I went to the movies alone. It was a one-stop BART ride with a short walk from my house. I met my best friend Jean at the movies; I was ten, and she was almost thirteen. She was standing behind me in the line for the bathroom during an intermission, and I told her she had beautiful hair. She and I started talking and became fast friends. I also did something rather dastardly. I looked over my shoulder and said, none too quietly; "I think the movie's starting." She looked at me as though I was crazy, and said in a whisper, "No it's not!" I grinned, shook my head no, grabbed her hand, and hauled her off to the bathroom since the line had vanished.

Jean adored me as much as I adored her, even though in her words I was "as hard as a New York hooker." I told her about Mother strangling me in the bathtub, and she was really nice to me about it. I am sure I told her about the pliers thing, too. She saw my mother being a terror, but my house was safer for her than it was for me, and I was glad she was there a lot. She got along with my father and with my brother as well. Better than I did.

Jean loved my family. Her family was conventional, and she felt alone and different around them. It wasn't just Jean: overall, the people I brought over *loved* my family. My family was amazing: they read, heck, *wrote* science fiction, my mother was famous, and everyone was eccentric. Frankly, my friends tended to fit into my family better than I did. Of course, they didn't see what I saw.

Mostly. I knew I had to warn people that my parents would probably be nude when they first came over. I also had to warn my friends to not go into the hot tub without a bathing suit and to make sure never to be alone with the grownups if they could help it. I also tried to tell them that anyone who wanted to give them drugs intended to separate them from their clothing.

Every form of alternative sexuality and spirituality was not only accepted but expected. Christians were derided, of course, and anyone who believed in God quickly learned to hide it around my family, lest they be subjected to a long, superior lecture meant to shame the believer out of faith.

My parents loved kids, especially if they had dependent personalities and reasonable intelligence. I had neither, and I refused to do what I was told. I was an enormous disappointment.

While my social life had begun to bloom, my relationship with my father was going very badly. He mentioned to me every week or so that he wanted to "babysit me" during my "first acid trip." By acid, my father meant LSD, or Lysergic Acid Diethylamide. It was never presented as a request but as a statement, as though it was a foregone conclusion that I would have one and the only thing to be determined was when and where. He was very disappointed and very angry with me for refusing to take acid with him. Why was it so important that I do so?

From the accounts of a few of his victims, including Jean a few years later, LSD was simply the means to establish a sexual connection with an otherwise unwilling partner. LSD would preoccupy them with unrelated images and mental experiences, compromise their memory, and immobilize them enough to make escape or protest impossible. This way, he could claim that anything they didn't like was a hallucination. His real hope was to make sex with him have a positive association.

I was nervous about my father's physical attentions. Most of it was made to seem accidental, like too-wet kisses or wandering hands when he managed to get a bunch of people in a group hug, but I was encouraged to create a hard denial in my mind. After all—said my mother—my father liked *boys* and would never bother with girls, who she claimed he thought were disgusting. Therefore the gooey kisses didn't mean *that*, and the wandering hands were accidental.

I was required to view his wish to babysit me on acid as perfectly benign and fatherly. I was required to ignore what I saw, and heard, and felt, even though my father used to tell me, all the time, "Incest is *Nicest* spelled sideways."

In any event, between my refusal to smoke pot with him, my refusal to take acid with him, and my refusal to go naked around the house, and the fact that my objections grew stronger over time and not weaker, my father came to the inescapable conclusion that he was not going to be able to seduce me. I went from being someone he loved to someone who had ruined his life. This was not your average refusal because to him I was supposed to be the bearer of his Grand Vision to the future. Getting me involved was an integral part of his plan; for me to be a prude destroyed the whole thing. If I could not be made to understand that sex all the time would eliminate all human problems, how would anyone understand it? My prudishness had ruined his life.

But I was not finished inadvertently spoiling his fun.

I would get very angry when people called him a child molester, even though I knew it was true. I knew my father regarded people my age as "romantic" targets. I was loyal to my father and hoped he would stop. I know this is absurd, but I thought I could get him to understand. Like a child, I tried to talk him out of what he wanted to do. I asked my father repeatedly why he didn't "pick on someone his own size." Why did it have to be kids? Why didn't he want a grownup? He was not interested in my perspective: He wanted what he wanted, and what he wanted was sex with children.

He was infuriated with me and felt betrayed. He told me, very clearly, that there was no reason that he would love me any more than any random child he knew. I cried when he told me this and pleaded with him to tell me it wasn't true. I told him we had blood ties and asked how couldn't it mean anything to him that I was his own daughter: His response was to sneer and to tell me that we did not have blood ties at all, but only "sperm ties."

It got worse from there. He decided that not only had I betrayed him and his vision but that I was "in league with [my] mother to put [him] in jail." He told me again and again that he would die in prison and that it would be all my fault. He let me know in no uncertain terms that he did not trust me and that he would never trust me again. I had crossed the line, and now I was one of *them*. I had become part of the enemy.

I didn't want him to hate me, and I was devastated by his rejection. I had believed my father loved me because he was the one who looked at me kindly and held me after my mother beat me up. I bonded to him. To her, never. He was the only kindness I knew. He was the sun in my sky, but the feeling was not mutual.

Still, I refused to let go of the illusion that he loved me.

My mother was walking along Prince St. near our house with me one day. She asked me if she could divorce my father, and I became distraught. I was so frightened and upset that I didn't know what to do. What would happen to me if he left? He was the only kind voice in the house and the only adult who didn't hit me. If he left, my life would be over. Of course, I begged and pleaded with my mother to not divorce him… as though I was a factor in the decision. She was very upset with me and blamed me for her misery, but at least this was not news.

Not long after that, my mother sent my brother and me to visit with our lesbian neighbor over near the corner of Prince and Deakin, about a block away. I had the sense at the time that Mother had sent us there not so that we would have fun but because the neighbor lady was very lonely and needed company. It almost seemed like we were to be "borrowed children", as if we had been taken out of a petting zoo to help her feel better.

The neighbor lady was hostile and angry while determined to "do this right." She did some crafts with us: something involving glitter and tongue depressors and a ceramic cup. I was aware that this was a very strange situation: I knew something was very, very wrong, but I did not know what.

A few days later she shot herself to death.

'I am half sick of shadows', said the Lady of Shalott.

—Alfred Tennyson, "The Lady of Shalott"

Chapter 17

My Strange Love of Faire
(1975–1977)

I don't know love. I was built to protect not to love, so there is no use for me other than this.

—Leeloo Dallas, *The Fifth Element*

I did everything I could to stay busy—and out of the house. Once I got involved in the Renaissance Faire, the Dickens Christmas Fair, and the SCA I was gone for thirty weekends a year at least. I had ballet lessons and swimming lessons, and I worked hard at everything I did. For years, I lost myself in work, too busy to notice how alone I was.

Ah, the Faire… the saving grace of my life. I began at the Renaissance Faire when I was nine, courtesy of my uncle Don. He had brought me into the Parade Guild, also known as St. Cuthbert's Guild. I was to be part of the Heraldic Animals parade, and he had helped me make a Cockatrice mask out of painted plaster over gauze strips over a wire armature, which I wore with the page costume Serpent had made for me; a cockatrice is a two-legged dragon with a rooster's head. I also carried what they called a "Jingle Johnny" in the parades, which was a long stick with four sticks at right angles covered with bells on the top.

When I was eleven, I started doing all three Faires: Northern Faire, Southern Faire, and Dickens Fair. Between the three of them, I was away for thirty weekends a year, and that meant I could have some space from the absolute insanity in that "home." Unlike school, which was populated with normal children, the Faire was full of the different, the misfits, the strange—people like me. What a blessing it was to finally be around other misfits and also to be somewhere that I did a number of things well enough to be noticed in a good way.

There was a lot of overlap between people who went to the Faire, where the primary the focus was improvisational theater, and the SCA, where the focus was hanging out with friends while in costume. Many of us spent every spare weekend either at the SCA or at the Faire as well as attending weeknight rehearsals, making costumes, learning new skills—even studying music, dance, or a host of related skills. In any event, we got to dress funny, talk funny, dance, sing, and hang out with other people doing the same things. I dragged all my friends to the Faire.

Not everything at the Faire or SCA was rosy.

I remember hauling my friend Jessica out of a tent at Southern Faire: She had been invited in there to see some of a man's drawings. I knew exactly what he meant to do to her, so I grabbed her by the arm, yanked her out, and screamed at him, "Leave her alone; she's a *virgin!*"

When I was ten, Donovan Duncan Adkison, a mostly blind photographer and masseur, invited me to his home. He gave me a conventional, capable massage and then made a pass at me. I politely declined, got my clothes on, and quickly left. I was aware that he had committed an ethical breach, and as such, I was not obligated to anything beyond politeness; I did not have to feel guilty or explain my departure. However, even though I could get away from Duncan, I would never have told my mother. She would have been furious with me. My father would have gotten That Look in his eye and rubbed his hands with glee. Even at that age, he would have wanted me to not be upset, but to integrate sexuality into every single relationship. Worse, he probably would have asked me why I left and no doubt reminded me what a prude I was.

Sadly, strange things happened at the SCA, too. When I was 12, I took medieval dance classes with Flieg a few blocks from my house in Berkeley. I was a good dancer, so I felt secure enough to be a bratty adolescent, roping others into doing the Bunny Hop amid all the medieval dances: pavanes and bransles (pronounced "brawl") and galliards. The result of this was Flieg inventing the "Bransle de Lapignette", or Bunny Bransle.

One day, Flieg drove me home from some SCA event or other, he gave me a hug goodbye, and then, to my horror, he jammed his tongue down my twelve-year-old throat. I managed to make my excuses, politely, and escaped before he tried anything else. I was very lucky that he decided to do this while parked in front of the orange church across from my mother's house rather than at the SCA event itself, where I might not have been able to find a way to get away.

After that, I avoided being near him if there was any possibility of being alone with him. I do not remember dance classes with him after, that, but it made a difference in my life. In an instant I went from being the teacher's pet to someone who could not be around my dance teacher any more, at least not in my mind.

I was dragged into a situation I didn't belong in and wanted no part of. He was an adult, I was a child, and now I felt used, soiled, as though he had used me to wipe his nose on.

I could not tell any other adult in either case, let alone the police. A child automatically has less credibility than an adult. I was certain that my objections would have been met with a condescending "You must have misunderstood" or worse, a denial. Besides, he hadn't "hurt" me. I had left before he could back up his words with actions. It was easier at that point to learn to identify dangerous situations and to get away before things got too weird. We kids could look out for each other, but there was no way to fight back legally if someone had bad intentions.

It made the world a little smaller.

Now some men will tell you that it is harmless to make a pass at a girl, all girls, every time, just in case they might get lucky. Here is the problem: when a man makes a pass, it permanently changes the relationship. Instead of Duncan being a kindly older man who was looking out for me, now he was one of the predators that I had to be wary of.

When I was eleven, I landed my first major theatrical role. I played Alice in Wonderland at the Dickens Fair. I prepared exhaustively both for the audition and for the part, reading all of Alice many times and discussing "The Annotated Alice" at length with my father. He loved the work of Lewis Carroll, and he and I spent a lot of time further annotating the book.

Of course, I realized many years later that my father had a bit too much in common with Lewis Carroll. This was not a shared interest based on wonderful literary devices and madcap humor: Lewis Carroll loved photographing little naked girls.

At the time, I didn't know that. All I knew is that my father and I had something to talk about which had nothing to do with my being a prude. I had been cast in large part because according to Sylvia, my beloved director, I was a dead ringer for the Tenniel engraving of Alice found in the books.

I loved playing Alice, and I did my best. There were many rehearsals, and Mother had to drive me to Novato for a fitting more than once when the costumes were being made. Once there was a problem with the costume—possibly it might have been delayed at the dry cleaners. Mother made me a shirt and skirt which she believed looked enough like the Alice costume to suffice. This was a kind act, but my response was not kind.

I was a rotten perfectionist and made no secret of my disappointment. The original blouse had a collar and buttons, and the skirt was pleated with tiny pleats and cut in gores, so it was very full at the hem. The costume was meant to be pale blue with white bands at the skirt hem and sleeve ruffles. Mother had made me a skirt and blouse of bright blue polyester knit with no white bands. The skirt was narrow and the wrong shape: straight from hip to hem. The blouse was made on a shapeless pattern with raglan sleeves and an elastic neckline and sleeve cuffs. Raglan sleeves are what one might find on a peasant blouse: instead of actual sleeves being set into armholes, the top edge of the sleeve forms part of a square neckline, and elastic holds the shirt in place.

I would always internally reference this afterward as being the reason I refused to let Mother ever sew anything for me again. No doubt Mother was furious with me for hating what she had made me on short notice. Yes, she had made me a costume, but it looked utterly wrong. In retrospect, my brutal honesty shocks me. I hope I am no longer so vicious. One might also reasonably conclude that my mother had poor eyesight and was doing her best.

In any case, my ability to sew was not lost on the Faire people around me who needed costume pieces, and I began to earn money sewing costumes. When I was twelve, I became the youngest person ever to appear on the Renaissance Faire's approved list for people who could be commissioned to make costumes. That meant the things I made were not only known to be well made but historically accurate enough to look right to the Faire patrons: natural fibers, concealed seams, period colors, naturally period shapes and designs, and awareness of sumptuary laws. No purple, no scarlet red, no cloth of gold unless you were royal, and no velvet unless you were noble!

Rohana worked at the Dickens Fair with me after I had learned to sew, and I got to make some dresses for our use. Recently, she showed me pictures of her daughter wearing a black-and-white plaid taffeta dress I had made back then, when I was twelve. It had a border of knife-pleated hard-pressed pleats: It was a thing of beauty, even all these years later. She remarked on how quickly I had cut it out and put it together. Mostly what I remember about that dress was the endless plaid-matching, where the seams have to line up one line on the plaid with the same one on the other side so it looks nice, not messy. She also saw my earlier experiments from the year before when I was eleven, where I had made some skirts with the wide wales on the corduroy going side to side instead of up and down—not a good look!

For all that I resented having to BART around so much, it might just have been a blessing in disguise. Mother owned an orange 1967 VW squareback station wagon, and later an identical one in white. On one trip to Novato for a costume fitting she got into a fifteen-car pileup, and on the way home another time, the car caught on fire just off University Avenue in Berkeley. My cousin Fiona was in the car that time, and I was in the back deck, as usual. I had to wake Fiona up and make her get out of the car so we could escape the fire. There were many car accidents with Mother at the wheel. When we were still in New York, she crashed, and none of us had our seatbelts on. All the SCA swords and things that were in the back of the car flew into the front of the car. We were okay, oddly enough. Bumps and bruises and scrapes, nothing more.

As Alice, I was part of several different stage shows and scenes. One included my aunt Tracy as The Red Queen and her friend Samantha as the White Queen. I admired them both tremendously as actresses and felt so honored to be cast opposite them.

At the end of the run, the director gave me an Alice in Wonderland doll, which thrilled me. I had never owned a doll. I don't really have a way to explain what it meant to me when Sylvia gave me that doll. After all, little girls usually have dolls, and know they are pretty and even believe that their parents will protect them. When Sylvia gave me that doll, it made me think that maybe someone in the world thought I was a little girl and that maybe even I deserved to have a doll.

At the Dickens Fair the following year I was given a different role, which seemed to suit my personality better than Alice. Alice was meant to be mild-mannered, quiet, and studious. I was quiet and studious, yes, but I was as mild-mannered as a wolverine, more of a demon than an ingenue.

The directors at the Dickens Fair set me to work leading the Father Christmas parade as Princess Mistletoe. That meant I had to be able to compel crowds of people to get out of the way, choose an appropriate pathway to keep a hundred or more people together, and keep a good pace, neither too fast nor too slow.

At this point, I was twelve years old. I became addicted to coffee that Dickens Fair and discovered it made me feel a whole lot better. I did not discover for many years that one reason coffee suited me so well was that it helped with my PTSD symptoms. I figured it just helped me stay awake since our workdays at the Fair were quite long at that point.

I wore a red military-style jacket covered with miles of gold braid and a short yellow satin skirt. Since my character was meant to be a Christmas doll, I wore white face, red spots on my cheeks, and bright green and gold eyeshadow. It was the most unusual stage makeup I had ever done to that point. My hair was done in braids across my head, and I had mistletoe woven in among them. The following year, I made a new Princess Mistletoe costume with a longer skirt, again loads of gold braid, and epaulettes on the shoulders with gold fringe.

I appreciated the necessity of wearing stage makeup, even if it was extreme. I wanted to dress like a girl and wear makeup, but my mother was absolutely opposed to anything which would "reinforce gender stereotypes." She could not object to my wearing stage makeup though. She even got me cold cream because the red circles on my cheeks would not come off any other way. After all, I was not a little girl.

I merely played one on stage.

Chapter 18

Wind-Up Dolls Don't Eat
(1977)

To be "Bone Chewing Bear", robbing the plates of every scrap of food you could find. Life got better as I got older and there was more money, but the earth could turn any day to seeing the big cat stalking in her skin. I flinch from hands and eyes and am very polite and patient day by day by…

—Mark Greyland, "Secret Keeper No More"

Food is disgusting, or so I keep thinking. Where my diabetic, morbidly obese Mother lived to eat, I had trouble getting myself to eat. These days I know I had a constellation of symptoms which amounted to some type of eating disorder. At the time, all I could articulate was that "food is disgusting."

But what does that mean?

There were two parts to my troubles with food: the starvation part and the depression part. The starvation part was worst when I was very small. I do not remember much except being very hungry and developing the attitude that if I needed food and she could say no, I could not endure feeling like that. I could not be at her mercy, or I would die.

I will not beg her for mercy or for food. No, I will not. Never again!

The depression part was stronger when there was enough food. Anhedonia, or the inability to feel pleasure, is very common in traumatized people. It never occurred to me that eating could be pleasant unless I was around my friends. Most of the time, eating had become a disgusting chore. I had a great deal of difficulty with hypoglycemia. I would not eat, or could not eat, and then I would get faint and shaky.

My mother ate too much. At 5'2 ¾" and 250 pounds, her weight was a huge issue in her life and one that she never managed to handle. Her chronic overeating and overindulgence in fats were two more habits that she could not drag me into, even once there was enough food for everyone. She read cookbooks, vegetarian magazines, and diet books obsessively, convinced she was doing everything possible to reduce her weight. After all, reading about weight loss is the same as actually losing weight, right?

This led to a lot of friction with my mother. Since she had no problem with eating, my inability to eat—coupled with my refusal to eat certain things—infuriated her. It is possible that despite her best intentions, she thought I was trying to show her up by being skinny and succeeding where she had failed. I did not see it that way at all. I just thought food was disgusting, and I could not begin to explain why.

My mother read many books on anorexia and railed against the "culture of thinness." I was not anorexic. I was simply growing and at that age I was all arms and legs. I didn't care about my weight. She accused me of anorexia, as if I had acquired the disease just to upset her. Worse, she accused me of being one of those "evil" girls who wanted to look good for a man. As if my lack of appetite had anything whatsoever to do with *that*, especially when I was just eleven!

Mother did not cook very often, and when she did, her cooking revolted me. She would make homemade soup. She would take a chicken carcass that we had eaten the chicken from the day before, boil it, and add potatoes and celery. It would be full of bones and have chicken grease floating on the top. It had more disgusting chicken skin than meat, and I simply could not face it. It was my observation—possibly unfair—that she would find ways to put lumps of fat into anything. She would butter everything that wasn't nailed down. She rarely used salt or seasonings because she was on a "low-salt diet" for her heart.

Sometimes she would put unseasoned chicken leg quarters in the oven on a cookie sheet, and then when they were done, she would set the sheet on top of the stove and expect us to grab a leg for ourselves. My father and brother would eagerly eat them, but I could not. I would usually not see them on the stove until they were cold, and they would stay there for days sometimes until the skin shrank and turned dark brown and translucent, and the bones stuck to the pan. I found the grease the chicken legs sat in to be unbearable. If hunger drove me to eat them, I would have to cope with nausea afterward.

There were times that I felt so angry I didn't know what to do because on the occasions when she made something worth eating, like red meat, she would give all the best of it to my brother Patrick. My brother's temperament is different than mine, and he chose to interact with our parents more than I did. She always maintained that although I was her "favorite", she liked him better, and I can easily see why she would like him better. I was the spitfire, either hiding or fighting her, whereas he did his best to be pleasant and agreeable. Patrick maintained that we were starved, and I can't deny that, but it was better by the time I was eleven. I was a workaholic even then. I made things, did homework, and did not poke up my head to interact with the family unless there was no alternative. Being perpetually busy meant that I was not usually aware of being hungry until it was painful.

Mother had very strong opinions on what I was supposed to like to eat. She was often angry that I refused to eat the fat on steak or the skin on chicken. She would scream at me in the supermarket about wanting boneless steaks without lumps of fat, even if the best ones, the breakfast steaks, were the cheapest of all. She would scream at me for wanting "succulent" meat with no bones in it.

She loved eating fat, which disgusted me. She said it tasted rich, which made no sense to me. Fat nauseated me in any quantity, and it made me feel anxious. It still does.

I refused to butter my bread—which infuriated her—and I would not eat any bread which she would try to hide butter on, whether toasted under jam or under poached eggs. She would talk about what an odd child I was for refusing to eat fat. She would tell anyone who would listen about how strange I was for hating butter on my toast. She eventually decided that either I would eventually become normal and butter my toast like everyone else, or I would stay scrawny.

I didn't want to be forced to eat fat because it reminded me of things I didn't want to think about. My hatred of fat approached a phobia. The truth of the matter is that fat or grease reminds me of creepy smiling adults with lube. Some things, after all, will not work on a child without lube and a good deal of physical force. I don't want to think about it. I also do not keep Vaseline in my bathroom, and I have a lot of trouble with opaque soaps and shampoos.

How could I refuse food when we had so little of it to start with? Maybe this sounds weird, but I cannot endure feeling vulnerable. If she can use food as a weapon against me, then she owns me. I cannot need something she can withhold, or she will never stop using it, as though I was a dog she was training.

What on earth did I eat when I couldn't cope with her food? I could usually find a can of something, even if it was a can of something weird. I ate a lot of sardines and tuna fish—more canned soup than anyone should—and even odder things. I would heat them up and season them. If she bought chicken hearts and gizzards, I would put them on a fork and cook them on the burner.

Why did we have so many cans? Back then, my mother would shop at what she called "The Used Bread Store." I thought this was hilarious. Its real name was "The Returned Bread Store." She would buy stale-dated bread and other stuff, especially a loaf which seemed to be flavored with prunes, which I loved, and she also bought mountains of dented canned goods, which were much cheaper than real food.

To be fair, there were also times where she cooked edible things. She made a lentil-tomato-potato stew flavored with curry, turmeric, and cinnamon, which I loved, and which I make for myself to this day. Sometimes she would make a beef stew that was wonderful. I have gleefully stolen her recipe.

There were even times she tried to help me. Many mornings I would wake up revolted by food and unable to eat. Mother would sometimes put raw eggs, milk, and a little sugar in the blender for me called it eggnog. I would usually be able to get it down.

There was a cookbook I used and loved which she had among her hundreds. It was *The Back-To-Cooking Cookbook*, and I use the brownie recipe to this day. The thing about that cookbook: it was hilarious! It was sarcastic, mostly full of stories about how bad eating processed food was and how unhealthy and pointless it all was. It suggested that the perfect murder could be committed by feeding one's husband lots and lots of shortening-laden biscuits; It made merciless fun of popular housekeeping magazines. Among all this barbed social commentary were simple, practical recipes. The only other one of my mother's cookbooks, other than *The Joy of Cooking*, which I stole from her with her knowledge and consent, was *To Serve Man*, a humorous not-quite-cookbook by Damon Knight, which featured cannibal recipes, grudgingly permitting the substitution of chicken and beef for people.

My mother's irritation with my physical condition went far beyond trying to tell me what I was supposed to enjoy. She accused me of having a host of ailments. When I drank a lot of water after exercise, she would tell me that I was pre-diabetic and that we should run to the doctor and get me a blood test right away. When we went to the skating rink, she would go on and on about how I had "weak ankles" when I was first learning to skate.

Yes, this ballet dancer magically had weak ankles after years of dance training.

I don't have to tell you that my ankles work just fine and that I am still not pre-diabetic, despite test after test after test. The actual ailment that I had was major depression and PTSD, which was called "shellshock" or "battle fatigue" back then and not diagnosed in children until years later. Of slightly more concern were PTSD seizures, which nobody had ever heard of back then. It would have made perfect sense for me to have inherited my father's epilepsy, but the EEG did not agree. I didn't have epilepsy either. I suppose I should be grateful that she knew that something was wrong and had some concern for me, but her concern did very little good.

Yes, something was very wrong. Yes, it was a problem for me every single day. And yes, she had a lot to do with it. My difficulties with food were just one more symptom caused by her ongoing physical and sexual abuse of me and her lifelong attempts to dominate me. This elephant in the room was dressed up as anything else from pre-diabetes to anorexia.

I have had to learn several different coping strategies over time because I have not gotten less weird about food. Sometimes I overeat, and sometimes I get too overwhelmed to cope with food at all.

Part of my trouble with food can be chalked up to depersonalization; if I don't experience myself as a human being and I can neither feel nor accept the feelings I have, I may not recognize that I am hungry or thirsty until it has become a problem.

Tick, tick, tick.
Wind me up and watch me go
Stick, stick, stick.
Stick me back on the shelf

Ever wonder what a doll thinks
Before she falls into the fire
Or is crushed beneath a tire

Break, break, break
Hear the clockwork break
Take, take, take
Your leave lest you hear her cry

The crunching of glass in her hollow chest
Can soon be mended at the shop
What you don't see is that
Something else has stopped.

Tick, tick, tick.

—Moira Greyland

Chapter 19

From the Looking Glass to the Funhouse Mirror (1977–1978)

'But I don't want to go among mad people,' Alice remarked.

'Oh, you can't help that,' said the Cat: 'we're all mad here. I'm mad. You're mad.'

'How do you know I'm mad?' said Alice.

'You must be,' said the Cat, 'or you wouldn't have come here.'

—Lewis Carroll, *Alice in Wonderland*

I am a trained pony.

In my family work, learning, and accomplishments were valued above everything else. Relationships were impossible. In the rest of the world, work is important, but relationships are also important. Why was I there? Why did I exist? No reason I could think of to be alive except to achieve, so Mother could point her finger at her "gifted" daughter.

I had always known that I was destined to create and that my entire worth was to be gauged by my output of creative acts. My empathy was worthless; my company was worthless; everything about me was worthless except for my ability to create. No kindness, no love, no connectedness counted; my personality was completely unimportant. My humanity was unimportant, and I didn't even get to have a gender. All that mattered is that I would create… something.

I was absolutely forbidden to be beautiful, sexy, or female unless I was onstage. After all, as far as my mother ever knew, sexy girls don't create, and any girl who gets a man instead of a quest is contemptible. I was used to service my parents sexually—and I know that sounds disgusting because it was—but I might as well have been invisible. I had no personality in their eyes other than evil.

I know that sounds contradictory because I was meant to perform sexual acts to please my parents. Remember that their issue was with gender roles, not sex. I was meant to *have* sex, but not to *be* sexy, let alone to be beautiful.

I was 12 when my mother abruptly became famous and successful. My mother seemed very happy to suddenly have money and behaved as though a great weight had dropped off her shoulders. It did not really alter our relationship in any meaningful way, but it allowed her to do some things that she had always wanted to do.

I hope this does not sound rude or mean. My mother was very busy with her writing and did not spend much time with my brother or me. In a way, this was a mercy, but in another way, it felt sad and lonely to me to not ever be near my mother, even though I knew she was dangerous. Once she had money, she realized she liked to spend it on my brother and me.

For the first time in my life I got new clothes. She took me to The Limited and let me pick out what I liked. I got a plaid shirt, two pairs of pants, and two T-shirts. She got me new underwear, which I had never had in my life. Always before then, everything had come from the second-hand store.

At that time, my mother had put me into Berkeley Alternative School behind Willard Junior High on Telegraph Avenue. For once, the misfits outnumbered the normals and I hit my stride. There were several Faire brats there, including myself, and although there was rather more academic work than there had been at the last two alternative schools, I got to do a lot of what I wanted to do. My friend Aria from the Faire and I co-directed Shakespeare's *Twelfth Night*. She played Viola, and I played Olivia. The costumes were very easy, of course, since we had tons of Faire stuff already.

I was cast as the female lead in the school musical, which was a parody of a Sam Spade story called *The Mystery of the Missing Link*. I had auditioned by singing a Jean Redpath song, probably "Tae the Weavers Gin Ye Go" or something like that. In retrospect, I do know how very odd that is! In any case, I got to play a slinky vamp in a black dress. By then, I had not let my mother come to any of my shows for years, so I didn't have to worry that she would see me wearing a dress and makeup and freak out. After all, it is one thing to dress up as a girl at the Faire in costumes from a hundred or four hundred years ago, but dressing up as an actual girl from modernity, especially a hot one? It would infuriate my mother and father both because gender roles, stereotypes, blah blah blah.

As long as I could remember, any time my mother caught me singing or saw me in a show, she would either give me inappropriate, exaggerated praise or she would rip me to shreds, telling me how horrible my performance was. I was either the best or the worst, which hurt more than I can say.

I believed her criticism of me no matter how vicious because I knew I was a kid and relatively untrained. Any performer worth her salt will take the criticism and try to improve, but the criticism my mother gave me was so vicious and so incomprehensible that there was no way for me to fix whatever it was that she was upset about. I knew, somehow, that what she was saying was not real and that it was not right, but I couldn't make the pain go away. I couldn't just discount her and pretend she was wrong. I had to be doing *something* wrong, but I didn't know what.

I couldn't believe the praise because it was so exaggerated and so incongruent with the criticism. I could not be both amazingly wonderful and completely horrible at the same time. So rather than continuing to jump in the blender, I decided I would not sing in front of her, and I began to refuse to let her come to my performances. I would ask my father to come, but never her. He would tell me the truth about my performance, whether I was good, bad, or merely okay.

Why did she agree to my wishes? I had become such a spitfire that I would scream back at her, and I would fight her tooth and nail. She probably figured that if she came to one of my shows and I saw her in the audience and I made a scene, it would not do her any good.

Even now, even though I have been a professional singer for decades, I cannot think about the things she said to me about my singing without my stomach twisting up. Even though she was not an authority on singing, as a mother, she was supposed to be an authority on *me*. I know that is ridiculous. In addition, although I will work like a demon if I have a show coming up, I don't sing for pleasure, and I don't sing unless I am rehearsing. It simply stirs things up. Again, I know that is ridiculous. People would say I am letting her live rent-free in my head, but I know what happens.

On a much more cheerful note, I had been earning money at the Faire and saving it up for some time. My mother offered to go in half and half with me and let me buy a horse. She found me one for sale in the Richmond Hills. Touche was not very tall, only 14.2 hands high. She was half Appaloosa and half Quarter horse, so she was compact and fast. As a show horse, she had been a wash; her previous owner gave me her green seventh-place ribbon and inexplicably also told me that she had been a bronc and that she liked to buck. This was probably the result of poor training. I have no idea who owned her before the girl who sold her to me, but I can understand why she was for sale: She liked to buck, and her mouth was ruined, exactly as her former owner told us.

I was an experienced rider, and I had taught riding, but I was not an experienced trainer by any stretch of the imagination, and my ideas on how to help my new horse with her issues were completely wrong.

The only time she ever unseated me was the result of mistakes I made based on my lack of training in, well, training. To begin with, I thought I could help her mouth heal by putting her in a comparatively gentle snaffle bit instead of the Western bit with the high curb her former owner used on her. I also thought she might be more comfortable in an English saddle.

I put her in a snaffle and an English saddle for a trail ride alone in the Richmond Hills. She ran away, and I could not induce her to slow down at all. I lost a stirrup, then a rein, and then my seat when she went around a turn. I landed in gravel on the back of my left shoulder and the side of my face. I walked back to the barn, and she was there, eating.

I didn't break my neck, but it could easily have happened. My neck was never the same after that, but it could have been much worse. I learned my lesson, and after that, I rode her in a Western saddle, and she never threw me again. I also put her into a hackamore, which sidestepped her ruined mouth. A hackamore does not have any bit at all; it doesn't hurt the mouth or teeth, but it puts unpleasant pressure on the nasal cartilage if the horse decides she wants to do something untoward. Horses don't argue with hackamores.

Not long after that, Mother had us move her to Skyline Ranch in the Oakland Hills, so I could get there myself via BART and bus. Mother did not want to spend her afternoons at the stable while I was riding, which I can understand.

She did bring me up a few times though. Once when she was there, a lady stopped her and told her to not let me ride Touche, exclaiming, "That horse is crazy! No child should be riding her!" My mother said only, "That's her horse!" When Mother told me that story, it did not occur to me that perhaps the lady at the stables had a point: My horse was not safe. No horse is "safe", of course, but the fact that I *could* cope with a horse who loved to buck did not mean that I *should* do such a ridiculously risky thing.

I have wondered from time to time why she allowed me so much freedom. Not only was I allowed to ride trail by myself, which in retrospect seems insane, but I had been going about on BART by myself since I was old enough to put money in the machine.

So in review: I can perform, but I can only be a girl onstage. I can be trusted in situations of appalling peril, like going everywhere alone, but my makeup must be micromanaged. I can *look* beautiful, but I can never *be* beautiful.

Chapter 20

The Stormqueen and the Queen Mother (1978)

Marion Zimmer Bradley is a great writer. Dorothy's mother is a bitch!

—Kallun of Clan Colin

When I was 12, my mother's book *Stormqueen* came out. She told everyone that the lead character, Dorilys, was based on me. Back then, I was still going by Dorothy, my middle name. When I read *Stormqueen*, I was horrified. The heroine went about zapping people to death with psychic lightning, and she got stuck in suspended animation because nobody could deal with her.

I wondered if my mother had ever met me. Not only was Dorilys a naïve ninny who got all freaked out in situations I had been fielding for years, but she had no ability to control her temper. There was a tiny grain of truth in the midst of Mother's tall tale: I had a temper, a truly terrible temper. Of course, my mother had been calling me an "evil child" for a very long time.

It is possible that my temper was the sole inspiration for the book and the rest was fiction since I didn't kill people. I just screamed and yelled a lot. Not only was I the sort of perfectionist which people rightly dread meeting, I had a typical artistic temperament. It might be surmised that I came by it honestly… or that I was simply a fiend from Hell, which was my mother's conclusion. But what did I actually do? I screamed and yelled and refused to do things; that was as far as it went. I did not do drugs, I always did my homework, and I worked hard in school and everything else I did. I did not blow up entire cities or stomp on them, Godzilla-style.

Mother made a huge fuss about how impossible I was to deal with, and I will agree… to a point. I fought her tooth and nail when I felt she was being unjust, and considering the form her abuse of me had taken, it felt rational to me to fight her rather than to surrender. If I was not being threatened, there was nothing to fight. My father and I did not fight. It is possible that the bottom line of my fiendishness was simply that I would not let her win, ever. Not even if she had beaten me to within an inch of my life. I would still be defiant. I could not see her as a legitimate authority because she was unjust. Oh, I had to obey her, but I did not have to pretend she was right.

I had friends who cared about me—lots of them. They overlooked my temper, or maybe I was not as much of a fiend as my mother claimed. Most of them had a much different perspective on her. In fact, most of my friends who met my mother were so appalled by her that they usually didn't tell me how they felt until much later, for fear of offending me. Other people, even strangers, observed her behavior and offered condolences.

I was working at the Northern and Southern Faire when I was twelve, and I was very busy. Already, my temperament was asserting itself there in a penchant for advancement and leadership. I became the youngest Journeyman and then the youngest Mistress in the history of St. Cuthbert's Guild, and I was entrusted to teach banner waving to those who carried banners in the parades, finally becoming Banner Captain. Although I was busy with St. Cuthbert's Guild, I also worked with other groups, including Court, where I played both a young noblewoman and an evil pastry cook. I also started to hang around with Clan Colin, the Scottish group at the Faire. I met my good friend Kat there.

My friend Kat let me stay at her house in San Francisco, a BART ride and a green cable car away from my school, and she would share her rice and beans with me and make me tuna sandwiches to bring to school. I adored her. Once she got a boyfriend, she was no longer able to have me over because she moved into his place, and I was only invited once in a while.

It was easy to be in different groups at the Faire. The difference between a peasant costume and a Scottish costume is a belted plaid, also called an arisaid, pinned at one shoulder and worn over everything else. I got into Scottish dancing there, and I started spending time at Duntamknackan, which was the house of the Chief of Clan Colin, Eoin Mackenzie.

Eoin MacKenzie did me a huge favor while giving me a rather substantial challenge. I told him I wanted to learn how to make kilts, so he gave me an old kilt of his to turn. He was left-handed, and kilts typically fasten on the right side, so my challenge was to take it apart and put it back together inside-out, thus hiding all the worn parts of the fabric. I would mend all the moth holes using military darns and hair-canvas, a fusible tailoring cloth used in wool jackets to add stability where necessary. I would also re-line it, hand-stitch all the pleats, and make new buckles and leather fittings and sew them on.

I let it sit in my mending basket for months out of sheer terror.

Once I finally got to it, it was not as bad as I anticipated, and by the time I was done, I knew more about kilt-making that I ever would have if I had simply gone from a pattern. After all, everything was where it was supposed to be already. I did not have to figure out how many pleats, or how deep, and I could measure their width at top and bottom rather than experimenting.

I was so fond of going to see the MacKenzies that I went there for an event when I should have been convalescing. I had to have my tonsils out since they were like golf balls and kept compromising my breathing when they got infected, which was many times a year. After I was sent home from the hospital, I hopped onto a bus to Petaluma—almost fifty miles away—and brought my sleeping bag to Duntamknackan, with my Tylenol and Codeine in my backpack. I was miserably sick and in pain, but it beat being home. My mother was not necessarily horrible when I was sick, but considering how quickly she could change, I didn't want to be a captive audience.

Once she told me that my face was very asymmetrical and that symmetry in a face was a measure of beauty. Since by this time I was so used to her assaults from years and years of experience, I didn't cry. Instead, I asked her, deliberately misunderstanding, whether she would prefer that I had two mouths or four eyes. As I hoped, she laughed, and I sent the conversation in another direction. Naturally, after that, I checked the mirror a million times afterward, convinced she was right and that my facial asymmetry meant I was not at all beautiful. I wonder what she thought I could *do* about having an asymmetrical face?

My mother had told me every variation on my failure to be beautiful many times long before. According to her, I was not beautiful, but "striking." She would also tell me that I was "handsome", which was simply weird, as though I had been a horse or a brigadier general. Other times she would scream at me for looking "sultry", whatever that meant.

She would tell her friends that I was "sullen", which might have had a grain of truth, speaking of a known pre-teen emotional attitude not a physical attribute. In any event, my appearance was not acceptable to her at all. These sorts of verbal attacks where she thought she was being truthful and helpful were an ongoing part of my life with her, as familiar and pleasant as weekly blood transfusions might be. You know what's coming, but that does not make it hurt any less.

I get it. I'm not beautiful. All those people who said I was over the years were *wrong*!

Mother knows best.

I wish I had been secure enough to not be affected by what she said to me, but she was my mother, and I was convinced that somewhere, somehow, she had to be right. Since I am a stage performer and I am of necessity completely aware of what I look like, I knew that if I put on my makeup in a certain way, people would *think* I was beautiful, even if the reality is that I was not.

I wonder what she would have said to me if I had been overtly deformed.

Don't get me wrong. I desperately wanted to be close to her, but emotionally she was very much like an automaton. She had an emotional life in her books, but in person with real people she was more like a series of tape loops, and her invariable conversational goal was to puncture any weakness or anything she could interpret as falling short in some way.

I eventually concluded that I liked thwarting her efforts to destroy or control me, and I loved excelling her at cooking, sewing, singing, foreign languages, dance, and a host of other things. I could tell she would always verbally rip me apart for the things I did better than she did, and amid my bruises and tears, I would laugh at her.

And laugh at her I did. When I was going to West Campus Junior High, I studied tap dancing since I would routinely take any kind of dance class I could. My mother absolutely despised tap dancing and called me "Baby Twinkletoes." I don't know if she thought this would shame me out of tap class, but what actually happened is that her words spurred me on to diligence. I practiced for many hours, always in the room above her bedroom. What could she say? I was doing my homework.

For as long as I could, I stayed anywhere but home.

If she saw me cry, she would hurt me. When I was younger, she would hurt me physically. When I was older, she would mock or humiliate me for crying. After all, according to her crying never did anyone any good. So I learned early to never let her see me cry and to brace myself if she did. Any vulnerability would expose me to harm since she was viciously competitive at heart, and vulnerability was weakness, and overpowering a vulnerable, weak person means *presto*—she wins!

Letting her know how I felt about more or less anything was the stupidest thing I could possibly have done. Trying to tell her about my life would simply put it on the chopping block, ready for the hatchet. Trying to talk to her about school would result in tape loops, but I was persistent and foolish… to a point.

In practice, I would confide in my father and talk to him about anything and everything. I would not talk to my mother unless there was some real-world problem I needed her to help me solve.

The last time my mother hit me, we had been driving somewhere in the car, and she had reached back into the backseat and whacked me hard in the face with the back of her fist. I complained to her, saying that she had promised she would never hit me again. When we got home, she got out of the car, stood there like a statue, and told me that I could hit her back. Naturally, I did not hit her, but I felt I lost all respect for her from that moment onwards; not for hitting me, but for believing that I was the sort of person who would hit my mother. For all that I have felt from time to time that I do not know who I am, there are some things that I *do* know about myself. I know that I do not hit my parents. Ever.

The last time she molested me, I was twelve years old, and I was able to walk away. We were in the living room upstairs in the Prince Street house, usually called Greenwalls, and we were near the unused fireplace—the wall near the kitchen. She had been badgering me about sex, as usual, and complaining at me. She told me she was going to show me how sexy she was, and she stuck her tongue in my ear. I can still feel it. I walked away: what on earth else could I do? I certainly was not going to do what she wanted and respond with amazed arousal and tell her that she was as sexy as she thought she was.

I was not going to bash her in the face, although the thought did cross my mind.

My mother would complain endlessly to Tracy and Diana about me. She did this instead of simply telling me that I had misbehaved. One day she told me that I was fresh, which meant "impertinent" or "rude" back then, and I asked her if she would prefer that I was stale. Even if we assume that I was the rudest child who ever drew breath, in retrospect it strikes me as silly that Marion went to my aunt to complain about this rather than address the issue with me.

My mother's view of me could not always be regarded as either accurate or reasonable. Nowhere was this more obvious to me than in a letter I received a few weeks ago from my friend Jane Beckman. Jane met me when I was a little girl and was around a lot when I was twelve to fourteen and involved in Clan Colin.

I will present the letter here, and I trust you will find it as illuminating and alarming as I did:

I first encountered MZB at a Darkover Con in Berkeley in 1978. It was a small and rather intimate affair, back then. I knew Moira (then Dorothy) from the group I hung with in the SCA. Various friends would bring her along. I was part of a conversation with several people when the topic turned to children. MZB started talking about how Dorothy was such a trial to raise because she "wasn't like other children." One of the other women laughed and said something about how they were always a trial. Marion's face darkened and she said "You have no idea. She has to be watched carefully and disciplined regularly. She's my little bad seed." I was somewhat shocked that someone would speak that way about her daughter, as Dorothy seemed like just a regular young teenager to me. (I think she had just turned 14.) I think I said "Hey, she's just a teenager."

She then started hinting that Dorothy had some sort of "powers" that had to be channeled and regulated. "It's a dangerous age. They discover sex, and can use it to call power. I know about these things." Um, yeah. There were also some comments that Marion and her brother were doing rituals to "keep her in check." I thought this was odd, but I also knew a lot of folks who believed that not only was Darkover real, but were using it like some sort of magical training, so why shouldn't the author believe in various laran powers?

However, I was getting to know Dorothy, and she seemed like just an average kid. And she seemed troubled by her family. By that point, I was starting to hear rumors, things like that Walter Breen was into "man-boy love" and that this was condoned by her mother. Little wonder that she was avoiding being home a lot. Over time, I started to learn enough to horrify me. By the time I had known Dorothy and her family for a couple years, I started making cynical comments that I could sell family secrets to the National Enquirer. In those days, there was a sense of powerlessness a lot of us felt, when we had an idea that there was abuse and sexual abuse going on. Making inquiries of authorities tended to result in skepticism and a shrug of "so what do you expect us to do? Can you prove this?" Times were different.

At one point, in a conversation with friends, someone talked about how great it must be to live with noted science fiction authors. Dorothy burst out "What's it ever done for me, except getting me raped at twelve?" and ran out of the room. Silence fell on the room. Kat and Jana and I started talking to people about whether it would be possible to wrest custody from Marion, as we believed there was abuse and sexual abuse going on, based on little half-hysterical comments that were occasionally made. She reacted badly to being touched, and often seemed on the verge of hysteria over something as simple as someone giving her a hug. There were also things like her saying she wanted to be a dominatrix, because then she could "get back at" the people who had abused her.

The authorities were not particularly helpful. Everything came down to "well, it would be her word against her parents, and do you think that she would be credible enough as a witness?" The problem is, when things were as "alternative" as not just her family, but our whole circle was, we all knew the authorities would just treat us all as a freak show, and it might make things even worse.

Dorothy hung around at other places where I was, including my "family" (the Bruners) at Dragon Run, with Clan Colin, with Serpent and Kathy, my boyfriend Dean, my best friends Jana and David, with my friend Kat, Renaissance Faire, and other places. I also got invited to Greyhavens now and then, and also was at Greenwalls (MZB's house) a couple times.

Marion wrote a lot of us into her books. My friend Jana is in one of the books. I'm in one of the books, looking like Marion but sounding like myself, some number of people we know had characters based on them. My friend David quoted things I'd said that showed up in books. We think Marion worked with real people she knew, rather than creating characters from scratch, and using her daughter was no exception.

When Stormqueen came out, Marion said openly that she had based the main character on Dorothy. Oh swell, a book about a little girl with occult powers who accidentally kills people. I thought it was a horrible thing to do to your child. Dorothy was upset. David tried to always diffuse it a little by going "Hey, Stormqueen! Killed anyone lately?" Dorothy would respond with "Yeah, it's going to be you!" and it would devolve into good-natured ribbing. But I could tell that underneath, it really upset her. But I started to realize that Marion really believed a lot of it. One time, when we were at Eoin MacKenzie's (with Clan Colin), a mug fell out of the loft and hit her on the head. It hit her pretty hard, and she was pretty dazed.

We wanted to take her to the ER, but needed parental permission for them to do anything other than give her an ice pack. Marion was called and expressly forbid it. She got really strange on the phone, very upset, and said she refused to let her go to the hospital where they would test her and "find out she's not human." What??? We started to realize that this was Marion's reality, somehow she had created some story about her daughter being some unhuman elemental being, and believed it enough that she wove the whole thing into Stormqueen. Around this time, I also heard from some of the Greyhavens folks that Paul and Marion were creating some sort of quasi-religious movement to acknowledge Dorothy as an elemental being and "keep her under control."

Then there was the SCA event at Lodi Lake. Dorothy had earlier been watching a little boy whom she had left back with his family household. He had wandered away, fallen into the lake and drowned. Later that day, my friend Ruth Bruner and I had a very distraught and hysterical Dorothy in our pavilion in crying fits saying: "My mother was right. I'm evil. I must have done something. I killed him. It was me. I don't know what I did, but it must have been me." We kept her with us and tried to calm her down and convince her that she didn't have some sort of unregulated psychic powers that would reach out and kill people she cared about.

About the last paragraph—it relates to an event that happened at an SCA event at Lodi Lake, CA (March Crown) when I was 13. I have mentioned Flieg. He was married but went around with another woman, Lee, who was married to someone else. Lee had a three-year-old son named Robin.

I had never thought of myself as a potential parent and had never spent any time with children before, and Lee let me look after Robin briefly. Robin wanted to play with the ducks at the lake, so I brought him back to Lee, telling her what he wanted to do and cautioning her to keep him away from there. I left the site with my friend Sterling to get some asthma medicine. When Sterling and I got back, we saw Lee and Flieg near the lake, and they asked me if I had seen Robin. I asked them if they had looked in the lake, and they said yes, they had.

Lee told me she had told Robin to find a big kid to play with after I left, which horrified me.

I went to the lake and found Robin, floating face-down in deep water, and apparently dead. I screamed bloody murder and grabbed the first large adult I could find. He dove into the lake and rescued Robin. He held Robin upside down by the feet, so the water ran out of his nose and mouth. The paramedics arrived and did everything they could to save him. They also treated me for shock. I was a wreck for the rest of the day.

I did not go into the lake because the water was deep where Robin was, and I was wearing about ten yards of skirts, long sleeves, a tightly laced bodice, and a Scottish plaid. I realized I would not be able to get him—or me—out if I went into the water in my costume. To this day I feel ashamed that I did not risk it because maybe the few seconds I would have saved might have made a difference. The man who went in after Robin took his shirt off before going in after him, which seems in retrospect to have been a very good idea—if he would not even risk keeping his shirt on, perhaps it was irrational of me to think I should have gone in wearing my costume despite the risk.

Initially, Lee and Flieg hailed me as a "hero" but then got mad because when the insurance people came to my house, I told them exactly what had happened, and Lee was found to be responsible for Robin's injuries, ending a multimillion dollar lawsuit against the SCA.

There was no happy ending. Robin lived until he was ten years old and never woke up. I saw him only once after that, and he could do nothing but breathe, unaided, noisily, while lying in his crib.

I had had lifesaving classes before then, which is how I knew that it would have been stupid for me to go into the water in my costume. Still, I have questioned myself so many times: could I have saved him? Should I have just gone in the water in my costume on the chance I could have saved him even if I could not save myself? Would the few seconds I might have saved by going in myself have made any difference?

After that, I was not able to go near lakes for many years. I was not able to make myself swim, nor was I able to even look at lakes. Years later, I told a boyfriend that my mind invented wall-to-wall sharks and other dangers when I thought of swimming into the ocean, even though I knew it was absurd. He told me, gently, that he thought that sharks were not the problem, but one little floating child.

Requiem for Robin

Little boy, blond, precious
Little boy sat in my lap
Little boy, just three summers
Settling down to take a nap

I'd never even held a baby
Till you came and cooed at me
I had never understood
How the love for a child could be

Lonely mother, foolish mother
Flirting with a new strange man
Once I'd given you back to her
Wouldn't give in to your demands

She told you run and find a big kid
So you'd not run off alone
But you toddled off to the water's edge
to play with ducks and pretty stones.

When I returned your worried mother
Asked if I'd seen you anywhere
I asked her if she'd checked the lake
She said she had, you weren't there

I made a beeline for the water
Found you floating, yellow and blue
My screams brought help, and in mere seconds
A man dove in and rescued you

For seven years you clung to life
You never woke, just wheezed and stared
Your father drank himself to death
And still the bitter scars we share

And Robin, Robin, safe in Heaven
Precious boy, now in God's lap
Know that here I still weep for you
Settling down to take a nap.

—Moira Greyland

Chapter 21

The Lisa of Two Evils
(1979)

King: But now, my cousin Hamlet and my son-
Hamlet: A little more than kin and less than kind.

—Shakespeare, *Hamlet*, Act 1 Scene 2

My stepmother Lisa moved in with us on August 24, 1979, when I was 13. Lisa, also known as Elisabeth Waters, was born in 1952 in Providence, Rhode Island. She was originally a fan of my mother's writing and an aspiring writer. Before she arrived, she mailed me a package when I was at summer camp: a nightgown, some chocolate chip cookies, and a very nice letter telling me how much she looked forward to meeting me. That was wonderful and gave me high hopes that she would be a good part of our family.

It was not to be.

Lisa was submissive and sweet to Marion, calling her "Breda" and worse, "Mommy." She treated my mother with veritable hero-worship, and it puzzled me. I was even more puzzled that this infantile behavior was so enthralling to my mother. I had been trained to never be feminine, never be child-like, and certainly to never be submissive. Why would Mother desire the very traits she worked so hard to beat out of me?

Lisa never objected to anything Marion did no matter how irrational or weird and treated her as though she was a goddess. One day, when Marion wore a particular skirt suit, Lisa told her that she looked like Kim Novak, inspiring her to parade about in the outfit.

But Marion looked no more like Kim Novak than she looked like the family dog. I am not trying to insult either my mother or the dog. My mother was perfectly plain. Her pictures are easy to find on the Internet. She was hugely overweight, and she had a flat, round face and nearly invisible blonde eyebrows, no eyelashes, stringy, dirty blond hair, and no physical grace or self-awareness in terms of how to move.

I was astonished. In direct contradiction to everything I had ever been taught, here was my mother preening like a sixteen-year-old girl in a prom dress. Lisa was feeding Marion's vanity with obvious out-and-out lies. It was incredible.

Why on Earth was Lisa flattering Mother, pretending she was sexy and pretty instead of focusing on her actual positive attributes? Why not be entranced with her intelligence, her quick wit, her occasional kindness, or her sense of fun? Why not talk to her about books and music, like my father did? Why would she lie to Mother if she really gave a hoot about her? Did they have anything resembling a genuine relationship, or was Lisa merely hoping to get both hands on the checkbook?

If Lisa loved Mother, why did she lie? At that point, I began to fear that the entire relationship was a theatrical sham.

Why is there an issue about someone looking the way they have always planned to look? Mother never paid any attention to her appearance and did nothing to improve it. She had always taught me that appearance did not and must not matter, and the only reason I was ever allowed to pay attention to my appearance was that I was onstage and my work depended on it.

Telling such a disingenuous, obvious lie was a huge warning sign to me that Lisa was not what she seemed. No friend would have told such a tall tale: how could a lover do so? After all, it was not as if Mother's looks were something she had ever set great store by, and she did nothing at all to try to improve them. If she brushed her hair, let alone washed it, it was a miracle.

To my astonishment, Marion didn't catch on to Lisa's deception. She was lapping it up like a kitten with a saucer of milk, making a ridiculous spectacle of herself. Mother even told me that if I ever wanted her to choose between me and Lisa, I wouldn't like her choice.

Although Mother and Father technically separated in 1979, it was not the sort of separation one might assume. The only thing that really changed about their relationship was the sleeping arrangements. After Lisa arrived, my father continued to live in the same house with Mother and Lisa, keeping the downstairs bedroom he had shared with Mother. Since he was no longer sexually interested in Mother, he was initially grateful that she had another target so she would not be harassing him for sex and threatening suicide over his abandonment.

My mother and father remained best friends. They still saw each other every single day and had tea together every morning. He still read her morning's work, and Mother and Lisa handled all the bills and other things for my father, managing his money and giving him an allowance from his paycheck. When he lost his job, they put him on the payroll, even though he didn't do much of anything for them. Mother felt that since he had shared everything with her, she should share with him.

However, things turned sour between my father and Lisa very quickly. Lisa was as sweetly Machiavellian to my father as she was to the rest of us. With Mother's blessing, she ended up managing all his money, and she gave him a tiny allowance out of what was left over.

Where Mother had let my father do as he liked, Lisa was a much fiercer taskmistress than Mother had ever been. Now she not only owned Marion and the two of us kids, but my father as well. He had been disenfranchised by someone who did not care about him the way Mother did. Lisa knew perfectly well that every bit of money she did not give my father she had access to herself; she was not about to let him have any more of his money than she absolutely had to. My father ended up having to beg for every cent, and he was never one to confront anyone to begin with. He was humiliated and afraid of Lisa and with good reason.

Where I could comfort myself with the knowledge that I was going to be able to do things that Lisa could never do, my father had no such comfort. In his mind and heart, he knew that he was a prisoner and that there would never be any escape for him.

I had seen Mother having love affairs before, and they did not involve one person acting the part of a perfect love-slave. Mother's relationship with Randall Garrett had been very different: no hero-worship, no stupid submission, and certainly no lies. Randall was not trying to get anything from her, and he had always seemed trustworthy to me. He was obviously attracted to my mother. Their relationship was egalitarian and based on love. And yes, this went on with my father's knowledge and consent.

Randall was nice enough, if a bit creepy. I got very upset once because he made an admiring sexual comment at me, and when I protested, Mother simply claimed he was paying me a compliment. He admired my mother's wit and her large bustline, which annoyed her. Mother eventually declined to marry him because he was a drinker, and he married another writer named Vicki Ann Heydron. Mother and Randall remained friends until his death from encephalitis.

Randall figured in one of Mother's favorite jokes. Since they were both science-fiction writers, they had briefly been friends with L. Ron Hubbard. They had been discussing with him how to create religions in their science-fiction worlds and were both appalled when Hubbard announced he was going to use this knowledge to create his own religion and get rich. Every time Hubbard's name was mentioned after that, Mother would say, "I knew him when he was a small-time crook!"

Because I had seen Mother in love before, and the way she acted and the way that Randall acted, I did not believe that Lisa was there for love, and I concluded sadly that she was not there because she cared about us. She was there because she saw a gold mine in my newly successful Mother. Nothing Lisa has ever done has counteracted this initial impression, although I have hoped and wished again and again that I was wrong.

Early on, Lisa slept with Mother in the upstairs room that used to be her office but was now done up as her bedroom. Lisa kept Mother in an erotic haze for the first several months while she consolidated her position. I walked in on them more than once while they were having sex. Where it was giggle-worthy when my friend Jean and I walked in on them, it was also extremely uncomfortable.

Lisa thought she had to explain to us exactly what kind of sexual conduct we had witnessed. It was appalling to hear Lisa mispronouncing various sexual terms which I will not repeat here. We knew what they had been doing, given what we had been exposed to over the years. The issue was not her explaining their sex life but the embarrassment of witnessing it at all. For me, to know a woman who called my mother "Mommy" was providing her with orgasms made me sick.

Is this, in the final analysis, what a daughter *does*? Is this what my mother wants a daughter to do? Had I simply been replaced because of my failure to sexually comply?

Mother had long complained about having to be "the heavy" because my father refused to discipline us in any way. She saw a golden opportunity to be "the good guy" when Lisa arrived by making Lisa be "the heavy." Mother put Lisa in charge of all discipline, sidestepping my father. My mother changed, overnight, from being an unholy terror—a random, frightening disciplinarian—to being an insipid, irresponsible marshmallow who followed Lisa around like a puppy. In terms of our day-to-day lives, this made things a lot worse for both Patrick and me. To begin with, Lisa had no history with us, and we had no reason to trust her. Both my brother and I had seen the same things about her relationship with Mother, and we both suspected her of being there only for Mother's money. From the way she fawned over Mother and how insincere she was, we didn't think Lisa actually believed a word she said.

Worse, Lisa warmed to the task of disciplining us and enjoyed it entirely too much. Mother thought, naively, that Lisa would love us in the same way that she did and that she would make all the right decisions to benefit us all. However, Lisa seemed to see us as competition for resources and knew that the more ground she gained with Mother, the more resources she would control. That meant that to gain status with Mother meant marginalizing my brother and me.

Neither Lisa's methods nor her attitudes were anything like what we had been exposed to; her values were completely at odds with everything we had ever been taught. She was sweetly caustic, like an ounce of lye mixed into a cup of nice, warm hot chocolate. To her, we had no manners and were dirty and ill-taught and didn't write thank-you notes whereas she was the pinnacle of perfection, having been raised in a "good family" in Connecticut.

We never heard the end of her "good family", which failed to explain her anxiety and dread over every communication with her mother. Why would a "good family" not make her feel loved and welcomed? I had seen good families, such as Serpent and Cathy, and I knew perfectly well that a good family was a happy, harmonious one, not one that folded napkins just so and wrote thank-you notes. On that basis alone, I knew she was a social climber. Only money could trump the social status she believed her "good family" gave her. I thought it was pathetic and repulsive. I had never met anyone in my life who made such claims or who tried to act superior based on the alleged social status of the family she apparently feared so much. Her parents worked straight jobs and had written no books. Really, the whole thing mystified me. How could her family be superior to anything if they hadn't created anything of lasting value?

Lisa was a big fan of Miss Manners and trotted her books out at every occasion. It was not only that our conduct and our manners were substandard, but the two of us as people did not meet her standard. Her fundamental dislike and contempt for us were as obvious as they were painful. Eventually, Patrick and I both went to Mother, suspecting Lisa's motives and complaining about her treatment of us. Mother could not believe that Lisa was so very different behind her back. She could not believe that her sweet, submissive "baby" would cut us to the bone.

Not long after Lisa arrived, they decided they wanted more privacy, so they moved into an apartment on Telegraph Avenue together, about three blocks from Greenwalls. I always thought of the apartment as "The Love Nest." Although I was relieved to not walk in on them *in flagrante delicto* anymore, their absence made its own set of problems. Both actual adults were now gone, and my father was allegedly going to care for my brother and me.

My father, though loving and kind, was no more fit to run a household than he was fit to run a marathon. Would he drive us anywhere? No, of course not. Help with homework? No. The idea of him paying bills? Preposterous. Going to the bank? Impossible. Putting out the trash once a week? Absurd. Cooking? Never. We cooked for ourselves and for him.

Mother and Lisa came over once a day and took care of some things, but it did not prevent the house from becoming completely unmanageable. It was a riot of cockroaches and filth. I was used to the chaos though. I was also used to finding my own food in the pantry and getting myself to wherever I needed to go. My father was helpless when faced with even the simplest real-world matters. Left to his own devices, he would work as close to 24 hours a day as he could manage, sleeping when he could not avoid it.

Here is an example of my father's coping skills: one day, my father's oven set the house on fire when he was alone. He called Lisa, and said, "The house is on fire. I am not kidding." Naturally, she told him to call 911, which had never occurred to him.

The cuckoo had landed, and it was time for the baby birds to hit the concrete. To Lisa, we were not welcome, we were not good people, and we were not worthy of the food it took to feed us. We did not take this lying down though. We staged a full-blown intervention with probably a dozen of us present downstairs in the carriage house before it had been rebuilt. The whole family tried to tell Mother that Lisa was corrupt and only out for her money, but Mother did not believe it and told us that even if every word was true, she would remain with Lisa.

By far the worst part of Lisa's attempted reformation of us began when Mother was still in her Lisa-induced sexual haze. She was trying to reform my awareness of my position in our family. I was supposed to accept her not only as my owner and superior but as my "older sister", which was ludicrous.

If one accepted Lisa's definitions, Lisa was right. I was not submissive but rebellious. I was not interested in what Mother wanted me to do but intent on leaving the house. I was not even interested in Mother's books, and dealing with her fans was difficult for me because they adored her, and I couldn't join them in hero-worship. If sycophancy is the measure of a daughter, I failed on every level.

Mother spoke often of how Lisa was a "better daughter" than I was. I was puzzled by this: biology is not earned, nor can it be altered through merit. But apparently, Mother thought that there were a set of things that a "good daughter" would do that I considered to be completely unreasonable.

To be fair, Lisa did some wonderful things. Rather than claiming a stopped clock is right twice a day, I must think Lisa did not want to be hated. She was complimentary about both my singing and my costumes, and she also did not always join in when Mother was verbally bashing my brains out on the things I did. Moreover, she once did something even more important and tutored me in math after I had a head injury.

When I was attending ninth grade at West Campus Junior High in 1979, I had two episodes of trouble. Since I was a bookworm with a big mouth, I was often beaten up at the Berkeley public schools I attended. One day, a girl chased me for a long way from school, insisting that she was going to beat me up. I ducked into a bank and explained the situation to the teller, who kindly let me call home. Mother came and got me from the bank, so the girl never got to beat me up. In this case, the story grew as she retold it until she claimed to have "rescued [me] from a pack of children in full cry!"

My mother loved to defend me at times, provided there was an audience and she could look properly heroic. My brother David used to say that to Mother, "truth is a lousy first draft."

The other time I got into trouble was on the way into class one day. A young man was standing outside my classroom as I was walking in, and I saw him kick the rear ends of the two girls ahead of me, which made me very angry. I told him clearly that he was not going to do that to me. He grabbed me by the throat and slammed my head against the door jamb until he knocked me out. I was not unconscious for long: I remember waking up flat on the floor in the school hallway.

I was taken downstairs to the infirmary and learned I had hit him back, although I do not remember doing so. He walked by my bed with a huge frown and a bloody split lip. I had sustained more damage though. The school nurse called my mother and she took me to the hospital. Although they feared a skull fracture, I only had a serious concussion. I was out of school for some weeks after that.

The school had interpreted the event which resulted in my head injury and his split lip as a "fight", even though it did not seem that way to me at all. We *both* were required to serve detention. I was not able to remain at school for long after returning. My head still hurt a lot, and I was dizzy and sick to my stomach for some time.

Lisa tutored me in math, which I had completely forgotten, from arithmetic to trigonometry and algebra within the space of about two weeks. That was a kindness on her part and an important one. She did not make a show of rescuing me; she just helped me with the actual problem which resulted from my being out of school.

I do not think either my father or my mother had ever helped me with homework.

Since I was not going to be able to finish out the year at West Campus, my mother decided to homeschool me. She called the school she created for me "Hollingworth School." She had Lisa teach me math and French, pretty much testing me on what I did on my own. Adrienne Martine-Barnes taught me sewing, which amounted to her looking at the things I did on my own, and Mother herself assigned me various papers to write on English topics, which amounted to her reading what I wrote. I wrote easily, and she never said much, although when she said something, it tended to feel like a switchblade. I knew enough to be very careful in what I wrote. She was vicious about free verse and to anything that was less than meticulous with words.

Doing schoolwork had never been a problem for me. Dealing with the other kids was the problem. Mother always called me a "self-starter" and knew I would easily complete any assignment they gave me. Mother only homeschooled me for half a year and then put me into Berkeley High School.

Like so many people with normal skill sets, Lisa wanted very much to sing, to write, to dance, to ice skate. Sadly, she had about as much artistic talent as a spare tire. As a dancer, despite many years of ballet lessons, she might as well have been a panda. As a skater, despite endless lessons, a starfish would have been more fun to watch. As a singer, no amount of voice lessons corrected the odd sounds she made. Eventually, she volunteered as a supernumerary for the San Francisco Opera, where she would stand in for a singer while they dealt with lighting and costuming issues or simply stand there in a costume and *not* sing.

It is possible that Lisa might have gotten involved with Mother so that she could become an author herself. It is a fact that she sold everything she wrote to Mother and then posthumously to Mother's estate. In effect, she sold everything she wrote to herself. Her two books were reviewed by her friends, which goes to show that they have more patience than I do. I read the first one, *Changing Fate*, and my overall impression was that her characters sat around making "To Do" lists, and during one particularly torrid love scene, the lovers held hands. The reviews themselves are online on Amazon. I thought they were worth noting, the way her friends all found something nice to say to the effect that either book was worth the electronic paper it wasn't printed on.

Lisa's verbal skills were good, as one expects from a well-read college graduate, and she made a reasonably competent editor. In fact, most of her contributions to the literary field involved editing all of Mother's "Sword and Sorceress" anthologies. Her writing reminded me of chewing on a battery: a series of weak shocks and a bad taste in one's mouth. Of course, that could be a result of hearing everything she wrote in her voice, which was annoying beyond belief. It is a different experience to read the writing of people you know. Mother was good, and Father was hilarious. Lisa was neither.

There was a time I did something awful to her, though it was nothing I had planned to do.

Lisa fancied herself a rider and wanted to come up to the stable on Skyline Ranch with me to ride my bratty horse. I was positive that Lisa would not be able to keep her seat and would end up in the mud. I was judging by her general physical coordination. If she could not dance, how could she ride? I figured that even if Lisa had had formal riding lessons and was a reasonably capable rider under normal circumstances, my horse would be more of a handful than she might expect. If you recall, my horse was not exactly a rocking chair.

Lisa had been at the dinner table when I discussed innumerable rides, so she could not have been unaware of my horse's temperament or behavior. It is entirely possible that she had decided that I must have been exaggerating and thought that maybe she could teach me a thing or two about riding.

Although from time to time I had brought other people to the stable with me, I did not ordinarily permit anyone to ride my horse. This was not out of selfishness but because I did not want to see anyone get hurt. However, Lisa was in the position of a parent, and I did not have the authority to forbid her. We went up to the stable together. I rode Western, with a nice big heavy saddle and a hackamore, so it would be impossible for my horse to fling me about. Lisa insisted on riding English, with an English saddle, her little helmet and jodhpurs and immaculate black boots.

I told Lisa my horse would be completely unmanageable in a snaffle and a cornflake of an English saddle, but she ignored my warnings. As might be imagined, Lisa's ride was very, very short. My horse took the opportunity to get some exercise, and Lisa went into the mud. It could have been a great deal worse; she was not hurt, merely muddy.

I brought another person to the stable that year: Heather Rose Hearn. I realized my mistake while we were there. I don't remember exactly what she said, but I realized she was a lot like my mother. Her heart seemed empty and jagged to me, and her basic outlook was cruel. No matter. She took up with my brother nearly immediately, eventually married him, and remained with him for the next several decades. The difficulty she caused him is inestimable. What a pity we so often end up marrying clones of our parents. I have felt at times that introducing the two of them was among the worst things I have ever done.

I have described the first evil in detail: Lisa manipulated my mother and laid the groundwork for her eventual theft of an empire, but the second evil dwarfs it. The first is only money whereas the second is blood and souls. Lisa feigned ignorance, refusing to stop my father from molesting children no matter how much I pleaded with her.

Here is what she said about my words:

MR. DOLAN: Have you, since this all came out with Kenny Smith, been made aware of any other allegations of Walter's molestation of children other than Ken Smith, the young boy down in L.A. Barry—I believe you referenced Sterling, and Glenn?

MR. BURESH: Let me have the question again. (Whereupon, the record was read by the reporter.)

ELISABETH WATERS: Moira was instantly convinced that Walter had molested every child he had ever been near, so to that extent, yes, I have heard other allegations.

Yes, the fact that my father only molested five other children on that particular list confirms how unreasonable I was.

Chapter 22

My Father's Imaginary Relationships
(1979–80)

I'm your wicked Uncle Ernie
I'm glad you won't see or hear me
As I fiddle about...

Down with the bedclothes
Up with the nightshirt!
Fiddle about...

—The Who, "Fiddle About", *Tommy* (1969)

In the next few paragraphs, I am not going to use quotation marks because if I do, I will run out, just like I am about to run out of facepalms.

Now that my father is free to pursue his own interests, he is pursuing them all over the house because they can both run faster than he could. Gregg was 13, and Barry was 12. Both boys were hookers, brought to him by his friends in clerical collars.

With my father in charge of Greenwalls, a new crowd started to come around. My father's friend, Archbishop Mikhail Itkin, was friends with two other priests: Reverend Richard Kihlstadius and Father Jim Dennis. The mission of these purported priests defies belief. While wearing clerical collars, they would pick up young boy hookers in San Francisco, feed them, bring them home with the promise of rescue, and use them for sex. Since what was happening amounted to the prostitutes having fewer johns with more safety and less money, a lot of them went along with it. Which is not to say it was reasonable or decent. It was horrible.

Several of these boy hookers would routinely come over to our house. Infuriatingly, just having a professional, sexually-available visitor or three was not enough for my father. He wanted to believe that the boys loved him, had a relationship with him, and wanted to have sex with him. Apparently, having to pay for sex made my father feel undesirable, and he hated spending the money. Some of the boys would settle for sandwiches and $20.00 bills, but even that much annoyed my father to no end. How could he get a child to be willing to have sex with him without having to pay him every time?

The answer is utterly repulsive.

He was trying to legally adopt a child named Barry, a twelve-year-old Native American boy prostitute. If I begin giving vent to my absolute outrage here, the story will never be told. It does not matter how long a child has been prostituted, he needs a parent, not a pimp or a john! Please understand that if I am relating these facts coldly, it is not because I do not care. I do.

The priests introduced Barry to my father with the idea that my father could adopt him *and* have sex with him. He was not an innocent child but as hard-boiled and self-serving as could possibly be imagined. The rumor mill claimed Barry thought he was getting a great deal because my family had money—at least more than his family did. Once more, the fact that Barry's innocence had been stolen due to his work as a prostitute does not excuse my father's victimization of him!

Barry's mother was in favor of the adoption. His father was in prison and money was tight. She seemed to think that for him to be involved with our family was so financially beneficial that nothing else mattered. I do not know whether she was aware of what my father was trying to do or not.

My mother's perspective was clear: As noted in her deposition, she tried to tell my father that if he adopted Barry, he would have to be a son but not a lover. All the testimony about Barry is in the appendix. One might think that it was kind and compassionate of my mother to try to insist that my father not sleep with Barry, but why would he deserve safety when my father's other victims did not? What was the real dividing line? Was it that Barry was physically very small and Mother thought he was being coerced? Why was it okay for *any* child to be a sexual target for my father?

In no way did my father ever intend to obey Mother or to end his sexual relationship with Barry. Instead, as always, he would tell Mother what she wanted to hear and then come complain to my brother and me about their conversations, even telling us what kind of a story he had cooked up to appease her and to shut her up.

I had no question in my mind whatsoever that my father was sleeping with Barry and I was appalled. I could not understand how Mother and Lisa could go along with an "adoption" like this. It was like watching a slow-moving train: the crash is inevitable and horrible to watch. Why didn't Lisa stop it? Why didn't Mother *do* something? Why was this just allowed to go on as though it was the most normal thing in the world? Moreover, why did Mother think for a moment that my father intended to obey her?

Meanwhile, my father's fame was increasing. He was the keynote speaker for NAMBLA's second conference in New York in 1979. I am still puzzled that anyone had any doubt about what my father was doing.

Perhaps this is unworthy and horrible of me, but I hated Barry. I hated him because he stole things from me, including the moonstone I had been given at my "puberty ritual", which had taken place shortly before. I hated him because he routinely went through my underwear drawer, which humiliated me. I hated him because he was mercenary and mostly seemed willing to be around my father to get his money.

I also hated Barry because he insisted on growing pot in my unfinished closet, doing his cultivating when I was away and hoping I would not find out. There were two closets in my room: one was for clothing, and one was unfinished and full of dirt and spiders and bare earth under the front steps of the house. I despised pot and had no respect for those who insisted on living stoned.

I felt torn between despising the carnal beast Barry was and pitying the child who was destroyed so young that prostitution seemed to him a small price to pay to live in my family.

Barry's "adoption" fell through, likely because he kept stealing from everyone. What I can't understand is why it didn't fall through because my father was sleeping with him. Why did my parents finally reject Barry instead of someone jailing my father? Why did the adoption agency suspect nothing? Did everyone just neglect to mention how Barry got there?

Mother and Father went through all the proper channels, filled out all the right forms and lied their brains out about what was actually going on. I don't know whether it was more a matter of the agency not looking closely enough to discern sexual abuse or my parents managing to lie convincingly while being "Famous, Important People."

One night after the adoption effort was over, Barry sneaked into the house and I found him there. I called Lisa and Mother over at the Love Nest, and they had him picked up by the police. Tragically, when the police asked him if my father had molested him, he denied it. That meant that later when he tried to report my father for molesting him, he was not believed.

Not every boy in our home was there for my father. Sterling was around a lot; he and I were very good friends. He was 16 to my 13, and I hero-worshiped him. He was tall, blond, and muscular. We spent a lot of time together at the Faire as well as at my house whenever he was there and could duck my father.

Sterling was safe. He respected me too much to paw me or to make passes at me until we actually decided to date when I was almost fifteen. While we were still just friends, we would spend nights at the Faire hanging out together, listening to Journey, and talking about everything and nothing. Sterling had a motorcycle when he was a little older and he rode us both up to Sonoma County on it. It was a wonderful ride and completely exhausting. I had never been on a motorcycle before.

When we got home from the ride, we flopped in a heap on the sofa in the living room. My uncle Don walked in and began mocking the two of us for our "display of disgusting heterosexuality." In context, this was absurd; we were sitting together in close contact, but we were not even kissing. Nor at that point would we have. Don was simply being a jerk and trying to make a point. I was supposed to understand that in this house, heterosexuality was not normal, and anything I did that was even remotely "heteronormative" would be mocked.

My father tried to induce Sterling to spend more time with him, mostly by offering sexual acts that I refuse to specify, and worse, speculating that I would not offer the same services, as if that were the coin of the realm. Sterling and I were friends, not lovers. I was furious that my father was trying to compete with me for Sterling's time.

MR. DOLAN: Okay. Had you ever discussed the topic of Walter and young boys with Marion Zimmer Bradley prior to the placement of Barry within the home in 1981?

ELISABETH WATERS: Yes, in 19—I think it was 1980, I saw a letter that Walter had written to his therapist, Dr. Morin, and he said that he missed Sterling—who was another one of the kids who hung around. He was a friend of Patrick's—not just because he was horny but because—I forget the rest, but that phrase struck me as so odd that I went and asked Marion about it.

Reading about the reality of my father's relationship with Sterling in Lisa's testimony after my father's death was devastating. How many times do I have to discover that a boy I loved was getting sodomized by my father? And will anyone be surprised that Sterling ate himself into nine hundred pounds of obesity and died in his forties of heart failure?

It was during this time that my brother Patrick went on a particularly bad acid trip. It was hardly surprising, but terrifying to watch. He was sitting in the living room on the folded-out sofa-bed, and screaming and yelling about the universe and the moon and the stars and how he hated women, "Fuck 'em all. Fuck 'em all!"

It is almost certain that my father gave him the acid, as usual, but he might have also had other drugs with it. His girlfriend Heather had a habit of mixing drugs, so any acid trip she gave him the drugs for might also include speed, and mushrooms. He did not ever do well this way, but that never stopped her.

I tried to talk to him, which was useless. Sterling was there with me, and we went for a long walk around Berkeley since there was nothing either of us could do to help. Someone called my uncle Don, who came over and decided that the way to help Patrick was to get him stoned. After all, if someone is out of his mind on drugs, more drugs will help, right?

Discipline with my father in the house was erratic. My brother and I had never gotten along, and I have already noted my propensity for biting him. I am not trying to excuse my conduct. One day I bit him, and my father backhanded me across the room. I thought his response was reasonable, even proportional. He had never hit me before that, nor did he do so again.

One day my brother punched me in the nose, no doubt because I said something or several somethings which upset him. He was not an experienced puncher, and he knocked me backwards into the door from the living room to the kitchen. Nevertheless, his punch broke my nose and also knocked me out when my head hit the door. He panicked and called 911.

The ambulance crew came upstairs to check me out. I was fine, but they noticed the lush, verdant six-foot-tall pot plant which grew next to the piano in the music room, easily seen from where I was on the floor. They told my brother that either he would allow them to confiscate it, or they would call the police, who would both confiscate it and charge him with a crime.

My brother spoke ruefully thereafter of how he had seen them admiring their new pot plant on their way back to the ambulance. For some reason, he did not believe they intended to throw it away. Did my father punish my brother for punching me? No, but I think he probably believed my brother had been punished enough with the loss of his precious pot plant.

I suppose one could make a twisted case for the benefits of my father's home-schooling. After all, Barry and my brother were learning how to cultivate plants and to cope with new and different kinds of challenges, and they were certainly learning a great deal about independence and crisis management.

There was another boy hanging around with my father at this time: Gregg, a prostitute and junkie. He had also been brought by the priests, but he was my age, 13, and a good deal taller than Barry. His back was crisscrossed with horrible scars from beatings with electrical cords that his mother had given him. He seemed to feel that no matter what my father wanted from him, he was glad to be anywhere he could have food, a bed, a safe place, and no beatings.

Gregg became a fixture in my father's life for many years, over my serious complaints. I remember hanging out with him when we were still 13, and he made kind of a whiny pass at me, begging me for sex, as though he thought I could save him from my father. I was irritated and refused him. After that, I wanted nothing to do with him. I did feel sorry for him, though.

Gregg was mixed up with another boy named Nick, who was a few years older than I was. I had a huge crush on Nick. He had a terrific smile, he was tall, dark, and handsome, and he radiated masculinity and presence. I couldn't imagine why he would spend any time with my father because he was mostly friends with Patrick and me. Any time my father caught me hanging around with Nick, he would freak out as though he owned Nick. I imagined Nick mostly stuck around for pot and food, and endured my father's company in exchange for that. There was much more to it, as I later learned, but I will let Nick tell that story himself.

One day I found Gregg in my father's bed, and I went to Mother and Lisa and told them. They didn't seem to give a darn what my father was doing with whom. Instead of calling the cops, Mother and Lisa moved back into Greenwalls and moved my father into the Love Nest, where he promptly turned it into even more of a bawdy house. Suddenly, there was nobody there to witness him having sex with anyone he wanted to, and nobody, not even me, to complain about his pot smoking. Now my father had all the privacy he needed to do what he had always wanted to do.

It should be noted that in Lisa's testimony, she remembered my complaint about Barry, but she totally forgot the reason she had made my father move into the Love Nest. When I asked her why she didn't do anything about Gregg being in my father's bed, she told me, "You never said they were in bed at the same time", as though that made the slightest difference. If Barry and Gregg had merely been taking an innocent nap in my father's bed, then why make my father move out of the house?

This is what Lisa said in her testimony despite her denials of what I had said:

MR. DOLAN: Elisabeth Waters in her 10-8-89 diary, which was given to the police, indicates the following: Quote, "And I feel like a total idiot for not having said anything back when I thought Walter was molesting [Sterling] ten years ago.

This was one example of many of Lisa creating some nauseatingly implausible story to explain how something obvious was miraculously something else. When I complained that Gregg was in my father's bed, perhaps she thought I was complaining that Gregg did not match the decor!

Our house was a flop-house. People slept all over the place all the time, and I was used to stepping over them. Such a trivial matter was nothing to complain about—unless they were in my bed. The idea that I would object to either Gregg or Barry occupying an empty bed is stupid and obviously untrue. The issue was sex, not real estate.

Lisa completely denied the reality that my father was having sex with both Gregg and Barry, possibly because she was afraid that legal action against Walter would compromise her meal ticket. When Lisa first arrived, I had been so full of hope that she would be more like a real mother. She had made me cookies, after all, and even tutored me in math, and she never said horrible things about my costumes or my singing. I needed so badly to have a mother who loved me. I needed her to see the insanity and stop it. Instead, she followed Mother into every bizarre fad, and behaved like an empty-headed nincompoop when there were people all around her who needed saving. What could be the purpose of turning a blind eye, not so much even to my brother and me, but to Nick and Gregg and Barry and Sterling and the rest of them?

It is also entirely possible that from the very beginning, all Lisa wanted was my mother's money. If that is the case, all I can say is that she earned it. On her back.

Chapter 23

Letters from Beyond the Grave (1980)

He broke my heart. You merely broke my life.

—Humbert Humbert, *Lolita*, Vladimir Nabokov

In 2008, many years after my father's death, I received a parcel from a family member. I was standing in my garage, next to a huge trash can when I opened the stack of letters which my father had written to his psychologist back in 1980. These letters described my father's sexual liaisons with young boys and his observations about these "relationships" and their endings. I read the letters and threw them away immediately afterward, not even wanting to bring them in my house. The contents made me feel sick. I did not transcribe them but wrote about them in my journal. I mention that, because the following does not include direct quotes from the letters, but my observation of the contents as I wrote them down in my journal that day.

Why was my father writing to a psychologist about the sexual crimes he had committed? And what kind of psychologist would tolerate such a thing? In Berkeley, one can find validation for nearly anything one's heart desires and find plenty of other people to hail the "revolutionary" mindset of those who follow their hearts. Or their gonads.

Back in 1980 and before, my father urgently needed competent mental health care for his paranoid schizophrenia and bipolar disorder, not to mention his catastrophic depression and suicidal ideation, but he neither sought nor found it. My father did not look for a psychiatrist who would treat the medical aspects of his condition, but a sex-positive, sympathetic therapist who would allow him to complain and validate his delusions. He certainly did not want anyone who would help him change.

He chose Dr. Jack Morin, PhD (1946–2013), the author of *Anal Pleasure and Health* and *The Erotic Mind*. Dr. Morin was openly gay and steeped in the bathhouse community in San Francisco. Dr. Morin is still celebrated throughout the "sex-positive" community for his assistance in improving people's experiences with anal sex. Forgive me for not wanting anything like that on my tombstone. The following is an excerpt from a tribute to Dr. Morin:

Inspired by Love and Guided by Knowledge: Remembering Jack Morin

Jack was a doctoral student in psychology, and his great ambition was to apply the principles of humanistic psychology to the study of sexuality and the practice of sex therapy. Sex therapy was still a new concept, and many in the field believed that it was their business to determine for the rest of us what was and was not "normal" sexual behavior.

Words like "perversion" and "deviance" still appeared in "scientific" papers on sexuality. Jack's mission was to change all of that. In a time when so many of his contemporary therapists pathologized minority sexual preferences, he wanted to respond to all of his patients from the humanistic principle of "unconditional positive regard." And in the field of sexology he wanted to replace ancient prejudices with scientific rigor.

—Tom Moon, MFT, 2013

Note the term "minority sexual preferences", and understand that it means bestiality, necrophilia, pedophilia, pederasty, and incest, among other things. Instead of confronting criminal acts in his clients head-on, Dr. Morin advocated "unconditional positive regard."

Note also how the word "normal" is put in quotes, as though incest and necrophilia are not abnormal, but merely different. According to this school of "thought", our objections to these things are merely the result of "ancient prejudices", not a sincere concern for our children and their lives, and also for the lives of any children they will have in the future.

I am puzzled that Dr. Morin did not insist that my father seek medical treatment. Instead, Dr. Morin went along with my father's idea that all his thoughts were vitally important and should be written down. This resulted in vast numbers of little notebooks: journals which my father wrote in every time some grand thought crossed his mind. My father also wrote many, many letters to Dr. Morin.

According to my father, his therapy ended when Dr. Morin informed him that if my father sent him any more letters about his sexual encounters with boys, he would have to talk to the police. Because of the Child Abuse and Neglect

Reporting Act, or CANRA, passed in 1980, Dr. Morin was now legally bound by the mandated reporter laws, and any failure to report current illegal acts would result in him losing his license to practice. My father made it sound as though Dr. Morin was very unhappy with the CANRA laws, presumably because he believed Dr. Morin approved of his activities.

I met Dr. Morin only once. My father brought me to a therapy session, presumably so he could demonstrate just how difficult and awful I was to deal with. It was clear from my father's comments that Dr. Morin had already heard at length about my father's animosity toward me, and he was prepared for my head to spin around while I would presumably be intoning ominous threats in Latin while burning crosses and projectile vomiting in Technicolor green. But I was not that interesting, and I made a very poor Antichrist. My father carefully avoided mentioning the real issue: my open opposition to his "relationships" with Barry and Gregg.

My father said very little about me during the session and seemed to think Dr. Morin could tell that I was evil. What could he have possibly have said to make his point to Dr. Morin about me in my presence? The topic itself would be a tar baby. My father would not want me to tell Dr. Morin that I hated Barry because he went through my underwear drawer and stole from me or that I was furious and disgusted that my father was trying to adopt his sex partner. Nor could he have said openly that he was angry that he kept having to drag Sterling and Nick away from me. That is certainly not a can of worms my father would have wanted to open anywhere. What could he have said? "Stop being female around the boys I want to have sex with!" "Don't let them like you!" "Stop being their friend!"

Maybe it will be obvious to a normal audience that most boys of 15 would much rather hang around with a 14-year-old girl than a 50-year-old man, but it was not obvious to my father. He was incensed over it and would have been more so if he had suspected that they spent time with him only out of obedience, not desire. He thought they should sexually desire him and choose him, and he regarded the attention they paid to me as infuriating disloyalty.

I read many unpleasant things about my father's obsession with pedophilia in the letters he wrote to Dr. Morin. He had an internal image of his ideal lover, who he called "The Golden Boy." The Golden Boy of my father's imagination was 12 years old, completely accepting of my father's physical appearance, totally compatible with him in bed, and would never, never, never refuse my father oral sex like his actual partners did. The Golden Boy would also never betray him by reporting him to the cops or robbing him like the others did. The Golden Boy would supposedly *want* sex with my father rather than simply enduring it like the real-life boys did. Their imagined sexual compatibility would supposedly heal my father's heart and finally bring him the peace he needed so badly.

According to Patrick Carnes' book *Contrary to Love*, most sexual addiction works this way: the fantasized sexual activity promises healing and relief which never comes. Even the most carefully planned reenactment of the chosen fantasy never satisfies. Like any sexual addict, my father was looking for healing in the wrong place. He thought that just one more episode of sex with "the right boy" would "heal" him. It is a repetition compulsion; like the drug addict thinking that this fix will make it all better, this acid trip will go back to that first trip and heal the wounds of all the others.

My father wrote about how jealous and spiteful I was. He also regarded me as being completely untrustworthy because I had told Mother about finding Gregg in his bed, which resulted in him having to move into his own apartment. I can understand how angry he was that I tried to stop him from sleeping with boys; I am not sure how or why I was spiteful. He didn't say. There was no limit to my evil. I was one more victimizer. Another person who failed to understand his Grand Vision. He had not yet given up hope on me though.

In his letters, my father expressed tremendous frustration and anger because he could not persuade my brother to have sex with Gregg. My brother only liked girls and would sooner have spent a celibate lifetime than slept with Gregg. Although this never mattered to my father, at the time my brother was 15 and already involved with the girl he would later marry. In my father's imagination, getting my brother to sleep with other boys his own age was a prerequisite to other sexual involvements which would eventually not be limited to people his own age.

What my father really wanted was for Patrick to be willing to have sex with him *and* Gregg, preferably simultaneously. It would have been a very different thing to have a willing, "consensual" relationship with his son than what happened when Patrick was too young to get away. Patrick did not discuss the details with me, but in 2014, he was beginning to have a lot of trouble with flashbacks of Walter molesting him. He had never forgotten what Mother did, but it seemed his mind could not handle the reality of having had two insanely abusive parents.

Walter never took my brother's relationships with women seriously. To him, my brother's wishes were an irrelevant distraction. It seemed as though my father regarded my brother's refusal to sleep with Gregg as disloyalty and filial disobedience. After all, a truly loyal son would have followed his father's Grand Vision, right?

At no time did my father ever regard heterosexuality as being real or legitimate. He believed all men who thought they were straight were merely "hung up" and the moment they were exposed to enough experience with other men, they would "embrace their natural homosexuality" and never bother with women after that. Obviously, my father felt that homosexuality was something which could be chosen by anyone who was willing to try it.

My father spoke at length in the letters of his "relationship" with Gregg; he loved Gregg, and Gregg loved him, or so he believed, but they were "sexually mismatched." I can only assume that this meant that Gregg was not compliant enough and refused some of the sexual acts that my father wanted. My father spoke of Gregg's mother as being "horrified and disgusted" by his sexual relationship with Gregg, but she never went to the cops.

If I talk about the utter gall of an adult claiming he is "sexually mismatched" with his child rape victim, I will become so angry that I start throwing things. Isn't it enough to force a child to endure repeated sexual hell without complaining about the quality of the services the child-victim is forced to provide? Maybe Idi Amin could require all his torture victims to scream in a particular key!

In the letters, my father wrote of his desperate pain and loss over Barry losing interest in him. According to my father, he was in love with Barry and wanted his feelings to be reciprocated. Barry had already been a child-prostitute for some time when he became involved with my father, and to him the "relationship" was all business. He was not interested in being my father's "Golden Boy." When my father did not give him enough money and presents to hold his interest, Barry left him and eventually reported him to one Inspector Bierce. Sadly, because Barry had previously denied being molested by my father, he was not believed by the police when he finally chose to talk.

My father never understood that he was victimizing these children; he imagined there was a relationship. It looked like one to him because the boys returned, had sex with him, and were polite. The boy prostitutes knew what he wanted of course, and as long as there was money, they would stay. What choice did they have? A known regular client in a home or an unknown person—possibly a more dangerous one—in a San Francisco alley or hourly hotel. To the children, it was an unavoidable financial transaction. To my father, it was a love affair.

Not only did my father desperately want these boys to love him and to want sex with him, but he expected them to "love him for himself." Since, in his own words, my father had been "tormented by young jocks" in school, he did not want to emulate them in any way lest he risk more rejection and more humiliation. He repudiated everything even remotely identified with masculinity other than sex. As a result, he absolutely refused to do anything to improve his physical appearance, his scent or his level of fitness. Yet he expected these children to desire him sexually, pot-belly and all, as insane as that might sound.

Ironically, the one person who loved and desired my father for himself despite his appearance was my mother, but he held her in contempt and often cited her appearance as an explanation for his revulsion with her.

My father never saw that where his book claimed that *Greek Love* was the cure for delinquency, the boys he defiled became *more* delinquent, not less. Gregg was hooked on heroin when they met and never kicked it, though he had some time on and off methadone. His victims robbed him routinely, which never surprised me even if I could not condone it. In a sense, he robbed them of far more: their hearts and souls and minds. They remained prostitutes. A few grew up to repudiate him.

Why could he not see that what these boys needed was *fathering*, not sex?

And here is the central problem with incest or child molestation: it monetizes parenting. Whether the child is a bacha bazi in Afghanistan, a child prostitute, or a molested son or daughter in America, the victim can end up roped into exchanging unwanted sexual favors for anything which looks or feels even remotely like parenting.

If a child is molested young enough, he will imprint on the first sexual act, much like a BDSM practitioner is triggered into his kink through arousal coupled with violence or bondage or shoes, or whatever it is. My father knew perfectly well that early sexual experience was needed in order to create a "gay child", and he took advantage of this. He often said that boys had to have experience with a man before they were old enough to be "ruined" by sexual attraction to a girl.

My father wrote in his letters about spending an entire night cuddling with Ian during a "coming of age" ritual for Nick and Gregg. Ian would have been about 12 or 13 at that point: the age my father thought was ideal. Ian still insists on my father's innocence, even though my aunt Tracy caught my father molesting him when he was much younger. Ian was never a prostitute. Why wasn't he protected by my family? I am beginning to suspect that the actual priority, trumping children, jobs, stability and everything, was male sexual privilege.

I would love to be disproved about this.

When I was ten years old, Walter became convinced that my mother and I were In League to Put Him In Prison, and that he would DIE there. He told me this again and again. He KNEW he was going to die, and that it would be All My Fault.

Therefore, he had to write, write, write and finish the book quickly before he faced his inevitable and tragic end.

"The book" was his gargantuan "masterpiece" called *The Cynic's Dictionary*, a greatly expanded imitation of Ambrose Bierce's *The Devil's Dictionary*. It contained unusual, contrary, and oft-humorous definitions of common concepts. It was so vast that Letter A alone was several hundred typewritten pages long, and it could not be edited for length due to the importance of the material. Walter would trot out parts of it as an answer to any and all questions as a final authority, and he claimed that "every word in it is true; more's the pity."

A central feature of my father's mental state was his belief that he did not have opinions, only facts. This lay beneath his entire delusional system. To him everything in his mind was true; therefore everything he thought was true. All his feelings were true, all his thoughts were true, and anything contradicting them was a lie.

He found such mundane choices as dinner to be nearly impossible to navigate because they involved opinions and desires, and he only had facts. The only "facts" he could draw from for something like choosing dinner amounted to "I have eaten this before and not died; therefore I can eat it again." Anything beyond that was not possible for him.

Although my father felt that "*The Cynic's Dictionary* was of vast, apocalyptic importance", he could not persuade anyone to publish it.

Seriously, who would read something—even a clever something—which is comparable in length to Webster's Unabridged Dictionary? Two hundred pages of clever and fun I can see. Two thousand pages of dated sociopolitical polemic from the Eighties, even dressed up with epigrams, wit, and puns? Spare me. It would have been unimaginably wearisome long before Letter B. Yes, we know: he hates Reagan, he hates Republicans, he hates straight culture, he hates nuclear families, and he loves sex with children. Do we really need to slog through any more of this?

Lest anyone think I am disparaging his writing wholesale, I am not. I draw stark contrast between his writing about personal matters—which was bizarre at best—and his writing about coins, which was splendid, witty, and unassailably accurate since it was based on facts about coins.

To illustrate this contrast further, I will add another excerpt of his writing at the end of this chapter which will demonstrate how very odd, limited, and ultimately self-pitying his own perspective was. Here are two examples of what may be found in his unpublished masterpiece. You can tell me whether you would want to read several thousand pages of this and whether you think that it would be likely to change the world into a grand utopia of free love and sex between all people:

Straight: adjective. Narrow. More like the cage than the bird, more like the wall than the vine or child that climbs it: more like the nightstick than the head it smashes.

Marriage: noun. For the man, a wife sentence: for the woman, a new name and address.

Anyone can see how *The Cynic's Dictionary* is destined to change the world into a utopia!

Or not.

I am including the following article written by my father not because it is especially edifying but because it might serve to illustrate his personality better than anything I could say. He wrote this to explain an eleven-month absence from writing his usual article, Bristles and Barbs, for *Coins* magazine. Note: "SBAs" are Susan B. Anthony one-dollar coins, and the Berkeley Soap Opera was the extended family in Berkeley we lived in. "Don't Make Waves!" is the way he felt he was obliged to suffer in silence, living in pain and endless misery.

Before I get to the main theme, let me publicly thank my well-wishers who have been inquiring about my health during the months I've been away from these pages and up to my eyebrows in the Berkeley Soap Opera ("Don't make waves!"). We are all at last over our major infections; I finally sent off the last installment (a 600 item bibliography) of the Encyclopedia of American Coins to Doubleday; we are no longer trapped carless in a house with four long-term house guests and all our major appliances out of order; the back door (vandalized by a burglar) has been replaced; I have had six narrow escapes from death in my car at the hands of loose nuts behind other wheels, who evidently don't believe in turn signals or making sure intersections are clear; one of our house guests was shot in the leg and given three minor jaw fractures by a mugger; another family member was abducted by a rapist and rescued by a friend at the last moment; we contacted authorities after my foster son was mugged, on the same day he was almost blinded by chemicals; we settled out of court with the hotel in whose elevator we'd been trapped for hours; I have been (permanently, I hope) cured of asthma by a group of psychic healers; I am finally off crutches, no thanks to the turkey who left an extension cord stretched across my floor. (Never a dull moment.)

And how've your last few months been?

—Walter Breen, "Bristles and Barbs", Coins, Vol. 28, No. 2 (February 1981), p. 68.

A few things stand out to me from this excerpt: I remember almost nothing of what he claims. During the time period in question, I never heard of anyone being shot in the leg, abducted or rescued, trapped in an elevator, or almost blinded by chemicals. To be fair, I was gone as much as I could be, but I still spent a certain amount of time at home and there should have been *something* said about such difficult events.

I do remember one thing, and only one, which keeps me from saying I remember nothing of his mystifying claims. I do remember my father being on crutches, and tripping over an extension cord is a reasonable explanation although I don't know how one could have ended up in his room without his knowledge or consent. After all, how many mysterious figures go into one's room in secret, install suspicious extension cords and leave?

Perhaps I was simply not close enough to him, or all these dramas mysteriously happened out of my sight, or somehow he forgot to mention any of it to me. Perhaps he was simply living in another space-time continuum, where dreadful things conspired against him at every moment.

His six near-misses behind the wheel? I think he was without any doubt the worst driver I have ever known. He would get so upset so easily that he would scream uncontrollably at other drivers for anything at all, and worse, he would ease off the brake pedal onto the gas pedal as though they were connected, and vice versa, which meant someone would invariably get whiplash from being his passenger. I would be willing to bet that all six near-misses were his own fault and the result of his own panic.

But more obvious to me is this: even if those events all took place within eleven months, I am still willing to bet that he spent every spare minute writing, even if he neglected the column he was asked to write. To me this is a lengthy, nonsensical rehash of the classic "Dog Ate My Homework" gambit, and I'm not sure why he even included it in a professional article.

Without a doubt he was a charming and charismatic writer, but his reality was distinctly different than that which happened in the lives of the rest of us. And no, the psychic healers did not cure his asthma.

Try to not look so surprised...

Something is rotten in the state of Denmark.

—Marcellus to Horatio, *Hamlet*, Act 1 Scene 4

Chapter 24

Religion of the Month Club
(1980–1982)

For the time will come when people will not put up with sound doctrine. Instead, to suit their own desires, they will gather around them a great number of teachers to say what their itching ears want to hear.

—*The Holy Bible*, 2 Timothy 4:3 (NIV)

For a batch of intellectuals like my parents, a new interest is usually all that is needed to drive any interpersonal stuff away. In that light, my parents' new interest in religion was quite enough to consume them all for some time and to distract them from anything as trivial as genuine dislike of one another, incompatible values, and the occasional felony.

Their interest in religion was more of a scholarly exercise than anything which could be confused with genuine faith in anything. After all, "sitting in a church does not make you a Christian any more than sitting in a garage makes you a car." Still, for my parents, who had money, books, and plenty of space, making their very own religion seemed a reasonable project. I am not claiming there is anything objectively wrong with their religious inquiry. The problem is that I do not believe for a microsecond that any of them believed in any part of what they were doing.

To say that my parents' interest in religion inspired the respect and admiration of their offspring is a slight overstatement. Where my brother and I tried hard to not openly guffaw at each new fad, the overall effect was about as impressive as watching a pair of toads endlessly trying on ball gowns. No, the cut doesn't matter. No, the color doesn't matter. No, the fit doesn't matter. Nothing is going to make a toad look good in a ball gown, and nothing is going to make a fake faith worthy of respect.

Greenwalls was a two-story Victorian house with external stairs front and back, and behind the house was a two-story carriage house which was initially unfinished, like a barn on the inside. When both floors of the carriage house were finished, the upstairs, always called the "Temple", became the nonprofit Center for Non-Traditional Religion. There was a giant pentagram painted on the floor, which might still be there under the linoleum, although I don't know what happened to the building once we were all gone.

Before the Temple was finished, Mother held rituals in our living room. There was also a tiny little room off the library at Greenwalls that was used as a magical room. It was small and narrow with almost no furniture except the altar. A candle was always burning, and this was very important to both of my parents, not just as the symbol of fire, but as a symbol of eternity. Also on the altar were a little dish of salt (earth), a chalice of water (water), and a knife (air).

My mother had a magic cabinet. It was five or six feet tall a foot and a half wide, and it was made of grey enameled metal with shelves. My father kept his geodes and other rocks and crystals in there alongside my mother's pictures and little statues, some silver jewelry, and the ritual knife. It was double edged with a Japanese wrapped-cord grip expertly done by Mother's friend Barry Green.

On the wall was a piece of paper hand-lettered by my father. It said:

Let none enter unless they
ACKNOWLEDGE
The Fatherhood of God
The Motherhood of Nature
and the Brotherhood of Man.

Yes, I know that is awfully pompous, but all their religious meanderings were pompous.

In 1978, my mother, my aunt Diana, my aunt Tracy, and several others had a coven which they called the "Darkmoon Circle." They had lots of rituals about which I remember little, except I thought that they were stupid, and I had to make several magical robes for them. The robes were simple: a long length of black fabric folded in half crosswise and sewn up both sides with a hole in the top for the head. There was a white cord tied at the waist, knotted at both ends.

What was the point of the Darkmoon Circle? The notion was that the "goddess" appeared in three aspects: "Maiden", "Mother", and "Crone" or "Wise Woman"; called collectively "The Triple Goddess." Someone joked that I was the unmaidenly Maiden, Lisa was the unmotherly Mother, and Mother was the foolish Wise Woman. Even now I fail to see the point, but one thing we all did during the ritual was to act the part of one of those three "goddesses", complete with really dopey lines, typed out and stapled in the upper left-hand corner.

I know that in other pagan rituals, the stated intention is to get the "spirits" or "gods and goddesses" to inhabit the bodies of the ritual participants and then for them to have sex with one another as though human beings were an earthly singles bar for disembodied spirits. Where I am certain that enough fancy language and historical references might make a "Great Marriage" seem less stupid, nothing could *make* it less stupid. My mother wrote about at least one of these "Great Marriages" in *Mists of Avalon* a few years later. In private, she joked about the possibility of invoking a spirit and then not being able to get it to do what she wanted it to do. It would have made a good plot device, I suppose, if one was writing a book.

To attempt it seems the height of idiocy.

Nonetheless, I had a "puberty ritual" with the Darkmoon Circle when I was 13, which took place in the hot tub and the living room at Greenwalls. We were all naked, or "skyclad", although there was no sex, and no attempts were made to get any spirits to show up that I recall. I was given a few gifts, including some needles and silk thread from Esther in a small leather bag, and a little moonstone from my aunt Diana wrapped in a square of white silk.

One thing I had difficulty forgiving my mother for are the new words she wrote for Mozart's incomparable *Ave Verum Corpus*. They are too stupid and banal to repeat here. Compare this to the part in Stanley Kubrick's *A Clockwork Orange*, where Beethoven's Ninth is ruined for Alex by its inclusion in the Ludovico Treatment, meant to "cure" Alex. There is no excuse to destroy good music.

Mozart was inspired by God, and anything Mozart wrote was much holier than anything which went on in my mother's Temple.

I noticed Mother and Diana wrote the pagan rituals with increasingly Christian language over time. Instead of Darkmoon Circle and Triple Goddess, we started hearing about the "Liturgy of the Mother" and the "Covenant of the Goddess." The latter, also known as "COG", was an organization Diana ran for years and years before she got mixed up with Asatru, or Norse paganism.

The rituals made me feel sick. It was almost as though my mother thought that inventing a bunch of nonsense would suddenly cause a new deity-to-order to leap into existence, ready to do the bidding of people.

Far from sanitizing it, the Christian-speak simply made the pagan stuff seem confused and lacking in identity. After all, if religion is meant to recognize ultimate reality, how can it be invented and reinvented by anyone with a Selectric typewriter and a Xerox machine? Yes, I know my parents would spend ages trying to talk anyone who would listen out of believing anything in the Bible and questioning the inspiration of the authors, but Mother never claimed inspiration, holy or otherwise, for the mindless twaddle she stuffed into the rituals we wasted our time with.

The "Aquarian Order of the Restoration" (AOR) met in the newly fixed up upstairs of the Temple. The objective of the AOR was to restore Goddess worship to the culture. Although the Internet claims my mother and father founded the AOR in the '50s or '60s, that is absurd considering they did not meet until 1962. I first remember my mother and father holding AOR rituals in the '80s; I was there.

Where the Internet claims my mother "initiated" others into the AOR, including Ramfis S. Firethorn, that was just my Uncle Don using yet another pseudonym. One notable use of all these pseudonyms is that it means the worst books my family has ever coughed up can be reviewed by lots and lots of people— or two people with lots and lots of pseudonyms, proving that nepotism is alive and well.

All I remember of the AOR rituals is that they were just as stupid as the Darkmoon Circle rituals, they included men unlike the Darkmoon Circle, and in a particularly awful moment in one ritual my uncle Don held a sword to my throat and swore me to secrecy about something or other.

I remember how horrified I was that men—mostly Don, my father, and Phillip (Phil) Wayne—were present at the AOR rituals. The last thing I wanted was to be either skyclad or in nothing but a thin magical robe around a bunch of fat, oversexed creeps—whether I was related to them or not!

When my parents had lost interest in Wicca and agreed that the objective of the AOR had been accomplished, they all turned their interests toward Christianity, or their interpretation of Christianity anyway. My parents felt that what they believed was far superior to anything that was actually in the Bible, and if they studied hard enough, they would be able to prove that their interpretation and revision was really the "right" one.

Mother didn't approve of how non-feminist the Bible was, and she certainly didn't believe in any of that anti-gay and anti-lesbian stuff. My father was passionately interested in religion, although his beliefs were unsupportable. He was committed to the notion that he could prove that Jesus was a pedophile and that John the Beloved Disciple was his teenaged lover: in my view, a hideous blasphemy.

My mother had been volunteering as a telephone "pastoral" counselor at the Pacific Center, a gay counseling center in Berkeley. When she discussed this with Mikhail Itkin, he persuaded her that she had a vocation for the priesthood.

First, a little bit about Mikhail Itkin:

"Archbishop" Michael Francis Augustine Itkin (aka Mikhail Itkin) was the protege of Bishop George A. Hyde. Father Hyde presided over the Eucharistic Catholic Church in 1946, the first Christian church in the United States to ordain gay people. He ordained Mikhail to the priesthood in 1957. Bishop Hyde and Itkin parted ways two years later because he quit ordaining gay people and backed away from his pro-gay stance.

Mikhail was a fan of gay sex, leather, and LSD. He had written an essay about spirituality and LSD which caught the eye of one Timothy Leary. He ran his own church, first called the "Primitive Catholic Church" (Evangelical Catholic), followed by about six other names, finally settling on "Western Orthodox Catholic" (Anglican Orthodox). After a long, "priestly" love affair with the San Francisco bathhouses, Mikhail Itkin died of complications of AIDS in 1989. In 2002, the Moorish Orthodox Church decided he was a saint. No doubt Heaven leapt into obedience at their whim.

For the next few paragraphs, I am going to set aside the use of quotation marks because if I use all of them that the subject matter requires, I will run out. You can imagine, if you like, someone trying to read the following passage in a self-important tone, with a straight face, or perhaps imagine me reading it, laughing my brains out. Suffice to say, it is very difficult to take one's parents seriously when they take leave of logic and reason, but you'd think I would be used to that by now. Here we go, with no quotes:

Mikhail helped my parents invent their very own Christian sect and called it Gnostic Catholicism. I know. I know. That's a bit like dry water or vegan hamburger. Mikhail had already ordained my father as an archbishop years before. His series of ordination classes culminated with him ordaining my mother as a priest and Lisa, Don, and Don's lover Kelson as deacons.

This is my belief about Mikhail and his farcical notion of "ordaining" the people in my house:

They are the kind who worm their way into homes and gain control over gullible women, who are loaded down with sins and are swayed by all kinds of evil desires, always learning but never able to come to a knowledge of the truth.

—*The Holy Bible*, 2 Timothy 3:6–7 (NIV)

I was required to go to Mother's ordination after years of watching her be a pagan priestess. I was repulsed, finding the entire thing to be idiotic. I have no idea whether she took it seriously or whether she regarded it as the equivalent of a new merit badge. When Mikhail laid hands on her during her ordination, there was a loud thunderclap. This was interpreted by my parents as a symbol of great and wonderful things; for me it seemed more a sign of divine disapproval. I halfway expected her to be struck by lightning.

The church horrified me. What went on inside seemed such a waste of time! There was no congregation: just them. No ministry. No people. Nobody was helped. The entire shaky edifice seemed built on the notion that they, as gay people, wanted to be ordained, and gosh darn it, they were going to be ordained.

I seem to recall that in other Christian churches, priests and deacons are there to preach the Gospel. They are there to share Christ, to confess their sins, to love one another, and to take Communion. Of course, Mother could not be bothered with anything like that. From what I observed, what mattered were the props and the costumes. Naturally, with my mother's money all of *that* was easy.

Where I cannot find even a shred of respect for the ersatz religious hats my parents stuck akimbo on their swelled heads, I can admire the artwork provided by the supporting cast.

Kelson, my uncle Don's gay lover and a phenomenally talented costumer, made splendid vestments for the new "church." He also made five stained glass windows for the Temple: one for each of the four directions, and a gorgeous likeness of the Yellow Submarine for my father. These were not kits. They were not simple. They were masterpieces. I know what goes into making stained glass (copper binding, soldering all the edges, cutting every single piece of glass to size) because I had taken a class in it, and Kelson kindly let me help while he was making the Yellow Submarine window.

I knew Kelson from before. He had showed me how to operate my industrial sewing machine. It went 5,000 stitches per minute, and it absolutely terrified me. He also showed me how to work with leather. I had designed a cat o'nine tails whip with a dowel, a long strip of inch-wide leather which I ran diagonally down the dowel and used to cover the tails and make the handle. He showed me how to sew leather with the industrial sewing machine and not hurt myself. I had a lot of experience working with leather lacing it up by hand, but only a very little bit of sewing—done with a triangular needle, waxed thread, and an awl with a hammer. I can think of few people in my lifetime who I know who have come anywhere near to Kelson's brilliance, talent, and vision. He died tragically young, also of AIDS.

Is God a shmoo?

Why am I talking about vestments and stained-glass windows and Kelson's brilliance? Because there was absolutely nothing of merit which went on in that "church" whatsoever other than yet another outlet for a most remarkable artist and artisan. A "Christian" "church" where Christ cannot be found, and where the Bible is merely a stage prop? Why not go to a restaurant and eat a meal of plastic fruit? What is the actual belief? Is God real, or did my parents believe that God was a "force" and presume it would become whatever they liked, as though Divinity was a shmoo?

What is a shmoo? It is an imaginary creature, popularized by the ancient comic strip Li'l Abner, which will do and be anything you need. Via Infogalactic:

> *Shmoos are delicious to eat, and are eager to be eaten. If a human looks at one hungrily, it will happily immolate itself—either by jumping into a frying pan, after which they taste like chicken, or into a broiling pan, after which they taste like steak. When roasted they taste like pork, and when baked they taste like catfish. (Raw, they taste like oysters on the half-shell.) They also produce eggs (neatly packaged), milk (bottled, grade-A), and butter—no churning required. Their pelts make perfect bootleather or house timber, depending on how thick one slices it.*

The upshot is this: if God is real, we do not have the ability or the right to decide what, or who, God is. If we are Christians, we do not have the ability or the right to decide that God is something other than what He has told us plainly that He is.

If people with no interest in Christian doctrine can be ordained as priests, our dogs also deserve ordination. After all, dogs live a life of service and poverty, depending entirely on their people from morning to night. They exhibit the qualities of patience, perseverance, unconditional love for all people, appreciation of the blessings in their lives, forgiveness, long-suffering, and wet noses. It is obvious that dogs possess Christian qualities and virtues in much greater measure than the ordained heretics found in my family.

The cake is a lie.

Imagine baking a chocolate cake, but you don't really like chocolate, so you substitute prunes. Wheat flour is too high in gluten, so you substitute cornmeal.

Sugar is unhealthy, so it is left out in favor of some molasses. Eggs are deemed undesirable, so applesauce is used instead. By the time the whole business is baked, calling it a chocolate cake doesn't make a lot of sense since the only resemblance to a cake is the general shape. If you bite into it expecting chocolate cake, it is not likely to be a pleasant surprise. Why not just call it a bizarre casserole rather than pretending it is a chocolate cake?

Similarly, if you want to be a Christian, but you don't like Christian doctrine and you substitute your own, are you a Christian or a generic mystic wearing a costume?

I had quietly become a Christian a few years before. When Jesus came to me speaking in a small, still voice, He told me that I was His and He would take care of me. I couldn't tell anyone, of course. I certainly couldn't go to church, let alone stop going to my mother's "rituals." One thing I do remember very distinctly is that I would get sick every single time I attended one of the rituals.

I would sooner have told my parents I had become a cannibal than admit I was a Christian. If my parents had found out, first they would have wondered who "corrupted me", and then they would have made merciless fun of me, possibly coming up with something more extreme. Both my mother and father had regularly railed against Christianity with many high-sounding intellectual arguments and condescension. I could not take the hours and hours of balderdash they would subject me to to talk me out of it, and I knew that they would view my conversion as a betrayal. I didn't dare come out of that particular closet for a very long time, and I acted like a pagan all through my teens so I wouldn't upset them.

It occurs to me that this is simply one more area of my life that they owned.

In any event, I make no claims of having been anything resembling a "good" Christian. It was more about what He did than what I did, because at that point I could do absolutely nothing. I am convinced He is the one who made it so that I became strong enough to speak out and eventually to bring my father to justice.

Where the "Priest Friends" had brought Barry and Gregg into the house, their pimping and pandering did not stop there. One day, my father's friend Richard Kihlstadius told me that the reason I was so moody and angry all the time was that I was sexually frustrated. This was absurd, and I did not give it another thought. I knew perfectly well that I was moody and angry because I was a teenager living in chaos, and the chaos interfered with my ability to get my homework done.

Then, Richard Kihlstadius brought a young man over to meet me. His name was Rick, and I found him to be frightening. He was a punk in leather and spikes, and he talked at length about how Sid Vicious had killed his girlfriend in the bathtub. Worse, he was in our bathroom doing something in the mirror when he was talking about that. I refused to talk to him, and I left. I was not sure why he was there or why he wanted to meet me if he idolized murdering girls.

The next time Richard brought a young man over, it was completely different. His name was Smiley. He told me as soon as we left the house that Richard had paid him to have sex with me, and I was aghast. He said he intended to give the money back and offered to take me out to dinner because he liked me like a girlfriend, not a friend or whatever Richard intended. Smiley even picked a place on Shattuck Avenue called Omnivore, and we walked right by it. I couldn't make myself walk inside though.

I really, *really* liked Smiley, and I was completely awkward and uncomfortable. Besides, my father had been telling me for ages that no man would ever want me and worse, that all women ever wanted from men was money. If I let Smiley take me out to dinner, I would just be one of *them*, those awful mercenary women. Was this a colossal joke with me as the butt of the joke? Was I being manipulated into acting like a normal girl so my father could become enraged with me for it?

Smiley and I walked around Berkeley, talking about everything for a long, wonderful time because I couldn't go along with letting him buy me dinner. Eventually, he walked me home.

I suppose that was my first date.

Chapter 25

The Breaking of Nick

By Nicholas Bosson

I was born in 1964, in the university town of Berkeley, California. By the time I had reached puberty, I had experienced the People's Park riots (firsthand) dropped acid (age 11), and been tossed between my divorced parents' houses a series of times. My mother left home when I was three—an act that my sister convinced me was my fault. I saw virtually nothing of her until the age of seven, when she rode in like an avenging angel and took me to live with my new stepfather. He had already raised three kids and seemed to have felt he had had enough of raising kids.

When I was 12, I met Patrick Breen. An artist, like me, with a mystical bent. It wasn't till a few years later that we became best friends. When visiting his house, Greenwalls I met his father, a man who welcomed me with open arms. He let me share his marijuana, something in short supply for a lad my age. The mother, Marion, was a kind enough woman to allow me to share their table. The family seemed to live solely on over-salted canned goods. She was so busy writing that a murder could have happened there without her knowledge. The entire house seemed to whirl about a center of fantasy and science fiction. I spent many hours with my mind in the clouds. I thought I had found home, a place where I could be who I thought I really was.

Well, that proved false. I was but one of the many young boys that Walter had "made comfortable." Comfortable enough to let my guard down. I wasn't an idiot, and neither was he.

He began with not so subtle comments concerning my physical beauty. I was an attractive boy. Having had some few dalliances at such an early age, I enjoyed the pleasures of the flesh; what teenager doesn't? But, they expect to experiment with others their age. At 14, a simple bus ride would give me an erection. I was the perfect target for cock-gobblers. Hell, if it was wet and warm, I would stick it in there, just to pleasure myself.

This must be a common tactic for child molesters, as most boys my age find themselves bereft of options. The girls, most of them, didn't want to appear to be sluts. The boys were too hung up with being labelled a "FAG". When Walter went down on me, without even asking, it felt good. Still, looking down, I realized that a repulsively ugly man was giving me head. I felt dirty. I wanted to hide this. But there were too many others that knew the truth for me to do that. It was not a secret what Walter was doing. He was akin to the Black Plague.

It seemed like many of the kids I had grown up with had been approached by him. Not only the kids knew about him; I discovered a lot of adults did as well! Namely Marion, and her live-in girlfriend Lisa. I personally saw a lot of Marion. The thing that can be said in her favor was that she doted on Patrick. She loved to touch his hair. She would call him her "Prince". Soon after, though, she would head back into her tiny study to write. Perhaps Patrick was her muse.

Dorothy, I remember, spent a lot of time upstairs when I first showed up. This became less and less as the years passed. Dorothy was a rambunctious kid with scarlet hair. She rarely left her room. I have to admit that I wanted to know her better. It was hard to get inside her armor, especially since I was dragged away by Walter each time we spent more than five minutes talking together.

Walter was… hungry. He craved attention.

I guess I should describe him to you, both mentally and physically. Please don't judge me. He liked to think of himself as Santa Claus. A long grey-black beard that reached his swollen belly. Eyes, a bit piggy. He had false teeth. Though he would bathe in the hot tub often, he had a scent. An old man scent. Being overweight, sedentary, and lacking a healthy diet, (remember the canned foods) he smelled of what he ate… cholesterol. And YES, I know what cholesterol smells like. It is often a joke that fat people wear Muu-muus. Walter wore Muu-mus. He preferred to be naked. Displaed his hirsute belly without a tad of shame. Well, God bless him for that, but he did it for all the wrong reasons.

Walter would not have hurt a fly. He was a coward. His voice high pitched, his giggle was girlish and his demeanor fey. He claimed his staunchly religious mother had placed clothes pins on his member if it ever became erect. He said he was a bishop, but I never learned of which church he hailed.

One summer my mother sent me off to a horse summer camp in Montana while they toured Europe. I got kicked out three weeks in.

My father was far too busy with his "new" family: a purely Swedish bastion on the edge of Wildcat Canyon. Tom Fogerty owned the mansion at the top of the street. Nice digs. My half-sister Jenny consumed most of their time. She eventually has become a thoracic surgeon, so I guess they did right by her.

Kicked out of summer camp. No parents or home to go home to. I ended up on the porch of Greenwalls begging for a place to stay. This is where things got out of control.

My old friends from school barely saw me, as Walter demanded the full extent of my time. I felt imprisoned. I met with nobody but that inner circle. A form of brainwashing, perhaps Walter intended, or just subconscious. I was daily indoctrinated into what Walter believed to be "MY" preferred way of life/sex. One problem: I truly loved women. They had everything I desired. I wanted their difference, their grace, their warmth. And I hated the feel of coarse hair! One night, Dorothy invited me into her bedroom. I reveled in her perfect form. I sucked her up like nectar. And thirty minutes later, I was back with Walter and surrounded again by "that smell." Thanks, kid.

A seed was planted. I had become so involved in a way of life I was no longer comfortable with, something that felt like a cat being petted backward. I drifted back to my old friends once again. But now there was a pall of distrust. "Is Nick trying to seduce us?" Most of the girls—YES! But not so much the boys: I had had enough. Still, I was not trusted. My closest friends knew better. I was lucky to have found a group of highly intelligent people, ones who took me at face value. I felt it difficult to relate to my true friends at Greenwalls (those of my own age).

Then one day, in the bathroom of Silver Ball Gardens, my friend injected me with methamphetamine. I wanted it. I loved it. Suddenly, I had the ability to complete my very dreams, or so it seemed. This became a problem, a problem that lasted 30 years. How can I explain this?

I was in a bubble. A steel bubble. One that I could escape at any time, but I was assailed by such feelings of guilt. If I were to not ever see Walter ever again, it would have been unfair to the others who were my true comrades. People like Patrick and Dorothy. I hung out with them, and we played the games that teenagers do, like Magick, role-playing games, (pre-computer) drawing, and painting. Dorothy began to slip away, perhaps because of an innate revulsion to what her father was doing?

At a certain point, Walter was forced to move out to an apartment on busy Telegraph Ave. I had started to go to a new school in San Francisco. There I met a young gay kid named Gregg. He had a lot of baggage concerning his mother.

He loved me. I am afraid that I did not feel the same way, but I still introduced him to all of my friends, including Walter.

Soon Gregg was a fixture in Walter's little crash pad. I deign to call it a home. Walter had a large bed in the central room where the sex happened. Two "priests", "Fathers" Jim and Richard Kihlstadius, began to make themselves regular fixtures there. They had been at Greenwalls also. Both were on the edge, if not over, 50 years old. They began to prey on us young boys with an even greater lust than Walter had ever shown. They were thoroughly addicted to sex. They wanted to fuck all day long, even after their sagging scrotums were empty of cum.

It was at this point that Walter became increasingly paranoid about the police. There was one certain officer who he would always bring up. He complained vehemently that men should be able to have sex with kids. He cited NAMBLA tracts and other like-minded organizations, purporting that since man/boy love had been practiced throughout history… it must be okay, utterly ignoring all arguments that might counter his beliefs.

Gregg began to petition Walter to urge me to be more affectionate to him. Gregg, I think, had started to figure out that I wasn't as into him. As I was now nearing 16, my life extended beyond Walter's apartment. Gregg took my place there and soon made me out to be some kind of devil. I really didn't give a damn. I had places now that I would rather be. Back with my friends from the underworld.

We were all interesting people. A lot of us were just teenagers, a few from "the older kids" (at that age, "older kids" were two or three years older than you). We had all met through friends or chance meetings. The majority were enamored with magick, or languages, or art. We knew who was one of us at first glance. If you had seen us holding court in the back of a Berkeley cafe, you would have said, "Those kids belong together."

It was a weird amalgam of children from different races and economic levels. It was our shared alienation, I think, that brought us all together. My friends all knew what was going on with Walter; Berkeley is a small town where news travels fast amongst natives.

We all know the seedy underbelly of this seedy little college town. The gossip of Berkeley's teenagers could have taken down many respected academics. We had our fingers on the pulse of that town, as all of us kids were insiders. Dinner table conversations, parents fighting, sisters fondled, sons propositioned, etc. An endless dirty fountain of burbling excrement. Believe me: universities are rife with socially-crippled intellectuals.

Walter was a numismatist, which, if you can believe it, is a field controlled by gnome-like men who would rather spend their time with coins in some dimly-lit study than having a merry conversation with their colleagues or family. Marion, an author, had none of the charisma of other fiction writers I had met. Most of the best loved to amuse crowds. They tend to be storytellers. (duh). Capturers of others' interest. Weavers of shared dreams. Walter's charisma had none of this. His "wife" neither. It was more planned out. Charisma in the form of orchestrating the emotions of those around them. Still even at this, they both lacked. The constant attempts by Walter to indoctrinate us into his felonious beliefs. Marion's blithe ignorance of affairs that only Helen Keller might not be aware of.

The sex was a tedious thing that I was beginning to be guilt-tripped into taking part in, be it Gregg, Walter, or these traveling priests. I had very little of my true self involved in the activities. Believe me: I am not one to hang around when chores are to be done.

Then one day Sterling dipped into Walter's wallet and the group pointed their fingers at me. Being accused of a crime I hadn't committed drove me further off and the catty little rumor mill took off.

I left! My friends at the cafe greeted me with pensive arms. The accusations had followed me to the only place I felt safe. So, what had been a disturbing drug problem before became extreme.

Years later, the ghost of Walter's whining bothered me. He had insinuated himself into every niche of my life that he had access to. I was running from myself when I should have been running from him.

I felt misrepresented. Most of my friends were hippy kids, and hippy kids were very leery of homosexuals, as most of us had suffered from their advances throughout our lives. Being the creatures that dwelt within the hedges of the campus, we had seen what lurks in the bocage: old jerks jerking off. We Berkeley kids had a few secret forts (well, not that secret) around the UC campus. The steam vents, down and over, the beach, the grove, Afghanistan, up and over, these were our secret names for various hiding places. Mostly we would go to these little Edens, (thank you, UCB gardeners) and be alone with each other reading poetry, throwing tarot cards, smoking pot, and sharing food (remember, we were teenagers). We would be perfectly at home, until an intruder happened by. The joy instantly gone, we would look at each other, thinking, "When is this guy gonna leave??"

Walter had taught me distrust. A nasty lesson, but necessary.

Do you know how stories are often given depth by character actors? Well, Greenwalls was full of these sorts. Odd bodkins who would do their rounds monthly, weekly. This always included Marion's house. I say Marion's house because the house was her caliphate.

And, oh the humorous sacks of water that came through those doors! Isaac, THE MAGICIAN, he was little more than an angry aging hippy who had never been cool. Izak, ha ha. Various female Renaissance Faire people of voluminous proportions. Mostly washer women or innkeeper's wives in their various personas during Northern Faire. Often the buxom cuddly hawkers during Dicken's Faire. They would come babbling through the door in their costumes. Playing their parts as if it were true. Method actors, I guess?

It wasn't until many years later in my life that I actually had enough insight to see how Walter had damaged me. Some would say, "But you invited it. You didn't fight back." Well, I spent a long time holding onto that same attitude. I woke up at night cursing myself for being the fool that I was. A thousand twitches, unexpected swearing at myself while others tried to avoid me. I had been broken. I would like to think of myself as a fine piece of china that has been glued together so many times that it was no longer of any use.

I remember one fellow named Andy, whose company I no longer keep, saying quite clearly in my earshot, "That Nick is a waste of human flesh." You might be able to imagine how that hurt. Adding on insult and injury daily I became a desperate addict. Anything to get out of myself... the boy who hadn't fought back. Still in the darkness when I had woken up from a serious drinking bout, I would feel the claws of remorse digging deep into my already-drained heart. Had you seen me in passing during this period, you would think to yourself, "He smiles. He jokes. He laughs. There is still something really wrong with this kid."

My mother tried to send me to an old-school (Freudian) psychologist. I made him angry when I told him that there was nothing he could do for me. I was set so firmly in my ways that nothing would be able to change me. I was perhaps 17 at the time, and had been kicked out of three very good schools. Somehow I could have one of the worst attendance records on campus, yet on test days... I would ace the entire test. I didn't like classrooms (unless they were art classes). My attention span was ridiculously short. Boredom was a constant battle. I could not bear to spend the whole day in class. For me, that style of learning just did not work. I taught myself. My choices of subjects were completely useless as to their career potential. I might have done better back in the days when kings had court magicians. I had little concern for the clothes I wore. If it hid my nudity, that was good enough. It confused me to see people spending inordinate sums of money on clothes; clothes to me were a thing that you found, not bought. My mother said that she had bad dreams of me being one of those guys who wore rags and picked through trash cans while cursing to themselves.

I was well on my way by 21. While living on the streets, I discovered a trick to find a warm sleeping place. You can enter into the crawl spaces under houses through the little panels where the gas meters were. I had been doing this for a while when one morning I was awoken by a man carrying a tray with eggs, toast, and coffee. He had shimmied under his house. Perhaps I had snored the night before? The man's name was Ric, and he was a nice stable fellow. He had a good sense of humor. Something probably hard tested by me. He said to me that morning that when I was done with breakfast he had a few chores he needed help with. This beat being bored and wandering around with nothing to do. I became a laborer. Construction paid well enough that I could stay stoned as much as I wanted.

I worked a few jobs until I was a bit older, and then my job opportunities dried up due to my erratic behavior or drug addictions. I threw my hands up in the air and went back to sleeping in garages and parks. Nothing had changed. I was back at ground zero. I saw no feasible future for myself. I hated myself. I don't think the damage would have been as incredibly crippling if it were not for the years of degradation I had experienced under the manipulation of Walter and his "friends".

This was a very impressionable time for me. Who has ever been certain of themselves when aged 14? I was a neophyte waiting for some kind of direction. I looked to the adults around me to prove or disprove what I was thinking. And O! How my mind could wander! These bestial old men had no idea of what I sought. They reversed gears on me and made me feel shallow for the depth of my trek, my reason for being.

One night I returned to Patrick after having been given a vial of pure LSD. The creepy old men had no idea what we were doing. It was a barely visible amount. We split it into two tiny sparkling piles. My friend had told me that pure LSD would actually produce light if you cracked a crystal of it. No shit! This stuff was good enough to prove that theory.

We snorted the two tiny piles, one a piece. My God! I had never had acid hit me that quickly. We were overwhelmed by a need to leave civilization. We ran, completely dazed, up into the Strawberry Canyon nature preserve. Our minds were tripping balls. There was no way we could find our fingers without opening our mouths. An extreme sense of expectation drove its dowel down our spines. We hunted the perfect place, and we found it!

A perfect bowl dug from the base of three giant oaks, and there at the bottom a few slabs of rock, as old as the hills. On one side of the bowl was a cliff covered in blackberry. The other side was a mossy rim to that sacred bowl. It was beautiful beyond words. The very crux of life. The Holy Grail. We spent the following hours traveling on a wave, then in a spiral, and finally a brilliant point of blinding light.

We came back home at sun up, weary and fully worn out. The universe had kissed our brows and blessed us as few had been blessed before. I tried to talk to Patrick about what had happened to us that night. He claimed to remember nothing. Nothing! Nothing!? The most intense spiritual journey of my life, and he had FORGOTTEN IT????

I am aware of my own sins. Not all that I experienced after my molestation could be blamed on Walter. But certain things were unquestionably tied to his attempts at forced indoctrination. I was an obvious drug addict. A lazy teenager I was.

If you have never attempted suicide, you may not understand what I am about to say.

Having watched through my rearview mirror the catastrophe that was my life, I decided that there was nowhere left to go. My life was over.

The sky lit like a fire under a cauldron. I slid down the wall to sit splayed on the floor. My head drooped so that the hair covered my eyes. Heavy stones seemed to be stacked on my face by all those I had ever known. My head rocked back. The cracks in the ceiling; a canvas for the hallucinating eye. I was not on drugs. Maybe that was the problem? NO! The problem was myself and what I had allowed others to do with me!

I remember looking up to the people who had affected my childhood view of the world. By the time I was 5, Berkeley was worldwide news. The rebels fighting against a war machine that was crushing its children under a juggernaut's wheels. I looked at the counter-culture spokesmen as heroes. I thought that long hair, incense, pot, and paisley were the medals that "our army" wore. In many ways I still hold to a lot of the values that the flower children espoused. Love, peace, and cooperation.

But underneath the exterior facade lay a huge dirty brown paper satchel filled with perversions, mental incompetents, and straight-up murderers on the run from the law. Drugs had drawn in some of the most despicable characters. Their idea of freedom was staying out of jail. Not the beautiful ideal based on our pioneer ancestors' driving spirit.

Here we were in one of the loveliest environments that God had created. The Bay Area is blessed with a warm climate year-round and a liberal political machine. It was behind this facade that Walter hid his wooly head. Wreathed in a purposeful guise as some kind of wizard, he drew young boys in with the promise of free marijuana and a permissive household. It is a complicated thing for teenagers to find somewhere to hang out. They spend most of their time scooting from one haunt to another. Finding somewhere you could do your own thing, have free grass, and access to the fridge? Shit, what healthy 15-year old could deny this flower ripe to be picked? But the more one took, the more one owed. It was not a one-way street.

The world was so much smaller then. A kind of closed loop filled with horrible old men and unpleasant older women. Women who had renounced their love of the masculine while emulating men in all their steps, their speech, their bearing. Men so utterly confused by years of hatred and abuse that they lived under Victoria's Thumb. Shadows revealed to me the horrors I had been shot full of. Thieves of pride. Insulters of what I needed at that age; a strong man. Someone to guide me. Teach me the ways of human life. Instead I had become a pawn in some private game of perversity. A hidden world, shy from prying eyes. Felony-grade shame, though claiming it all was proper, and the children suffered. Oh, how they suffered.

Let me tell you about Father Jim. He dressed like a priest (which denomination is your guess as well as mine). As a young boy very interested in the mystical, I was the perfect patsy; a mark waiting for a con-man's light touch. To gain my attention he told me that he would teach me magic, though his conception of magic was quite staid compared to mine. I wanted to break the cork off of the Universe, drink its entire contents, wipe my mouth with my sleeve, and sigh in contentment. His intentions were based on one thing… sex.

Now, I have had friends who were very interested in the lovely smoothness of erotic sensations, a beautiful thing. Something you share with your loved one; a complete act of trust, and a sharing of the glories of our odd circumstances riding within bodies capable of so much.

Jim had a sickness. He saw sex as others might any addictive substance or act. He was driven by a beast upon his back. How can I claim to know what drove him? You get quite close to someone whose hemorrhoid-infested asshole is being shoved in your face. A kind of deeper understanding. Judge not a man by his words, but his deeds. Thus we can assume that Jim had very little concern about certain strictures laid down by our forebearers: no murder, no theft, and DON'T FUCK CHILDREN.

His friend Richard also claimed to be a priest. I must say, I was a pretty trusting lad. He was younger than Jim but driven by the same perversion of spirit. Lots of tall talk about how he had been some kind of adventurous martyr. Most of his games are dulled by the fog of age. I still wake up late at night confused and startled by what I had done. Things that my young body was trained to perform. So little of my self resided there. I shut it out of my mind.

I was a holy sacrifice. This made it bearable. Some dream of lessons to be learned and selfish demons fed. In shame I scream!

Richard had me splayed on my back downstairs at Greenwalls, in the kids' area, between the other bedrooms, right in the middle of the floor. I remember that floor like it was yesterday.

Thinly laid artificial astroturf glued messily to the floor. Beneath it hard, flat cement.

I was on my back, as I said, and oh how that carpet raked my back. Along with the cold concrete I was pretty miserable. Richard offered me an inhalant called "Locker Room". Remember, I was on my back. The stuff came in a tiny jar that you would take the lid off of and have a sniff of the vapors. Well, that is, if you're standing up. Try this on your back, and the bottle empties a corrosive and probably carcinogenic liquid into your sinuses and throat. I swear I felt as if I was going to die. I struggled, but Richard was in the throes of passion. He had no concern for me. He had seen the little jar glug into my nose. Any idiot would know that I might be in a mild state of DYING. He just kept up the rhythm.

If it were not for my age I might have died. No wonder he left in such a hurry. I repeat. I was a dumb kid.

Armchair Psychology

by Moira

Nick is a wonderful young man. Talented, creative, and brave beyond words. Most of my father's victims cannot admit they were hurt, cannot talk about what was done to them, and in many cases cannot even admit the reality. Many are dead now; others have disappeared without a trace. Thankfully, Nick is alive and can tell us his frank and incisive insights about what it was like to be sexually violated and even turned over to other predators by a man who promised mentorship and love when he had been abandoned by his own father.

Transcribing his words has been painful. I love Nick dearly, and reading what happened meant I wanted to punch my father and those "priests" in the nose and throw them out of several high windows for what they subjected him to, between the brainwashing and the utter disregard for him other than as a sex toy. It is easy to see that for a young man, the need for a father figure is so strong that he will go through nearly *anything*, including massive and unforgivable sexual exploitation, for even a semblance of it.

Like nearly all victims of sexual abuse, Nick blames himself. He was manipulated, seduced with the semblance of "fathering", and brainwashed with much the same rubbish that was "taught" to me. Every time he wanted a girl, the brainwashing was renewed. The only peer-to-peer relationship he was "allowed" to have was the brief sexual connection with another boy, which he really did not want, let alone the externally imposed emotional trappings. Nick needed a father figure. He didn't need to be another boy's mommy; but my father knew that the day Nick got a girlfriend, he would stop being sexually available to him and to his friends. Therefore, establishing and maintaining the "born that way" lie was essential to my father's continued orgasms at Nick's expense. I hope you can see that even though Nick takes total responsibility for what happened, he never had a chance to escape. He was played by older men who were completely focused on playing him and had spent years learning to do so with other victims.

Nick blames himself for his long, long addictions, and yet, unlike many, he has left them all behind. Addiction is nearly universal among traumatized children and teens because it provides a way to handle overwhelming feelings and create some feelings of pleasure in a situation where such things are almost impossible to feel, and cannot be trusted anyway. Anhedonia (being incapable of experiencing pleasure in anything) is characteristic in major depression, but it is *enormous* in traumatized people. Imagine trying to enjoy things while always being in a mild-to-moderate state of fight or flight. One's attention is always, unconsciously, on the threat behind that door over there, even if the only threat is really the pervert who is now dead or distant. Our brains adapt, and the adaptations of PTSD are often permanent, making the injury done to him even more heinous.

Despite what anyone might have supposed, he has been married to the same woman for a great many years, and he walks dogs for people while painting prolifically and running a Facebook page for other artists. I will not pretend his life is easy or wonderful. Yet unlike so many of my father's victims, he is alive, speaking out, and has developed and maintained a loving marriage, something which has eluded many of my generation.

In the last paragraph, "Locker Room" is either amyl nitrite or butyl nitrite, also known as "poppers." When a tiny amount is inhaled, it can enhance sexual pleasure. Nick is quite right; poured into one's nose, he could have been very seriously hurt. The base is acetone and it would have assuredly destroyed the epithelial cells in the nostrils and sinuses.

I believe that both Richard and Jim are dead, so I can't kill them again even though reading this account makes me want to. Jim used to recite a "poem" which I think expresses the truth of the gay movement and how it is hardly exclusive to one sex or age or even species:

> *I am a dirty old man.*
> *I make love wherever I can.*
> *Little boys, little girls, little sheep, little squirrels...*
> *I am a dirty old man.*

Chapter 26

Flings, Fosterlings, and Folly
(1979–1982)

I can't think of anyone who's done more good than Marion has, for more people.

—Debbie Notkin, Other Change of Hobbit Bookstore

Let us review:

My father was living in the apartment on Telegraph Avenue, using his privacy to his own advantage and the disadvantage of every young man he could induce to join him. My mother and Lisa were now back at Greenwalls, sharing a bedroom and using the living room in ways a living room was never intended to be used.

I did not want to live with my father and his continual abuse of young boys. I also did not want to live with my mother and Lisa. Between their oppressive control, repulsive conduct, and what I saw as never-ending hypocrisy, I would rather have slept on the subway. I was gone as much as I could possibly manage, but when I had to come home, there were many unpleasant things in the house I had to step over.

My parents had always insisted to me how much they loved children. Now that Mother was making some money, she could get some more children to hang around under the pretense that she would rescue them. Not all of them were underage, and not all of them were seduced, but none of them should have been seduced. Moreover, if one is going to devote time and resources to caring for foster children (or "fosterlings", as I always called them), it makes no sense at all to create an intolerable atmosphere for them. I was horrified when the orgies began.

Yes, orgies. Let us not spend more than a moment imagining the gruesome picture of middle-aged fat people committing consensual adultery in the living room. Let us not imagine the total number of showers taken in the week preceding any of these orgies, but I am certain it is less than the total number of human beings. And here I thought that in our enlightened family, male-female interaction of that type was out of style. Where once Mother had complained bitterly of my father "passing her around like a plate of cookies", she was now passing herself around.

Phil was a neighbor who had moved in two houses down with his wife Joanne and their friend Cynthia McQuillin. Cynthia was a folksinger and recording artist of some note and not involved in any of the rubbish found in this chapter. I do not know what happened to Joanne, but Phil became sexually involved with both Mother and Lisa. They would tape a sign on the door from the kitchen to the living room which read: "Do Not Enter." I would leave. It was either that or wait for my homework to be disturbed by noises which defied description.

One day, I was sitting in the car about 50 feet in front of Greenwalls, near Phil Wayne's house. Mother and Lisa, who were about to drive somewhere with me, told me that they had to go on a drug called Flagyl to treat trichomoniasis, a venereal disease. They told me that they had caught the disease from Isaac (yes, *that* Isaac) or from his transgendered then-wife Celine.

Why on earth was my mother having sex with a man who had asked her permission to have sex with me when I was six? Did she have feelings for him, or was she simply willing to get naked and trade microorganisms with anyone willing to do so? How could a mother have feelings for a man who slept with little children?

Oh wait… why am I even asking that?

Isaac was certainly not her only partner who had unusual ideas about the age of consent. I must have been some kind of fuddy-duddy to want my mother to be protective of me. Apparently, since I was no longer even a potential source of sexual contact, my mother had to gather her rosebuds where she might—even if some of these rosebuds were tainted with metaphorical nuclear waste.

I am going to think about something other than Isaac and my mother before I start throwing things. I am trying as hard as I can to not feel anything at all right now.

Lisa told me that Phil had gotten her pregnant and added with obvious pride that he would have married her if she had not had an abortion. She felt her abortion was necessary because she had severe endometriosis.

Yes, I know. The whole business is absurd. How can Lisa even have a conversation with me like that? She was sexually involved on a long-term basis with my mother and would have married Phil, who was still married to Joanne. She aborted Phil's child. Why wasn't she using birth control? How can anyone living in the last several decades be unaware of the most routine consequences of sex?

Anodea hung around a lot. She was a masseuse, a painter, and later on she was my father's dealer, too. When Phil got her pregnant, Mother talked her out of having an abortion. She married Phil, briefly. Their "wedding ceremony" was typical of the pagan weddings of the day: they vowed to love each other "until they died or until love died." After all, what could be better for a child than for his parents to stay married only as long as they felt like it?

They now are both married to other people.

Despite her involvement with my mother, Lisa was a Puritanical little thing. She was obviously scared of men, absolutely avoided dressing in a way which would have ever made her seem attractive, and wore her religion like a twisted halo. Yes, religion. Before she got to Greenwalls, she had been very Christian, and she continued that despite all the pagan rituals, ordinations, and orgies.

One might recall that calling a dog's tail a leg does not make it a leg.

What had happened to Mother and Lisa being lesbians now that all these guys were involved? Although my father regarded homosexuality as being "natural" to all people, back then nobody doubted that people could function sexually with people regardless of gender; all that was required was a willingness to get naked. It was regarded as a choice, a preference, which could be altered by experience. The assumption was that anyone who tried gay sex would prefer it, so the goal was to make sure they tried it before they got too "hung up."

These days some people call this "sexual fluidity" and claim it is "more the person than the plumbing." Why would a preference for gay sex be more natural, more inborn, and more compelling than a preference for straight sex?

My mother did not seem to think there was any contradiction between iden-tifying as a lesbian while having sex with men, women, and sadly children. One of my teenaged friends, Cyndi, ended up in the orgies. She had first been mixed up with Phil, then later with Lynx, and after that with my mother. She told me that Mother had crashed the car because she had been staring at Cyndi's breasts. Mother claimed in her testimony that it had been Cyndi's fault, that Cyndi kept putting her hand on her knee. A semi-truthful account of one of the orgies appears in Lisa's testimony below.

MR. DOLAN: Would you call four people together having sex an orgy?

ELISABETH WATERS: No, I don't think I would.

MR. DOLAN: Have you ever defined this particular episode of these four people together as an orgy?

ELISABETH WATERS: I don't remember.

MR. DOLAN: How old was Cyndi when this occurred?

ELISABETH WATERS: 19, to the best of my knowledge.

MR. DOLAN: Who was involved in this particular group activity?

ELISABETH WATERS: Cyndi, Phil, Anodea and Marion.

MR. DOLAN: And there was a fourth party, as well?

ELISABETH WATERS: That is four people.

MR. DOLAN: Were you involved in it?

ELISABETH WATERS: No.

MR. DOLAN: Did you witness it?

ELISABETH WATERS: Not really.

MR. DOLAN: Could you explain, please?

ELISABETH WATERS: I was over at Philip and Anodea's house visiting them, and Cyndi was over there for some reason or another. I think she was chasing after Philip. I think she was having an affair with Philip at the time. And Marion was coming over, and I made some stupid joke about if you really want to make Marion happy, why don't you jump her when she comes through the door and have sex with her. Probably the stupidest and most tasteless thing I ever said in my entire live, but I never expected them to take me seriously, and when Marion did, they did it. I just sort of rolled over on the other side of the room and closed my eyes and pretended to be asleep.

Lisa claimed that first she suggested the orgy for Mother's benefit and then she went to sleep and didn't participate. No doubt if she went to a bar, she'd drink water; if she went to the grocery store, she'd wander the aisles with an empty cart; and if she went to the opera, she'd wear earplugs.

I know that Lisa claimed Cyndi was 19 at the time of the orgies, but I do not believe she was. She had troubles with her own family: when I first met her, she had bruises all over her legs from some violent episode. We were friends back then. I was fifteen and we were close in age. Her place in our family was not that of an independent adult but that of an older child who still required care. It might have seemed to her that initiating a sexual relationship with my mother would guarantee an ongoing connection, in the simian way I mentioned above.

In most parts of the universe, if a teenager makes a pass at an adult, then the adult is obligated to say *no* and preserve the relationship's nonsexual boundary for the good of the child. Sadly, in my family if a teenager makes a pass at an adult and the adult is one of my parents, the parent is bound not only to take advantage of the teenager but to blame her! Not one shred of attention is given to the welfare of the child or the circumstances which might lead a child to do such an unwise thing!

Cyndi was not the only teenager that my mother chose to support. Despite her dislike of any and all aspects of caring for me, my mother was absolutely convinced that she loved children, and she took in every waif and stray she could find. I resented them. It hurt so much to see Mother casually replace me as though I was just a button on a coat. It hurt so much to be told day after day that they were better children than I was because they were conforming to her ideology and doing what they were told.

Marion would pay for their college and support them, often train them in writing, and spend mountains of time with them. To her credit, she put a lot of people through college. Not everyone made it. After all, living with Mother was very much like being with someone who would pay you handsomely and only ask you to eat arsenic in return. One or two of the fosterlings did well. One became the editor of a major magazine and another reached her dream of becoming a veterinary technician.

Lisa tried to convince me I was no different than any fosterling and that my birth in the family gave me no rights at all. My father had already made it clear that he felt that I should have no precedence over any child he met anywhere. In practice though, I was less important than the fosterlings since they had something my mother and father wanted: either direct sexual access, or sycophantic respect and admiration. I had nothing like this to offer my parents. I think it is disgusting to rank one's children according to what services they can provide. Or at all.

What do you do when your mother and her lesbian lover are having orgies in the living room?

What happens when you have absolutely no connection to your family and are afraid of being at home? What do you do when you feel you are safer on a

BART train than in your own bedroom? What do you do when your bedroom is Grand Central Station, and anyone will walk through there in the middle of the night for any reason at all?

What do you do when you are afraid, ask for help, and you are jeered at? What do you do when you are terrified of being alone and the only response is humiliation? What happens when you know you are an inconvenience to your mother and an obstacle to her sex life?

You leave. I had a backpack, a BART pass, and enough money to refill it. It was clear to me that this was no place to do my homework.

If anyone wants to know why I do not intend to become a writer: I shudder to think what Mother would say about my writing.

9. To The Critic

Trite and true
Rhymes for you
I mete out meter
Never sweeter

The poison inside
You'd only deride
Your love is a farce
Affection is sparse.

You murder with words
I ran, they're unheard
Unseen and unfelt
The scars on my pelt
Remain to this day
Without going away

I retreat to within
Never feeling my skin
Till I trip or I stumble
Still taking a tumble
I bumble through life
With the slash of your knife
Still fresh in my brain
Unendurable pain!

How can I escape
From your long-ago rape
Except to break free
You no longer own me

——YOU BITCH!!!!!

Chapter 27

The Cat that Walks by Himself
(1979–1982)

I am the Cat that walks by himself, and all places are alike to me.

—Rudyard Kipling, *Just So Stories*

I was already out of the house for thirty weekends a year, and with the SCA it was more than that. Coming home at all was intolerable. Coming home was not a relief, not a safe place, not a place of comfort or familiarity. It was a swamp of unpredictability and chaos, even if I have painted it as being funnier than it seemed at the time.

The stupid things my parents were doing changed every day, as did the cast of characters. If I came home and no stranger was in my bed, I would sleep. If a stranger was in my bed, either I could rouse the person them or look for a couch. Food? Who knows? Cans of this and that, as usual. Shower with who-knows-who wandering into the bathroom? Jam something under the door and make a LOT of noise if any strangers were walking around. Hope that nobody is high and crazy, and if someone is, have a plan to leave in a hurry and a backup place to stay.

I was in school, of course. I was studying the usual subjects in school, plus some unusual subjects on my own time. I was studying heraldry and blazoning—Medieval coats of arms and identifying what is on them. I also studied Scots and Irish Gaelic on the bus on the way to school and taught myself to sing in both of them. One teacher allowed me to do the "children's book" we had been assigned in Scots Gaelic. It was displayed for some time at the Berkeley Public Library. I also read almost all of Dickens and most of Shakespeare on my lunch hours at school. I regarded the subjects I studied on my own to be ever so much more interesting than the stuff at school.

Some of my teachers were very patient and allowed me to twist other assignments in a way that I liked. My German teachers were quite taken with me. German was easy because I had already memorized Mozart's opera *Die Zauberfloete* (*The Magic Flute*) in German when I was ten. This gave me a huge head start in vocabulary. I was offered a trip to Germany and a scholarship, but I wasn't interested. To me, German was a tool I would use for opera. In any event, one German teacher allowed me to learn and recite Lewis Carroll's *Jabberwocky* in German for an exam.

Yes, it is just as weird in German as it is in English. In English, the first verse of Jabberwocky goes thus:

'Twas brillig, and the slithy toves
Did gyre and gimble in the wabe
All mimsy were the borogoves
And the mome raths outgrabe.

In German, it is:

Es brillig war. Die schlichte Toven
Wirrten und wimmelten in Waben.
Und aller-muemsige Burggoven
Die mohmen Raeth ausgraben.

I took a sewing class, along with fencing, English, and other expected classes. This was self-serving of me: I planned to use the class time to get some work done. I had no expectation that the teacher would have anything much to teach me since I had already been sewing professionally, and the rest of the class would be making aprons and pot holders.

The things I made were not what one might have expected. I made a white Victorian ballgown for the Dickens Fair with a satin underlay below white eyelet lace for the bodice, a lightweight canvas lining, and a three-tiered skirt. It was gorgeous. I also made a corset from a pattern one of the ladies at the Renaissance Faire had given me.

Stupidly, I showed the ballgown to my mother. I had put a narrow black velvet ribbon around the knife-pleated Bertha neckline and my mother went insane because she hated my wearing black. She thought it meant I was depressed and that was *not* okay. She screamed and yelled and I cried. I knew perfectly well that what I had made was glorious and did not need her "help", but she absolutely forbade me to keep the ribbon on it, so I had to find a way to appease her. She would not allow me to wear it or keep it with the black ribbon.

Adrienne, who had acted as my sewing teacher when I was being home-schooled, came over and brought me to her house. I was still sniffling and crying. She gave me some brown velvet ribbon to use on the neckline so my mother would calm down. It was wider: an inch wide as opposed to the ¼ inch black velvet ribbon I had chosen, but it looked okay. To this day, I cannot figure out why my mother was so upset over the ribbon.

My mother used to humiliate me in public, often reducing me to tears in front of my friends. Whether she thought I was impervious to her words or whether she was unaware of the effect they would have on me, I have met very few people in my entire life who were willing to commit such obvious and vile verbal assaults on anyone anywhere, let alone in front of a large audience.

Was she screaming at me for crashing the car or burning the dinner? No. It was usually because I had either stayed up until 10 PM or slept till 7 AM, for which she claimed that I had "wasted the whole day." Although it could be noted that she was a morning person who woke at 3 AM and retired at 8, her schedule did not justify burning me at the proverbial stake.

She seemed to think that everyone witnessing her tirades would sympathize with her, which added to my pain. I found out eventually that this was not the case and that at least one person who watched her was horrified and angry with her conduct. She had attacked me in front of one Bret Culpepper, who was to me the handsomest young man I knew. After she was done and had stalked off in a dramatic huff, he and a few of his friends came close to me, touched my arms and asked me if I was all right. I was stunned. I was afraid that he would laugh at me, but he and his friends responded with care and concern and reminded me that I was a human being.

Bret sent me his recollections about her:

Moira's mother demeaned her all the time and told her she was worthless, and a mistake, and things like that. There was a time when I just wished to sock her right in the jaw and knock her arse out because of it! She seemed like a broken record, as it was the same nonsense over and over again, as I recall.

Eventually, I learned that she would scream at me no matter what I did, and I quit letting it run my life. I had been commissioned to make a ballgown for another girl, and it was a marvel in peach, apricot, and pale brown satin. As before, I cut it out by eye with a ruler and a piece of tailor's chalk. It was utterly exquisite with the girl's dark hair and olive skin. When Mother started in on me about everything she decided was wrong with it, I knew that she was not telling the truth. I knew I had made a beautiful dress in beautiful colors, and I was being paid to make it. I was not about to keep on letting Mother run roughshod over my heart.

I took metal shop and learned how to work copper and brass, even to weld steel. I joked that I was the only girl in town who owned and used an anvil. I would bring a little box of rings to history class with two pairs of pliers and make chain mail. This was very stupid of me. Making chain mail was engrossing and kept the lectures from boring me to death, but I did not absorb enough of the material to do well in class. I also made a little double-edged knife, which I wore as an ornament, holding a feather in my homemade, crocheted, fuzzy blue tam o' shanter.

I also fenced, which became my favorite thing ever. I loved fencing. At Berkeley High I took weightlifting along with fencing, and I was also required to run. Lifting weights was easy. Running and I have never been friends; it is by far the easiest way for me to get an asthma attack. I would carry Primatene Mist with me. The only medical intervention I had ever had for my asthma was the occasional emergency room visit if an asthma attack was too bad. I simply tried to cope with the running: run slow, hyperventilate, take breaks, self-treat the asthma attack, and move on with my life.

It was much the same with Irish dancing, which I was doing every week at the Starry Plough, an Irish pub in Berkeley, a few blocks from Greenwalls. An Irish dance would go on for a vigorous three minutes, and then there would be time for me to catch my breath.

Where I could manage a three-minute fencing bout, ferocious activity for a very brief stretch of time with a rest afterward or a three-minute dance, I could not manage running for twenty minutes at a stretch. Running would invariably knock me out.

I was the intramural champion at Berkeley High that year. I cannot take total credit though. I was much, much stronger than the other girls due to my broad shoulders, good upper-body strength from weight training, and very long arms and legs that conferred reach, an advantage in fencing. I routinely beat everyone I fenced with in my class, both boys and girls. I was aggressive, even ferocious, in my basic approach to fencing. I routinely broke blades on people, which is a bit unusual. I was angry, and I had found a way to be angry and violent and win.

My final opponent in the championship was a little Asian girl with perfect form—and absolutely no way to cope with me. I would beat her sword out of her hand simply because I was strong. A "beat" is a fencing move where you strike the base of their foil with the base of yours and if you are strong enough, it will disarm your opponent. It is as much an intimidation move as anything else. She lost and was very upset with me. So was the teacher, who gave me two warnings for excess violence on the strip before giving me the championship.

My opponent had another way of coping with me: her boyfriend was a much more advanced fencer than I was, and he knew epee and saber. We had a bout where he used epee rules, and he beat the holy hell out of me with a maneuver called a "fleisch", which involved running past me and sticking me in the back. I was so astonished that he ran past me that I didn't know what to do. In foil fencing, we stay on our own side. These days, of course, I would do a reverse lunge, put my left hand on the floor, get my body below the place he was targeting, and hit him with a stop thrust as he ran by.

I did not like myself very much. My violent feelings terrified me, and my warlike attitude was not limited to fencing class. Perhaps relatedly, I carried my foil everywhere. One day I was on the bus going through downtown Oakland, a man on the bus asked me if that was a real sword. I asked him if he would like me to run him through so that he could find out.

My father was furious at me for adopting such a warlike sport. I was supposed to be a boy or to be as masculine as I could manage, but I wasn't supposed to be *that kind* of masculine. In our family, sports were derided, strength in males was derided, lifting weights was derided, and fighting? I might as well have told my father I was going to work for Anita Bryant or Operation Rescue!

For those of you who were not born back then, Anita Bryant was a pro-family advocate who virulently disagreed with homosexual conduct, and Operation Rescue was an anti-abortion group. In my family, homosexuality was "natural" to the exclusion of being straight, and abortion was a "right" that did not involve the murder of anything but a "clump of cells." These days, Planned Parenthood is selling these clumps of cells to people who want specific clumps, like brains, kidneys, and eyes…

I know in retrospect that my father's issue was with women being feminine and men being masculine. Masculinity and femininity are marks of adulthood, and his interest was in those who were not adult. When people have a secure identity, it is much harder to get them into bed. Keeping me from being feminine *or* masculine in an adult way meant I would remain dependent on him for my identity, and I would continue to let him tell me what to think. His continuing hope that I would become a willing sexual partner relied upon my lack of an adult identity, coupled with the faint hope that he would one day be able to convince me to use the kind of drugs which would incapacitate me. Or "raise my consciousness", as he might have said.

I loved making things and learning things, and I worked day and night. Working obsessively was much easier than thinking about my life or my family. I lived out of my backpack, and I stayed with anyone who would allow me a couch.

Serpent and Cathy took me in as much as they could, and that was a huge blessing. Cathy would make dinner, let me help with the dishes, and help me with my homework. At 10:00, she would make sure I went to bed. She would put Classical Barbra on the stereo, tuck me in and tell me, "You are A Sleep!" I would tell her that she was the big sleep and I was the little sleep. Those were blissful days, while they lasted.

Then Serpent got malignant melanoma and died very suddenly. He went from being fine to being wasted and horribly sick within a few weeks. Cathy couldn't endure having me around anymore because of her grief. She moved to Newfoundland, half a world away.

At the same time, because nobody could take me all the time, I stayed with my director, Sue Honor, and with a few other Faire directors. I also spent a lot of time with my wonderful friend and Faire sister Kat Krischild.

As I mentioned before, Kat and I met at Clan Colin at the Faire and played Scottish Faire sisters. She was in her early twenties and I was thirteen. She would let me stay at her tiny one-room apartment and even let me sleep on the floor with her while never, ever taking advantage of me. She made me tuna sandwiches in the morning when I went to school in Berkeley and shared her rice and beans with me in the evenings.

When Kat got a boyfriend, she moved and couldn't have me over anymore. I was very sad about it and I missed her terribly. We still hung out sometimes: her new SCA household, "House Ostrov", had meetings. House Ostrov's coat of arms was a heraldic joke, meaning "A turn for the worse." The shield was black and red, divided lengthwise up the middle. A white tern was flying left, toward the black half.

Armchair Psychology

I coped with a preposterous situation at home by becoming a workaholic. Although I am expected to uncritically accept the nonsense going on at home, the "crimes" I am openly punished for amount to putting the wrong ribbon on a ballgown or staying up too late. My father is disappointed with me for becoming "warlike."

The actual reason my mother is angry with me is probably a combination of my emotional withdrawal from her, my attitude of contempt toward her and Lisa, which is probably visible even though I am polite, and my increasing absence.

After all, here she is presenting herself as such a kind mother willing to care even for the children of strangers, but I would rather sleep *anywhere* than home. I have voted with my feet. Even if we ever discussed it—and we never did—I have rejected her.

Chapter 28

Hunting Girl
(1980–1984)

The long restless rustle of high-heel boots call...

And I'm probably bound to deceive you after all.

—Ian Anderson, Jethro Tull,
"One White Duck / 0^{10} = Nothing At All",
Minstrel In The Gallery (1975)

When I started having boyfriends, my mother was furious. One might imagine that a normal mother would want her daughter to focus on school and not dating, but that was not her concern. Not in the least. My mother thought that sexual preference should reflect politics, and so if I was ever to be a feminist of the least merit I had to be a lesbian.

Naturally, my father agreed. After all, if I was a lesbian, all his problems with me would be over. My father would scream irrationally at me for allegedly stealing his boyfriends. In practice, this meant that any time a boy he liked looked at me, I had "stolen" him even if they had come over to see me in the first place. In my father's imagination, if I didn't like boys, they would all want to be with him rather than out looking for other girls.

My mother insisted that she would be such a good mother to a lesbian and was furious and hurt when I told her I was straight. She shouted at me about this, demanding to know how I could possibly *know* I was straight? She insisted that I *had* to try it the other way before I could call myself straight.

In a 1988 video interview, Marion talked about not believing me when I told her I was straight. She thought I was making it up. She viewed me as a sellout to the male establishment and therefore no better than a breeder or a whore.

Oh yes. A breeder. "Breeders" were those mindless straight people who existed only to have children and who never thought deeply like she did. In retrospect, it seems so idiotic. What does that mean? The second you get married and have children, your brain retroactively turns off?

I don't know why she was saying those things to me. "Try it the other way", as though she had not been sticking her tongue in my ear not long before? Had she forgotten everything she had done to me? Was I supposed to have become a lesbian because of her early efforts with me? Was I supposed to conclude that forcing me to tell her she was sexy and do the things she demanded meant I would be sentenced to a life of wanting her? Was I to seek out her nauseating hobbies voluntarily?

Maybe she really believed that since I, as a child, "didn't have erogenous zones", none of the stuff she did to me counted as sex. Maybe she and my father did not anticipate that sex with children does not always twist them in the way you want them twisted.

To me, the idea of being a lesbian sounded about as appealing as chocolate-covered oysters.

Besides, I liked boys. They looked nice. They smelled nice. It felt wonderful when they talked to me. Smiley made me suspect that men might like me. The men at the Faire dispelled all doubt. Once I had grown out of my coltish self and gotten a figure, the male attention began in earnest. I had a tiny waist, and I was busty, and my hair was very long. They told me I was beautiful, and oh, how I wanted to believe it.

Long before I ever had a boyfriend, my mother told me that if ever I decided to sleep with someone, I should bring them home so that I wouldn't "fall into the hands of a sadist." I thought that that was very compassionate and kind and reasonable of her, and I believed her.

When I took her at her word and brought someone home, she went out of her mind, calling me a slut and a whore.

One kindness my friend Kat did for me very early on: when she found out I was being chased by boys and was considering becoming voluntarily sexually active, she took me to Planned Parenthood and helped me get on the Pill. I did not ask my mother take me to the doctor if I needed birth control because of her inconsistency. She might have taken me to the doctor, and she might have gone out of her mind with screaming.

Initially, I absolutely did not want to give in to sexual pressure from a boy no matter how much they liked me. At the Faire after hours, I would wear a pair of jeans which were so tight that they were impossible to remove unless I decided to help. That way if I did something stupid, like drink from someone's hip flask, I would be impossible to rape without a discouraging level of effort.

I would often wear too many clothes, which is a classic symptom of sexual abuse. It probably seems absurd that while I was considering becoming sexually active, I was also wearing way too much clothing. I was also perpetually cold though. I know now what I didn't know then: being cold is my most frequent kind of flashback, bringing horrible images. Avoiding being cold has often required much of my attention because it is so distressing.

I wanted my first chosen sexual experience to have love and romance and all that stuff that young women normally want, but the first time I had sex voluntarily, I had gotten scared and said no, four days before my fourteenth birthday. The boy, who was sixteen, did not care about my having said no, and he forced me. It hurt physically, and then it hurt emotionally, and it made me feel helpless and worthless and stupid. I had been in love, and now that was over, too. I would never see him the same way again. No doubt the boy felt he had the right since I had agreed to "go all the way" in advance. I never went to the police or thought of it as anything but simply my own fault. I should have figured out a way to say no in advance.

I wondered why anyone would ever have sex at all if it felt like that.

I never wanted to feel that helpless ever again. I decided that rather than me being at the mercy of a predatory man, I would be the predator. I thought maybe sex would be less terrifying and painful with someone else. I tried. Several times. And it wasn't. And it was a disaster. All I could be at 14 was an older man's dirty little secret with "no strings attached."

I was already emotionally stronger than most of the men I interacted with, and I became a complete and total bitch. In response to the old joke: "Will you respect me in the morning?" I would say, "Did I respect you in the first place?"

There were plenty of men who liked swaggering, strong women who wanted to be in charge. Sadly, the kind of man who wants a strong child of fourteen is not the kind of man who wants to protect her—or feels he can. In a way, by trying to act the part of a man, I set myself up to find unsuitable men. I thought I was protecting myself with my strength and my swords. I was wrong.

After a few disasters, I had a string of boyfriends coming from the Faire. I was involved with a very nice young man who worked at a chocolate shop in Berkeley and drove us around on a scooter. His mother was a darling, and she let me make a pair of blue jeans with her Viking sewing machine. Sherman would make us a drink which was lovely: blueberry juice and Perrier, which he called "Berrier." I made a pale blue plaid soft wool tailored suit at his house, and it was gorgeous… until someone at my house threw the skirt in the wash, which turned it into a pot holder.

When I was almost 15, I met Ole. He was tall and blond with a beard and hair to his waist. He looked like a painting from an Irish historical book. He was 23 and very romantic, at least initially. My strength appealed to him. He saw me leading a parade and was smitten. We had a lot in common: we were both interested in Irish history and Irish dance, folk music and the Faire. I moved in with him in San Francisco. I was in love.

My mother had no objection whatsoever to my moving in with a man eight years older than I was when I was barely fifteen. She spoke of it as "marrying me off" and immediately began to pressure me to give her grandchildren. She told me, again and again, that I should have children young while I could still enjoy them. I was aghast. I told her unequivocally that I thought I would be a terrible mother and that I was not going to have children ever. Considering my experiences, how could she think for one moment that I would have any idea how to be a good mother to anyone?

Ole worked as a tax collector, and I would come to meet him for lunch at City Hall in San Francisco sometimes. One day, I was walking through the plaza in front of City Hall wearing a floor-length circle cloak I had made: black wool and lined with grey fake fur. It was raining, and the darned thing probably weighed over ten pounds. A panhandler came up to me and started harassing me for money, very aggressively. I whacked him in the face with a corner of my very wet cloak, and he ran away.

I continued to attend high school in Berkeley while I was living with Ole in San Francisco. The commute involved a bus from the far end of San Francisco and then BART from downtown San Francisco, under the bridge and the Bay all the way to Berkeley High. The trip took a very long time, and it ended up seeming rather ridiculous. I got thrown out of my last English class for correcting the teacher's spelling, took the equivalency, and left high school in the middle of eleventh grade.

I was working full time on my costuming business, which I called Choose Your Century, and as soon as I was out of high school I started thinking about going to college.

Ole was aware that our relationship was illegal and over time this began to make him uneasy. He made me buy an adult bus pass so that it would be less obvious that he was running around with a child. He also stopped sleeping with me not too long after we moved in together; we were more like roommates. Maybe he thought that he could not be arrested if he was not currently committing statutory rape. I felt very rejected and hurt though.

It is possible that I drove Ole insane, and he simply didn't want to break up with me. I was a temperamental terror, and most of what I did while we were together was sew costumes and do my homework. I also ran our household, paid the bills, bought our groceries, and balanced the checkbook. I used to buy him beer at the supermarket, and I was never carded. Not once. I used to do our laundry down the street, and I would cut out Faire costumes on the large, flat floor at the laundromat.

Since Ole had stopped sleeping with me, I felt free to do more or less whatever I wanted to with whoever I wanted to. What a worthless layabout I was—as rotten as can be imagined! To illustrate the point, I will quote an aria from Ariadne Auf Naxos. Zerbinetta is a coquette and a layabout like I was, and she is trying to comfort Ariadne, recently deserted by Theseus. Ariadne is planning to die of grief. Zerbinetta counsels her to take another lover and offers her own story. I am including the German because that is how I think of it.

So war es mit Pagliazzo und Mezzetin
Dann war es Cavicchio, dann Burattin,
Dann Pasquariello! Ach und zuweilen
will es mir scheinen, Waren es zwei!

Doch niemals Launen immer ein Müssen
Immer ein neues beklommendes Staunen:
Daß ein Herz sogar sich selber nicht versteht

That's how it was with Pagliazzo and Mezzetin,
then there was Cavicchio and Burattin,
Then Pasquariello! Oh, and sometimes
if I remember correctly, there were two!

But it was never out of a caprice, always a need,
each time a new, uneasy shock to realize
that a heart can't even understand itself.

—Zerbinetta, "Grossmaechtige Prinzessin"
Ariadne Auf Naxos, Richard Strauss

I was intoxicated with my own ability to captivate people, and I never thought through what I would do once somebody fell in love with me. I even did what my mother had wanted me to do all along, although I didn't do it very well.

I really hurt a girl named Becky when I was 15. She was beautiful and sweet and everything a lesbian could have wanted. She fell for me after seeing me at a con and wrote to me. I wrote back, and we began a relationship. I knew how to act like a butch lesbian because I was raised with lesbians, but I felt like I was playacting. I just didn't have what it took to be her girlfriend.

Her friends scared the living daylights out of me. So many stories of how one girl or another got the hell beaten out of her by her jealous butch girlfriend. If you're going to involve yourself with a bad imitation of an alcoholic, battering husband, why not just marry an actual alcoholic, physically abusive man? What is the advantage of being a lesbian if the sexual dynamics are just as awful as they are in a bad straight relationship?

I left Becky without explanation. I was a failure at being a lesbian and she deserved better than me. That is certain.

Around that time, I met my best friend Elizabeth Rousseau at Ann Healy's Irish dance studio in San Francisco. I wanted to be a step dancer. These days we would think of "Riverdance" for what I was doing. Irish country dancing was done in multiples of two, three, or six, and I was already good enough at that to teach it. Step dancers have to remember a great deal of choreography, execute intricate footwork and high kicks with perfect form, and demonstrate physical agility. I became a solo dancer at the Renaissance Faire, as did she. Elizabeth was, and is, a phenomenally good dancer.

I was living in Laussat Street in San Francisco, and I was 16 years old to her 17. I was doing a great deal of commissioned sewing at the time and many of our visits revolved around sewing, blueberries, Milano cookies, and lots and lots of coffee. She did embroidery on linen which was stunningly beautiful and made tatted lace, even making me a collar and cuffs for an Irish competition dance dress which belonged in a museum. She was, and is, an artist, and she has become a molecular biologist. I hung around with her, and less often with her sister Pam, who also worked at the Faire.

That year, I wore an Irish dress I had made; it incorporated design elements of a corset so that I would not be adding an extra few layers of fabric to the dress. The bodice was double-lined with a sturdy grade of canvas as well as the medium blue fabric which lined the rest of the dress. Underneath the front closure, which was pewter hook-and-eye fastenings with Celtic interlace, I had built an extra pair of flaps with lacing so that I would be laced down invisibly and the bodice would close over the top. I didn't care for the look of visible lacing, and I despised lacing down the back because of the nightmare of costume changes. The dress was black velvet over a medium blue underdress. The overdress had panels of dark red velvet in tie-shapes, with the large ends both up and down, to emphasize the hourglass shape, and it had a lot of silver Celtic interlace which I had laid out with my trusty ruler and tailor's chalk. It sparkled with gems.

At the Renaissance Faire, I fenced at the fencing booth every chance I got—dress and tight lacing and all—I once challenged the entire Queen's Guard to have a bout with me. Two declined: the oldest and wisest two. The rest came. I beat all but one.

Did they let me win? I hope not!

In any event, I had made all of them favors of blue velvet ribbon, and the ones I had beaten got a square of chainmail sewn beneath the blue velvet roses on their favors whereas the ones I did not fence and the one I did not beat simply got blue velvet roses. What is a "favor"? At the Faire, it was a tradition for women to give men ribbons to signify their favor, and these ribbons were often sold at the Faire. I made my own. They were not always given to men one was dating; it was a friendly thing as often as not, and some men had a huge collection of favors on their doublets or jackets. The ones I made were distinctive and not much like the ones which were sold.

Yes, all that nonsense was going on while I was still living and working the Faire with Ole. We even got "handfasted." Handfasting was allegedly a Celtic tradition, performed by the chieftain of the tribe in remote locations where there was no priest. We believed it was a marriage, meant to run for a year and a day. Historically, handfasting was more like a betrothal, and if it were happening as it had back then, the engaged couple would never have behaved as though they were married.

Most of what I remember about our handfasting was what I made for us to wear. For him, it was a dark green Irish kilt made of really good wool, with a Scottish jacket in black and silver with a silk shirt. Mine was a dark blue and grey velveteen riding habit, with an off-white silk shirt and petticoat underneath. Both the skirt and the petticoat had a train with a loop, so the length could be managed easily. An Irish band played for us, Ole smashed cake in my face, and I danced with my old Irish country dance teacher Terry O'Neill, which was wonderful fun.

Ole and I had been handfasted, and I don't really know why I went along with it. Our relationship was already over long before, and we were basically roommates. Several things happened that made me eager to leave San Francisco and eventually, him.

One day while coming back on BART from a step dance competition which I had won, Ole and I were mugged. We were living on Laussat Street in the Haight-Ashbury district of San Francisco, which was not a safe area at all in those days. He had walked down to meet me at BART, and as we walked back to our apartment, five guys came around the corner very quickly and grabbed us. I did not see what they did to him, though later he told me they had a knife to his throat. I was pushed backward against one of the short cast-iron fences with the points on top, and I immediately started screaming for help. They demanded money, which I did not have, and Ole told me to give them my backpack. I was very much against this because in my backpack was both my Red Sonja costume, which I set great store by, and also the first-place medal I had just won at my very first step dancing competition.

Meanwhile, Ole was preoccupied with other things. I already knew that Ole preferred women with enormous boobs despite his interest in me. I was only a 32DD, which was nowhere near as large as the women in his fantasies. Eventually, I found out that he wanted to *be* the large-breasted woman in his fantasies when he left his water balloons to leak on my shoes in our closet along with some female clothing I did not recognize. When I found this out, I went to visit my friend Elizabeth, and I laughed and I cried, and then I laughed and I cried some more. I knew then that I could never be the real object of his sexual fantasies, and I would remain second place to what, water balloons?

Ole had a good friend, Duncan, whom I had known from before. I thought he was a real scumbag because although I had extricated myself from his immodest proposal when I was ten, I figured I would not be the only very young girl he would attempt to victimize. Once again, the stuff we put up with via the Renaissance Faire was just unbelievable.

Duncan had been accused of rape and his girlfriend Laura was incensed with me because I said unequivocally that I believed the accusations. Ole didn't stand with me though until Duncan actually went to jail for rape. The best he could come up with was, "I always kinda believed Dorothy." I had been nearly ostracized from our small circle of friends for refusing to pretend that I believed Duncan was innocent.

Duncan was known in that time as "The Telephone Rapist" because he would call his victims and demand that they do things in their windows where he could watch them from outside. Worse, he assaulted my friend Elizabeth on the massage table, and she was too frightened to take any action against him.

Over time, Ole became impossible to live with because he became increasingly more dependent on alcohol. Shortly before my eighteenth birthday, Ole drove drunk with me in the car. We had been staying at his father's house for Christmas and we drove home Christmas night. He told me that he had had a little something to drink before he left, and he commenced weaving all over the road. I tried to remain calm and asked him what kind of a little something. He told me he had had some beer, some Laphroaig whiskey, and an impressive list of spirits, which made the problem all too clear.

I asked him to get off the road so I could call my father. He said no. He wanted to drive home himself. I repeated my request more firmly, and he insisted he was going to make it to the next big city. I demanded he pull off the road right now because he was not safe to drive.

So he stopped, very angrily, and pulled into an all-night restaurant because it was quite late. I called my father, who drove down immediately to get me. And get me he did; remember my father hated alcohol with a passion. The idea that I was in the car with a drunk driver was much more distressing to my father than the idea that I, an underage girl, had been living with a much older man for a few years.

In any event, our relationship did not survive that. I could not forgive him for driving drunk with me in the car. I told him the next morning that I was leaving, and he told me that I had been gone for some time. After that, he drove drunk with Elizabeth in the car. She managed to persuade him to get off the road, and he made a big deal about how at least she had let him "be a *man* about it!"

Soon afterward, Ole married a woman he had met when we were first together, and five years later she left him an AA pamphlet along with divorce papers.

Chapter 29

The House on the Hill and the Tacky Mansion (1984–1987)

Before they learn to say my name
I heard them wailin' tryin',
Some I detest, because I know
Politeness has me lyin'!

Mariah, Mariah
They call my name Mariah
Maria, or Myra,
Or anything but Moira.

—Moira Greyland, with apologies to Loesser and Loewe

I changed a few things after I left Ole and turned eighteen. First, I took back my own name. I had gone by Dorothy since I was six because nobody could pronounce Moira, and I was trying to make it so the kids had one less reason to tease me. Now that I was about to go to college, I figured that the social consequences of having an unusual name would be trivial. I discovered that I preferred to tolerate mispronunciations of my name rather than correcting them. These days, the few who find my name impossible to pronounce call me Mimi. It is "MOY-Ruh", by the way.

I also cut off more than a foot of red hair, which I regretted very much. My hair had been red from henna since I was about 12, and I decided it was not going to stay that way. Hair dyed with henna cannot be colored anything else, nor can any color near it be evened out. I was advised that if I wanted to be done with my red hair and go back to my natural dirty blond, I would need to cut it off, so I did. I hated my hair until it grew out a bit, and I decided to go white-blond at the advice of Sebastian, the best hairdresser I had ever known.

I moved in with my friend Geraldine from the Faire. Geraldine was the mother of Sterling and Aaron, whom I had been friends with since I first came to Berkeley as a small child. Geraldine was a fascinating character. She was highly intelligent, erudite, and expert in everything related to historical reenactment as one might find at the Renaissance Faire. I also liked her very much as a human being and enjoyed her company very much.

She had a lovely house. Truly, it was a marvelous place to live, out in the wild part of Lafayette on top of a hill. It was a half-timbered Elizabethan reproduction house, and it looked as though it would have been perfectly at home at the Renaissance Faire. I rented a room from Geraldine, and she also let me use the entire attic for my sewing. I needed a fair amount of room between my sewing machine, my industrial sewing machine, my overlock machine, and the inevitable overworked ironing board. When making costumes, it often seemed to me that the time spent with the ironing board would always exceed the time spent sewing. I did a lot of sewing while listening to Jethro Tull, and reveling in the view of the gorgeous green hills out the window.

I did not own a stick of furniture other than my bed, so Mother bought me an unfinished dresser and a nightstand, which I eventually sanded and stained. I put my fencing foils and mask above the doorway inside the door skull-and-crossbones fashion. My room had a little doorway with a right-turn entrance and two steps down. It was the first time I had lived alone, and it was very freeing. I loved it there.

At Geraldine's house, I could practice for several hours a day since I was utterly undisturbed and nobody would be bothered by my endless scales. I had a small upright piano in Geraldine's attic which my mother had gotten me when I began studying at the Conservatory.

I was single, and I dated—briefly—a man I had known for years. He visited me at Geraldine's house, and we had a glorious picnic in her front yard. He was a real adult—even had a job and a car—and I found him to be handsome, charismatic, and irresistible.

But I left him the same day as our picnic.

I didn't stop dating him because I didn't care about him. He told me he was in an open marriage and I pressed him for details, saying I needed to talk to his wife and make sure she was okay with him seeing me. He told me his wife was sick, and he didn't want to upset her. I was shocked that he intended for the two of us to betray her and disgusted that he would participate in such a moral travesty.

I had a very odd "Berkeley" moral code at that time. Open relationships and polyamorous relationships were something I had seen a lot of, and they did not surprise me, but I was beginning to change my mind about participating in that way. I did not want to be used as comfort for a man having trouble in his marriage. Since then, every time a man has approached me and told me he was in an "open relationship", I figured it was code for "I'm lying to my wife."

I fail to see the point of a polyamorous relationship. Since stability, home-making, and eventually children are the point of a pair-bond, to have an extra woman around merely means one relationship or more is going to end. I have seen it too often, and I have had too many poly people weeping on my shoulders over some romantic mishap or other. Just no.

I loved the house on the hill and I would have stayed there for a long time, except for something I could never have predicted.

Geraldine's son Aaron had friends who had come to stay in one of the spare bedrooms. Their Rottweiler had bitten their infant daughter, and although they were not happy about it, their "punk" sensibilities meant that their dog was acceptable as he was. He would never receive any correction or training no matter how vicious his behavior. One night, that dog and I faced off on the way from my car to the house after I came home from rehearsal. Although it seemed that the dog and I stood there for an hour with him growling and me trying hard to look bigger, I'm certain it was merely the scariest ten seconds I had had in recent memory.

I became convinced after that encounter that if I was going to live there, I should carry a gun, and then I decided that if I needed to carry a gun to live there, I needed to live somewhere else.

I called my mother, and she told me that the upper floor at my father's Oakland house was vacant so I could move in there. I was on reasonably good terms with my mother and father—at least as good as might be expected with time and distance and a complete lack of daily contact. My last significant contact with my father had been him rescuing me from Ole's drunk driving.

I had high, if false, hopes.

I would never have lived with my mother and Lisa again under any circum-stances. At least I was clear about that. I knew that coping with my father would not be as difficult. I would have to take care of him since left to his own devices, he would have nothing but chocolate cake and chocolate milk. When he would go to the bank, if there was a line, he would stand there and scream; ditto with the grocery store. I would be taking a load off Mother and Lisa by stepping in, quite enough to compensate for the financial burden I would create by living in his house. I also thought the commute to classes in San Francisco would be a lot easier from Oakland than from Lafayette.

My father's house was a duplex of sorts with an upstairs and a downstairs. It had a large horseshoe driveway, and it looked like a cheap, dilapidated version of a plantation mansion with gigantic pillars. It was in a marginal to downright frightening part of town, across the street from a cemetery a few blocks away from Mills College. I would not have walked anywhere outside that house for all the tea in China. I can imagine that a hundred years ago the area might have been considered most elegant and exclusive, and the house would have been the height of fashion.

But not when we were there. Not by any stretch of the imagination.

Every so often when I came home, I would discover young gentlemen climbing the fruit trees outside the house, in such a way that they could see into my kitchen via the sliding glass doors. I let them take all the fruit they wanted. I did not realize at the time that they were "casing the joint." Not long after that, both the upstairs and the downstairs were broken into and robbed expertly. Since neither of us had especially grand possessions, they only got my father's wonderful stereo system, my ornamental knives, and my meager jewelry collection.

I did not own any more furniture than I had before, so the apartment was glaringly empty. I had two bedrooms, and one of them held my sewing stuff. I had to get a kitchen table and a chair or eat on the floor.

The house did not stay empty. Although my father owned nearly as little furniture as I did, he owned a vast—and I mean *vast* library—much too vast for his downstairs apartment to encompass. Arguably, it needed an entire house of its own and maybe a staff to care for it. Dealing with my father's library became my task.

I came up with a cheap solution which involved cinder blocks and pine boards, dozens of them. Soon, my upstairs was as full of his books as his own place was. I hated cinder blocks—vaguely ornamental 12-inch square by 4-inch thick hunks of filigree-shaped concrete. I hate keeping hundreds of linear feet of books stacked up in rows to make my living room look like the stacks in a tiny, remote library!

Yes, in Berkeley books are the thing. If you don't have at least enough books to fill every wall in your house, you are not a credible intellectual. If you are allergic to dust, that does not matter. If your house is uncleanable, that does not matter. You *must* have your books, and your books define you. Wherever you go, they will follow you like a papery anchor around your neck.

Over the next few decades, I gradually reduced my own book collection from thousands of books to hundreds. I have kept a lot of music—mostly operatic scores—but the hundreds of e-books I have now do not require schlepping or cinder blocks and boards, and I do not miss the physical ones a bit.

I know, I know. I am a heretic. How *dare* I not decorate my house in Early Book?

I mentioned I had high hopes that things would be better with my father. Well, they were in some ways. Regardless of what I had been taught I ought to feel and to value, I still wanted very much the same things that every other little girl on earth wanted.

When I was very little, my friend Jean and I would play dress-up like little girls do, and I asked my father, "How do I look?" He gave me a look of something approaching disgust and told me that he was "not aware enough of the cultural conventions to give a fair answer." At the time it hurt because I wanted my Daddy to think I was pretty and to protect me. Heck, it always hurt. I wanted to be Daddy's Little Girl instead of the monster who was ruining his life and "stealing" his boyfriends.

When I lived with my father, I was still the same person. I needed my father to protect me and even—unreasonably—think that I was pretty. I knew in my head that this would never happen, but my heart never quite gave up. I don't remember how it came up, but one day, downstairs in that tacky mansion, my father was talking about my appearance. He told me that I was very androgynous.

Androgynous.

I was 5'6" and 36-22-36. I dressed as well as my tailor's craft and my mother's provision would allow me, doing my best to emulate a Forties movie star. I know now that I was about as androgynous as Barbie, but back then it was a blow. I was expected to be sexual, not sexy. Apparently in my father's universe, children were sexy, but adult women, as I had become, were nothing.

To him, as a woman, I was nothing. I should have expected it, but I never really gave up hope.

Make no mistake, he made no secret of his admiration for my intelligence, my musicality, and my sense of pitch. He was my biggest fan in terms of my singing. But to see me as a woman, a daughter, *his* daughter, even a female person of any description? That was not going to happen.

So I was what? An intelligent, androgynous blob of nothing who could sing but was neither male nor female?

Even though my father did nothing for my sense of myself as a female human being, he could be very kind and even loving in other ways. My wisdom teeth were all impacted, so I had to have my wisdom teeth out. The procedure was going to be long and difficult. Since Novocaine did not work very well on me, I had to be put under at the small dentist's office my mother had found. When I woke up afterward I asked for my father, who had driven me there. They told me I could see him when I could walk out to see him.

I stood up right away—terrible mistake. I fell over on my face as though I had been a tree. I couldn't even break my fall with my hands. I was nauseated for weeks from the pentathol, and my lower lip and chin were numb for a year from the fall.

My father, bless him, did his best to tend me when I was sick. When I was well enough to try to eat again, I asked him to fry me some potatoes, and he completely went to pieces. Apparently, cooking was not something he could do. His care for me when I was sick was wonderful. He could hand me yogurt, jello, and pudding, but it all went to hell in a handbasket when I needed actual food.

I was still working at the Southern Renaissance Faire. That year, there were both good and bad things which went on. On the good side, I was fencing. Oh fencing! How I loved it. After hours, a bunch of us would get together and grab anything resembling fencing gear, including sabers, shinai (Japanese bamboo practice weapons for Kendo), and masks. I would routinely fence with a mask, a T-shirt, shorts, and a fencing glove, and we would pound on each other for ages.

My father was still horrified that I was fencing. Fencing is warlike, and my being non-feminine in his imagination didn't mean that I could do masculine things that he did not like. I was forbidden to be either male or female.

Eventually, my harp teacher put a stop to my fencing. I showed up to a lesson with my inner arm all cut up from where the glove didn't cover it, and she told me I could not possibly play the harp while I was risking injury. She ended my sewing for the same reason. I didn't care. I wanted to play the harp so badly that I was willing to give up sharp objects.

I got to the Faire all kinds of ways and stayed at all kinds of places. The Faire bus only ran during the Faire weekends, so we had to arrange for transportation to workshops on our own. That year during workshops, I stayed with people I did not know well and ended up being given a ride from a house in Pasadena to the Faire site in Agoura, which limited my choices about how I would go where and with whom. The person who gave me a ride to the Faire raped me. It went on for a long, horrible time. He got to be the human, and I got to be the blow-up doll. If I saw him again, I don't know what I would do, but I hope I never see him again. I did nothing because I was trapped there, and I had no way to get back to the house I was staying at but with him.

I know. It is very common for child sexual abuse survivors to be raped as adults partly because we tend to have horribly bad boundaries and partly because we don't see warning signals. It didn't hurt; a lot of it was my fault. It never occurred to me to make sure I knew what the address was where I had left my car. It never occurred to me to question the person who drove me to the Faire. I had no backup plan. I was an idiot.

Part of the trouble with counterculture organizations is that it is easy to assume that since we are all part of the same community, we have shared goals and therefore safety. These are stupid assumptions but very common ones. Naturally, a counterculture organization is going to be a perfect place for a predator to hide precisely because of the expectation of safety and partly because counterculture organizations are full of victims who do not fit in in "straight" society and have poor boundaries from their victimization.

Now, of course in a normal family, I would have had some recourse. Not in mine. I screwed up my courage and told my mother what I didn't dare tell the police. I had been raped, and I didn't tell anyone.

My mother sighed and pouted and complained that I got more sex than she did.

Yes, she really, really did.

I can still make no sense of her response unless taken in the blunt context of her years-long quest to blame me for her sexual frustration. It hurt so much to hear that from her. Stupid me, wanting my mother to love me and show concern for my safety and bodily integrity! As though a rape had anything to do with sex other than gross physical mechanics! Might as well compare eating dinner at a five-star restaurant with being forcibly intubated and fed that way!

Why would Mother choose this moment to grumble about her sex life? Here is one clue I didn't see: Lisa had secured her position and no longer needed to provide those kinds of services to get Mother's cooperation. Lisa had moved out of Mother's bedroom and into the library, installing a lock on the door.

Of course, in a normal family a mother does not bitch at her daughter about her sexual frustration, but we were very, very far away from normal.

My being in closer contact with my parents had some other notable side effects. Mother was friends with three people in a group marriage: Deborah, her husband Richard, and Deborah's girlfriend Phyllis.

Deborah was a kind, gentle earth-mother working as a chiropractor. She was kind, nurturing, motherly, and never inappropriate in the least. She was the glue holding the entire unsteady edifice together, and she always welcomed me and treated me kindly. Phyllis was a strange, masculine physicist whose great passion turned out to be repairing bicycles. She was intelligent, which is the usual root of my folly.

Deborah's husband Richard was a hopelessly inadequate man who did Rolfing—a sort of massage—for my family when they visited. Richard touched me in a way I hated during a Rolfing session and ignored my objections. I found him less appealing than a plate of slugs and his professional ethics reprehensible. It seemed there was no way to get out of the Rolfing my mother had paid for. Next time, I wore my underpants and told him not to touch me there, but he insisted on working on my "pelvic floor" muscles anyway.

I never came back. I didn't shoot him. Not even when my friend Kat told me that he had done "everything but" with her while pretending to be faithful to Deborah since they wanted a child. Yes, these are the kind of stupid shenanigans which go on in polyamorous relationships. Fidelity is *negotiated*, and even then it is lied about. You'd almost think that infidelity as the basis of a relationship might lead to more and more of itself.

I hated Richard.

Phyllis was quite taken with me. I was 18, and she was 36. I had a strong personality, which meant that men and women with daddy-issues got hooked on me very easily. I stupidly let my infatuation with my own attractiveness to let me captivate her. Once she was in love with me, I couldn't figure out how to get out of the situation. I realized she now thought we had a relationship and I didn't want to upset her. I was stuck because of my bad boundaries.

I can't stand having sex with women. It is a chore, like being forced to perform for my mother. Our "relationship" was over almost before it began. As soon as Phyllis felt sure of me, she began to treat me very badly, always wanting to tell me how unhappy she was with me. Phyllis was like a tapeworm, causing great pain and wasting without an obvious cause. Emotionally, she was difficult to the point of seeming insane.

I am sure I was not nearly involved enough and that I caused her a lot of pain and disappointment. Here I was, a usually-straight person, trying to make the best of a bad situation. I probably was not acting at all as though I was in love with her, and as such, she was very unhappy with me. I have no doubt that as a lesbian lover, I was a complete and total failure. I couldn't make sense of her complaints. In the case of a normal complaint like "You're standing on my foot" or "You left the cap off the toothpaste", I could do something to fix it. Her complaints were not about what I had done as much as how I always thought and felt the wrong things. I didn't call her enough, and I didn't say the right things when I called. I had no idea how to give her what she wanted, and I stopped wanting to try very quickly. I am certain she sensed my lack of commitment and interest.

I stayed with Phyllis and Deborah and Richard in Southern CA a few times instead of camping out. Some weeks I drove, and once I flew. It might have been for a Faire TV commercial, I don't remember. As I was getting ready to leave to fly south, Phyllis called me on the phone. I don't remember anything much about the phone call other than that I had done several things wrong and she was unhappy with me, and my last words to her were "Mea culpa, dammit!" I had no idea how to do right what she thought I had done wrong. Our interactions hurt so much I didn't know what to do.

It was clear to me I had made a mistake, and I didn't know how to extricate myself from it. I had no idea how to get out of having sex with her. I couldn't figure out how to tell her that and make it stick. For me, there is nothing quite so non-aphrodisiac as a guilt trip.

One day, Phyllis came to see me at the Faire. I hadn't expected her to come, and as always, I had a heavy performance schedule with back-to-back shows and parades with no break at all until 2 PM. She waited for me at Celt camp for five hours until she passed out from hypoglycemia.

I was horrified. I knew that this was meant to cause me to feel guilty and to do... what? I had no idea. I didn't feel guilty, though, but furious and disappointed. Phyllis was 36. How could she allow herself to pass out from hunger instead of taking care of herself? Moreover, how could she place the responsibility for that on me?

She came to, declined the medical assistance that I offered to get her, and still swaying, told me her sad tale about How Long She Had Waited For Me, and How Sad It All Was. I told her that my schedule was very heavy, and if she had told me ahead of time when she was going to arrive, I could have let her know when I would be free, but no, that was not enough.

How can men *stand* women? If that is what we do, then seriously, how has the species survived?

Now, what I didn't have the gumption to tell her is that in my heart our relationship had been over from the moment she screamed at me over the phone.

I have had many female friends, and they do not act that way. If women can be decent human beings with their clothes on, and they turn into raving lunatics with their clothes off, they had better keep their clothes on.

Phyllis still had a final salvo, a final volley, a final way to Express Herself and to get me to do whatever it was she wanted me to do provided her aim was to get me to suffer. She said, "I thought you'd be happy to know Deborah miscarried the baby."

Why on earth would I be happy? I wasn't happy that Deborah lost a child she wanted. I was horrified that Phyllis said that to me. If her aim was to get me to suffer, it worked; if her aim was to get me to feel sorry for her, it completely failed. Now not only had she staged a dramatic scene which left me completely unmoved, but she obviously wanted me to feel pain, and for what?

I concluded that she was out of her head, too dangerous and too damaged. I finally managed to get up the nerve to break up with her. What a relief!

The only clue I ever had to why Phyllis was so twisted came from Deborah. She told me that Phyllis had tried to tell her about some heinous abuse she had suffered, and Deborah had succeeded in convincing her it had never happened. This was not a good idea. Years later Deborah confided in me how wacky Phyllis had been and how betrayed she felt by her. They have had no contact at all in years.

One result of my breakup with Phyllis was that I could no longer maintain my pretense of being a lesbian or even bisexual to my mother. I came out of the closet and admitted that I was straight. At first she was upset since this had been a very big deal to her, but since I was over 18, she did not seem to think she could do anything about it. In an interview, she said that she had thought I was kidding. How could I possibly grow up in a family like ours and end up straight? Eventually, she laughed it off. She said she was going to write an article for *True Confessions* magazine.

Imagine my SHOCK! My HORROR!!
The day I found out my DAUGHTER was a
HETEROSEXUAL!!

That fall, I directed an Irish music and dance show at the Renaissance Faire. I made costumes for all the major cast members, choreographed, danced, sang, helped to write the script, and otherwise did way too much. I became so burned out that I quit sewing for a long time after that.

Ole, Duncan, and Laura were all in the show. I was the director, and Laura decided she could do the job better. We quarreled, and she wrote a nasty letter to the director of the Faire about how dreadful I was. He was puzzled, but I felt betrayed and devastated.

I quit the Faire and started college. Apparently, after getting rid of me Duncan, Laura, and Ole could not decide which one of them was going to run the show, and *they* quarreled. I also quietly spoke to Elizabeth and told her that if she wanted to direct the show next year, all she needed to do was to announce auditions and rehearsals at the Renaissance Faire workshops, and it would be her show. She did, and she directed the show for the next three years.

Meanwhile, my father and I were still living in the tacky mansion in Oakland. Between the burglaries and the tree-climbing, I began to feel as though that house was no place for man nor beast. By that time, Mother had made a great deal of money with *Mists of Avalon*, and she intended to buy my father a house.

I wanted to live in North Berkeley because it would be safe, but Mother wanted us to live closer to her. She let me house-hunt with him but then bought Walter a house just half a block away from hers. This was the same block we had all been on since arriving in California in 1972.

And so, like the bad penny which keeps turning up, I found myself back in Berkeley once more, three blocks from Ashby BART and a host of bad memories. I should have stayed in Lafayette, but if I had, this would have been a very different story indeed.

Chapter 30

The Ermine Violin
(1984–1987)

Dr. McCoy: "They're nice, soft, and furry, and they make a pleasant sound."

Spock: "So would an ermine violin, but I see no advantage in having one."

—"The Trouble with Tribbles", *Star Trek: The Original Series*

I started taking voice when I was still staying with Serpent and Cathy and I had had many voice lessons, fully expecting to become a professional singer one day. I could not face singing in front of my mother because she tended to say horrible things to me that made me think Hitler was to peace and freedom what I was to singing. My voice lessons had ended when I left home because I could not get to my teacher on my own, but I kept on singing and performing every chance I got.

While I was living with Ole, I had auditioned for the San Francisco Conservatory of Music. I sang *The Clancy Brothers* version of "The Wind that Shakes the Barley", which was nebulous in terms of tempo. I did not have an accompaniment, nor had I prepared for my audition with my previous voice teacher. I did not sing in a way that demonstrated I had the faintest idea what I was doing, musically. After my audition, they told me that they were not going to unleash another singer on the world who could not count. They required me to take a year of piano before they would let me take voice, a decision I understood completely.

I am not a good pianist, as my mother would be the first to tell you. These days, when I am leading masterclasses or rehearsals or teaching voice lessons, I will simply take a conductor's bow, and say, "I am The World's Worst Pianist. Thank you very much!"

My lessons at the Conservatory left me quaking in my boots. My piano teacher, Scott Fogelsong, either disliked me or thought he could inspire me with harsh strictness. When I did something well, he would snarl at me, "I'll show you something you *can't* do." When I did something badly or hesitated, he would sneer and tell me, "I am counting the spots on the ceiling while I am waiting for you to play." He would even pound my fingertips into the keys, very hard. I ended up so intimidated I could barely talk to him, but I persisted because I wanted to take voice again.

I can chalk up a lot of the stuff Dr. Fogelsong did to dopey old-school peda-gogical stuff. After all, he sounded a lot like my mother, who had always insisted I had no touch for the piano and practically yanked the chair away every time I got near it.

I could not have been 100% hopeless because I learned to play all 24 scales at four octaves. I could do that and play the pieces he asked me to play. My piano lessons with him left me absolutely cold, but like I had with math, I forgot everything after I was away from him. My hands worked well enough that I could play, but I was a terrible reader, slow and inefficient.

Dr. Fogelsong did do me one enormous favor though. He insisted I learn rhythm from a book and tested me on assignments from the rhythm book every single week. Of course, learning from a decidedly old-school teacher led me to an awareness of the difficulty with this mindset, and it helped me to eventually devise a new teaching method which would not leave anyone quaking in their boots.

After the year of piano lessons, I was allowed to begin voice lessons with Dorothy Barnhouse. She taught me to sing different things, including a few of the *Songs from the Hebrides* by Marjorie Kennedy Fraser, art songs, and small operatic things. She was going to bring me straight into the Conservatory vocal program as a voice major, but I made a very poor decision. I thought it might be better to go to a regular university to get an education which included subjects other than music. Over her strenuous objections, I applied to San Francisco State and was accepted on the basis of my SAT scores.

There were both good and bad things about San Francisco State. I met a young man, Kristoph, and we became close very fast. We were both singers, and he was a tenor. He also played guitar and oboe and his voice was like John Denver's, but better.

The vocal program at San Francisco State was not good, and I found out about this the hard way. My voice teacher, Dr. Barlow, was a baritone with a tenor extension who had long performed as a tenor. His self-concept was that he was a tenor who was losing his top, but looking back on him as a voice teacher, I see a baritone who managed to sing as a tenor for many years.

The result of his vocal difficulties was that he obliged nearly all his female singers to sing either mezzo-soprano or full contralto, and the result was laryngitis, emotional devastation, and long-standing dysfunction. Of course, he was not the only factor in this equation. My mother, who paid the bills and was a Famous Author, might have had some influence on him. She was a very high soprano, and she wanted me to be a mezzo-soprano to sing Adalgisa to her Norma.

I tried. Oh yes, I tried.

My perspective on this as a voice teacher is different than my perspective as a student; back then, all I knew is that what he was asking me to do hurt my voice and over time destroyed it. Not only did he have me singing contralto repertoire but Wagner, which is too heavy for any singer under 20—even under 30! I understand now that he heard the dramatic potential in my voice and thought since in his view I would end up singing Wagner, why not today?

A dramatic voice does not refer to acting, but physical characteristics; a dramatic voice can produce a huge crescendo and a lot of sound whereas a more lyric voice will not. However, speaking as a voice teacher, a sensible teacher will hear dramatic potential in a voice and stay light, light, light until the voice is fully trained. Letting a dramatic voice blast away will destroy the voice. Imagine that you are a trainer and that your new prospective bodybuilder is born to be a heavyweight lifter: you can see it in his body and bone structure. Do you begin with 500-pound weights? *No!* Naturally, you build up his strength gradually and carefully, being sure to avoid injury. The bodybuilder may *want* to lift the heavy stuff today, but a sensible trainer will never allow it since what matters is long-term health and what the body can do a year from now, not what we can demand from our bodies today.

It was almost funny during my voice lessons with Mr. Barlow; he would warm me up to F or G above high C, which is impossible for most sopranos let alone any alto of any description. Instead of simply working with that part of my voice, he would ask me if I was all right. He liked to say that all high voices would naturally "find their way down." He thought that because he was losing his top, all tenors would eventually be baritones; thus, all soprano voices would eventually be altos, so why not hurry everything along?

From a pedagogical standpoint, I can see his point only from the perspective of Vennard, who believed that nearly all soprano voices would be contained in very short bodies: 5'3" and under, and they would invariably have short necks. At 5'6" with a long neck, I didn't fit. Of course, at 6'0", Joan Sutherland didn't either!

The real bottom line for a voice is not the size of the body but the size of the larynx and the length of the vocal folds (vocal cords), which are not related to height but to genetics. We can determine where a voice likes to be by where it—and the singer—is most comfortable. The voice will work best where it belongs. Issues with high notes are dealt with through teaching position and breath, and issues with low notes are dealt with the same way. For a very young student—and any teen is a baby from an operatic perspective—we ideally stick to the middle, with no extremes of range on either end.

The long and the short of it is that I received appallingly bad voice lessons for two semesters and ended up barely able to sing at all. Between *O Thou That Tellest Good Tidings to Zion* from the *Messiah*, and *Agnus Dei* from Bach's *B Minor Mass*, *Senta's Ballad* from *The Flying Dutchman* and *Allmacht'ge Jungfrau* from *Tannhauser*, I was vocally wrecked. He even had me sing Wagner's *Wesendonk-Lieder*, which as a voice teacher I would no more give to a young opera singer than I would demand she sing while walking a tightrope. What all these songs have in common is they are *loud!*

If a singer does not have both support and technique, which I did not have—let alone the correct type of voice—she will invariably create appalling tension at the level of the larynx. A sensible voice teacher will assign light music to a young singer and only increase the weight of the repertoire when the voice is very well-developed and can handle the music without strain.

There are huge numbers of soprano voices out there. Real mezzo or alto voices are a much rarer thing. One reason I know this is that I train and audition around twenty sopranos to one real alto.

Most "altos" in choirs are sopranos who do not understand breath well enough to be able to reliably access their tops. The result is usually pushing in the lower registers as identification with the wrong classification buts up against physical reality, and a set of coping dysfunctions must be used to create the desired low, loud sounds.

In college there are nearly *no* voices that have any business singing dramatic music of any sort, and assigning Wagner or even Puccini to young sopranos does them a disservice. Bellini, Donizetti, oratorio, straight art songs, Mozart by the bucketful, heck, even Gilbert and Sullivan would produce better results much more quickly.

Dr. Barlow was going through many changes besides his voice. He was leaving his wife of nineteen years and his daughter because he had fallen in love with a man. He was also most inappropriate with the young men in my family who came to him for lessons. One managed to rebuff him and manage the situation, but Dr. Barlow was also inappropriate with my brother Patrick, telling him to "let [his] throat relax, like there was a cock in it." That was my brother's first and last voice lesson with him, and who can be surprised?

If I had known what he had done at the time, I would have ended my lessons with him and gone to the department head to complain. It is ethically unforgivable to try to seduce a student. Pardon me for not being surprised when I heard, many years later, that Dr. Barlow had lost his life to AIDS.

After two semesters with Mr. Barlow and chronic laryngitis, I protested and got another teacher who let me sing in a register which I could actually sustain without pain. My new teacher, Kathryn Harvey, had me singing *Lucia di Lammermoor*, *Violetta* from *La Traviata*, and all the normal dramatic coloratura repertoire: Bellini, Donizetti, and Verdi. I was in loads of opera workshops, of course, singing stuff like "Susanna" from *Nozze di Figaro* and "Musetta" from *La Boheme*. The music was easy and felt good, and it no longer hurt when I sang. I learned huge amounts of music and had a blast. She had high hopes for me and called me "the Callas" when she talked with other people about me.

Kathryn would tell me that I could sound like Joan Sutherland and I could sound like Maria Callas, but I had no idea how to sound like Moira. Her observation about me was correct, although I do not know if she understood the depth or importance of what she had said to me. The truth was that I had no self, nothing to sing about.

I was not allowed to be me. If I was allowed to be me, I would matter. If I was allowed to be me, I could protest what had happened in my house or what had happened to me, and my protestations would actually matter, but I did not matter. My father's past crimes did not matter, my pain did not matter, the bellyful of things I tried to forget never mattered.

I was a shell, a doll, a mask, singing someone else's music and pretending the joys and pain of other people instead of talking about my own, or even admitting it.

In therapy circles, they call this "dehumanization", but I did not understand that yet.

My mother wanted me to sing opera and although I loved opera, singing was emotionally painful, and I did it mostly because it seemed to be what I had to do to please her. My mother expected me to become the famous opera singer she had always wanted to be, and my life had to be devoted to that forever. I did not understand then that if my heart was not in it, my voice would not be in it either.

All that mattered was my mother's dream.

While I was at San Francisco State, I chose to do something that changed my life forever. I took up playing the concert harp. I had a wonderful harp teacher with impeccable harp technique, Vicki DeMartini. Go to see her at Cliff House in San Francisco, if you like. She is probably still there.

As a harp student, I proved to have all the aptitude for the harp which I never had for the piano. In order to learn the harp, one must have the ability to mimic a set of very small motions with tremendous precision and to recreate identical movements very, very quickly. All that I lacked on the piano, all the pain and terror I felt... none of that was there on the harp. The harp and I became fast friends; it was probably the easiest thing I ever learned. I didn't figure out exactly how odd of a harp student I was until I became a harp teacher and saw people learn in months what I had learned in minutes.

This was a musical situation that, at last, my mother could not destroy. She knew absolutely nothing about the harp, and the one time she laid hands on it in front of other people, she plunked tunelessly on the strings and told us all that she had "played the harp in a past life." She never even tried to critique my harp playing since she had no knowledge which would have allowed her to do so. This meant that I was totally free to play the harp without fear. And play I did!

Why is impeccable technique on the harp important? Because the harp is one of the few instruments that can really hurt you if you don't play it properly. The harp is asymmetrical; it sits on the right shoulder and brings the right arm high with the right hand often near the ear, and the left hand and arm overextended in front of you as far as it will go if you are playing the concert harp. If one does not use the fingers in such a way as to access forearm muscles instead of hand muscles, the risk of carpal tunnel is exceptionally high. In addition, if you are not rigorous about posture, the harp will bend your spine to the left, twist your neck, and drop your left shoulder. The pain involved from allowing any of these things to happen is appalling and progressive.

These days, I tell my students that the harp will turn them into a gnome if they do not take care to sit very straight. Much of my practice with harp students has involved correcting painful hands, painful backs, and the slow playing that results from wrong technique of one sort or another, usually claw-fingers, which curl into themselves instead of coming flat into the palm.

Playing the harp was a guilty pleasure. It was something I was doing, at last, for me.

My aunt Diana had given me a small, wire-strung Witcher harp, and I brought it to my first harp lesson. Neither my teacher nor I could figure out how to make it hold still on my lap. The string spacing on a wire-strung harp is very narrow, and the technique is very different than what is used on a gut strung concert harp or Celtic/Folk harp. I love the sound of the wire-strung harp, but I opted to learn to play the concert harp instead.

My first harp was a rented black Troubador I. A Troubador is a tall, stable Celtic harp with concert spacing and tension. That means that it will feel like a concert harp while being both more portable and far less expensive. Folk harps with different spacing and tension can feel very "squishy" to a player accustomed to concert harps. Some people prefer that squishy feel because it takes very little effort to produce a sound, but if you play a squishy harp too hard, it will make a horrible rattling sound. When the strings vibrate, they will slap against the harmonic curve and the other strings. We call this "overdriving" a harp.

I was and am a "power" player. Most self-taught harpers cannot produce any appreciable volume because the usual way of playing if you don't have a teacher is to pluck the strings with sharply curved fingers, which is painful and tiring even if you do it very softly. Playing with concert harp technique means you can play both very loudly and very softly with no appreciable difference in effort. This works best on a harp with concert spacing and tension. You can only reliably get a wide range of possible dynamics (volume) on a harp which is not squishy.

A good way to observe the difference between "claw hands" and functional harp hands is to snap your fingers and notice where your fingertips go. My harp teacher had me snapping my fingers for the first few weeks so that I could get the proper motion down. When your fingertips go flat into the palm, the muscles used are all forearm muscles, not the comparatively much weaker hand or finger muscles. It is the musical equivalent of "lift with your legs, not with your back."

I outgrew the Troubador very quickly. I loved the feel, the size, and the stability; I was annoyed at the harmonic limitations. I outgrew the simple music which is possible on a folk harp. I wanted to be able to use more keys and more sharps and flats, to play actual classical music without having to leave things out or make ridiculous modifications to avoid accidentals.

A folk harp like the Troubador has a full set of sharping levers, which means that one can play in a wide variety of keys, but only those with naturals and sharps unless you retune the harp to another key like Eb, with 3 flats tuned in and then you always have levers engaged, which means that the strings sound slightly tinnier. One way to handle the lack of keys available on a folk harp is to use sorta-enharmonic keys; instead of six flats, I would use one sharp, and instead of three flats, I would play in four sharps. It would put the whole piece up a half step, but it meant I could play more things, and since I usually played alone, it made no especial difference whether I was on the original pitch or half a step higher.

A pedal harp or concert harp uses seven foot pedals—one for C, one for D and so forth—which enable rapid key changes and accidentals (sharps and flats) while one is playing. On a folk or Celtic harp, we have to take our hands out of the strings every time we want to use an accidental and reach up and change it by moving a lever at the top of the string.

What a relief that I had rented the Troubador harp, so I could discover which direction I wanted to go before buying something!

When Mother became very wealthy from *Mists of Avalon,* she bought me a harp. It was a beautiful second-hand Salvi Diana, which cost a lot less than it would have cost new.

For those who do not eat, drink, and breathe the harp, a Salvi Diana is a 47-string full sized concert harp—the sort you'd see in an orchestra. Salvi is an Italian company which makes concert harps. The other major concert harp company is Lyon & Healy. At my teacher's home, I had had the chance to try both her Lyon & Healy and her Salvi, and the main difference is that to me, the pedals on the Salvi were smoother and quieter. The Lyon & Healy also had a long, rectangular piece from top to bottom in the back over the string holes where the harp sat on the collarbone, and the corners digging in drove me a little bit nuts. Rather than play with a washcloth between the harp and me, I preferred the Salvi.

The harp became a new universe to me and a great and unimaginable blessing. To my future audiences, I would say that I learned to play harp while playing hooky from my voice lessons. This was a nod to the fact that I was supposed to become an opera singer, but the harp was where I was happiest.

I began performing in local opera companies, premiering Michael Masumoto's *Echo and Narcissus* in Berkeley. Afterward, I auditioned for the Marin Opera and joined them for a production of *Romeo et Juliette* by Gounod. Again, I sang in the chorus, but I was also chosen to be the understudy for Stephano, a brief coloratura role with one aria and one scene: an invented role which exists to start the fight between the Capulets and Montagues.

I joined the Marin Opera again for its production of *Madama Butterfly*, but even though I had again been moved into a more prominent position, I decided against continuing, preferring to rejoin the Renaissance Faire and play the harp and sing there. I was not very attentive to my auditions and even ignored a callback from the Oakland Opera.

I changed my mind eventually, and I spent a glorious year singing with the chorus of the Lamplighters. The Lamplighters are a famous and very old San Francisco opera company which specializes in the music of Gilbert and Sullivan: comic operas, operettas, and a very few musicals.

We began with *Iolanthe* and then went on with the *The Gondoliers*, *Where's Charlie*, and finally the Lamplighters Annual Gala, which always has a theme and is original. That year, we were poking fun at corporate raiders, so *Iolanthe's* "dainty little fairies" became "dainty secretaries."

I had to audition for every show, which was fine. The competition increased, and by the time we were doing *Where's Charlie*, I was one of only four sopranos chosen for the chorus. Each show had up to seventeen performances and a three-month rehearsal cycle for a year-round schedule.

When I sang *Iolanthe* with the Lamplighters, I noticed I had let my weight climb a little, so I ate less, went to the gym, and worked hard. By the time *Where's Charlie* rolled around, I had become quite slim again. My family was furious. After all, being heavy is good, desirable, and feminist, and fat bodies are "beautiful." How dare I pander to the male establishment by deliberately losing weight?

Yes, Virginia. Being fat in Berkeley is no accident. If you want to upset feminists, lose weight; they will lose their minds. The only way my mother could begin to cope with it was by telling herself that as a performing artist I had to look a certain way. After all, who cares about health? Men love thin women, so being thin is hateful and evil and impossible. Can you imagine losing weight and having the people around you be both appalled and critical? I *must* be anorexic because all thin girls are anorexic, and I must be on my way to death, hospitals, and insanity. What a terrible crime I had committed!

I enjoyed my time with the Lamplighters very much, but I decided not to continue. Kristoph and Margaret and I formed a Celtic band, Magic Fire. I chose all the repertoire, doing what I usually do. We began with one show with me as lead singer, which went very well. Afterward, Margaret decided she wanted to take turns being the lead singer with me. Rather than argue with her about it, I opted to leave the band and go solo. Once I left, they changed the name to Avalon Rising, and Kristoph has been a very capable front man. The band has been active ever since.

I did exactly one solo vocal performance after I left Magic Fire and before I left Berkeley. I went to an open mic with Jonnie at La Val's Pizza in North Berkeley. It was downstairs and very crowded. I sang a Pentangle piece a cappella, "When I Was in My Prime" as recorded by Jacqui McShee. I got a standing ovation to my complete shock. I was accustomed to being very successful onstage through personality, but this piece was nothing but singing.

Just me.

Chapter 31

The Goldfish Bowl
(1985–1988)

How I wish, how I wish you were here.
we're just two lost souls
swimming in a fish bowl
year after year
Running over the same old ground:
what have we found?
The same old fear.
Wish you were here.

—Pink Floyd, "Wish You Were Here", *Wish You Were Here* (1975)

That song is the origin of the name my father gave our new house on Fulton Street: The Goldfish Bowl. One might imagine that the futility implied within the lyrics could have been an impetus to change something about our lives. If things are impossible and pointless, do something else! Sadly, my father and I differed on an important issue; he felt he was a helpless victim, blown about by every wind while I am convinced each of us can and must take steps to improve our own lives. Indeed, many members of our family persisted in predictable folly, and the problems I stepped in to resolve were of the most basic nature. They were the sorts of things that any reasonable adult should have been able to do.

Mother now had piles of money, which had enabled her to buy my father a house, but Lisa still kept my father on a short financial leash. He had to choose between groceries and his marijuana. I negotiated with her to let him have what he wanted. He was miserable and agitated without his pot, and adding to his misery helped no one. After all these years, he was not likely to give up his dependence on pot-smoking, and I saw no point in arguing the matter with him.

When we first moved in, the movers had put his bedroom downstairs next to the front door, accessible through glass-paned double doors. He was completely convinced that Mother had put him in that room to spy on him, and he felt like a caged animal trapped by a hostile trainer. He was the goldfish in the bowl, and she would look in through the glass and make sure that he wasn't doing anything wrong.

I understood how helpless he felt, and in my usual meddling way I helped him move upstairs into a real bedroom. The room he had been in was more of a formal dining room, right off the kitchen. It is likely that Mother simply wanted to save him the trouble of going up and down staircases, but what good would it have been to say that to him?

My father's friends would routinely drop in day and night at any hour, and he felt incapable of telling them not to. I instituted a "Call Ahead" rule. I told all his friends when they visited that he was very busy with writing, and I asked them to call before they came over to ask if it was a convenient time for a visit. When I had initially discussed this with my father, he had expressed relief that the endless interruptions of his work would stop, but he was also afraid that his friends would be angry with him.

I asked him to blame me for the rule, and to let them call me any name they wished and be angry with me. That way he would have the benefit of the emotional space and time and not have to weather any storms. Naturally, I was sharply criticized for this rule, which didn't bother me a bit. I could cope with criticism much more easily than my father could, and besides, I did not want visitors at 3 AM.

I took care of the household stuff, including all the chores and cooking, which I expected. I was used to him, and I put up with his beliefs, tirades, paranoia, and fearfulness as the price of admission. He was still my dearest friend, or so I thought, and the nearest thing to a parent I had ever had.

I was going to college and no longer working at the Faire. I was lonely and culture shocked because I had chosen to separate myself from my community of the past nine years. I was living in much closer quarters with my father now, and dealing with his endless paranoia and misery at being closer to Mother.

During this time, I spent more time with Mother and Lisa than I should have. I certainly saw and heard a great deal more than I wanted to. Mother was not able to have a truthful relationship with Lisa, precisely like their early interactions might have indicated. Mother would triangulate a lot of interactions between herself and either Lisa or me in an attempt to get either one of us to give her back some of the power she had given away. Mother would essentially say to me, "Oh, bad old Lisa runs my life, Moira!" Conversely, she would say to Lisa, "Oh, bad old Moira forced me to do whatever you are currently objecting to, Lisa!" I was astonished to watch Mother playing these games because I had always regarded her as being so powerful.

The two of them communicated through money. Mother would buy anything she wanted to for my brother and me, and she didn't want Lisa to tell her what to do. Every time Mother spent money on us, she would act like a naughty child getting away with something truly dastardly, and Lisa would fume and sulk.

Mother gave me plenty of money for voice lessons and music. Her success had made her very wealthy, but she never cared about money and gave it away as readily as if it was a heap of old socks. She felt providing for me to become a musician was very important; she was convinced of my talent. In that way, I was very lucky.

When Mother bought me a concert harp after *The Mists of Avalon* became a bestseller, Lisa was incensed. She claimed that Mother couldn't give it to me and tried to find ways to take it back. As the years went by, Lisa's financial shenanigans became even more toxic and deadly.

Mother was diabetic and not interested in taking steps to reverse it. As noted, she hated exercise and refused to do it. She would claim that she had lots of "hard muscle" beneath her fat and that she was not really that overweight, but she became insulin dependent and her mental status began to decline. She was over 250 lbs and wore a size 24. I saw no evidence of hard muscle anywhere, except perhaps between her ears. Her early cognitive deficits were probably also the result of frequent mini-strokes, or TIAs.

She had many ideas about healthy eating, none of which resulted in health. Mother read a lot of vegetarian magazines, toyed with becoming vegetarian, and denigrated what she felt was the Western tendency toward chronic overconsumption of protein. Left to her own devices, she would eat toasted white bread with butter and jam and leave off the butter if she was feeling virtuous. If the jam was labeled "no sugar", she thought it could not possibly be a problem for her diabetes. Of course, not adding sugar to a compound which already contained a huge amount of naturally occurring fructose didn't change its effect on her blood sugar.

She was feeding her daily appetite with the sugar found in bread and jam instead of proper meals. This resulted in more hunger, more empty calories, and chronic poor nutrition coupled with dangerous obesity. Her blood sugar was out of control, and she was not able to adequately care for herself. One day when we were out together, she told me, "I can have coffee and a doughnut. My blood sugar is only 400."

I tried to intervene and I would take her grocery shopping. I thought that if she had yogurt and eggs around, she might have been able to resist the toast and jam and perhaps even start dealing with her health and her weight. However, nothing helped her cognitive decline.

One day Mother, my friend Elizabeth Rousseau, and I were driving home across the Bay Bridge, and Mother hit another car. She was confused and couldn't figure out how to get the car started again, so I got into the front seat and drove us home. When we got there, Mother told Lisa that the steering had failed and then that the brakes had failed. Kristoph checked the steering and the brakes and said that they both were fine. Then Mother told Lisa that I had made her crash the car, even though I had been in the back seat when it happened. Mother also insisted that I was a dangerous driver—and my having caused this crash proved it. When I left, Mother and Lisa were both pleading with me to "drive carefully", as though I really had caused the whole thing myself.

I was very upset because I had fixed the problem that I was now being blamed for. If I had had a shred of perspective at the time, I would have been able to laugh it off. In retrospect, what had happened was that Mother's strokes and multi-infarct dementia were beginning to severely affect her ability to drive. Instead of confronting Mother about her driving, Lisa chose to let me take the proverbial hit and colluded with Mother on blaming me for something I did not do.

My friend Elizabeth was puzzled by what Mother was saying, but she didn't feel she could contradict my mother. We were able to talk about it in whispers out of earshot. It was just another instance of the adults in my house being completely outrageous. I felt hurt by the whole thing. I was being blamed and mischaracterized when I had literally done nothing wrong and my only goal had been to help.

My mother, Lisa, and I used to see a chiropractor together: He was a kind man who did a lot to help the neck pain I was always stuck with due to head injuries and migraines. He felt I was chronically stressed and exhausted, and much of his treatment of me amounted to shoulder and neck massage since I tended to get spasms.

I went to the chiropractor with Mother and Lisa the day after the accident which Mother had blamed me for. I was acting as the chauffeur, as I had so often. All the way there they were telling me about what a dangerous, unsafe driver I was. When we arrived, I was still quietly distraught from listening to their twin tirades, and I lay on the chiropractor's table with the tears running into my ears. He laid his hands on my forehead and stayed with me until I calmed down. God bless him for that.

From my perspective now I can see how silly the whole thing was. Lisa knew how to drive. If I was so unsafe, it would have been a simple matter to have her drive rather than to lecture me as though that could somehow make me a better driver. Lisa apparently wanted to demonize me while validating Mother's impossible version of events. The triangle turned again, and this time I was a villain the two of them could agree on.

I was used to being the villain by then, and I added one more villainous act to my collection: I told Mother that it was time for her to stop driving. I told her that if she did not voluntarily stop, I would go to her doctor and tell her about all the crashes, and her doctor would stop her. She agreed, though unwillingly.

Mother finally had one big stroke when we were coming back from the grocery store. She dropped the bag of groceries she was carrying, and I got her into the house. She could not talk. I made sure that she got medical help, and I spoke to her, saying, "I know you can understand me, and I know you're still in there." She nodded her head furiously *yes*.

Mother was severely affected by the stroke, but over time some of the effects became less. She stopped dragging a foot, her face looked more normal, and she became able to talk again, but there was still significant brain damage. I attribute her healing from her strokes in part to her lifelong habit of reading an entire book every day. Typically, she would write from 3–6 AM, then meet with my father, then do errands, and then read for the rest of the day, usually retiring no later than 8 PM.

Around the time that Lisa established financial control over my mother, she did some genealogy and discovered she was my mother's ninth cousin and my ninth cousin once removed. From that day forward, she referred to my mother as her "cousin" and me also, which felt like sandpaper on my ears. How many "cousins" step in and own the lives and financial empires of their "cousin"?

The slight to my mother infuriated me. How could Lisa deny the twenty-odd years she spent with my mother and pretend they were never lovers? Why would a "cousin" edge out my father from his own home? How could Lisa twist the nature of her relationship in a dishonest attempt to explain how she got her fingers in Mother's estate? Kissing cousins, perhaps!

Lisa began having a straight relationship with a man named Raul under

Mother's nose. Predictably, Raul was put on the payroll, so he had a reason to be there day and night.

Raul was the perfect companion for Lisa. He was a beetling man, timid, angry, and odd. He and Lisa shared an interest in ice skating. He would watch videos of the little girl skaters at night at Greenwalls, which made no sense to me. He was all too happy to agree with Lisa on absolutely anything. When the two of them began to travel together, Lisa told me that she and Raul were utterly virtuous and claimed that although they shared a bed, there were pillows between them. Given her long and interesting sexual history, I was completely unconcerned with whether she was building a pillow fort or using the pillows as a place to rest a few dozen sex toys.

I didn't care who she was sleeping with, and I didn't know why she wanted me to think her sleeping arrangements with Raul were so virtuous. Mother cared a lot, though, but loved Lisa too much to show her how hurt she was.

How could Lisa expect Mother to watch her carrying on with Raul every day as though it was the most normal thing in the world? And most of all, how could she expect Mother to go along with her pretense and never show a broken heart—the one I know she had? From our conversations, she would have done anything to please Lisa, including endure her betrayal.

Less savory, though, were the financial goings-on. Raul and Lisa would have Mother sign papers, and they would put a piece of grey cardstock over the papers with a cutout a little smaller than a 3x5 inch card. That was large enough for Mother to sign but not large enough for Mother to know or read what she was signing.

Chapter 32

Boundaries, Bathrooms, and Betrayal (1989)

You always hurt the one you love
The one you shouldn't hurt at all
You always take the sweetest rose
And crush it till the petals fall

—The Mills Brothers, "You Always Hurt the One You Love"

My father was everything to me. He was my best friend: much more of a parent to me than my mother had ever been, and in many ways he was the only person I could talk to. Multilingual, multi-instrumental, polymath, punster, author amd brilliant beyond dreams of brilliant, he had fields of expertise about which I knew nothing. His friends said that he had forgotten more than they would ever know.

He got my jokes and could follow anything I said no matter how weird. He was a punster like me, and when we got going with the puns, the proverbial rafters would shake with our laughter. We had common interests, lots of them: we both loved languages, classical music—especially opera—and he and I would joke in a few languages at once. He would even accompany me on the piano while I sang opera.

His approval and his love made the sun rise. Living with him meant I was with the person I cared about most, and I didn't care that I had to do everything around the house to take care of him, I was hardly the first daughter to be in the position of caring for a parent who had severe limitations. Considering his brilliance, it would have been very strange for him to have no limitations; the handicapped genius is a trope.

Even more than that, he believed in me. No matter what kind of wackiness he said when his friends were around, I knew he thought that my life was important and that he believed I would do important things. He made me feel not only special, but essential.

Of course, my feelings about him are idealistic and might even be completely wrong. I cannot say for certain whether he loved me or simply accepted my company because I took care of him. He had the ability to make people feel special, and for him to point this in my direction did not mean he thought any more highly of me than any stranger.

I also knew and accepted deep down that there were limits. I knew my father would choose his beliefs over me, his other friends over me, and certainly his sex life above me. It was almost as though I could borrow what passed for his love provided he did not have anything else more pressing to do.

If there were any other men around, I abruptly went from being his beloved daughter to being the Antichrist. Women, according to him, were only interested in monopolizing male attention, and this was a reprehensible, almost intolerable, evil. Very few women, he thought, had even a small amount of intelligence, and it often seemed as though I was tolerated only because he thought I was a little bit unusual in this regard.

He regarded my mother as intelligent but not especially so and spoke of her disparagingly at nearly every turn. Most of the things he said conveyed contempt, even hatred, and deep, deep fear. He spoke at length of how disappointed he was in their sex life and how repulsive she was. Most notably, he regarded himself as totally under Mother's power, little better than her slave. He felt any freedom he had needed to be stolen from her, his owner, when she was not looking, and that his life ended where her influence or presence began.

Despite this overly dramatic, self-pitying assessment, he and Mother continued to see each other every morning for as long as he was a free man. No matter how much he complained, he would still read her work every morning as he had for decades. Many times, his talk about her amounted to "I hope she still has a few good books left in her", acknowledging her unfortunate stroke-related mental decline which began shortly after *Mists* was completed.

I had become accustomed to his tape loops about her, about women, heck, about how bad all women were. I was under the impression that if I acted as unfeminine as possible around him, he might not extend his hatred of women to include me. I loved him and I simply adjusted to his foibles. It was not as though I could do anything about them.

Yes, I know in retrospect that his entire set of beliefs were absurd and self-serving. His self-concept of having absolutely no power was not only untrue, but it amounted to complete abdication of responsibility. He let Lisa handle all his money and then lived in fear because she would play games with the money.

He also did nothing whatsoever for the sake of his physical health. He absolutely disdained any form of vegetables and took no care with his diet other than to eat whatever was handed to him which was cooked and void of most produce. I could sooner imagine him floating on a cloud than exercising. To him, exercise belonged to the category of overtly masculine activities, all of which were anathema to him.

My relationship with my mother had never been good and living near her was making things much worse. My interactions with my mother hurt. They hurt a lot, and I didn't have the faintest idea how to make any of that better. She had become infatuated with Cabbage Patch Dolls and bought a lot of them. This amazed me. I was never allowed to have dolls as a child, and I could not understand why Mother would want them as an adult. She seemed to delight in how ugly her dolls were.

Mother used the dolls, especially her favorite doll, Miranda, as a way to communicate hostility to me and Lisa. She pretended to have relationships with these dolls, and insisted that they talked to her. She would tell me "Miranda is a better daughter than you…" Worse, when she called home from traveling out of town to talk to Lisa, she would tell her to "Give Miranda my love." Lisa would express intense hurt over this because the love was never for her, only for the dolls.

Naturally, it was impossible to take Mother to task for her bizarre conduct. She had already begun to go into multi-infarct dementia, and it was tacitly understood in our household that we do not jiggle the crazy people, even when they hurt you. We simply adapt and cope.

I believed Mother really was trying to be hurtful. She had told me many times that her words had no impact on anyone, so she had to find a way to make sure they did. The goal of her cruelty was to teach the rest of us how to behave, as though our hoped-for improvements would stop her attacks, which she considered to be truthful, reasonable criticism.

I did not get along with Lisa and had panic attacks nearly every time I was around her. She would write me poison pen letters, and she would speak sweetly with bitter barbs hidden in her words. She held the purse strings although Mother made the decisions. She did her best to keep me away from Mother and behaved in a way that I found to be erratic and punitive. She communicated with me through money. Years later, she claimed she had taught me to balance a budget. I told her that the only thing she had ever taught me was to be afraid.

I felt so much panic and rage between Mother's blatant attacks and Lisa's sweetly charming barbs that I decided to see a counselor, Jane Conger. Jane began to teach me about boundaries—an unpopular subject in our family. I would not have dared to mention to anyone else that I was learning about boundaries. The resulting lecture would have been both infuriating and useless.

Jane was maternal, gentle, beautiful, and kind. I trusted her. I told her that in our family, I was considered to be evil, which I was inclined to believe but couldn't put my finger on why. One day I showed her my school ID picture, hoping that she would recognize the evil and help me understand. What was I doing that was so evil? Could I be evil without acting evil? Was evil just my nature, and would I have to wait for it to show up one day?

She looked at my picture and told me I looked like a rosy-cheeked cherub.

I was astonished.

I realize in retrospect that to Jane, it was reality. I was not evil. I was trying hard to do exactly what my mother wanted me to. I tucked the possibility that maybe I was not evil into a safe spot in my heart and set it aside to think about later. Jane knew perfectly well my mother had simply projected her own evil onto me.

Jane's therapeutic strategy for me was perfect. We did bibliotherapy, reading every book which she thought might conceivably help me. We started with all the works of Alice Miller, notably *The Drama of the Gifted Child*, which fit like a glove.

But that was only part of the story.

I had been having a lot of distress for a long time over several things which were normal for my father but which I could never quite accept as normal for me. Almost invariably, Walter went naked around the house. As you may recall, nudity to him was simply part of his enlightened sensibilities. According to him, people who have truly transcended their limited sexual and emotional morality feel no need to wear clothing, or so the story goes.

It never seemed that way to me. Where he might have felt supremely comfortable wandering around the house with all of his procreative equipment waving in the breeze, it was awful for me. I hated nudity: both his and his expectation that I would also walk around undressed. Naturally, my refusal to go naked meant he would call me a "prude." Maybe he thought that the seven thousandth time he said it would finally convince me of the error of my ways and get me to strip.

His insistence on nudity made me feel uneasy because I was aware of his sexual interest in everything which breathed and I was afraid that one day I might breathe around him. It also made me uneasy because it meant that if ever I had another person there with me, be it roommate, date, or guest, that person would be "treated" to the sight of his yards of naked flesh, pot belly, grey hair, dangling participles, and all sorts of sights which nobody should have to see. Yes, I will spare you details of his shingles rash and whatever single-celled organism it was that was cooking in reddish patches on his inner thighs.

From the time I was a child, I was as accustomed to the sight and smell of Walter's genitals as his face. He expected me to play with them, of course. When I was younger, I would flee from him when he was naked and this did not please him, although at least he did not try to give me uncomfortable lectures on the subject.

I was also distressed by the fact that whenever there was more than one person around, he wanted sloppy group hugs and kisses which were a little bit too wet and too feely for me to be able to cope with. Naturally, for me to back away from them meant I was a prude. For me to object was unthinkable. I was trapped, and I had to learn ways to escape before I could be grabbed and roped in.

He routinely used the bathroom while having conversations with people, left the door open, and expected the conversation to continue. If I had attempted to "leave the scene" while he did his business, again, I would have been a prude. It goes without saying that it is pretty weird that I knew exactly how he folded his toilet paper and which hip went up when he used it. Suffice to say he was as modest as a barn cat, and even less concerned with the opinions of others.

I told Jane about the sloppy kisses and the never-ending nudity and how uneasy and sick they made me feel. She was appalled, which I understand better now than I did then. Remember that I had been taught that nudity was normal and I was the prude. It was only in the houses of friends that I saw the reality: nobody else went around naked, especially not in front of guests. She did not see my father as a great revolutionary figure but as a dangerous sex addict, and I suspect she knew I needed to be removed from that situation as quickly as possible.

Next, Jane suggested I read Patrick Carnes's book *Contrary to Love*, which is an exploration of the pathology of sexual addiction. Again, the book fit like a glove.

Jane wanted me to understand that my father treated sex like a drunk might treat alcohol. She did not believe in his Grand Vision but recognized a self-serving delusional system. She saw him as a dangerous person as well as a sex addict and was not happy that I was living in the same house with him. She wanted me to understand that his conduct was completely abnormal.

She recommended that I go to my father and ask him if he would consider changing his conduct.

I did, with massive trepidation. I do not know when I have ever been so frightened by anything before. I screwed up my courage, walked up to my naked father where he was standing right outside my bedroom door, and I asked him to please wear a bathrobe around the house if he didn't want to get dressed. I also asked him to please, please, please close the bathroom door.

A normal person would have accepted my request and been embarrassed for upsetting me. My father's response was completely different.

He went bananas.

"It's the thin end of the wedge!" he shouted at me. I had never seen him so angry with me in his life. I had betrayed him and nothing I said now could make it better. I was wrong, so wrong, absolutely, completely, irrevocably wrong! Even *thinking* about such a thing was wrong, and how *dare* I speak to him that way? I was no daughter! Indeed, I was no better than the straights and the Christians he railed against. I had learned nothing. I had betrayed him by even asking, and how *dare* I think that my paltry wishes and needs could compare to his Grand Vision for the world?

By asking him to keep his clothes on I was telling him that I was not going to bring his philosophy to the world and that I, his great hope for the future, had abandoned his dreams in favor of all the people he hated. Instantly, I had gone from being part of "us", one of a tiny number of people he trusted, to being part of "them", part of the hated straight community. In retrospect, although it makes me feel sick to say it, I was saying that I would never become his willing sexual partner. He would never babysit me on acid, he would never "initiate" me into anything with anyone, and there would be no group sex involving me.

I was now the enemy.

When I asked him to close the bathroom door and to wear clothing in the house, I was admitting that his sexual presence was unbearable to me—which was the truth. Not only that, but I was saying that his Grand Vision of sexualizing all relationships was something I could not support and did not agree with. I didn't fight back: I withdrew, and I knew I had blown it. He would never understand, and I had no business jiggling the crazy person. It was my job to adapt and to cope, not to try to change him.

Did he wear clothes around the house from that point forward? Did he close the bathroom door? Of course not! Not that I expected he would. He didn't have opinions, after all, only facts, and that I was attempting to go against his facts. This could never be allowed. I was wrong, and I needed to be educated, corrected, and taught the deadly error of my ways. I had failed, more profoundly than I had ever failed in my life.

Jane Conger was furious. She thought I had the right to privacy and the right to be free from never-ending subtle sexual overtures from my father. I didn't understand myself as having rights at all. She thought it was unreasonable for me to have to live in a place where my father was inflicting sloppy kisses on me. What she was seeing was incest on the hoof, and my one paltry attempt to defend myself had gone down in flames.

In retrospect, I wonder if she was indirectly testing him. Did he have a conscience somewhere with an iota of concern for his daughter? His response was certain. His priority was his Grand Vision, and I was not even on the radar. My needs were irrelevant, my feelings an affront. My opinions needed either to be corrected or eliminated. I did not exist as a person except to serve him, and if I could not be the right person—the person he expected me to be—I was a justified target for raging, screaming, and utter hatred.

Unfortunately, more pressing and dangerous was my father's ongoing interest in boys. My father still wanted to have sex with anything male, young, and breathing. Naturally, I had told Jane about Gregg, who was now 23 and of legal age. There was nothing I could do about what my father had done to him when he was younger, but I knew that there had been others and that there would be others, and I felt so trapped, like this was another atrocity waiting to happen.

My father had been "confiding" in me for years about his sexual encounters, to my utter horror. He did not talk about current events. I told Jane that when I was 18, he had told me about kissing a little boy and called it "eight minutes of ecstasy", weeping with fear that he would never again be so happy and wanting to die if he could not. I was disgusted but too cowardly to say so, or even to say much of anything, and I had no idea when this had happened or who the child was.

Jane told me that she would only go to the police if something was happening right now which would endanger a child. I was relieved to know that. I loved my father, and I had no wish to harm him, and I wanted to keep him out of trouble if there was a way, but I silently agreed with her that I *would* come to her if he ever decided to molest a minor under our roof and I found out about it. For me it was an incredible relief to know that someone cared about the children chewed up by our house.

And then my father informed me that we were going to have a house guest.

Chapter 33

My Ultimate Crime
(1989)

I kiss the part that's nearest.

—Walter Breen

My father had met Kenny, the eight-year-old son of Mary Mason and stepson of author Stephen Goldin in 1985 at Westercon 38, a science-fiction convention. Four months later, at another convention in November, my father started molesting him. Some of the specific information about his crimes is taken from my father's confession.

In 1989, my father invited Kenny to visit us for a week. Mary Mason had heard rumors that my father was a pedophile. Mary told me in a phone call after my police report that she asked my mother, Lisa, Aunt Tracy, Aunt Diana, and Uncle Don if it would be safe to have Kenny over and if there was any truth to the rumors about my father. They all told her that my father was safe. She also said that my mother and Lisa specifically told her not to ask me because I was crazy and hysterical.

Mary agreed to let Kenny come over for the week long visit. She had been studying psychology, and she decided to instruct my father in good boundaries, just in case. She told my father to never let Kenny sit on his lap. She told him to not be naked around him. She even told him to not sleep in the same bed as Kenny and not to kiss him on the lips.

Yes, I know. I know.

My father was about as interested in observing her boundaries as an active alcoholic would have cared about hearing how to not get drunk. "Don't open the bottle of wine. Put down the corkscrew. Don't take the beer out of the fridge. Don't pour the whiskey into the glass, and above all, don't drink it." Of course, my father told her exactly what she wanted to hear because he did not want to derail the visit by alerting her to his actual intentions.

Kenny came to our house for a week in early July of 1989. My boyfriend Jonnie and I had provided bedding for Kenny and a room of his own. My father and Kenny were gone for the first few days since my father took him to Monterey Bay Aquarium over 100 miles away and other places that would be fun for a child. I had been told that Kenny was nine, and he seemed very small and young for his age. I found out later that he was eleven. Certainly, the amusements my father sought for him were much more geared toward a child than even a preadolescent, judging from the types of toys my father bought him.

On July 5th, Kenny and my father were at home instead of traveling. I walked into my father's bedroom and he was holding Kenny upside down by his feet. He was hugging him and touching him all over, and saying, "I kiss the part that's nearest." Worse than that, his porn books were out: comic book porn and a book I remembered well from my own childhood called *Show Me!*

How I hated that book! I remembered it vividly since my father had insisted I read it repeatedly when I was very small. It was a black and white artistic picture book, probably 14 by 18 inches, full of pictures of graphic sexual activity—including full penetrative sex—being explained by adults to a child. Worse than that, the child is initially disgusted and upset and the adults persuade him how normal it all is.

I was horrified by what I saw my father doing to Kenny. I did not even try to confront him because I knew he would just freak out, and then Kenny would cry, and my father would freak out more, and God knows what would happen to Kenny if he was in a room with my father when he was emotionally compromised. I feared he would become violent. I left the room, and Jonnie and I left for Westercon in Southern CA in a huge hurry.

As we drove, Jonnie and I talked about what my father had done. Jonnie told me that Kenny's bedding was unused, and that was the final straw for me: my father had clearly been sleeping with Kenny. As soon as we got to a safe place with a phone, I called Jane Conger, and she put me on hold to call CPS. They told her to call the police because this absolutely could not wait.

Mary Mason came and got Kenny, and I had to tell my father over the phone what I had done. This prospect caused me about a million times as much trepidation as I had felt about asking him to close the bathroom door. I was trembling and shaking all over when I called him. I said, "Daddy, I did something, and I'm afraid you'll never forgive me." He said, "I love you, and no matter what it is, I will always forgive you." That was the last time he ever spoke to me with love in his voice.

I told him, "Daddy, I told the police about you and Kenny."

He started screaming at me. "Asshole" was among the milder things he said. It was not the foul names he called me that made the biggest impression but the nature of the crime he accused me of committing. He called me a murderer—his murderer. He disowned me. I was no longer his daughter. I was a parricide: a father-killer. I was nothing to him. I was dead to him. I betrayed him. I betrayed everything he ever taught me. I killed him. I killed his dream. I killed everything he ever loved. I was a monster. I was a failure. I had single-handedly destroyed his life, and he was going to die in prison, and it was all my fault.

I could no more have convinced him that Kenny was in danger from the sexual contact he was intent on having with him than I could have convinced him that we were both standing on Mars. He insisted that I only reported him to the cops out of "vengeance", which I found bizarre. Had he concluded that I had been harboring some insane grudge for years, and for what? I did not have enough of a concept of a self to even begin to be angry with him for violating me, but he seemed to think I had been saving up my revenge on him for raping me all those years before. I was not aware of being angry, let alone seeking any kind of "vengeance."

On the contrary, I felt like I had fallen on my own sword and ruined the most important relationship in my life with the person I treasured most.

When Jonnie and I came home from Westercon, I saw my father in person. I tried twice to talk to him, and he shouted and screamed at me and stomped around. I fainted from terror, like an absurd Victorian heroine. Twice this happened, and I realized we were at the point of no return.

I could no longer live with him.

I had been desperately frightened that he was either going to rape Kenny or that he had already done so. He viewed my fears as intolerable. Not because I was wrong about his intentions but because I was interpreting his acts wrongly: to him it was not rape but the fulfillment of his philosophy, destined to save Kenny from delinquency. All he cared about was what he felt was my "betrayal" of him and his Grand Vision. He had no concern for Kenny at all because what he was doing was "right", as his book made so clear. All he had done, in his view, was to "bring more love into the world", and I was trying to stop him.

Meanwhile, what I had told Jane Conger was nowhere near enough for the cops. They were convinced that there were more victims, and they began calling me around the clock. They said on my answering machine that they would arrest me for obstructing justice if I did not call them back, meet with them in person, and make a formal statement.

When I listened to their messages, I panicked and called Mother. I told Lisa that the cops wanted to talk to me and that I was afraid and really needed to speak to my mother. Lisa answered the phone, and she absolutely refused to let me speak to her. Yes, Mother was there and no, I couldn't speak to her.

There was only one thing I could do: handle this myself. I called the cops back and agreed to meet with Officer Harris from the Berkeley Police Department. We met at a little cafe on Shattuck Avenue and I gave her the names of 22 kids I suspected he had had sexual contact with. I told her everything I could remember about the drugs, about my father's Grand Vision, about what he did in the hot tub, and about our whole family's strange attitudes about sex.

After my police report was complete, I went and sat with Jonnie at the Good Earth Restaurant in Berkeley, devastated with what I had done. I was torn in two. I knew my father would never speak to me again, never forgive me, and probably never even regard me as his daughter ever again. I knew the most important relationship in my life was over, and I wanted to die. Even so, Kenny didn't deserve to be raped by my father, and his safety had to come ahead of all other concerns.

While the TV played images from Tiananmen Square—the young man facing the tank—I told Jonnie that since I had betrayed my father I deserved to die. I told him I was going to have to kill myself since what I had done could never be forgiven. Jonnie disagreed with me. He said emphatically that I was not going to kill myself, but we were going to leave, immediately. We went home, threw clothes and my Troubador harp into the car, and left very quietly.

Chapter 34

Climbing out of Hell
(1989–1993)

You mocked me once, never do it again! I died that day!

—Buttercup, *The Princess Bride*

After my police report in July of 1989, Jonnie and I vanished without a trace. I could no longer be anywhere near my father. He obviously, loudly, despised me. I was receiving death threats from his friends. As far as I knew, Greyhaven had circled the wagons, insisting my father was innocent, and my brother Patrick was furious with me. Patrick seemed to think that my father had been arrested without evidence or witnesses but on my word alone. Nobody was the slightest bit concerned about Kenny except his mother. People were even asking if there was a way to discredit him to save my father.

Lisa was less than no help. My friend Elizabeth, who was staying with my mother at the time, told me that Lisa was going around claiming that I was hysterical, lying, crazy, and that I had "made the whole thing up for attention." Here is what Lisa said in her deposition:

MR. DOLAN: About the fourth line down you write—the third line down. 'I thought she was being hysterical—after all, God knows she has plenty of reasons to be angry with Walter.' What did you mean by ', God knows she has plenty of reasons to be angry with Walter'?

ELISABETH WATERS Walter always preferred boys to girls. He always favored Patrick over Moira. He favored Moira's boyfriends over Moira. I think she resented that he didn't love her because she was a girl.

MR. DOLAN: Okay. So prior to Kenny Smith being molested, did you have any understanding that Walter favored Moira's boyfriends over Moira?

ELISABETH WATERS Moira—Walter favored any boy over Moira. Walter didn't like girls.

MR. DOLAN: *You indicate in the next paragraph, 'Sure, Walter was acting weird, but Walter always acts weird.' What did you mean by, "Walter was acting weird—'Sure, Walter was acting weird'?"*

ELISABETH WATERS *Walter generally acted paranoid, nervous, twitchy, suspicious, and he was acting that way.*

MR. DOLAN: *Anything else?*

ELISABETH WATERS *No, I think that about covers it.*

MR. DOLAN: *Did you think that any of Walter's interactions with children were geared in the sense that you have used the word 'weird' here before—strike that. Did you think any of Walter interactions with young boys were 'weird'?*

ELISABETH WATERS *No.*

MR. DOLAN: *You indicate here, 'And I certainly didn't think Walter was stupid enough to molest a child—especially in front of Moira.' What did you mean by that?*

ELISABETH WATERS *Well–*

MR. BURESH: *Other than what it says. You want her to paraphrase it?*

MR. DOLAN: *Sure, what was she thinking when she wrote that?*

MR. BURESH: *If you recall.*

ELISABETH WATERS: *Well, aside from the idea that I certainly didn't think Walter was that immoral, on top of that, I didn't think he was that stupid. I mean, he must have known that Moira was going to object.*

I suppose it never occurred to Lisa that Walter believed everything he was doing was good and right or that I had walked in on Walter unannounced. After all, I had made this same complaint before and for the same reasons!

After Jonnie and I left, we stopped in Santa Cruz to stay with two friends, Tarik and Carolyn. While we were there, I broke down. I had a flashback of my Mother beating me up, and I did not understand what was happening to me. I found myself pleading with them, saying "Please don't hit me!" I was fully conscious while this was happening and I was horrified at my own behavior, even though I didn't think at the time that I could stop it. I knew I was behaving irrationally and that they were not the ones I was afraid of. I was embarrassed and thought I was losing my mind, but I got over it within a few minutes.

Months later, my mother told me she had tried to beat me to death twice and she had "locked herself in a closet" to stop herself from killing me. I had no memory of either episode outside of flashbacks, my hands over my head, and my voice saying, "Don't hit me Mommy!" I was appalled both by what Mother told me, and why: Mother wanted me to sympathize with her over what an evil child I had been and how terrible her life had been while she was caring for me.

The next day, Jonnie and I left Tarik and Carolyn's house. We drove to Los Angeles to stay with other friends, and then we got to house-sit for friends of theirs. While house-sitting in Los Angeles, I got pneumonia. I had never been so sick in my life. I was coughing up blood and pieces of skin from my throat. It is possible my immune system was compromised from the shock. I also started to have flashbacks around the clock, which had never happened to me before I left home. Most of them were about Mother molesting me, which I had been aware of as an older child. The flashbacks added more details, as though turning a brief memory of a few seconds into a few minutes.

Apparently, distance from my family had opened the floodgates. Being in the shower was out of the question because any sensation on my chest made me hysterical and, once or twice, catatonic.

There were times when I could not stand to feel the air on my skin because it would provoke flashbacks. I felt so filthy and so soiled because of what had happened to me. I irrationally thought that anyone would be able to tell by looking at me that I had been defiled.

The worst flashbacks, though, were the ones about my father. I needed to think of him as safe Santa Claus not creepy Santa Claus, and this was no longer possible. The things I remembered were yucky and intrusive, but my flashbacks included a lot of things I had forgotten. Violence, whispered threats like "don't talk or I'll kill you!"

My symptoms were so bad that I got a therapist. I literally could not speak when I tried to tell her what my father had done. I couldn't even write down what he did. I could draw pictures, and they were not much help either, amounting to scary Santa with his private parts scratched out.

I stopped being able to drive because I couldn't stop crying. I could not talk. I could not sit alone at home.

I could still write though. I wrote these poems across the street from my boyfriend's work, sitting in a fast food place. These are poems I wrote right before I went into the hospital:

1. *The Song of Screams*

Ghosts
This torn
piece of paper
looks like I
feel
the part that's
left is quite
ordinary
the right is
gone.
No reason
only half-
thoughts half-heard
unnoticed and
blowing away
but bound to the
spine though tattered
If you look at it
quickly enough it
almost looks whole
It might fool you
it's fooled me before
but only until I wanted
to write on the part no longer there
empty and shredded, illusory
substance—use from uselessness
agony shrieks hollowly from
what is left of my soul
I too can be crumpled up and thrown away
Dying, I feel I might just disappear
wordless

—1989 Moira Breen

2. Demons

I had a flashback this morning, an image of what was,
the screams I couldn't scream then
Dying in my throat, my body rigid, defiled
Heartbroken with betrayal, guilt and grief.
Can I ever go back knowing what they did to me so very long ago?

My mind is a broken record of pain and shame
Humiliation of incest, early defilement
Someone else's unwanted sweat
The filth in the soul that can never be cleansed
Except by blood—may I be spared.

My choice is triage—live a lie or leave my parents forever.
An unintentional tragic heroine
Spills her coffee as she leaves her body
Not for the last time.

I eat, drink, work and sleep in a bubble of numb oblivion
Sometimes the cure is worse than the disease,
my hand shakes and my breathing intensifies
as I struggle to write instead of to scream.

—1989 Moira Breen

3. Carnage

Again I sing my cheerful song
What can I control today
I'll sort the books, I'll file the files
Pretend that nothing's wrong

But then my bubble bursts
My illusion of contented control disappears
And I dissolve in tears
Confusion and helpless rage

But still I sort, still I file
Cheeks wet and makeup streaming
My friends wondering why I act so oddly
Strangely knowing better than I do that it's time for me to rest
Once in awhile I do

I tell myself "it's done, I'm better, I won't be there again"
I know I'm stable now, I haven't wanted to die
For at least a week—or was it yesterday?
And then a nightmare comes, a lonely scream.
If I wait to face the demon in my dreams, I face it alone.
My mother's in my bed again, I throw her off repulsed
And scream until my voice is gone and run and then
Awake with my beloved—that is you, thank God!
I feel your face for whiskers—can I be sure it's really you
And not that sickening monster who spawned me?

But where is my cheerful song now?
When do I get to control my life again?
When can I get back to life rather than being
the prisoner of my own racking sobs
When can I run away again?

—1989 Moira Breen

I had applied to Long Beach State and was awarded a double scholarship in harp and voice. The man who auditioned me for the opera program, Michael Carson, was very pleased with my talent and was intent on making sure I did well. He let me into the program two weeks after classes had begun. I still had pneumonia, but I could still sing. It was an enormous relief to be accepted back into school; perhaps my life was over but I could still do what I was supposed to do.

When we left, we had been forced to leave my concert harp behind since it would not fit in my car. My mother's accountant told me Lisa did not ever intend to return it to me but was going to learn to play it. Then Lisa tried to give it to Kristoph's wife Margaret, who refused to accept it. I asked Margaret to please detune it and to lock it in its case so that it would become too much trouble for Lisa to deal with.

I had never been so angry in my entire life. I had gone through an insane ordeal, and I had lost my home, my father, and my family. Now I was losing my harp too, and it was more than I could take. I remembered this passage from *Gurrelieder*, where King Waldemar screamed at God. It seemed to me that Lisa was also taking my only lamb, robbing me of the only thing I had left that meant anything to me:

Herrgott, weißt du, was du tatest, als klein Tove mir verstarb?
Triebst mich aus der letzten Freistatt, die ich meinem Glück erwarb!
Herr, du solltest wohl erröten: Bettlers einz'ges Lamm zu töten!
Herrgott, ich bin auch ein Herrscher, und es ist mein Herrscherglauben:
Meinem Untertanen darf ich nie die letzte Leuchte rauben.
Falsche Wege schlägst du ein: Das heißt wohl Tyrann, nicht Herrscher sein!

Lord God, do you know what you did when you killed my little Tove?
You drove me from the last place where I was happy.
Lord, you should blush! You killed a beggar's only lamb!
Lord, I am also a ruler, and this is what I know of ruling:
I never steal the last light from my subjects.
You are going down the wrong path: you are a tyrant, not a ruler!

—Waldemar, *Gurrelieder*, Arnold Schoenberg

Both Jonnie and I were working at Major Video, later Blockbuster Video. I could still work, but when nobody was in the store, I would curl up in the fetal position behind the desk. This was extremely embarrassing to me, even though nobody ever saw me do it. At this point, my therapist told me that if I would not let her put me in the hospital, she would commit me.

I talked to my boss and told him I needed to be in the hospital and why. He told me to go and get the help I needed and that he would gladly hire me back as soon as I was ready to come back.

Lisa's story about me making up my father's crimes had fallen to pieces after I left. Mary Mason saw Lisa at a convention and told her what my father had done to her son. She expressed relief that I had saved Kenny from any more abuse. In November of 1989, Mary Mason filed suit against my mother and Lisa for criminal negligence because they had told her that my father was safe while obviously knowing he was not.

At this point, Lisa knew she had been wrong about me and my father. To her credit, she decided to try to find me. She looked me up in phone books until she found me living in Anaheim. She told me that I was right about my father and she was sorry. She said that Mary Mason had called me a hero for saving her son and confirmed that what I had said about his molestation was true. She said she wanted to help me and asked me what I needed?

I told her I needed to be in the hospital. She agreed and used my father's money to put me into a small psychiatric hospital in Laguna Hills, CA. I was on the unlocked side because I came in voluntarily, and I was not regarded as a danger to myself.

There was counseling in the hospital, food at predictable times, and therapy groups. One of the first things they did for me was to bring a biofeedback machine into my room because I was in such utter terror so much of the time. The hope was that if I could learn to bring my own heart rate down, it might help me sleep.

Early on during my hospital stay, I had an assessment which was done on the locked side due to a shortage of rooms, to my utter terror. The people over there were very different than the people on the unlocked side; they seemed drugged, there was a lot of yelling, and I was very distressed to even be there for an assessment.

At the end of this very long assessment the doctor asked me, almost offhand-edly, what my father had done to me, knowing I had not been able to say a word about it. I blurted out "He raped me", and I ran out of the room, stumbling, crying, and clinging to the walls like an idiot. Still, this was the first time I had been able to say anything about it, so in a way it was a relief. The stumbling was ataxia: a poor or staggering gait, which was simply another symptom which showed up when I was having trouble with my flashbacks.

I sat in my room and cried and drew until Dr. Hirz came to see me for the first time. He was a psychiatrist, all tweed, silver hair, and silver eyes. I told him I was a real mess. He was very nice and kind to me even though my hair was wet with tears and looked like I hadn't brushed it in a month.

I had several issues which I barely understood. For me, self-care had become almost impossible. I couldn't bathe because the water terrified me so much, and the best I could do was to scrub myself while partially dressed with a wet washcloth. Nakedness terrified me. I couldn't eat because food overwhelmed me and made me panic. I dissociated, feeling like I was not in my body. It felt as though I did not have a body at all and this could become so severe that I would become catatonic. I could not figure out how to move.

I was diagnosed with Complex PTSD, severe panic disorder, and post-incest syndrome.

Quoting from the article at http://criminal-justice.iresearchnet.com/crime/domestic-violence/post-incest-syndrome/:

Love puts aside the parent's needs to attend to those of the child. Incest, however, is a supremely selfish act. Where love nourishes, incest takes. Incest creates emotional abandonment by sabotaging the caregiver role. To be violated by those who are supposed to love them best teaches children that they are not worth loving.

Unconditional love is given without strings. It teaches children that they are valued, with no expectations. Incest, however, teaches children that they must earn 'love.'

Nonpossessive love allows children to be their own persons, to own their own lives. Incest victims, however, learn that they are extensions of abusers. Even their bodies do not belong to them. This destroys victims' ability to develop physical or emotional boundaries (where one person ends and someone else begins). Survivors frequently do not understand that all relationships have boundaries, where those boundaries should be, or how to establish them. Incest teaches children to be victims. Powerlessness leads to 'learned helplessness'—paralysis, crippling passivity, and resignation.

The difference between PTSD and Complex PTSD is that one can get PTSD from one event, and it is very troublesome but curable. Complex PTSD appears in cases where there is torture, captivity, or imprisonment, long-term, repeated traumas, and often multiple perpetrators. It is much, much harder to cure, which annoys me greatly. I am accustomed to being able to solve my problems, and it infuriated me to learn I had an issue that I could not simply fix.

During our time working together, Dr. Hirz did things which I would never assume any psychiatrist would do for anyone. Every single time I saw him, he gave me something to eat. My issues with food were severe, and if I avoided eating for long enough, I would become hypoglycemic. His feeding me was a way of demonstrating that I deserved to be alive, even if my mother and father had not fed me carefully or frequently or well.

At the hospital, the doctors told me that the difference between me and those who are sicker than I am is that I have what is called an "observing ego." I can see myself from an outside perspective. I can recognize, as it were, when I am being an idiot, when I am not acting appropriately, and even when I am having symptoms. It is a relief to be able to distinguish between "The world is ending and I am dying" and "I'm having a panic attack."

As might be expected, Dr. Hirz tried me on every SSRI known to man. None worked, for reasons that are clearer now than they were then: PTSD tends to disrupt the dopamine systems more than the serotonin system.

Early on in my hospital stay I met another harpist, Rodney, who was in the room two doors down from mine. His mother showed and groomed dogs all over the country, and she offered to get my harp for me because she had a dog show in Northern CA. Since Lisa was now talking to me and obviously wanted my approval, I managed to persuade her that it was a good idea to give me back my harp. I do not know how I spoke to Lisa about this calmly. She had alternated between threats about learning to play my harp herself and give it to other people with stories about the insurance not allowing it to be moved, but it was obvious she had kept it from me because she wanted to.

Rodney's mother told me about her encounter with my father. She knocked on my father's door, and he answered wearing nothing but a towel. She told him she was there to pick up my harp. He said, "Oh dear..." shut the door, and was gone for several minutes. She knocked again, and he answered the door still wearing only a towel. Again, he said, "Oh dear..." and disappeared for several minutes. Once more, they repeated the same performance. Eventually, my father said okay, let her in, and showed her where the harp was. They brought it down to me in the hospital, and I kept it there with me in my room.

Then Lisa came to visit me. I was ambivalent and anxious about seeing her at all. I had been angrier with her for taking my harp than I had ever been about anything she had ever done to me, but I felt obligated to see her because she had made it so I could be in the hospital to begin with.

The visit was a disaster. Lisa told me that Mother had "molested" her too and that she was no longer sexually involved with her. I found it hard to accept that Lisa had been a victim since she had been 26 when she came to live with us. She also told me that the reason she didn't believe me when I turned my father in to the cops was that she couldn't believe my dad "would be stupid enough to do that again."

She knew he had done it before, and she had done nothing. Of course she knew. She knew because I had told her. She knew because she acted atrociously on that knowledge, not by calling the cops, but by giving my father a private place to stay.

Lisa mentioned the time my mother twisted the skin on the back of my hand with her fingernails and drew blood. Lisa demonstrated this on my hand, for what reason I cannot imagine. My doctors intervened and threw her out, forbidding her from ever returning to the hospital.

Mother had given up on me becoming the famous opera singer she wanted. I was now 23, and Tracey Dahl, the youngest girl ever to win the Merola opera contest in San Francisco, was also 23. Since I could not beat her, I would never be what Mother wanted. I decided I was going to become a professional harpist and play for weddings and parties.

I was in the hospital for ten days, and then I was in what they called "partial hospital" for a few months afterward. "Partial hospital" is where you live in your own home but come to the hospital during the day for therapy groups. Over time, seven days a week would be reduced to one and then none. While I was an inpatient, I had been given passes to attend my college classes, although I had had to reduce my schedule to 6 units that semester.

While I was still in partial hospital, I was beginning to go to SCA events. I met Velma Cameron, a Celtic harpist and singer. I introduced myself to her and told her I was a beginner. I asked her to listen to me and tell me if she thought I could begin performing. I played and sang for her, and she told me that not only was I not a beginner, I could be a professional performer right now.

I called a local tea shop and arranged for a performance. While I was there, a woman asked me to come and play at her home. I protested and said I only knew a few songs. She said she didn't care and hired me anyway. From that day forward, I had more harp work than I knew what to do with. When I was about to be discharged, the hospital hired me to perform an event there. I played Irish music for their reception on the concert harp, and I sang. My performances were very much like the music from Celtic Woman, except I played a concert harp.

Chapter 35

Prison for Him and Hell for Me
(1990–1993)

And whosoever shall offend one of these little ones that believe in me, it is better for him that a millstone were hanged about his neck, and he were cast into the sea.

— *The Holy Bible*, Mark 9:42 (NIV)

On April 23, 1990, after a long investigation, my father was finally arrested by the Berkeley Police for his crimes against Kenny. Very few people wanted to testify against him no matter how much they knew. Some loved him; some didn't want to rock the boat. For his male victims, talking about the specifics of what he had done to them was so excruciating as to be impossible. Many of the victims, including Sterling, denied everything until after my father was dead.

In May my mother divorced my father. Mother told me she still loved my father, and she did not want to divorce him at all. She told me she only divorced him because Lisa had insisted on it. She also told me that if she could have traveled alone, she would have gone to visit him in jail every single day. Lisa insisted on the divorce to prevent Mother from losing the house and half the profits from *Mists* in the civil lawsuits which came from his offense.

This is from Lisa's journals in her deposition:

MR. DOLAN: Look to 10/16/89. Do you see where you say, 'The divorce is going to make a lot of extra work, but it beats losing the house in a messy lawsuit.' At the end of the first second full paragraph?

ELISABETH WATERS: Yes.

To be perfectly fair, when Mother found out my father had molested yet another kid, she was furious and yelled and screamed, but she never indicated to me that she stayed angry with him for this, let alone that she was angry enough to divorce him.

MR. DOLAN: I'm going to read to you from the 10-9-89 entry of Elisabeth Waters:

'Marion always said she'd divorce Walter if he did this again. She seems to think that he molested both Glenn and Gregg, but she was rather startled when I told her about the letter to Dr. Morin about Sterling. She said that she thought Walter thought of Sterling as a son.'

MR. DOLAN: Did you undertake any activity to ensure that Walter Breen would not molest young boys at this property that you rented to him?

MZB: As I say, at the time Barry was there. I told him Barry was off limits, and I told him Gregg was off limits.

My mother knew what my father liked to do. She seemed to draw a line at the boys she liked, whereas my father preferred to fuse fathering and sex.

Walter felt no shame and no remorse over his acts:

ELISABETH WATERS: Okay. First, I asked him why his bank account was overdrawn, and he said he had written a check for $5,000 to hire a lawyer because Officer Harris wanted to talk to him, and at that point I began to really seriously believe he was guilty of the accusations made about his behavior with Kenny. A couple of days later I asked him if he really performed oral sex on Kenny, and he said, 'yes.' No, actually he asked me who told me, and I said Mary Mason did, and he said he didn't know she was talking about it, and I said, 'Well, she did to me.' So he didn't actually say, yes, but he didn't deny it. And then sometime later, I forgot how the subject originally came up, but I said, 'How could you do that to an 11 year old?' And Walter said, 'He was 12.'

MR. DOLAN: Anything else?

ELISABETH WATERS: You mean like his exact words?

MR. DOLAN: Correct.

ELISABETH WATERS: 'He was 12 and besides he wasn't a virgin.'

MR. DOLAN: Okay. Anything else that he said that you can recall in any of these three conversations regarding whether or not he actually molested Ken Smith?

ELISABETH WATERS: Well, he seemed to think that it didn't matter because Kenny didn't care about it and Mary didn't care about it; that it was okay because Kenny and Mary didn't object.

On June 8, 1990, in Alameda County Superior Court, my father pleaded guilty to one felony count of lewd and lascivious acts with a minor under the age of 14. This was not the crime I witnessed but a previous offense which he had committed against Kenny in Berkeley between August 6–12 in 1988. Sadly, my father had been molesting Kenny for some time.

After he was arrested I told my mother that my father had raped me. I took a chance, considering her response the last time I had tried to tell her about anything like that, and I regretted it even as the words were coming out of my mouth. To my surprise and relief, my mother was angry with him, not me. She told me she had been out of town on the weekend of my father's birthday when I was five years old. I think she remembered how much it hurt when her own father had raped her. She told me later that she had hoped he would leave me alone since he preferred boys.

She confronted him immediately, bursting into the room where he was having a massage and yelling at him about having raped me. My father denied her accusations. She said, "Shall I believe someone who has never lied to me or someone who has never told me the truth?" Marion later told me that she reminded Walter that he didn't remember much of that time period, and he finally agreed with her. For some reason, that restored peace between them. She wasn't concerned about what he had done to me, only about the fact that she was right and he was wrong.

My father's denial puzzled me since he was generally truthful in his fashion. The only thing I can conclude is that he expressed again and again that he never seduced or raped anyone, but the children always seduced *him*. So maybe, in his imagination, I had done the same thing.

At the age of five.

After all, Lisa did not ask my father if he had raped Kenny. She only asked if he had performed oral sex on him. Maybe if Mother had rephrased her accusation as a clear statement of physical actions, my father would have cheerfully admitted it. In any event, I never went to the cops. It was enough that my mother knew.

On October 17, 1990, Mary Mason, Kenny's mother, filed a civil complaint against my father, asking for $500,000 in exemplary and punitive damages. Mary Mason claimed that the molestation began in April of 1986 when Kenny was 9 and that there were six separate episodes.

My father was sentenced to three years of probation on November 30, 1990.

Three years of probation for six life-destroying episodes of sex with a little child. Three years. Sadly, at that point the law saw my father as a first offender. Back then there was no Internet, and the investigation was limited to our local area. Among the six Johnny Does identified as victims, nobody wanted to testify no matter how bad their injuries were.

But my father's legal difficulties were only beginning. Kenny was not his only victim, but the only one who had talked up to that point.

I am going to use pseudonyms in referring to the next victim. I am in touch with him, and he does not want his name publicized. He already went through too much, and he does not need to have his privacy violated. For the purposes of this book, my father's next victim will be referred to as Jack Smith, and his father will be called John Smith.

My father had stayed as a house guest at the house of John Smith and Jack Smith for several coin conventions in Southern California over a period of several years. One day, John Smith mentioned my father to a friend since my father was a huge celebrity in coin-collecting circles. John Smith's friend had heard about my father's arrest. He reacted with horror and said, "You mean Walter Breen, the *child molester?*" John Smith went to talk to Jack Smith, now twelve. He told his father what my father had done to him, starting at the age of seven. Jack Smith was now twelve.

John Smith wasted no time and called the police. He filed a criminal complaint against my father, who was charged with eight felony counts of lewd and lascivious acts with a minor under the age of 14. My father faced six years of prison per count plus fines for a possible 48-year prison sentence. He was arrested on September 24, 1991, at Superior Stamp and Coin Galleries in Beverly Hills and brought to the Los Angeles County Jail. He was never released after that.

On September 26, 1991, my father was arraigned in Los Angeles County and pleaded not guilty. On the same day, Alameda County revoked my father's probation and issued a "no bail" bench warrant. If Los Angeles County ever released him, Alameda County would pick him up immediately and hold him without bail. Alameda and Los Angeles agreed to hold him without bail at the Los Angeles County Jail and to transfer him to Alameda County when it was time for him to appear in court there for his probation violation.

On October 28, 1991, my father pleaded not guilty to all charges at a preliminary hearing in Los Angeles Municipal Court. Detective David Berglund testified that my father met Jack Smith in the fall of 1986 while waiting for the same plane flight. The complaint stated that my father molested Jack Smith at his father's house in West Los Angeles from June of 1987 to January 1991. Most of the dates of my father's overnight visits coincided with the Long Beach

Numismatic, Philatelic and Baseball Card Exposition, held three times annually. My father was bound over for trial in Santa Monica Superior Court and held in lieu of $200,000 bond.

The Los Angeles police undertook a thorough investigation of my father's criminal background, and the prosecutor put together an ironclad case against him. Not only did they have all the details of his 1990 arrest and felony conviction, but they dug up his 1954 arrest in Atlantic City. This destroyed the notion that he had been a "first offender." It was obvious that my father was a habitual offender. In fact, my father's probation officer had regarded him as having a 100% chance of recidivism.

The police contacted me as part of the investigation and asked me to decipher some portions of my father's journals. My father, if you recall, had written down his every thought at the instruction of Dr. Morin, and he had hundreds of little spiral-bound books full of incriminating things. Naturally, my father had instructed me and my brother to burn his journals if he was ever arrested.

I realized much later that I had been my father's only confidant about his sexual activities other than Dr. Morin. That was why my brother Patrick had denied any wrongdoing on my father's part, and asking him to testify did no good: Patrick simply did not know.

The journals were written in calligraphic script, often with a heliotrope (pinkypurple) chisel-point pen. From long experience, I could read my father's appalling handwriting. I spoke as much "Walterese" as anyone else alive, and I could decipher his abbreviations and codes. For example, "M" was my mother. "M" followed by a treble clef (a musical symbol) indicated me.

I was saddened to see the things he wrote about me. I was a worthless piece of garbage who had been locked in a looney bin. He never knew me, he didn't love me, he should never have trusted me, and he would never forgive me. Yeah. I got it. I'm evil. Big surprise, and I can cry later.

I was baffled by the things he said about his long-term boy-lover Gregg. My father said, with absolute rage, that Gregg had turned against him. Worse, Gregg now perceived himself as a child victim rather than a willing lover. My father was outraged at Gregg's "betrayal."

After all, how dare the Thanksgiving turkey protest the carving knife?

I was also relieved, if saddened. I had tried to intervene on Gregg's behalf ten years before but had gotten nowhere. Now Gregg was finally old enough to stand up for himself and apparently no longer cared that my father would be mad at him, which was the whip keeping the rest of us in line.

Gregg's repudiation of my father made perfect sense to me. I know it might seem weird that Gregg would keep returning, but my father didn't beat Gregg like his mother did. Ongoing sexual abuse must have seemed more bearable than beatings with electrical cords. Once Gregg was an adult, that comparison became irrelevant. Gregg got rid of both Tweedledum and Tweedledee, both the batterer and the rapist.

On November 27, 1991, my father pleaded innocent to all charges.

On Christmas Eve, December 24, 1991, my father was transferred to the hospital wing of the Santa Rita Jail in Oakland for a hearing on his Alameda County probation violation. It never took place, though. My father was too ill to participate, and the hearing was rescheduled for July 14, 1992.

He had been sick for a long time. Our family masseuse, Dr. Jane Robinson (now James Robinson), had asked my father repeatedly to seek emergency medical help for an obvious huge growth in his abdomen. My father had absolutely refused, which made members of my family suspect that he was committing a form of suicide. After all, a fast-growing mass was not likely to be anything other than cancer. Once my father had been arrested, he was given no choice about his medical care.

On March 17, 1992, at Highland Hospital in Oakland, my father had a grapefruit-sized malignant tumor removed from his abdomen. The seven-hour surgery also took half his colon and several feet of his small intestines. He had metastases all over his internal organs, and the diagnosis was Stage 4 liver cancer, terminal and inoperable.

My brother was interviewed by a coin magazine on March 23. He told them about my father's cancer and that the family would be meeting with the doctors to decide on the next step, whether chemotherapy, radiation, or nothing. My father wrote to *Numismatic News* on March 25, 1992, confirming the cancer and stating he had first noticed the lump in December.

My father was confined to a wheelchair for the rest of his life after his surgery. He continued to work on several writing projects until his death, including a revision of his *Complete Encyclopedia of U.S. and Colonial Coins.*

On July 14, 1992, while being held in a prison infirmary in Dublin, CA, my father was sentenced to three years in prison for his probation violation in Alameda County. Then he was returned to the Los Angeles County Jail for a pretrial hearing at the Santa Monica Superior Court on August 3, 1992, where he changed his plea to No Contest. On December 15, he was sentenced to ten years in prison for the eight felony counts of lewd and lascivious acts with a minor under the age of 14.

His book *Greek Love* had come up during one of the hearings, and he had reportedly tried hard to convince the judge that what he had done to his victims was right and that the laws should reflect that. The judge did not agree and sentenced my father to a total of thirteen years in San Quentin. The judge noted his total lack of remorse and concern for the victims and determined that he was too dangerous to even be allowed into a hospice to die. Even though he was terminally ill, wheelchair bound, and almost blind from cataracts, the judge believed, correctly, that he would reoffend from his hospital bed.

My father was in the Los Angeles County Jail when he was sentenced. He was then scheduled to be transferred to San Quentin and was placed in the custody of the California Department of Corrections.

When the American Numismatic Association found out about my father's crimes, the Board of Governors expelled him from membership in the association. My father had been regarded as one of the most famous researchers and authors in the field of numismatics for more than 40 years. He wrote over twenty books and hundreds of numismatic articles.

Before he died, he wrote two poems about his cancer. I will leave it up to you to judge their literary merit. Their relationship to his life and his crimes is clear: he thinks he has nothing to regret.

Cancer

In silent stealth unseen invaders spread
unplanning through each niche and convolution
digging in to eat and multiply
uncaring that they kill the hosts that feed them,
until no death rays nor pollutant poisons
can stop these armies, and their reign of terror.
Usurping the gift of immortality,
they only perish when their host world dies.

Paradox

Dear God,
I'm not afraid of you—
only of those who claim to speak for you.

I'm not afraid of death—
only of those who act out "Don't die, suffer!"
I'm not afraid of hell—
only of its too-earthly imitations.
When a book that claims to show your words
says that wisdom begins by fearing you,
why do I not fear you?
Because, dear God, you know in full already
what I am inside—
unlike those who claim to act for you.

My father died on April 27, 1993, in the prison hospital at Chino Penitentiary. He did not survive long enough to be transferred to San Quentin.

Chapter 36

An Opera and a Funeral
(1991–1993)

My father was a child molester
His daughter was the lone protester
She's long since fled
He's jailed, now dead
And now she weeps and plays the jester.

—Moira Greyland

While I was in the hospital, I was living in an apartment in El Toro by myself. I was such a mess of fears that it was impossible for me to turn off the lights at night and any sound sent me into panic. I was doing some work as an extra in a few movies, which meant I met more people, including handsome men, and ran into more of my own propensity for stupid conduct. I decided to get a boyfriend. I realized that I was incapable of living alone, and if I persisted, I would probably end up having endless one night stands to stave off my terror and insomnia.

I chose poorly. I chose a highly intellectual harpist, who ended up being—guess what?—another sex addict. He wanted me to dress a certain way, very sexy with high, high heels and red lipstick. He believed, as some fetishists do, that women become sexually aroused from wearing high heels. I told him he would do better offering to rub the feet of women wearing high heels because they hurt. Naturally, he could not endure this at all and angrily denied that this was even a possibility.

The problem with fetishism is that the other person does not exist. To him, I was not a woman but a prop: a mannequin or dressmaker's dummy meant to look a certain way. I didn't matter. My shoes mattered: five-inch stiletto heels. My lipstick mattered: bright red. At the heart what mattered to him was his fantasy, and I didn't think there was any reason for me to be involved. Eventually, I left the shoes and the lipstick on the bed and told him to leave me out of it.

No doubt he would find much to be angry about with me and less to forgive me for.

Of course, that is not the whole story. I was a rotten girlfriend. I fell in love with another man, and naturally my liberal background did not instruct me in how very much men hate it when their girlfriends want two boyfriends. After all, polyamory and consent... but he didn't consent, so I had to leave one—or both. So I left both.

To be fair, I had no business trying to be in a relationship with one man, let alone two. What I really needed was a babysitter, not a boyfriend. I was consumed by my pain and tormented by flashbacks and was only out of the hospital because I was stable enough to care for myself, not because I was all better.

Michael, the man I loved, had brought me to visit his parents, Richard and Maryellen Bancroft, and they remained in my life for the next few decades. I called them Mom and Dad, and I lay my continued health and sanity at their feet. God bless them both, my guardian angels. They lived on a ranch in Riverside with fifty elderly horses and a flock of chickens and one of guinea hens and a few ducks.

Richard wrote unpublished science fiction, modeling his favorite heroine, Lady Barbara, on me. It is from him that I learned that men can love women as daughters with their clothes on. I made him a pecan pie, and he wrote me a poem. He had been an electrical physicist, and he had fought in Korea. He was aghast at the things my parents had been up to, and we would talk for hours and hours.

Maryellen cooked and taught me things. She was relentlessly cheerful and worked all the time. She was still running irrigation and feeding the horses into her eighties. I say of her: "Maryellen doesn't say 'I love you.' Maryellen holds you when you vomit." And she did. She nursed me through a bout of rubella, and I can't tell you how many flashbacks. She showed me decisively that love is what you do, not what you say. She had a fantastic sense of humor, though utterly without pretense or silliness. We would laugh and laugh... She met my mother on one occasion, and she certainly made an impression! She helped me learn to laugh at a lot of things which certainly are better laughed at than taken seriously.

Even though I was a complete wash as a girlfriend, professionally, I hit my stride. I got hired to play twice a week in a restaurant in Costa Mesa: Mother's

Market. My employers noticed that people would sit there holding hands and not eating by the hour when I sang, so they decided to have me only playing the harp. This meant I needed to learn two hours of instrumental harp music very quickly, and within two weeks I did. I began to get hired at other venues, and I became an established professional harpist in Southern CA.

Meanwhile I was trying to mend fences with my family, no matter how stupid that sounds. I wrote to my father in prison before he died and offered to visit him. He wrote back to me and told me he prayed I would return to sanity and realize the harm I had done to my family. He told me not to come if I was going to moralize at him. In utter fury, I wrote back and told him that I would never see him again. And I did not.

Yes, the harm *I* had done to my family, as though molesting children was the most natural thing in the world! Hoped I would return to sanity and repent… putting a felon in prison for destroying the life of not one but many children? Was I wrong for refusing to see him? Maybe. What could I possibly have accomplished by seeing him? Would he forgive me and love me again? No. Not even if I gave in and agreed with his ideas, which I would never do. Would I persuade him that he had harmed the batch of us? No. He staked his life on his Grand Vision, and he was not about to give it up for me.

I transferred to the University of Redlands and continued studying harp and voice. My teacher, Patricia Gee, was a delight. She gave me Mozart concert arias and had me accompany her on the harp when she sang. I had arrived on campus knowing nobody, and I auditioned for and got the lead in the school opera, *The Merry Wives of Windsor*. The performance took place in April of 1993. The show was amazing, and the papers called me "Outstanding!"

Then everything went back to Hell. Right before the first rehearsal of Beethoven's Ninth, I got a message from my mother telling me to call back right away. She said it was about my father.

I felt my blood chill. I knew he was dead, even before I called her back.

When I called, I told Marion I needed to make this a very short phone call because I had to get to rehearsal. She told me it could wait. I told her no, not even if it was about my father dying it couldn't wait. She sputtered and said it was just a rumor, and she didn't know for sure, and Richard Kihlstadius was probably wrong. I got off the phone, feeling devastated and in shock, and went to rehearsal. I told the director that my father had died and that there was no way I could do the show.

That night, I dreamed I saw my father. I was sitting behind a black desk in an office with a window, and he was walking across the hallway in front of me. I saw him through the window. He was wearing one of his rainbow shirts, and he was transfigured with heavenly light. I asked him if he was okay, and he said yes. I asked him if he was dead, and he said he was. He told me he had to see Yeshua. Suddenly, I woke up, crying, but feeling at peace.

My feelings of peace did not last. Later that morning, my mother confirmed his death. I went to Northern CA for his funeral. I was very apprehensive and expected either shunning or a lynch mob. There were two services: one at St. Mark's Episcopal in a little chapel and one at Greyhaven. At the service at St. Mark's, I borrowed Margaret's Celtic harp, and I sang *"Starry Starry Night"* for him. To me, it fit both because of his artistic nature and because I was convinced that he had committed suicide by ignoring his cancer. I never sang it again.

Later I wrote this:

Don't touch me 'cause I'm not alive
I'm not in a body, I'm not really here
If I lie still enough I can get to that other place.
But you keep disturbing me and saying "wake up! Wake up!"

And my tears have run to the back of my neck.
I don't want to wake up. Ever.

I'm trying to find my Father, have you seen him?

See, we had a fight and he left before we could make up.
He's six feet tall with a halo of grey hair
Looks like Santa—Wait—Don't say that to me!
Don't say that he's a pile of scattered ashes and bits of bone.

I mean my Father! You can't tell me that anyone
Would throw him on the fire and roast him like a Christmas goose!
I mean Walter, my Father! If I look hard enough I'm sure to find him.

He's just over the center divider, in the center of the noose,
Over the cliff and behind the Valium,
Under the razor and in front of the trigger.
Please don't let me find him.

—2003 Moira Stern

After the service, the celebrant introduced me as one of the bereaved and treated me like a human being, which surprised me. My father had died without forgiving me. I had been disinherited, of course, and I was aware that my brother blamed me for his death. I was surprised at civility from anyone, let alone kindness and respect.

The second service, at Greyhaven, was presided over by my uncle Paul. We passed the French bread and chocolate around the circle, celebrating my father's life with the things he liked to eat.

Everyone was invited to talk about him, one by one, but both my mother and I were silenced by Paul's booming voice, "We are to remember *only* the good!"

Short list, that. Everyone talked about how brilliant he was. My uncle Don noted that my father had the gift of making people feel special. We do not need to notice what a poison pill that was in the seduction of his young victims. Gifted young people want above all to talk to intelligent people who will understand them; my father used this to notch his proverbial bedpost.

Professor Nathan Hellerstein, a friend of my father's, told me that Patrick had had my father cremated. He and my brother scattered his ashes in Mendocino County, not wanting me there. I was heartbroken over his death and hurt even more that now there was no place I could go to visit him. Maybe that seems ridiculous, but it is how I felt.

My friend Jean told me that some awful things had happened to my father while he was incarcerated. The other inmates hung a sign on his wheelchair saying "Chester the Molester" and beat him savagely. The next year, an ambulance driver told me he had transported my father and had beaten him up in the ambulance for what he had done to kids. Walter had been placed in the general population even though the judge knew what the other prisoners would do to a child predator. She also told me that my father had forgiven me at the end over my brother Patrick's nearly hysterical objections.

I asked to be made co-executor of my father's will. The court granted my request, puzzled that I had been disinherited, and viewed me and my brother as equals in the eyes of the law.

I asked for only three things. I asked for two books: *The Lives of a Cell* by Lewis Thomas and *The Annotated Alice* by Lewis Carroll, which my father and I had further annotated when I played Alice In Wonderland. I also asked for my strobe harp tuner, which I had left at his house by mistake when I moved out. He had refused to give my tuner back to me while he was still alive.

I gladly signed off on the rest of the estate. I had no interest in my father's money. Patrick got half, and Kenny got the other half. I doubt that any amount of money could ever compensate Kenny for what he had gone through, but I was glad he had something, and I was not about to interfere.

I had to finish college after the funeral. I had taken eleven units of incompletes, and I had to take twenty-two units to graduate. I auditioned for both Yum Yum and Katisha in the opera production, and I was told that although I had done the strongest audition for either role in the whole process, they were not going to cast me because I had been the star of the last show, and someone else needed to have a turn.

I thought that was fair enough. Besides, I had a project due: I had to produce an opera myself. I chose *The Impresario* by Mozart, and I sang a huffy, hysterical diva: Madame Goldentrill. The part is known for outrageously high notes: several high F's (F above high C). I *loved* producing the show, and I certainly did a lot of opera production after I left college.

I didn't get along with my harp teacher at Redlands. Her philosophy was that the harp was to be used to uplift, never to entertain, and I was already a very busy professional harpist. When I did concerts, I was a silly, fun, talkative performer, and my audiences loved me. My harp teacher called me a "cheap showman." I told her no; I was a very expensive showman, but it hurt. She declined to let me perform at her house-classes where her beginners were performing, saying, "I know what *you* can do." I even sent her all my surplus harp jobs since I had more work than I knew what to do with. She was displeased and told me I should not market myself so much, and I should leave my success up to God and not try so hard. After that, I decided not to continue studying with her. My audiences loved me, and I had such fun performing; I was not about to change my style of performance.

I determined that a harp degree would not magically make me into a harpist. I was already a harpist, and the piece of paper would only be paper. Nobody who has hired me to perform or teach harp has ever given a fig whether I had a harp degree. They only cared that I could play or that I could make them play better and that I could make their hands quit hurting. On the other hand, the vocal degree was something I needed to help me stand out among the zillions of other voice teachers, and the material I was learning would only make me a better singer.

I had to return some months later to sing my senior recital. I chose Poulenc's *Les Fiancailles Pour Rire* (*Laughable Betrothals*) and dedicated one song to my father. I did not expect anyone to understand. It was enough that I understood since I was only singing it for him.

Je ne peut plus rien dire, ni rien faire pour lui.
Il est mort de sa belle, il est mort de sa mort belle
Dehors, sous l'arbre de la Loi.
En plein silence, en plein paysage, dans l'herbe
Il est mort inapercu, en criant son passage
En appelent, en m'appelent
Mais comme j'etait loin de lui E que sa voix ne portait plus
Il est mort seul dans les bois Sous son arbre d'enfance
Et je ne peut plus rien dire. Ni rien faire pour lui

I cannot say anything, nor do anything for him.
He died quietly, he died his beautiful death
Outside, under the tree of the Law.
In total silence, in open country, in the grass.
He died unnoticed, crying out as he died.
Calling out, calling for me
But because I was far from him and his voice no longer carried
He died alone in the woods, beneath the tree of his infancy
And I cannot say anything more, nor do anything for him.

—"Dans l'herbe (In the grass)" *Les Fiancailles pour rire*,
Francis Poulenc, lyrics by Louise de Vilmorin

Chapter 37

The House of the Rising Sun
(1994)

There is a house down in New Orleans they call the rising sun
And it's been the ruin of many a poor girl and me, oh God, I'm one

—The Animals, "The House of the Rising Sun", *The Animals* (1964)

Mother gave me a lavish graduation present. She bought me a house in the El Sobrante Hills, and I was expected to come back to Northern CA after graduation. She also bought my brother a house, a huge duplex across the street from the Goldfish Bowl. I kept the picture of my new house on the refrigerator and looked at it every day. I had a massive amount of work to do, between the incompletes and my classes, and I wrote and went to class all day, every day. I graduated, scheduling my senior recital after my graduation. I moved into the new house and began setting up auditions with opera companies.

Then Lisa dropped a bomb on me: She presented me with an amortization table, asking me to give her $2,500.00 per month for the house. She ignored the fact that Mother had bought the house for me as a graduation present and insisted that Mother could not do any such thing. I had to get her a huge pile of money and fast.

I ended up doing something I never thought in my whole life that I would do. I went to work as a dominatrix in a place I will call "The House of the Rising Sun." It was fast, it was reliable, and it was disgusting. "Dominatrix" is interchangeable with "dominant", "dom", or "mistress". Many of us who worked as doms also had to "switch" or work as "subs", or "submissives". Dominants and submissives collectively practice what is known as BDSM, or Bondage & Discipline and Sado-Masochism. The BDSM community is often called "The Scene."

In my job, I met adult babies who wanted to wear diapers, people who wanted to be spanked or dress up in women's clothing, and many other things that I will not discuss. We did not offer sex or allow any intimate contact at all. This was specifically for people who were turned on by pain or humiliation, and we provided only the pain and the humiliation.

It was probably the strangest few months of my life.

Any place where people practice BDSM can be called a "dungeon" with the lighthearted, mostly joking idea that people will be chained to cold stone walls and subjected to the sort of medieval imagery found in Robin Hood movies. Some people will even fix up their houses to reflect some portion of this, but the House was far more suburban, at least when I was there. Our rooms looked like normal rooms but with eyebolts for shackles at odd points on the bed, boxes full of "toys" which ranged from feather dusters to... well, I would like to say entire chickens, but that would not be entirely accurate.

We had a lot of rules meant to establish our physical safety. The most important rule for anyone involved in BDSM is to have and agree on a safe-word. A safe-word is a code word which means "STOP." Some people use "Yellow" for "SLOW DOWN" and "Red" for "STOP."

Many people in powerful professions and positions of leadership would end up sexually submissive. Judges, doctors, policemen, and presidents of major corporations were among the typical submissives we would see in our work. On the job, they would make literal life-and-death decisions. In their fantasy lives, they finally didn't have to be in charge.

As one might imagine, there was a great deal of pathology, not only in the beaters but in the beatees. Some were harmless and hardwired for bondage but had no drive to escalate anything to a pathological level. Others were criminal and terrifying, and we might expect to see a few of them on *Forensic Files* or *Law and Order* one day. Naturally, the submissives, whether clients or professionals, would have a history of heinous abuse of one sort or another. Every single professional dom or sub I ever met had been sexually abused. Every single one.

A lot of funny business went on at the House. If a man came to the House and tied up a submissive and then raped her, he might be barred from the House or merely barred from seeing the girl he had assaulted. The policy was to never call the police for anything, and this was the eventual cause of my departure. I was aware of a few incidents which caused a lot of harm, but nothing was done. It is unthinkable to tolerate crimes so that a place of business can be protected.

Most of the professional doms and subs working at the House were "lifestylers", people who personally enjoyed BSDM and practiced it in their own private lives. Men who were happy to be "houseboys" would hang around the house, doing housework for the privilege of being near the dominant mistresses. Usually, a lifestyler would begin as a client and then gradually become more and more involved in The Scene through making friends with a dom or two. I made friends with the lifestylers who hung around the House, and they eventually invited me to "play parties". A "play party" is a party where people get together to talk, hang out, and chain each other up. People do not usually have sex at play parties, partly because it is almost universally the rule and partly because sex is not really the point of BDSM. Going to play parties might give someone the idea that lifestylers never had sex at all, even though I am certain they did. I appreciated the small nod to modesty, though.

As a lifestyler, I was a wash. I played the role of the dominatrix, but not especially well. I found the whole thing very difficult to take seriously, and I found nothing about being in charge even remotely erotic. It was simply a normal part of my life which reflected the lack of good leaders in my family.

I made friends with other lifestylers and learned a lot about how people get twisted the way they do. I met a very nice man and dated him for some time. I learned a lot about how people would get started in kink. Everyone remembered their triggering episode. Almost invariably, the first time that bondage, or shoes, or spanking became eroticized for them, they were children.

One man who spent a lot of time around the House was the sub of one of the leading dominatrixes there. She routinely beat him and subjected him to terrible humiliations, even demonstrating this to neophytes. He told me privately that he was accustomed to tolerating a lot of pain. His father had thrown him through the wall on more than one occasion and given him multiple broken bones. He confided in me that he was not really interested in BDSM at all but didn't want to upset the woman he was dating. He ended up marrying someone outside The Scene, or what we would call a "vanilla" woman. Was he denying his true nature? I doubt it. He simply went in another direction, and I admire his insight.

One place that lifestylers would meet and "play", aside from "play parties", was Bondage-A-Go-Go at the Trocadero Transfer in San Francisco. This was an event on Wednesday nights, roped off from the rest of the venue, and we would come in costume, wearing leather, fishnets, and a host of other odd things. We would put on exhibitions of whipping, bondage, and so forth.

One thing I witnessed, not once but many times, was a girl who came to Bondage-A-Go-Go, probably ninety pounds dripping wet. She chose to be tied up and whipped to blood and bruises not once but repeatedly by a seven-foot-tall transvestite. The master of the "dungeon" eventually threw her out because he was afraid that she would die. She had been whipped unconscious more than once, and naturally there were judgments about her mental state. Nobody had the slightest concern about the whipper, though, just the whippee. Why was she the crazy one? She consented. They both consented.

She could have died.

What did her "consent" to being beaten unconscious mean? Is this merely a "preference" that we should "respect" and "celebrate"? If she died, would we be expected to "celebrate" that as well? Must her desire for this practice be regarded as more important than her life? The parallels to anorexia and any other life-threatening lifestyle are obvious.

It occurred to me that consent does not work as an arbiter of morality. Consent does not take about three hundred things into account, and it cannot.

A notion I call the "Doctrine of Consent" is common to all nontraditional sexual communities which I have personally encountered. The Doctrine of Consent claims that anything you want to do to another person is just fine provided everyone consents.

This is, as one might imagine, an idea which dovetails with the "Witches Rede": *An it harm none, do as ye will.* It sure sounds good, doesn't it? So much better than all those rigid rules found in religion which only exist to limit people's sexual expression, right?

The good part of BDSM relationships is the focus on negotiation and bringing hidden relationship dynamics into the open. The bad part of BDSM relationships is that the "doctrine of consent" is a bunch of hooey, and relationships based on it can be both pathological and dangerous.

Here is the trouble: consent is a funny thing. Although most decent human beings will acknowledge that children cannot legally consent to sex, many adults give consent under less than free circumstances.

The fact is that many people, myself included, cannot set appropriate limits—especially with people who have committed prior bad acts. If we have a history of enduring violation of one sort or another, our "no" might be broken. This is not only common to abuse victims but other adults.

In many group or "open" relationships, the man wants another woman. His original partner is manipulated into accepting that her jealousy is "immature." She consents because her husband has tacitly let her know that he will reject her unless she lets him have sex with another woman whether she is brought into it or not. Does her consent mean she genuinely wants this to happen or that she simply does not have a choice?

Her approval from her partner is now contingent on her going along with his "open-mindedness."

What about the BDSM relationship where one person wants something but the other person is not sure? To what degree is there consent, and to what degree are people going along with manipulation, pressure, and even tacit emotional coercion? The threat of abandonment is a powerful thing.

Arguably, my father's victim Gregg could have legally given consent to my father raping him once he turned 18, and he only withdrew his consent and repudiated him when he was 23. Was every single episode of sexual abuse coerced or only the ones before the day Gregg turned 18? Or had Gregg merely become so accustomed to tolerating rape that he did not see any other options for himself?

Eventually, I realized that my anger and other people's desire to be hurt did not make it okay for me to strike them. It did not matter how much they wanted pain. Their consent could not make my actions acceptable. We don't hit people. I don't hit people. It is wrong.

The end of my participation with BDSM was when I realized that the "doctrine of consent" was baloney. The fact that someone gives me permission to hit them does not make it okay for me to do so.

I found it nearly impossible to take anything about the dynamics of BDSM seriously. When I thought of dominant women and submissive men, I imagined a roomful of little boys desperately trying to please their mothers, and a roomful of damaged women treating their sons disgracefully. When I thought of dominant men and submissive women, I saw insecure, violent men whose ordinary dominance in their outside relationships was not enough to make them happy.

If we are to regard BDSM as healthy or normal and that acting out these fantasies would help us to understand ourselves, then the next chapter should be healing of some sort. I didn't see healing taking place.

If we view BDSM as psychodrama, meant to reenact a psychological trauma with the goal of mastering it, we might expect growth, insight, increased personal understanding, and personal transformation. Instead, what we see is what amounts to a repetition compulsion being turned into a personal ritual, where a trauma one might not even remember fully is eroticized. In such a ritual, the trauma is not integrated, the injury is not understood, and the psychological genesis of the trauma is not rejected, but rather reenacted. Instead of discovering that a beating made you eroticize violence, or hot water, or shackles, and then deciding to walk away from the things which had been done to us, we simply were meant to accept that we would be aroused through bad acts and allow this arousal to dominate our lives as though no other arousal would ever mean anything.

The thing which interested me was the backstory—the *actual* need. In the case of the typical submissive male fantasy, he goes through some sort of physical torment at the end of which time, either the woman standing in for "Mommy" will give him affection or be pleased with his compliance, or if he is twisted too far to even dream of that, he will have the "privilege" of licking her boots.

What I wanted to know was this: was there ever a way out? Could "Mommy" ever be pleased to the degree that the abasement was no longer needed? Would this ever deescalate instead of escalating? Could the tormented child ever become an adult with neither the need to please a person who was willing to hurt him nor the willingness to hurt anyone else?

What about the fantasies, which seem harmless but represent non-harmless things, and often escalate?

Imagine a submissive male. His fantasy is to be dominated by a 50-foot tall woman whom he calls a "goddess." He has rehearsed this fantasy to the point that he is incapable of arousal without it. He imagines himself as a tiny little man only a few inches tall. The "goddess" will not only dominate him but literally crush him underfoot. Strawberries crushed under her twisting high heeled shoe will help him visualize the spurting blood and complete his excitement.

The "goddess" in his fantasy is sexually turned on by committing murder, and he can only please her by dying. I invite those of you who have a particularly strong stomach to look up "crush" and ask yourself whether the mice can consent.

Over time, I observed that female dominants were invariably angry. The complaints would always be the same. Sure, the dominant woman wanted to be strong and in charge, but she didn't want her partner to be an irresponsible twit. She would find the parallels between her situation and that of a mother and son to be vile and infuriating.

On the flip side, male dominants were invariably insecure. It is very easy for a strong man to find an ordinary woman to date, and the way men and women typically operate already puts him in charge. If he is incapable of taking charge and gets mixed up with dominant women, he might be angry and frustrated while not knowing a way to make a different relationship.

But this is not the same as a man who eroticizes being dominated, or worse, eroticizes injury to another person. If a man needs to humiliate women or subject them to violence and pain, he is not strong. He is dangerous.

The worst of that lot I ever met was a man who claimed he had been a prison guard. He wanted to put me in handcuffs and interrogate me. My arms are long, so I brought my hands to the front, which annoyed him a lot. He was cold as ice. The thought that a former prison guard would be turned on by humiliating and terrorizing a female "prisoner" disgusted and appalled me. I refused to ever see him again, of course.

What about the guy who wanted a girl who looked like a preteen and wanted her to wear a Catholic school uniform? Is seeing a professional an alternative to acting out on a pedophilic impulse, or is it simply going to strengthen the fantasy? Are we to conclude that men with dangerous fantasies must take them out with professionals rather than becoming offenders?

We do not lose our impulses by acting them out. We strengthen them.

What is a man really looking for in a strong woman? Maybe he is a strong man who wants a strong partner, or this is the most common idea.

Among most of the men who sought me out for my strength, they wanted me to do what they did not want to do. Either they wanted to abdicate the traditional masculine role or to feel like a child again. Some men see sex as entertainment, and the strong woman he seeks will care for herself and pretend to need nothing from him. Certainly, a strong woman will never trouble a man by having children.

But this model does not work for women no matter how strong we are. These role reversals negate any possibility of "happily ever after", and no amount of strength will ever destroy all our dreams. Role reversals do not lead to the happiness they promise, and they often do not even lead to anything resembling mutual respect.

I remember walking into Bondage-A-Go-Go at the Trocadero Transfer in San Francisco and seeing a woman dressed in red. She informed me that she was a dominant goddess and that men worshiped her. "How boring," I thought to myself. After all, if women are so superior, why on earth would we pad about in uncomfortable leather and stiletto heels? Why would we not be devoting ourselves to bettering whatever it was that made us so superior in the first place? And even more specifically, exactly what would make a woman superior, and in what way? One might as well say that a cat is superior to a dog. They are different.

It is more likely that this "superiority" routine comes from feelings of inferiority. We can never truly control anyone, and any sense of fear and insecurity can make that lack of control seem almost unbearable. BDSM slaps a veneer of pretend-control over the reality of no actual control at all. Perhaps the silly notion of "I am superior" would avoid any dates with any man who would refuse to go along with such an absurd routine while making an easy path for men who were at least willing to appear to be controllable.

Women rarely realize that men are a whole lot smarter than we think they are, and they are more than willing to go to considerable lengths to get us to go along with what they want. Men are used to having to deal with the irrational antics of women. Pretending to be submissive to get laid is not rocket science but a standard tactic used by men who might not otherwise be chosen. I see a woman claiming she is a goddess, and what I hear is a little girl saying, "I want you to do *this* for me, Daddy!"

I was grateful for my time at the House and in the Scene, even if I would never have anything to do with it again. I got to talk to a lot of people about the psychological dynamics involved in strength, weakness, dominance, and control, and I began to see what my parents had done in a slightly different light. Viewed only in the context of the "Doctrine of Consent", my mother had done a lot of nonconsensual BDSM and criminal intergenerational acts on me, even if I knew deep down I would never even try to confront her over what she had done.

Chapter 38

Marriage, Merriment, and Mother (1994–1999)

Our mother who aren't in Heaven, hollow be her fame...

—David Bradley

I fell in love and got engaged.

My mother was delighted. Lisa withdrew the amortization schedule for the house on the condition that I would give her my entire inheritance.

One decision I had made when I moved back to Northern CA was that I was going to be in my mother's life. I believed in forgiveness, and I thought that she was old and sick and that I could do some good by being there with her. I understood that she was not easy to get along with, and I thought if I could only anticipate what she would do, I would be able to cope with it.

I was wrong. I could no more cope with her ongoing verbal abuse than I could fly. But I tried.

I would talk to Mother about whatever she felt like. I weathered her verbal jabs. My job was to protect her. I would steer her away from anything that would trigger her into rumination, tears, and tape loops. She was incapable of introspection. It had never been her strong suit, but the dementia made it worse. She could not understand the bad things in her life. She wanted to blame, to rage, and sometimes if she was upset enough, to drink.

She repeated her story about trying to beat me to death twice to my future husband, who was appalled. He was more appalled the day we came home, and my neighbor handed me my cat, Carlotta, dead in a cardboard box, telling me she had been hit by a car. I cried, and my mother laughed and mocked me savagely for crying over a cat.

One day, he drove her somewhere, and she lectured him on the merits of Communism through a long, long traffic jam. She then soiled her diapers while not wearing any and showed no concern whatsoever for the mess she had made. Of course, I cannot say whether she was unaware, too embarrassed to speak, or simply not worried.

We planned a traditional wedding rather than the "dress up in Faire costume" sort of thing most of my family did. I thought since a marriage was a real thing, it should reflect our real lives, not a fantasy. We had bridesmaids and groomsmen, and Lisa took charge of much of the planning, paying for it with Mother's money. One of my bridesmaids was an unusual size, so I got to make her dress out of the same fabric as what we had for the rest of the bridesmaids. I paid for our wedding venue by playing the harp at an outdoor garden spot for ten weeks during their Sunday brunches.

We had a joint attendant's party at my house the night before the wedding. A few of my friends asked me to play the harp. When I sat down to play, Lisa started noodling on the harpsichord. Instead of confronting this rudeness outright, I did something passive-aggressive and vicious.

I offered to accompany her while she sang.

She proceeded to create auditory hell while I put on my best Sphinx-like poker face and behaved as though the noises she made were the most natural thing in the world. The men who were sitting outside came and closed the window. After she was done making sounds, I played the harp and sang for my friends. After she was out of earshot, my friends asked me quietly why I had let her sing and wondered why I had been so calm when she had done so. I laughed and laughed.

The *only* saving grace of living around Lisa had been that she was utterly talentless in a household full of people who did things. She might have stolen my mother and my inheritance and my peace of mind, but she could not sing to save her life.

The wedding was gorgeous. We had prerecorded orchestral music and traditional vows. I walked down the aisle to *Le Cygne* by Saint-Saens, which I still adore. My cousin Ian's wife Elizabeth told me she wished she had had a non-costume wedding.

We set up housekeeping and went to church every week.

I continued to stay in close touch with Mother and Lisa, and I ended being almost a referee between them. Lisa was intent on making Mother seem Christian to the public and dragged her to the Episcopal church every week. Mother confided in me that she only went for the music and to keep Lisa from getting upset with her. She told me that she would have been much happier leading rituals at Stonehenge, but Lisa would not hear of it.

I did not sense that Lisa felt the slightest concern for Mother's immortal soul. It seemed that all that mattered to Lisa was that any pictures of Mother in the paper would be of her going to church. I suspect Lisa wanted to distance both herself and Mother from paganism because of the ongoing legal troubles.

Mother was not Christian. She had been telling me she was not Christian since I was old enough to figure out what she meant by "6,000-year-old Jewish fairy tales" and "outdated screwing license" and "God is a bedroom snoop and a kitchen snoop." She told me that she had turned her back on God when He didn't save her from her daddy, so why should she bother with Him now.

To be fair, it is unlikely that she would have written the books that she did if she had been even remotely Christian. They would have been intolerable to her, as they have been to some of her Christian readers. The "intergenerational sexuality" alone makes many people's skin crawl. There is also a clear anti-Christian bias, not only because of the invariably demonized paternalistic elements but because of the schism between the controlled sexuality allowed by the Church and the considerably more liberal sexuality she herself advocated.

I very much wanted Mother to become Christian, and I took her to church many times in her later years. I have no idea whether she ever converted or whether she merely put up with going to church to have a visit with me.

Even more offensive to me by then was Lisa's campaign to deny and whitewash her relationship with my mother. After making like a cuckoo and doing her best to drive off not only my father but both my brothers and me, Lisa was going around calling herself my mother's "cousin." She even openly addressed Raul as her "boyfriend." Mother was expected not to be hurt by this, but she was. Maybe Lisa didn't care that Mother was crying, but she was.

Apparently, calling herself Mother's "secretary" did not adequately explain Lisa's presence.

Lisa decided she never had been a lesbian—that is true—but how could Lisa be with my mother for twenty years and lie about the nature of their relationship? It is wrong to pretend that that the woman who gave her life to you is nothing but a distant relative!

I felt sorry for Mother. It is one thing to have your relationship break up, but to deny it ever existed is a cruelty which seems unimaginable to me. I do not know whether Lisa denied their relationship to Raul. I had always assumed that Raul would know everything. Maybe Lisa felt she could only seem adequately virginal if she denied her entire history with my mother and the rest of the sticky cast of characters.

I had begun a teaching practice, training harpists and singers and working locally as a harpist. My husband told me it was his dream to live in Truckee in the snow, among the beautiful trees. Then, to be closer to his work, we moved yet again to Sparks, NV, and I went back to school. I began a master's degree in vocal performance.

I also grappled with being profoundly suicidal.

I know a girl with bright blue eyes
She's frightened of the dark
She'll never say what happened
"Just some guys out on a lark..."

Three years ago I met her
To this dusty stone she's gone
I know she hurt, I know she ached
But her friends had done her wrong.

She had an ancient sorrow and
She needed friends to hear
She listened to the wrong advice
And now she's disappeared.

They quoted her a country song
That prompted her to do a wrong
The song said to 'get over it'
So in this waiting room I sit

Before her blue eyes closed for good
She handed me a folded note
I blew my stack, I punched the wall
I read her scribbled, sad misquote

"No one will listen, no one cares,
I've got to solve my own affairs
I'll give the Eagles tat for tit
Just tell them "she got over it!"

—Moira Greyland, "She Got Over It"

In 1998, Mother and Lisa were embroiled in civil suits about my father's molestation of Kenny. They were both charged with negligence. My mother and

Lisa countersued Mary Mason and claimed that she knew what was happening all along.

I was called on to testify about Mother and Lisa, and the lawyers and the court reporter came to my counselor's office to take down my testimony. Their lawyers were so horrified by what I told them that they quit and had to be replaced. Apparently Mother and Lisa didn't bother to tell them the full details of the case.

To make a long story short, Mother and Lisa lost and dropped their counter-suit. Reading their testimony was a long piece of hell. Mother knew. Lisa knew. Some of what they knew horrified me. Here is a piece of testimony that might have changed my feelings about being around either one of them if I had known about it beforehand: Lisa knew my mother had molested my brother.

MR. DOLAN: Is there any particular reason why you did not relate what Patrick had told you, to Marion Zimmer Bradley?

ELISABETH WATERS: At the time, we were all so traumatized that I didn't want to add to anybody's trauma anymore than they were already traumatized, and Patrick was an adult at that point, and whatever Marion may have done to him in the past was clearly over.

The lawsuits were over in 1999, and Mother died soon afterward of a massive heart attack.

She did not die in her own home as she had always wanted to. Lisa was having an elevator put into the house and she had moved Mother into a disgusting little apartment in the pits of Oakland. I was there once, and it was as Spartan and cold as might be imagined.

Mother could not be counted on to eat regular meals or to control her blood sugar. She could not change her own diapers without leaving them all over the floor. She did not see well enough to prepare an injection of insulin. If she had to inject herself, she might be able to do so without breaking a needle, but it was doubtful. She had a toe amputated because of her diabetic peripheral neuropathy. She was suffering from multi-infarct dementia as well as high blood pressure and congestive heart failure.

It did not surprise me at all that my mother died very soon after being left alone in that awful place and expected to care for herself. Either she got a shot wrong, forgot several shots, let her blood sugar go sky-high, or forgot to eat. In any event, on September 25, 1999, my mother had a heart attack and died.

Her funeral was a large affair. I had been asked to sing *Ihr habt nun Traurigkeit* from the Brahms Requiem, and the choir at the church joined me. Lisa and the other sycophants were front and center, and my brother David and I were way, way, way off in the back. My brother Patrick, now called Mark, did not attend and wanted nothing to do with Mother. He did not even acknowledge any efforts to contact him.

One might think it is a singular achievement to alienate all three of one's children.

Mother wanted to have her ashes scattered at Glastonbury Tor in England. Lisa had her cremated and packed up her ashes in a Tupperware container. She told me again and again that she would find herself talking to my mother's ashes. Eventually the ashes were taken to Glastonbury and scattered. Yet I find myself puzzled at the notion that my mother's final resting place was a piece of Tupperware for the months before Lisa got rid of her by figuratively throwing her off a building.

Given that Lisa was already in the habit of having Mother sign things covered in that gray folder with the rectangular hole in it, and given that Mother's writing style differs considerably from Lisa's, it is my considered opinion that Lisa wrote Mother's will. It is also possible that she simply wrote what Lisa told her to. It hurt that my brother and I were referred to as "strangers" in the will rather than as her children. It was also baffling that the will was full of effusive praise of Lisa, the sort of praise that Mother simply did not give, but Lisa got what she had wanted all along. She got half the estate, and the San Francisco Opera got the other half. After all, I had made Esau's bargain, and I had my house. It was my job to take care of myself after that, and that was just fine.

What I couldn't square was excluding my two brothers. David was on SSI, and the only thing he ever had from my mother was a new pair of shoes and some dental work. My brother Patrick, who was calling himself Mark by that time, had two little kids, and he had suffered a lot at Mother's hands. Understandably, he had wanted nothing to do with either Mother or Lisa after our father had died. Was it just because they didn't try to get my father out of jail? No. Lisa took Mark's house from him, too. It took a little longer, but she managed it. Mother did nothing, either because she didn't know or because she didn't want to upset Lisa.

For some reason, after Mother had died, Lisa found herself to be unwelcome everywhere. Greyhaven didn't want her around. I certainly didn't want anything to do with her.

But I did want to speak to my brothers. I had seen David at the funeral, but Patrick was nowhere to be found.

I wrote to my brother Patrick again and again in the years since my father went to prison and died. No response. Eventually, in 2003, I wrote to him with great fury and told him that if I had been the evil maniac he seemed to think I was, why did I give him our father's entire estate except for two books and my strobe harp tuner?

He finally wrote me back.

He had found evidence which turned my father's hoped-for innocence into an impossible dream. After Father had died, Patrick was the one stuck dealing with his estate. He found horrible things in my father's room. Kiddie porn, "art books" of naked children, pictures by the stack. He called all such items "dead bats" and although occasionally lamenting the fact that the obviously priceless rare items could not be sold, he would dump them in the trash where they belonged. After all, what else could one do with a dead bat?

Notable among the dead bats, though, my brother found position papers for NAMBLA. They were originals, which had obviously been written on my father's Selectric typewriter. They also went in the trash, where they belonged. There was a mountain of moldy books and papers in the recently flooded basement of the Goldfish Bowl, and they also went the way of the dead bats.

But the miracle had happened. My brother finally understood what our father had done. He changed his name to Mark Greyland in response, wanting nothing to do with our father's name. He had also attempted the geographic cure and moved to New Zealand.

We corresponded through email for years and through chat programs.

My eldest brother David and I had not seen each other in some time. He was 6'6" and always wore black, including black nail polish. I loved him very much. He sent me a card which I kept for a very long time, with a photograph of a little grey kitten on the cover. Inside he explained this: He saw me always as being very much like the little grey kitten, except my claws were always stuck to the ceiling as though I was in mortal terror. He described how he never wanted to distress me or upset me when I had so much going on with our mother. He described her hilariously as "our mother who aren't in heaven, hollow be her fame."

Two days before he died, we had a long, long phone call. We spoke briefly the next day, and then he was gone, dead in his fifties of a heart attack.

Chapter 39

Aftermath: What Has the Past Done to Now?

Little girl lies in her bed at home
Desperately wishes she was alone
No way to cope with what's horribly real
So her heart, overloaded, forgot how to feel.

And what has our past done to now
And what is still haunting and hunting you now?
Are you wide-eyed and staring? Do you feel past caring
Oh, what has our past done to now?

And what can we do about now?
Can we pick up the shreds of our life to save now?
The grief that we're dodging, Our pain is dislodging
Are we brave enough to save now?

—2003 Moira Stern, "What has the past done to now?"

After the lawsuits were over and my parents were both dead, I still had wounds to nurse and a lot of healing to do. Even though I no longer had to live in fear of their words or shenanigans, my neurological system had been altered by what I went through when I was young. I wish I could simply wave a magic wand and say, "It's all behind me now", but that would not be realistic.

I wish I could tell everyone who has asked me whether writing my books or my poetry is cathartic, "Yes, it is all better now. Catharsis fixes everything." But it doesn't.

I have Complex PTSD, which means I am stuck with a variety of symptoms which make me feel like an idiot. Since the symptoms don't look very good in public, it would be very easy to avoid being around people, but I love people, and most of them are very understanding. I have had to learn a variety of ways to handle my symptoms. I have also learned to view them differently over time.

I have mentioned being afraid of the dark, which is absurd for a teenager, let alone for an adult, but it is something that I have never been able to shake. If I am in a situation where I need to sleep in the dark, I will usually feel very agitated, and I will need to resort to one of several coping mechanisms to handle my feelings, which usually involve counting or breathing. More likely, I will turn on the light and try to sleep with it on, or just not sleep at all.

Sometimes these symptoms can be a bad startle reflex, or dissociation, which means I don't feel like I'm in my body. Dissociation can result in PTSD seizures or even catatonia, but it isn't as dire as it sounds. Often, if I go to bed, my brain will simply reset itself, and I'll be better in the morning.

I startle terribly, which means if someone comes up behind me or touches me unexpectedly I will jump and often shout. When I was a teenager, I used to hit people who startled me, which was awful for them and for me. These days I have more self-control, and I can catch myself more quickly. I can laugh at myself these days, and I certainly don't hit people who startle me anymore, but still, it is embarrassing to be startled, and it makes me feel silly.

I still have flashbacks which are disgusting. Out of nowhere, I will remember things that happened long ago. I will suddenly feel as though I am three, or six, or eight, even if I know perfectly well that I am an adult, and I am not there, and the people who hurt me are dead. The memories are vivid, and often multisensory. I might feel a sensation on my skin, or smell something, or remember what was happening back then as vividly as if it were happening right now. Sometimes they are very brief, and sometimes they last a bit longer. The aftereffects of flashbacks can be longstanding. While I wrote a few of the chapters of this book, I had hundreds of flashbacks. I became so overwhelmed with symptoms at one point that I had to use long successions of coping mechanisms to handle the distress I was feeling. I had to count my breaths, or count slowly backward from 100 to take a shower or to get dressed and undressed. I would sometimes even have to remind myself of where I was.

A host of relatively ordinary things will trigger me into symptoms. What is triggering? Originally, "trigger warnings" were used mostly in therapy chat rooms for PTSD patients. A post talking about childhood sexual abuse would say, "Trigger warning: CSA", then several blank lines, and then the writing would start. The point was to give each survivor an opportunity *not* to read stories that would upset them. When we are triggered, it means we are reminded of our own trauma to the point that we are having symptoms.

Sometimes being triggered can make us feel quite sick. What happens to a normal brain when it has the "fight or flight" reflex triggered is that it goes on for long enough to get out of trouble, with a release of epinephrine and cortisol. A PTSD brain has forgotten how to shut off the release of epinephrine and cortisol, and our "fight or flight" response goes on for hours instead of minutes. Over time, bathing in stress hormones takes a terrible toll on our health.

I cannot be still. I work all the time, or I type all the time. I have to do something with my hands all the time, or I will literally—not figuratively—rip off my skin. I don't like this about myself, and I wish I could mend it, but since I have not yet figured out a way, I simply stay busy. When I was little, I read and then learned to sew and make things. I spend too much time on Facebook, or I embroider for ten hours at a stretch. I wish I could stop the agitation, but until I find a way, I'll accept it, keep breathing, and keep busy in a way that will not harm me.

Do I sit around all day long thinking about my father and mother? No, not at all. If I did, I might actually feel something. Most of the time I feel nothing, or I feel agitation. Some days I vacillate between uncontrollable tears and feeling numb or frozen. Sometimes being triggered amounts to being jolted into feeling *anything*.

Many people believe that talking about trauma will heal it. It can. Sometimes talking about things can help, either by robbing the stories of their power to isolate us or by letting us know that we won't die or be rejected if we admit what we have gone through. Sometimes talking will lead to a catharsis, which can either bring relief, or ironically, trap us in further pain through triggering. But the most important part of the talking which we can do about our pain is the sort of talking which involves replacing lies with truth.

That is why I have written this book: I needed to eventually realize that I was not evil and that I did not kill my father. It is so easy to believe the lies our parents tell us, especially if there is no way to challenge them with truth and reality.

People wonder why people who went through sexual abuse end up so broken. Why can't we suck it up and leave it in the past? The reason is that although we almost never think about it directly, it affects everything in our lives. We choose weird relationships because our models are our parents, and later our models become our abusers. Every choice we make because of emotion is suspect because our emotions are broken. We tend to be frozen. Or at least I am. I can thaw around other people and feel like maybe I can be normal here and there, but when something reminds me that I am not normal, it makes me want to run away and hide so nobody will see how abnormal I am.

A better model for "getting over" trauma might be to view it more like an amputation than a broken bone. Whereas broken bone will heal and often be nearly as good as new, an amputation creates a set of problems which require daily adaptation. We will never go back to what we might have had or what a normal brain is supposed to be like. But many people learn to cope beautifully with amputations, and we can learn to deal with our new, different brain.

Forgiveness is supposed to make everything all better. Does it?

No book on trauma would be complete without a few platitudes about forgiveness and about how it makes everything All Better. Add a few inspirational quotes and a bandage slapped over the gangrene, and *presto*—Instant healing!

More likely, instead of instant healing, the result of pressure to forgive will be a survivor who no longer feels safe about talking and has now identified you as a person who does not understand.

The truth is that forgiveness can help some, but it is neither the beginning nor the end of healing, and it cannot be used instead of other things, any more than one would try to treat a brain tumor with a cast. Obviously, the right treatment at the wrong time or the wrong treatment at the wrong time can do no good at all.

One reason I found it difficult to forgive my parents, though I went through the motions of doing so thousands of times, is that I never really understood that they had done anything to me that I could have a say about. I knew that what they did hurt me, but my sense of self was wrapped up in pleasing them, and I couldn't really figure out that I had anything resembling a right to not be hurt. It was more like I was a pet or a doll, and if I said the wrong thing, they would hate me.

Forgiving them means that I have a self, I am separate from them, and they did me an injury. I can take this to understand the Biblical instruction to forgive another way. If I must forgive, then I must realize I have a self. I must realize I am separate from them, and I must acknowledge that they hurt me. It is as much for me as for them.

I understand why it feels so hollow to forgive: I have no problem at all with never even getting mad at what they did to me. My response is frozen in time. I cannot even begin to forgive them for what they did to other people, which is why I was able to take action against them when a child was in danger.

I have been told so many times to forgive, but forgiving the people who hurt me will not change my startle reflex, or make it so I could be around loud noises without going to pieces, or suddenly watch *Sybil* or *The Wicker Man* without becoming hysterical. Seriously, if someone came into a hospital with a head injury, nobody would tell that person to "forgive." Instead, the trauma team would be stabilizing the patient and making appropriate medical interventions!

Saint Paul had a thorn in his side which he prayed would be removed from him, and his prayer was not answered:

> *I was given a thorn in my flesh, a messenger of Satan, to torment me. Three times I pleaded with the Lord to take it away from me. But he said to me, "My grace is sufficient for you, for my power is made perfect in weakness.*

> —*The Holy Bible*, 2 Corinthians 12:7–9 (NIV)

From this I observe that if Saint Paul can live with an infirmity, so can I. If I can learn from this infirmity and shine a light on it for other people, it is worth it, many times over.

None of us said anything, so why am I talking now? Because the elephant in the living room is bigger than the living room now. It has grown over time. I can no longer keep her secrets. I can no longer pretend to be a radio, pretend only to be the singer of other people's songs, with the center of my life being a screaming void with nothing in it but pain and sorrow.

I will not go on pretending to be what she wanted me to be. I will not be a stranger in my own life, only doing what she wanted me to do and keeping her secrets so she could be perfect and famous, and I could hold all the agony in my heart where nobody would see it.

I am a singer without a voice. This impossible contradiction has left me feeling deep futility in all my ways. I don't know what I want to do because I don't know who I am. I don't know who I am because I am not allowed to be who I am. After all, if I told the truth about myself, she wouldn't like it…

I want my heart back

February 7, 2005

Good morning Mother
Will I please you today
Or will I find myself sobbing in a corner again
Forgetting as fast as I could what I still don't want to hear
The sound of my voice screaming again, as though I didn't know how to talk
Don't hit me Mommy!

The chorus of my life.
I can't live with that little voice
Don't hit me Mommy!
I'm sorry! I'm sorry!
And instead of that voice being real
I have become unreal
The woman of iron, who feels only strength
But I look deep in my heart and find a to-do list.
And I don't care about myself, or this list of things that I must become.
I don't care what I do, nor who I am,
As long as I don't have to feel anything
As long as I don't have to hear that little voice
Mommy stop it! Mommy don't hit me!
Please please stop it! I'm sorry! I'm sorry
I'll never do it again!
And I don't even know what I did.
I will never know what I did
What could I do to make me deserve to die
And I don't remember anything except my screams
And her self-satisfied confession.
"I tried to kill you twice, but I stopped myself.
You were a terrible child"
So now I have done what Mommy wished
And slaughtered all traces of me.
I am merely a shell, meekly doing her bidding
And trying to be famous in the way that she wished
Because if Mommy wants me dead
Who am I to argue?
I must have argued
I begged her to stop
And I can't stand the thought of my weakness
I can't stand to think that I couldn't have stopped her
Mommy don't kill me! Stop it Mommy
Please stop it, please!
And the thing I can't even understand
Could it be she was wrong?
Could it be she was cruel?

Could it be I have strangled my own heart
Out of obedience to a crazy illusion?
A sham of a mother?
If so, then I want my heart back.

I love "Still in Saigon" by The Charlie Daniels Band because it describes PTSD so well: the isolation, the feelings, the utter powerlessness to stop the adaptations that one does not want.

Chapter 40

The Blog Heard Round The World (2014)

Children are brainwashed into believing they don't want sex.

—Marion Zimmer Bradley

In addition to raising my family, I had been directing operas and playing the harp and singing for some years now. I routinely performed all over the country, as well as at science-fiction conventions, where a lot of people knew me for one reason or another. Deirdre Saoirse Moen arranged for me to play a concert at a convention, and so when I heard from her in June of 2014, I thought maybe it had to do with the harp again, but it was not.

Deirdre was writing to ask me about my late mother. Tor Books had Leah Schnelbach write a puff piece on Marion Zimmer Bradley to commemorate her June 3 birthday. Deirdre was surprised and understandably angry that Tor, which published several books by my mother, failed to mention anything about the scandal of her husband's criminal conviction, preferring to simply paint her as a great feminist hero. Deidre blogged about Marion, and in doing so, quoted her 1999 court testimony:

MR. DOLAN: And to your knowledge, how old was [Glenn] when your husband was having a sexual relationship with him?

MZB: I think he was about 14 or possibly 15. I'm not certain.

MR. DOLAN: Were you aware that your husband had a sexual relationship with [Glenn] when he was below the age of 18?

MZB: Yes, I was.

MR. DOLAN: Can you tell me why you would publicly state that Walter was not a pedophile when you knew that he had been having sex with a minor child?

MZB: Because, as I said, [Glenn] did not impress me as a minor child. He was late in his teens, and I considered him—I think he would have been old enough to be married in this state legally, so I figured what he did sexually was his own business.

Glenn was 10 and 11 at the time in question. The lawyer also asked Marion questions about some things Elisabeth Waters had written in her diary:

MR. DOLAN: Elisabeth Waters in her 10-8-89 diary, which was given to the police, indicates the following: Quote, "And I feel like a total idiot for not having said anything back when I thought Walter was molesting [Sterling] ten years ago. I guess it was just another case of," quote, "Don't trust your own perceptions when the adults are telling you you're wrong."

MR. DOLAN: I'm going to read to you from the 10-9-89 entry of Elisabeth Waters.

"Marion always said she'd divorce Walter if he did this again. She seems to think that he molested both [Glenn] and [Gregg], but she was rather startled when I told her about the letter to Dr. Morin about [Sterling]. She said that she thought Walter thought of [Sterling] as a son."

MR. DOLAN: Where did you have this discussion with David where he thought he was too old for Walter?

MZB: When he was 15 or so.

MR. DOLAN: So at the time that David was 15, David informed you that he believed that your then husband was not propositioning him because at that point David was too old for Walter's tastes?

MZB: I think that's what he said. To the best of my memory, that's what he said.

MR. DOLAN: So you were curious enough to ask your own son whether your husband had made a sexual proposition to him?

MZB: I wouldn't say I was concerned enough. I would simply say the matter came up in conversation.

After all, doesn't every mother discuss whether her new husband has molested her son, as a matter of casual conversation?

Deirdre wrote to me and asked me for my perspective on the subject. I told her a very few details about what happened, and agreed to let her reprint my emails and my two poems.

Hello Deirdre.

It is a lot worse than that.

The first time she molested me, I was three. The last time, I was twelve, and able to walk away.

I put Walter in jail for molesting one boy. I had tried to intervene when I was 13 by telling Mother and Lisa, and they just moved him into his own apartment.

I had been living partially on couches since I was ten years old because of the out of control drugs, orgies, and constant flow of people in and out of our family "home."

None of this should be news. Walter was a serial rapist with many, many, many victims (I named 22 to the cops) but Marion was far, far worse. She was cruel and violent, as well as completely out of her mind sexually. I am not her only victim, nor were her only victims girls.

I wish I had better news.

Moira Greyland.

I sent an addendum in a second email:

It should also be noted that Walter was convicted on 13 counts of PC 288 A, B, C, and D.

Oral sex was the least of anyone's worries.

Moira Greyland.

Mother's Hands

(in "honor" of my mother, Marion Zimmer Bradley)

I lost my mother late last year
Her epitaph I'm writing here
Of all the things I should hold dear
Remember Mother's hands
Hands to strangle, hands to crush
Hands to make her children blush
Hands to batter, hands to choke
Make me scared of other folk
But ashes for me, and dust to dust
If I can't even trust

Mother's hands.
They sent me sprawling across a room
The bathtub nearly spelled my doom
Explaining my persistent gloom
Remember Mother's hands.
And hands that touched me way down there
I still pretend that I don't care
Hands that ripped my soul apart
My healing goes in stop and start
Never a mark did she leave on me
No concrete proof of cruelty
But a cross-shaped scar I can barely see
The knife in Mother's hands.
So Mother's day it comes and goes
No Hallmark pretense, deep red rose
Except blood-red with her actions goes
It drips off Mother's hands.
The worst of all my mother did
Was evil to a little kid
The mother cat she stoned to death
She told to me with even breath
And no remorse was ever seen
Reality was in between
Her books, her world, that was her life
The rest of us a source of strife.
She told me that I was not real
So how could she think I would feel
But how could she look in my eyes
And not feel anguish at my cries?
And so I give you Mother's hands
Two evil, base, corrupted hands
And lest her memory forget
I'm still afraid of getting wet.
The bathtub scene makes me see red
With water closing over my head
No little girl should fear to die
Her mother's fury in her eye!

But both her hands were choking me
And underwater again I'd be
I think she liked her little game
But I will never be the same
I'm still the girl who quakes within
And tries to rip off all her skin
I'm scared of water, scared of the dark
My mother's vicious, brutal mark.
In self-admiring tones she told
Of self restraint in a story old.
For twice near death she'd beaten me,
And now she wants my sympathy.
I've gone along for quite awhile,
Never meant to make you smile
But here and now I make my stand
I really hate my mother's hands.

—2003 Moira Stern (Moira Greyland)

They Did Their Best

The cry of our day is to smile as we say
Something pat that sounds like understanding
And those of us left who still cry when bereft
Risk guilt trips upon our heads landing

For the party line now is to claim that somehow
Everybody somehow did their best
So the ones who did wrong goes the new New Age song
Aren't to blame, we should lay this to rest.

But it's lies, there are villains who are still out there killing
Or else for our courts there's no need
Our jails are not filled with innocents willed
By a system corrupted with greed.

My mother did her best, yes she really did her best
To drown me for not being her willing lover

My daddy did his best, oh he really did his best
And forced his preteen boyfriends to bend over.

Some people are sick, like to make people suffer
Some people just turn a blind eye
But pretending a monster is ribbons and lace
May condemn a small child to die.

My husband was a cop and much child abuse had stopped
Like the mom who put her baby on the stove
She threw him out of sight but the smell she couldn't hide
And she didn't come out smelling like a rose.

Did that mommy do her best? Would you tell that little one
"Forgive her dear, she must have been insane"
Would you tell that to those burns, To that lie will you return
And hurt those shining eyes so full of pain?

A victim does his best, a victim does her best
To love and live and give up grief and malice
But when we had no love, but what came down from Above
It's surprising we have not become more callous.

And how to learn to cope And not give up all my hope
Is painful far enough without your lies
But if you had seen me then With blood pouring off my skin
Would you have turned a deaf ear to my cries??

And told me "Mommy did her best, yes, she really did her best
So stop crying and stop bleeding and forgive her
To cut you she's the right, and to throw you out of sight
And not love you till you sexually deliver!!

—Moira Greyland

I had no idea how famous Deirdre Saoirse Moen was, and I didn't really think that my reply to her would be read very widely. I had no idea that my words would travel to 92 countries around the world and provoke articles in many major news outlets, including *The Guardian*, *Die Welt*, and *Entertainment Weekly*. Since then, I have called Deirdre's blog "The Blog Heard Round the World."

A great many comments on Deirdre's blog were addressed as letters to me. Many of the comments broke my heart because they were from people who had been sexually abused themselves, usually by their parents, and many began with the words "I never told anyone about this before." A lot of people were furious with my mother, and some even burned her books. You may recall that I had never spoken out about my mother before because so many people regarded Marion as having been so good to them and such a positive influence.

I was, in fact, so intimidated by the thought of publicly criticizing my mother that when I recorded my album of harp music, *Avalon's Daughter*, I only allowed myself a tiny jab of the sort no one would understand unless I told them. I dedicated the album:

"To my mother, who taught me to follow my dreams, no matter what."

Only my friends could have an inkling of the misery and agony that was contained in that *"no matter what."*

Chapter 41

I Break my Silence
(2014–2015)

And I remembered that I was Bagheera,
And no man's plaything…
And I broke the silly lock with one swipe of my paw,
And I have lived in the jungle ever since.

—Bagheera the panther, *The Jungle Book,* Rudyard Kipling

"The Blog Heard Round the World" was read widely, and I was contacted by another child of gays, Katy Faust. Katy Faust was an angel. She prayed for me, and with me, and reached out again and again, so very gently. Now I was no longer alone in what amounted to the worst secret of my life, the thing I could never tell anyone.

Katy introduced me to the rest of the COGs, or Children of Gays, the six people who had submitted amicus briefs to the Supreme Court. They opposed the Obergefell case, which purported to legitimize gay "marriage." When I talked to them and read their stories, I laughed. I cried. I felt both validated and devastated. I wanted to punch the wall and jump for joy at the same time.

I was baffled and overwhelmed to discover that my experience was not unique and that I had many commonalities with other children of gays and lesbians. I found out that nearly all of us had tried to be gay or trans or both and that many of us had been sexually abused. I also found out that we all felt guilty for not being more like our parents. We also all had issues with the lax sexual boundaries in our homes, even if we were not directly sexually abused.

All six of the COGs who had gone to the Supreme Court routinely received hate mail and harassment at work for having the gall to not fit in with what was expected of us and even more, for daring to dissent. We are supposed to *adore* being the children of gays and to live for the chance to be gay parents ourselves.

Do I condemn gay people? *No.* Do I hate them? *No.* Do I agree with what they believe or what they do? *No.*

But saying "No" is not allowed. In my family, the slightest dissent amounted to complete, unequivocal betrayal.

I did not agree with the basic philosophy of the people who had raised me. I did not agree with gay marriage. I also thought that the whole "born that way" thing was ridiculous since so many of the gay people I knew kept turning into straight people when they got older.

This puts us into a bind; we love our parents, and we are expected to support their lifestyle. If we cannot agree, we know we must not talk about it because it will break their hearts. However, we must find a way to be alive as well and to eventually, somehow, tell the truth of our beings.

Would I expect my family to agree with my right-wing politics or regard them as evil betrayers if they did not? No, of course not. Tolerance only goes one way, says the Left. They have determined Truth, and for me to dissent makes me an evil bigot.

Only among the right-wing is dissent acceptable and tolerance expected. One might notice the parallel between adults and the children. Patience is expected of adults and the right wing, and rigidity and temper is expected from children and the Left.

In a normal family, children grow up and begin to disagree with their parents and even to rebel as they form their own opinions. The children of gays are not permitted to do this because it is too threatening to the adults. Since the adults have what amounts to protected victim-class status, any dissent from us would be morally equal to kicking puppies.

Children of gays are parentified. We are expected to compensate for our parents' inability to tolerate difference and expected to suppress our own growth so we do not threaten the reality our parents must uphold.

For now, it is enough to know I am not alone. I am not the only child of gays who feels this way. In fact, many of us went through the very same things, whether we were molested or not.

Rather than talking about what they said to me in confidence, I invite you to find out what they have said for themselves.

Professor Robert Oscar Lopez is the son of two lesbians. He teaches English, and he recently was harassed out of his tenured professorship for daring to dissent from the orthodoxy about gay marriage. He is passionate about the rights of children. Professor Lopez writes at http://englishmanif.blogspot.com.

Heather Barwick, co-author of an amicus brief to the Supreme Court opposing gay marriage, has this to say:

Same-sex marriage and parenting withholds either a mother or father from a child while telling him or her that it doesn't matter. That it's all the same. But it's not. A lot of us, a lot of your kids, are hurting. My father's absence created a huge hole in me, and I ached every day for a dad. I loved my mom's partner, but another mom could never have replaced the father I lost.

I grew up surrounded by women who said they didn't need or want a man. Yet, as a little girl, I so desperately wanted a daddy. It is a strange and confusing thing to walk around with this deep-down unquenchable ache for a father, for a man, in a community that says that men are unnecessary. There were times I felt so angry with my dad for not being there for me, and then times I felt angry with myself for even wanting a father to begin with. There are parts of me that still grieve over that loss today.

—Heather Barwick, "Dear Gay Community: Your Kids Are Hurting", *The Federalist*

Heather's words really spoke to me because I wanted a real father every day of my life: one who would love me and protect me, not one who would judge me on my sexual compliance.

Katy Faust offered to let me tell my story and to host it on her blog, Ask the Bigot.

I have been asked to tell my story

by Moira Greyland

I was born into a family of famous gay pagan authors in the late Sixties. My mother was Marion Zimmer Bradley, and my father was Walter Breen. Between them, they wrote over 100 books: my mother wrote science fiction and fantasy, and my father wrote books on numismatics: he was a coin expert.

What they did to me is a matter of unfortunate public record: suffice to say that both parents wanted me to be gay and were horrified at my being female. My mother molested me from ages 3–12. The first time I remember my father doing anything especially violent to me I was five. Yes he raped me. I don't like to think about it. If you want to know about his shenanigans with little girls, and you have a very strong stomach, you can google the Breendoggle, which was the scandal which ALMOST drummed him out of science-fiction fandom.

http://breendoggle.wikia.com/wiki/Breendoggle_Wiki

PLEASE do not click this link lightly. It is very distressing. I am not kidding.

More profoundly, though, was his disgust with my gender despite his many relationships with women and female victims. He told me unequivocally that no man would ever want me because all men are secretly gay and have simply not come to terms with their natural homosexuality. So I learned to act mannish and walk with very still hips. You can still see the traces of my conditioning to reject my femininity in my absolute refusal to give in and my outspokenness, and my choice to be a theatrical director for much of my life. But a good part of my outspokenness is my refusal to accept the notion that "deep down I must be a boy born in a girl's body." I am not. I am a girl reviled for being a girl, who tried very hard to be the "boy" they wanted.

Suffice to say I was not their only victim of either gender. I grew up watching my father have "romances" (in his imagination) with boys who were a source of frustration because they always wanted food and money as a result of the sex they were subjected to, and didn't want HIM. (OF COURSE!) I started trying hard to leave home when I was ten, after the failure of my first suicide attempt, and to intervene when I was 13 by telling my mother and her female companion that my father was sleeping with this boy. Instead of calling the cops, like any sensible human being, they simply moved him into their apartment, which I called "The Love Nest" and they moved back into our family home. Certainly being in an apartment by himself gave my father ever so much more privacy in which to do what he wanted to do.

Naturally that made things much worse. I had already been couch-surfing at the home of my directors from the Renaissance Faire for some time, but nobody could take me all the time. As might be imagined, where my father was, there were teenaged boys, drugs, and not a whole lot of food, though I wasn't really starved in my teens once my mother's books began to sell really well. I lived all kinds of places as a teen, though I moved back in with my father when I started college.

One day he brought an eleven year old boy to stay with us for a week, with his mother's permission, which horrified me. I made sure he had a room and bedding. When I saw my father holding him upside down kissing him all over, and saw the porn books out, I called my counselor who had already agreed to call the cops if I ever saw anything happen, and my father was arrested. For that offense, he was given three years of probation. However, word got around, and a man who had given him a place to stay in Los Angeles realized his son was of the age to be a target, and asked questions, which resulted in my father's conviction on 13 counts of PC 288 A, B, C, and D. (Suffice to say that these are varying kinds of forcible sexual offenses that should never be committed on anyone, let alone a child!)

He died in prison in 1993, after my initial report in 1989. It should be noted that far from being a first offender, his first arrest had been in 1948, when he was 18. (I am accepting the birthdate he believed was correct, not the one in the public record, since he insisted his mother had falsified his birthdate to get him into the Army sooner.)

As might be imagined, although my mother was perfectly well aware of my father's crimes, and so was my "stepmother", I was disbelieved almost up to the moment of his conviction, and discounted as "hysterical". Again, much of that is in the public record: my mother's cold indifference and my stepmother's pretense of complete lack of responsibility is sickening in and of itself. Her words ought to suffice. She knew what he wanted to do.

At no time did I try to get justice for myself, because in my moral structure I was the protector of others and I loved my father very much. So although I thought I could forgive my father for what he did to me, in no way did I think it was my place to forgive him for what he did to someone else, and his latest victim was not a hooker, but an innocent child who was very badly hurt.

In any case, where my family had closed ranks around my father to protect him, more recently they've closed ranks around my nameless male relative, who stands accused of molesting his ex-boy-lover's kids, whom he thinks of as his "grandchildren" as he "adopted" his boy-lover as his "son." Yes I know, that is so sickening it is hard to read, and I am very sorry. Once more I am marginalized, called "crazy" and "hysterical" because after all, why would someone with a long history of molesting teenaged boys keep doing it? So as I did when I turned my father in, I've moved away. I made a police report, as did my students, who were horrified by what he said about his "grandkids."

Now it should be noted that boy lovers do not think of what they are doing as "molestation." To them it is sex, they imagine it is consensual, and any objections will certainly be overridden by the orgasms they are certain they can produce, and it is the shame of these orgasms that silences the boy-victims, and persuades them they "must" be gay. (Regardless of subsequent heterosexual marriages and children.)

Apparently, 33 reports against my nameless male relative for pedophilia were not enough, and he'll skate on all this. Not my circus: not my monkeys. I did what I could, and I am easy to find, if ever I am needed to testify. Pardon my fatalism, but serial sexual offenders don't stop, and there is likely to be another victim. Either someone will come forward, or he'll offend again, or perhaps, being that he is older, he'll pass on before he ever has any consequences.

Between the time of my reports of father's offense and my nameless male relative's, I went and got a Bachelor of Music Performance, and had a career as a wedding harpist and singer, then I married and had children, then I got a Master of Music Performance, and since 2007 I have mainly taught voice and harp and directed operas with two opera companies I founded: one in Southern CA and one in Northern CA. I also made an album of Celtic music. Yet I've always been dissatisfied with my career: artists need to tell their story, and mine was rather too ugly to be told.

Yes, I stupidly returned to Northern CA. My beloved cousin's wife was dying of cancer and I wanted to be part of a family, hoping that since my father was dead his evil might have died with him. I was wrong.

Last June, (2014) a blogger named Deirdre Saoirse Moen asked me if there was any truth to the rumors about my parents, and I told her yes, that both of them had molested me and my brother as well as a HOST of other children, and I sent her two poems that I had written about that, never having breathed a word about what they had done to me in public before.

She printed my emails and poems on her blog, which promptly went to 92 countries around the world, to my utter shock. I was flooded with letters from survivors of sexual abuse, all of which I tried to answer promptly with sympathy and warmth, (which knocked me out, emotionally, in a way I can barely describe!) Everyone who wanted to send money, I asked them to send it to RAINN (Rape Abuse Incest National Network) and there were even anthology authors associated with my mother who turned over every cent of their royalties from her to charity. Other people burned their copies of her books, because they couldn't stand to sell them and make any money off her evil. Still other people deleted her works from their Kindles and iPads.

The reason I have given, and stand by for not talking is this: I know many people found value in my mother's books, and I did not want to harm them or disturb their lives. Thus my shock and embarrassment at how far this story went. Ironically, the survivors who benefited from her books have found more strength in standing against abuse than with her, and my admiration for them is ongoing!

Naturally, there was a lot of debate about her and my father. Every time someone tried to doubt my story, a hundred people would shout them down. The age-of-consent creeps came out and were also shouted down. I was, to my shock, believed. After watching what had happened to Woody Allen's daughter, I had no expectation of anything other than a virtual public execution were I so stupid as to speak out, but in a way, my mother "protected" me with her OWN WORDS. She had testified, blandly, when accused of molesting me, that "children don't have erogenous zones" and didn't bother denying tying me to a chair and attacking me with a pair of pliers, claiming she was going to pull out my teeth. With her cold admissions, nobody could put much of ANYTHING past her.

In any event, since the truth came out, the pedophilic themes in her books became very obvious to people who had previously chalked them up to history or the license granted to an author of fiction. My father had written, with her editorial assistance, a book of apologetics for sex between adults and children called "Greek Love" under the pseudonym "J.Z. Eglinton." All of a sudden, nobody could have any question about what had been so obvious to me all along.

So what has changed since last June? Since my (and others) report of my nameless male relative back in November and my decision to go No Contact with my family due to their response, it began to dawn on me that maybe the gayness WAS an issue. Naturally, I had been brought up to be completely tolerant. Years ago I read Satinover, who believed that gays were largely "pansexual" that is, preferring sex with EVERYONE of EVERY age and EVERY gender rather than wanting to be limited to one person, and he regarded it, credibly, as a moral and ethical problem, rather than a sexual "orientation." I can't tell you how many lesbians I know who simply hate men, or who have been raped and can't face sex with men because of that. For me, my research about homosexuality was almost a guilty secret: me thinking the unthinkable. After all, gayness had always been presented to me as the natural state: I was "hung up" and a "prude" because despite my mother's pleading with me to "try it the other way" and "how could I possibly know I was straight?" I just couldn't hack being gay myself.

My observation of my father and mother's actual belief is this: since everyone is naturally gay, it is the straight establishment that makes everyone hung up and therefore limited. Sex early will make people willing to have sex with everyone, which will bring about the utopia while eliminating homophobia and helping people become "who they really are." It will also destroy the hated nuclear family with its paternalism, sexism, ageism (yes, for pedophiles, that is a thing) and all other "isms." If enough children are sexualized young enough, gayness will suddenly be "normal" and accepted by everyone, and the old fashioned notions about fidelity will vanish. As sex is integrated as a natural part of every single relationship, the barriers between people will vanish, and the utopia will appear, as "straight culture" goes the way of the dinosaur. As my mother used to say: "Children are brainwashed into believing they don't want sex."

I know, I know. The stupidity of that particular thesis is boundless, and the actual consequence is forty-year-olds in therapy for sexual abuse, many, many suicides, and ruined lives for just about EVERYONE. But someone needed to say it. Will anyone hear it? There were six Johnny Does at my father's trial, who would not testify, and two victims, who did. One of the victims I am in touch with. He was silenced so fiercely by fans of my mother years ago that he is not able to talk about it to this day. I don't know the fate of all the Johnny Does, but I do know one of them is dead in his forties from an eating disorder, never having been able to talk about what happened, and I know at least one of the people on the list of 22 names I gave the cops as a potential abuse victim died from suicide last year. I also know a number of victims of my father who would not testify because they love him. As a personal note, I can understand why: of my parents, he was by far the kinder one. After all, he was only a serial rapist. My mother was an icy, violent monster whose voice twisted up my stomach.

A very brief note on my "stepmother:" She now denies ever having been gay, after 22 years with my mother, and she has married a man. So what was was she "born"? Was she born gay, and is now living in "denial" of her "true nature" as the gays would have it, or was she besotted in a childish way with my mother, who did what celebrities do, and took advantage of her innocence and emotional infantility? She was 26 when she got involved with my mother, and told me later she felt she had been "molested" by my mother. I can't use that word for her: she was 26. But she DID call my mother "mommy", and most of the emotional content of their relationship was an attempt to prove that she was a "better daughter" than I was: a competition that for me, was over before it began. I am my mother's daughter. It is a biological reality. Giving my mother orgasms does not make my stepmother a better daughter, simply a fool. And as it can be noted now, she MUST be the "better daughter" because I blew the whistle. I don't speak to her.

This March I met Katy Faust online: one of the six children of gays who filed an amicus brief with the Supreme Court opposing gay marriage. We corresponded, and I left CA. I am still reeling from the death of my last bits of denial. It IS the homosexuality that is the problem. It IS the belief that all sex all the time will somehow cure problems instead of creating them that is the problem.

So I have begun to speak out against gay marriage, and in doing so, I have alienated most of even my strongest supporters. After all, they need to see my parents as wacky sex criminals, not as homosexuals following their deeply held ethical positions and trying to create a utopia according to a rather silly fantasy. They do not have the willingness to accept the possibility that homosexuality might actually have the result of destroying children and even destroying the adults who insist on remaining in its thrall.

From my experience in the gay community, the values in that community are very different: the assumption is that EVERYONE is gay and closeted, and early sexual experience will prevent gay children from being closeted, and that will make everyone happy.

If you doubt me, research "age of consent" "Twinks", "ageism" and the writings of the NUMEROUS authors on the Left who believe that early sexuality is somehow "beneficial" for children.

Due to my long experience with the BSDM community (bondage/discipline, Sado-Masochism) it is my belief that homosexuality is a matter of IMPRINT-ING, in the same way that BDSM fantasies are. To the BDSM'er, continued practice of the fantasy is sexually exciting. To the gay person, naturally, the same. However, from what I have seen, neither one creates healing. My mother became a lesbian because she was raped by her father. My father was molested by a priest—and regarded it as being the only love he had ever experienced. There are a vanishingly few people who are exclusively gay, but far more who have relationships with people of BOTH genders, as my parents and other relatives did.

What sets gay culture apart from straight culture is the belief that early sex is good and beneficial, and the sure knowledge (don't think for a second that they DON'T know) that the only way to produce another homosexual is to provide a boy with sexual experiences BEFORE he can be "ruined" by attraction to a girl.

If you're OK with that, and you might not be, it is worth your consideration. If you think I am wrong, that is your privilege, but watch out for the VAST number of stories of sexual abuse AND transgenderism that will come about from these gay "marriages." Already the statistics for sexual abuse of children of gays are astronomically higher compared to that suffered by the children of straights.

http://www.frc.org/issuebrief/new-study-on-homosexual-parents-tops-all-previous-research

Naturally my perspective is very uncomfortable to the liberal people I was raised with: I am "allowed" to be a victim of molestation by both parents, and "allowed" to be a victim of rather hideous violence. I am, incredibly, NOT ALLOWED to blame their homosexuality for their absolute willingness to accept all sex at all times between all people.

But that is not going to slow me down one bit. I am going to keep right on speaking out. I have been silent for entirely too long. Gay "marriage" is nothing but a way to make children over in the image of their "parents" and in ten to thirty years, the survivors will speak out.

In the meantime, I will.

My blog post was nominated for a Hugo in 2016. After it came out, a lot of people wanted to hear the rest of my story. This book is the result.

Chapter 42

The Last Closet

After I met Katy Faust online and recognized that I was not alone, my sense of myself changed considerably. I stopped being willing to pretend that I agreed with the things I did not agree with, and I came out of The Last Closet. I started speaking out, openly criticizing what I consider to be stupid philosophies, foolish moral relativism, and what now strikes me as utterly reprehensible immorality.

After all, the one thing which could not be questioned regarding this issue is that *every single child* of gay parents with whom I spoke had certain things in common. Those with only same-sex parents in the home ached for their missing parent and longed for a real father, and nearly all of us had been sexualized far too young. I had both biological parents in the home, but both refused to act like traditional parents. I needed my father to protect me and to see me as a girl instead of refusing to protect me and seeing me as an amorphous nothing who competed with him for boys. I needed my mother to love me and hold me and comfort me instead of being a terrifying, angry dictator.

Worse than that, I was expected to not want them to love me and protect me, or to act like normal parents. I was supposed to be *happy* that they were doing their own thing, no matter what they did to us.

And yes, I have heard all the customary protestations. "Your parents were evil because they were evil, not because they were gay", but I disagree. The underlying problem is a philosophical one that is based on beliefs that are not only common to gay culture but to popular culture. And this is the central belief:

All Sex is Always Right No Matter What.

Let us consider that a bit. Our society has now endured fifty years of this philosophy, and what we have is fatherless households, single motherhood, far more children being abused, and children sexualized at ever-younger ages because families are no longer intact. You may recall that I mentioned a study in the preface which supported my own personal experiences: we children of gays are more depressed, less functional, and less likely to graduate than our peers. The safest place for a child to be is in an intact family with a married mother and father. Exchange that for *any other* family structure, and the sexual abuse rates invariably climb.

Here is the relevant paragraph again just in case you don't recall it. Given this reality how in Hell can you ask *anyone* to endure gay parenting, or try to pretend it is good when it is the cause of so much misery? Please note that LMs means Lesbian Mothers, IBFs are Intact Biological Families, and GFs means Gay Fathers.

> *[T]he NFSS found that, when asked if they were ever touched sexually by a parent or other adult, the children of LMs were eleven times more likely to say "yes" than the children from an IBF, and the children of GFs were three times more likely to say "yes." The children of IBFs were the least likely of all family types to have ever been touched sexually: only 2% reported affirmatively (compared to 23% of LMs who replied "yes"). When asked if they were ever forced to have sex against their will, the children of LMs were the worst off again—four times more likely to say "yes" than the children of IBFs. The children of GFs were three times more likely to have been forced to have sex than the children of IBFs. In percentages, 31% of LMs said they had been forced to have sex, compared with 25% of GFs and 8% of IBFs. These results are generally consistent with research on heterosexual families. For instance, a recent federal report showed that children in heterosexual families are least likely to be sexually, physically, or emotionally abused in an intact, biological, married family.*

—"The Kids Aren't All Right: New Family Structures and the 'No Differences' Claim", *Public Discourse*

For me, the problem is not only the fact that my gay parents molested and raped and abused me. That problem is compounded by the cultural taboo on me talking about that or blaming their conduct on their sexual inclinations.

Over time, I have talked to a lot of people whose lives have been touched by homosexuality. I became friends with former gay people, as well as former trans people. I was surprised because according to what I had been taught, they are not supposed to exist. Joseph Sciambra, who was a gay porn star in the 1980s, gave up the gay lifestyle and now ministers to homosexual men. He endures daily hate mail sent to him by angry gays, which are balanced by the grateful letters he receives from other formerly gay men whom he has inspired to leave the lifestyle.

You can read Joseph's story at http://josephsciambra.com.

The first time I met a former transsexual was a man I'll call Frank, whom I had known since my teens. I met him again at a convention and he was talking about having left Scientology. He was extremely heavy and riding in an electric wheelchair. We stayed in touch for some time after the con, and eventually he told me he was making preparations for transgender surgery. I was a bit surprised, but we continued to stay in touch.

Eventually he told me he had become a Mormon, which I vehemently opposed, and we often argued about Scripture. I was wrong to object though, and fortunately he took it in stride. He ended up losing over 100 pounds and finally managed to ditch the wheelchair. He also abandoned the idea that he was a woman, decided against surgery, took up ballroom dancing, and married a nice Mormon girl.

If I had been a proper Berkeley girl, I would have chided him for trying to go against "who he really was", but I am certain he would not give up his new life for anything! I did not become a Mormon, but I do think that he found something he absolutely needed in that church. It is possible that after the overwhelming control found in Scientology, he could only have found an appropriately rigid and all-encompassing framework among the Mormons. God bless them too!

A woman I will only call Sandy spent many years convinced she was really born a boy. She had gender-reassignment surgery but subsequently changed her mind, as many do. Now she is having a terrible time trying to change her sexual identification back because while doctors are supposed to be endlessly supportive of people transitioning away from their birth sex, they are not supposed to help those wanting to return to it.

More information about former trans people can be found at http://www.sexchangeregret.com and http://www.help4families.com.

I was brought up to be completely tolerant of every possible sexual variation, and the wish to be loving and accepting of all people has stayed with me. Meeting former gay people and former trans people and hearing how furious their friends are about them leaving the lifestyle opened my eyes. They find themselves in a new closet because they are not supposed to be able to reject the lifestyle. What all former gays and former trans have in common is the reality of hate mail and fury from former friends who cannot stand the fact that they were able to leave.

It is, after all, supposed to be impossible to leave.

The underlying idea is this: "Homosexuality is normal. Heterosexuality is stultifying. If anyone enters it, they are growing. If anyone goes back to heterosexuality, they are hung-up and ridiculous, and they must be corrected until they stop trying to leave."

Tolerance only goes one way. It means that anyone who leaves the gay or trans lifestyle or dares to speak out against homosexuality and gay marriage is a fair target for persecution.

This is wrong.

People who have left the gay and trans lifestyle also deserve love and support because our humanity is more important than the ideology their silence is meant to maintain. That is the bottom line. Do we value people, or do we value ideology? If an ideology is good, that does not justify destroying or silencing people in order to support the ideology. Freedom of speech means that we all get a say, even if what we say is not universally accepted.

Now that I have left the closet and I am speaking out, I will be criticized, but I nevertheless hope to give strength to other people who need to speak out. If we are to take the one worthwhile thing from the gay community—something that is also common to the Christian community—which is the command to love and accept everyone, then that means ex-gays, ex-trans, and even the disaffected children of gays deserve to be heard as well.

And I want you all to be able to tell your stories.

God bless you all,
Moira Greyland

Appendix A: The Breendoggle and the Loyal Opposition

I have included the text of the Breendoggle in its entirety to spare you the trouble of looking it up online. This is a tough read, no doubt, but worth it not only to see how committed and blatant my father was in his pursuit of sex with minors, even toddlers, but also to see just how impotent the response to him was. There was both a sense of "somebody has to do SOMETHING" and a sense of "we can't be mean to a fan; we're all outcasts, and we have to stick together."

Here you can see the frog being boiled. In this case the frog is the horrified onlookers and the victims, who are arguably being boiled to this day. Please note that this was written in 1964, and my father was not stopped from his ongoing offenses until I turned him into the cops on July 5, 1989, 25 years later!

THE GREAT BREEN BOONDOGGLE
OR
ALL BERKELEY IS PLUNGED INTO WAR

This article is most emphatically a Do Not Print, Do Not Quote and Most Especially Do Not Blab My Name When You Mention This Letter Substitute. It is written for two different purposes:

(1) To put together the facts in some coherent manner to send to Jack Speer for advice

(2) To put together an account of recent stirring events in Berkeley to send to my friends for information purposes and/or to ask for advice. The account is long enough to make the writing of individual letters burdensome, particularly as I want to send it to a fair number of people.

As most stories do, this one has its roots in the past. It goes back to the very day when Walter Breen first arrived in Berkeley—almost four years ago. At first sight—even before Walter's statements and behavior largely confirmed this to most fans—Walter was assumed to be a homosexual. But no one cared. It was assumed that Walter had this facet under control and besides his sex life was felt to be no one else's business—consenting adults and all that.

In the beginning the only anti-Walter people were the Gibsons and Danny Curran. Joe let it be known that he kept a loaded revolver on his mantel and that if Walter ever showed up at the Gibsons, he would use it. And of course Walter was one of the main people Joe had in mind when he wrote that SHAGGY article. Danny also lost no opportunity of putting Walter down. I once accused him of being Square. Danny said, "Hell, it's not that. You know I have homosexual friends. But I think Walter is a shit. And this is a handy club to hit him with."

So, at first Berkeley was indifferent to Walter's sex life. This gradually began to change. There were two main causes for this. At a GGFS meeting at the ———', S—— walked into her son's bedroom—age 13—to find him in bed with Walter with Walter's arm around him. They were watching TV. (Walter is incredible.) S—— wasn't about to take this. She didn't make a scene at the time, but from then on, someone else was anti-Walter. Thenceforth the —— kids were under instructions to retire into their room and barricade the door with furniture whenever Walter was in the house. They did too. S—— wanted to ban Walter from the house entirely but Alva felt great reluctance to reject any fan.

Most people were rather amused by this incident, feeling that the kid could say "No" and even if he said "Yes" the experience probably wouldn't hurt him any. After all, Walter is so child-like himself that it would be just as if the kid were playing around with another kid. And quite apart from the sexual connotations some people were outraged that an adult could prefer the society of children to that of adults, as Walter does.

The second cause was Walter's sex play with 3-year old P—— ——. He had her trained up to the point where she would take off her clothes the minute she saw him. He would then "rub her down" and all that. I recall one occasion—a fairly large gathering at the Nelsons—in which he also used a pencil, rubbing the eraser back and forth in the general area of the vagina, not quite masturbating her. (Walter is incredible.) Many people were somewhat displeased by this— most particularly her parents. No one thought he was actually psychologically damaging P—— (she being so young)—obviously —— and —— would have interfered if they thought he had been—but the spectacle was not thought to be aesthetically pleasing. Years later Walter found out about the reaction and said, "But why didn't somebody say something! I wouldn't have dreamed of doing it if I'd thought someone *objected*."

There was of course more than one incident of sex-play with P—— ——. That was just the most spectacular one. I thought "Walter obviously isn't going to stop this as P—— grows older and more appealing. Sooner or later D—— is going to think she's being hurt. Now D—— as do most bohemians—may think it's approaching immorality to reject anyone for any reason, and particularly any fan, but *killing* in certain circumstances is perfectly moral. Now I wonder..." However, it didn't come to that. D—— let it be known that Walter was to stop this forthwith.

After this there were quite a few anti-Breen embers in Berkeley. But things jogged along for awhile. There were more and more Walter Breen stories (some of them screamingly funny) but no one's attitude changed. Then came the G—— episode. G—— was ten years old and Walter was seeing a hell of a lot of him. (And still does; he recently gave G—— a 10-gear bike; the standard quip is "One gear for each position."). Rumors kept growing that Walter was having an affair with G——. One fan said that he had surprised them engaging in sex. Upon being closely questioned, however, it developed that G—— and Walter were seated side by side on the couch in an unlocked, open room (Walter is incredible) and the guy came into the room suddenly. Walter leaped up and ran into the bathroom, clutching his open fly. The guy didn't actually see what they were doing, but drew his own conclusions.

At least three different fans have reported glowing descriptions of sex with G—— given them by Walter. (Walter is incredible.) One account: "G—— and I began with mutual masturbation and worked up to 69. Then G—— wanted to try buggering me, so I let him. Then I buggered him."

This is all very vivid and on the whole people were more shocked than amused. However, almost all Berkeley fans dislike G—— so no one cared much. "Who cares what happens to the little bastard?" But some felt that G—— was a little bastard because he is troubled and going through a most difficult time at home and that particularly under these circumstances Walter wasn't at all good for him.

Also about this time Walter was seeing another kid, 7-year old G2——. G2—— is the son of the girl Danny was living with at the time and Danny told Walter to keep the hell away. This wasn't too effective as the kid would still sneak off to see Walter, but Walter got all excited about it. He said that Danny had "betrayed" him. It is difficult to see how this could be a betrayal since from the beginning Danny and Walter have made no bones about intensely disliking each other. Danny's attitude was more or less: "If anyone who has a kid lets Walter even speak to it, he should have his head examined." Most people in Berkeley seem to think this is a reasonable attitude.

Walter was also upset about Danny's trying to deprive him of G2—— because "The kid's too young! All I can do is to *cuddle* him for Christ's sake." The parental idea though seems to be—quite apart from the possible damage of the "cuddling"—that although as a general rule Walter isn't interested in pre-puberty kids of either sex, if he's "cuddling" one and no one else is around, a sudden temptation or aberration may seize him.

But Walter has further said, "I never even *seduce* a teen-ager. The kids *always* seduce me!" That is as may be. But one teen-ager, leaving Walter's place after the first day of a proposed week's stay said, "Walter *may* always be the one who's seduced, but he makes it goddamn clear he's available."

However, Walter got quite upset about the whole G2—— matter. He seemed to think that Danny's action was somehow connected with G—— (Danny would have done the same if G—— had never been heard of), that Danny was actively spreading his "rumors" about Walter and G—— (Danny didn't have to, everyone else was) and that the story was causing not only Berkeley fandom, but all of West Coast fandom to reject Walter. (At that time Walter's status was the same as it had been for years; fans objected much more to his previous dealings with P—— than to his supposed affair with G——).

So, for months Walter was going around saying that Danny was responsible for his "rejection". Now he's changed his mind and is say[ing] that Al Halevy and Sid Rogers are responsible for his "persecution"; he's even promoted Sid so that according to him she is one of the Three Big Bitches of Fandom, the others being G. M. Carr and Christine Moskowitz. Ho hum. Perhaps all this is connected with Subbud. (An East Indian Cult that is quite the thing now a days.) I understand that when Walter was "opened" in Subbud he gained two primary insights:

(1) His Way of Life is absolutely correct and that he on no account should change it and

(2) He is far too tolerant of other people and subservient to their wishes, but nevertheless he is always being betrayed. (Walter is incredible.)

But now at last to our main story. Perhaps due to Subbud's reassurance, Walter's recent behavior has been getting many Berkeley parents not just alarmed, but semi-hysterical. If Walter is in the same room with a young boy, he never takes his eyes off the kid. He'll be semi-abstractedly talking to someone else, but his eyes will be on the boy. And if the kid goes to the bathroom, Walter gets up and follows him in. (Walter is incredible.)

Again when people complained about this, Walter said that if he had the least idea that anyone *objected*..... Knowing Walter I can readily believe that he was completely oblivious to the obvious signs of strong objection. Those who say

Walter is a child are right and as a child he is completely oblivious to other people's desires and wishes unless hit on the head with them.

By now there were three main attitudes in Berkeley:

(1) Walter is evil and should be locked up.

(2) Walter is sick and should be helped—against his will if necessary.

(3) Walter is an intelligent and nice guy. None of this is important. He loves and understands children.

About this point Al Halevy decided that whether Walter is evil or sick is irrelevant; there is no reason why we have to put up with him and we should excrete him. As is Al's wont, he waxed very enthusiastic about this project. He encountered stout opposition, but he also fanned the Anti-Breen embers into full flame.

The proposed excretion of Walter was discussed all around Berkeley. The suggestion was also made that we expel Walter from the Pacificon II as well, since we were expecting a large number of young teen-agers and shouldn't let Walter make the convention his Happy Hunting Ground—that after all we owed some protection to the kids we were gathering in. However, in the first place Walter had attended four previous Worldcons without untoward incident and was in fact usually sharing a room with several other fans. In the second place while we could of course cancel Walter's membership, if we did so without telling fandom why, there would be a big row. And if we told why, Walter would sue for slander and libel and we didn't have $75,000.00.

It was pointed out that truth is a defense in a case like this. So it is, but Walter would probably sue anyway. And even though we have all sorts of evidence establishing the main facts, if not each individual instance, we'd still be out several hundred dollars in lawyer's fees even after we'd won the case.

Here's the evidence we have, some of it being pretty good.

(1) Eyewitness accounts of his sex play with P——, following T—— into the bathroom (possibly similar things with other children), Walter's being in bed with B——, and of the time he and G—— were surprised on the couch. Cross-examination might minimize some of these, but not all I think.

(2) Somewhat guarded admissions by Walter in TESSERACT and other fanzines and somewhat less guarded ones in the Cult. But the most damaging ones are very guarded indeed as in TESSERACT where he defended abstractly teachers having sex with their teen-age male pupils, saying "What is *really* wrong with this?" But of course he has always claimed in public that this was an intellectual discussion and he didn't really believe that.

(3) Statements by Walter in letters (some of those letters have been destroyed, but fortunately not all. Can someone testify to the contents of a letter they threw away, Jack?) They range from admission of his relationship with G——, rhapsody about the joys of 69-ing with a couple of young New York fans, glorification of boy love in general, on downwards. Besides the destroyed letters a further difficulty is the reluctance of many people to bring this correspondence to light. But this would diminish somewhat in the case of a genuine suit.

(4) Quite a number of Statements made by Walter in person to three of four different people—particularly about the G—— affair, but also his homosexuality in general. But again a reluctance to testify is manifest. Not refusal—reluctance.

As word of these discussions began to leak around fandom we got a rumor back that at least one other convention committee had been planning to expel Walter, not telling why, but expelling him at the last moment before the convention so he wouldn't have time to kick up too much of a fuss. (They said—apropos of some homosexual remarks on child molesters, "If even the homosexuals won't accept him, why should we?") However, they chickened out at the last moment.

I didn't see any point in expelling Walter from the clubs here. I thought it would cause more fuss and mess than it was worth. I thought the best way to handle the situation was to have those people who objected to Walter—mostly parents—ask him not to come around. Ben agreed. Alva agreed saying that he wanted to protect his kids of course, but that the situation was adequately handled at his house by having them barricade themselves in their room. Danny said that it was outrageous for the kids to have to do this in their own home. After two more weeks of discussion with various people Alva finally decided to bar Walter from his own house at least.

Halevy finally decided to form a committee to investigate the "Breen situation", which would talk to Walter and all concerned, and then, if they thought the situation called for it, present formal charges at a club meeting, giving Walter ample time and opportunity to prepare a defense if he chose to do so. However, Al was shortly to leave for Israel, and he decided to defer doing anything until he got back, his theory being that Walter had been around for three or four years, three or four months wasn't going to make that much difference. So he left without doing anything.

But before leaving Al talked to so many people about this and some of them became quite stirred up. The counter theory was developed: "If Walter's dangerous enough to get rid of in three or four months, he's so dangerous he should be gotten rid of now!"

The Clintons were especially upset. they had just moved to Berkeley from the Peninsula and the GGFS had just been shoved onto them, Ed being the new president and Jessie the new secretary-treasurer. They felt that the whole Breen mess was being shoved onto them too, as they were continually being urged to Do Something about Walter. They felt that the people who had known Walter for years should have done something, not left it to newcomers.

And they swung between two points of view. "We must protect T——" and "We're all kooks. Walter is just a little kookier than the rest of us. Where will it all end if we start rejecting people because they're kooky?" So they swung from on the one hand proposing that if Walter wasn't to be expelled, then the banning from individual homes should be extended so that club meetings were only held in such homes, and on the otherhand calling the whole series of discussions "McCarthyite" and "Star Chamber". "I don't want Walter around T——, but if we do such a horrible thing as expelling him, I'll quit fandom."

Oh, people were really excited. There was a hell of a lot of mishmash and a lot of confusion between whether Walter deserved to be expelled and the methods suggested for doing this on the one hand and on the other, confusion between what was talked about—including many wild statements and impractical ideas— and what was actually seriously proposed as procedure for handling the situation.

Some people said that banning Walter from individual homes wasn't enough as he would still be in and around Berkeley and could see and entice the kids any time as he did with G——. And that no one was worried about Walter's raping the kids, but his seducing them. If this is the main fear, it is difficult to see how expelling him or even running him out of fandom would improve the situation either.

On this point Walter later said that if he really is as bad as all that, it's rather immoral for fans to be only concerned with protecting fannish children, leaving him perfectly free to prey on the rest of Berkeley. I gather that some people have the same idea—only from a different point of view.

Jerry and Miriam belong to the violently anti-this-persecution-of-poor-Walter faction. (They're not exactly pro-Walter though since they have been amongst the fans most disgusted at Walter's self-centeredness, obtuseness and behavior.) And just about this time Miriam got a brilliant idea: if Walter knew how people were reacting to and about him, he would voluntarily stay away from club meetings and all this unpleasantness could be avoided. She called up Ray Nelson and asked him to tactfully tell Walter. Ray did.

Walter was annoyed that all these parents so bent on protecting their children hadn't given him the *slightest* hint that they objected to his behavior. He does have a point. Plenty of non-verbal hints were given, but he might have been told off in so many words. Some have answered this point by saying that anyone in his right mind, even if he thought this behavior O.K. himself, would know that it is not socially acceptable. (But Walter is incredible.)

Walter said that he wasn't mad at anyone—except Al and Sid—and would stay away from club meetings at least "until all this dies down," but that if this Witch Hunt were carried to the point where he was excluded from the Pacificon II, well then, Marion Zimmer Bradley would stay away too. And if this wasn't enough to stop the committee, he would also sue for Defamation of Character. (I guess he's made too many noises about evil Moskowitzes suing for libel and slander to sue for libel and slander himself.)

Walter also brought forth the point that since he has been in a mental hospital and discharged, he was the only person in Berkeley fandom who was certified sane. I don't see the relevance of this, but there it is.

And of course Walter is writing to his correspondents, telling them all about how he is being evilly persecuted in Berkeley. And all because little children *insist* on climbing all over him.

Some people got quite irritated by Miriam's action. These divide into roughly two groups: Those who want to "get" or "help" Walter and are afraid that this solution will let things die down and he will still be around indefinitely and those who wanted to quiet things down and hush the whole Matter up before Marion Zimmer Bradley learned about it. Many of us like Marion and all this is not a very pleasant welcome to Berkeley for her. Not to mention the fact that it's going to severely strain her relations with almost all Berkeley fans, since naturally she will defend Walter. If under the circumstances there are any relations to strain, that is.

There are also two main sets of opinion about Marion's coming. One is: "Maybe she'll reform him. He may have had mistresses before, but he's never been fully committed to a woman. Besides, maybe she'll keep him so busy he won't have time for other outlets." Most of us think this is cloud 9 dreaming of the worst sort. For one thing there can be only change if there is a desire for change. Walter is extremely well satisfied with himself the way he is. The other position is "It'll only be a short time until she comes to her senses. Obviously she knows about Walter and accepts him, but let's see what happens to tolerance-in-theory when he starts making passes at her 12-year-old son."

And of course many people think Marion can't *possibly* know what she is getting into. "Doesn't she have some friend who can warn her?" But most of us think that this would be a thankless, not to say impossible, task. We feel that she most probably at least knows about some of Walter's affairs with adolescent males but believes in tolerance and also believes Walter when he says, "The kid always seduces me." We feel that she also believes that "Walter loves and understands children" and would put down anything she heard about Walter's activities with children and adolescents to distortion, exaggeration, lying and/or evil-intented persons. After all, presumably she loves the guy and has a little faith in him...

And the chain reaction keeps going on. More and more Berkeley fans keep hearing all the gory details and rush in to put in their 2 cents worth. And as the rumors keep trickling out, letters crying "Expel the bastard" keep coming in. At every party or meeting there's one or more hassles about Walter. And the discussions go on for *hours*. Most of us are thoroughly bored and disgusted. Just the other day Alva said, "If I hear the words "Walter Breen" or "WB" just once more, I'll puke. I know exactly what he means.

And nearly every Berkeley fan is irritated or disappointed or annoyed at at least one other Berkeley fan—and mostly at two or three or four—because of things said and positions taken in the Breen Boondoggle. I tell you the Martin affair can't even begin to compare to it. Next week: "East Lynn".

But to some extent we are regaining our sense of humor about it all. At a recent Little Men gathering at the Clintons one of the kids was trying to get me to play with him and Jessie said, "We don't want any of that around here: evil old men cuddling little boys. We won't have any of that in our house." All factions roared.

Any number of clashing viewpoints appeared in this account, so perhaps it's just as well to put down here exactly what mine is. I had a very good correspondence with Walter for some six months before I met him. I felt he was a friend and felt myself committed to him. (Walter can be quite different in letters; see his l.o.c.'s.) When I met him and suffered an intense shock: I found him self-centered to the point of egomania, deliberately and consciously exploitative of everyone with whom he came in contact, and possessed of an "You're entirely for me or you're entirely against me syndrome." Naturally I disliked him. However, because of the correspondence I felt intensely guilty for doing so and leaned over backwards to remain friendly with him. This lasted for about two years. By then his behavior had been such that I stopped feeling guilty. Soon afterwards I stopped disliking him. Now I feel very sorry for him. But I must admit that oft times his behavior with children mitigates my pity. Also I do not particularly enjoy his going around saying "Donaho is a homosexual." I suppose, however, I should take this for a compliment. Being called a homosexual by Walter is something of an accolade to him. The list of fans he has bestowed this accolade on is indeed impressive.

I think Walter is sick, extremely sick. And if he is evil, it's because he's sick. But I certainly don't want to hurt him. If anything is to be done to or about Walter, it should only be done because it's necessary to protect others, not to hurt Walter. If Walter is not damaging others he should be left to go on his peculiar way in peace. Although of course those of us who don't want to associate with him certainly don't have to.

But I do think Walter is dangerous to children. I'm not *entirely* sure of this, but I think so. I know from Walter's own statements that he has had sexual relations with children of both sexes of the age of puberty or older. I know from observation that he "cuddles" and has sex play with younger ones. But what I'm not so sure about is whether or not this sex actually hurts the kids.

Oh, of course I have an intense emotional reaction against this sex—after all I'm a product of this culture, but also I'm not conventionally religious and I think that everyone should have a free sex life. But not with children. But does it hurt the chlidren?

Of course Walter doesn't rape children or physically damage them. But he's very good at seduction. He's an adult meeting children on their own level and thinking in their own terms. They find this irresistible. All children seem to flock to Walter like bees to honey—even when he's given them no more cuddling or play than a normal affectionate adult would.

But I tend to think that normal, healthy, emotionally-secure children will not be damaged or much affected by Walter. The only trouble is: how many of this kind of children can be found in our society? And I'm reasonably certain that children lacking love and emotional security at home, even if they are partially neglected only and/or those who have disturbed attitudes towards sex—almost inescapable in our society—will be affected and most probably harmed. Also, while Walter can evidently be most tender and loving when it suits his purposes, he has had sex with young teen-age girls without using contraceptives—again by his own statements—and he had behaved quite brutally to some of his lovers after he has tired of them.

So, Walter is dangerous to children. What business is this of mine? I don't have any children. Well, I think everyone should have a certain amount of social responsibility, if not to society as a whole, at least to their friends and acquaintances and towards a friendship group like fandom. I think that I would be a coward and a shirker if I didn't at least try to do something about the danger that I think Walter represents.

I came to this conclusion most reluctantly. I have no axe to grind. And quite apart from my emotional reluctance, I expect some of my friends to get mad at me if I do anything about Walter. Others will be "disappointed" in me because of my "persecution" of Walter, poor innocent Walter who loves and understands children. Also I rather expect some damage in my race for TAFF in 1965.

While many people of course want to get Walter committed and out of circulation entirely, my own goals are more modest. I want to perform a surgical operation, separating Walter and fandom.

I'm certainly not going to protect or defend Walter or even try to argue with those who want to commit him. Nevertheless I shrink from this myself.

Walter is a human being. He has rights. But those rights do not extend to hurting children. They do extend to letting him defend himself. And as a matter of face he is defending himself quite well. If it weren't for the possibility of a suit, some such account as this would be going to all fandom.

We have evidence, sure, and according to a preliminary statement from Jack Speer, quite good enough, provided the people to whom Walter has told things would testify to this in court. But there is considerable reluctance to do so of course. And you start pushing people in a case like this, you wind up holding the bag.

And as I see it, there's no reason per se for excluding Walter from the Pacificon. He's evidently always been perfectly well-behaved at conventions. (If he hadn't been, I'm sure he would have boasted about it. Walter is incredible.) If he is excluded without fandom being told WHY, he would still be around and something of a martyr.

If we tell Why, we get sued. This is expensive even if we win. We should win, but there's always the possibility that we won't.

So, what the hell can we do?

If any of you have any advice or arguments to offer: Air Mail it.

Mailing List: F.M and Elinor Busby, Ed & Jessie Clinton, Dick and Pat Ellington, Dick Eney, Bill Evans, Joe & Robbie Gibson, Rog and Honey Graham, Al Halevy, Jerry and Miriam Knight, Betty Kujawa, Dave and Ruth Kyle, Norman Metcalf, Bob Pavlat, Dav Rike, Alva and Sid Rogers, George Scithers, Larry and Noreen Shaw, Jack Speer, and Ben Stark.

Appendix B: Mother's Complete Deposition (1998)

"Truth is a lousy first draft."

—Marion Zimmer Bradley

My annotations are in parentheses, and in italic. I have replaced [Victim X], [Name A], and [Johnny Does 1–4] with names, to the best of my knowledge and belief. I have also removed page numbers and margin numbers. The original documents with the numbers are available online.

DEPOSITION OF MARION ZIMMER BRADLEY, 8/10/98

IN THE SUPERIOR COURT OF THE STATE OF CALIFORNIA
FOR THE COUNTY OF ALAMEDA

KEN SMITH, Plaintiff, vs. MARION ZIMMER BRADLEY, ELISABETH WATERS, and DOES 1 through 10, Defendants.

DEPOSITION OF MARION ZIMMER BRADLEY Monday, August 10, 1998

REPORTED BY: JANINE P. BRANCO, CSR No. 10372

SHALLENBERGER REPORTING SERVICES - (415) 771-1988

PLAINTIFF'S EXHIBITS

2-page 7-29-98 "NOTICE OF TAKING DEPOSITION OF DEFENDANT MARION ZIMMER BRADLEY."

2-page undated document entitled "The Loyal Opposition."

19-page 7-22-89 "BERKELEY POLICE 57 DEPARTMENT UNIVERSAL REPORT FORM."

BE IT REMEMBERED THAT, pursuant to Notice of Taking Deposition and on Monday, August 10, 1998, commencing at the hour of 11:01 a.m. thereof, at 2121 Russell Street, Berkeley, California, before me, JANINE P. BRANCO, a Certified Shorthand Reporter of the State of California, personally appeared MARION ZIMMER BRADLEY, a Defendant herein, called as a witness by the Plaintiffs, having been by me first duly sworn, was examined and testified hereinafter as set forth.

APPEARANCES OF COUNSEL

For the Plaintiffs Ken Smith and Mary Mason

THE LAW OFFICES OF CHRISTOPHER B. DOLAN

655 Montgomery Street, 16th Floor, San Francisco, CA 94111

By: CHRISTOPHER C. DOLAN and SCOTT BONAGOFSKY, Attorneys at Law

For the Defendant Marion Zimmer Bradley

CAUDLE, WELCH, UMIPEG & BOVEE

1390 Willow Pass Road, Suite 200, Concord, CA 94520

By: M. HENRY WALKER, Attorney at Law

For the Defendant Elisabeth Waters

HAIMS, JOHNSON, MacGOWAN & McINERNEY

490 Grand Avenue, Oakland, CA 94610

By: LAWRENCE A. BAKER, Attorney at Law

ALSO PRESENT: MARY MASON, BELLE ROMERO

PROCEEDINGS

MR. DOLAN: This will be the first exhibit. (Plaintiffs' Exhibit 1 was marked for identification.)

EXAMINATION BY MR. DOLAN

MR. DOLAN: Please state your full name for the record.

MZB: Marion Zimmer Bradley.

MR. DOLAN: Ms. Bradley, my name is Christopher Dolan. I'm an attorney who represents Kenneth Smith in this case, and Mary Mason currently in this case. I am here today to take your deposition. You understand that?

MZB: Yes, I do.

MR. DOLAN: I am going to go through some of the rules of a deposition. Have you ever had your deposition taken before?

MZB: My lawyer went over it with me the other day.

MR. DOLAN: Okay. Have you ever had your deposition taken before?

MZB: No.

MR. DOLAN: I'm going to go over those rules just because I need to make sure that we're all clear on them. But before I do so, do you know what day it is today?

MZB: I believe it is Monday.

MR. DOLAN: Okay. Do you know what month it is?

MZB: I think it is—it's either July or August. I do tend to lose track since the kids are out of school.

MR. DOLAN: I understand. Do you know where we are today, what the address of this place is?

MZB: I don't think I know the street address, but it's between Telegraph and Shattuck on Russell.

MR. DOLAN: And what are your children's names?

MZB: My oldest son's name is David Bradley. My second son is named Patrick Russell Breen. And my third, youngest daughter's name is Laura Evelyn Dorothy Breen.

MR. DOLAN: And what was your maiden name?

MZB: Marion Eleanor Zimmer.

MR. DOLAN: The rules of the deposition are as follows: The first rule of a deposition is that everything we do here is orally, so therefore the court reporter must have oral statements made by all the people in attendance today.

MZB: In other words, I say yes instead of nodding.

MR. DOLAN: Please.

MZB: Thank you.

MR. DOLAN: Instead of using movements or hand gestures or anything we may do in normal conversation, we need full and complete English words. "Uh-huh" and "huh-uh" don't translate well.

MZB: I say "yes" or "no" or "maybe," "I don't know."

MR. DOLAN: Thank you. The other rule of a deposition is we need to let one person finish talking before the other one begins because the court reporter can only take the writing of one person at a time. So if you will wait until I finish speaking before you begin speaking, I will afford you the same courtesy.

MZB: I've been a school teacher. I know that. I always try to get the kids to finish talking before— talking before the next one starts.

MR. DOLAN: Very good. The other thing is I don't want you to guess or speculate as to anything, but I am entitled to your very best recollection.

MZB: If I don't know the answer, I will just say "I don't remember."

MR. DOLAN: You have to let me finish speaking before you begin speaking. That's the rule we just went over that school teachers follow. Okay?

MZB: Yes; I'll try.

MR. DOLAN: So I don't want you to guess or speculate, but I am entitled to an estimate or an approximation. So if you can't remember something exactly, I am entitled to your best estimate, however small it may be, your recollection, so long as it's not a guess. The difference between the two can be summarized as follows: We're sitting at a table. I may ask you the length of this table, and although you have not measured it, you might be able to estimate it.

MZB: I would say it's about eight feet.

MR. DOLAN: If I were to ask you the length of the conference room table in my office, that would be a guess because you have not been there.

MZB: I would just say I don't know.

MR. DOLAN: Very good.

MZB: Thank you very much.

MR. DOLAN: If you do not understand a question that I ask of you, I'll ask that you please have me rephrase it because I'm not here to trick you today. I want to make sure that you completely understand before you answer. All right?

MZB: Thank you. Yes, I understand.

MR. DOLAN: Are you under the influence of any medications today?

MZB: Well, I have taken insulin, which I am steadily on for diabetes; and I am steadily under the influence of the antidepressant Amipromene, which I take one every night.

MR. DOLAN: Okay. And are you under the influence of any other medication within the last 24 hours?

MZB: None whatsoever.

MR. DOLAN: Are either–

MZB: Except that I'm wearing a patch of....

MR. DOLAN: Nitroglycerin?

MZB: Yes.

MR. DOLAN: Do any of the medications that you have just described for me impair your ability to recall events?

MZB: I don't believe so.

MR. DOLAN: At the end of your deposition, when it concludes, you will have the opportunity to review and read this deposition and make any changes that you feel are appropriate or necessary.

MZB: Thank you.

MR. DOLAN: I must caution you, however, that if you make substantive changes to your deposition, I have the right to comment to the jury that you have changed or altered your testimony. So we'd like to get your best testimony today.

MZB: I'll try.

MR. DOLAN: In that regard, if you think, geez, I need to change something as we sit here, please let us know so we can make those changes now. Okay?

MZB: In other words, have my second thoughts not a month or a week from now.

MR. DOLAN: You're entitled to have them whenever you have them. I'm just letting you know there will be repercussions.

MZB: It's most convenient to have them right now.

MR. DOLAN: Please.

MZB: All right. I'll do my best.

MR. DOLAN: You're entitled to take a break anytime you need to. We have a very limited time because we're doing this in limited amounts of time because of your medical condition, so I would request if you need a break, let us know. We're not here to inconvenience you or harm you in any way. Okay?

MZB: Thank you.

MR. DOLAN: However, I must caution you that if there is a question pending, meaning you've got a question asked and not answered, and you request a break before answering it, I may place on the record that you are breaking on a pending question, and I may draw an inference at the time of trial that you have been coached on your answer by your lawyer during that break. You are entitled to still do so, I'm just merely advising you beforehand there may be re–

MZB: In other words, it's okay to do it, but you have to know about it.

MR. DOLAN: That's fine. Or if you do ask for a break after I've asked a question and you have not given an answer, I may ask a jury to draw an inference that you were coached during the break. Okay?

MZB: Uh-huh.

MR. DOLAN: Can you identify the woman to my right (indicating)?

MZB: No. I don't know her at all.

MR. DOLAN: Have you ever seen her before?

MZB: Not to my knowledge or belief.

MR. DOLAN: Do you have any idea or recollection who she is?

MZB: No; I'm afraid not.

MR. DOLAN: Let the record reflect I pointed to Mary Mason.

MR. DOLAN: Are you currently residing with Elisabeth Waters at this residence?

MZB: Yes, I am. No, not at this one. At the one over an Rose or whatever that street it is. Ashby and Grove. No Prince and Fulton.

MR. DOLAN: Do you have a residence on Prince Street?

MZB: Yes.

MR. DOLAN: Do you know the address of that residence?

MZB: 2221.

MR. DOLAN: How long have you been a resident in the home where we are now?

MZB: Not at all. I have just bought the place, and I believe we are not going to be able to keep it.

MR. DOLAN: When did you purchase this place?

MZB: Within the last month.

MR. DOLAN: So you're not living here at all?

MZB: No.

MR. DOLAN: Where are you living?

MZB: Over in the house at Ashby—Prince and Fulton.

MR. DOLAN: Prince and Fulton?

MZB: Yes; where I lived for the last 30 years.

MR. DOLAN: Do you know why we're having your deposition here today?

MZB: I believe it is because it was more convenient to come over here, but I'm not really certain.

MR. DOLAN: If at any time during this deposition you feel you're becoming unable to answer questions clearly because of anything medical or psychological, we have to ask that you let us know that so that we can try to make sure we're getting testimony that could be credible in court.

MZB: Will do so.

MR. DOLAN: Do you understand that although we're in your living room of this vacant house today that this particular deposition has the same force and effect as if it were being taken in front of a judge and jury?

MZB: Yes, I do.

MR. DOLAN: And you have sworn to tell the truth under penalty of perjury?

MZB: Yes, I have.

MR. DOLAN: I'm going to be asking you some very uncomfortable questions today, and I apologize for doing that in advance. This is an uncomfortable case.

MZB: Well, this is the law.

MR. DOLAN: Okay. I just want you to know that there is nothing personal in my questions to you today. And if they cause you discomfort, I apologize, but it is my job on behalf of my client to do the hard job of asking these questions.

MZB: Thank you.

MR. DOLAN: When did you first become aware that your husband had been sexually involved with boys under the age of 18 years old?

MZB: I have–

MR. WALKER: Objection. That lacks foundation.

MR. DOLAN: You may answer.

MZB: I was about to say that I had read some things that he had written on the subject, but unfortunately, I believed from the very beginning that it was a sort of an intellectual position, a sort of a feeling that it was something that was talked about in Greek literature and was sort of a testing position.

MR. DOLAN: Did you know that he had a relationship with [Glenn]?

MZB: I became aware of it, yes.

MR. DOLAN: When did you become aware of it?

MZB: About that time.

MR. DOLAN: What time?

MZB: Shortly after we were married. At that time I treated [Glenn] like one of my own children. He and my son David used to go swimming together and such.

MR. DOLAN: And to your knowledge, how old was [Glenn] when your husband was having a sexual relationship with him?

MZB: I think he was–

MR. WALKER: Objection. That lacks foundation. She never testified she was aware they had a sexual relationship.

MR. DOLAN: You may answer.

MZB: I think he was about 14 or possibly 15. I'm not certain.

MR. DOLAN: Were you aware that your husband had a sexual relationship with [Glenn] when he was below the age of 18?

MZB: Yes, I was.

MR. DOLAN: Did you know that about the time you were married to your husband?

MZB: Shortly afterward. It was quite shocking to me.

MR. DOLAN: How did you find that out?

MZB: I believe he mentioned it.

MR. DOLAN: Who mentioned it?

MZB: Walter.

MR. DOLAN: And what did he tell you?

MZB: Well, he told me that he and [Glenn] were sleeping together. And I said that I had believed that was an intellectual position. He told me it was not. I was very upset.

MR. DOLAN: So back in the 1960s you knew that it was not just an intellectual position for Walter; correct?

MZB: I knew that intellectually. I didn't have any physical awareness of it.

MR. DOLAN: Didn't Walter tell you that he was sleeping with [Glenn]?

MZB: He did. But you know how it is when you're told something, and everything people say needs people to say it and one to hear it. At that time I don't think I was emotionally or intellectually capable of hearing it.

MR. DOLAN: But you do recall hearing it?

MZB: Yes, I do recall hearing it.

MR. DOLAN: What else did Walter tell you on the subject of his relationship with [Glenn]?

MZB: I know that he gave him a bicycle.

MR. DOLAN: When did he give him the bicycle?

MZB: It was before I had come to live with him.

MR. DOLAN: Do you know where [Glenn] lives now?

MZB: I have not seen or heard of [Glenn] since he was—since about three years after we were married. I presume he is still alive somewhere, but, that is, I have not heard anything to the contrary.

MR. DOLAN: Did Walter ever discuss with you at length the various sexual activities that he would undertake with [Glenn]?

MZB: No.

MR. DOLAN: Did Walter ever tell you that he thought it was a mutually desired situation between [Glenn] and himself?

MZB: I had read that in his book.

MR. DOLAN: Which book?

MZB: He wrote a book called "Greek Love" under the name of John Eglington.

MR. DOLAN: And you reviewed some of the manuscripts of that book before it was published?

MZB: Yes, I did.

MR. DOLAN: And did you contribute by doing proofreading?

MZB: I did proofreading, yes.

MR. DOLAN: Did you do some editorial work on that book?

MZB: I attempted to, but I found out afterward that everything I had done had been thrown out by the publisher, Robert Bashno (phonetic).

MR. DOLAN: But you did attempt to make some editorial changes to that book as it was being written?

MZB: Yes, I did.

MR. DOLAN: And at that time you were also aware that he had a sexual relationship with [Glenn]?

MZB: Yes.

MR. DOLAN: Did you ever talk to [Glenn]'s mother about–

MZB: No.

MR. DOLAN: You have to let me finish.

MZB: Sorry.

MR. DOLAN: Did you ever talk to [Glenn]'s mother about the sexual relationship between Walter and [Glenn]?

MZB: No.

MR. DOLAN: Did you ever talk to the police about a sexual relationship between Walter and [Glenn]?

MZB: I don't remember. I know that I talked to a lawyer Walter had at the time.

MR. DOLAN: And who was that lawyer?

MZB: I don't remember her name. She was a lady.

MR. DOLAN: And what did you and the lawyer talk about?

MZB: About his book.

MR. DOLAN: Can you tell me the context of your conversation, please?

MZB: Largely that I had heard that [mother of Glenn] had said that she had nothing to complain about in [Glenn]'s relationship with Walter. And I thought that, well, because [Glenn] would come—he had been accused of stealing milk out of refrigerators, and he would come to dinner with us, and he obviously hadn't eaten for a long time.

MR. DOLAN: How did you hear that [mother of Glenn] had no complaints about the sexual relationship between your husband and her minor child?

MZB: She told me.

MR. DOLAN: So you did speak with her about this?

MZB: Yes.

MR. DOLAN: And when did you speak with her about this?

MZB: It was, as I say, shortly after we were married.

MR. DOLAN: And what was the nature of the conversation with [mother of Glenn] regarding your husband's sexual interactions with her son?

MZB: I don't remember that we spent any time on it. Mostly she was telling me that I was not a good writer, that I was a commercial hack, and that she was a great and artistic poet. I told her that at least I could feed my kids on what I did, and that if she had kids to feed, she'd probably do it too or—that is, write commercially.

MR. DOLAN: What about the subject matter between the sex of your husband and her son did you discuss that led you to believe that she had no complaint about this sexual relationship?

MZB: I think what she said almost exactly was"I find nothing to complain about," but I can't remember exactly. That was, I think, about 25 or 30 years ago.

MR. DOLAN: Was this sex occurring ever in your home?

MZB: Not that I—No, not to my knowledge.

MR. DOLAN: Was [Glenn] ever spending the night at your home?

MZB: Yes; but he slept with my older son.

MR. DOLAN: Did you ever hear a report from Moira [Glenn] was found in Walter's bed?

(My mother and Mr. Dolan have the names garbled. Glenn was there before I was conceived. I complained about Gregg in 1979 and afterwards.)

MZB: No, I didn't. I don't think Moira knew [Glenn] from Adams or Fox.

MR. WALKER: I would like to remind you here of an agreement we had.

MR. DOLAN: I know about it. I'm not going there.

MR. WALKER: Okay.

MR. DOLAN: I'm going to be very respectful of that. I'm going to be very respectful of her.

MR. WALKER: Okay.

MR. DOLAN: Did you ever talk to [Glenn] about the sexual relationship between [Glenn] and Walter?

MZB: Not to my memory, no.

MR. DOLAN: Did you ever report this sexual relationship between your husband and a minor child to the police?

MZB: Not to my knowledge.

MR. DOLAN: Can you tell me, were you aware that it was illegal for your husband to be having sex with a minor child?

MZB: No, I was not. I believed at that time—I know you told me not to volunteer anything. But I did seriously believe at that time that a teenage boy was old enough to make his own judgments in this matter. They let a girl get married when she's 12, and I thought that a boy of 14 or 15 would certainly be old enough.

MR. DOLAN: So it was your personal opinion that a boy of 14 to 15 years old was old enough to make decisions about having sex with a 50-year-old man?

MZB: Yes, I was. I believe so. He was not 50 at the time.

MR. DOLAN: How old was he?

MZB: 30. He and I were the same age. I've been told since that he was two years older than that, but I believe that that was what his mother told him.

MR. DOLAN: Did you have any other discussions with [mother of Glenn] about the sexual relationship between your husband and her minor child?

MZB: No.

MR. DOLAN: Did your husband ever pay any money to [mother of Glenn], as far as you know, to settle any disputes between her and himself regarding sex between himself and her minor child?

MZB: No.

MR. DOLAN: When did your husband give a bicycle to this child?

MZB: I think it was about three months before I came to join him.

MR. DOLAN: Do you know where this woman lives now, [mother of Glenn]?

MZB: No. I don't even know if she's still alive.

MR. DOLAN: Do you know if your husband ever wrote any poems that he published about his sexual relationship with [Glenn]?

MZB: I never saw them if he did.

MR. DOLAN: Okay.

MZB: I know that he translated some Italian work on the subject because he had me help him with the translation.

MR. DOLAN: Did you ever—strike that. To your knowledge, was the subject of your husband's sexual relationship with [Glenn] the basis for the "Boondoggle"?

MZB: Yes; I think so.

MR. DOLAN: Can you briefly describe for us your understanding of what the "Boondoggle" was?

MZB: There was a young man up in—I think it was in Washington, not D.C., up north in Washington, and he wanted the—to be the recipient of what they call the Big Pond Fund, which sent a man overseas to the convention in England. Walter also had been nominated for that. And Jack Sphere was—the other man was afraid that Walter would get it, so he published this thing about Walter being all of these things, a pedophile, and guilty of this, that and the other, and everything—everything up to and including the Civil War.

MR. DOLAN: Did you ever publicly defend Walter in terms of his not being a pedophile?

MZB: Yes, I did.

MR. DOLAN: And was that during the "Boondoggle"?

MZB: Yes.

MR. DOLAN: Can you tell me why you would publicly state that Walter was not a pedophile when you knew that he had been having sex with a minor child?

MZB: Because, as I said, [Glenn] did not impress me as a minor child. He was late in his teens, and I considered him—I think he would have been old enough to be married in this state legally, so I figured what he did sexually was his own business.

MR. DOLAN: The "Boondoggle" was partly—the subject matter was directed partly towards the sexual relationship with [Glenn] and Walter Breen; correct?

MZB: As far as I can remember, yes.

MR. DOLAN: And did you—Was the existence of that sexual relationship part of Walter's defense in the "Boondoggle"?

MZB: As I say, it was a long time ago. I don't emember whether I denied it or whether I said that it was nobody's business.

MR. DOLAN: But you did one of the two, either denied it or said it was nobody's business?

MZB: That's right.

MR. DOLAN: At what point do you personally believe that it's inappropriate to have sex with a minor child?

MZB: At this point I have no opinion on the matter.

MR. DOLAN: Did you ever publish any documentation regarding the "Boondoggle" in any of the fanzines?

MZB: Not that I remember.

MR. DOLAN: Did you ever publish anything in the fanzine called "The Loyal Opposition"?

MZB: I don't remember. I may have, but I....

MR. DOLAN: Did Bill Donaho publish something that you considered to be a slander about you?

MZB: Yes, he did.

MR. DOLAN: And what was that?

MZB: Well, as far as I remember, there was a cartoon. Bill Donaho is a big blowhard. The only time I ever met him he was very rude to me, and I didn't like him.

MR. DOLAN: And what was the subject matter of the cartoon that you felt was a slander of you?

MZB: It was a picture of some character standing around saying, "Why don't you two get started while I make up the fire" or something. I don't remember very clearly.

MR. DOLAN: Was there anything that Bill Donaho said that led you to believe that he was claiming you were a person who could only drag Walter down to deeper depths of depravity?

MZB: I have no idea.

MR. DOLAN: I'm going to show you a document that we're going to mark as Plaintiffs' No. 2. (Plaintiffs' Exhibit 2 was marked for identification.)

MR. DOLAN: I'm going to ask you to look at the first page of Plaintiffs' 2. It's a two-page document from a fanzine entitled "The Loyal Opposition."

MZB: Oh, yes. I vaguely remember.

MR. DOLAN: Would you look at Page 2 where your name appears?

MZB: Yes.

MR. DOLAN: Did you write these two paragraphs here? And please take the time to read it, if that will be of help to you.

MZB: He's lying in his teeth. The scandal's so unbelievable that I cannot repeat it here.

MR. DOLAN: What was the scandal?

MZB: It was—Well, as I say, it was that cartoon showing—showing David and me and Walter, and Walter was supposedly saying, "Why don't you two get started while I get things locked up" or something of that sort.

MR. DOLAN: "Get started" referencing a sexual act?

MZB: I think that was implied.

MR. DOLAN: When you said "David," are you talking about your son?

MZB: My oldest son, yes.

MR. DOLAN: That was the item that you were thinking could not be sent through the U.S. mail?

MZB: Something like that. At that time I had been in—I believed very firmly that obscene matter was not fit to be sent through the mail. There had been a big scandal about it.

MR. DOLAN: Have you yourself been arrested for sending obscene things through the mail?

MZB: Yes.

MR. DOLAN: When was that?

MZB: While I was living in Texas.

MR. DOLAN: And what was the documentation that you sent through the mail that was—caused you to be arrested?

MZB: One that caused me to be arrested was a young man with whom I had been corresponding for many years, whose name was Dean Boggs, had asked me some questions—having no brothers or sisters—about female anatomy, and I drew him a picture to illustrate. It was a picture that one might have found on the pages of an anatomy or biology textbook.

MR. DOLAN: How old was Dean Boggs at the time that you sent him this graphic drawing?

MZB: I think he and I were within a few weeks of each other in age.

MR. DOLAN: How old were you?

MZB: I think I was about 32. It was the year before I married Walter.

MR. DOLAN: Did you plead guilty to that charge?

MZB: Yes, I did.

MR. DOLAN: In what county of Texas was this?

MZB: I don't remember. It was in the county—I think it was up in a town called Rochester. And at the time I was going to college in Abilene, and the hearing was held there.

MR. DOLAN: Were there any other items that you had sent through the mail that had likewise been intercepted?

MZB: Not that I can remember.

MR. WALKER: I don't think that she testified that anything was intercepted.

MR. DOLAN: Do you know how the mail was found to be obscene by the authorities?

MZB: Personally I think they were—strike that. I believe that they illegally examined some of my letters.

MR. DOLAN: Okay. So, to your understanding, those letters were intercepted by the post office?

MZB: I believe so. At the time I believe that first-class mail was supposed to be inviolate. I think the matter was still under question at the Supreme Court at that time.

MR. DOLAN: Was there any other mail that you know of that was intercepted of yours around that time?

MZB: I believe they took a book that I had sent to me from France. It was Vladimir Nabokov's "Lolita," which was later judged to be quite permissible.

MR. DOLAN: It's actually been put on Showtime and HBO last week, as a matter of fact, with Jeremy Irons as the leading man.

MZB: I saw the old James Mason version.

MR. DOLAN: Right. If you look at this document in front of you again, in the second paragraph it says in here, "Anyone who defends Walter Breen is worse than Walter." Do you see where you've written that?

MZB: Where?

MR. DOLAN: Well, it's actually in the–

MZB: Oh, yes.

MR. DOLAN: –third sentence.

MZB: I was quoting Bill Donaho.

MR. DOLAN: Were you at that time defending Walter Breen?

MZB: Yes, I was.

MR. DOLAN: And how were you defending Walter Breen?

MZB: By saying that whatever it was was nobody's business but his.

MR. DOLAN: And, to your knowledge, did you ever publicly during that defense of Walter Breen state that it never happened?

MZB: I don't remember, but I don't think so.

MR. DOLAN: Who's [Barry]?

MZB: Oh, he's a little kid who was living around our property at that time.

MR. DOLAN: How old was [Barry]?

MZB: I think he was about 13, 14.

MR. DOLAN: To your knowledge, did your husband ever have a sexual relationship with [Barry]?

MZB: I don't know. At that time I believed Walter was completely impotent.

MR. DOLAN: My question is not whether you believed Walter was impotent, but did you ever receive any facts or information that led you to believe that Walter was having a sexual relationship with [Barry]?

MZB: No, I did not.

MR. DOLAN: Did your daughter ever report that [Barry] had been found in Walter's bed?

MZB: She did.

MR. DOLAN: Did you find that odd?

MZB: No. Walter had shared a bed with me on many occasions perfectly innocently.

MR. DOLAN: You knew that Walter was a pedophile at that time?

MZB: I knew it. Intellectually, yes, I knew it.

MR. DOLAN: And you knew that he was sharing a bed with a 13-year-old boy at that point; correct?

MZB: Yes. But, as I say, I believed Walter was impotent and nothing that could bother anyone could happen.

MR. WALKER: Now, when you say "sharing a bed," I think she was testifying about one occasion. I don't think–

MZB: Same occasions.

MR. WALKER: I don't think you've asked–

MR. DOLAN: Sharing a bed one time or more with a 13-year-old boy—we're going to get into in more detail here.

MR. WALKER: I just want to make sure the record is clear what you're asking her. Ask her a good question, and she'll give you the answer.

MR. DOLAN: My questions are good. I like my questions.

MZB: I was starting–

MR. WALKER: You don't have to answer. Let him pose a question, and then you can answer.

MZB: All I was going to say is that on one occasion I shared a house—I shared a bed with about seven other people, but we were all having a party overnight at the—I think it was up at the—what's the name? I've forgotten her name. I drew a blank. The lady and her husband were hosting an overnight party, and there were about 14 people there. And I think about nine of us piled into bed together.

MR. DOLAN: How many of those were children?

MZB: Four or five, I think.

MR. DOLAN: So you've shared a bed with minor children before too?

MZB: Well, they were all little girls.

MR. DOLAN: At the time were you aware that [Barry] was in Walter's bed on more than one occasion?

MZB: No, I was not.

MR. DOLAN: Did you make any attempts to adopt [Barry]?

MZB: Yes.

MR. DOLAN: Through what agency did you attempt to adopt [Barry]?

MZB: I think it was the Alameda County Children's Protective Services or something to that effect. It was a long time ago, and I don't really remember much about it.

MR. DOLAN: Did you have to undergo any kind of interviews or evaluation for the fitness of being adoptive parents?

MZB: Yes. We went to a class for counseling for adoptive parents.

MR. DOLAN: And at what time frame was this that you had heard the report that [Barry] had been in Walter's bed?

MZB: I don't remember.

MR. DOLAN: Can you give me an estimate or approximation?

MZB: No; I really can't. That was a long time ago.

MR. DOLAN: Was it when you were living at 2221 Prince Street with Walter?

MZB: Yes.

MR. DOLAN: Was it prior to your—you and Elisabeth moving out of 2221 Prince Street?

MZB: I don't remember.

MR. DOLAN: Was it in the 1980s?

MZB: It may well have been.

MR. DOLAN: Was it before Ken Smith's molestation was reported?

MZB: I never heard of Ken Smith. I mean, I'm told now that I know who he was, but I don't have any clear memory of him.

MR. DOLAN: Do you recall the fact that Walter was arrested for the molestation of Ken Smith?

MZB: Yes.

MR. DOLAN: Was the fact that Walter was in bed with [Barry] known to you before Ken Smith was arrested?

MZB: Yes.

MR. DOLAN: Strike that. I'm going to ask the question again. Was the fact that Walter was in bed with [Barry] known to you before Walter was arrested for the molestation of Ken Smith?

MZB: Yes.

MR. DOLAN: Was the fact that Walter was in bed with [Barry] known to you before you rented him the premises known as the goldfish bowl?

MZB: No.

MR. DOLAN: So you found that out after you had rented him the goldfish bowl?

MZB: Yes.

MR. DOLAN: And were you aware that he was found in bed with [Barry] at the goldfish bowl?

MZB: No.

MR. DOLAN: Where was he found in bed with [Barry]?

MZB: I don't remember.

MR. DOLAN: Okay.

MZB: I thought of [Barry] as a little boy that came over the house, and he used to sit on my lap.

MR. DOLAN: Did you think [Barry] was of the age to make decisions whether or not he could have a sexual relationship with Walter?

MZB: I was sort of ambivalent about that. [Barry] was like a stray cat that somebody put out on the street, and I think he was surviving any way he could.

MR. DOLAN: That would include having sex with older men?

MZB: Probably.

MR. WALKER: Objection. Asks for speculation.

MR. DOLAN: I just asked her–

MR. WALKER: I don't think that that's–

MR. BAKER: Argumentative.

MR. DOLAN: Did you get the answer?

THE REPORTER: Yes.

MR. DOLAN: Was [Barry] surviving by having sex with older men?

MR. BAKER: Argumentative.

MZB: I don't know.

MR. DOLAN: Did you ever talk to [Barry]'s mother?

MZB: No.

MR. DOLAN: Did you ever talk to his parents at all about this proposed adoption?

MZB: Yes. His mother came to see us on one occasion, and she paid more attention to the cat than she did [Barry]. She just said, "Oh, hello, [Barry]," and then she never looked at him or talked to him again.

MR. DOLAN: Did you talk to her at all?

MZB: Very little.

MR. DOLAN: So your testimony just given two seconds ago that you didn't speak to her was incorrect?

MZB: Yes; I spoke to her formally.

MR. DOLAN: Did you tell her that your husband and her child had been in bed together?

MZB: No, I did not.

MR. DOLAN: Why didn't you?

MZB: It didn't occur to me that it was important.

MR. DOLAN: Did you ever disclose to her that your husband was a pedophile?

MZB: I never thought of him that way.

MR. DOLAN: Did you ever tell her that your husband had a sexual relationship with a minor boy named [Glenn]?

MZB: No.

MR. DOLAN: Did you ever have any knowledge that your husband had been arrested in Atlantic City for lewd and lascivious acts with a minor?

MZB: No, I did not know that.

MR. DOLAN: Do you know who Kevin [Langdon] was in New York?

MZB: Yes.

MR. DOLAN: Who was Kevin?

MZB: He was a young man. At that time there were many multiple marriages, and at that time Walter and Kevin formed a triangle. It went on only for a short time.

MR. DOLAN: Okay. How old was Kevin?

MZB: I think he was 21 or 22.

MR. DOLAN: Let's get back to [Barry] for a minute. Did you ever have to fill out any paperwork to adopt [Barry]?

MZB: I don't remember.

MR. DOLAN: Did you ever disclose to the Berkeley—or strike that—the Alameda County Youth Authority, who you think it was, that your husband was a pedophile?

MZB: No.

MR. DOLAN: Did you conceal that from them?

MZB: I didn't think about it.

MR. DOLAN: Did the police ever investigate your husband's relationship with [Barry]?

MZB: No.

MR. DOLAN: To your knowledge, did the Berkeley Police ever investigate your husband's relationship with minor children prior to this incident with Ken Smith?

MZB: Not that I know of.

MR. DOLAN: To your knowledge, did the police investigate the issue surrounding the "Boondoggle"?

MZB: They did not.

MR. DOLAN: Did you ever tell your daughter that your husband preferred young boys between the ages of 9 and 10?

MZB: I don't think so.

MR. DOLAN: Can you deny that as you sit here today?

MZB: I don't remember doing so.

MR. DOLAN: Okay. But you can't deny it specifically never happening?

MZB: Correct.

MR. BAKER: Objection. Asked and answered.

MR. DOLAN: You can answer.

MZB: No, I don't remember any such thing.

MR. DOLAN: All right. If your daughter testified under oath that you told her that your husband preferred boys between the ages of 9 and 10, would you be able to deny that conversation?

MZB: Yes.

MR. BAKER: Objection. Speculation.

MR. WALKER: And Counsel, we've already talked about this.

MR. DOLAN: We talked about—we can step outside if you want.

MR. WALKER: Let's step outside.

MR. DOLAN: Pardon us. (Mr. Dolan, Mr. Bonagofsky, Mr. Walker and Mr. Baker exit and return.)

MR. DOLAN: If your daughter were to testify that you had spoken to her and told her that Walter preferred sex with boys between the ages of 9 and 10, would you be able to deny that conversation ever taking place?

MR. BAKER: Objection. Asked and answered. Speculation.

MR. WALKER: I'll join in the objection.

MR. DOLAN: You can answer.

MZB: I would say that I deny it absolutely.

MR. DOLAN: Okay. How many times did [Barry] stay over at your house?

MR. WALKER: I think that lacks foundation. I don't think she testified that he stayed over.

MR. BAKER: Join.

MZB: I don't remember.

MR. DOLAN: Did [Barry] stay over at your house?

MZB: I don't remember.

MR. DOLAN: So you don't know either way?

MZB: (Shakes head.)

MR. DOLAN: Is that a"Yes"?

MZB: I would say that I do not know.

MR. DOLAN: Okay. Whose [Johnny Doe 2]?

(Johnny Doe 2 is either Eric Worth or Michael Vaughn.)

MZB: Oh, he's some—he's a neighbor up the street.

MR. DOLAN: Does he still live up the street?

MZB: That was many years ago, but I think probably he does.

MR. DOLAN: Okay. Do you know his mother's name?

MZB: No.

MR. DOLAN: Do you know where up the street they lived from you?

MZB: No; just somewhere up the street.

MR. DOLAN: To your knowledge, was there ever any accusation that Walter was having a sexual relationship with [Johnny Doe 2]?

MZB: I never heard it if there was.

MR. DOLAN: Have you ever spoken to any of the parents of any minor children, informed them that Walter would never harm them?

MZB: I don't remember.

MR. DOLAN: Have you ever told any of the parents of minor children that Walter was not a pedophile?

MZB: I don't remember the subject has ever come up.

MR. DOLAN: So you don't remember either way; correct?

MZB: Uh-huh, I don't remember either way.

MR. DOLAN: How old was [Cyndi Beckett] when you began having a sexual relationship with her?

(I suspect Cyndi Beckett was Cyndi June, formerly Cyndi N'ha June)

MR. WALKER: Objection. Argumentative and lacks foundation.

MR. DOLAN: I'll rephrase.

MR. DOLAN: Did you ever have a sexual relationship with [Cyndi Beckett]?

MZB: No.

MR. DOLAN: Did you ever participate in an orgy with [Cyndi Beckett]?

MZB: Depending on what you call....

MR. DOLAN: Did you ever participate in an orgy with Elisabeth Waters, [Cyndi Beckett] and Philip Wang?

MZB: No.

MR. DOLAN: Was she ever present during a sexual act that you were involved in with other people?

MZB: She might have been.

MR. DOLAN: Elisabeth Waters has testified to being involved in an orgy with you and [Cyndi Beckett]. Do you deny that ever took place?

MZB: I neither deny nor affirm it. I simply don't remember any such event.

MR. DOLAN: Did you ever have sexual relations with [Cyndi Beckett]–

MR. WALKER: Objection. That's been asked and answered.

MR. DOLAN:–of any kind.

MR. BAKER: Objection. Asked and answered.

MR. DOLAN: You can answer.

MZB: Not that I can remember. I was riding once in a car with her, and she kept putting her hand on my knee. And I shoved her hand off my knee, and we hit the curb. We hit the curb and blew a tire.

MR. DOLAN: Did [Cyndi Beckett] come to live with you?

MZB: Yes.

MR. DOLAN: How old was she when she came to live with you?

MZB: I think she was 18 or 19.

(No, she was 16.)

MR. DOLAN: How old was Elisabeth Waters when she came to live with you?

MZB: 28.

(No, she was 26.)

MR. WALKER: Counsel, were you asking when [Cyndi Beckett] came or when Elisabeth Waters came?

MR. DOLAN: When Elisabeth Waters came and lived with you, how old was she?

MZB: 28.

MR. DOLAN: Is she your cousin?

MZB: Yes.

MR. DOLAN: And what is she, your first, second cousin, what?

MZB: Ninth. A friend of ours has a hobby doing genealogy, and we looked it up and found out that we were cousins in the ninth degree, that we had a common ancestor on the Mayflower.

MR. DOLAN: Other than—well, strike that. Did [Glenn] ever live with you?

MZB: No.

MR. DOLAN: Did he ever stay over at the house when you were there with Walter?

MZB: I don't remember.

MR. DOLAN: Did [Barry] ever live with you?

MZB: No.

MR. DOLAN: Did you ever have him stay over?

MZB: Wait. Excuse me. Strike that. Yes, he did. He was downstairs in a room between—that was one reason that we made him leave was because we said he had to go to school and he had to respect the girls' privacy. We had a young friend living with us then named [Jane Doe 1], and he was always popping into the girls' room when they were dressing.

(Jane Doe 1 was Rohana? Heather? Elizabeth Rousseau??)

MR. DOLAN: Is that [Jane Doe 1] ?

MZB: No. That's a girl called [Jane Doe 1]. She was in my daughter's second grade with her, and they were in dancing class together.

MR. DOLAN: And she lived with you for a time period?

MZB: Yes.

MR. DOLAN: Other than [Barry] living with you for a time period, did any other minor children—young boys live with you?

MZB: Let me think. Not that I can remember.

MR. DOLAN: Whose idea was it to adopt [Barry]?

MZB: As I remember, Walter and I were talking it over together that he had become like a son in our household and that why shouldn't we try it.

MR. DOLAN: Did any members of the community oppose this proposed adoption?

MZB: I don't remember them opposing it.

MR. DOLAN: Do you know if there were any background investigations done by the Alameda County Youth Authority of you or your husband regarding this?

MZB: I don't think so.

MR. DOLAN: Was Elisabeth Waters living at the house at the time [Barry] was going to be adopted?

MZB: Yes.

MR. DOLAN: Did you know of Walter's pedophilic ways?

MR. WALKER: Lacks foundation.

MR. DOLAN: Did you ever know about Walter's pedophilic ways?

MR. BAKER: Objection. Lacks foundation. Misstates her previous testimony.

MR. DOLAN: Did Elisabeth Waters ever come to you and raise any questions about Walter's behavior with young children?

MZB: Not until this thing came up with whoever it was.

MR. DOLAN: With who?

MZB: I'm trying to remember. Some—they've alleged some kid I wouldn't know from Adam.

MR. DOLAN: Ken Smith?

MZB: I think that may be the one.

MR. DOLAN: Sean [redacted]?

MZB: I don't know. As I said, I have no memory of any of it.

MR. DOLAN: Has anyone told you that you have memory problems with certain areas of your memory?

MZB: Yes.

MR. DOLAN: And who told you that?

MZB: My doctor.

MR. DOLAN: Which doctor?

MZB: My heart specialist. I can't remember his name at the moment.

MR. DOLAN: Do you know who Ian Studebaker is?

MZB: He's my nephew.

MR. DOLAN: To your knowledge, did Ian Studebaker ever complain that Walter had—

MZB: No.

MR. DOLAN: Did Tracy Blackstone ever complain about the fact that Walter had inappropriately touched Ian?

MZB: Not to me.

MR. DOLAN: Do you know if she complained about it to anyone else?

MZB: I have no idea.

MR. DOLAN: Did Tracy state that Ian couldn't come over to the house unless you or Elisabeth were there?

MZB: I don't know. She made that statement about her daughter Fiona.

MR. DOLAN: Okay. She told you she didn't want Fiona coming over to your home unless you or Elisabeth were there?

MZB: That's what she said.

MR. DOLAN: Did you ever ask her why?

MZB: No. I thought Tracy was just—well, Tracy's a funny person.

MR. DOLAN: What did Tracy say to you?

MZB: As far as I know, she just said—Tracy said Fiona couldn't come over here unless Elisabeth or I were there. And I thought it was simply because we were all coming in and out. There were quite a lot of people around.

MR. DOLAN: To your knowledge, did Walter ever have underage boys, meaning boys under the age of 18, in the hot tub at your house at 2221 Prince Street?

MZB: Not to my knowledge.

MR. DOLAN: Did–

MZB: David was there sometimes.

MR. DOLAN: Did Elisabeth Waters ever discuss with you any concerns that she had that Walter might have been molesting [Sterling]?

MZB: No. I thought [Sterling] was Moira's boyfriend.

MR. DOLAN: Did you ever insist to Elisabeth Waters that Walter was incapable of molesting [Sterling]?

MZB: I can't remember, but it doesn't sound like the sort of thing I would say.

MR. DOLAN: Elisabeth Waters in her 10-8-89 diary, which was given to the police, indicates the following: Quote, "And I feel like a total idiot for not having said anything back when I thought Walter was molesting [Sterling] ten years ago. I guess it was just another case of," quote, "'Don't trust your own perceptions when the adults are telling you you're wrong.' Marion insisted that Walter was incapable of it, and she was 22 years older than I and married, while I was very ignorant about sex." Does that refresh your recollection at all as to whether you had a conversation with Elisabeth Waters about the molestation of–

MZB: If she says so, it probably happened.

MR. DOLAN: Okay. Do you have any—Does that refresh your recollection about that conversation?

MZB: No. I don't remember the conversation at all.

MR. DOLAN: Having had that read to you, do you recall telling Elisabeth that, that Walter would be incapable of molesting [Sterling]?

MZB: No, I don't.

MR. DOLAN: Do you know if Walter was incapable of giving oral sex to minor boys?

MZB: I have no idea. I know nothing at all about oral sex. I broke up both my own marriages over it.

MR. DOLAN: What was that last part?

MZB: I said I broke up both my own marriages over it.

MR. DOLAN: Did you ever talk to [Sterling]'s parents about any of this?

MZB: I don't think so.

MR. WALKER: Any of what, Counsel?

MR. DOLAN: Any of these issues regarding pedophilia.

MZB: No. I never met his father, and I knew his mother only as part of SCA.

MR. DOLAN: The Society for Creative Anachronism?

MZB: That's right.

MR. DOLAN: Do you know what the syntax dictionary?

MZB: No.

MR. DOLAN: Do you know who had it last?

MZB: I haven't any idea.

MR. DOLAN: Did you ever see a letter from Dr. Morin about [Sterling]?

MZB: Who's Dr. Morin?

MR. DOLAN: Dr. Morin was one of Walter's psychologists.

MZB: I can't remember any such letter. I don't believe I ever knew him. As far as I know, I never met the man.

MR. DOLAN: Who's [Gregg]?

MZB: The name doesn't ring a bell.

MR. DOLAN: I'm going to read to you from the 10-9-89 entry of Elisabeth Waters. "Marion always said she'd divorce Walter if he did this again. She seems to think that he molested both [Glenn] and [Gregg], but she was rather startled when I told her about the letter to Dr. Morin about [Sterling]. She said that she thought Walter thought of [Sterling] as a son." Let me ask you a few questions about that statement. Does that refresh your recollection about a letter from Dr. Morin?

MZB: Yes, it does.

MR. DOLAN: Can you now tell me what you recall?

MZB: Yes. I can remember discussing the fact that he thought of him as a son because Moira and Patrick both thought of [Sterling] as a brother.

MR. DOLAN: Did you talk to Walter about any sexual activity between himself and [Sterling]?

MZB: It never occurred to me.

MR. DOLAN: It didn't occur to you to talk about it?

MZB: No. I wouldn't even have thought about it.

MR. DOLAN: Do you recall the letter from Dr. Morin now?

MZB: I never saw any such letters.

MR. DOLAN: Did Elisabeth ever tell you about a letter to Dr. Morin about [Sterling] that Walter had written?

MZB: No.

MR. DOLAN: Did you ever tell Elisabeth that you thought Walter had molested both [Glenn] and [Gregg]?

MZB: I can't remember. I don't believe I ever discussed it with Elisabeth, but I might have in passing.

MR. DOLAN: If Elisabeth states that you discussed it with her, do you deny having those discussions?

MZB: No, I wouldn't deny it. But I think she might have written in her diary and forgotten to read it to me or something. Elisabeth does not have the greatest memory in the world either.

MR. DOLAN: I've noticed. Do you have any recollection of anybody named [Gregg] ever being over at the house?

MZB: I think Moira had a boyfriend of that name.

(No, I never did. Gregg was involved with my father, never with me.)

MR. DOLAN: Do you have any understanding as to whether [Gregg] was ever molested by Walter Breen?

MZB: I wouldn't have inquired into the matter or thought about it.

MR. DOLAN: Did you know that Walter had a lot of young boys over at the house?

MZB: No. I didn't notice. I was never over at the goldfish bowl.

MR. DOLAN: How about when he was living with you?

MZB: Well, he had friends, yes.

MR. DOLAN: Young boys?

MZB: Occasionally.

MR. DOLAN: Did Walter have an unusual number of young boyfriends for a man of his age?

MZB: I wouldn't think so.

MR. DOLAN: Did you state that you would divorce Walter if he ever did this again?

MZB: Yes, I did.

MR. DOLAN: What did you mean by doing this again?

MZB: I meant if he ever molested a young boy again.

MR. DOLAN: And when you say "again," who were the other young boys that you were talking about him molesting?

MZB: [Glenn] especially.

MR. DOLAN: Any others?

MZB: I can't remember any offhand.

MR. DOLAN: Are you aware of there being others?

MZB: There might have been. I would not have inquired into the matter.

MR. DOLAN: But to your knowledge, there might have been others besides [Glenn]?

MZB: There might have been.

MR. DOLAN: But you didn't specifically inquire into that?

MZB: At the time I did not. I can look back now and see there might have been, but I didn't know at the time.

MR. DOLAN: Did you ever warn any people in the general public about Walter's tastes for young boys?

MZB: No.

MR. DOLAN: Did you know that Walter was attending conventions where lots of young children were?

MZB: I think he had only been to coin conventions, and they sort of flocked around him like—like bees around honey. He was an expert on coins and an authority on the subject.

MR. DOLAN: Okay. Did Walter ever attend science-fiction conventions?

MZB: Once or twice.

MR. DOLAN: Did you pay for his attendance at those conventions?

MZB: Yes, I did.

MR. DOLAN: As somebody who was paying for his attendance at those conventions, did you ever warn people at the convention that Walter was a pedophile?

MZB: No.

MR. BAKER: Objection. Argumentative.

MR. WALKER: I'll join that.

MZB: I did not.

MR. DOLAN: Did you ever warn any of the people at the convention about Walter's tastes in young boys?

MZB: No.

MR. BAKER: Objection. Lacks foundation.

MZB: Never occurred to me.

MR. DOLAN: You were aware that Walter had a sexual appetite for young boys?

MZB: I suppose I was.

MR. DOLAN: Did you ever warn people at the conventions of Walter's sexual appetite for young boys?

MZB: No, I did not.

MR. BAKER: Same objections.

MR. DOLAN: Indeed you defended Walter's expulsion from a convention on the basis of pedophilia, didn't you?

MR. BAKER: Objection. Argumentative.

MZB: Yes, I did.

MR. DOLAN: So in addition to never warning people, you actually defended his presence there, didn't you?

MR. BAKER: Objection. Argumentative.

MR. WALKER: Asked and answered.

MR. DOLAN: You can answer.

MZB: I thought it was his own business.

MR. DOLAN: Okay.

MZB: And we did not discuss the subject, as far as I can remember.

MR. DOLAN: Did he attend these coin conferences as an employee of yours?

MZB: No, he did not. I had no interest in the coin business.

MR. DOLAN: I'm talking about the science-fiction conventions.

MZB: No, he did not.

MR. DOLAN: Why did you pay his way, then?

MZB: Because he was my husband. He had shared things with me when we were very poor; and then when I got money, I shared things with him.

MR. DOLAN: Maybe we could take a break. Are you okay?

MZB: Yes, I'm fine.

MR. DOLAN: Was Walter an employee of yours during the time that he attended these conventions?

MZB: No.

MR. DOLAN: Was he ever an employee of yours?

MZB: I believe he wrote some articles for the magazine.

MR. DOLAN: Did you ever pay him as an employee?

MZB: No. I paid him for what he wrote and was printed in the magazine.

MR. DOLAN: Was he ever paid a salary by you or your company?

MZB: I don't think so. I don't remember very clearly. I seldom think much about money at all.

MR. DOLAN: Okay.

MZB: The thing is that when we were very broke, he was always very good about sharing his poverty with me; and then when I began to make money, I shared everything I had with him.

MR. DOLAN: I'm looking for some guidance here. We okay here?

MR. WALKER: I mean, we only have about five more minutes left. Are you okay to keep–

MZB: Yeah, I'm fine.

MR. DOLAN: I'm going to take a break for two minutes, and I'll take my five minutes, and we'll be out of here. Okay?

MR. WALKER: Okay.

MR. DOLAN: I just need to talk to Scott for a moment. (Mr. Dolan and Mr. Bonagofsky exit and return.)

MR. DOLAN: Did you ever tell Elisabeth Waters that children didn't have erogenous zones?

MZB: I may well have.

MR. DOLAN: Do you have the belief that children don't have erogenous zones?

MZB: At the time I believed it.

MR. DOLAN: And what time was that?

MZB: I think it was probably when my own kids were young.

MR. DOLAN: Are you aware of Walter writing any posthumus letters to Ken Smith?

MZB: Posthumus letters?

MR. DOLAN: There is some indication that he had written letters to be delivered posthumously.

MZB: I thought if he wanted it–

MR. DOLAN: Did you ever receive such a letter?

MZB: No.—he would have written it to me.

MR. DOLAN: Did you ever state to your daughter that these young boys got what they deserved?

MZB: I don't remember.

MR. DOLAN: You don't remember either way?

MZB: No.

MR. DOLAN: All right. Did you attend the Westercon 4 on Halloween weekend in 1982?

MZB: I believe so.

MR. DOLAN: Did you attend the Westercon 5 in 1985 on Halloween weekend?

MZB: I don't remember.

MR. DOLAN: Do you have records of what conferences you attended?

MZB: No.

MR. DOLAN: Did you attend the 1984 Nebula Awards?

MZB: I probably did. I attend—you'd have to tell me when it was held. I go to them if they're anywhere within my traveling capacity.

MR. DOLAN: Okay. In New York, the 1984 Nebula Awards.

MZB: No.

MR. DOLAN: Were you aware that Ken Smith was spending time with Walter Breen over at the other home that you rented to Walter Breen?

MZB: I never saw Ken Smith and, to the best of my knowledge, I never heard of him.

MR. DOLAN: Did you speak to the police following the arrest for the molestation of Ken Smith?

MZB: I don't remember, but I don't think so. I probably would have remembered it.

MR. DOLAN: There are statements attributed to you in the police report following the molestation of Ken Smith.

MZB: I don't remember them.

MR. DOLAN: If you had spoken to the police, would you have been truthful and correct to them?

MZB: Yes, I would.

MR. DOLAN: The police officer records, quote, "I asked"—and this is on page—it's not listed by page, but it's Report No. 89-42141, which has been provided previously to counsel. And it's a date of–

MR. WALKER: Do you have a copy of that right now?

MR. DOLAN:-- 2-6-90. Let's mark this as the next in order. It's going to be the fourth page back. (Plaintiffs' Exhibit 3 was marked for identification.)

MR. DOLAN: I'm going to show you what's been marked as Plaintiffs' Exhibit No. 3, and I'm going to refer you to Page 4, the last paragraph of Plaintiffs' Exhibit No. 3, Page 4. Quote, "I asked if she knew Ken Smith, and she said met him in the fall of 1988, briefly because Breen had brought him over, but that she does not know his family." Does that refresh your recollection as to whether or not you had met Ken Smith?

MZB: I don't remember him.

MR. DOLAN: Okay. So you don't remember either way?

MZB: No, I don't. I've been racking my brains back and forth, but I can't remember ever meeting Ken Smith.

MR. DOLAN: In 1990, in that same page, you told the officer you did not think that Breen was actually engaging in sexual activity with young boys.

MZB: I believed that at the time.

MR. DOLAN: At that time you knew that he had sexual activity with [Glenn] when [Glenn] was under the age of 18, didn't you?

MZB: Yes, I did. But as I said, [Glenn] was a teenager, and, as I remember, this was some little kid around 10, 12 years old.

MR. DOLAN: Would 12 years old be too young, in your opinion, then?

MR. BAKER: Calls for speculation.

MR. WALKER: Join.

MZB: No opinion.

MR. WALKER: Counsel, I think we're just about done with the hour and–

MR. DOLAN: Sure. We'll set up a another date. Thank you for your time. We were going to suspend but not conclude your deposition today. Okay?

MZB: Yes, sir.

MR. DOLAN: Have a good day, ma'am.

MZB: You too.

(Whereupon, the deposition adjourned at 12:01 p.m.)

I, the undersigned, hereby certify that the witness in the foregoing deposition was, by me, duly sworn to tell the truth, the whole truth and nothing but the truth in the within-entitled cause.

That said deposition was taken in shorthand by me, a Certified Shorthand Reporter and a disinterested person, at the time and place therein stated, and that the testimony of said witness was thereafter reduced to typewriting, by computer, under my direction and supervision. I further certify that I am not of counsel or attorney for either or any of the parties of the said deposition, nor in any way interested in the event of this cause, and that I am not related to any of the parties thereto.

IN WITNESS WHEREOF, I have hereunto set my hand, this 25th day of August 1998.

Janine P. Branco

25 CSR #10372

DEPOSITION OF MARION ZIMMER BRADLEY, 12/14/98

IN THE SUPERIOR COURT OF THE STATE OF CALIFORNIA
FOR THE COUNTY OF ALAMEDA

KEN SMITH, Plaintiff, vs. MARION ZIMMER BRADLEY, ELISABETH WATERS, and DOES 1 through 10, Defendants.

DEPOSITION OF MARION ZIMMER BRADLEY VOLUME II Monday, December 14, 1998

REPORTED BY: JANINE P. BRANCO, CSR No. 10372

EXHIBITS

2-page 6-6-54 typewritten document.

1-page 2-1-86 document entitled "Rental Agreement."

BE IT REMEMBERED THAT, pursuant to Notice of Taking Deposition and on Monday, December 14, 1998, commencing at the hour of 11:24 a.m. thereof, at 200 Marina Boulevard, Room 1102, Berkeley, California, before me, JANINE P. BRANCO, a Certified Shorthand Reporter of the State of California, personally appeared MARION ZIMMER BRADLEY a Defendant herein, called as a witness by the Plaintiff, having been by me first duly sworn, was examined and testified further hereinafter as set forth.

APPEARANCES OF COUNSEL

For the Plaintiff Ken Smith

THE LAW OFFICES OF CHRISTOPHER B. DOLAN

655 Montgomery Street, 16th FloorSan Francisco, CA 94111

By: CHRISTOPHER B. DOLAN, Attorney at Law

For the Defendant Marion Zimmer Bradley

CAUDLE, WELCH, UMIPEG & BOVEE

1390 Willow Pass Road, Suite 200 Concord, CA 94520

By: M. HENRY WALKER, Attorney at Law

For the Defendant Elisabeth Waters

HAIMS, JOHNSON, MacGOWAN & McINERNEY

490 Grand Avenue Oakland, CA 94610

By: LAWRENCE A. BAKER, Attorney at Law

ALSO PRESENT: BELLE ROMERO

EXAMINATION BY MR. DOLAN (Resumed)

MR. DOLAN: Ms. Zimmer Bradley, we're going forward with your deposition today based upon the limitations that have been imposed by your doctors and your counsel; so we will have no more than one hour today of deposition. Do you understand that?

MZB: Yes, I do. Thank you.

MR. DOLAN: I've also agreed with your counsel not to delve into particular areas during this session of your deposition. Do you understand that?

MZB: Well, I think I know what you mean.

MR. DOLAN: Okay. I will not be asking any questions about your relationship with your daughter. Do you understand that?

MZB: Yes.

MR. DOLAN: I reserve my right to do so at a future date; okay?

MZB: Okay.

MR. DOLAN: Who is the president today?

MZB: William Clinton.

MR. DOLAN: Do you know who the vice president is?

MZB: I am not sure.

MR. DOLAN: Do you know who the governor of the State of California is?

MZB: The last I heard it was Willie Brown.

MR. DOLAN: Okay. And do you know who was elected governor recently?

MZB: Gray Davis.

MR. DOLAN: Do you know what party Gray Davis is a member of?

MZB: I think he's a democrat.

MR. DOLAN: Do you know what day today is?

MZB: December 12th or 13th, 1998.

MR. DOLAN: Do you know what day of the week it is?

MZB: Monday.

MR. DOLAN: How many children do you have?

MZB: Three.

MR. DOLAN: Where is your home when you're not living in this hotel?

MZB: 2223—2223 Fulton Street, Berkeley, California.

MR. DOLAN: Okay.

MZB: It's just—it's just—It's between Shattuck and Telegraph almost exactly.

MR. DOLAN: Do you have another home that you own besides that one?

MZB: Yes, I do. We just purchased a place on Fulton Street.

MR. DOLAN: Okay. Where do you live when you're not living here?

MZB: I live at Fulton Street, not—yes, I live at the Fulton Street house.

MR. DOLAN: Do you ever live on Prince Street when you're not living here?

MZB: Well, it's on the corner of Prince and Fulton. They run into each other.

MR. DOLAN: What are your children's names?

MZB: My oldest son is named David Steven Bradley; my second son is Patrick Russell Breen; and my daughter is named Moira Stern. She's married to Robert Stern.

MR. DOLAN: Do you have a nurse here today?

MZB: Yes.

MR. DOLAN: What is your nurse's name?

MZB: Belle.

MR. DOLAN: Do you know where Moira lives?

MZB: At the moment I think she's living somewhere in Novato. She's going to the university there to work on a master's degree.

MR. DOLAN: The reason I was asking you those questions is to try to determine whether or not you're–

MZB: Whether I'm oriented in time and space.

MR. DOLAN: Right. Are you feeling sufficiently oriented in time and space to go forward with your deposition today?

MZB: Yes; I think so.

MR. DOLAN: Have you seen any physicians in the past week that have indicated that you're unable to go forward with this deposition?

MZB: No. I've seen three physicians. None of them have mentioned the deposition.

MR. DOLAN: And do you have any knowledge of why we cannot go forward with your deposition today?

MZB: No.

MR. DOLAN: Very good. I'm going to go over the rules of a deposition with you again, even though we've gone over them once before–

MZB: Yes.

MR. DOLAN: –just to make sure we're both familiar with the rules of a deposition; okay?

MZB: Okay.

MR. DOLAN: The first rule of a deposition is I do not want you to guess or speculate as to anything that's said here today. Do you understand that?

MZB: Yes, I do.

MR. DOLAN: I understand that you've had some strokes and that you may have some memory problems, but I don't want you to guess or make anything up merely to be helpful today.

MZB: If I don't remember something, I just say I don't remember it.

MR. DOLAN: That will be fine. Thank you. The second thing is we need to talk in turn, only one person talking at a time because the court reporter can only take down written statements of one person at a time. So if you'll wait until I finish my questions before you begin your answers, or wait for the attorneys to finish their objections before you begin your answers, that will be very helpful to us today. Will you do that?

MZB: Yes; I'll try to do so. I can't guarantee it. I tend to—people ask me things, and I tend to speak without thinking.

MR. DOLAN: Okay. That's fine. Everything that's done here today needs to be said in a full English language spoken word. We have to use English, and we have to avoid grunts and groans, but use "yes," "no" or any other combination of words that you feel suitable or appropriate. Do you understand that?

MZB: I'll do my best.

MR. DOLAN: If you do not understand my question, ask me to help you understand the question. Tell me you don't understand the question or somehow otherwise let us know because if we receive an answer to a question, I will assume that you understood the question asked of you. Is that clear?

MZB: Yes, it is.

MR. DOLAN: At the end of the deposition process, you'll have an opportunity to review the booklet that's being typed by the woman to my right, to your left. You'll have an opportunity to make any changes in the transcript you'd like, that reads a lot like a script or a novel like you may have written in the past, and you can edit it and make changes to it. I must caution you, however, that if you edit it or make changes to it of a substantive nature, I can comment on that at trial, or any other lawyer can comment on that at trial in order to make you look bad or to show that you may not be truthful or to say your memory is not very good. So if you think of something you need to change today, please try to do that today so that we can avoid the embarrassment later on. Is that clear?

MZB: Yes, it is.

MR. DOLAN: Have you read your last session of your deposition?

MZB: Well, yes. But since it was—all the questions were on one page and the answers on another, I found it very confusing.

MR. DOLAN: Okay. Is that your deposition or your Interrogatory answers; do you know?

MZB: I don't know the meaning of those words.

MR. DOLAN: Okay. A deposition is the booklet that's being written up by the court reporter to our right. It's a question-and-answer thing. It reads a lot like a script. And this is a copy of your deposition from the first session, which has questions and answers (indicating). Did you read something like that?

MZB: No. The one that I saw had the questions on one page and the answers on another one and nothing but numbers on them to keep them straight with.

MR. DOLAN: Something more like this that I'm showing you, your responses to requests for–

MZB: Yes.

MR. DOLAN:–admissions?

MZB: Yes.

MR. DOLAN: Okay. Is there any reason that you're aware of why your deposition should not go forward today?

MZB: None that I'm aware of.

MR. DOLAN: Are you living in this hotel currently?

MZB: Yes, I am.

MR. DOLAN: And for how long have you been residing in this hotel?

MZB: Two weeks.

MR. DOLAN: Do you have any understanding of how long you expect to reside in this hotel?

MZB: Hopefully we'll be out of here in another week. They have a—they have a place for me for—a temporary one at a disabled apartment.

MR. DOLAN: Very good. Have you been traveling out of the hotel anywhere to go to conventions or to any types of events?

MZB: No, I have not. I have been taken out to lunch once or twice. That is about all.

MR. DOLAN: Okay. When did you first start living with Walter Breen?

MZB: In, I think it was, 1963.

MR. DOLAN: And how did you come to know him prior to 1963?

MZB: We had been corresponding. We were both members of what at that time was known as Science Fiction Phantom. We both were readers of science fiction, and we would write to each other and discuss the stories and the writers, and occasionally other items of interest. Naturally we found we had interests in common and began speaking to each other frequently on the telephone.

MR. DOLAN: Had you met personally prior to corresponding with him?

MZB: Not at first. I met with him about the middle of the time.

MR. DOLAN: Where did you first meet him?

MZB: New York City.

MR. DOLAN: Did you understand him to be living there at the time?

MZB: Yes, I did.

MR. DOLAN: Were you living in New York City at the time?

MZB: No, I was not. I was living in Albany with my mother and father.

MR. DOLAN: Have you retained any of the correspondence that you initially had with Walter?

MZB: No.

MR. DOLAN: Okay. When did your relationship develop in terms of years to the time that you two began to live in the same city?

MZB: I—I am a little doubtful, but what happened was that we had been talking to each other frequently on the telephone, and then I decided to leave my home and move to the University, to Berkeley, University of California t do graduate work there, and he said that I could stay with him, and I accepted the invitation. And when I went out there we moved in together.

MR. DOLAN: When you say you moved out there, is that New York or California?

MZB: California.

MR. DOLAN: So the first time that you lived with Walter was in California?

MZB: Yes. We had met several times before that but briefly.

MR. DOLAN: When you came to California, did you live with anyone other than Walter?

MZB: Yes. For a time I lived with Miriam Knight.

MR. DOLAN: And that is whom in relationship to you?

MZB: Well, she's just another lady that I met through Phantom. She was married to a friend of mine.

MR. DOLAN: She still alive?

MZB: I don't have the slightest idea. I haven't seen her in years. When Walter died we went to Las Vegas to wait out a divorce. Marium agreed to keep my son and took care of David during the six weeks I was in Novato.

MR. DOLAN: And her last name was Night, N-i-g-h-t?

MZB: K-n-i-g-h-t.

MR. DOLAN: And do you know where she lived the last time that you knew of her to be in existence?

MZB: The last time I knew of her she had—I think she had a child. I remember that she and I and Grania Davis were all expecting children at the same time. I'm trying to remember. I think she was living in an apartment in Berkeley.

MR. DOLAN: Do you know if she ever changed her name from Knight to something else?

MZB: I don't remember.

MR. DOLAN: So you began living with Walter sometime in 1964—is that right?—in Berkeley or–

MZB: I think it was very early in '64.

MR. DOLAN: When did you marry him?

MZB: '64. Later in the year, about June.

MR. DOLAN: Prior to marrying Walter did you ever discuss his relationship with any young men under the age of 18?

MZB: I think the subject may have come up in passing, fleetingly. Certainly very little impression on me.

MR. DOLAN: When you say the subject "may have come up in passing, fleetingly," can you tell me what you can recall about the subject coming up prior to your marrying him?

MZB: Maybe at that point we were discussing civilization and the fact that young men among the Greeks—well, the women, of course, at that time were idiots and uneducated and living in Perdock, and so the men had emotional and friendly relationships with members of their own sex, and that formed the topic of conversation. It was an interesting subject. We talked about it a bit.

MR. DOLAN: And at that point did Walter confide to you that he had sexual relationships with young men?

MZB: He did.

MR. DOLAN: And do you have an understanding of the names of any of those young men?

MZB: No.

MR. DOLAN: Did he give you an indication of how many occasions he had sexual relationships with different young men?

MZB: No. We did not talk much about it. I gather it was something that just came up now and then.

MR. DOLAN: So it was your understanding it was something that Walter would engage in now and then?

MZB: Yes.

MR. DOLAN: You understand that these sexual relationships were with young men under the age of 18?

MZB: I didn't know.

MR. DOLAN: Did you form any understanding as to the approximate age of the young men with which Walter was having sexual relationships?

MZB: No, I did not. He was in his 30s, so I naturally assumed they would be in their 20s or 30s also.

MR. DOLAN: Didn't you come to know about [Glenn] prior to marrying Walter?

MZB: Yes, I did.

MR. DOLAN: You knew he was under the age of 18, didn't you?

MZB: Yes.

MR. DOLAN: So when you said naturally they were in their 20s to 30s, you knew of at least one that they weren't 20 to 30?

MZB: Yes; I knew of that one exception.

MR. DOLAN: Did you inquire as to any other exceptions?

MZB: No, I did not.

MR. DOLAN: Did you prior to marrying Walter Breen inform him that he was to have no sexual contact with your minor children?

MZB: It never occurred to me one way or the other.

MR. DOLAN: To your knowledge, did Walter ever have sexual contact with your son David?

MZB: I asked David one time about it, and he told me one of Walter's friends had propositioned him and that he said no, and so the friend said, "Okay. Let's go ride the merry-go-round."

MR. DOLAN: Okay. Tell me when you and David had this conversation.

MZB: I think it was sometime in '64. Might have been early '65.

MR. DOLAN: And how old was David at that time?

MZB: I think he was 13 or 14.

MR. DOLAN: Do you know the name of the person who propositioned him?

MZB: Yes, I do. His name was Robert Bashlow.

MR. DOLAN: Could you spell–

MZB: B-a-s-h-l-o-w.

MR. DOLAN: What occasioned you to ask your son David about whether or not he had been propositioned by anyone?

MZB: Because I knew Robert Bashlow, and I knew that anything with two legs which got in his vicinity was likely to be propositioned.

MR. DOLAN: I didn't hear the last part.

MZB: I said that anyone in his vicinity of either gender was likely to be propositioned. I never paid much attention because my attitude was well no harm in asking as long he takes no for an answer.

MR. DOLAN: So your—So your understanding at that time in 1964 is that there was nothing inappropriate about an older man asking a minor for sex so long as the young boy said no?

MZB: As long as the young boy is given plenty of opportunity to say no.

MR. DOLAN: At that time did you also believe if the young boy had said yes that would be okay then?

MZB: I had not thought a great deal about the matter, but I suppose yes, that is a fair statement.

MR. DOLAN: Okay. Did you ever ask your son whether Walter propositioned your son? We've mentioned now about this other gentleman, Mr. Bashlow, but did you ever ask your son whether Walter ever propositioned David?

MZB: It came up a few years ago.

MR. DOLAN: Tell me how it came up.

MZB: Well, somebody was talking about it, and afterwards I said to David, "Did Walter ever say anything to you about it?" and he said, "No. I was too old. I didn't pay much attention to it." He wrote me a letter saying that Walter had been a very good stepfather to him. I think his exact words were that when it came to stepfathers he got the pick of the bisque.

MR. DOLAN: He had the what, the pick of the basket?

MZB: Pick of the bisque.

MR. DOLAN: Where did you have this discussion with David where he thought he was too old for Walter?

MZB: When he was 15 or so.

MR. DOLAN: About 15?

MZB: Yes.

MR. DOLAN: That's when you discussed this with him?

MZB: Yes.

MR. DOLAN: So at the time that David was 15, David informed you that he believed that your then husband was not propositioning him because at that point David was too old for Walter's tastes?

MZB: I think that's what he said. To the best of my memory, that's what he said.

MR. DOLAN: Was that consistent with your understanding at that time that David at the age of 15 would be too old for Walter's tastes in partners?

MR. BAKER: Objection. Lacks foundation.

MR. DOLAN: You can answer.

MR. WALKER: I'll join in that.

MR. DOLAN: You can answer.

MR. WALKER: Go ahead and answer it, if you can.

MZB: I don't know.

MR. DOLAN: Did you ever undertake any inquiry after David said that to find out exactly what Walter's tastes were in terms of young men?

MZB: No.

MR. DOLAN: Did it trouble you at all that your son—that your husband was interested in boys under his age?

MZB: No, it didn't. At that time my husband and I were very in love, and I had no reason to suspect that his interests lay anywhere else.

MR. DOLAN: But you had asked your son that question?

MZB: It came up in conversation.

MR. DOLAN: How did it come up in conversation?

MZB: I haven't the least idea.

MR. DOLAN: To the best of your recollection, how did this come up in conversation?

MZB: I'm sorry. I can't remember. It was just something we were talking about.

MR. DOLAN: So, was a topic of conversation in your family Walter's interests in young boys–

MZB: It could have been.

MR. DOLAN:–back when your son was as young as 15?

MZB: Yes.

MR. DOLAN: When was your son born?

MZB: 1950, I think.

MR. DOLAN: And it was a topic of conversation such that you asked your son whether Walter had ever propositioned him; correct?

MZB: Yes.

MR. DOLAN: And so you were concerned enough to ask your own son whether your husband had propositioned him sexually?

MZB: I wouldn't say I was concerned. I meant the subject had come up and I was curious.

MR. DOLAN: So you were curious enough to ask your own son whether your husband had made a sexual proposition to him?

MZB: I wouldn't say I was concerned enough. I would simply say the matter came up in conversation.

MR. DOLAN: Okay. When your son indicated that he had been propositioned by Robert Bashlow, did you do anything to prohibit Mr. Bashlow from coming in contact with your son?

MZB: No. I think I might have thought it was funny.

MR. DOLAN: So you thought the fact that an older man propositioned your then 13-year-old son was funny?

MZB: I thought Robert Bashlow was a pretty funny individual.

MR. DOLAN: And you took no steps to prevent your son from coming in contact with a man who you knew had propositioned him?

MZB: Considering that David was almost six feet and Bashlow, as I remember, was about five foot, one, I didn't worry about it.

MR. DOLAN: You're saying your son was six feet tall at the age of 13?

MZB: Pretty near.

MR. DOLAN: So the question again is–

MZB: He's now six foot, six.

MR. DOLAN: The question is: Did you undertake any action to prevent any further contact between Robert Bashlow and your then 13-year-old son after you learned that Mr. Bashlow had sexually propositioned your son?

MR. BAKER: Objection. Asked and answered.

MR. WALKER: I'll join in that objection.

MR. DOLAN: You may answer it.

MR. WALKER: You can go ahead.

MZB: Well, I would say that—that that was much more David's business than anyone else.

MR. DOLAN: So you didn't do anything to prevent Mr. Bashlow, did you, from coming in contact with your son?

MZB: No, I did not.

MR. BAKER: Objection. Asked and answered.

MR. DOLAN: Did you discuss it with your—please take your water.

MR. WALKER: I'm going to join in that last objection.

MR. DOLAN: Did you discuss this proposition of your then 13-year-old son by one of Walter's friends with Walter?

MZB: The subject may have come up in conversation.

MR. DOLAN: Okay. To the best of your recollection, tell me how that subject may have come up in conversation.

MZB: Well, I think one of us would have said to the other, Do you know what that idiot Bashlow has done now?

MR. DOLAN: Okay. I don't want you to guess or speculate. Do you recall what Walter said in any regard regarding the issue of Robert Bashlow propositioning your 13-year-old son for sex?

MR. BAKER: Objection. Speculation.

MR. DOLAN: You can answer.

MR. WALKER: I'll join in that. You can answer.

MZB: All I know is that Bash—that Bashlow's regarded largely as a laughing stock by most of our friends.

MR. DOLAN: Right. Okay. My question is a little bit more specific, though. Do you recall Walter saying anything to you on the subject of Bashlow propositioning your 13-year-old son?

MZB: As I said, I think he said something like, Do you know what that idiot Bashlow has done now? and then he recounted a story.

MR. DOLAN: Did he express any—To your knowledge, did he express anything that you understood to be disapproval to what Mr. Bashlow had done?

MZB: I think at the time he shared my belief that David was perfectly old enough to make his own decisions of that sort.

MR. DOLAN: Okay. So at that time it was your belief that a 13-year-old child was perfectly able to make their own decisions regarding sexual contact with adults?

MZB: Oh, really, a-13-year-old child? I wasn't a child at 13, were you?

MR. DOLAN: The question—Could you read back the question for her, please? (Record read by reporter.)

MR. DOLAN: Do you have the question in mind?

MZB: I never thought that I was very intelligent, but this—my opinion at the moment was that 13-year-old young people were quite old enough to decide what they wanted to do.

MR. DOLAN: Okay. Did you have any understanding at that time as to whether the law was in contrast with your opinion on the issue of 13-year-old children making decisions about sex with adults?

MZB: I don't think I ever inquired into the matter.

MR. DOLAN: I'm going to show you some pictures, and I'm going to ask you if you can identify anybody in these pictures.

MZB: No. Let me see here. No. At first I thought this was a picture of David in his teens, but it's not.

MR. DOLAN: To your knowledge, have you seen a picture of that boy before in the pictures? Have you ever seen that boy?

MZB: Not to my memory, no.

MR. DOLAN: Looking at the pictures of the young boy in those pictures, do you think that boy is of the age to make decisions whether or not he should be having sex with adults?

MR. BAKER: Objection. Speculation.

MR. WALKER: I'll join in that. And also lacks foundation. She's never seen those pictures before.

MR. DOLAN: Okay. I'm just asking you, does it appear the ages of those young boys in those pictures are of the age to be making decisions as to whether they should be having sex with adults?

MR. BAKER: Objection. Lacks foundation. She doesn't know the boy. She's never even seen the picture.

MR. WALKER: Just a second. We don't even know what age that is.

MR. BAKER: It's also vague. Speculation.

MZB: What I was going to say is that I'm not a psychological counselor or a school teacher.

MR. DOLAN: Right. You indicated, though, that you think children at a particular age are able to make decisions whether or not they're going to have sex with adults. That was your personal belief; right?

MR. BAKER: Objection. Asked and answered.

MR. WALKER: I'll join.

MR. DOLAN: You may answer.

MR. WALKER: Go ahead.

MZB: I would say that my personal opinions are not at issue in this matter.

MR. DOLAN: Okay. I would disagree with you, and I would ask you to answer my question.

MZB: I would say that you are entitled to your opinion, sir.

MR. DOLAN: I'm asking your opinion.

MZB: My opinion is my opinion.

MR. BAKER: She's already answered it.

MR. DOLAN: She's refusing to answer the question.

MR. BAKER: She's already–

MR. WALKER: She has already answered that.

MR. DOLAN: Are you of the understanding that children at some particular age are capable of making decisions about whether or not to have sex with adults?

MZB: I never claimed to be of great psychological knowledge, but on the surface of it I thought so at the time.

MR. DOLAN: Right.

MZB: What I think now has no relevance.

MR. DOLAN: Okay. Well, at what time did you think it was appropriate for children to begin to make the decision whether or not to have sex with adults?

MZB: I don't believe I speculated.

MR. WALKER: At what time are you talking?

MR. DOLAN: She said "at the time."

MR. WALKER: Okay. But you're asking the question. You have to make your question better. I'm sorry.

MR. DOLAN: At the point you indicated at the time you had an understanding of when children could begin to make decisions regarding sex with adults, what time are you referring to, what time period?

MZB: I would say that in their middle teens most teenagers are perfectly capable of deciding what they want.

MR. DOLAN: Okay. When did you come to form that opinion in time? Was it in the '60s? The '70s?

MZB: During my own teens, in the '40s and '50s.

MR. DOLAN: All right. And did you retain that opinion in the '60s?

MZB: I don't know when I began to change my opinions.

MR. DOLAN: Do you have any knowledge if you began to change your opinions prior to marrying Walter Breen?

MZB: I don't know.

MR. DOLAN: Well, at the time that your son had informed you that he had been approached by Mr. Bashlow, you still were of the opinion that he at the age of 13 could make that decision; right?

MR. BAKER: Objection. Asked and answered.

MR. WALKER: Join in that. You can go ahead.

MZB: I would say that—as I say, Robert Bashlow was enough of a laughing stock that I never took anything he did seriously as a danger to anyone, including a kitten.

MR. DOLAN: The question I asked you, though, is different, which was: At the time that that incident happened between Robert Bashlow and your son, did you believe that a 13 year old could make decisions as to whether or not it was appropriate to have sex with an adult?

MR. BAKER: Objection.

MR. WALKER: Same objections.

MR. BAKER: Asked and answered about ten times now.

MZB: I certainly think that David knew what he was doing at that time and if Bashlow said anything to him that he didn't like he could have broken Bashlow in two with one hand, so I never took it very seriously as a danger.

MR. DOLAN: Okay. If the 13 year old wasn't six feet tall, did you have any opinion that child, let's say a four-foot-tall 13 year old, it would be appropriate to proposition them for sex?

MR. BAKER: Objection. Vague. Lacks foundation. Compound.

MR. WALKER: I'll join those objections.

MR. DOLAN: You can answer. You may answer it.

MZB: I did not speculate on the matter. If it came up, it came up very briefly and crossed my mind very quickly.

MR. DOLAN: How tall was [Glenn]?

MZB: I don't remember.

MR. DOLAN: Did you ever meet him?

MZB: Yes.

MR. DOLAN: Can you recall about how tall he was at the time that Walter Breen was having a sexual relationship with him?

MR. BAKER: Objection. Speculation.

MR. WALKER: Lacks foundation.

MR. DOLAN: She testified at the last deposition that she knew he was having a sexual relationship with him. Foundation was laid in the first deposition.

MR. DOLAN: So how tall was [Glenn] at the—to your knowledge, at the time that Walter was having a sexual relationship with him?

MR. BAKER: Objection. Speculation.

MR. WALKER: Same objection. And Chris, for the record, I don't know how many months ago that deposition was. I don't have it in front of me. She doesn't have that knowledge in mind unless you ask her about it—unless you tell her about it.

MR. DOLAN: You still remember saying that Walter had a sexual relationship with [Glenn]; right?

MZB: Yes, I do.

MR. DOLAN: You just testified to that about 15 minutes ago?

MZB: Yes. [Glenn] was in our house a great deal.

MR. DOLAN: Due to the fact that he was in your house a great deal, how tall was he?

MR. BAKER: Objection. Speculation.

MZB: I think he was about five foot, eight.

MR. DOLAN: Did you think he was big enough to ward off something he didn't want too?

MR. BAKER: Objection. Speculation. Vague, ambiguous. Lacks foundation.

MR. WALKER: Same objections. I'll join.

MR. DOLAN: You may answer.

MZB: I don't believe I speculated on the matter.

MR. DOLAN: Okay. So is size a determining issue in your mind as to whether or not a minor was capable of deciding whether or not they should be having sexual contact with an adult?

MR. BAKER: Objection. Speculation. Foundation. Vague, ambiguous.

MR. WALKER: Same objections.

MR. DOLAN: You may answer.

MZB: I didn't do any speculating.

MR. DOLAN: I didn't ask you if you speculated. You indicated earlier that you didn't worry about your son David because he was six feet tall and could break Mr. Bashlow in half. Do you remember that?

MZB: Yes.

MR. DOLAN: So I'm asking you: Is your determination or understanding of when a child was able to make decisions regarding sex with an adult based on the size of that child and ability to physically defend themselves?

MR. BAKER: Same objections.

MR. WALKER: Same objections.

MZB: That would be one consideration.

MR. DOLAN: What other considerations would there be?

MZB: The general maturity of the child in question, the fact whether the adult was the kind of person to be threatening. If the adult was generally a non-threatening person, I think my attitude would have been no harm in asking if he takes no for an answer.

MR. DOLAN: Okay. And did you consider Walter to be non-threatening?

MZB: I certainly did.

MR. DOLAN: So, did you feel, then, there was no harm in Walter asking young children to have sex with him so long as he would take no for an answer?

MZB: Yes.

MR. DOLAN: And until—down to what age would that be okay?

MZB: I don't believe I ever considered the matter much.

MR. DOLAN: So–

MZB: It would have come up and been dismissed from my mind in a matter of moments.

MR. DOLAN: As you sit here today, do you ever recall forming an opinion what would be a minimum age it would okay for your husband to proposition young boys?

MZB: I never stopped to think about it.

MR. DOLAN: You never gave it any thought?

MR. BAKER: Objection. Asked and answered.

MR. WALKER: Same objection.

MR. DOLAN: Did you ever come to a point where you kind of consciously pushed that out of your mind and made a decision not to think about Walter's interaction with young boys?

MR. BAKER: Objection. Vague. Asked and answered. Speculation.

MR. DOLAN: You may answer.

MR. WALKER: Same objections.

MZB: I can only say I don't remember.

MR. DOLAN: And my question is a little different. Did you come to a point in time after you were aware of Walter's interest in young boys that you sort of made a conscious decision not to think about that subject?

MR. BAKER: Same objections. Asked and answered as well.

MR. WALKER: Same objections.

MR. DOLAN: Pardon me?

MZB: Yes.

MR. DOLAN: Do you have the question in mind?

MZB: You mean did I ever come to such a conclusion?

MR. DOLAN: I'll ask it again. Did you ever come to a point in your life where knowing about your husband's interest in young men, young boys, that you consciously made a decision that your sort of going to turn your head the other way and not think about it?

MR. BAKER: Same objection.

MR. WALKER: Same objections.

MZB: No, I did not come to such a decision consciously to turn away from it.

MR. DOLAN: Did you ever ask your daughter Moira if Walter had ever propositioned her?

MZB: What?

MR. DOLAN: Did you ever ask your daughter Moira if Walter ever propositioned her?

MZB: I don't think I understand. Are you trying to—seriously asking me if my husband propositioned my daughter? If you are seriously asking that question, I can only say no, she did not say anything about it to me until considerably later, after this was all over with.

MR. DOLAN: My question was somewhat different, which was: Did you ever ask your daughter whether Walter had ever propositioned her?

MZB: No, I did not.

MR. DOLAN: But you did ask your son?

MZB: Yes; because—because I thought that Walter had a thing about young boys, which is not to be taken as being acceptable in this situation, and therefore I asked.

MR. DOLAN: Did you ever ask Patrick whether Walter had ever propositioned Patrick?

MZB: No, I did not.

MR. DOLAN: Is there any reason why you felt differently about asking—well, strike that. Can you explain why you asked your son David that question but you didn't ask your son Patrick that question?

MZB: Yes. Because when we met Walter David was nine. I think when we first met Walter David was nine or ten. When I married him he was 13, and I understood that Walter liked boys that age. Patrick was a baby. Walter saw him born. It never even crossed my mind.

MR. DOLAN: Okay. Back in 1964 did you ask Walter whether he was still engaging in sexual acts with [Glenn]?

MZB: I did not.

MR. DOLAN: Did you make a conscious decision not to ask him about his relationship with [Glenn]?

MZB: Yes; because [mother of Glenn]—the subject came up between us. And before you ask, I do not remember how it came up, but somehow or other it came up, and [mother of Glenn] had said that she had no complaint to make about Walter's relationship with her son.

MR. DOLAN: Okay. So at some point you had a discussion with [mother of Glenn] regarding the sexual relationship between Walter and her son; right?

MZB: Yes.

MR. DOLAN: And did you ask her how she felt about it?

MZB: I think she volunteered that. She said Walter's influence on her son had been a good one all around.

MR. DOLAN: Based upon what she had said to you, did you form any opinion as to whether or not Walter's relationship with [Glenn] was good for [Glenn]?

MR. BAKER: Objection. Speculation. Vague.

MZB: I did not.

MR. WALKER: Same objection.

MR. DOLAN: Did you ever ask [Glenn] how he felt about the sexual relationship with Walter?

MZB: All I have to say on that point is that once [Glenn] was a big strong boy, and if he had any objections, he could have tied Walter into a bow knot.

MR. DOLAN: My question is: Did you ever ask [Glenn] about how he felt about the relationship with Walter?

MZB: No, I did not because, as I say, he was big enough to take care of himself.

MR. DOLAN: The discussion with [mother of Glenn], did it happen after you were married to Walter?

MZB: Yes.

MR. DOLAN: So you knew that the relationship with [Glenn] was still going on after your marriage to Walter?

MR. WALKER: Objection. That misstates her testimony.

MR. DOLAN: At the time that you had the discussion with [mother of Glenn], did you understand that Walter and [Glenn] were still sexually involved?

MZB: No.

MR. DOLAN: Why were you having a discussion with [mother of Glenn] about the subject?

MZB: Oh, you know how women are, they talk about anything that comes up.

MR. DOLAN: So at the time that you were having a discussion with [mother of Glenn], did you have any understanding as to whether or not Walter and [Glenn] were still sexually involved?

MR. BAKER: Objection. Asked and answered.

MR. WALKER: Same objection.

MR. DOLAN: You may answer it.

MZB: I'm sorry. Could you repeat the question?

MR. DOLAN: Sure. At the time that you had the conversation with [mother of Glenn], did you have any understanding as to whether or not Walter and [Glenn] were still sexually involved?

MR. BAKER: Same objections.

MR. WALKER: Same objections.

MZB: I don't believe I gave the matter any thought.

MR. BAKER: Asked and answered.

MR. DOLAN: So, did you ever tell [mother of Glenn] what your opinion was on the relationship between Walter and her son?

MZB: No, I did not.

MR. DOLAN: Did you ever form the opinion that it was okay for Walter to have a sexual relationship with [Glenn] when [Glenn] was under the age of 18?

MZB: No, I did not.

MR. DOLAN: Prior to marrying Walter, were you ever made aware that Walter had been arrested for lewd and lascivious acts?

MZB: No, I was not.

MR. DOLAN: Were you aware that in 1954 he had been arrested as a disturbing person for molesting a child under the boardwalk?

MZB: No, I did not.

MR. DOLAN: I'm going to show you a document that we're going to mark as plaintiff's next in order, which was produced by your counsel previously in this litigation. (Plaintiff's Exhibit 4 was marked for identification.)

MZB: If you'll pardon my saying so, this whole thing seems useless. The man is dead, and he's up before a judge much more sterner than any judge in California courts.

MR. DOLAN: You're still with us, that's why we're asking questions, because you're a defendant in this litigation. Do you realize that you're a defendant in a lawsuit?

MZB: No, I did not. It never occurred to me that anyone could think in those terms.

MR. DOLAN: As you sit here today, have you ever been informed that you're defendant in litigation?

MZB: Well, you're informing me now.

MR. DOLAN: Prior to me informing you, have you ever understood that you're a defendant in a lawsuit?

MZB: No.

MR. WALKER: Objection. That calls for attorney-client privileged information.

MR. DOLAN: Well, I'm just asking prior to my telling you, did you understand that you're being sued because of the molestation of Ken Smith?

MR. WALKER: And only answer—Don't answer anything that has to do with any discussions that you've had with any of your attorneys.

MR. DOLAN: Okay. If Elisabeth Waters told you you were being sued or your daughter told you you were being sued or you a saw document that led you to believe, with your name on it, that you were being sued, anything other than your lawyers actually sitting you down and saying, "Hey, you're being sued." Prior to sitting down in this room today, did you understand that you were a defendant in a lawsuit?

MZB: Not entirely.

MR. DOLAN: Do you understand now that you're a defendant?

MZB: Yes, I do.

MR. DOLAN: Can you answer my question, then? I'm asking you as a defendant in this lawsuit, were you aware of how that document came into your possession that was given to us by your counsel?

MZB: What is this?

MR. DOLAN: It's a two-page document. Just please take a look at it, and I'll ask you some questions once you've had an opportunity to review it.

MZB: I have no memory of ever having seen that.

MR. DOLAN: Okay. Do you have any understanding of where your attorneys got this document they gave to us?

MZB: No.

MR. DOLAN: Do you keep a file of Walter's on Walter in your possession at your home anywhere?

MZB: No.

MR. DOLAN: At any point prior to today did you know that Walter Breen had been arrested for molesting children under the boardwalk in 1954 in Atlantic City?

MZB: No, I did not. I didn't even know he had ever been in Atlantic City.

MR. DOLAN: Okay. In your last deposition you indicated that you had not seen [Glenn] since three years following the marriage with Walter Breen. Do you recall that testimony?

MZB: Yes, I do.

MR. DOLAN: During the three years that you did see [Glenn] during the marriage, was [Glenn] a frequent visitor at your home?

MZB: Yes, he was.

MR. DOLAN: Okay. To your knowledge, was he engaging in sexual activity with Walter during the three years that he was a visitor at your home?

MZB: I have no idea.

MR. DOLAN: Did you ever so inquire knowing that Walter had previously had a sexual relationship with [Glenn]?

MZB: I did not.

MR. DOLAN: Did you ever do anything to protect [Glenn] from any type of sexual contact with Walter Breen during the three years that he was a guest in your home following your marriage?

MZB: Oh, please. The idea of me protecting little [Glenn], good heavens.

MR. BAKER: Objection. Lacks foundation as well as argumentative.

MR. WALKER: I'll join in those objections.

MR. DOLAN: Did you ever do anything—I'll ask the question again because I would like an answer to the question. Did you ever do anything to protect [Glenn] from sexual contact with your husband during the three years following your marriage that you knew [Glenn] was around your home?

MZB: It never occurred to.

MR. BAKER: Same objections.

MR. WALKER: Same objections.

MR. DOLAN: It never occurred to you is your answer, that it was necessary?

MR. BAKER: Same objections.

MR. DOLAN: You never asked [Glenn] if it was okay with him; right?

MZB: I never asked [Glenn] because I knew perfectly well that if anything was wrong he could come to me. We were on terms that—I mean, he was in my house. He was getting milk from my refrigerator. He was eating at our table. If anything had been wrong, he would have come to me and said, Marion, there is something wrong. I'm quite sure he would have.

MR. DOLAN: So, as long as he didn't come to you and say, Marion, there is something wrong, you felt no need to inquire?

MZB: No.

MR. BAKER: Objection. Argumentative.

MR. WALKER: I'll join in that.

MR. DOLAN: Did you ever—Did it ever bother you that your husband might be sleeping with this boy?

MR. BAKER: Objection. Argumentative. Lacks foundation.

MR. DOLAN: You may answer.

MR. BAKER: Same objections.

MZB: I never gave it any thought.

MR. DOLAN: Pardon?

MZB: I never gave it any thought. At that time I was newly married to my husband. I was pregnant, and I was very happy with him.

MR. WALKER: You can just let him ask the questions, and then you can give the answers, but you don't have to volunteer anything.

MZB: Okay.

MR. DOLAN: During those three years did Walter and you have any other boys under the age of 18 in the home?

MZB: Not to my knowledge.

MR. DOLAN: Did you ever talk to Walter about whether or not he was still having sex with [Glenn] after your marriage?

MR. BAKER: Objection. Asked and answered.

MR. WALKER: Same objection.

MR. DOLAN: Go ahead.

MZB: I did not.

MR. DOLAN: Did you ever say to Walter, I don't want you to be having sex with anybody else now that we're married?

MR. BAKER: Objection. Argumentative.

MR. WALKER: I'll join.

MZB: I did not.

MR. DOLAN: Did you ever say anything to Walter about, you know, Walter you need to be careful. This might be illegal?

MR. BAKER: Objection. Argumentative.

MR. WALKER: Same objection.

MZB: It never occurred to me.

MR. DOLAN: Did you ever discuss with Walter the legality or illegality of having sex with boys under the age of 18?

MZB: I did not.

MR. DOLAN: Did you ever discuss it with anybody prior to Ken Smith's molestation being made known to you?

MZB: Not—Yes.

MR. DOLAN: Okay. Who Did you discuss that with?

MZB: With my daughter, Moira.

MR. DOLAN: When did you discuss it with Moira?

MZB: I think it was—It was shortly before her marriage.

MR. DOLAN: Before what?

MZB: Before her marriage.

MR. DOLAN: Okay. And what was the reason that you and Moira discussed that?

MZB: She made an allegation that her father had molested her.

MR. DOLAN: Was that before or after Ken Smith's molestation was reported to the police?

MZB: I have no idea.

MR. DOLAN: Do you know if your daughter was married before or after Ken Smith's molestation was reported to the police?

MZB: I thought I did, but I'm sure I don't.

MR. DOLAN: Are you still focused on the questions? Are you having any difficulty answering now? Are you mentally—are you still here in time and space?

MZB: Yes. I'm trying to make up a time line in my mind.

MR. DOLAN: Okay. Very good. Other than your discussion with Moira prior to her marriage regarding the legality or illegality of Walter's contact with minor children, did you ever discuss that topic with anyone else?

MZB: I can't think of anyone.

MR. DOLAN: When you and Walter were thinking about adopting [Barry], did you ever have a discussion with Walter saying, Walter, if we adopt [Barry] you can't have sex with him?

MZB: Yes, I did.

MR. DOLAN: Okay. Tell me about that.

MZB: I just told him flat out that if we adopted [Barry] he would be our son and nothing else. That it was not to be a boyfriend or anything of that sort.

MR. DOLAN: At that point did you have any concerns that Walter might be having sex with [Barry] such that it caused you to tell Walter that?

MZB: I did not. I was just sort of vaguely thinking back on our whole background.

MR. DOLAN: And when you say your "whole background," what do you mean by that?

MZB: Of everything that had happened since I had first met Walter and everything everyone else had said about him.

MR. DOLAN: Now, you said that he would be your son and nothing else. Do you think that would put him in a different category than other young boys?

MR. BAKER: Objection. Argumentative.

MR. WALKER: I'll join in that. And vague and ambiguous.

MR. DOLAN: You may answer it.

MZB: I don't believe that I formulated it in any way.

MR. DOLAN: What did you mean by your statement to Walter that he would be our son and nothing else?

MZB: That if he had any idea in his mind that the boy might be a subject for his—his sexual interests, he should put that right out of his mind right away.

MR. DOLAN: Okay. And why would–

MZB: That if he ever had such an idea, and I wasn't accusing him of it, that he should not continue thinking that way.

MR. DOLAN: All right. And did you think that—Was that solely because he was going to be adopted by you?

MZB: Yes.

MR. DOLAN: So if he wasn't to be adopted by you, then you would not have had this conversation with Walter about this boy being a part of his sexual interests?

MR. BAKER: Objection.

MR. WALKER: Objection. That lacks foundation.

MR. BAKER: Speculation.

MR. WALKER: Speculation.

MR. DOLAN: You can answer it.

MZB: I didn't speculate on my husband's affairs. We were no longer living together at that time, and I paid very little attention to what was going on.

MR. DOLAN: Okay. You weren't living together. Where was Walter living at that time?

MZB: He was living a couple of doors up the street.

MR. DOLAN: In the gold fishbowl?

MZB: Yes.

MR. DOLAN: So at the time that he was living in the gold fishbowl and you were aware that [Barry] might be adopted by you, you told Walter that he could not be a subject of Walter's sexual affection; is that correct?

MZB: Yes.

MR. DOLAN: And did you understand that [Barry] might be spending time at that other premises where Walter was living?

MZB: Yes, I did.

MR. DOLAN: Okay. And did you feel that you had some responsibility to [Barry] to tell Walter—

MZB: Yes. That if we had adopted [Barry], he would have been our son.

MR. DOLAN: So, did you feel you had some responsibility to [Barry] to tell Walter no sex with [Barry]?

MZB: Yes. I laid down the law very firmly.

MR. DOLAN: All right.

MZB: It was one of the reasons we—we eventually split up.

MR. DOLAN: What do you mean by that?

MZB: He was very upset with me. He said I didn't trust him, and, of course, I didn't.

MR. DOLAN: So you didn't trust Walter around young boys at that time, did you?

MZB: At that point, no.

MR. DOLAN: And do you know approximately what year that was?

MZB: I am afraid I couldn't tell you.

MR. DOLAN: Can you give me an estimate or approximation?

MZB: I think I began to think differently of him about—about 1975 or '6.

MR. DOLAN: Okay. So sometime—Was it sometime around then that [Barry] came along?

MZB: I think it was after that.

MR. DOLAN: Approximately how long after that?

MZB: I couldn't tell you.

MR. DOLAN: Can you give me an estimate or an approximation, was it before 1980, between '80 and '85, anything you can do to help me?

MZB: It might have been.

MR. DOLAN: Might have been which?

MZB: Might have been between '80 and '85. [Barry]—I saw [Barry] a few weeks ago.

MR. DOLAN: Okay. So you were concerned that Walter might have some inappropriate sexual relationship with [Barry] over at the other house?

MZB: Yes.

MR. DOLAN: And you told him that that was completely prohibited; right?

MZB: Yes.

MR. DOLAN: And how old did you understand [Barry] to be at that time?

MZB: I thought he was about 12 or 13.

MR. DOLAN: And how big was [Barry]?

MZB: He was small and fragile.

MR. DOLAN: So, did you feel you had a responsibility at that time to protect [Barry] from Walter?

MZB: Yes, I did. More than anybody else I felt very protective toward [Barry].

MR. DOLAN: And what was—made you feel that more than anybody else you had a responsibility to [Barry]?

MZB: Well, when he was around he'd come sit on my lap sometimes and things like that, so I developed a certain feeling that he didn't have any other family and that I'd take care of him.

MR. DOLAN: Did Walter ever refuse to agree to your condition that he not have sex with [Barry]?

MZB: He didn't. No, he didn't.

MR. DOLAN: Did he ever agree to it?

MZB: I don't remember. I don't think he said in so many words no, I will not have sex with [Barry]. I think he said something like, You don't have to worry about that or something.

MR. DOLAN: Was this topic of sex with [Barry] at all one of the reasons why [Barry] was never adopted?

MZB: Not that I know of.

MR. DOLAN: What was your understanding as to the reason why [Barry] wasn't adopted?

MZB: I believe that his—his father was in prison, wanted to maintain a relationship with him and didn't want him adopted.

MR. DOLAN: Were you ever interviewed by the people at CPS regarding the adoption?

MZB: Yes, I was. We went and attended a couple of classes on adoption.

MR. DOLAN: Did they ever ask you whether either of you had ever had any problems with sex with minors?

MZB: The question did not come up. Of that I am perfectly sure.

MR. DOLAN: What makes you say you're perfectly sure of that?

MZB: Because I think I would have remembered that.

MR. DOLAN: Did you ever inform them that Walter had had a sexual relationship with [Glenn]?

MZB: No, I did not.

MR. DOLAN: Did you ever tell them that you were concerned about Walter perhaps having a sexual relationship with [Barry]?

MZB: No, I did not.

MR. DOLAN: Why didn't you?

MZB: I think the only answer I can make to that is that it's quite obvious that you have never been in love.

MR. DOLAN: Can you explain that further? I don't understand your answer.

MZB: Simply that the subject did not come up even in my mind. It came up briefly, and I mentioned it, and that was the end of it.

MR. DOLAN: So the subject did come up in your mind enough for you to raise it Walter; correct?

MZB: Yes.

MR. DOLAN: But you didn't raise it with the child protective authorities?

MZB: No.

MR. DOLAN: And you're saying that's because of your love for Walter?

MZB: I don't know if by then it was love or just a general sense of protectiveness.

MR. DOLAN: So, was you're not telling CPS an effort to protect Walter?

MZB: I suspect it must have been.

MR. DOLAN: As you sit here today, do you believe that you're not telling CPS was in an effort to protect Walter?

MR. WALKER: Objection. Asked and answered.

MR. DOLAN: You may answer it.

MZB: I suspect it must have been.

MR. DOLAN: Okay. How are you doing? You need a break?

MZB: No. I'm all right.

MR. DOLAN: Are there any other boys that you told Walter you're not to have sex with that boy?

MZB: Well, Moira at one time complained that Walter was coming on to one of her boyfriends.

MR. DOLAN: Okay.

MZB: And I went up to Walter's house and I said, "Look, this is not a good thing to do."

MR. DOLAN: Okay. Which boyfriend was that; do you remember?

MZB: I think his name was [Gregg] something.

(No, Gregg was not my boyfriend. But Walter made passes at Sterling and Nick and every other young man who was near him.)

MR. DOLAN: [Gregg]?

MZB: It could have been.

MR. DOLAN: Okay. Did Moira ever—So Moira said to you she was afraid that Walter might be trying to have sex with [Gregg]?

MZB: Yes.

MR. DOLAN: Okay. Approximately when was this?

MZB: I don't remember the date. I think at that time it was—she was at University of California then.

(I never went to University of California.)

MR. DOLAN: How old did you understand [Gregg] to be?

MZB: I thought he was 17 or 18.

(When I complained about Gregg, he was 13.)

MR. DOLAN: Did you ever ask him, [Gregg], about what was going on?

MZB: No, I didn't. But I mean, the two of them were going around together, and he looked to be 18 or 19.

MR. DOLAN: And did you tell Walter not to have sex with [Gregg]?

MZB: I just said that Moira would not approve.

MR. DOLAN: So it was based upon Moira being unhappy with the situation?

MZB: Yes.

MR. DOLAN: Did you ever tell Walter when he was living in the gold fishbowl that he was not to have sex with minors in that home?

MZB: I never mentioned the matter.

MR. DOLAN: You were the landlord there, weren't you?

MZB: I owned the house.

MR. DOLAN: Did you lease it to Walter?

MZB: No. I let him live in it because he needed a place to live.

MR. DOLAN: So it's your testimony that you never leased it to him?

MZB: Not formally, no.

MR. DOLAN: Okay. Let's mark this as plaintiff's next in order. (Plaintiff's Exhibit 5 was marked for identification.)

MR. DOLAN: It's already been marked as Plaintiff's 3 to Elisabeth Water's deposition, but we'll just mark it for this one too.

MR. DOLAN: See your signature on this document?

MZB: Oh, yes.

MR. DOLAN: Okay. What's the date of that document at the top?

MZB: February '94.

MR. DOLAN: Actually, it says '86, doesn't it?

MZB: I can't tell. Yes, I guess it does say '86.

MR. DOLAN: Having seen this document, do you want to change your testimony as to whether or not you formally leased that premise to Walter Breen?

MZB: I can only think that it's something that somebody stuck in front of me and said, sign this, and I saw Elisabeth's name was already on it and signed it. I was not aware of what it was.

MR. DOLAN: Prior to 1986 did you know that Walter Breen had had sex with minor boys?

MZB: Yes. I have said that on several occasions now.

MR. DOLAN: And you rented that place to him anyways; right?

MZB: Well, he needed a place to live.

MR. DOLAN: Okay.

MZB: What was I supposed to do, throw him out in the street?

MR. DOLAN: I'll withhold my comments.

MZB: Well, I–

MR. DOLAN: Did you undertake any activity to ensure that Walter Breen would not molest young boys at this property that you rented to him?

MZB: As I say, at the time [Barry] was there. I told him [Barry] was off limits, and I told him [Gregg] was off limits.

MR. DOLAN: Okay. But the other ones weren't off limits?

MZB: I never knew there were any others there.

MR. DOLAN: Did you ever tell him it would be off limits to molest young boys on your property?

MZB: In those words, no.

MR. DOLAN: Did you ever tell him that he was not to have young boys on your property?

MZB: I did not tell him that in those words, no.

MR. DOLAN: Did you know that he had young boys on your property?

MZB: I did not.

MR. DOLAN: You knew that he had [Barry] there?

MZB: Yes. Well, that was different. [Barry] was there because of both of us.

MR. DOLAN: You knew he had [Glenn] there; right?

MZB: No; [Glenn] never came to that place–

MR. DOLAN: Okay.

MZB:–to the best of my knowledge and belief.

MR. DOLAN: You knew he had Ken Smith there, didn't you?

MZB: I don't know who Ken Smith is or who he was. I wouldn't know Ken Smith from—well, I would know President Reagan because I saw him on T.V., so I can't say I wouldn't know him from President Reagan.

MR. DOLAN: Do you recall telling the police you met Ken Smith when Walter brought him around?

MZB: Yes, I do. I mean, sometime after he had been living in the gold fishbowl for quite awhile.

MR. DOLAN: You knew that he had Ken Smith over there; right?

MZB: Well, he came in one day with Ken Smith, so I assumed it.

MR. DOLAN: So you assumed at some point after Walter moved into the gold fishbowl and you rented it to Walter that Walter had Ken Smith over there; right?

MZB: Yes.

MR. DOLAN: Did you ever tell Walter, You can't molest Ken Smith over there?

MZB: I didn't know him from Adam or Fox.

MR. DOLAN: But you met him and knew Walter had him over there and–

MZB: Oh, yes.

MR. DOLAN: Did you ever tell Walter, Ken Smith is off limits?

MZB: It never occurred to me. I think what I probably thought was that was up to Ken Smith to tell him if he didn't want to.

MR. DOLAN: So at that point you believed it was up to Ken Smith to tell him if he didn't want to have sex with Walter?

MZB: Yes.

MR. DOLAN: Can we take a couple-second break? We're getting pretty close to our hour, but I want to take a two-minute break. Just two minutes.

MR. WALKER: Okay. Well, I mean, we have about two minutes left in the deposition.

MR. DOLAN: Actually, my stopwatch shows that I have about seven minutes left, and I hope you'll give me two minutes' credit. And I'm giving you time off with my client's deposition. I mean, I wouldn't jam you on two minutes here. I'm trying to be polite.

(Whereupon, the deposition adjourned at 12:24 p.m.)

I, the undersigned, hereby certify that the witness in the foregoing deposition was, by me, duly sworn to tell the truth, the whole truth and nothing but the truth in the within-entitled cause. That said deposition was taken in shorthand by me, a Certified Shorthand Reporter and a disinterested person, at the time and place therein stated, and that the testimony of said witness was thereafter reduced to typewriting, by computer, under my direction and supervision. I further certify that I am not of counsel or attorney for either or any of the parties of the said deposition, nor in any way interested in the event of this cause, and that I am not related to any of the parties thereto.

IN WITNESS WHEREOF, I have hereunto set my hand, this 29th day of December 1998.

Janine P. Branco

25 CSR #10372

Appendix C: Lisa's Complete Deposition (1997)

(My annotations are in parentheses, and in italic. I have replaced [Victim X], [Name A], and [Johnny Does 1–4] with names, to the best of my knowledge and belief.)

DEPOSITION OF ELISABETH WATERS - 10/16/97

IN THE SUPERIOR COURT OF THE STATE OF CALIFORNIA
IN AND FOR THE COUNTY OF ALAMEDA

KEN SMITH, Plaintiff, vs.

MARION Z. BRADLEY, ELISABETH WATERS, and Does 1 through 10 inclusive, Defendants.

DEPOSITION OF ELISABETH WATERS Thursday, October 16, 1997

REPORTED BY: KARLA SHALLENBERGER, CSR No. 10752

SHALLENBERGER REPORTING SERVICES - (415) 771-1988

PLAINTIFF'S EXHIBITS

Deed of trust note

Quit claim deed

Rental agreement

Copy of interview with J.Z. Eglinton

Employment agreement

11/15/89 letter from Ms. Waters to Mr. Breen

Personal journal entries of Ms. Waters 10/20/89

BE IT REMEMBERED that pursuant to Notice of Taking Deposition, and on Thursday, October 16, 1997, commencing at the hour of 10:15 a.m. thereof, at the Law Offices of CHRISTOPHER B. DOLAN before me, KARLA SHALLENBERGER, a Certified Shorthand Reporter in the State of California, there personally appeared ELISABETH WATERS, called as witness, who being by me first duly sworn, was hereafter examined and testified as hereinafter set forth.

APPEARANCES

LAW OFFICES OF CHRISTOPHER B. DOLAN,

655 Montgomery Street, 16th Floor, San Francisco, CA 94111,

represented by CHRISTOPHER DOLAN, Attorney at Law,

appeared as counsel on behalf of Plaintiff.

BURESH, KAPLAN, JANG, FELLER & AUSTIN,

2298 Durant Avenue, Berkeley, CA 94704,

represented by SCOTT BURESH, Attorney at Law,

appeared as counsel on behalf of Defendant.

RAMSEY & DURRELL,

755 Sansome Street, Suite 350, San Francisco, CA 94111,

represented by JUSTINE DURRELL, Attorney at Law,

appeared as counsel on behalf of Defendant.

ALSO PRESENT: Scott Bonagofsky

EXAMINATION BY CHRISTOPHER DOLAN:

MR. DOLAN: Would you please state your full name for the record?

ELISABETH WATERS: Elisabeth Waters.

MR. DOLAN: Do you have a middle name?

ELISABETH WATERS: No.

MR. DOLAN: Have you ever been known by any other names?

ELISABETH WATERS: Yes.

MR. DOLAN: Please tell me those other names.

ELISABETH WATERS: My parents christened me Nancy Elisabeth Waters.

MR. DOLAN: Other than being christened Nancy Elisabeth Waters and the current name of Elisabeth Waters that you use, have you used any other names?

ELISABETH WATERS: No.

MR. DOLAN: Do you have a handle, as we have come to know it, I don't know what the proper name is, but a name within the circles that either the Society for Creative Anachronism or any other science fiction circles that would give you a name other than Elisabeth Waters that you're recognized by?

ELISABETH WATERS: No.

MR. DOLAN: No?

ELISABETH WATERS: No.

MR. DOLAN: Have you ever had your deposition taken before?

ELISABETH WATERS: Yes.

MR. DOLAN: Can you tell me when?

ELISABETH WATERS: I believe it was in 1993.

MR. DOLAN: Was that in relationship to a property dispute between Marion Zimmer Bradley and Patrick Breen?

ELISABETH WATERS: Yes, it was.

MR. DOLAN: Do you have a copy of that deposition still in your possession at your home?

ELISABETH WATERS: I do not believe so, no.

MR. DOLAN: Have you ever been deposed on any occasions other than that one?

ELISABETH WATERS: No.

MR. DOLAN: I am going to go over with you the rules of a deposition just so that we are clear on them even though you may have had the opportunity to speak to one or more of your attorneys on this matter, okay?

ELISABETH WATERS: Okay.

MR. DOLAN: Before I do that, do you have any legal training whatsoever of an official nature; i.e., have you ever attended any classes in any law schools?

ELISABETH WATERS: No.

MR. DOLAN: A deposition is a question-and-answer period, and although it's being conducted in a somewhat informal atmosphere here in my office, it is the same as if it were being conducted in front of judge and jury in a court of law, and it carries the same weight as trial court testimony; do you understand that?

ELISABETH WATERS: Yes.

MR. DOLAN: You have sworn to tell the truth under the penalty of perjury today, and I just want to make sure that you understand that the penalty of perjury in California includes both fines and incarceration if you were found to be untruthful or dishonest during this deposition; do you understand that?

ELISABETH WATERS: Yes.

MR. DOLAN: Everything that is said in this room will be recorded into a booklet. The court reporter, at my left, is typing everything now, and it will be transcribed into a booklet of questions and answers that you will have an opportunity to review at some point in the future. Because everything is transcribed, everything that is said in this room needs to be done audibly, and everything said in this room will be recorded in that booklet; do you understand that?

ELISABETH WATERS: Yes.

MR. DOLAN: Therefore, I would ask that you please give me audible English language answers to my questions. Yes, no, or any other string of words you may wish to put together. If you wish to have a private conversation with anybody, do not do it in this room because it will not be considered private if it is done in my presence or in front of this court reporter. There is a room available for you and your counsel if at any time you need to talk to them; do you understand that?

ELISABETH WATERS: Yes.

MR. DOLAN: One thing that we're doing very well, and I thank you for, is that we need to wait, one before the other in terms of speaking. So if you would kindly wait until I finish my questions before you begin your answers, I will likewise try to do the same. Your attorney may have advised you that it's often good to pause momentarily so if there's another attorney who wishes to make an objection, they may do so; do you understand that?

ELISABETH WATERS: Yes.

MR. DOLAN: I do not wish you to guess or speculate as to anything in this deposition. I only want your best testimony or your best recollection; however, I am entitled to estimates or approximations and any basis of information which you may have which is not a guess; do you understand that?

ELISABETH WATERS: Yes.

MR. DOLAN: I'll give you an example of the difference between a guess and an estimate. I may be able to ask you to estimate the length of the table in this particular room, and you might be able to do that based upon your personal observation and your experience. If I were to ask you the length of the dining room table in my home, you would be unable to do that because you have never been there, so do you understand the difference?

ELISABETH WATERS: Yes, I do.

MR. DOLAN: If you do not understand a question, I'll ask that you please ask me to rephrase the question, and I'll somehow help you to understand the question. Otherwise, if I get an answer to a question, I will assume that you have understood the question as it was asked to you; do you understand that?

ELISABETH WATERS: Yes.

MR. DOLAN: If at any time today you need to take a break for any reason, to use the facilities, to get a beverage or to speak with your attorneys, you are free to do so. However, I must ask that you please do not interrupt a question pending to break to talk to your attorneys or to do something. I would request that I please get an answer before we take that break. I cannot force you to do so; however, I need to let you know that if you do break during a question and answer pending, I may draw an inference as to what happened in that time period between the question and the answer and present that to some jury at trial; do you understand that?

ELISABETH WATERS: Yes.

MR. DOLAN: You will have an opportunity to review your deposition and to make any changes that you think are necessary or appropriate once it's completed. You will receive the booklet, and you can review it and make changes. However, I would ask for your best testimony today because if you make any changes to your deposition, I can comment, or any lawyer can comment on that at trial and ask the jury to draw an inference therefrom that there's a reason why you have gone back and changed your testimony, and it may affect your credibility. So I would ask that you give me your best testimony today, and if you have any changes in the testimony that you think up later on during the day, please let us know while we're still on the record because that will minimize any type of impact that a change in your testimony might have later on; do you understand that?

ELISABETH WATERS: Yes.

MR. DOLAN: Okay. Are you under the influence of any medications today which would impair your ability to recall events as they occurred in 1979 through to the present day?

ELISABETH WATERS: No.

MR. DOLAN: Are you suffering from any organic or physical defects of your brain or body which would impede your ability to remember events that occurred in the time period 1979 through the present day?

ELISABETH WATERS: No.

MR. DOLAN: Do you know of any reason why your deposition cannot go forward today?

ELISABETH WATERS: No.

MR. DOLAN: Are you suffering from any serious emotional difficulties, related to anything at this point, which would impede your ability to give your best testimony today?

ELISABETH WATERS: No.

MR. DOLAN: Please tell me where you were born.

ELISABETH WATERS: Providence, Rhode Island.

MR. DOLAN: How long did you live there?

ELISABETH WATERS: About a year and a half, I believe.

MR. DOLAN: How many children in your family?

ELISABETH WATERS: Three.

MR. DOLAN: Where do you fall in that framework?

ELISABETH WATERS: I'm the eldest.

MR. DOLAN: What were the names of your brothers and sisters?

ELISABETH WATERS: My sisters are Ellen and Julie.

MR. DOLAN: What are their last names please?

ELISABETH WATERS: Ellen is still Ellen Waters, and Julie is Mrs. Larry Robinson.

MR. DOLAN: Where do they live currently?

ELISABETH WATERS: Ellen lives is New Canaan–

MR. DOLAN: Connecticut?

ELISABETH WATERS: Yes.

MR. DOLAN: It is a small world.

ELISABETH WATERS: Yes, I know.

MR. DOLAN: And?

ELISABETH WATERS: And Julie lives in Raleigh, North Carolina.

MR. DOLAN: Where in New Canaan does Ellen live?

ELISABETH WATERS: Frogtown Road.

MS. DURRELL: Excuse me just a minute. Elisabeth, can you speak up a little bit because I'm really having a hard time hearing you. Thanks.

MR. DOLAN: And what does Ellen do in New Canaan?

ELISABETH WATERS: She's a teacher at King-Low-Heywood-Thomas School.

MR. DOLAN: You probably know this by now seeing how thorough you were on some of the things I saw in your documents on astrology related to other lawyers and things. I'm from New Canaan, Connecticut and lived my whole life there, and I'm actually somewhat of an oddity that I'm the fourth generation of five who lived there. We were poor Irish potato farmers that came over, and I'm intimately familiar with the Frogtown Road. What is the address of Julie in Raleigh, North Carolina, please?

ELISABETH WATERS: I don't remember the exact street address.

MR. DOLAN: Do you have the name of the street?

ELISABETH WATERS: I think it's Van Dyke Avenue, but I'm not positive.

MR. DOLAN: Where did you move after Providence, Rhode Island?

ELISABETH WATERS: I don't remember. I was a baby. I believe it was Staten Island.

MR. DOLAN: And how long were you there?

ELISABETH WATERS: I think about maybe six months.

MR. DOLAN: Where did your family move to next?

ELISABETH WATERS: 54 Halsey Drive, Old Greenwich, Connecticut.

MR. DOLAN: And how long did your family live there?

ELISABETH WATERS: Until the fall of 1968.

MR. DOLAN: And where did they move after that?

ELISABETH WATERS: 379 Cascade Road, Stamford, Connecticut.

MR. DOLAN: North Stamford, Connecticut?

ELISABETH WATERS: Yes, right along the line.

MR. DOLAN: Between Ponus Ridge, going over the High Ridge Road?

ELISABETH WATERS: Uh-hum.

MR. DOLAN: How long did you live there?

ELISABETH WATERS: They're still living there.

MR. DOLAN: Okay. How long did you live there?

ELISABETH WATERS: Well, first I was in boarding school for three years. Then I was in college for four. Then I went back and lived with them—let's see, I went to Katie Gibbs in Norwalk the summer after I graduated from college, which would have been the summer of '75, and then I went to graduate school at the University of New Haven, so I lived with them during that, so I lived with them until August 24th, 1979, when I moved to Berkeley.

MR. DOLAN: Okay. Did you receive any degree from graduate school at the University of New Haven?

ELISABETH WATERS: Yes.

MR. DOLAN: And what was that in, please?

ELISABETH WATERS: Computers and information science.

MR. DOLAN: Was that a Masters or Bachelors?

ELISABETH WATERS: Master of Science.

MR. DOLAN: My parents met at Katie Gibbs. My father was a recently graduated attorney and was taking typing, and my mother was also, and they met in the typing class at Katie Gibbs?

ELISABETH WATERS: New York or Norwalk?

MR. DOLAN: Norwalk, it may have been New York. Who knows. Okay. What boarding school did you go to?

ELISABETH WATERS: St. Anne's.

MR. DOLAN: Where is that located?

ELISABETH WATERS: Charlottesville, Virginia.

MR. DOLAN: What college?

ELISABETH WATERS: Randolph Macon College.

MR. DOLAN: That's in Virginia, isn't it?

ELISABETH WATERS: Yes.

MR. DOLAN: Was it still a women's college then?

ELISABETH WATERS: You're confusing the two.

MR. DOLAN: Okay.

ELISABETH WATERS: Randolph Macon Women's College is in Lynchburg. The one I attended is Randolph Macon College, which is in Ashland.

MR. DOLAN: In 1979 you moved to Berkeley; is that correct?

ELISABETH WATERS: Actually, Oakland.

MR. DOLAN: Where was your first residence in Oakland, please?

ELISABETH WATERS: 6617 Telegraph Avenue, Apartment 3.

MR. DOLAN: And who lived there with you, please?

ELISABETH WATERS: Marion moved into my spare room when she came back from England.

MR. DOLAN: Anyone else ever live there with you?

ELISABETH WATERS: No.

MR. DOLAN: How long did you live at 6617 Telegraph Avenue?

ELISABETH WATERS: About two years.

MR. DOLAN: Did either of Marion's children ever stay with you at that address?

ELISABETH WATERS: I believe Moira did once or twice when Marion was away at convention.

MR. DOLAN: When Marion was actually in residence at 6617 Telegraph Avenue, Apartment No. 3, did either Patrick or Moira Breen ever stay in the apartment with you?

ELISABETH WATERS: No.

MR. DOLAN: Who was taking care of the children when you were living at 6617 Telegraph Avenue, if you know?

ELISABETH WATERS: In the daytime Marion and I would go over to the house. It's a few blocks away from the house on Prince Street, and Marion was the daytime parent, and then at night Walter was there with the children because Walter was nocturnal. He would sit up all night writing.

MR. DOLAN: So this would be roughly the '79 to '81 time period?

ELISABETH WATERS: Yes.

MR. DOLAN: Did you have any permanent house guests at the 6617 Telegraph Avenue, Apartment 3 address? And what I mean by "permanent" is anyone who stayed there for more than three nights during that time period.

ELISABETH WATERS: No.

MR. DOLAN: Did you have any frequent guests? And what I mean by "frequent" is guests who came over on a regular basis, i.e., like once a week.

ELISABETH WATERS: No, it was a two-bedroom apartment. I had one bedroom. Marion had the other.

MR. BURESH: Your "no" answer was sufficient. You don't have to explain your answer.

MR. DOLAN: Was there an office in that apartment?

ELISABETH WATERS: No.

MR. DOLAN: Did you and Marion Zimmer Bradley ever share a bedroom in that apartment?

ELISABETH WATERS: No.

(I saw them in bed together in that apartment and at the Prince Street house, and so did my friend Jean.)

MR. DOLAN: Did you and Marion Zimmer Bradley ever share the same bed in that apartment?

MR. BURESH: I'm going to object to the question, and all questions along this line, as an invasion of the witness's privacy and also because it's not reasonably calculated to lead to the discovery of admissible evidence. Subject to that objection, I am going to allow the witness to answer to the extent that she feels comfortable, and so I'm going to allow the witness to go ahead to that extent.

MR. DOLAN: I'm not asking if you ever had sexual relations with her. I'm just asking whether you ever shared the same bed.

MR. BURESH: Well, that's a matter of characterization.

MZB: No, I don't think we did.

MR. DOLAN: Have you ever shared the same bed with Marion Zimmer Bradley?

MR. BURESH: Can we have a stipulation that I have continuing objection to this line of questions subject to what I just got through saying.

MR. DOLAN: Certainly. I'm not necessarily agreeing to your objection, but I understand you don't have to say it every time.

MR. BURESH: Thank you. Give me the question back, please.

MR. DOLAN: Did you and Marion Zimmer Bradley ever share the same bed?

MR. BURESH: I'll also object on the basis that it's vague and ambiguous.

MS. DURRELL: Overbroad.

MZB: I think we may have some times. It was a long time ago, and I don't remember very well.

MR. DOLAN: Have you and Marion Zimmer Bradley ever been romantically involved?

ELISABETH WATERS: Yes.

MR. DOLAN: From what time period?

ELISABETH WATERS: 1978 to about 1985, I think.

MR. DOLAN: Where did you live after living at the Telegraph Avenue address, please?

ELISABETH WATERS: 2221 Prince Street.

MR. DOLAN: Is that where you currently reside?

ELISABETH WATERS: Yes.

MR. DOLAN: Do you recall when you moved into 2221 PrinceStreet?

ELISABETH WATERS: It was when Moira was 15, so that would have made it 1981.

MR. DOLAN: When you moved into Prince Street in 1981– strike that. Have you ever lived at any other addresses on Prince Street?

ELISABETH WATERS: No.

MR. DOLAN: So when I refer to Prince Street, you'll know that I'm talking about 2221 Prince Street?

ELISABETH WATERS: Yes.

MR. DOLAN: When you moved into Prince Street, who was living in the dwelling at that time?

ELISABETH WATERS: Marion and I and Moira and Patrick.

MR. DOLAN: Do you know where Walter was living?

ELISABETH WATERS: Yes, he moved to our apartment.

MR. DOLAN: Have you ever lived in any addresses since– strike that. Have you ever lived in any addresses other than Prince Street since 1981?

ELISABETH WATERS: No.

MR. DOLAN: Are you familiar with a home called the "goldfish bowl", referenced as the goldfish bowl?

ELISABETH WATERS: Are you referring to 3031 Fulton Street?

MR. DOLAN: I believe that's what I'm referring to, yes.

ELISABETH WATERS: Yes.

MR. DOLAN: Do you know that to be commonly known as the goldfish bowl?

ELISABETH WATERS: Yes.

MR. DOLAN: Have you ever lived there?

ELISABETH WATERS: No.

MR. DOLAN: Is there another one that's 2024 Fulton Street that was owned by Marion at one point?

ELISABETH WATERS: That was 3024 Fulton Street that was owned by Marion and Patrick.

MR. DOLAN: Did you ever live there?

ELISABETH WATERS: No.

MR. DOLAN: Is it your testimony that since 1981 you have always resided at the Prince Street address except for trips to conventions and business or family and whatever?

ELISABETH WATERS: Yes.

MR. DOLAN: Could you please list any parties who live at the Prince Street address while you resided there other than yourself, Marion, and Patrick?

ELISABETH WATERS: Well, Moira was living there when we first moved there.

MR. DOLAN: Okay.

MR. BURESH: That's no constraint as to time on this; this is the entire time she has lived there, all the people who have lived in the house throughout the entire time she lived there?

MR. DOLAN: Let's take this here. We'll break it down. I got a feeling.

MR. DOLAN: Let's take from '81 to '85.

ELISABETH WATERS: All right. In 1981 it was Marion and me and Patrick and Moira. In 1982, Moira moved out to live with some friends, and a fosterling called Cynthia Becket moved in. She lived with us until I think early '84, and she got married in 1984. Then there was another fosterling Kathryn Krischild. I'm sorry, what time period were we?

MR. DOLAN: '81 to '85.

ELISABETH WATERS: Elizabeth Rousseau may have moved in during that time period. Generally, a lot of the kids' friends would come and stay with us for various periods of time.

MR. DOLAN: Any others that you can recall from '81 to '85?

ELISABETH WATERS: Let's see, there was a child named Barry who was there briefly. He was a runaway and Social Services temporarily placed him with us, but that didn't work out, and we had to ask Social Services to take him back.

MR. DOLAN: Any others during that time period?

ELISABETH WATERS: Not to the best of my recollection.

MR. DOLAN: Do you recall anybody named [other name] ever living there?

ELISABETH WATERS: I remember a boy named [Gregg]. I think he was one of Moira's boyfriends. [Gregg] and Nick and Patrick and Moira hung around together when– about the time when Moira was 15 and Patrick was 16, but he didn't live there. He lived in San Francisco with his mother.

(Lisa is claiming that Gregg was my boyfriend???? He was gay!!)

MR. DOLAN: Do you know if [Gregg] ever spent the night there?

ELISABETH WATERS: At Prince Street? Not to the best of my knowledge, no.

MR. DOLAN: Anyone else during the '81 to '85 time period that lived in the home?

ELISABETH WATERS: Not that I recall off the top of my head.

MR. DOLAN: Does [full name of Cyndi Beckett] have another name she was known by?

(Is Cyndi Beckett Cynthia Beckett, AKA Cyndi Nha June?)

ELISABETH WATERS: She was later [Cyndi Beckett].

MR. DOLAN: How old was [Cyndi Beckett] when she lived at the Prince Street address, if you know?

ELISABETH WATERS: 18, 19 and 20.

MR. DOLAN: Do you know her birth date?

ELISABETH WATERS: October 5th, 1963.

MR. DOLAN: How old was Kathryn Krischild when she lived there; do you know?

ELISABETH WATERS: I think she was a couple of years older than the rest of the kids. [Cyndi Beckett] was a year older than Patrick, and I think Kat was a couple years older than that.

MR. DOLAN: Do you know where Kat lives now?

ELISABETH WATERS: Shattuck Avenue, Berkeley.

MR. DOLAN: Do you know where on Shattuck?

ELISABETH WATERS: I think it's 3024.

MR. DOLAN: Do you know her phone number?

ELISABETH WATERS: Not off the top of my head.

MR. DOLAN: Do you know where [Cyndi Beckett] lives now?

ELISABETH WATERS: No.

MR. DOLAN: Do you know if she's known by any other names?

ELISABETH WATERS: She married [Mr. X], so she might be known as [Mrs. X[.

MR. DOLAN: Do you know if she was ever known as [Nickname]?

ELISABETH WATERS: Not to my knowledge. Certainly not during the time I knew her.

MR. DOLAN: Do you know if Miss Krischild is known by any other names?

ELISABETH WATERS: I don't believe I have ever heard any other names for her.

MR. DOLAN: Do you mind if we break for a minute?

(Whereupon, a recess was taken.)

MR. DOLAN: Do you know if Miss Krischild is known by any other names?

ELISABETH WATERS: I thought I just answered that, no.

MR. DOLAN: You may have.

ELISABETH WATERS: No.

MR. DOLAN: Do you know where Lisa Rousseau lives?

ELISABETH WATERS: Somewhere in San Francisco. I don't know the exact address.

MR. DOLAN: Do you know what street?

ELISABETH WATERS: No.

MR. DOLAN: Do you know who she lives with, if anyone?

ELISABETH WATERS: No.

MR. DOLAN: Do you know if she is known by any other names currently?

ELISABETH WATERS: Not to the best of my knowledge.

MR. DOLAN: Do you know if she's married?

ELISABETH WATERS: I believe she is not.

MR. DOLAN: Do you know where Barry lives?

ELISABETH WATERS: No.

MR. DOLAN: How old was Barry when he lived at the house?

ELISABETH WATERS: 12.

MR. DOLAN: How long did he live there?

ELISABETH WATERS: A couple of months, I believe.

MR. DOLAN: How old was [Eric] during the time period '84 to '85?

ELISABETH WATERS: Who?

MR. DOLAN: Is that his last name, [Eric], do you know?

ELISABETH WATERS: I don't know anyone by that name.

MR. DOLAN: Do you know what [Eric]'s last name was?

ELISABETH WATERS: You mean the [Eric] that hung out with Moira and Patrick?

MR. BURESH: The witness has testified that he didn't live there.

MR. DOLAN: Okay. Well, he was there in and out.

MR. DOLAN: How old was [Eric]–

MS. DURRELL: I'm going to object, that misstates the witness's testimony.

MR. BURESH: Why don't you just say what you said before about [other name]'s presence at the house.

ELISABETH WATERS: Maybe he was there three or four times. I didn't see much of him.

MR. DOLAN: Okay. Do you have any idea how old he was?

ELISABETH WATERS: I believe he was 15. As I said, I thought he was Moira's boyfriend, and she was 15.

MR. DOLAN: Were you ever advised by Moira that [Gregg] was found in Walter's bed?

ELISABETH WATERS: No.

(Yes. I told her that Gregg was in Walter's bed.)

MR. DOLAN: At any time prior to today, has Moira ever told you that [Gregg] was in Walter's bed?

ELISABETH WATERS: Not to the best of my recollection.

MR. DOLAN: Did you ever live at Prince Street before moving to Telegraph Avenue for any period of time?

ELISABETH WATERS: No.

MR. DOLAN: Did you ever visit there?

ELISABETH WATERS: While I was–

MR. DOLAN: Prince Street?

ELISABETH WATERS: Oh, you mean before I moved out there?

MR. DOLAN: Yes.

ELISABETH WATERS: No.

MR. DOLAN: Have you ever heard of a man by the name of [Glenn]?

ELISABETH WATERS: I think I have heard the name. I have never met him.

MR. DOLAN: How have you heard the name [Glenn]?

ELISABETH WATERS: If he's the one I'm thinking of, he was somebody that Walter was accused of molesting back in the early '60s or something. I don't really know much of anything about it.

MR. DOLAN: When did you first hear that Walter had been accused of molesting [Glenn] in the early '60s?

ELISABETH WATERS: I think it was sometime in the '80s. It was some sort of science fiction fan feud that Marion told me had happened back around the time she and Walter were married.

MR. DOLAN: Did Marion ever tell you that Walter had had a sexual relationship with [Glenn] before they were married?

ELISABETH WATERS: No.

MR. DOLAN: Did you ever hear Marion make such a statement to anyone that Walter had had a sexual relationship with [Glenn] before they were married?

ELISABETH WATERS: When we told her about Kenny, she said that she thought he might. I don't remember her exact words, but she seemed to think there was a possibility then that he had molested [Glenn], but that wasn't until October of 1989.

MR. DOLAN: So in October of '89 when you told her that she may have molested Ken–

ELISABETH WATERS: That Walter may have molested Ken.

MR. DOLAN: Strike that. I'm out of it from this car thing. I'll start over again. In October of 1989 when you told Marion that Walter may have molested Kenny, she told you that she thought there was a possibility that Walter may have also molested [Glenn]?

ELISABETH WATERS: When we told her that Walter had molested Kenny—by then we were pretty sure—she seemed to think that if Walter was capable of molesting Kenny then perhaps he had also molested [Glenn].

MR. BURESH: [Name 1] or [Name 2]? We've got two names here. I know they're in the police report.

ELISABETH WATERS: Possibly both of them.

MR. BURESH: Are you confusing [Name 1]with [Name 2] in your answers?

ELISABETH WATERS: No.

MR. BURESH: Okay.

ELISABETH WATERS: [Glenn] I knew. [Gregg] I didn't.

MR. BURESH: Okay.

MR. DOLAN: Did she ever tell you that Walter may have possibly molested [Glenn]?

ELISABETH WATERS: Didn't I answer that?

MR. DOLAN: I'm trying to–

MR. BURESH: We talked about [Glenn] and now we're talking about [Name 2]. Why don't we get the names straight?

ELISABETH WATERS: I thought we were talking about [Name 2].

MR. DOLAN: Who is [Name 2]?

ELISABETH WATERS: [Name 2]is the kid in the Breen boondoggle, which was a big fannish scandal back when I was in grade school in Connecticut.

MR. DOLAN: Okay. And [Name 1] is the boy who was referenced as possibly being the boyfriend of Moira's, correct?

ELISABETH WATERS: Yes.

MS. DURRELL: Is that– excuse me, is that [Glenn]?

MR. DOLAN: No, I think I have that wrong. It's [other name].

ELISABETH WATERS: Yeah, I think his last name is [other name] or something like that.

MR. DOLAN: I think I got the two mixed up because they both begin with G. I'll try to be more careful.

MS. DURRELL: Let me ask then, this testimony that's been going on about [Glenn], is that a separate [first name] from [other name]?

MR. DOLAN: It's [Glenn] and [other name].

ELISABETH WATERS: We have been– at least I have been talking about [Glenn].

MR. DOLAN: Right, okay. Let me start over again.

ELISABETH WATERS: Okay.

MS. DURRELL: Maybe you should take few days off before you continue.

MR. DOLAN: I have been told that. Let's sort of clean this up here.

MR. DOLAN: [Glenn], when did you first hear about him?

ELISABETH WATERS: I think it was sometime in the 1980's.

MR. DOLAN: Okay. Do you know approximately when?

ELISABETH WATERS: No.

MR. DOLAN: Was it before Kenny Smith was reported as being molested?

ELISABETH WATERS: Yes.

MR. DOLAN: How long before Kenny Smith had been reported as being molested had you heard about [Glenn]?

ELISABETH WATERS: I don't know.

MR. DOLAN: Can you give me an estimate or approximation?

ELISABETH WATERS: Five years plus or minus three.

MR. DOLAN: How did you hear about [Glenn] in that time period that you just referenced?

ELISABETH WATERS: Somebody referred to some old fannish scandal. It was a fan feud. Apparently Walter and some other fan were in competition for some fannish award, and the fan accused him of molesting [Glenn], and there was a police investigation, and the police apparently cleared Walter, and there was– I gather people argued about whether Walter should be something called FAPA, which I believes stands for Fantasy Amateur Press Association. And it's a sort of round-robin news letter, although why anybody would want to be in it is a mystery to me, but apparently it was a big thing to Walter and Marion.

MR. DOLAN: Okay. Do you know if Walter was ever banished from Worldcon as a result of this?

ELISABETH WATERS: As a result of what?

MR. DOLAN: The episode with– the accusation regarding [Glenn]?

ELISABETH WATERS: Not that I ever heard.

MR. DOLAN: Do you have any information of whether Walter Breen was excluded from the 1964 Worldcon?

ELISABETH WATERS: I have no knowledge of that.

MR. DOLAN: Were you aware of the fracas that was happening regarding this issue at any time when you yourself were a younger child before you became involved with the Zimmer Bradley Enterprises?

ELISABETH WATERS: Are you asking if I knew about that before I met Marion?

MR. DOLAN: Correct.

ELISABETH WATERS: No, I did not.

MR. DOLAN: Did you know if Walter was ever blackballed from the FAPA waiting list?

ELISABETH WATERS: I believe he was. I think that was a–

MR. BURESH: The question was whether you know, not what you believe. We are venturing into speculation here. The question is whether you know.

MR. DOLAN: Do you have any reason to believe that Walter was ever blackballed from the FAPA waiting list?

ELISABETH WATERS: I don't think so, no.

MR. DOLAN: Did anyone ever tell you that Walter was excluded from FAPA?

ELISABETH WATERS: I got the impression from what Marion said about it that he was for a time or that there was some big debate as to whether or not he should be admitted.

MR. DOLAN: Who was it in the 1980's that brought this issue regarding [Glenn] to your attention?

ELISABETH WATERS: I don't remember. I think it may have been Marion.

MR. DOLAN: Can you tell me everything you can recall regarding the discussion that concerned [Glenn] at that time in the 1980's?

ELISABETH WATERS: I think we were discussing science fiction FANDOM feuds and how silly they were. That's really all I remember.

MR. DOLAN: What do you remember about the discussions specifically concerning Walter's conduct, if any, with [Glenn]?

MR. BURESH: Other than what she has already testified to?

MR. DOLAN: Right.

ELISABETH WATERS: Other than what I have already testified to, nothing.

MR. DOLAN: Did Marion ever give you any opinion of her own at that time as to whether or not she thought the charges had any basis to it?

ELISABETH WATERS: At that time, no.

MR. DOLAN: At a later time, did she?

ELISABETH WATERS: I have already mentioned the conversation in October of 1989.

MR. DOLAN: Can you tell me with specificity what happened in that conversation in 1989 regarding [Glenn]?

ELISABETH WATERS: Raul and I picked her up at the airport, and while she was gone we had found out that Walter really had molested Kenny, so on the way home from the airport we told her, and she was very upset, and she said that if Walter was capable of that, then maybe he molested [Glenn] and [other name] as well.

MR. DOLAN: Anything else that she said about that?

ELISABETH WATERS: That she was going to divorce him.

MR. DOLAN: Anything else?

ELISABETH WATERS: I think that's about it.

MR. DOLAN: Did she give you any indication of whether she had ever told Walter that if he did this again she was going to divorce him?

ELISABETH WATERS: She said something about, she had always said that if he did this again, she would divorce him, but I'm not sure whether she was talking to him or to herself.

MR. DOLAN: You heard her say the words, though, "If he did this again, I was going to divorce him"?

MR. BURESH: The exact words, or words to that effect? I don't know what your question is.

MR. DOLAN: The best I can get.

MR. DOLAN: What was your best recollection regarding what she said in that regard?

ELISABETH WATERS: My best recollection is that she said, "I always said if he did this again I would divorce him."

MR. DOLAN: Had you ever heard her say that before?

ELISABETH WATERS: No.

MR. DOLAN: Have you ever heard her say that after that time that she was riding in the car on the way home?

ELISABETH WATERS: No.

MR. DOLAN: Approximately what date is this date that you picked her up at the airport?

ELISABETH WATERS: I believe it was October 9th, 1989.

MR. DOLAN: When she was using the word "again," did you ask her what do you mean by "again"?

ELISABETH WATERS: No.

MR. DOLAN: Did you have any understanding as to what she meant by the word "again"?

ELISABETH WATERS: No.

MR. DOLAN: Did you undertake any inquiry of any type whatsoever to find out what Marion meant by the words, "if he did this again"?

ELISABETH WATERS: No, I did not.

MR. DOLAN: Since that time have you ever come to understand what Marion meant when she said, "If he did this again, I would divorce him"?

ELISABETH WATERS: No.

MR. DOLAN: And you have never asked Marion what she meant by that, have you?

ELISABETH WATERS: No.

MR. DOLAN: Have you ever discussed it with Raul, that particular phraseology of what Marion said?

ELISABETH WATERS: Not to the best of my recollection.

MR. DOLAN: Have you ever discussed it with anyone else?

MR. BURESH: Besides her attorney?

ELISABETH WATERS: My attorney.

MR. DOLAN: Okay. I won't call that a waiver.

MR. DOLAN: Going back to this thing that has come to be known as "the boondoggle", have you ever heard it called that?

ELISABETH WATERS: Yes.

MR. DOLAN: When I use the word the "boondoggle", I'm talking about this episode that occurred at some point in FANDOM regarding Walter's alleged acts of molestation of children; do you understand that?

ELISABETH WATERS: Walter's alleged acts of molestation with [Glenn]. I never heard that there were any other children involved.

MR. DOLAN: Okay. Do you know if there are any documents that concern this alleged act of molestation with [Glenn] from the boondoggle?

ELISABETH WATERS: None that I know of.

MR. DOLAN: Do you know if the Worldcon has a governing body there, an organization that runs it?

ELISABETH WATERS: Yes.

MR. DOLAN: And what is the name of that organization?

ELISABETH WATERS: I believe it's called The World Science Fiction Society.

MR. DOLAN: Where is The World Science Fiction Society located?

ELISABETH WATERS: I don't know.

MR. DOLAN: Did you ever send in registrations for Worldcon?

ELISABETH WATERS: Yes.

MR. DOLAN: Where did you send them to?

ELISABETH WATERS: To whatever convention committee is running the Worldcon that year.

MR. DOLAN: Do you know if they're a business or a corporation, The World Science Fiction Society?

ELISABETH WATERS: I don't know. I have never really paid all that much attention to the business end of how it's run.

MR. DOLAN: Do you know who the current president of that society is?

ELISABETH WATERS: No.

MR. DOLAN: Has Marion ever been the president of that society?

ELISABETH WATERS: No.

MR. DOLAN: Do you know where the current committee is located for the next Worldcon?

ELISABETH WATERS: I believe the next Worldcon is in Baltimore.

MR. DOLAN: Do you know how I could find out who the parties are associated with the Worldcon organizing committee for Baltimore?

ELISABETH WATERS: I believe they have a Web page.

MR. DOLAN: Do you have any other ideas of how I could locate them besides a Web page?

ELISABETH WATERS: Locus Magazine, that's L-o-c-u-s. They have convention lists, and you just look through the listing for them.

MR. DOLAN: Where is Locus Magazine out of?

ELISABETH WATERS: It's published out of Oakland.

MR. DOLAN: Do you know if they have a publishing office or editorial office there in Oakland?

ELISABETH WATERS: Yes.

MR. DOLAN: You indicated that the police investigated Walter for this issue regarding [Glenn] and cleared him; do you know what police you were talking about?

ELISABETH WATERS: No. Marion just said that they had. I don't know it of my own knowledge.

MR. DOLAN: Do you have any understanding as you sit here today which police department that may have been?

MR. BURESH: Are you asking her to speculate?

MR. DOLAN: No, I asked for her understanding.

MR. BURESH: As to what it may have been? I'll object. Calls for speculation.

MR. DOLAN: Do you have any understanding as to what police department investigated Walter at that time?

MR. BURESH: Asked and answered. I mean, if you got any. I mean, do you know where it happened?

ELISABETH WATERS: No, I don't know.

MR. DOLAN: Okay. Is there anyone that you know who I could speak to who would have better information than you on this issue of the boondoggle?

ELISABETH WATERS: I think most of the people who were involved in it are dead by now. So, no, I'm afraid I don't.

MR. DOLAN: Would Marion have more information on the boondoggle than you?

ELISABETH WATERS: In her present condition, I'm afraid not.

MR. DOLAN: Were any of the other members of Greyhaven involved with the science fiction community back at the time of the boondoggle?

ELISABETH WATERS: I don't know.

MR. DOLAN: Have you ever discussed the boondoggle with anyone other than Marion?

ELISABETH WATERS: Not that I recall.

MR. DOLAN: Do you know if Walter has been investigated by any other police other than the Oakland police, the L.A. police, and whatever police may have investigated him in the [Glenn] issue?

ELISABETH WATERS: I don't know that Walter was ever investigated by the Oakland police.

MR. DOLAN: The Berkeley police, excuse me.

ELISABETH WATERS: There was that thing in Atlantic City that came up in the stuff you sent us, but other than that, I don't know.

MR. DOLAN: When did you first learn about Walter's arrest for the lewd and lascivious behavior in Atlantic city?

ELISABETH WATERS: When you sent us the information.

MR. DOLAN: Did you ever discuss that with Marion?

ELISABETH WATERS: Not to the best of my recollection.

MR. DOLAN: Did you ever hear Marion talk about Walter's arrest in Atlantic City?

ELISABETH WATERS: Wasn't that in 1954?

MR. DOLAN: I am just asking in—

MR. BURESH: Well, regardless of when it was, he's asking—

MR. DOLAN: Did you ever hear Marion talk about it?

MR. BURESH: Also I'm presuming all of these questions are directed to conversations that were outside the presence of counsel.

MR. DOLAN: Yes.

ELISABETH WATERS: No, I never heard Marion discuss it. And since it would have been about 10 years before she met him, there is no reason she would have known about it.

MR. BURESH: I move to strike.

MR. DOLAN: The question was just, have you ever heard her discuss it?

ELISABETH WATERS: No.

MR. DOLAN: Are you aware if Walter Breen has ever been investigated by any police agencies other than the ones that we have identified as the Atlantic City police, the ones who investigated the [Glenn] issue, the Berkeley police, and the Los Angeles police?

ELISABETH WATERS: To the best of my knowledge, that's all.

MR. DOLAN: Do you know if Walter has ever been investigated to your knowledge by any child protective services?

ELISABETH WATERS: Well, when we got Barry as a foster child, there was the investigation, I think, that was run by Child Protective Services because we were certified as a foster home for this child.

MR. DOLAN: Were you involved in that process at all of the investigation?

ELISABETH WATERS: I think they asked me a few questions.

MR. DOLAN: Did they ask you any questions about Walter Breen and his sexual activity?

ELISABETH WATERS: No.

MR. DOLAN: Did they ask anything about child molestation in any way?

ELISABETH WATERS: No.

MR. DOLAN: At the time that they investigated you, did you have any knowledge as to whether or not Walter Breen had any particular beliefs regarding the age of consent for sexuality?

MR. BURESH: I'll object to the form of the question. You said, "At the time they investigated you." I don't know if you mean this particular witness or who you are talking about.

MR. DOLAN: I will rephrase it.

MR. DOLAN: At the time the Child Protective Services investigated the suitability of the family for placement of a child, did you have any understanding as to Walter Breen's idealogy regarding the age of consent as it concerned children?

MR. BURESH: Age of consent for sexual conduct?

MR. DOLAN: Yes.

MS. DURRELL: Do you understand the question?

ELISABETH WATERS: I don't think so.

MR. DOLAN: At the time that you were—that your family unit was being, shall we say, "investigated," for lack of a better word, for suitability of placement of a foster child—do you understand when I'm saying that part?

ELISABETH WATERS: Yes.

MR. DOLAN: During that time when this was going on and you were talking to the Child Protective Services people who were doing that investigation—we are focusing on that time period, okay?

ELISABETH WATERS: Okay.

MR. DOLAN: At that point did you know Walter Breen had written the book Greek Love?

ELISABETH WATERS: No.

MR. DOLAN: At that point did you have any understanding as to whether Walter Breen thought that the "pedophilic tradition of education," as it's been referred to in his writings, was appropriate?

ELISABETH WATERS: I have never seen any writings of Walter which refer to the pedophilic tradition of education, and I don't know what that term means.

MR. DOLAN: At that time did you have any understanding as to how Walter felt regarding sex between men and boys?

ELISABETH WATERS: I do not believe so, no.

MR. DOLAN: At that point were you aware that Walter had written any works whatsoever on the subject of sex between men and boys?

ELISABETH WATERS: No.

(We are seriously expected to believe that Lisa knew nothing of my father's open conduct or writing.)

MR. DOLAN: Had you ever discussed that topic with Walter Breen at any time prior to the placement of Barry with the family?

ELISABETH WATERS: No.

MR. DOLAN: Had you ever discussed that topic with Marion at any time prior to the placement of Barry with the family?

ELISABETH WATERS: No.

MR. DOLAN: To your knowledge did Marion Zimmer Bradley ever alert the Child Protective Services that Walter Breen had written the book Greek Love?

ELISABETH WATERS: I don't know.

MR. DOLAN: To your knowledge–

ELISABETH WATERS: Oh, to my knowledge, no, she didn't.

MR. DOLAN: Were you present when they discussed the placement of Barry with the family, Marion and CPS?

MR. BURESH: When you say "they discussed."

MR. DOLAN: I said "Marion and CPS". I just clarified that.

MR. BURESH: I'm sorry.

ELISABETH WATERS: No, no.

MR. DOLAN: Were you present when– did CPS discuss it with Walter, the placement of that child with the family; do you know?

ELISABETH WATERS: I don't know. I would imagine they must have, but I don't know.

MR. DOLAN: Who was present when you discussed the placement of this child with the family?

MR. BURESH: With Child Protective Services?

MR. DOLAN: Yes.

ELISABETH WATERS: I'm not even sure, now that I think of it, that it was an oral discussion. I think they may have just had us fill out questionnaires.

MR. DOLAN: Do you know if you still have copies of those questionnaires?

ELISABETH WATERS: No, we don't. I don't know if we ever did.

MR. DOLAN: Do you know what agency placed this child?

ELISABETH WATERS: I wouldn't know the proper name, but the kid was from San Francisco, so it would have been whatever agency had jurisdiction over runaway kids in San Francisco.

MR. DOLAN: Do you have any records whatsoever in the home that you're aware of there on Prince Street that relate to the placement of this child with the family?

ELISABETH WATERS: No, we do not.

MR. DOLAN: Do you know if it was a public or private agency that placed the child within the home?

ELISABETH WATERS: I believe it was public.

MR. DOLAN: Do you know if anybody within the family alerted the agency that placed this child in the home that Walter Breen had written the book Greek Love?

ELISABETH WATERS: No, I don't know. That was the question, wasn't it, did I know?

MR. DOLAN: Do you have any knowledge as to whether Marion Zimmer Bradley was aware that Walter Breen had written the book Greek Love prior to the placement of this child within the family?

MR. BURESH: Let me hear the question back again, please.

MR. DOLAN: Do you have any knowledge as to whether Marion Zimmer Bradley was aware that Walter Breen had written the book Greek Love prior to the placement of this child in the family.

MR. BURESH: I'm not sure what the time frame refers to, whether it refers to when she knew or when Marion knew or–

MR. DOLAN: I'm just asking if she has any knowledge as she sits here today as to whether or not Marion was aware prior to the placement of this child within that family that Walter had written the book Greek Love.

ELISABETH WATERS: Yes.

MR. DOLAN: Can you explain that answer for me?

ELISABETH WATERS: Yes, I believe she did know that he had written the book Greek Love.

MR. DOLAN: Do you have any knowledge as to whether or not the boondoggle had occurred before or after this child was placed within the family?

ELISABETH WATERS: It was before.

MR. DOLAN: Do you have any knowledge as to whether Marion Zimmer Bradley alerted the CPS workers that Walter had been accused of molesting [Glenn] prior to this child being placed within the family?

ELISABETH WATERS: I do not have knowledge of that.

MR. DOLAN: Do you know if anybody within the family unit notified CPS that Walter had been accused of molesting [Glenn] prior to the placement of this child, Barry, within the family unit?

ELISABETH WATERS: I have no knowledge of that.

MR. DOLAN: Prior to the placement of this child, Barry, within the family unit, and this is sometime you said in the 1981 to '85 time frame; is that correct?

ELISABETH WATERS: I believe it was in 1981.

MR. DOLAN: Okay. Prior to 1981, did you have any understanding as to Walter Breen's opinions on the issue of sex between men and boys?

ELISABETH WATERS: No, not really.

MR. DOLAN: Not really? Did you have any idea whatsoever what his beliefs were on that subject?

ELISABETH WATERS: I don't know, at some point I knew that he had written a book about man-boy love throughout history, but I didn't have any idea whether that reflected on his actual current opinions.

MR. DOLAN: Okay. Had you ever discussed the topic of Walter and young boys with Marion Zimmer Bradley prior to the placement of Barry within the home in 1981?

ELISABETH WATERS: Yes, in 19– I think it was 1980, I saw a letter that Walter had written to his therapist, Dr. Morin, and he said that he missed Sterling—who was another one of the kids who hung around. He was a friend of Patrick's—not just because he was horny but because– I forget the rest, but that phrase struck me as so odd that I went and asked Marion about it. And Marion said that Walter had been completely impotent since Moira was two, so I thought that Walter was just bragging to his therapist, you know, the way teenage boys brag to their friends about having scored with their girlfriends when they haven't, because Walter was about that immature.

MR. DOLAN: Was this prior to the placement of this child within the home, Barry?

ELISABETH WATERS: Yes.

MR. DOLAN: Do you know why Walter was seeing this therapist, Dr. Morin?

ELISABETH WATERS: No.

MR. DOLAN: Do you know who was paying for that therapy?

ELISABETH WATERS: Walter was.

MR. DOLAN: Do you still have a copy of that letter?

ELISABETH WATERS: I never had the letter in my possession. I saw it on the music room floor.

MR. DOLAN: Do you know if a copy of that letter still exists in the possession of anyone within the Breen family or Zimmer Bradley family?

ELISABETH WATERS: No, I would certainly very much doubt that it would. I don't know that.

MR. DOLAN: Do you ever see that letter at any time after the point that you showed it to Marion?

ELISABETH WATERS: I didn't show it to Marion. I saw it, and I asked her about it, but, no, I never saw it again.

MR. DOLAN: Did Marion and you ever have any discussions other than what you have just described to me regarding that letter at that time?

ELISABETH WATERS: I think I mentioned it again in October of 1989 when she was talking about boys Walter might have molested. But basically, no, you know, I said this looks weird. Marion said, no, this is impossible and forgot about it for 10 years.

MR. DOLAN: Who was Sterling?

ELISABETH WATERS: Sterling was a friend of Patrick's.

MR. DOLAN: What was his full name?

ELISABETH WATERS: I believe his last name was [redacted].

MR. DOLAN: Did you ever see Walter and Sterling together?

ELISABETH WATERS: Yes.

MR. DOLAN: Where did you see?

ELISABETH WATERS: I mean, Sterling hung around the house a lot. He didn't like his stepfather, so he spent a lot of time at our house.

MR. DOLAN: What time period was this that Sterling was hanging around the house?

ELISABETH WATERS: 1979 to 1981, maybe.

MR. DOLAN: During the time period 1979 through 1981, did you ever see Sterling interact with Walter?

ELISABETH WATERS: Could you be more specific? What do you mean by "interact"?

MR. DOLAN: Did you ever see them touch?

ELISABETH WATERS: No.

MR. DOLAN: Did you ever see them in the hot tub together?

ELISABETH WATERS: I don't remember. A lot of people went in the hot tub. We usually all went in as a group.

MR. DOLAN: Do you ever remember seeing Walter naked in the hot tub with any young boys at any time?

ELISABETH WATERS: Well, I think I remember seeing Walter naked in the hot tub with Anodea and Philip and Alex, and Alex was an infant.

MR. DOLAN: Any other young children that you saw Walter naked in the hot tub with?

ELISABETH WATERS: Walter always went in the hot tub naked, and sometimes Patrick and Moira and Ian and Fiona and the adults from Greyhaven and Marion and I would all be there.

MR. DOLAN: Did you ever see Walter alone in the hot tub naked with any young children?

ELISABETH WATERS: No.

MR. DOLAN: Do you ever see Walter naked in the hot tub with Ken Smith?

ELISABETH WATERS: No.

MR. DOLAN: Do you ever see Walter touch Sterling physically in any way?

ELISABETH WATERS: Not that I recall.

MR. DOLAN: After reading this letter regarding Sterling, did you ever ask Sterling whether Walter was touching him in any inappropriate ways?

ELISABETH WATERS: Not until 1989 or 1990, and I asked him then, and he said Walter didn't.

MR. DOLAN: Back at the time that you read the letter, did you undertake any investigation to see whether Walter was acting inappropriately with Sterling other than the discussion that you have mentioned with Marion Zimmer Bradley

ELISABETH WATERS: No.

MR. DOLAN: Did you ever call Dr. Morin?

ELISABETH WATERS: No.

MR. DOLAN: Did you ever ask Walter about the letter?

ELISABETH WATERS: No.

MR. DOLAN: Why not?

MR. BURESH: I'll object to the question. It assumes facts not evidence. It assumes there was some reason why she didn't do.

MR. DOLAN: Is there any reason why you didn't ask Walter about the letter?

ELISABETH WATERS: I was cleaning the music room, and I found it on the floor. I picked it up and put it with the rest of his papers. It wasn't as if he had shown it to me, or it was really any of my business.

MR. DOLAN: Did you think that that letter was odd?

ELISABETH WATERS: I thought that practically everything Walter did was odd.

MR. DOLAN: Did you think that letter was odd?

ELISABETH WATERS: Yes.

MR. DOLAN: Do you think that letter– did that letter cause you any concern at the time you read it about the welfare of Sterling?

ELISABETH WATERS: No.

MR. DOLAN: Why did you ask Marion about it then?

ELISABETH WATERS: It just–

MR. BURESH: Objection, it's argumentative.

MR. DOLAN: You can answer.

MR. BURESH: Go ahead. You can answer the question.

ELISABETH WATERS: It just seemed weird.

MR. DOLAN: Did it seem more weird than other things that Walter was doing?

MR. BURESH: I'll object to the question as vague and ambiguous, and I instruct the witness not to answer.

MR. DOLAN: You say it was weird; what do you mean by "weird"?

ELISABETH WATERS: How did you feel when you moved from New Canaan, Connecticut to the Bay Area?

MR. DOLAN: Liberated.

ELISABETH WATERS: I felt confused. I felt culture shock. Everything seemed strange.

MR. DOLAN: Okay. Did the fact that Walter was talking about being horny around an underage boy seem more weird than the other things that Walter was doing?

ELISABETH WATERS: No.

MR. DOLAN: Would Walter talk about being horny in relating to underage boys in other context during that time period?

ELISABETH WATERS: No.

MR. DOLAN: And so that didn't seem any different to you than Walter's other behavior?

ELISABETH WATERS: I don't understand the question.

MR. DOLAN: I'm trying to understand. Did you think it was normal behavior, as Walter behaved, to talk about being horny with an underage boy?

ELISABETH WATERS: Yes, because I thought it was sort of teenage, "I'm so great", "I score", type thing.

MR. DOLAN: Okay. And that was normal for Walter to act in that manner?

MR. BURESH: In what manner? I'll object to the question, vague and ambiguous as to "that manner."

MR. DOLAN: Was it, from your observations of Walter, was it normal for him to be acting in that teenage kind of manner saying, "I'm great", "I scored"?

ELISABETH WATERS: From my observations of Walter, it was normal for him to be acting very immature.

MR. DOLAN: Had you ever heard Walter acting immature regarding sexuality or sexual issues before this letter you saw of to Dr. Morin?

ELISABETH WATERS: Not to the best of my recollection.

MR. DOLAN: Had you ever heard Walter discuss sexuality in any way with you prior to reading this letter addressed to Dr. Morin?

ELISABETH WATERS: No.

MR. DOLAN: What were the other things that Walter did which were as weird as what you read in this letter?

ELISABETH WATERS: Well, he went naked a lot. He didn't– he didn't really seem like a normal father. It's like nobody really respected him. It's more as if he were a pet people tolerated. You know, he knew coins, and he knew music, and that was about it.

MR. DOLAN: And what weird thing, though, I mean, other than being like a pet who people tolerated, what activities, what things did you see or hear him do which were as weird as stating in his letter to his therapist that he missed this young man and not just because he was horny?

MR. BURESH: Object to the question, assumes facts not evidence, mainly that there were things that were done that led her to believe that he was weird.

MR. DOLAN: She stated earlier that it wasn't much weirder than the other things he did.

ELISABETH WATERS: Well, one day his house caught on fire and he called me instead of the fire department.

MR. DOLAN: Okay. What else?

ELISABETH WATERS: I really don't know. He just always seemed weird to me.

MR. DOLAN: Did you, at that point, tell Marion that you– and when I say– strike that. At the point that you read this letter and brought it to Marion's attention, did you indicate any concern for the welfare of Sterling to Marion?

ELISABETH WATERS: Well, Sterling was a big strapping kid, and I figured that if Walter tried anything Sterling didn't like, Sterling would flatten him.

MR. DOLAN: How old was Sterling at that time?

ELISABETH WATERS: 15, 16.

MR. DOLAN: The question was, did you indicate any concern to Marion at the time that you mentioned this letter to Dr. Morin to her about the welfare the Sterling?

MR. BURESH: Other than the fact that she brought it to Marion's attention?

MR. DOLAN: Yeah.

ELISABETH WATERS: Other than that, no, I don't think so.

MR. DOLAN: Is there anything else that you can recall about the conversation with Marion other than what you said, I found this letter that Walter wrote that says this, and Marion saying he's impotent.

MR. BURESH: Other than what she has already testified to?

MR. DOLAN: Right.

ELISABETH WATERS: That's all I remember.

MR. DOLAN: Did the subject ever come up again between the time that you first discussed it with Marion then and the time that Kenny was reported in 1989?

ELISABETH WATERS: No.

MR. BURESH: I don't know what subject you're talking about. The subject of Sterling and the Dr. Morin letter?

MR. DOLAN: The subject of the Dr. Morin letter and Sterling ever come up again?

ELISABETH WATERS: No, it did not.

MR. DOLAN: Did the subject of a possible molestation of Sterling ever come up again between the time of that letter and the time that Kenny's molestation was reported?

MR. BURESH: Object to the question, misstates her testimony, assumes facts not in evidence.

MR. DOLAN: Did the subject of any improper conduct or possible improper conduct between Walter and Sterling ever come up between the time of talking with Marion about that letter and the time Kenny's sexual molestation was reported in 1989?

MR. BURESH: Same objection.

MR. DOLAN: You can answer unless you're instructed not to answer.

MR. BURESH: I just wish you would rephrase the question because the subject was the letter to Dr. Morin. He said he was– he missed him because he was horny.

ELISABETH WATERS: Not just because he was horny.

MR. BURESH: Not just because he was horny. Now whether that implies improper conduct or not is the assumption that's built into the question. It's not coming from what the witness said, so I think it's a mischaracterization of her testimony, and it assumes facts not in evidence. So I would ask that the question be rephrased. As to the current question, I'll instruct the witness not to answer.

MR. DOLAN: Did you ask Marion, at the time that you showed her this letter, whether she thought that Walter might be doing anything improper with Sterling?

ELISABETH WATERS: Yes.

MR. DOLAN: Okay. Between the time that you had that discussion with Marion and the time that Kenny's molestation was reported, did the subject of Walter possibly doing something improper with Sterling ever come up again?

ELISABETH WATERS: No.

MR. DOLAN: Are you aware of any other letters that Walter wrote that in any way referenced anything sexual about children?

ELISABETH WATERS: No.

MR. DOLAN: Did you ever read any of Walter's diaries?

ELISABETH WATERS: No.

MR. DOLAN: Have you ever seen any of Walter's diaries?

ELISABETH WATERS: I think I saw part of one when– during the police investigation when they were trying to find somebody who could decipher the darn things. I couldn't.

MR. DOLAN: Did you ever see Walter's diaries at the goldfish bowl?

ELISABETH WATERS: I might have seen some of them on a bookshelf someplace. I don't really remember.

MR. DOLAN: Do you have any knowledge of where those diaries are today?

ELISABETH WATERS: I believe Patrick has them.

MR. DOLAN: Did you ever touch those diaries personally yourself?

ELISABETH WATERS: No.

MR. DOLAN: Were you ever aware of any instructions to burn Walter's diaries?

ELISABETH WATERS: Certainly no such instructions were ever given to me.

MR. DOLAN: Were you ever aware of there being any instructions like that?

MR. BURESH: At any time including up to the present time?

MR. DOLAN: Yeah.

ELISABETH WATERS: I have heard that Moira has written or said something that she had instructions to burn his diaries if the police came.

MR. DOLAN: Were you ever aware of that before the report of Kenny Smith's molestation in '89?

ELISABETH WATERS: No.

MR. DOLAN: Did you ever clean out the goldfish bowl of any papers or articles of Walter Breen's?

ELISABETH WATERS: Yes, in 1993 after they gave you the lease and moved out.

MR. DOLAN: What did you do with those papers?

ELISABETH WATERS: I gave them to Jonathan Chase, who is the lawyer handling Walter's estate.

MR. DOLAN: Did you throw any of Walter Breen's papers out at that time?

ELISABETH WATERS: I think we recycled some old Numismatic News, like newspapers but not any personal papers.

MR. DOLAN: When you went through his property in 1993, did you ever see any pornographic material?

ELISABETH WATERS: There was some photographs. I think the top one on the stack was a naked man, and I sort of looked at them and went, "yuck," and passed them to Raul, and said "Should we turn these over to the police?" And Raul went through the top couple and he said, "yes." So we called the police, and the police officer came out and took them, and he told him that Walter had been arrested for child molesting, and that Cynthia Harris had been the investigating officer, and they should probably go to her.

MR. DOLAN: Who was the officer that you turned them over to?

ELISABETH WATERS: I don't remember. It would have been the officer, whoever they sent out.

MR. DOLAN: How big was this stack of photographs?

ELISABETH WATERS: About half an inch, maybe three-eights of an inch.

MR. DOLAN: Do you know if there are any photographs in there of men with boys?

ELISABETH WATERS: No, I don't know. I didn't look at them.

MR. DOLAN: Did you know what was on any of the other pictures other than the top one?

ELISABETH WATERS: No.

MR. DOLAN: Did Walter have any pornographic magazines in the house in '93 when you went through his personal effects?

ELISABETH WATERS: No.

MR. DOLAN: Did you know if Walter had any letters written to any young children in his personal effects when you went through them in 1993?

ELISABETH WATERS: No.

MR. DOLAN: Did you read any of Walter's letters when you went through any of his personal effects in 1993?

ELISABETH WATERS: I sort of flipped through stuff enough to sort it, to sort out the tax papers from the other stuff, the other junk.

MR. DOLAN: Did you ever see any letters written to Ken Smith in there?

ELISABETH WATERS: No.

MR. DOLAN: Were you ever aware of any letters that Walter wrote to be delivered to Ken Smith posthumously?

ELISABETH WATERS: At one point in October of '89, as to the best of my recollection, Walter said that he had written to Kenny, but I don't believe the letter was ever delivered.

MR. DOLAN: Do you know who had possession of the letter?

ELISABETH WATERS: I would imagine Walter did.

MR. DOLAN: Did you ever see it?

ELISABETH WATERS: No.

MR. DOLAN: Did he ever tell you who had possession of it?

ELISABETH WATERS: No.

MR. DOLAN: Getting back to this time period sometime in– well, before 1981 when you saw the letter from Dr. Morin, prior to that, had you ever seen anything that caused you any concern about Walter's conduct around young boys?

ELISABETH WATERS: No.

MR. DOLAN: How long did Barry live with you?

ELISABETH WATERS: Some months, I don't remember exactly.

MR. DOLAN: Do you know if Walter ever acted in any way inappropriately with Barry during that time period?

ELISABETH WATERS: To the best of my knowledge, no.

MR. DOLAN: Has anyone ever made any allegations that you're aware of that Barry acted– strike that. –that Walter acted inappropriately during that time period?

ELISABETH WATERS: Barry got arrested or picked up or something about a year later and apparently then he said something, but nobody believed him because the police had already talked to him before, and he denied it.

MR. DOLAN: Do you know where Barry got picked up or arrested?

ELISABETH WATERS: I think it was San Francisco.

MR. DOLAN: Do you remember Barry's last name?

ELISABETH WATERS: [redacted].

MR. DOLAN: How do you spell that?

ELISABETH WATERS: [redacted].

MR. DOLAN: Do you know where his parents live?

ELISABETH WATERS: No.

MR. DOLAN: Do you know anybody that was a family relative of his; did you ever come to know where they live?

ELISABETH WATERS: He had a mother. She came to visit him once while he was living with us, but other than that, I know of no relatives.

MR. DOLAN: Do you know where the mother came from?

ELISABETH WATERS: Not really. I would guess San Francisco, but that's just a guess.

MR. DOLAN: Do you know his middle name?

ELISABETH WATERS: No.

MR. DOLAN: Do you know his date of birth?

ELISABETH WATERS: No.

MR. DOLAN: Do you recall if he had a birthday during the time that he was living with you?

ELISABETH WATERS: I think not.

MR. DOLAN: Was he white, black, Mexican, any particular race?

ELISABETH WATERS: I believe he was mixture of white, black and Miwok Indian.

MR. DOLAN: Did you ever hear anything about Barry other than what you just described about being arrested a year later?

ELISABETH WATERS: Some years later when Marion had a stroke—I don't remember whether it was the '87 stroke or the '89 stroke—he showed up on the doorstep one day, and he said he heard she was sick and he came by to say, to give his best wishes for a speedy recovery.

MR. DOLAN: Did you ask him where he was living at that time?

ELISABETH WATERS: No.

MR. DOLAN: Do you have any understanding where he was living at that time?

ELISABETH WATERS: No.

MR. DOLAN: Do you have any understanding what his occupation was at that time period?

ELISABETH WATERS: No.

MR. DOLAN: Do you know if he ever enlisted in the military?

ELISABETH WATERS: No.

MR. DOLAN: Do you know if he had any brothers or sisters?

ELISABETH WATERS: No.

MR. DOLAN: Do you know anybody who might know where Barry is located now?

ELISABETH WATERS: No.

MR. DOLAN: Do you know anybody who kept in any contact with Barry?

ELISABETH WATERS: No.

MR. DOLAN: Do you know where he was picked up on this charge a year after, you said San Francisco, was it?

ELISABETH WATERS: I don't really know.

MR. DOLAN: How did you hear that he had been picked up on a charge a year later?

ELISABETH WATERS: Somebody phoned me, but I don't remember who.

MR. DOLAN: Do you know if it was someone from a police organization?

ELISABETH WATERS: I don't remember.

MR. DOLAN: Can you tell me what was discussed in the conversation, to the best of your knowledge?

ELISABETH WATERS: I think it was not the police. I think it was probably some, some—somebody who knew the family, and they said that Barry had been picked up and that he was saying that Walter had molested him.

MR. DOLAN: What did they say about the issue of Walter molesting Barry?

ELISABETH WATERS: Nothing. They just said that Barry was claiming that.

MR. DOLAN: Did you ask Marion about that?

ELISABETH WATERS: No, I don't think so. Marion may have been away at a convention or something.

MR. DOLAN: Did you ever discuss the possible molestation of Barry with Marion Zimmer Bradley at any point up to the time that Ken Smith's molestation was reported to the police?

ELISABETH WATERS: No.

MR. DOLAN: Did you undertake any inquire pre the investigation after hearing that Barry had alleged that Walter Breen had molested him?

ELISABETH WATERS: No, I didn't. Why should I? The police were doing it.

MR. DOLAN: How did you know the police were doing it?

ELISABETH WATERS: Because if he was picked up and he was telling the police that Walter had molested him, presumably the police were investigating this.

MR. DOLAN: Did you say anything back to the person who said to you that Barry was accusing Walter of molesting him?

ELISABETH WATERS: I believe I said that Barry always was a liar.

MR. DOLAN: Did you ever talk to Patrick or Moira about whether or not Barry's alleged statements to the police that Walter was molesting him were true or not?

ELISABETH WATERS: No.

MR. DOLAN: Were you ever contacted by the police regarding the investigation on Barry's allegations of child molestation by Walter Breen?

ELISABETH WATERS: No.

MR. DOLAN: Were you ever contacted by the Child Protective Services in any way regarding the allegations by Barry that Walter Breen was molesting him?

ELISABETH WATERS: No.

MR. DOLAN: Did you ever apply for another foster child through the same group?

ELISABETH WATERS: No.

MR. DOLAN: Any particular reason why not?

ELISABETH WATERS: Well–

MR. BURESH: Object to the question. It's argumentative, assumes facts not in evidence. I instruct the witness not to answer. You'll have to rephrase the question. If somebody says they didn't do something, and you say, "why didn't you do it?", that's just not a fair question.

MR. DOLAN: Why didn't you apply for another child, for a foster child?

MR. BURESH: Same objection.

MR. DOLAN: Are you instructing her not to answer?

MR. BURESH: Yes.

MR. DOLAN: Mark it.

(Whereupon, the previous question was marked for the record.)

MR. DOLAN: You didn't apply for another child through a foster service, correct?

MR. BURESH: Let me just ask, when you say "you," do you mean Elisabeth, personally, or Walter and Marion? So you're asking her to speak on behalf of the whole family?

MR. DOLAN: Who applied for the child?

ELISABETH WATERS: You mean Barry?

MR. DOLAN: Yeah.

ELISABETH WATERS: We didn't exactly apply for Barry. After Barry came to live with us, Social Services did the investigation so he could stay.

MR. DOLAN: How did Barry come to live with you?

ELISABETH WATERS: A friend of Walter's brought him.

MR. DOLAN: Who is the friend of Walter's who brought him?

ELISABETH WATERS: His name was Richard Khilstadius.

MR. DOLAN: Do you know if he was a priest or clergyman of some sort?

ELISABETH WATERS: Yes.

MR. DOLAN: Do you know where he is currently?

ELISABETH WATERS: I believe he lives somewhere in San Francisco, but I haven't seen him in years.

MR. DOLAN: When he brought him, did Mr. Khilstadius in any way indicate whether or not Barry was a child prostitute?

ELISABETH WATERS: Not that I heard of.

MR. DOLAN: Did he ever have any discussions with you or Walter about Barry being sexually inappropriate in any way?

ELISABETH WATERS: No.

MR. DOLAN: So if I understand it, Richard Khilstadius brings Barry to live with the people living at 221 Prince Street?

ELISABETH WATERS: 2221.

MR. DOLAN: 2221?

ELISABETH WATERS: Yes.

MR. DOLAN: And at some point then, there's an application made for him to become a foster child; is that correct?

ELISABETH WATERS: Yes.

MR. DOLAN: And who filed the application?

ELISABETH WATERS: Well, since Barry was a ward of the court, in order for him to stay with us, the paperwork had to be sorted out, and that was just a matter of sorting out all the paperwork.

MR. DOLAN: Who sorted out all the paperwork?

ELISABETH WATERS: I don't know.

MR. DOLAN: Were you involved in that process?

ELISABETH WATERS: Not directly.

MR. DOLAN: Do you know if any documents were filed with any courts regarding Barry being put into the custody of the group there on Prince Street?

ELISABETH WATERS: I don't know.

MR. DOLAN: Were you in any way designated as a legal guardian of Barry?

ELISABETH WATERS: No.

MR. DOLAN: Do you know if Marion was?

ELISABETH WATERS: I believe Marion and Walter were jointly. Actually, this may have been '80 rather than '81 because it was when– it was before– it was when Marion and I were still living on Telegraph Avenue, and Walter was living on Prince Street, so it may have only been Walter who was designated as the guardian. I really don't know.

MR. DOLAN: Can you tell me anything else about the conversation you had with this unidentified party who called you to tell you that Barry was making allegations that he had been molested when he was living on Prince Street?

ELISABETH WATERS: No.

MR. DOLAN: Can you tell me anything more about who this person might have been who placed this call to you?

ELISABETH WATERS: No.

MR. DOLAN: Were there any other children living at Prince Street at the time that you received this call about Barry's allegations other than Moira and Patrick?

ELISABETH WATERS: I don't remember if it was Moira and Patrick. No, I don't remember exactly when this call was. It was over a year after Barry left, so I guess it would have been Moira and Patrick.

MR. DOLAN: Any other children living there at that time that you're aware of?

ELISABETH WATERS: I think not.

MR. DOLAN: Did you ever discuss these allegations of Patrick— strike that. Did you ever discuss these allegations of Walter molesting Barry with Walter?

ELISABETH WATERS: No.

MR. DOLAN: I may have asked you this. Did you ever discuss them with Marion?

ELISABETH WATERS: No.

MR. DOLAN: Did you ever discuss it with anybody after you had the phone call?

ELISABETH WATERS: No, not that I recall.

MR. DOLAN: Through the present time, other than perhaps with counsel, have you ever discussed the issue of this phone call regarding Barry's molestation?

ELISABETH WATERS: No.

MR. DOLAN: So at this point in time, you read this letter regarding Walter's statements on Sterling, correct?

ELISABETH WATERS: Yes.

MR. DOLAN: And you've heard, at least, an allegation of Barry that Walter was molesting him, correct?

ELISABETH WATERS: Yes.

MR. DOLAN: At this point are you getting at all concerned about Walter's interaction with young boys?

ELISABETH WATERS: No.

MR. DOLAN: At this point you're also aware that Walter has written the book Greek Love, correct?

ELISABETH WATERS: I'm not sure I was aware of it that soon. I think it was a couple years later that I learned about that.

MR. DOLAN: Didn't you indicate that prior to [Barry] coming to live there that you were aware that Walter had authored articles on the issues of men and boys like those contained in Greek Love?

MR. BURESH: Let me hear the question again, please.

ELISABETH WATERS: I'm not aware—

MR. BURESH: Before you answer, let me hear the question read back. (Whereupon, the record was back by the reporter.)

MR. BURESH: Okay.

ELISABETH WATERS: I have no knowledge that Walter wrote articles. I know he wrote Greek Love. I don't remember exactly when I learned he wrote Greek Love, and I did not read Greek Love until I found a copy for Officer Harris in 1989.

MR. DOLAN: Okay. But at this time you read Walter's letter to Dr. Morin, correct?

ELISABETH WATERS: I saw a paragraph of it.

MR. BURESH: And by "this time," you're referring to the time of the phone call regarding Barry?

MR. DOLAN: Sure.

MR. DOLAN: And you have heard a phone call regarding an allegation of molestation by Barry, correct?

ELISABETH WATERS: Yes.

MR. DOLAN: Do you undertake any investigation at that time to find out whether or not Walter Breen was acting improperly in a sexual manner with any of the people who were on the property at Prince Street?

MR. BURESH: Other than what she has already testified to?

MR. DOLAN: Other than– the only thing I have never heard you testify to is that you asked Marion about the letter?

ELISABETH WATERS: Uh-hum.

MR. DOLAN: Other than asking Marion about the letter, did you do anything after hearing about Barry's allegation of molestation to inquire as to whether or not Walter Breen was acting inappropriately with any children on any of the properties owned by Marion Zimmer Bradley?

ELISABETH WATERS: The only property owned at the time was 2221 Prince Street, which was owned jointly by Marion and Walter, and the children living in it were Walter's own children, so, no.

MR. DOLAN: Did you inquire in any way to find out whether or not Walter was acting inappropriately with the numerous guests that you said were often there who were friends of Moira's and Patrick's?

ELISABETH WATERS: No.

MR. DOLAN: Do you guys want to take a break at this point? We have been going for a while.

MR. BURESH: It's up to the witness. (Whereupon, a recess was taken.)

MR. DOLAN: Do you know if Richard Khilstadius has ever been accused of child molestation?

ELISABETH WATERS: Accused by whom?

MR. DOLAN: Anyone.

ELISABETH WATERS: I think I sort of heard vague gossip that he might be, but I never heard that anybody actually accused him.

MR. DOLAN: Who did you hear vague gossip from that Richard Khilstadius might be a child molester; who did you hear that from?

ELISABETH WATERS: I don't really remember.

MR. DOLAN: Did you ever discuss that with Marion?

ELISABETH WATERS: No.

MR. DOLAN: Did you ever discuss it with anyone?

ELISABETH WATERS: No, I was brought up to believe that other people's sex lives were none of my business.

MR. BURESH: You're volunteering.

ELISABETH WATERS: Sorry.

MR. DOLAN: What other fosterlings lived at the house in the '81 to '85 time period besides Barry and [Cyndi Beckett], anyone?

(Cyndi Beckett is Cyndy Nha June?)

ELISABETH WATERS: I think Kat Krischild.

MR. DOLAN: Is Kat Krischild a female?

ELISABETH WATERS: Yes.

MR. DOLAN: Do you know how old Kat Krischild was when she lived there?

ELISABETH WATERS: You already asked me this, and I already answered this.

MR. DOLAN: Humor me, please.

MR. BURESH: I wrote that one down.

MR. DOLAN: I may have too.

ELISABETH WATERS: I remember, I believe she was in her early 20's.

MR. DOLAN: How old was Elizabeth Rousseau when they moved in there?

ELISABETH WATERS: I think 18.

MR. DOLAN: Do you know if Marion Zimmer Bradley and [Cyndi Beckett] ever had any sexual relationships?

ELISABETH WATERS: I think there was one incident.

MR. DOLAN: Was that an orgy?

MR. BURESH: Do you want to define "orgy" for the witness?

MR. DOLAN: It's been talked about in this litigation so far that it involved more than [Cyndi Beckett] and Marion Zimmer Bradley; it may have involved two other partners?

ELISABETH WATERS: Yes, I believe it did.

MR. DOLAN: Do you know when that occurred?

ELISABETH WATERS: I believe it was in 1983.

MR. DOLAN: Do you know where it occurred?

ELISABETH WATERS: It was at Philip and Anodea's house.

MR. DOLAN: Was there any special occasion; was it Marion's birthday or anything?

ELISABETH WATERS: No.

MR. DOLAN: Do you know who arranged it?

ELISABETH WATERS: It was a sort of spontaneous thing.

MR. DOLAN: Did you have any role in arranging that?

MR. BURESH: Assumes facts not in evidence. There's no evidence that anybody arranged anything.

MR. DOLAN: Did you have any role in that coming about?

MR. BURESH: In what coming about; the get together or the orgy?

MR. DOLAN: The orgy.

MR. BURESH: Okay.

MR. BURESH: Have we decided on the term "orgy" yet?

MR. DOLAN: Like I said, more than two parties involved.

MR. DOLAN: How many parties were involved in the sexual activity?

ELISABETH WATERS: Four.

MR. DOLAN: Do you consider four people involved in a sexual activity to be an orgy?

MR. BURESH: Object to the question. It's irrelevant, not reasonably calculated to lead to the discovery of admissible evidence. Who cares what she characterizes it as.

MR. DOLAN: You can answer.

MR. BURESH: No, I'll instruct the witness not to answer.

MR. DOLAN: What do you call four people together having sex?

MR. BURESH: Object. As if she calls it anything. It really doesn't matter, Chris.

MR. DOLAN: Well, I'm trying to use a word that she wants me to define.

MR. BURESH: How about "group sex"?

MR. DOLAN: Would you call four people together having sex an orgy?

ELISABETH WATERS: No, I don't think I would.

MR. DOLAN: Have you ever defined this particular episode of these four people together as an orgy?

ELISABETH WATERS: I don't remember.

MR. DOLAN: How old was [Cyndi Beckett] when this occurred?

ELISABETH WATERS: 19, to the best of my knowledge.

MR. DOLAN: Who was involved in this particular group activity?

ELISABETH WATERS: [Cyndi Beckett], Phil, Anodea and Marion.

MR. DOLAN: And there was a fourth party, as well?

ELISABETH WATERS: That is four people.

MR. DOLAN: Were you involved in it?

ELISABETH WATERS: No.

MR. DOLAN: Did you witness it?

ELISABETH WATERS: Not really.

MR. DOLAN: Could you explain, please?

ELISABETH WATERS: I was over at Philip and Anodea's house visiting them, and [Name A] was over there for some reason or another. I think she was chasing after Philip. I think she was having an affair with Philip at the time. And Marion was coming over, and I made some stupid joke about if you really want to make Marion happy, why don't you jump her when she comes through the door and have sex with her. Probably the stupidest and most tasteless thing I ever said in my entire live, but I never expected them to take me seriously, and when Marion did, they did it. I just sort of rolled over on the other side of the room and closed my eyes and pretended to be asleep.

MR. DOLAN: Were there any other people in the room besides yourself and those four?

ELISABETH WATERS: No.

MR. DOLAN: Were there any children present at the time?

ELISABETH WATERS: No.

MR. DOLAN: Was [Name A] still living at the house at that time?

ELISABETH WATERS: At Prince Street?

MR. DOLAN: Yes.

ELISABETH WATERS: Yes.

MR. DOLAN: Do you know if Marion and [Name A] ever had a physical relationship besides that one occasion?

ELISABETH WATERS: I'm pretty sure they didn't because Marion was really mad at me for that. She said [Name A] had been trying to crawl into her bed for months, and until then, she had successfully avoided her.

MR. DOLAN: Did Kat Krischild and Marion ever have a sexual relationship, as far as you know?

ELISABETH WATERS: As far as I know, no.

MR. DOLAN: How about Elizabeth Rousseau?

ELISABETH WATERS: No.

MR. DOLAN: Did anyone ever mention anything to you about a young boy being in Walter's bed at Prince Street?

ELISABETH WATERS: There was one night while Marion and I were still living at Telegraph Avenue when Moira called in the middle of the night and said that Barry was in Walter's bed. This was after Social Services had taken him back and he was out on the streets again, and Walter didn't know he was there, but Moira had gotten up in the middle of the night and found them there and called us. And because Barry had been coming back and bothering Moira prior to this, I had told him the time before that if he ever came back again, I would call the police. Marion and I got up and got dressed and came over to Prince Street, and I did call the police. And the police came, and they woke up Barry, and they asked him what he was doing in Walter's bed. And he said he was sleeping there because he knew that Walter wouldn't be there, and then the police sent Marion and me out of the room, and they talked to Barry.

(That is not what my concern was.)

MR. DOLAN: Did the police ask you any further questions about what Barry was doing in Walter's bed?

ELISABETH WATERS: No.

MR. DOLAN: How long after Barry had moved out did this occur?

ELISABETH WATERS: Six months, maybe.

MR. DOLAN: Did Moira indicate to you that she thought there was something inappropriate going on between Barry and Walter?

ELISABETH WATERS: No, she was just furious to find him on the property.

MR. DOLAN: Did you ever ask Walter what Barry was doing in his bed?

ELISABETH WATERS: No.

MR. DOLAN: Was Walter home when the police came?

ELISABETH WATERS: Yes, I believe he was working in the music room, which is upstairs at the other end of the house.

MR. DOLAN: Do you know if the police interviewed Walter at all about what Barry was doing in his bed?

ELISABETH WATERS: I think they must have, but I don't remember for certain.

MR. DOLAN: Did Barry have his own bed when he lived at the house?

ELISABETH WATERS: Yes, of course.

MR. DOLAN: What was the room that Barry occupied when he was living in the house?

ELISABETH WATERS: It was one of the downstairs bedrooms. The bedrooms are sort of– there is a room, and there are two bedrooms off of it, and he was in the middle room. Patrick's bedroom was off one side and Moira's bedroom was off the other.

MR. DOLAN: And where was Walter's in relationship to those?

ELISABETH WATERS: After that there is the laundry room, the hall, the bathroom and Walter's room.

MR. DOLAN: Was anybody living in Barry's room the night that he was in Walter's bed?

ELISABETH WATERS: I don't remember.

MR. DOLAN: As far as you know, was Barry's bed available for Barry to sleep in the night that he was found in Walter's bed?

ELISABETH WATERS: I don't know, but Moira would have found him there much faster because it was right next to her room, so if he was trying to hide from Moira, Walter's bed was a better bet.

MR. DOLAN: When you say "hide from Moira," why would he be hiding from Moira?

ELISABETH WATERS: Because Moira hated his guts and didn't want him on the property, and he wasn't supposed to be there. I mean, he had committed an unlawful entry, for starters.

MR. DOLAN: Was he arrested for that, do you know?

ELISABETH WATERS: The police took him away. I don't know if they finally arrested him.

MR. DOLAN: I've got to make a call. Excuse me, please. (Whereupon, a recess was taken.)

MR. DOLAN: Would you read the last question and answer for me. (Whereupon, the record was read by the reporter.)

MR. DOLAN: Were you ever notified by anyone that there were any young boys in Walter's bed other than Barry on any occasion?

ELISABETH WATERS: No.

MR. DOLAN: And you never undertook any investigation after Barry was found in the bed to find out why he was there, correct?

ELISABETH WATERS: No– I mean, yes, that's correct.

MR. DOLAN: Okay.

ELISABETH WATERS: No, I did not investigate.

MR. DOLAN: Were you ever aware of Walter being alone in his bedroom with any young boys?

ELISABETH WATERS: No.

MR. DOLAN: We sort of covered who was there from 1981 through 1985. When did Walter move over to the goldfish bowl?

ELISABETH WATERS: 1987. Sorry, no, wait a minute. I guess it was 1985.

MR. DOLAN: Let's go on to another topic here. Do you have any information that would pertain to Marion Zimmer Bradley having any sexual interaction with Moira Stern?

ELISABETH WATERS: No.

MR. DOLAN: Have you ever heard that issue discussed at any time?

ELISABETH WATERS: I have heard Moira say some things about it.

MR. DOLAN: What have you heard Moira say about it?

ELISABETH WATERS: She said that one time her mother fondled her breasts while she was in the shower.

MR. DOLAN: Anything else?

ELISABETH WATERS: That Moira said to me, no.

MR. DOLAN: Okay. Did you ever ask Marion if any of that was true?

ELISABETH WATERS: Yes.

MR. DOLAN: What did Marion say?

ELISABETH WATERS: She said that children before the age of puberty didn't have erogenous zones.

MR. DOLAN: Anything else she said to you?

ELISABETH WATERS: No.

MR. DOLAN: When did she tell you that?

ELISABETH WATERS: When I asked her if– when I said that Moira was– when I said that I had been visiting Moira in the hospital, and that Moira had said that Marion fondled her breasts in the shower.

MR. DOLAN: How old was– strike that. What year was this that you had this discussion with Marion Zimmer Bradley?

ELISABETH WATERS: I guess it would have been around 1990.

MR. DOLAN: Did you ever ask Marion if she actually did fondle Moira?

ELISABETH WATERS: No.

MR. DOLAN: Did you ever inquire of Marion whether there was any truth about Moira's statement that Marion had been touching her breasts when she was in the shower?

ELISABETH WATERS: No, I just told her Moira had said that, and she said that children that age didn't have erogenous zones.

MR. DOLAN: Did you ask her what she meant by that?

ELISABETH WATERS: No.

MR. DOLAN: Did you find that to be an odd statement by Marion Zimmer Bradley?

MR. BURESH: Object to the question. Instruct the witness not to answer. It's vague and ambiguous.

MR. DOLAN: I don't think that is grounds for an instruction not to answer. Are you instructing her not to answer on the grounds of vague and ambiguous?

MR. BURESH: If I object to the question, I can instruct the witness not to answer. If it's vague and ambiguous and it's an improper question, I don't see why the witness should be forced to answer it.

MR. DOLAN: I just want to know if you are instructing the witness not to answer on the grounds of vague and ambiguous?

MR. BURESH: Yes.

MR. DOLAN: Mark it, please. (Whereupon, the previous question was marked for the record.)

MR. DOLAN: Did the statement by Marion Zimmer Bradley that children did not have erogenous zones cause you any concern of any type?

ELISABETH WATERS: No.

MR. DOLAN: Had you ever heard Marion Zimmer Bradley make that statement before?

ELISABETH WATERS: No.

MR. DOLAN: Had you ever heard Marion Zimmer Bradley make any statements to that effect before?

ELISABETH WATERS: No.

MR. DOLAN: Before this time that Moira was in the hospital, had you ever heard anything within the family about allegations that Marion Zimmer Bradley had molested Moira?

ELISABETH WATERS: No.

MR. DOLAN: Other than this statement made by Moira in the hospital that Marion had molested her, have you ever heard or seen or read any allegations of molestation by Moira Breen against her mother Marion Zimmer Bradley?

MR. BURESH: Is there a time frame on this question? I'm sorry, any time up until today?

MR. DOLAN: Yeah.

MR. BURESH: Okay.

ELISABETH WATERS: You mean like the stuff I read last night?

MR. DOLAN: I don't know.

MR. BURESH: He means anything that's in your head as of today including the police report that you have reviewed, the Moira documents, the letters that you produced, et cetera, et cetera.

MR. DOLAN: Anything.

ELISABETH WATERS: Well, there were some documents that she produced at the deposition that I sort of skimmed through last night, and I think there was something in there about that, and it was vague and sort of crazy sounding.

MR. DOLAN: Okay. Before last night, had you ever read or heard anything other than just the statement that Moira had made in the hospital that her mother had touched her breasts that in any way alluded to Moira being molested by her mother as a child?

ELISABETH WATERS: No.

MR. DOLAN: So it's your testimony that prior to yesterday, the only thing you had ever heard regarding Moira Breen having allegations against her mother of molestation was this one statement that her mother had touched her breasts when she was in the shower?

ELISABETH WATERS: Yes.

MR. DOLAN: Did you ever investigate with anyone to find out whether there was any truth to the allegation that Marion Zimmer Bradley had touched Moira Breen's breasts when she was in the shower?

ELISABETH WATERS: With whom would I have investigated it?

MR. BURESH: Just answer the question.

ELISABETH WATERS: No.

MR. DOLAN: Did you ever talk to Marion about it in any more detail other than the two sentences you indicated that Moira said this and Marion responded back that children don't have erogenous zones?

ELISABETH WATERS: No.

MR. DOLAN: Okay. Did that satisfy your– strike that. Did you find Marion's answer to be a satisfactory answer to your question of why did Moira say this?

MR. BURESH: I will object to the question, on the grounds of vague and ambiguous.

MR. DOLAN: Did you ask Marion, "Is there any truth to the allegation that Moira has made that you touched her breasts when she was in the shower"?

ELISABETH WATERS: No, I did not ask her that.

MR. DOLAN: What exactly did you say to Marion?

ELISABETH WATERS: That I had been visiting Moira in the hospital and that Moira had complained that Marion had touched her breasts when she was in the shower once.

MR. DOLAN: Okay. And Marion's response was that children that age don't have erogenous zones; is that correct?

ELISABETH WATERS: Yes.

MR. DOLAN: What age did you understand that she was talking about?

ELISABETH WATERS: Nine.

MR. DOLAN: So do you understand that Moira alleged that Marion had done this when she was about nine?

ELISABETH WATERS: Yes.

MR. DOLAN: How did you come to that understanding?

ELISABETH WATERS: I believe Moira told me.

MR. DOLAN: So what was the full extent of what Moira told you when she talked to you about the alleged act of Marion touching her breasts?

ELISABETH WATERS: She said that when she was about nine she was in the shower and Marion touched her breast.

MR. DOLAN: And that's what you related to Marion, correct?

ELISABETH WATERS: Yes.

MR. DOLAN: Did you ever have any discussions with Marion, other than the one where Marion said that children of that age don't have erogenous zones, concerning the molestation or the alleged molestation of Moira?

MR. BURESH: I'm sorry. I've got to hear that again.

MR. DOLAN: I'll do it again.

MR. BURESH: I didn't get it.

MR. DOLAN: Other than that conversation where you just related to us where you said that Moira had told you that Marion touched her breasts in the shower when she was nine and Marion replied that children that age don't have erogenous zones, did you ever discuss with Marion Zimmer Bradley at any time up to the present day any allegations of molestation with Moira Breen?

ELISABETH WATERS: By Marion?

MR. DOLAN: Yes.

ELISABETH WATERS: No.

MR. DOLAN: And it's your testimony that through the present day that the only information up through last night in reading Moira's information produced at the deposition, that you were aware of any acts of molestation between Marion Zimmer Bradley and Moira Breen; is that correct?

ELISABETH WATERS: To the best of my knowledge and recollection, that's the only alleged act of molestation of which I have heard prior to last night.

MR. DOLAN: Did you ever read the police reports prior to last night?

ELISABETH WATERS: Yes.

MR. DOLAN: Did you ever read any of those allegations of molestation by Marion Zimmer Bradley against Moira Breen in any of the police reports?

MR. BURESH: Object to the question. You are certainly welcome to show the witness the portions you're referring to. She said what she said, so you're assuming facts not in evidence. I have got the police report right here, and we can certainly–

MR. DOLAN: We will go over it later, line by line.

MR. DOLAN: Did anyone ever tell you that Patrick Breen had been molested by Marion Zimmer Bradley?

ELISABETH WATERS: Not exactly.

MR. DOLAN: Okay. Could you explain your answer, please?

ELISABETH WATERS: When the investigation about Kenny was going on, I went to Patrick, who was trying very hard to stay out of this, and asked if Walter had ever molested him, and Patrick said, "No, which is more than I can say for my mother and some of my baby-sitters."

MR. DOLAN: Anyone else ever make any statements that might have led you to believe that Marion Zimmer Bradley may have molested Patrick Breen?

ELISABETH WATERS: No.

MR. DOLAN: Did you ask Patrick at all what he meant by that statement?

ELISABETH WATERS: No.

MR. DOLAN: Did you find that statement to be at all unusual?

MR. BURESH: Object to the question. I really don't know what it means. Did she find it to be unusual?

MR. DOLAN: Did you find it an unusual statement that Patrick said "that's more than I can say about my mother," when you were asking him the question?

MR. BURESH: Object to the question because the word "unusual" is vague and ambiguous.

MR. DOLAN: You can answer it.

MR. BURESH: Instruct the witness not to answer.

MR. DOLAN: Mark it. (Whereupon, the previous question was marked for the record.)

MR. DOLAN: Did you feel that it was– strike that. Did you have any concerns about Patrick's statement that that was more than he could say about his mother?

MR. BURESH: Let me hear that again, please.

MR. DOLAN: I'll do it again.

MR. DOLAN: Give me the conversation between you and Patrick again, please, regarding the question of whether Walter had ever molested him and what his response was.

ELISABETH WATERS: I asked if Walter had ever molested him, and he said, "No, which is more than I can say about my mother and some of my baby-sitters."

MR. DOLAN: Did the fact that he said– did his reply cause you any concern whatsoever that he may have been molested by his mother?

ELISABETH WATERS: Yes.

MR. DOLAN: Okay. Did you inquire to him any further about what he meant by that statement?

ELISABETH WATERS: No.

MR. DOLAN: Did you undertake any investigation whatsoever to determine whether or not Marion Zimmer Bradley had ever molested her son, Patrick?

ELISABETH WATERS: No.

MR. DOLAN: Did you ask Patrick anything more on the subject of whether he was ever molested by his mother?

ELISABETH WATERS: No.

MR. DOLAN: Did you ask Moira about it ever?

ELISABETH WATERS: No.

MR. DOLAN: Did you ask Walter about it ever?

ELISABETH WATERS: When Moira said that Walter raped her when she was five, I asked Walter about that.

MR. DOLAN: But did you ever ask Walter whether or not he had any facts that would lead him to believe that Marion Zimmer Bradley had molested Patrick?

ELISABETH WATERS: No.

MR. DOLAN: And you never asked Marion whether she molested Patrick; is that correct?

ELISABETH WATERS: No, that is correct, I did not ask her.

MR. DOLAN: Did you ever tell her what Patrick had said?

ELISABETH WATERS: No.

MR. DOLAN: Why not?

MR. BURESH: Objection.

MR. DOLAN: Is there any particular reason why you did not relate what Patrick had told her– told you to Marion Zimmer Bradley?

ELISABETH WATERS: At the time, we were all so traumatized that I didn't want to add to anybody's trauma anymore than they were already traumatized, and Patrick was an adult at that point, and whatever Marion may have done to him in the past was clearly over.

MR. DOLAN: Did you have any understanding as to what frame in time that this alleged molestation of Patrick had occurred?

ELISABETH WATERS: No.

MR. DOLAN: Did you ask anyone to find out or– strike that. Did you ask Patrick how old he was when this alleged molestation occurred?

ELISABETH WATERS: No.

MR. DOLAN: So you did nothing further to inquire about this alleged act of molestation by Marion Zimmer Bradley against Patrick; is that correct?

ELISABETH WATERS: That's correct.

MR. DOLAN: Other than the allegation by Moira and Patrick that Marion molested them, did anyone else to your knowledge ever make any allegation that Marion Zimmer Bradley had molested them?

ELISABETH WATERS: No.

MR. DOLAN: Did you ever make any statement to Moira Breen that Marion Zimmer Bradley had molested both of you?

ELISABETH WATERS: No. I was 25 when I met her.

MR. BURESH: No, just answer the question.

ELISABETH WATERS: No.

MR. DOLAN: Did you ever make any statement to Moira Breen that if she had had the opportunity, she would jump in bed with her mother again?

ELISABETH WATERS: No.

MR. DOLAN: Now, you indicated that Moira also had told you at some point that she had been raped by her father when she was five; is that correct?

ELISABETH WATERS: Yes.

MR. DOLAN: When did she tell you that?

ELISABETH WATERS: After the investigation with Kenny started.

MR. DOLAN: What did she tell you about suffering rape at the hands of her father?

ELISABETH WATERS: She said that she was five years old, and it was his birthday and that he said she was his birthday present, and he raped her.

MR. DOLAN: When did she tell you that, approximately what time frame, as best you can, month and year?

ELISABETH WATERS: October, November. I don't know. Sometime in '89.

MR. DOLAN: And did you do anything to investigate the truthfulness of that statement?

ELISABETH WATERS: I asked Walter.

MR. DOLAN: What did Walter tell you?

ELISABETH WATERS: He denied it.

MR. DOLAN: Please tell me the full substance of the conversation as best you can recall?

ELISABETH WATERS: I asked if it was true that he raped Moira when she was five, and he said, "No, of course not," and that she was a liar, and I said, "But isn't that the period of your life you don't remember much of?" And he said, "yes."

MR. DOLAN: Did you ever ask Marion about Moira allegations that Walter had raped her?

ELISABETH WATERS: No.

MR. DOLAN: Did you ever discuss Moira's allegation that Walter had raped her with Marion Zimmer Bradley?

ELISABETH WATERS: I think Moira told her sometime, a couple of months later.

MR. BURESH: That's not the question he asked you.

ELISABETH WATERS: I'm sorry.

MR. DOLAN: Did you ever discuss it?

ELISABETH WATERS: I don't think so.

MR. DOLAN: Has Moira ever recounted to you any other episodes of sexual abuse that she suffered at the hands of either her mother or her father other than the ones you have identified?

ELISABETH WATERS: Not that I recall.

MR. DOLAN: Are you aware of any– strike that. Are you aware of what the term "satanic ritual abuse" means?

ELISABETH WATERS: I believe so, yes.

MR. DOLAN: Has Moira Breen ever told you that she believes that she was a victim of satanic ritual abuse?

ELISABETH WATERS: Yes.

MR. BURESH: I would like the witness to define what she means by "satanic ritual." I don't know what the term means exactly. I would like to make sure, for the record, that both questioner and answerer are talking about the same thing.

MR. DOLAN: What do you understand satanic ritual abuse to be?

ELISABETH WATERS: People who worship Satan who, as part of their ritual, abuse children or, I suppose, adults would count too.

MR. DOLAN: Have you ever worshipped Satan?

ELISABETH WATERS: No.

MR. DOLAN: Have you ever observed any satanic rituals?

ELISABETH WATERS: No.

MR. DOLAN: Have you ever participated in any satanic worship services?

ELISABETH WATERS: No.

MR. DOLAN: Have you ever practiced Wicca?

ELISABETH WATERS: No.

MR. DOLAN: Have you ever practiced black magic?

ELISABETH WATERS: No.

MR. DOLAN: Have you ever practiced paganism?

ELISABETH WATERS: I have attended some pagan rituals, and I was active for a while in the Dark Moon Circle. I was sort of tagging after Marion while she was doing research for Mists of Avalon.

MR. DOLAN: Did Moira Breen ever indicate to you that she felt that she had been the victim of satanic ritual abuse?

ELISABETH WATERS: Could you give me a time frame?

MR. DOLAN: Ever.

ELISABETH WATERS: Yes.

MR. DOLAN: When?

ELISABETH WATERS: After all of the investigation with Kenny.

MR. DOLAN: After or during?

ELISABETH WATERS: After the investigation with Kenny started.

MR. DOLAN: Can you give me an approximate time frame when you had this discussion with Moira?

ELISABETH WATERS: I think it was while he was in the hospital, with the CPS in Laguna Hills.

MR. DOLAN: Give me a month and year, please?

ELISABETH WATERS: I don't remember.

MR. DOLAN: Can you give me a year, please?

ELISABETH WATERS: I think it would be 1990.

MR. DOLAN: Do you recall whether it was winter, spring, summer or fall?

ELISABETH WATERS: Not too many seasons in Southern California.

MR. DOLAN: As we know these things in the East Coast, I guess.

ELISABETH WATERS: I really don't remember, I'm sorry.

MR. DOLAN: Were there lights on palm trees? Could you please tell me what Moira Breen told you about her belief that she had been a victim of satanic ritual abuse?

ELISABETH WATERS: She said that some men in white robes tied her up and hung her on the wall and poured hot coffee on her and spilled, I think, spilled hot wax on her skin and killed a baby in front of her and killed a grown-up in front of her and gave her something to eat and told her—something to eat—some funny meat and told her it was her baby brother, and she has never had a baby brother. She said a lot of stuff, and none of it made sense.

MR. DOLAN: Did she tell you whether she had been sexually assaulted by any of those people during the satanic ritual abuse?

ELISABETH WATERS: Not that I recall.

MR. DOLAN: Did she tell you where she believed the satanic ritual abuse had occurred?

ELISABETH WATERS: No.

MR. DOLAN: Did you ever come to learn from any source where she believed the satanic ritual occurred?

ELISABETH WATERS: No.

MR. DOLAN: Have you ever read any letters addressed to Marion Zimmer Bradley from Moira Breen regarding the satanic ritual abuse?

ELISABETH WATERS: I think so. There have been so many letters. It's hard to remember them all.

MR. DOLAN: Do you open all Marion Zimmer Bradley's mail?

ELISABETH WATERS: Yes.

MR. DOLAN: How long have you been doing that?

ELISABETH WATERS: Well, I started working for her full-time in 1986, and I was working for her part-time before that.

MR. DOLAN: Have you been opening her mail full-time since 1986?

ELISABETH WATERS: Yes.

MR. DOLAN: Do you read all of her mail?

ELISABETH WATERS: If it's a personal letter from somebody she knows, I will just look at the top and open the envelope enough to see if it's personal, and then I will just toss it on to her.

MR. DOLAN: Have you read Moira's letters to Marion Zimmer Bradley?

ELISABETH WATERS: Some of them. I did not routinely read everything Moira wrote to Marion because that was mother-daughter correspondence, not business correspondence.

MR. DOLAN: Did you ever ask Marion about any of these allegations of satanic ritual abuse?

ELISABETH WATERS: I don't remember. I might have told her that Moira was saying this stuff.

MR. BURESH: I don't want you to speculate about what you might have done. You're fine. For Mr. Dolan's sake, if you want to try and jog your memory and pause and think about it, but please don't say what you might have done.

MR. DOLAN: Do you have any recollection whatsoever? I am entitled to know that. It doesn't have to be crystal clear.

ELISABETH WATERS: Actually, no, I don't recall discussing it with Marion.

MR. DOLAN: Have you ever discussed the topic of satanic ritual abuse with Marion?

ELISABETH WATERS: As regards to real people or as regards to her books?

MR. DOLAN: Start with real people?

ELISABETH WATERS: With real people, no.

MR. DOLAN: Has she written any books on satanic ritual abuse?

MR. BURESH: Wait a minute. Any books in which that topic comes up? You said a book on that subject.

MR. DOLAN: Has she ever written any books where that topic is discussed or incorporated into the theme?

ELISABETH WATERS: Yes, it's in some of her occult novels.

MR. DOLAN: What are the names of those novels?

ELISABETH WATERS: Dark Satanic, The Inheritor, actually The Inheritor– well, sort of, Witch Hill. That's all I can think of at the minute.

MR. DOLAN: Do any of those novels involve the satanic ritual abuse of a young girl?

ELISABETH WATERS: No.

MR. DOLAN: Do any of them involve a young heroine who was abused by satanists?

ELISABETH WATERS: No.

MR. DOLAN: Do any of them involve a young woman?

ELISABETH WATERS: There is a character in The Inheritor named Emily who is rather loosely based on Moira, in that she was a music student, and a very talented one. And there is a character in the book named Simon who is dating Emily's older sister, and he was an adapt, I guess, a white adapt, and then he was in a car accident and injured his hand. And he was a piano player, and this upset him very much, and he was willing to do just about anything to get the use of his hand back, so he could go back to playing the piano. He hypnotized Emily. He was teaching her to play the harpsichord and that was part of the teaching. He took her to, what sounds like a sort of pseudo-Rosicrucian ritual where she just sat there. She was their token virgin and was sitting under the rose, whatever that means. And that was all he did to Emily. What he did later in the book was try to sacrifice a child who was mentally defective and was one of the older sister's patients. The older sister was a therapist. And the good guys came in and told him this was a really bad idea, and he decided not to do it, and then smashed his hand completely so that he would never be attempted to do this again, so he sort of repented and returned to the light.

MR. DOLAN: Do you know when this was written?

MS. DURRELL: Excuse me just a second. What book was this?

ELISABETH WATERS: The Inheritor.

MR. DOLAN: The Inheritor.

ELISABETH WATERS: Sometime in the 1980's.

MR. DOLAN: Before Ken Smith–

ELISABETH WATERS: Yes.

MR. DOLAN: –had been identified as being molested?

ELISABETH WATERS: Yes.

MR. DOLAN: And before Moira had told you about the satanic ritual abuse?

ELISABETH WATERS: Yes.

MR. DOLAN: Do you know where Marion got her research on the satanic ritual abuse?

ELISABETH WATERS: She read the Golden Bough. She read the books on the order of the– I think it's called The Order of the Golden Dawn. She's read Alisdair Crowle's work, and then I think they made a lot of it up. After all, she was writing fiction.

MR. DOLAN: Do you know if there was ever any satanic rituals performed at Greyhaven?

ELISABETH WATERS: I don't know. I don't go to Greyhaven very often. I haven't been there in years.

MR. DOLAN: Is your answer that you don't know if it was ever practiced at Greyhaven?

ELISABETH WATERS: To the best of my knowledge, none of the people at Greyhaven are Satanists.

MR. DOLAN: The question is, do you know whether satanic rituals were ever performed at Greyhaven?

ELISABETH WATERS: No.

MR. DOLAN: You brought up an interesting issue of– and I was going to do it later on. What documents did you review in preparation for your deposition today?

ELISABETH WATERS: The police report. I glanced through those things from Moira.

MR. DOLAN: Don't look to him to help you out. He's going to remain remarkably silent throughout this part of it.

MR. BURESH: I'm happy to– I'll tell you what I showed you. Maybe now is the time to break simply because we seem to be running out of mental steam.

MR. DOLAN: Okay.

MR. BURESH: She knows what she reviewed.

MR. DOLAN: I just want to ask one short series of questions before we break, if we can.

MR. BURESH: Well–

MR. DOLAN: Did you keep diaries through most of the time between 1979 and 1989?

ELISABETH WATERS: No.

MR. DOLAN: When did you start keeping a personal diary?

ELISABETH WATERS: I don't keep a personal diary.

MR. DOLAN: There were some diary entries that were turned over to the police?

ELISABETH WATERS: That was a police report that I wrote specifically for Officer Harris.

MR. DOLAN: So those things that you were reporting, writing down starting on 12, October '89 roughly, were done specifically to be handed over to the police?

ELISABETH WATERS: Yes.

MR. DOLAN: Do you keep– did you keep any personal journals whatsoever between 1979 and 1989?

ELISABETH WATERS: No.

MR. DOLAN: Did you keep any items like the things that were on the computer and turned over to Officer Harris, just little mental thoughts, on the computer between 1979 and 1989?

ELISABETH WATERS: No.

MR. DOLAN: Did you turn over to Officer Harris all of your thoughts and notes that pertained to the molestation of Ken Smith?

ELISABETH WATERS: Yes.

MR. BURESH: Well, just so I'm clear on the question. Written or recorded thoughts and notes?

MR. DOLAN: Right, right.

ELISABETH WATERS: Yes.

MR. DOLAN: Have you, other than the items that you turned over to Officer Harris, have you, in your possession, any documents that you would have authored that relate to the molestation of Ken Smith other than what you have turned over to me by your attorneys?

ELISABETH WATERS: No.

MR. DOLAN: We can break now and come back. (Whereupon, the lunch recess was taken.)

AFTERNOON SESSION

MR. DOLAN: Can you give me the last question and answer, please. We were talking about your diaries. Never mind. Or lack there of.

ELISABETH WATERS: One clarification in what I was reading in preparing for the deposition, when I said "the police report," I meant my portion of the police report.

MR. DOLAN: Okay. That's those documents that you gave to the police?

ELISABETH WATERS: Yes, not the entire report.

MR. DOLAN: Let me ask a question before we delve further. There was a $57,000 loan following the divorce of Walter Breen and Marion Zimmer Bradley, if I remember correctly, that was part of the marital dissolution. Do you recall anything pertaining to that?

ELISABETH WATERS: I imagine that would be this was–

MR. BURESH: If you're imagining then– I don't want you to imagine.

ELISABETH WATERS: I'm not imagining.

MR. BURESH: All right.

ELISABETH WATERS: Are you talking about a loan where Marion owed the money to Walter?

MR. DOLAN: Yes, and it was to be paid in three equal payments through the time period 1993?

ELISABETH WATERS: Yes, she bought out his half of the house.

MR. DOLAN: Do you know if that loan was ever paid off?

ELISABETH WATERS: Yes, of course it was.

MR. DOLAN: The only reason I ask is I never saw satisfaction of the loan in the papers that were provided to me, but I saw documentation pertaining to the loan.

ELISABETH WATERS: Oh, I see. We don't have all the papers. Heavens know where they all got to. It would be on file at the courthouse.

MR. DOLAN: Is that part of the settlement agreement between the lawsuit with Patrick and Marion Zimmer Bradley regarding the houses at all?

MR. BURESH: If you know.

MR. DOLAN: If you know.

ELISABETH WATERS: I mean, the– wait a minute. We're talking about Marion buying out Walter's interest in Prince Street, aren't we?

MR. DOLAN: Correct.

ELISABETH WATERS: That had nothing to do with anything with Patrick. That was part of the divorce.

MR. DOLAN: To your knowledge though, this $57,000 was paid to Walter before his death?

ELISABETH WATERS: Oh, yes.

MR. DOLAN: What year did Walter die?

ELISABETH WATERS: 1993.

MR. DOLAN: Do you know of any documentation that exists that would verify the payment of that loan?

ELISABETH WATERS: There is on file. In the courthouse, there should be the– whatever they call it. What do they call it when they finally transfer?

MR. DOLAN: A quitclaim deed, or something like that?

ELISABETH WATERS: Reconveyance. Because I remember Walter lost– that's right, Walter lost the papers, and we had to go through hoops to get that reconveyance done.

MR. BURESH: Let me just ask a question on this subject. Mr. Dolan has characterized this as a loan. To your knowledge was there a loan involved?

ELISABETH WATERS: Define "loan".

MR. DOLAN: Well, I believe you indicated it was a loan, actually, not myself. I just said there was $57,000. She said there was a loan between Walter and– on the house which had to do with her buying the interest of the house?

ELISABETH WATERS: I think it would probably be more accurately characterized as "a mortgage," since it was secured by the property. It was an exchange for his half of the house.

MR. DOLAN: Do you recall drafting the papers for that mortgage, loan, whatever, do you recall?

ELISABETH WATERS: I remember Camille LeGrand did it.

MR. DOLAN: The reason I am asking is I have, in the documents that you provided to me, an interspousal transfer deed dated 1990. There was also a document that was the loan agreement which called for payments past the 1990 period that the interspousal transfer was entered. I was wondering if there were any documents which closed that loop and show that it actually had been paid. That's– I'll show you these documents so that you're not relying on my representations. Do you have the note? What date do you have on the quitclaim deed there?

ELISABETH WATERS: September 17th, 1985. Oh, this is the other property. This October 17th, 1985, is the 3031 Fulton property.

MR. DOLAN: Okay. But looking at the February 9, 1990, document for the interspousal transfer deed, can you tell me which property that relates to?

ELISABETH WATERS: That would be 2221 Prince.

MR. DOLAN: And that part of the deed was conveyed in 1990, correct?

ELISABETH WATERS: Yes.

MR. DOLAN: Was that the deed that you were talking about there was some difficulty in filing, or is there another deed?

ELISABETH WATERS: There may be another deed. There were so many of them. I just remember there was one where Walter was supposed to have the papers, and Walter lost the papers.

MR. DOLAN: There was a note secured by a deed of trust that was provided to me that I'll show you now, which is– we can mark as Plaintiff's 1 to this deposition. (Whereupon, Plaintiff's Exhibit No. 1 was marked for identification.)

ELISABETH WATERS: I think what happened was that this one was paid off early, but I would have to go back to the bank to get checks or canceled checks or copies of checks or whatever.

MR. DOLAN: Do you know when Walter Breen died in 1993?

ELISABETH WATERS: April, toward the end of April.

MR. DOLAN: Do you know if any documentation exists that shows that note, Plaintiff's Exhibit 1, was satisfied?

ELISABETH WATERS: There must be some somewhere.

MR. DOLAN: Okay. Do you know if the note was paid directly to Walter, was it paid to somebody who had power of attorney, or was it paid to his estate; do you recall?

ELISABETH WATERS: Well, it can't have been paid to his estate because it was paid before he died. To the best of my memory, and I can not swear absolutely to the truthfulness of this, what tended to happen is that Marion and Walter, if they were lending each other money, would write up a note, and as soon as the money came in they would pay it off, so this was probably paid off way early, and, therefore, would have been—let's see, when was Walter arrested in '91?

MR. DOLAN: He appears to have been arrested in—according to the police reports here, roughly in August of 1991.

ELISABETH WATERS: That sounds right. So if it was paid off before then, it would have been paid directly to Walter. After he was arrested, he gave his power of attorney to his son, Patrick.

MR. BURESH: Are you talking about the Los Angeles arrest?

ELISABETH WATERS: Yes, one that put him in jail and prevented him from managing his own affairs.

MR. DOLAN: Did you ever hold power of attorney for Walter after his arrest in Los Angeles County?

ELISABETH WATERS: I never held power of attorney for Walter at all.

MR. DOLAN: Were you ever an owner of the property in which Walter Breen resided?

ELISABETH WATERS: Which one?

MR. DOLAN: Are you an owner of any of the properties either on Prince Street or Fulton Street?

ELISABETH WATERS: At present– wait a minute. Let's get a time period here. Are you asking if I was an owner of 3031 Fulton or 2221 Prince?

MR. DOLAN: Let me ask you this question: Prior to 1989, were you an owner on any of the properties, either 2221 Prince Street or Fulton Street?

ELISABETH WATERS: I was a part owner of 3031 Fulton.

MR. DOLAN: And that's where Walter Breen was residing?

ELISABETH WATERS: Yes.

MR. DOLAN: And what time were you a part owner of 3031 Fulton Street?

ELISABETH WATERS: From the time we purchased it until, I believe, the summer of 1990.

MR. DOLAN: When did you purchase it?

ELISABETH WATERS: It was just on here. October 17th, 1985.

MR. DOLAN: Who purchased the– that's the goldfish bowl, correct?

ELISABETH WATERS: Yes.

MR. DOLAN: Who was it that was actually involved in the purchase of the goldfish bowl?

ELISABETH WATERS: Well, Marion's CPA, Janette Burke, was the one whose idea it was, and she thought Marion should get into real estate, and Marion and I bought it jointly with Marion holding an 80-percent share and me holding a 20-percent share, and Camille LeGrand did the agreement for that.

MR. DOLAN: Was title ever in your name, do you know?

ELISABETH WATERS: You mean when it was bought, yes.

MR. DOLAN: The deed?

ELISABETH WATERS: Yes.

MR. DOLAN: Is it your testimony that through some time in 1990 you remained a part owner of the property on Fulton Street?

ELISABETH WATERS: Yes.

MR. DOLAN: I am going to show you what we'll marked now as Plaintiff's Exhibit 2. (Where-upon, Plaintiff's Exhibit No. 2 was marked for identification.)

MR. DOLAN: Which was a document, I believe you looked at, and I'm identifying the 1985 time frame when you purchased the property; is that correct?

ELISABETH WATERS: Yes.

MR. DOLAN: Do you know what this document was designed to accomplish, this quitclaim deed, why it was drafted?

ELISABETH WATERS: Because Marion and Walter, though both separated, were still legally married, and so Walter would not have a claim on the property.

MR. DOLAN: And that was when; when was that drafted?

ELISABETH WATERS: 1985.

MR. DOLAN: Does your name appear anywhere on that document?

ELISABETH WATERS: No.

MR. DOLAN: Do you have any understanding as to why your name was not included on the document if you were a part owner?

ELISABETH WATERS: No.

MR. DOLAN: Okay. But to your knowledge, you were a part owner on the property between 1985 and 1989, correct?

ELISABETH WATERS: Yes.

MR. DOLAN: And that was the time period wherein Walter Breen was residing at that property, correct?

ELISABETH WATERS: Yes.

MR. DOLAN: I'm going to show you a document that we are going to mark as Plaintiff's 3, which is a rental agreement. (Whereupon, Plaintiff's Exhibit No. 3 was marked for identification.)

MR. BURESH: Do you know what exhibit number that was?

MR. DOLAN: You don't have them numbered. Oh, in what category it comes, yes. Exhibit No. 22.

MR. DOLAN: Have you ever seen Plaintiff's Exhibit 3 before?

ELISABETH WATERS: Yes, of course, that's my signature on it.

MR. DOLAN: That was my next question. Did you indeed sign that document?

ELISABETH WATERS: Yes.

MR. DOLAN: Did you rent the property that you were part owner of to Walter Breen in 1986?

ELISABETH WATERS: Yes.

MR. DOLAN: At the time that you rented the property to Walter Breen in 1986, were you aware that he had authored the book Greek Love?

ELISABETH WATERS: I don't remember.

MR. DOLAN: The time that you rented the property to Walter Breen in 1986, were you aware of the allegation that had been made against him by Barry?

ELISABETH WATERS: Yes.

MR. DOLAN: At the time that you rented this property to Walter Breen in 1986, were you aware of the allegation that had been raised against Walter regarding his molestation of [Glenn]?

ELISABETH WATERS: I don't believe so.

MR. DOLAN: At the time that you rented this property to Walter Breen in 1986, were you aware that Walter Breen had been the subject of some controversy at the Worldcon regarding the molestation of a child?

ELISABETH WATERS: No.

MR. DOLAN: At the time that you rented the property to Walter Breen in 1986, were you aware of any allegations against him that he had molested his own children?

ELISABETH WATERS: No.

MR. DOLAN: At the time that you rented the property to Walter Breen in 1986, were you aware in any way about Walter Breen's beliefs concerning sex between men and children?

ELISABETH WATERS: No, I don't really think so.

MR. DOLAN: I want you not to guess or speculate. To remember if you can give me your best testimony as to whether or not at that point in time you had any knowledge whatsoever regarding Walter Breen's ideologies concerning sex between men and boys at the time that you rented him this property in 1986.

ELISABETH WATERS: Well, I think at this point I knew he had written Greek Love, but I wasn't sure. I didn't know exactly what the book was about.

MR. DOLAN: Did you have any understanding, even though you weren't sure exactly what it was about, did you have any understanding as to whether or not the subject matter of that book involved relations between men and young boys?

ELISABETH WATERS: I understood it involved relations between men and young boys in ancient Greece.

MR. DOLAN: At that time, did you have any understanding as to why Walter had written that book?

ELISABETH WATERS: No.

MR. DOLAN: At this point–

ELISABETH WATERS: For money, I suppose.

MR. BURESH: Don't guess, please.

ELISABETH WATERS: Sorry.

MR. DOLAN: At that time, did you have any understanding whatsoever regarding Walter Breen's idealogy on the age of consensual sex between people?

ELISABETH WATERS: I'm sorry, would you rephrase the question?

MR. DOLAN: At that time in 1986, did you have any understanding as to what Walter Breen's beliefs were regarding the age of consensual sex between people?

ELISABETH WATERS: I think I may have heard him say that he thought the age of consent should be lower than 18.

MR. DOLAN: Did you ever ask him what age he thought it should be lowered to?

ELISABETH WATERS: No, I told him I didn't agree with him.

MR. DOLAN: So prior to renting the property to Walter Breen, you had heard him say that he believed that he thought the age should be lowered below 18?

ELISABETH WATERS: Yes, I believe so.

MR. DOLAN: Did you have any further discussions with him on that issue at any time prior to renting him the property in 1986?

ELISABETH WATERS: I don't think I had a discussion with him on the issue. I think I heard him arguing with Marion about it.

MR. DOLAN: Okay. Can you tell me what you can recall about his argument with Marion on the issue of the age of consent being lowered below the age of 18?

ELISABETH WATERS: I think he said something vaguely sympathetic about NAMBLA, and Marion said—N-a-m-b-l-a—and Marion said that you were always seeing dirty old men march for the right to have sex with young boys, but you certainly didn't see young boys marching for the right to have sex with dirty old men. She was very cross with him.

MR. DOLAN: Do you recall anything else that transpired during that conversation between Walter and Marion?

ELISABETH WATERS: Well, no, that's sort of ended the conversation. Walter didn't– doesn't–

MR. BURESH: You have answered the question, I'm sorry.

MR. DOLAN: Do you know how the subject came up between the two of them?

ELISABETH WATERS: No.

MR. DOLAN: Did you ever know Walter to be a member of NAMBLA?

ELISABETH WATERS: No.

MR. DOLAN: Do you ever know Walter to be a member of the Mattachaine Society?

ELISABETH WATERS: No.

MR. DOLAN: Was Marion ever a member of NAMBLA?

ELISABETH WATERS: To the best my knowledge, no.

MR. DOLAN: Was Marion ever a member of the Mattachaine Society?

ELISABETH WATERS: No.

MR. DOLAN: Have you ever been a member or supporter NAMBLA?

ELISABETH WATERS: No.

MR. DOLAN: Have you ever been a member or supporter of the Mattachaine Society?

ELISABETH WATERS: I don't know what the Mattachaine Society is, and, no.

MR. BURESH: Let's go off the record one second. (Discussion off the record.)

MR. DOLAN: Have you, at any time, come to learn that Walter may have been a member of NAMBLA?

ELISABETH WATERS: No.

MR. DOLAN: Have you ever heard of a journal called One?

ELISABETH WATERS: No.

MR. DOLAN: Have you ever–

ELISABETH WATERS: Sorry. It was in the interrogatories, but prior to that, no.

MR. DOLAN: Have you ever heard of a journal called Two?

ELISABETH WATERS: No.

MR. DOLAN: Were you ever aware of Walter giving any interviews under the name of J.Z. Eglinton?

ELISABETH WATERS: No.

MR. DOLAN: Have you ever read any interviews regarding Walter's authoring of the book Greek Love?

ELISABETH WATERS: I think I may have seen one once.

MR. DOLAN: I am going to show you a document that we are going to mark as Plaintiff's next in order, which will be Plaintiff's No. 4. (Whereupon, Plaintiff's Exhibit No. 4 was marked for identification.)

MR. DOLAN: I'm going to ask you– it's a two-page exhibit. (Discussion off the record.)

MR. DOLAN: It is a document entitled An Interview with J.Z. Eglinton, E-g-l-i-n-t-o-n, by Martin Denison, D-e-n-i-s-o-n. I have highlighted two portions on it which were not highlighted at the time that it was originally generated, and I will be happy to make a photocopy without these for introduction in the record if counsel has any objection to it, but this is the only copy I currently have with me. I'm going to ask if you have ever seen that document before?

ELISABETH WATERS: It looks vaguely familiar. I may have.

MR. DOLAN: Do you recall when you may have seen that document before?

ELISABETH WATERS: Probably in '89 with all the rest of the stuff.

MR. DOLAN: This document– strike that. Do you know if Marion Zimmer Bradley had read Greek Love?

ELISABETH WATERS: I think she read parts of it. I don't know that she had read the whole thing.

MR. DOLAN: Were you aware that Greek Love was dedicated to Marion Zimmer Bradley?

ELISABETH WATERS: Not until I found a copy for Officer Harris.

MR. DOLAN: Do you know if Marion Zimmer Bradley was aware that book had been dedicated to her?

ELISABETH WATERS: I don't know.

MR. DOLAN: Marion Zimmer Bradley was an owner of the property rented to Walter; is that correct?

ELISABETH WATERS: Yes.

MR. DOLAN: Do you know if Marion Zimmer Bradley had read the book Greek Love prior to renting the property to Walter Breen?

ELISABETH WATERS: You're asking do I know for sure?

MR. DOLAN: Yes.

ELISABETH WATERS: I don't know for sure, no.

MR. DOLAN: Prior to renting the property to Walter Breen, is it correct that you and Marion Zimmer Bradley had discussed the letter that had been sent to Dr. Morin?

ELISABETH WATERS: As I mentioned earlier, I had asked her about this in 1980, and by then we had long since forgotten about it.

MR. DOLAN: I move to strike as nonresponsive. The question was, prior to renting the property in 1986, had you and Marion discussed the letter sent to Dr. Morin?

MR. BURESH: I'm going to object to the question as being asked and answered. She has all ready testified to the best of her knowledge of when that took place, and now you're asking her to reference a point in time, and you're asking her the same question over again. I suggest you go back in the record and look at her testimony then, but you're now asking the same question over again.

MR. DOLAN: I'll ask a different question.

MR. DOLAN: At the time that you rented this property to Walter Breen, you knew that he had written a letter to Dr. Morin, correct?

ELISABETH WATERS: I had long since forgotten about it.

MR. DOLAN: But you had knowledge of that letter prior to renting the property to Walter Breen, correct?

ELISABETH WATERS: I had had knowledge of it, yes.

MR. DOLAN: And so had Marion Zimmer Bradley, correct?

ELISABETH WATERS: Assuming she was listening to me when I talked to her, yes.

MR. DOLAN: Well, she had actually responded to you then?

ELISABETH WATERS: Yes.

MR. DOLAN: So can you draw a conclusion as to whether or not she was listening to you?

MR. BURESH: Object to the question. Instruct the witness not to answer. Go on to the next question.

MR. DOLAN: Well, do you have any facts at your disposal as to whether or not Marion Zimmer Bradley was listening to you at the time that you told her about Dr. Morin's letter?

MR. BURESH: Asked and answered.

MR. DOLAN: You can answer.

MR. BURESH: I instruct the witness not to.

MR. DOLAN: She's now saying she doesn't know whether or not–

MR. BURESH: She said she presumed that she did, and she has already testified what she said that was a response. You're badgering the witness. Instruct the witness not to answer.

MR. DOLAN: Mark it. (Whereupon, the previous question was marked for the record.)

MR. DOLAN: So prior to renting this property to Walter Breen, do you have any facts at your disposal as to whether Marion Zimmer Bradley knew that Walter had written the letter to Dr. Morin that we discussed earlier?

MR. BURESH: Objection. Instruct the witness not to answer.

MR. DOLAN: On what grounds?

MR. BURESH: Asked and answered.

MR. DOLAN: I'm asking a different question. I never asked this question of her. I did ask a different question that may identify the space in time, but I am entitled to ask a different question that relates it to another item. I have never asked her that question before, Mr. Buresh, and you'll find it's not in the record.

MR. BURESH: That's fine. We can talk to the judge about it.

MR. DOLAN: Mark it, please. (Whereupon, the previous question was marked for the record.)

MR. DOLAN: Prior to renting this property from Walter Breen, did Marion Zimmer Bradley know that Barry had been found in Walter's bed?

MR. BURESH: Objection, asked and answered. You already talked about the time frame of Marion Zimmer Bradley's knowledge of that, and you're asking her the same question again. I instruct the witness not to answer.

MR. DOLAN: Mark it. (Whereupon, the previous question was marked for the record.)

MR. DOLAN: Prior to the renting of the property by Marion Zimmer Bradley to Walter Breen, do you have any facts at your disposal to know that– strike that. Prior to Marion Zimmer Bradley renting this property to Walter Breen, do you have any facts at your disposal which would indicate to you that she had known Walter had been accused of child molestation?

MR. BURESH: Other than what she has already testified to?

MR. DOLAN: No.

MR. BURESH: Then I object to the question as being asked and answered, and I instruct her not to answer.

MR. DOLAN: Mark it. (Whereupon, the previous question was marked for the record.)

MR. DOLAN: Do you have any knowledge as to whether or not Marion Zimmer Bradley knew that Walter Breen had been accused of child molestation prior to renting this property to him in 1989?

MR. BURESH: Same objection, same instruction.

MR. DOLAN: Mark this. (Whereupon, the previous question was marked for the record.)

MR. DOLAN: You're not allowing me to ask her that whether prior to renting the property, which is the issue of this litigation, the question of whether the woman who rented it to him knew that the man that she was renting it to was accused of child molestation; you're not allowing me to ask that.

MR. BURESH: This morning, in great detail, we went all through of these instances of what Marion might have known and what she knew, and you asked the witness many questions about the time frame of when this knowledge might have been obtained, and now you're taking one point in time, this 1986, and you're asking her the same series of questions all over again. That's asked and answered.

MR. DOLAN: It is relevant to an issue directly at issue in this litigation as to whether she rented her property to someone she knew had been accused of pedophilia.

MR. BURESH: I agree with that.

MR. DOLAN: And I'm entitled to ask that question in the way I want to ask it. It is a different question than on this date did she know this, on that date did she know that. I am asking in 1986, did she know this.

MR. BURESH: I respectfully disagree with your analysis, and we'll have to let somebody else decide this issue.

MR. DOLAN: And what is the reason for your instructing her not to?

MR. BURESH: What I have already said, asked and answered.

MR. DOLAN: That question has never been asked and the record will show that. Different questions may have been asked. Mr. Buresh, you know I'm entitled to ask different questions of her.

MR. BURESH: You asked the same question in a different form.

MR. DOLAN: I have never asked her in 1986.

MR. BURESH: You can do the same thing with 1987, 1988. You can put any date in the calendar and ask her the same questions all over again.

MR. DOLAN: This is a definitely important point in time.

MR. DOLAN: Prior to this point in time in 1986, did you know that Walter Breen had been accused of child molestation?

MR. BURESH: Same objection, same instruction.

MR. DOLAN: Mark it. (Whereupon, the previous question was marked for the record.)

MR. BURESH: Why don't we just have a continuing objection to this, and we'll have to take this to the judge.

MR. DOLAN: Ultimately we are. I am just going to make sure that the record is very clear that you're telling me that I have asked these questions before, and the judge can see how I'm being obstructed from inquiring on a very important point. That's why I am making the record here. I understand that you're not going to let her answer the question, but I am entitled to continue to try and make it different.

MR. BURESH: Well, what I would like you to do is categorize the question so that we can take it to the judge that you want to use this point in time to ask the same questions you were asking before about knowledge of his propensities.

MR. DOLAN: Well, I'm not going to categorize it that way. That's the way you would like it categorized. My questions are on the record.

MR. DOLAN: Why did you rent a property to a gentleman you knew had been accused of child molestation?

MR. BURESH: I will object to that question. Instruct the witness not to answer.

MR. DOLAN: On what basis?

MR. BURESH: It's lacking foundation, assumes facts not in evidence and it's argumentative.

MR. DOLAN: You have just told me I can't ask her if she knew this man had been accused of child molestation prior to February 1986. You're now telling me I can't ask her why because I have already asked her and she's answered?

MR. BURESH: You don't need to pound the table, Chris.

MR. DOLAN: Well, I'm getting frustrated.

MR. BURESH: I know you are.

MR. DOLAN: And I have asked her, and you said it's asked and answered that she knew that he was a child molester– had been accused of child molestation prior to this. Now I'm asking her, why did you rent property to him if you knew that he had been accused of child molestation?

MR. BURESH: Argumentative, instruct the witness not to answer.

MR. DOLAN: Prior to renting the property to Walter Breen, did you know that he had been accused of child molestation?

MR. BURESH: Don't answer the question.

MR. DOLAN: Why did you rent this property to Walter Breen if you had knowledge that he had been accused of child molestation?

MR. BURESH: Objection, argumentative. Instruct the witness not to answer.

MR. DOLAN: Argumentative is not a reason to instruct not to answer, and we can break now, because I'm going to go find you the law, and I'll show you the only reasons you're allowed to instruct someone not to answer. Argumentative is not one of them. I just want to make sure it's clear on the record that this is becoming obstructive. (Whereupon, a recess was taken.)

MR. DOLAN: Prior to renting the property to Walter Breen, did you and Marion Zimmer Bradley discuss his fitness as a tenant?

ELISABETH WATERS: No.

MR. DOLAN: Prior to renting the property to Walter Breen, did you and Marion Zimmer Bradley in any way discuss any allegations of Walter being a child molester?

ELISABETH WATERS: No.

MR. DOLAN: At the time that you rented the property to Walter Breen, did you have any concerns about renting the property to a gentleman who was– who had been accused of child molestation?

MR. BURESH: Same objection, same instruction.

MR. DOLAN: What was the objection?

MR. BURESH: Same objection.

MR. DOLAN: I don't know what it is though.

MR. BURESH: It's the one I made to the same–

MR. DOLAN: Is it asked and answered? I never asked her if she had any concerns about renting to an alleged child molester.

MR. BURESH: Well, it's the same question in a different form. You asked what her suspicions were, what her predilections were, and now you're picking this date, which I understand is a significant date from your standpoint. It's the same series of questions, and I think we are just beating a dead horse here because we are going in front of a judge, and the judge is going to decide this issue.

MR. DOLAN: Mark it, please. (Whereupon, the previous question was marked for the record.)

MR. DOLAN: Did you interview any other possible tenants for the goldfish bowl location that was ultimately rented to Walter Breen?

ELISABETH WATERS: No.

MR. DOLAN: Did you interview Walter Breen for the residence as a tenant?

ELISABETH WATERS: No.

MR. DOLAN: Did anyone object to Walter Breen being rented that premises prior to the time that Ken Smith was reported as being molested, and not making that pregnant with the fact that someone may have objected to it at that time?

ELISABETH WATERS: No.

MR. DOLAN: Did you ever hear any rumors of Walter Breen's molesting of any children other than the ones that have been previously identified in this deposition today?

ELISABETH WATERS: No.

MR. DOLAN: Have you, since this all came out with Kenny Smith, been made aware of any other allegations of Walter's molestation of children other than Ken Smith, the young boy down in L.A. Barry– I believe you referenced Sterling, and [Glenn]?

MR. BURESH: Let me have the question again. (Whereupon, the record was read by the reporter.)

ELISABETH WATERS: Moira was instantly convinced that Walter had molested every child he had ever been near, so to that extent, yes, I have heard other allegations.

MR. DOLAN: Did any parents, prior to the molestation of Ken Smith, ever tell you that they wouldn't let their child stay over at the house unless you or Marion were there?

MR. BURESH: I've got to hear that one again. I'm sorry.

MR. DOLAN: Did any parents, prior to the molestation of Ken Smith, ever tell you that they did not want their child staying over at the house unless you and Marion were there?

MR. BURESH: This is calling for statements made by parents to you.

ELISABETH WATERS: Yes.

MS. DURRELL: And the time frame on this is confusing.

MR. DOLAN: Prior to the molestation of Ken Smith?

ELISABETH WATERS: It wasn't me and Marion. It was me or Marion. Tracy said that she didn't want the kids from Greyhaven staying over there unless Marion or I was there because she didn't consider Walter grown up enough to take care of children on his own.

MR. DOLAN: Did she have a son, Tracy?

ELISABETH WATERS: No.

MR. DOLAN: Was Ian related to her in some way, Ian Studbaker?

ELISABETH WATERS: He's her husband's bastard.

MR. DOLAN: So it is her husband's son?

ELISABETH WATERS: Yes.

MR. DOLAN: Did Tracy ever tell you that she didn't want Ian—you or Marion as you put it—staying at the house until you or Marion were there?

ELISABETH WATERS: No, she wasn't talking about Ian. She was talking about Fiona. She let me and my boyfriend Philip have a slumber party for Fiona and a few of her friends, but she wouldn't have let Walter do it.

MR. DOLAN: Did any parent, prior to the molestation of Ken Smith, ever express any reservation about having their child at Prince Street for any reason that you're aware of?

MS. DURRELL: Excuse me, Chris, you keep saying, "prior to the molestation."

MR. DOLAN: Prior to the identification of– prior to the '89?

ELISABETH WATERS: Okay.

MR. DOLAN: So prior to the date of '89 that Ken Smith's molestation was reported?

ELISABETH WATERS: No, Tracy was the only one.

MR. DOLAN: Did Tracy ever discuss with you any allegation of molestation of her son, Ian, or the bastard son of her husband, Ian?

ELISABETH WATERS: Call him her nephew. You see– let's see. Tracy is married to Paul. Diana is married to Don. Don and Paul are foster brothers, and on Ian's birth certificate it says he is Diana and Don's. It's just biologically he's Paul's, so nephew will do. What was the question?

MR. DOLAN: Did Tracy ever tell you that she had any concerns about Walter's interaction with Ian?

ELISABETH WATERS: No, she did not.

MR. DOLAN: Did Diana ever talk to you about my concerns she had about Walter's interaction with Ian?

ELISABETH WATERS: No.

MR. DOLAN: To this day are you aware of any allegations that Walter may have molested Ian?

ELISABETH WATERS: Moira said that Tracy said that she heard Ian say once, "Don't touch me there, that tickles."

MR. DOLAN: Do you know if Walter ever had any overnight guests who were underage children at the property you rented him?

ELISABETH WATERS: I believe that Mary Mason sent Ken to stay with him.

MR. DOLAN: Okay. Any others that you're aware of?

ELISABETH WATERS: No.

MR. DOLAN: Are you aware of whether Walter was entertaining any young men under the age of 18 in the home that you rented to him other than Ken Smith from the time period 1985 through the report of Ken Smith's molestation in 1989?

ELISABETH WATERS: No.

MR. DOLAN: Did you ever find Walter Breen in a room alone with a young boy at Green Walls at the time between 1985 and 1989?

ELISABETH WATERS: No.

MR. DOLAN: Did you know that Ken Smith was staying alone with Walter Breen at Green Walls between 1985 and 1989?

ELISABETH WATERS: He wasn't.

MR. DOLAN: Who was there?

ELISABETH WATERS: Marion and I lived at Green Walls.

MR. BURESH: You mean the goldfish bowl?

MR. DOLAN: I'm sorry. The goldfish bowl?

ELISABETH WATERS: Well, I don't think he would have been alone. Moira and whatever boyfriend she was living with then would have been there.

MR. DOLAN: Were you aware at the time that Ken Smith was staying at the residence rented to Walter between 1985 and 1989, that Ken Smith was staying there?

ELISABETH WATERS: No.

MR. DOLAN: Did you ever see Ken Smith on the property at the goldfish bowl?

ELISABETH WATERS: No.

MR. DOLAN: Did you ever see Ken Smith on the property at Green Walls, which is the Prince Street address?

ELISABETH WATERS: To the best of my recollection, no.

MR. DOLAN: Do you know if Ken Smith and Walter ever used the hot tub at the Prince Street address?

ELISABETH WATERS: I do not remember their ever doing so, but it's quite possible that they did.

MR. DOLAN: Let's sort of switch gears here. When did you first meet Mary Mason?

ELISABETH WATERS: At the Worldcon in Boston in 1989.

MR. DOLAN: Is it your testimony that you never spoke with Mary Mason prior to Worldcon in Boston in 1989?

ELISABETH WATERS: I believe I phoned her in July to tell her the police wanted to talk to Kenny.

MR. DOLAN: Prior to the report of molestation of Ken Smith, did you ever talk to Mary Mason?

ELISABETH WATERS: No.

MR. DOLAN: Did you know who Mary Mason was prior to the report of the Ken Smith molestation in 1989?

ELISABETH WATERS: Not that I recall.

MR. DOLAN: Had you ever talked to Ken Smith at all prior to the molestation– the report of molestation in 1989?

ELISABETH WATERS: No.

MR. DOLAN: Had you ever seen Ken Smith at any science-fiction conventions prior to 1989 when his molestation was reported?

ELISABETH WATERS: No.

MR. DOLAN: Had Ken Smith ever assisted you in any of the MZB Enterprises prior to his report of molestation in 1989 that you're aware of?

ELISABETH WATERS: No.

MR. DOLAN: Did you know if Ken Smith had ever occupied any of the hotel rooms which were rented by MZB Enterprises at any time prior to his molestation in 1989?

ELISABETH WATERS: MZB Enterprises didn't rent hotel rooms.

MR. DOLAN: Okay.

MR. BURESH: Listen to the question.

MR. DOLAN: Okay, were there hotel rooms rented for the different conferences for the employees of Marion Zimmer Bradley or Marion Zimmer Bradley Enterprises, whatever they were?

MR. BURESH: By Marion Zimmer Bradley Enterprises?

MR. DOLAN: By Marion Zimmer Bradley or Marion Zimmer Bradley Enterprises?

ELISABETH WATERS: No.

MR. DOLAN: Did you pay for Walter's hotel rooms at these conferences?

ELISABETH WATERS: No.

MR. DOLAN: Did you have an employment agreement with Walter?

ELISABETH WATERS: Yes.

MR. DOLAN: Let's mark this as Plaintiff's next in order. (Whereupon, Plaintiff's Exhibit No. 5 was marked for identification.)

MR. DOLAN: It comes out of your Exhibit No. 23. It's a two-page exhibit called, "Employment Agreement."

MR. DOLAN: Do you know who drafted this employment agreement marked as Plaintiff's Exhibit No. 5?

ELISABETH WATERS: I'm sorry, was that a question?

MR. DOLAN: Do you know who drafted this agreement that has been marked as Plaintiff's Exhibit No. 5?

ELISABETH WATERS: I did. I copied it from his previous employment exhibit with First Coin Investors, pretty much.

MR. DOLAN: And do you see on the second page of that where it talks about expenses for travel?

ELISABETH WATERS: Yes.

MR. DOLAN: Did you reimburse Walter for expenses for travel that were involved with the MZB Enterprises?

ELISABETH WATERS: No, because those weren't business travel. When we're talking about travel here, we are talking about numismatic travel.

MR. DOLAN: So Walter's attendance at coin shows– I mean, at science fiction fairs was not something that was part of his business?

ELISABETH WATERS: Correct.

MR. DOLAN: So is it your testimony that prior to 1989, the time in 1989 that he was reported for the molestation of Ken Smith, his job duties did not include attendance at science fiction or fantasy conventions?

ELISABETH WATERS: That is correct.

MR. DOLAN: Let's mark this as Plaintiff's next in order. (Whereupon, Plaintiff's Exhibit No. 6 was marked for identification.)

MR. DOLAN: It has highlight markings on it. If you have–

MR. BURESH: A clean copy.

MR. DOLAN: Yeah.

MR. BURESH: Give me the number again.

MR. DOLAN: Exhibit 11.

MR. BURESH: What is it, a letter from Walter?

MR. DOLAN: To Walter. We'll make a copy and give you one back.

MR. BURESH: I don't think I have it in this one.

MR. DOLAN: 15 November '89.

MR. BURESH: Is it after the employment agreement?

ELISABETH WATERS: Yes.

MR. DOLAN: Yes. And after the will. We'll make a clean copy.

MR. DOLAN: I'm going to show you what's been marked as Plaintiff's 6 and ask you if you drafted that document?

ELISABETH WATERS: Yes.

MR. DOLAN: Did you send that document to Walter?

ELISABETH WATERS: Yes.

MR. DOLAN: If Walter's duties did not include attendance at science fiction or fantasy conventions as part of his employment, why did you send him a letter in November of 1989 telling him that his duties no longer include traveling to science-fiction conventions?

MR. BURESH: Well, it doesn't say that.

ELISABETH WATERS: It doesn't say "no longer." It says, "do not include". It's clarifying that point to make it absolutely clear.

MR. DOLAN: It says, "Therefore, effective immediately and until further notice, your job duties do not include attendance at any science fiction or fantasy convention."

MR. BURESH: The question is argumentative and misstates the record.

MR. DOLAN: I haven't asked a question yet.

MR. DOLAN: Why did you send this letter to Walter Breen telling him that effective immediately his job duties did not include traveling to science fiction and fantasy conventions if, indeed, his job duties never included those?

MR. BURESH: I'm going to object to the question. It assumes facts not in evidence and misstates the record. The duties as stated on the employment agreement, Exhibit 5 says, "Employee shall update the Darkover Concordance, work on the magazine as requested, and undertake other projects as assigned. These may include numismatic work, as long as such work does not involve numerical grading of coins."

MR. DOLAN: What is the objection?

ELISABETH WATERS: Actually, his duties did not involve travel at all.

MR. DOLAN: Then what was the need for sending the letter in November of 1989 telling him that effective immediately, and until further notice, your job duties do not include attendance at any science fiction or fantasy conventions?

MR. BURESH: Objection, assumes that there was a need.

MR. DOLAN: You can answer.

MR. BURESH: If you want to explain to him why.

MR. DOLAN: Scott, please.

ELISABETH WATERS: Camille LeGrand suggested that we do this just to make the paper trail absolutely clean. To make it very clear that he was not attending conventions as our employee.

MR. DOLAN: Had Walter ever attended a convention as your employee?

ELISABETH WATERS: No.

MR. DOLAN: Had Walter ever facilitated the business of the MZB Enterprises at any time during the science-fiction conventions?

ELISABETH WATERS: You mean, like sat at a dealer's table or something?

MR. DOLAN: Yes.

ELISABETH WATERS: Not to my knowledge.

MR. DOLAN: Had he ever helped move boxes of books or anything like that?

ELISABETH WATERS: No.

MR. DOLAN: Did Walter in any way during any of these science-fiction conventions represent MZB Enterprises?

ELISABETH WATERS: No.

MR. DOLAN: Do you know if during his discussion– did Walter ever appear on any panels?

MS. DURRELL: I'm going to object. That's vague and ambiguous. I don't understand that question.

MR. DOLAN: During the science fiction or fantasy conventions that Walter attended, do you know if he ever sat on any panels where he spoke to audiences?

ELISABETH WATERS: I don't know.

MR. DOLAN: Did you ever?

ELISABETH WATERS: He may have. I don't know.

MR. DOLAN: Did you ever listen to Walter talk to any audiences?

ELISABETH WATERS: No.

MR. DOLAN: Did Walter stay in the same room with the rest of the people who were employees of Marion Zimmer Bradley at these conventions?

MR. BURESH: Sleeping in the room?

MR. DOLAN: Same room– let me ask this question.

MR. DOLAN: Would the family often rent a suite of rooms when you went to these conventions?

ELISABETH WATERS: No, we all had individual rooms.

MR. DOLAN: Did Walter and Marion ever share a room at these conventions?

ELISABETH WATERS: Not as late as this. Probably they did when they were first married.

MR. DOLAN: Do you know from the time period 1985 to 1989 whether Walter and Marion ever shared a room at a science-fiction convention?

ELISABETH WATERS: I don't know.

MR. DOLAN: Do you know if at any time during 1985 to 1989, Walter and Marion had continuous rooms, room that were connected in any way at the science fiction and fantasy convention?

ELISABETH WATERS: No, if they weren't sharing a room, there is no reason they would have had adjoining rooms.

MR. DOLAN: The questions is, do you know?

ELISABETH WATERS: No, I do not know.

MR. DOLAN: Why did you write here in this letter– well, you spoke to Camille LeGrand before writing this letter, correct?

ELISABETH WATERS: Yes.

MR. DOLAN: What did Camille LeGrand tell you about the writing of this letter?

MR. BURESH: I'm going to object to the question. It invades the attorney/client privilege. Instruct the witness not to answer.

MR. DOLAN: That has been waived. It says, "I have talked to our lawyer, Camille LeGrand, yesterday regarding liability of MZB Enterprises for your behavior at any conventions or shows you attended. She informs me that MZB Enterprises is not responsible," and she goes on to indicate what they talked about.

MR. BURESH: I don't consider that to be a waiver of the privilege.

MR. DOLAN: Mark it please. (Whereupon, the previous question was marked for the record.)

MR. DOLAN: Did Camille LeGrand, quote, "inform you the MZB Enterprises is not responsible for anything that Walter had already done"?

MR. BURESH: Same objection, same instruction as to all communication between Camille LeGrand and this witness.

MR. DOLAN: Mark it. (Whereupon, the previous question was marked for the record.)

MR. DOLAN: Did someone inform you that once you had good reason to believe that Walter was capable of violating the law in the course of his association with children you meet at the functions, that MZB Enterprises could be liable for future behavior in any situation in which he was acting as your employee?

MR. BURESH: Let me hear the question again, please. (Whereupon, the record was read by the reporter.)

MR. BURESH: The same objection, same instruction.

MR. DOLAN: I'm not asking what any lawyer told you. I'm asking, did anyone ever tell you that?

MR. BURESH: In the context of this letter, same objection, same instruction.

MR. DOLAN: I'm not asking her the context of this letter.

MR. DOLAN: I am just asking, did anyone ever tell you that MZB Enterprises could be held liable for the actions of Walter Breen once you knew that he might be molesting children?

MR. BURESH: Same objection, same instruction. It's not reasonably calculated to lead to the discovery of admissible evidence.

MR. DOLAN: Certainly, there may be a claim if he was involved somehow in the molestation of children as an employee.

MR. BURESH: What somebody told her about that is of no relevance. Same instruction, same objection.

MR. DOLAN: I just want to make sure I understand for the record, please, which objections are you making, attorney-client privilege, or you just don't want her to answer?

MR. BURESH: Attorney-client privilege, and also all the objections that I just got through stating, which is not reasonably calculated to lead to the discovery of admissible evidence.

MR. DOLAN: At the time you wrote this letter, were you aware that Marion Zimmer Bradley Enterprises could be held liable for the activities of Walter Breen if he were to molest someone after the allegations had been raised regarding Ken Smith?

MR. BURESH: Object to the question assumes facts not in evidence and calls for a legal conclusion. You're grilling her on the law here.

MR. DOLAN: No, I'm not. I'm asking her if she had knowledge or awareness. I'm not asking her the status of the law.

MR. BURESH: Her own knowledge or awareness of potential vicarious liability is of no meaning in this case. Either they're vicariously liable according to what the law is or they're not. Her understanding–

MR. DOLAN: This isn't a proper objection, Scott. A proper objection is foundation, the form of the question or attorney-client privilege, but this colloquy is not appropriate, and I will ask you please to refrain from doing it. If you're going to instruct her not to answer, go ahead and do that.

MR. BURESH: I have, and now you started the colloquy.

MR. DOLAN: I am just trying to make sure that we please keep to the CCP. We have been pretty good at it in doing this so far, and I don't like it when we start having this other stuff.

MR. BURESH: I don't either.

MR. DOLAN: Did you ever have an understanding that once you were aware that Walter Breen may have molested a child, that MZB Enterprises could be held liable for any further acts that he undertook in molesting a child?

MR. BURESH: I'm going to object to the question. Calls for a legal conclusion, and it's also not reasonably calculated to lead to the discovery of admissible evidence.

MR. DOLAN: Are you instructing her not to answer?

MR. BURESH: No, she can go ahead and answer the question.

MR. DOLAN: I'll have it read back, please. (Whereupon, the record was read by the reporter.)

MR. BURESH: I want to talk to my client.

MR. DOLAN: Please let the record reflect that they're breaking during a pending question. (Discussion off the record.)

MR. BURESH: I'm going to instruct the witness not to answer the question.

MR. DOLAN: On what basis, please?

MR. BURESH: Same basis.

MR. DOLAN: Which one, attorney/client privilege or it calls for a legal conclusion? I just want to be clear, Scott; that's all.

MR. BURESH: I have stated three different objections to this line of questioning. Invasion of attorney-client privilege, calls for a legal conclusion, and is not reasonably calculated to lead to the discovery of admissible evidence.

MR. DOLAN: I just want to be very clear that you understand my question. I'm not asking if an attorney told you anything. I'm asking, did you understand? I'm not asking if you, as a lawyer, just as you as a person; if you had any understanding at this time in 1989 as to whether or not, once you knew that Walter Breen was capable of molesting children, that Marion Zimmer Bradley Enterprises could be held responsible if he did so as an employee? Is it the same instruction not to answer?

MR. BURESH: Correct.

MR. DOLAN: Please mark that. (Whereupon, the previous question was marked for the record.)

MR. DOLAN: At some point did you become concerned that Walter's behavior might cause liability for MZB Enterprises? Unless your lawyer objects, please look– I understand that you're looking at him, but unless he objects, I'm entitled to an answer.

ELISABETH WATERS: After I found out what he had done to Kenny, yes, I became concerned that his behavior would cause future liability.

MR. DOLAN: Were you concerned that it might cause the loss of one or more of the houses as well?

ELISABETH WATERS: Well, since he and Marion owned 2221 Prince Street as husband and wife, I was concerned that it might cause the loss of that house if he were sued.

MR. DOLAN: Was that one of the reasons why the title to 2221 Prince Street was transferred over to Marion solely?

ELISABETH WATERS: That was done as part of the divorce because she was the one living there.

MR. DOLAN: The question was, was that one of the reasons why that property was transferred over to Marion Zimmer Bradley?

ELISABETH WATERS: I don't know. I was not a party to the divorce negotiations.

MR. DOLAN: Was it your testimony that you never contacted Camille LeGrand regarding the divorce?

ELISABETH WATERS: I called her secretary to set up an appointment.

MR. DOLAN: Did you participate in any way whatsoever in terms of the handling of the divorce other than calling the secretary of Camille LeGrand to set up an appointment?

MS. DURRELL: I'm going to object. That's overbroad, vague and ambiguous as to "handling the divorce proceedings."

MR. DOLAN: You may answer.

ELISABETH WATERS: I believe I helped draw up the list of assets and sort out what was community property and what wasn't.

MR. DOLAN: Did you have any understanding as to whether or not one of the motivating factors in divorcing Walter Breen was to protect Marion Zimmer Bradley for any liability for his conduct?

MR. BURESH: Object to the question.

ELISABETH WATERS: I'm sorry, could you rephrase the question. I don't quite understand it.

MR. DOLAN: Did you finish your objection?

MR. BURESH: I was going to state the grounds for my objection. It's not reasonably calculated to lead to the discovery of admissible evidence, and I'll also object based on what the witness said that it's ambiguous and unintelligible.

MR. DOLAN: Do you have any understanding that one of the motivating factors for Marion Zimmer Bradley to divorce Walter Breen was to protect herself from any liability for the actions of Walter Breen in molesting children? You keep looking at your counsel, which you're free to do, but this is a deposition that is really controlled by me asking you questions and not your counsel sort of controlling the gate of information.

ELISABETH WATERS: Well, after he's objected to the last five or six, I want to be sure. So I can answer this?

MR. BURESH: Yes.

MS. DURRELL: Also, you feel free to look at your attorney.

ELISABETH WATERS: Thank you. My understanding of the reason why Marion divorced Walter was that she was so angry to discover that he really was a child molester that she just didn't feel that she could live with him anymore.

MR. DOLAN: The question was, was one of the reasons why she divorced Walter Breen, as far as you know, in an effort to protect herself from liability for his actions in molesting children?

ELISABETH WATERS: No.

MR. DOLAN: Did you ever hear Marion Zimmer Bradley state, "If Walter ever did this again, I would divorce him"?

MR. BURESH: Asked and answered.

MR. DOLAN: You can answer unless you're instructed not to.

MR. BURESH: Well, other than what she has already testified to?

ELISABETH WATERS: We went over all that this morning.

MR. BURESH: I'm going to object. It's argumentative. Instruct the witness not to answer.

MR. DOLAN: I asked her, did she ever hear Marion Zimmer say this; that's argumentative?

MR. BURESH: In light of the fact that you asked the question this morning and in light of the context, yes.

MR. DOLAN: No, I'm allowed to re-ask certain questions in certain ways at different times to probe an issue.

MR. BURESH: No, you're not.

MR. DOLAN: You guys are obstructing me now, and I'm trying to play this fair, but we will be in front of a judge mega times on this because this is not something I engage in. I am asking her questions to probe on an issue of why this woman divorced her husband.

MR. BURESH: You're asking her the same question repeated times.

MR. DOLAN: I am not asking repeated times and the record will bear that out. I know when I'm asking repeated times, and I'm not.

MR. BURESH: We went into that.

MR. DOLAN: The record will bare it out, and it will be in front of a judge, and I will seek sanctions, and it's unfortunate.

MR. DOLAN: Did Marion Zimmer Bradley ever tell you that if Walter ever molested children again she would divorce him?

ELISABETH WATERS: No.

MR. BURESH: You just asked that.

MR. DOLAN: That's all I want to know.

MR. BURESH: Object to the question. You're going to have to look at me and give me time, just as Chris told you at the beginning, especially when I'm objecting like this.

MR. DOLAN: Do you know if Marion Zimmer Bradley ever met Mary Mason prior to the report of molestation of Ken Smith in 1989?

ELISABETH WATERS: To the best of my knowledge, Marion has never actually met Mary Mason, aside from perhaps talking to her at a convention as a fan, which is different from meeting someone as a person and establishing a personal relationship.

MR. DOLAN: To your knowledge, do you know if Marion Zimmer Bradley has ever discussed the issue of Ken Smith in any form with Mary Mason?

ELISABETH WATERS: To the best of my knowledge, she has not.

MR. DOLAN: Do you know if she has ever discussed Ken Smith's molestation with Mary Mason after it was reported to the police?

ELISABETH WATERS: To the best of my knowledge, she has not.

MR. DOLAN: Do you have any doubt in your mind as to whether or not Walter Breen molested Ken Smith?

ELISABETH WATERS: Well, yes, I do have a little bit. When I read the police report, I could tell that Kenny was lying to Officer Harris.

MR. DOLAN: So do you believe that Walter Breen molested Ken Smith?

ELISABETH WATERS: I believe he may have done it once, but I don't believe all the stuff that's in the police report.

MR. DOLAN: Did you ever investigate to find out if he had done it more than once?

ELISABETH WATERS: No.

MR. DOLAN: After you rented the property to Walter Breen in 1986, did you ever hear any allegations of child molestation against Walter Breen up and through the time that he was reported to the police?

ELISABETH WATERS: Until he was reported for molesting Kenny, no.

MR. DOLAN: Do you know if there are any letters that exist between Walter and Marion from the time period that they were courting?

ELISABETH WATERS: No, I know of no such letters.

MR. DOLAN: Did you look for any such letters when you were providing your response to the request for production of documents?

ELISABETH WATERS: Yes, I did.

MR. DOLAN: When you were providing your response to the request for production of documents, did you go through all of Marion Zimmer Bradley's papers and effects as well?

ELISABETH WATERS: Yes.

MR. DOLAN: Were the responses that you provided to the request for production of document only those documents which you had in your personal possession, or were they also the documents that Marion Zimmer Bradley had in her possession?

ELISABETH WATERS: Both. Since I'm her secretary, most of her documents are in my possession.

MR. DOLAN: Do you know if any documents exist that you did not go through that are owned by Marion Zimmer Bradley– strike that. Do you know if there are any documents owned by Marion Zimmer Bradley that you did not go through in formulating your responses to the request for production of documents?

ELISABETH WATERS: I don't believe so.

MR. DOLAN: Did you talk with Marion Zimmer Bradley when you were putting together your responses to the request for production of documents?

ELISABETH WATERS: Yes, I did. She went into the hospital the next day.

MR. DOLAN: Do you think those two were connected?

MR. BURESH: Well, I will let her answer. Objection, it calls for an opinion, an expert opinion, but go ahead. If you've got an opinion.

ELISABETH WATERS: Yes, I think there is a connection. She had a heart attack when she found out what Walter had done. Having to relive one of the most traumatic times of her life could not have been good for her health.

MR. DOLAN: Prior to having her heart attack, was she able to manage her financial affairs?

ELISABETH WATERS: Yes.

MR. DOLAN: Prior to having her most recent heart attack, was she able to remember events that occurred between 1985 and 1989, as far as you know?

ELISABETH WATERS: Define "most recent heart attack".

MR. DOLAN: Well, you indicated that when you were filling out your request for production of documents she had a heart attack and she went into the hospital?

ELISABETH WATERS: No, she went into the hospital. She didn't have a heart attack.

MR. DOLAN: Okay. Prior to her going to the hospital the most recent time, let's say that, when you were doing the request for production of documents, was she able to remember events which occurred between 1985 and 1989, as far as you know?

MR. BURESH: Objection, calls for an expert opinion. Calls for speculation.

MR. DOLAN: You can answer.

ELISABETH WATERS: Some of them.

MR. DOLAN: Was Marion Zimmer Bradley having difficulty remembering events– strike that. Did you witness, see or hear anything that would lead you to believe that Marion Zimmer Bradley was having difficulties remembering events that occurred between 1985 and 1989 before she was admitted to the hospital this last time?

ELISABETH WATERS: I don't know. She's a science fiction writer. Her brain has always been on another planet, and more recently she's just been less and less interested in daily life. She turned more of it over to me to manage. I don't know what she can remember or can't remember.

MR. DOLAN: Has she ever told you that she has memory problems?

ELISABETH WATERS: No.

MR. DOLAN: Have you ever witnessed anything about Marion Zimmer Bradley prior to being admitted to the hospital this last time that led you to believe that she was having memory problems?

ELISABETH WATERS: Well, yeah, she had a couple of strokes.

MR. DOLAN: And how did that affect her memory that you were able to observe?

ELISABETH WATERS: Well, while she was having these strokes, she would insist she was fine when she couldn't walk across the room. This last time when she was in the hospital visiting— when the visiting nurse called to arrange to come out and asked to verify her street address, they had the address wrong. Marion had given them the wrong address. It's hard to tell sometimes what's loss of memory and what's just loss of interest.

MR. DOLAN: Do you have any personal belief as to whether or not Marion Zimmer Bradley's memory has been affected by her stroke?

MR. BURESH: Objection, calls for an expert opinion.

MR. DOLAN: I'm just asking her belief.

MR. BURESH: Her personal beliefs are irrelevant. Go ahead. I'm not going to argue.

MR. DOLAN: She said she saw her on a day-to-day basis.

ELISABETH WATERS: I think her cognitive function has been affected by her strokes. I'm not sure to what extent her memory has.

MR. DOLAN: Were you ever informed that Walter was giving drugs to children?

ELISABETH WATERS: Moira said that he used to give her marijuana to put in the spaghetti sauce to cook for him.

MR. DOLAN: When did Moira tell you this?

ELISABETH WATERS: Sometime when she was in her late teens, I think.

MR. DOLAN: Did you find that to be inappropriate?

ELISABETH WATERS: Well, I didn't think that you should give drugs to children, so, yes.

MR. DOLAN: Did you ever ask Walter about it?

ELISABETH WATERS: No.

MR. DOLAN: Did you ever undertake any investigation to find out whether or not Walter was giving drugs to children after Moira had reported that to you sometime in her teens?

ELISABETH WATERS: No.

MR. DOLAN: Do you have any understanding– strike that. Did you learn that information from Moira that Walter was giving her drugs to put in the spaghetti sauce prior to renting him the premises in 1986?

ELISABETH WATERS: I think so.

MR. DOLAN: Did you ever learn any information about Walter Breen giving drugs to anyone other than Moira Breen?

ELISABETH WATERS: I believe that Patrick Breen used marijuana as a teenager, but I don't know where he got it.

MR. DOLAN: Do you have any information as to whether or not Walter Breen ever smoked marijuana with Patrick Breen when Patrick Breen was under the age of 18?

ELISABETH WATERS: I never saw either of them smoke marijuana, but they smelled funny a lot.

MR. DOLAN: Do you have any information as to whether or not they ever smoked marijuana together, whether or not you actually saw them; you may have heard something or someone has told you?

ELISABETH WATERS: No.

MR. DOLAN: Did you ever smoke marijuana– well, I won't ask that question. Did you ever see Walter Breen smoking marijuana in your presence?

ELISABETH WATERS: No.

MR. DOLAN: Did you have any information as to whether or not Walter Breen ever gave drugs to any of the friends of Moira and Patrick Breen?

ELISABETH WATERS: No.

MR. DOLAN: Have you ever been told that by anyone?

ELISABETH WATERS: No.

MR. DOLAN: Were you at all concerned about renting an apartment in 1986 to Walter Breen if you knew that he was using marijuana?

ELISABETH WATERS: No.

MR. DOLAN: Were you at all concerned about the rental of the apartment to Walter Breen if you knew that he was giving marijuana to his children prior to 1986?

ELISABETH WATERS: By 1986 his children were adults, so that was not a concern if, in fact, he was giving them marijuana.

MR. DOLAN: Okay. Was your and Marion's departure from the Prince Street address connected in any way with the episode of finding young boys in Walter's bed?

ELISABETH WATERS: What departure from the Prince Street address?

MR. DOLAN: I'm just going from what Moira told us. She indicated that you and Marion departed Prince Street after a young boy was found in Walter's bed, and I'm wondering if you have any information about that allegation by Moira?

ELISABETH WATERS: If she's talking about when she was complaining about Walter's behavior with [other name] in 1981; that was when Walter left Prince Street, and Marion and I moved in.

MR. DOLAN: Okay. What behavior are we talking about relating to [other name] in 1981?

MR. BURESH: Well, what behavior is she talking about or are you talking about?

MR. DOLAN: She just mentioned, "behavior with [other name] in 1981." What behavior are you referencing?

ELISABETH WATERS: Moira complained that her father was trying to steal her friends.

MR. DOLAN: Did Moira complain that her father was trying to seduce her friends?

ELISABETH WATERS: No.

MR. DOLAN: Did Moira complain that her father was trying to steal her friends in any way relate to anything of a sexual nature?

ELISABETH WATERS: No.

MR. DOLAN: Did Moira ever complain to you that she felt her father was trying to pick up her friends in a sexual manner?

ELISABETH WATERS: No.

MR. DOLAN: Did Moira ever complain to you that she thought her father and [other name] were engaged in sex together?

ELISABETH WATERS: No.

MR. DOLAN: Did anyone ever inform you that they believed that Walter and [other name] were engaged in sexual conduct?

ELISABETH WATERS: No.

MR. DOLAN: Did you ever talk to Walter about Moira's belief that Walter was trying to steal her friends?

ELISABETH WATERS: No.

MR. DOLAN: Did you ever ask Moira what she meant by that?

ELISABETH WATERS: No.

MR. DOLAN: Did you undertake any investigation to find out what Moira meant when she said Walter was trying to steal her friends?

ELISABETH WATERS: No.

MR. DOLAN: Had you ever heard that Moira was of the belief that her mother attacked her with a pair of pliers?

ELISABETH WATERS: I think the story you're talking about is that her mother tied her to a chair and threatened to pull out her teeth with pliers but did not actually touch her.

MR. DOLAN: Had you heard that story before?

ELISABETH WATERS: Yes, from Marion. She was deeply ashamed of it.

MR. DOLAN: When did you hear that story?

ELISABETH WATERS: I don't remember. Sometime in the 1980's.

MR. DOLAN: Was it prior to 1989?

ELISABETH WATERS: Probably.

MR. DOLAN: What did Marion tell you about that episode?

ELISABETH WATERS: That Moira kept biting Patrick, and she couldn't think of any way to stop her, so she tied her to a chair and threatened to pull out all of her teeth with pliers, and Moira became hysterical, and Marion untied her and let her go, and Moira never bit her brother again.

MR. DOLAN: Did Marion ever tell you about any other story where she tied up her children?

ELISABETH WATERS: No.

MR. DOLAN: Did she tell you any other stories that were similar to the threat of physical abuse of the children if they did not behave?

ELISABETH WATERS: No.

MR. DOLAN: Did you ever see Marion attempt to take a knife to herself?

ELISABETH WATERS: No.

MR. DOLAN: Did you ever see Marion attempt to take a knife to anyone else?

ELISABETH WATERS: No.

MR. DOLAN: Did you ever see Marion claw at her own face?

ELISABETH WATERS: No.

MR. DOLAN: This is stuff that's all in Walter's letters to the police.

MR. BURESH: I know. I am just wondering what the relevance is.

MR. DOLAN: I'm just trying to find out about the stability of one of the defendants regarding her own child and other people, which I think is at issue in this litigation.

MR. BURESH: That's pretty broad, but anyway, I don't want to argue with you right now. Let's wait for another question.

MR. DOLAN: Do you have any knowledge as to whether or not Marion ever tried to beat Moira to death?

ELISABETH WATERS: I think it highly unlikely, and certainly I never saw her strike Moira.

MR. DOLAN: Did the family take in any other fosterlings other than Elizabeth Rousseau, Kathryn Krischild, [Cyndi Beckett] or Barry that you know of?

MR. BURESH: I'm going to let the witness answer. I'm objecting that it's been asked and answered. Go ahead.

ELISABETH WATERS: Well, we didn't actually have fosterlings, but there were other people who lived in the household from time to time.

MR. DOLAN: Any of those minor children?

ELISABETH WATERS: No.

MR. DOLAN: Who were the other people who lived in the household from time to time from the time period from 1980 through 1989?

ELISABETH WATERS: Greg Harder stayed with us for a while. He was Kat's boyfriend. H-a-r-d-e-r. Let's see. Kristoph Klover, K-r-i-s-t-o-p-h, K-l-o-v-e-r. That's all I recall off the top of my head.

MR. DOLAN: Do you know where Greg Harder lives now?

ELISABETH WATERS: No, Kat broke up with him years ago as far as I know.

MR. DOLAN: Do you know where his family was from?

ELISABETH WATERS: No.

MR. DOLAN: Do you know where Kristoph Klover lives now?

ELISABETH WATERS: In Oakland.

MR. DOLAN: Do you know where in Oakland?

ELISABETH WATERS: I think it's Truman Street.

MR. DOLAN: Did you ever have a romantic relationship with either of these two people?

MR. BURESH: Objection, instruct the witness not to answer. Invasion of privacy and not reasonably calculated to lead to the discovery of admissible evidence.

MR. DOLAN: Were you ever emotionally involved with either of these two people?

MR. BURESH: Same objection, same instruction.

MR. DOLAN: I'm entitled to probe if there might be bias when I get to these witnesses later on, Scott. That's all I'm asking. I'm not asking about sex. She doesn't have a right to privacy on emotional relationships, only sexual ones.

ELISABETH WATERS: You're asking if I was trying to have an affair with my housemate's boyfriends?

MR. DOLAN: No.

MR. BURESH: You can go ahead and answer whether you had an emotional relationship with either of those two.

ELISABETH WATERS: No.

MR. DOLAN: Did Marion ever discuss with you any of her beliefs regarding the age of consent?

ELISABETH WATERS: Yes.

MR. DOLAN: Can you tell me when she first discussed that with you?

ELISABETH WATERS: No, not the exact date. But she said repeatedly that anyone who molested a child under the age of puberty should get the death penalty.

MR. DOLAN: Do you know what she meant by the age of puberty?

ELISABETH WATERS: Puberty, as in physical puberty.

MR. DOLAN: No, I am wondering if you have any understanding of what she believed the age of puberty was?

ELISABETH WATERS: I understood her to mean physical puberty.

MR. DOLAN: Ages like–

ELISABETH WATERS: 13.

MR. BURESH: Well–

MR. DOLAN: I'm asking if she had an understanding.

MR. BURESH: –the question assumes a fact not in evidence, namely that there is an age, a specific age of puberty that's the same regardless of the individual.

MR. DOLAN: I'm asking if she has any understanding what Marion Zimmer Bradley's definition of puberty is as she used it in that sentence?

ELISABETH WATERS: My belief was that she meant physical puberty. After that she was content to see them thrown in jail.

MR. DOLAN: Okay. And I'm asking you if you have any understanding of what Marion Zimmer Bradley's definition of physical puberty was in terms of chronological ages?

ELISABETH WATERS: It varies from person to person.

MR. BURESH: He's asking if you have an understanding of what Marion meant, and if you do have an understanding of what she meant, you can tell him, and if you don't, you can tell him.

ELISABETH WATERS: I'm sorry, could you repeat the question? It just didn't quite make sense.

MR. DOLAN: Sure. You indicated that Marion thought that anyone who had sex with a child under the age of puberty ought to be thrown in jail, correct?

ELISABETH WATERS: Yes.

MS. DURRELL: No, she said the death sentence.

ELISABETH WATERS: Death sentence. Past puberty should go to jail.

MR. DOLAN: Past puberty should go to jail?

ELISABETH WATERS: Yeah, in other words if you molest a 16 year old, you should go to jail. If you molest Kenny, you should get the death penalty. And I asked her if she included Walter in that, and she said, yes.

MR. DOLAN: Did Marion Zimmer Bradley ever tell you that she believed that the age of consent should be lowered?

ELISABETH WATERS: No.

MR. DOLAN: Do you know why– did Marion Zimmer Bradley visit Walter Breen after he had been arrested for molestation of the boy in L.A?

ELISABETH WATERS: I think she went to see him once in–

MR. DOLAN: Can you explain– strike that. Did you have any knowledge as to why she went to visit Walter Breen when she believed that anybody who got caught molesting a child under the age of puberty should be killed?

MR. BURESH: Object on the basis it's argumentative. If you just lop off the second part after the second and ask if she knows why Marion went down to visit him, that would be fine. Otherwise, it's argumentative, and I'm objecting and instructing the witness not to answer.

ELISABETH WATERS: She–

MR. BURESH: No, he hasn't changed the question yet.

MR. DOLAN: Did her beliefs regarding people who molest children under the age of puberty, to your knowledge, ever change?

ELISABETH WATERS: No.

MR. DOLAN: Can you explain why then she went to visit Walter Breen?

MR. BURESH: Same objection.

MR. DOLAN: You said if I cut it off.

MR. BURESH: You didn't. You said–

MR. DOLAN: And now I'm asking.

MR. BURESH: You didn't cut it off, you joined it up again.

MS. DURRELL: You just put it in front instead of at the end, Chris.

MR. DOLAN: It's a different question.

MR. DOLAN: The question is, do you have an understanding as to why she went to visit Walter Breen?

MR. BURESH: That's fine. He wants to know if you have–

MR. DOLAN: My question— please don't interpret my question, Scott. I don't want you interpreting my question. My question speaks for itself. If she doesn't understand, she can ask me.

MR. BURESH: Ask the question then.

MR. DOLAN: The question was asked, and it will be read back. (Whereupon, the record was read by the reporter.)

ELISABETH WATERS: Yes, he was in Highland Hospital in the jail ward, and they just found out that he had terminal cancer.

MR. DOLAN: Did Walter continue to work for MZB Enterprises after the charges of molestation came up on Ken Smith?

ELISABETH WATERS: Yes.

MR. DOLAN: Did Walter continue to work for MZB Enterprises after he pled guilty to the molestation of Ken Smith?

ELISABETH WATERS: Yes.

MR. DOLAN: Do you know why Walter Breen continued to work for MZB Enterprises after he pled guilty to molesting a child under the age of puberty?

ELISABETH WATERS: Because, unfortunately, when I wrote his contract, I didn't put a clause in it to allow us to fire him under those circumstances.

MR. DOLAN: Had anyone told you that you couldn't fire Walter Breen before the termination of his contract?

MR. BURESH: Other than an attorney?

ELISABETH WATERS: Well, no, but the contract was written with a specific term and did not provide for firing him.

MR. DOLAN: So was it your understanding that you couldn't fire Walter Breen before the expiration of his contract?

ELISABETH WATERS: Yes.

MR. DOLAN: Where did you get that understanding from?

MR. BURESH: Assuming that she got it from somewhere.

MR. DOLAN: Well, it had to come from somewhere.

ELISABETH WATERS: My own very imperfect understanding of the law.

MR. DOLAN: Did you ever have any discussions with Marion Zimmer Bradley about Walter being alone in the company of young boys prior to the molestation of Ken Smith?

ELISABETH WATERS: No.

MR. DOLAN: Did you ever talk to [Glenn]?

ELISABETH WATERS: No.

MR. DOLAN: Do you know where he resides now?

ELISABETH WATERS: I never met him in my life. He was gone long before I moved out.

MR. DOLAN: Was [Glenn] around the house at some point before you moved out?

ELISABETH WATERS: He was the one back in the 1960's?

MR. DOLAN: Correct.

ELISABETH WATERS: I didn't move out until 1979. I never met him.

MR. DOLAN: I didn't know if you were talking about moving out—moving out here or moving out of there to another place. I was trying to understand that. Did you ever meet Sean?

ELISABETH WATERS: Not to the best of my recollection.

MR. DOLAN: Do you know who Sean is?

ELISABETH WATERS: I believe he's the guy that Walter was accused of molesting in Los Angeles.

MR. DOLAN: Are you aware of any of the charges regarding Sean and Walter Breen?

ELISABETH WATERS: Child molesting.

MR. DOLAN: Are you aware of any charge involving molestation which occurred when Sean was in Berkeley?

ELISABETH WATERS: No.

MR. DOLAN: Are you aware of whether there were any allegations of Sean was molested in the hob tub at Green Walls?

ELISABETH WATERS: No.

MR. DOLAN: Was Walter prohibited from having guests after the allegations of– strike that. Was Walter prohibited from having young boys as guests at the goldfish bowl after the charges of molestation were brought concerning Ken Smith?

ELISABETH WATERS: Yes.

MR. DOLAN: Was that done in writing or verbally or how?

ELISABETH WATERS: It was part of his probation. He wasn't allowed to be with people under 18.

MR. DOLAN: Well, that may have been after he was pled out. My question was after the charge arose regarding Ken Smith. Let me ask a different question. After the charges regarding Ken Smith arose, did you undertake any activity to prohibit Walter Breen from having any young children on any of the premises owned by yourself or Marion Zimmer Bradley?

ELISABETH WATERS: I believe Marion did.

MR. DOLAN: Do you know how that was done?

ELISABETH WATERS: I think she wrote him a letter.

MR. DOLAN: Do you know where that letter is today?

ELISABETH WATERS: No.

MR. DOLAN: Did she keep copies of most of her correspondence?

ELISABETH WATERS: No, usually not.

MR. DOLAN: Do you know what the letter said?

ELISABETH WATERS: No.

MR. DOLAN: Did you read that letter?

ELISABETH WATERS: I don't remember.

MR. DOLAN: Did Marion draft her own correspondence, or did you draft it, for the most part?

ELISABETH WATERS: Well, since part of her correspondence is answering her fan mail, I do most of it, but for her own personal correspondence, she usually does it.

MR. DOLAN: Do you recall whether you prepared the letter sent to Walter or Marion did?

ELISABETH WATERS: Marion did.

MR. DOLAN: Did you know what the contents of the letter was in any way?

ELISABETH WATERS: I gathered she was saying she was very angry with him and disgusted by his behavior and didn't want– I think she said she didn't want him on the property at Green Walls.

MR. DOLAN: Anything else?

ELISABETH WATERS: (Witness shakes head.)

MR. DOLAN: Do you know if she still undertook any activity to remove him from the property at Green Walls?

ELISABETH WATERS: She told him she didn't want him on the property.

MR. DOLAN: Do you know if he ever came back to the property at Green Walls?

ELISABETH WATERS: Yes, he did. She calmed down later or something, I guess.

MR. DOLAN: Did you have any understanding as to why Marion Zimmer Bradley would permit this gentleman who pled guilty to child molestation back on her property?

ELISABETH WATERS: Well, he was her ex-husband and the father of her two young children, and she was, after all, fond of him. He used to come over in the afternoons and have a cup of tea with her, but he didn't bring other people with him after that.

MR. DOLAN: After the allegations of Ken Smith came up, did you ever discuss with Walter his molestation of any other children?

ELISABETH WATERS: No.

MR. DOLAN: After the allegations of molestation with Ken Smith came up, did you ever discuss with Walter the allegations of molestation of Ken Smith?

ELISABETH WATERS: I asked him if he was true, and he didn't deny it.

MR. DOLAN: Anything else?

ELISABETH WATERS: Practically every word I said to him on the subject of sex is in the police report.

MR. BURESH: Would you like to review that in order to answer the question?

MR. DOLAN: She hasn't indicate she cannot remember. The only reason to have her review something is to refresh her recollection. I don't– I'm not going to allow her to review documents at your direction at this time.

ELISABETH WATERS: Okay. First, I asked him why his bank account was overdrawn, and he said he had written a check for $5,000 to hire a lawyer because Officer Harris wanted to talk to him, and at that point I began to really seriously believe he was guilty of the accusations made about his behavior with Kenny. A couple of days later I asked him if he really performed oral sex on Kenny, and he said, "yes." No, actually he asked me who told me, and I said Mary Mason did, and he said he didn't know she was talking about it, and I said, "Well, she did to me." So he didn't actually say, yes, but he didn't deny it. And then sometime later, I forgot how the subject originally came up, but I said, "How could you do that to an 11 year old?" And Walter said, "He was 12."

MR. DOLAN: Anything else?

ELISABETH WATERS: You mean like his exact words?

MR. DOLAN: Correct.

ELISABETH WATERS: "He was 12 and besides he wasn't a virgin."

MR. DOLAN: Okay. Anything else that he said that you can recall in any of these three conversations regarding whether or not he actually molested Ken Smith?

ELISABETH WATERS: Well, he seemed to think that it didn't matter because Kenny didn't care about it and Mary didn't care about it; that it was okay because Kenny and Mary didn't object. (Whereupon, a recess was taken.)

MR. DOLAN: Back on the record, please.

MR. DOLAN: Did Walter, in his documentation, indicate that he corresponded with Marion Zimmer Bradley from the mid '60s up until the point of their marriage? Do you know if any of those letters are still in existence?

ELISABETH WATERS: Not to my knowledge.

MR. DOLAN: If they did exist, do you know where they would be kept as far as the structure of Marion's home?

ELISABETH WATERS: Yes, in the files that I went through to prepare for the document production.

MR. DOLAN: Did you see any such documents as those when you were looking through those files?

ELISABETH WATERS: No.

MR. DOLAN: Who was Vince Morgante?

ELISABETH WATERS: I don't know.

MR. DOLAN: Do you know why he was receiving $50 payments from Walter each month when you were paying Walter's bills?

ELISABETH WATERS: No.

MR. DOLAN: Do you know who Margaret was that was referred to on the rental receipts?

ELISABETH WATERS: Which rental receipts?

MR. DOLAN: It says, "Davis, Margaret." Is that Margaret Davis, or do you know who that relates to there?

ELISABETH WATERS: Yes, I know who Margaret Davis is, but what rental receipts are we talking about?

MR. DOLAN: It says, "Rental receipts; Davis, Margaret; rent x/i 75."

ELISABETH WATERS: Oh, she and Kristoph were living with Walter, and they were paying part of the rent.

MR. DOLAN: She was Margaret Davis then; that's her full name?

ELISABETH WATERS: Yes, Margaret Davis.

MR. DOLAN: Do you know where Margaret Davis lives now?

ELISABETH WATERS: With Kristoph Klover. They're married.

MR. DOLAN: Okay, and you gave me a place where you thought they were living earlier; where was that again?

ELISABETH WATERS: Truman Avenue in Oakland.

MR. DOLAN: Do you know who Joan Sandberg is?

ELISABETH WATERS: Joan Sandberg, was she one of Moira's therapists?

MR. DOLAN: Well–

MR. BURESH: He's asking you if you know, and if you don't know, just say you don't know.

ELISABETH WATERS: The name sounds familiar, but I don't remember offhand.

MR. DOLAN: There's some payments to a Joan Sandberg included in this documentation. I was just wondering if you knew who that was?

ELISABETH WATERS: Where are they?

MR. DOLAN: On the next page, "Sandberg, Joan." It begins with "cash" at the top of the document. I don't want to touch your documents. This next page here, down at the bottom, second paragraph up, third– fourth line up.

ELISABETH WATERS: Okay, that would be Moira. That would be one of Moira's therapists. And from the coding on Vince Morgante, he must have been some doctor Walter was seeing.

MR. DOLAN: Did Marion Zimmer Bradley keep a journal as far as you know?

ELISABETH WATERS: No.

MR. DOLAN: Do you know if she kept any documentation regarding the allegations against Walter of pedophilia?

ELISABETH WATERS: No.

MR. DOLAN: When you were first made aware that there might have been some sort of a problem with Walter molesting Ken Smith?

ELISABETH WATERS: When I talked to Mary at the Worldcon.

MR. DOLAN: Had you heard from Moira, or anybody before, that there had been a report made to the police?

ELISABETH WATERS: Yes.

MR. DOLAN: When did you first hear that there might have been some molestation of Ken Smith?

ELISABETH WATERS: Well, I heard that Moira had told the therapist who told the police sometime in July.

MR. DOLAN: How did you learn that?

ELISABETH WATERS: I don't remember, somebody must have– I think maybe Marion told me.

MR. DOLAN: Did Moira ever call you directly to tell you that?

ELISABETH WATERS: Not that I recall.

MR. DOLAN: Do you ever recall Moira trying to get in touch with Marion to talk about this issue and you preventing her from doing so?

ELISABETH WATERS: If Moira called Marion and I didn't let her talk to Marion, it would have been because Marion wasn't home. I was not in the habit of coming between the children and their mother.

MR. DOLAN: So is it your testimony that you first heard about the molestation of Ken Smith from Marion Zimmer Bradley?

ELISABETH WATERS: To the best of my belief, I first heard about the allegation that Kenny had been molested from Marion, yes.

MR. DOLAN: Do you know how Marion had learned of it?

ELISABETH WATERS: From Moira, I assume.

MR. DOLAN: Please don't assume.

ELISABETH WATERS: Sorry.

MR. DOLAN: Do you have any knowledge as to how Marion learned about this?

ELISABETH WATERS: I believe she said Moira had told her.

MR. DOLAN: Did you ever talk to Moira directly about the report of molestation of Ken Smith at any time prior to first speaking to the police about it– you first speaking to the police about it?

ELISABETH WATERS: I wrote to her, but I didn't speak to her. She moved, and I didn't have her phone number, and she wasn't speaking to me.

MR. DOLAN: Did you say the first time you ever talked to Mary Mason about it was at the Worldcon?

ELISABETH WATERS: Aside from the phone call telling her that the police wanted to talk to Kenny. The first time I talked to her about the actual molestation was at the Worldcon, yes.

MR. DOLAN: When did you talk to her about the police wanting to talk to Kenny?

ELISABETH WATERS: That must have been sometime in July.

MR. DOLAN: Who would you have spoken to regarding the molestation prior to talking to Mary Mason in July?

ELISABETH WATERS: I really don't remember. All I remember is that somebody told me that the police wanted to talk to Kenny, and since I'm the person in the family who's organized enough to be able to look in the SFWA directory which had Mary's phone number, I got delegated to call Mary and tell her the police were looking for her kid.

MR. DOLAN: Did you have any understanding is to why the police were looking for her at that time?

ELISABETH WATERS: Because Moira said that Walter was molesting him.

MR. DOLAN: And you learned that Moira said that Walter was molesting him from whom?

ELISABETH WATERS: I believe it was from Marion.

MR. DOLAN: And who did you learn– who was it that you learned from– who was it–

ELISABETH WATERS: From whom.

MR. DOLAN: –from whom did you learn that the police wanted to talk to Kenny?

ELISABETH WATERS: I don't remember.

MR. DOLAN: Had you talked to the police at that time at that point prior to calling Mary Mason?

ELISABETH WATERS: No.

MR. DOLAN: How did you know that the police wanted to talk to Mary Mason or Kenny?

ELISABETH WATERS: I believe Marion must have told me.

MR. DOLAN: Did you have any understanding at the time where Ken Smith was?

ELISABETH WATERS: With Walter.

MR. DOLAN: Okay. Prior to the call from—or from learning from whoever that there had been an allegation that Walter was molesting Ken, did you know that Ken was with Walter?

ELISABETH WATERS: I don't believe so.

MR. DOLAN: Did someone tell you that Ken was with Walter?

ELISABETH WATERS: At some point around the time of WesterCon, or right before or right after, somebody said that Kenny was going with Walter to Disneyland after the convention and was going to stay with Walter for a month. And then right after the convention, Moira came out with these accusations and nobody seemed to know where Kenny and Walter were, so I called Mary assuming that she, at least, would know where her child was, and then that was about all I heard until I ran into Mary at Worldcon in September.

MR. DOLAN: Who was it that told you that Kenny and Walter were going to spend a month together?

ELISABETH WATERS: I don't remember.

MR. DOLAN: Do you have any recollection whatsoever of how you came to understand that?

ELISABETH WATERS: No.

MR. DOLAN: But you knew that before Moira had said that Kenny was being molested, correct?

ELISABETH WATERS: I think so. I'm not positive.

MR. DOLAN: Did someone tell you to call Mary Mason?

ELISABETH WATERS: I believe Marion did.

MR. DOLAN: Can you tell me everything you can recall about the conversation where Marion informed you that Walter had been accused of molesting Ken?

ELISABETH WATERS: Marion said that Moira had blown the whistle on her father, and I looked at her blankly, and I said, "For what?" And she said that Moira was saying that Walter was molesting Kenny, and then I guess she said the police wanted to talk—were looking for Kenny and nobody knew where to find him, so I got my SFWA directory, and I called Mary Mason.

MR. DOLAN: Did you ask Marion whether she thought it could be true?

ELISABETH WATERS: No, she didn't sound as if she thought it were true.

MR. DOLAN: Okay. Did you have any further discussions with her regarding Walter and the molestation of Kenny or any other children at that time?

ELISABETH WATERS: Not until she got back in October.

MR. DOLAN: So Walter, who was a tenant of yours, as well as her ex-husband, had been accused of molesting a child, correct?

ELISABETH WATERS: Yes.

MR. DOLAN: And the only conversation that occurred between the two of you was Marion saying that Moira had blown the whistle on Walter and had accused him of molesting Kenny; is that correct?

MR. BURESH: Object to the question as being augmentative and asked and answered. If you want to ask the question again, go ahead.

ELISABETH WATERS: Yeah, that was pretty much what I remember. You know, this was–

MR. BURESH: You have answered the question.

ELISABETH WATERS: –this was a long time ago.

MR. DOLAN: You spoke to Mary Mason, what did you say to her?

ELISABETH WATERS: Just that the police wanted to talk to Kenny.

MR. DOLAN: Did you tell her why?

ELISABETH WATERS: I believe so.

MR. DOLAN: Do you recall what you said to her in that regard?

ELISABETH WATERS: I think I said that the police thought that Walter was molesting Kenny, and they wanted to talk to Kenny and–

MR. DOLAN: Did you say anything else to her?

ELISABETH WATERS: No.

MR. DOLAN: Did Mary say anything to you?

ELISABETH WATERS: "Okay."

MR. DOLAN: Did she tell you where she thought Kenny was?

ELISABETH WATERS: No.

MR. DOLAN: Did you have any further conversation with her at that time?

ELISABETH WATERS: No, I think, as I recall she just said, "okay," and hung up.

MR. DOLAN: Did you try and locate Walter?

ELISABETH WATERS: Did I try and locate Walter?

MR. DOLAN: Uh-hum.

ELISABETH WATERS: No, I had no way of locating Walter.

MR. DOLAN: Did you talk to Walter at all after– did Walter call or anything?

ELISABETH WATERS: No.

MR. BURESH: Well, let's get the time frame down.

MR. DOLAN: That day, did you talk to Walter at all?

ELISABETH WATERS: No, Walter didn't turn up at home for another couple of weeks, I think.

MR. DOLAN: Did you undertake any activity to try to locate Walter in the couple of weeks before he returned home?

ELISABETH WATERS: No.

MR. DOLAN: Were you at all concerned that Walter might be molesting this child?

ELISABETH WATERS: It was my understanding that once I had told his mother that the police wanted to talk to him, and she had acknowledged receipt of this information, that she would take steps to remove her child from Walter's custody and talk to the police, and certainly that's what any reasonable parent would do.

MR. DOLAN: Did you have any reasons– the question was, did you have any concerns after receiving this information that Walter was molesting Kenny?

ELISABETH WATERS: No, I assumed that Mary had removed him from Walter's presence immediately.

MR. DOLAN: Did you ever talk to Ken about the alleged acts of molestation by Walter at that time?

ELISABETH WATERS: I have never talked to Ken at all.

MR. DOLAN: Did you ever talk to Moira about it; after her mother told you Moira has blown the whistle, did you ever call Moira up and say, what's going on here or anything?

ELISABETH WATERS: No.

MR. DOLAN: Did you undertake any investigation, other than calling Ken Smith's mother, to find out whether or not these allegations were true between the time that you were first notified of it by Marion Zimmer Bradley and the time that Walter returned home several weeks later?

ELISABETH WATERS: No, the police were investigating.

MR. DOLAN: Did you talk to Raul about it at all?

ELISABETH WATERS: I might have, quite possibly. I talked to Raul a lot.

MR. DOLAN: Is Raul an ex-police officer?

ELISABETH WATERS: Yes.

MR. DOLAN: Did Raul give any advice as to how to handle the situation?

ELISABETH WATERS: When I found out that Walter really had molested Kenny, and I wanted to go running straight down and tell Officer Harris everything I knew; Raul told me to wait until she got to me and not impede the flow of her investigation, and that's why I kept the journal for her.

MR. DOLAN: Did you talk to Camille at all on the day that you heard that Walter was molesting– may be molesting Kenny?

MR. BURESH: Without disclosing any content of any conversation with Camille.

ELISABETH WATERS: I'm sorry, did I talk to Camille when?

MR. DOLAN: LeGrand, on the day that you were informed that Moira had blown the whistle on Walter?

ELISABETH WATERS: No.

MR. DOLAN: Did you ever talk to her at any time between the time that you were informed that Walter might be molesting Kenny and the time that you talked to the police?

MR. BURESH: Again, without divulging the content of any communications.

ELISABETH WATERS: I'm just trying to remember the timeline. Yes, I did, because by that time Marion was back and filing for divorce.

MR. DOLAN: Okay. Is it your understanding that Marion was filing for divorce before you spoke to the police?

ELISABETH WATERS: Yes.

MR. DOLAN: Did anyone instruct you that you should keep diaries during that time period?

ELISABETH WATERS: No.

MR. DOLAN: Did anyone review those diaries prior to your handing them to the police?

ELISABETH WATERS: No.

MR. DOLAN: Did you show them to Raul?

ELISABETH WATERS: I don't believe so. I might have, but I don't remember that I did.

MR. DOLAN: Did you show them to your lawyer?

MR. BURESH: Objection, calls for attorney/client communication.

MR. DOLAN: Well, she said she didn't prepare them at the request of her attorney or for her attorney. I'm just asking if she showed it to her attorney; that's all I want to know.

MR. DOLAN: Did you show them?

MR. BURESH: Then it becomes an attorney/client communication, so don't answer the question.

MR. DOLAN: Did you show them to anybody prior to showing them to the police?

MR. BURESH: Other than an attorney.

ELISABETH WATERS: To the best of my recollection, no.

MR. DOLAN: When did you first speak with the police?

ELISABETH WATERS: I don't remember the exact date. I will have to look at the– where is it? Here it is. October 20th, 1989.

MR. DOLAN: What page are you looking at?

MR. BURESH: They don't have page numbers.

ELISABETH WATERS: It's the third from the end of the police report.

MR. DOLAN: Thank you. Did you, at that time, give information to Officer Harris on 10/20/89?

ELISABETH WATERS: Yes.

MR. DOLAN: Where did you meet with Officer Harris?

ELISABETH WATERS: In her office at the police station.

MR. DOLAN: Did you give Officer Harris any documents at that time?

ELISABETH WATERS: Yes, the journal that I wrote that is appended.

MR. DOLAN: Did you also give her forms from the Veterans Administration?

ELISABETH WATERS: Yes.

MR. DOLAN: Did you understand that those forms indicated that Walter had a preference for young boys?

ELISABETH WATERS: No.

MR. DOLAN: Had you ever seen those documents prior to the date that Ken Smith had been molested?

ELISABETH WATERS: I don't know when Ken Smith was molested.

MR. DOLAN: The date that the molestation of Ken Smith was reported, had you seen those documents prior to the date that Ken Smith had been reported as being molested?

ELISABETH WATERS: To the best of my recollection, we got that packet of documents from the V.A. in April of '89.

MR. DOLAN: Do you know why you got them in April of '89?

ELISABETH WATERS: I was doing genealogical research.

MR. DOLAN: And when you got them in April of '89, did you read them?

ELISABETH WATERS: Yes, some of them, yeah, I certainly started reading them.

MR. DOLAN: Did you, in April of '89 when you read those, did you have any impression as to whether or not Walter Breen had expressed a preference for young men in those documents?

ELISABETH WATERS: No, I did not.

MR. DOLAN: Did anybody else read those documents between April of '89 and the time that Kenny Smith's molestation was reported?

MR. BURESH: To your knowledge.

ELISABETH WATERS: I think Moira might have.

MR. BURESH: I don't want you to you guess or speculate.

ELISABETH WATERS: Sorry.

MR. BURESH: Please, I know you're trying to be helpful.

MR. DOLAN: If you have any reason to believe, though, I'm entitled to know.

MR. BURESH: That's right, of course.

MR. DOLAN: If you do think, if you're not guessing or speculating.

ELISABETH WATERS: I think Moira did because I was doing the genealogy for her.

MR. DOLAN: You provided him with some documents at that time; is that correct?

ELISABETH WATERS: Who?

MR. DOLAN: Her, Officer Harris, some documents marked "Personal journal"?

ELISABETH WATERS: Yes.

MR. DOLAN: Do you know how many pages of documents you provided of your personal journal to Officer Harris?

MR. DOLAN: Do you have clean copies?

MR. BURESH: The answer is, no, I do not have. Well, wait a minute. Yeah, I think I do.

ELISABETH WATERS: Nine pages.

MR. DOLAN: Can we use that?

ELISABETH WATERS: And you can tell when I provided them to her because they're signed and dated.

MR. DOLAN: Sure.

MR. BURESH: You have got what I sent you, the police report?

MR. DOLAN: I have them. I just—

MR. BURESH: Did you mark the other copy, the one I just sent you?

MR. DOLAN: Last night I may have marked these up, but I know I have a clean copy. It's just a matter of—

MR. BURESH: I'm going to give you what I have. I've got a clean copy.

MR. DOLAN: I'll make a copy and give it back to you.

MR. BURESH: How many pages, nine pages?

ELISABETH WATERS: Nine pages.

MR. BURESH: This one is marked, I mean, everything is clean except for the one page. Let me see if I can get you that one clean page.

ELISABETH WATERS: What page is it?

MR. BURESH: It would be— or here's a clean set.

MR. DOLAN: Thanks. Mark this as Plaintiff's next in order, which would be Plaintiff's 7.

MS. DURRELL: You said there's nine pages of it?

ELISABETH WATERS: I think so. (Whereupon, Plaintiff's Exhibit No. 7 was marked for identification.)

MR. DOLAN: I'm going to show you a group Exhibit that's been marked as Plaintiff's No. 7. It's a nine-page document. I would like you to look at the first page marked 10/5/89. Did you ever keep any personal journals of any type whatsoever prior to 10/5/89?

ELISABETH WATERS: No, I told you that right before lunch, remember?

MR. DOLAN: I sometimes re-ask questions to make sure I've got a clear answer on this.

MS. DURRELL: That's the document I don't have, 10/5/89.

MR. DOLAN: Did you ever keep any notes other than these personal journals regarding the events surrounding the alleged molestation of Ken Smith?

ELISABETH WATERS: No.

MS. DURRELL: This is 10/20/89. It's here, sorry.

MR. DOLAN: Was there anyone else present with you when you spoke to the police on 10/20/89?

ELISABETH WATERS: No.

MR. DOLAN: I may have asked you this; did anyone edit these journal entries before you gave them to the police?

ELISABETH WATERS: No, can't you see the typos still in them.

MR. DOLAN: About the fourth line down you write– the third line down. "I thought she was being hysterical—after all, God knows she has plenty of reasons to be angry with Walter." What did you mean by ", God knows she has plenty of reasons to be angry with Walter"?

ELISABETH WATERS: Walter always preferred boys to girls. He always favored Patrick over Moira. He favored Moira's boyfriends over Moira. I think she resented that he didn't love her because she was a girl.

MR. DOLAN: Okay. So prior to Kenny Smith being molested, did you have any understanding that Walter favored Moira's boyfriends over Moira?

ELISABETH WATERS: Moira– Walter favored any boy over Moira. Walter didn't like girls.

MR. DOLAN: You indicate in the next paragraph, "Sure, Walter was acting weird, but Walter always acts weird." What did you mean by, "Walter was acting weird– Sure, Walter was acting weird"?

ELISABETH WATERS: Walter generally acted paranoid, nervous, twitchy, suspicious, and he was acting that way.

MR. DOLAN: Anything else?

ELISABETH WATERS: No, I think that about covers it.

MR. DOLAN: Did you think that any of Walter's interactions with children were geared in the sense that you have used the word "weird" here before– strike that. Did you think any of Walter interactions with young boys were "weird"?

ELISABETH WATERS: No.

MR. DOLAN: You indicate here, "And I certainly didn't think Walter was stupid enough to molest a child—especially in front of Moira." What did you mean by that?

ELISABETH WATERS: Well–

MR. BURESH: Other than what it says. You want her to paraphrase it?

MR. DOLAN: Sure, what was she thinking when she wrote that?

MR. BURESH: If you recall.

ELISABETH WATERS: Well, aside from the idea that I certainly didn't think Walter was that immoral, on top of that, I didn't think he was that stupid. I mean, he must have known that Moira was going to object.

MR. DOLAN: Down in the later paragraph there you indicate, "I don't think he wanted to hurt Kenny—I think he just thinks that laws against sex with children are designed to prevent children from having any fun." When did you come to the understanding that—or the belief that Walter thinks that laws against sex with children are designed to prevent children from having any fun?

ELISABETH WATERS: I think it was probably listening to one of his arguments with Marion over NAMBLA. And by the way, hyphen, hyphen is a dash. It's just the way it's typed.

MR. DOLAN: When did these arguments over NAMBLA occur?

ELISABETH WATERS: Over the course of the '80s.

MR. DOLAN: Tell me–

ELISABETH WATERS: I think there was one around '87 because when I was looking for stuff for Officer Harris, I found a canceled check to NAMBLA that looked like it might have been for a book or something, so he had gotten a book from NAMBLA, and if Marion had seen it, that would have sparked an argument.

MR. DOLAN: Can you recall what transpired in the argument where you heard Walter saying to her something that led you to believe that the laws against having sex with children are designed to prevent children from having any fun?

ELISABETH WATERS: He just seemed to feel that the laws restricting children's behavior were an infringement of children's rights.

MR. DOLAN: When you say "children's behavior," are you talking about children's sexual behavior?

ELISABETH WATERS: Children's sexual behavior, children's ability to take drugs, children's ability to drive cars—I mean, Walter was a nut.

MR. DOLAN: And you knew this back in 1987 that he held these beliefs; is that correct?

ELISABETH WATERS: Yes, I believe so.

MR. DOLAN: Did you hear about– and Marion Zimmer Bradley heard Walter expressing these beliefs back in 1987 as well; is that correct?

ELISABETH WATERS: I believe so, yes.

MR. DOLAN: And, indeed, she debated these beliefs with him, according to your testimony, right?

ELISABETH WATERS: She strongly disagreed, yes.

MR. DOLAN: And did he strongly advocate those positions in those arguments with her?

ELISABETH WATERS: No, any time she strongly disagreed with him, he shut up and went away.

MR. DOLAN: After learning that he held these beliefs in 1987, did you do anything to remove him from the premises that you were renting to him?

MR. BURESH: Asked and answered.

MR. DOLAN: I have never asked this. This just came up now, Scott. I never even knew about this before.

MR. BURESH: Didn't you ask her whether she ever took steps to remove him from the premises at any time?

MR. DOLAN: It's a different question. You can't block this line of questioning. If you do, I will move for the judge—you're obstructing me. I am asking her a whole series of separate questions on something that just came up. If you're going to say asked and answered, this is really questionable as to good faith. I'll fight this one to the end.

MR. BURESH: If the witness has testified that she never took steps to remove him from the premises at any time, then it's redundant to ask her that same question in light of any other event.

MR. DOLAN: I am allowed to ask questions the way I want to ask them, Scott, not the way you want them asked, or if I ask a question, it doesn't forestall me from asking a different question later on. That is just cross-examination, and you know that, and I know that.

MR. BURESH: It's badgering the witness by asking the same question over and over.

MR. DOLAN: Are you instructing her not to answer?

MR. BURESH: Yes.

MR. DOLAN: Please mark that. We are going to go to the mat on that one. (Whereupon, the previous question was marked for the record.)

MR. BURESH: Let me ask the witness a question. Did you ever take steps at any time to remove Walter from the Fulton Street property?

ELISABETH WATERS: No.

MR. BURESH: Okay.

MR. DOLAN: Did it concern you that a man who advocated beliefs that laws against sex with children were designed to prevent them from having fun was living in your property?

ELISABETH WATERS: I felt there is– I felt, and still feel, that there is a difference between belief and behavior. I did not necessarily equate the one with the other, so, no, it did not concern me. Walter expressed a lot of crazy beliefs.

MR. DOLAN: Did you know, around that time in 1987, that Walter also believed children should be allowed to have drugs?

ELISABETH WATERS: I think you mean 1987.

MR. DOLAN: I did say 1987, didn't I?

ELISABETH WATERS: I thought you said 1997. Yeah, I think I did.

MR. DOLAN: Okay. Did it concern you that a man who thought that children should be allowed to have drugs was living on your premises?

ELISABETH WATERS: I didn't think making him move would change his views.

MR. DOLAN: Okay. Did you do anything to try to make him change his views?

ELISABETH WATERS: I told him I thought he was an idiot.

MR. DOLAN: But you continued to allow him to live on your premises, correct?

ELISABETH WATERS: Berkeley–

MR. BURESH: Objection, argumentative.

MR. DOLAN: Are you instructing her not to answer? (Discussion off the record.)

ELISABETH WATERS: Berkeley has very strict eviction laws. You can't evict someone just on their beliefs, or their personal beliefs, if he was not acting on them. I would actually have to prove that he was dealing drugs on the property in order to evict them.

MR. DOLAN: Do you ever undertake any investigation to find out whether he was giving drugs to children at that time?

ELISABETH WATERS: No.

MR. DOLAN: Did you ever undertake any investigation to find out whether he was acting out his beliefs that children should not be denied the opportunity to have sex?

ELISABETH WATERS: I believed he was impotent. I assumed he was not.

MR. DOLAN: Did you undertake any investigation to find out whether he was acting out those beliefs on your property?

ELISABETH WATERS: No.

MR. DOLAN: At any time prior to the molestation of Kenny Smith in 1989, did you undertake any investigation to find out whether Walter Breen was acting out his belief regarding sex with children on your property?

ELISABETH WATERS: No.

MR. DOLAN: Could you please refer to your 10/8/89 entry. Before we go there, let me just ask you this: The nine pages that are included as Plaintiff's 7, did you author those?

ELISABETH WATERS: Yes.

MR. DOLAN: Are those true and correct copies of the documents that you authored and surrendered to the police?

ELISABETH WATERS: Yes.

MR. DOLAN: Let's turn to 10/8/89.

ELISABETH WATERS: Uh-hum.

MR. DOLAN: On 10/8/89, were you satisfied beyond any reasonable doubt that Walter was guilty of molesting Ken Smith?

ELISABETH WATERS: Yes.

MR. DOLAN: And at that point you– did you take any steps to remove him from your premises?

MR. BURESH: Objection. Instruct the witness not to answer.

MR. DOLAN: On what basis?

MR. BURESH: Asked and answered, argumentative, badgering the witness.

MR. DOLAN: Please mark it. (Whereupon, the previous question was marked for the record.)

MR. DOLAN: Do you see here where you say, "If it can all be sorted out quietly, that's fine with me– "; what did you mean by, "If it can all be sorted out quietly"?

ELISABETH WATERS: If Walter can plead guilty without Kenny having to testify.

MR. DOLAN: You indicate here, "God knows, enough people have been hurt already." Who were you referring to when you said enough people?

ELISABETH WATERS: Kenny, Moira, me, Mary Mason—Marion, who was going to be as soon as she found out—Patrick, and there's probably others, but those are the ones that come to mind immediately.

MR. DOLAN: Did you tell Anodea, Philip and Phyllis not to leave their children with Walter unchaperoned?

ELISABETH WATERS: Anodea, yes.

MR. DOLAN: Did you tell them that?

ELISABETH WATERS: Yes.

MR. DOLAN: Who is Anodea?

ELISABETH WATERS: Anodea is a friend of mine, and she and Philip have a son together.

MR. DOLAN: What is Philip's last name?

ELISABETH WATERS: Wayne.

MR. DOLAN: Is that the same Philip that was involved in the group experience we referenced earlier?

ELISABETH WATERS: Yes.

MR. DOLAN: Prior to 10/8/89, have you ever warned them about leaving their child alone with Walter?

ELISABETH WATERS: Not with Walter, but I did warn them about leaving their child alone with another child molester.

MR. DOLAN: Who was that?

ELISABETH WATERS: His name was Gary. I forgot his last name. I found out in 1985 that he was a convicted child molester, and Anodea had been dating him, so I talked to Anodea and Philip about it then.

MR. DOLAN: Was this fellow a friend of Walter's?

ELISABETH WATERS: No, Walter didn't know him, as far as I know.

MR. DOLAN: Who was Phyllis?

ELISABETH WATERS: Phyllis Nelson is a friend of the family. She and Debra and Richard Wheeler lived– at that time lived together, and they had two children, so basically I just called everybody in the immediate circle who had children.

MR. DOLAN: Did any of these people say that they thought Walter may have molested their children?

ELISABETH WATERS: No.

MR. DOLAN: Where do Anodea and Philip live?

ELISABETH WATERS: Anodea lives in Sebastopol, I think, and Philip, I think, is in Fremont.

MR. DOLAN: What is Anodea's last name now?

ELISABETH WATERS: Judith.

MR. DOLAN: And Philip lives where, I'm sorry?

ELISABETH WATERS: I think it's in Fremont.

MR. DOLAN: What was the name of their child?

ELISABETH WATERS: Alex.

MR. DOLAN: Where does Alex live?

ELISABETH WATERS: With Anodea.

MR. DOLAN: And who is Phyllis?

ELISABETH WATERS: Phyllis Nelson. I just told you.

MR. DOLAN: Where does she live?

ELISABETH WATERS: They were living together in a house in Mar Vista.

MR. DOLAN: Do you know where in Mar Vista?

ELISABETH WATERS: Walgrove Avenue. And I understand that she's recently gotten a condominium and moved out, but I don't know where.

MR. DOLAN: What was their child's name?

ELISABETH WATERS: They have two daughters, Sarah and Rose.

MR. DOLAN: Do you know where they live?

ELISABETH WATERS: Sarah, I believe, is at Reed College in Oregon, and Rose is still home with her mother.

MR. DOLAN: Did you think Walter was molesting Sterling 10 years prior to 10/8/89?

ELISABETH WATERS: No.

MR. DOLAN: Did you ever go to Marion and say you thought that Walter was molesting Sterling?

ELISABETH WATERS: We went over all this this morning. Yes, I talked to Marion after I found the letter to Dr. Morin, and she said Walter was impotent, so at that point I naturally believed that Walter was not molesting Sterling, and I talked to Sterling later and Sterling–

MR. BURESH: It's okay. We did talk about it this morning.

MR. DOLAN: You indicate here at the end of this, "I'm really angry about all of this; I feel I've been used to help cover up something I would (underlined) never willfully have countenanced." What did you mean that you felt that you had been used to cover up something?

ELISABETH WATERS: Well, as you have no doubt heard, despite the fact that I was brought up to believe that sex belongs within the bounds of holy matrimony, when I moved out to Berkeley I bought into "the sex is okay as a recreational activity between consenting adults lifestyle," and I outgrew that. By 1985 people were calling me a prude and complaining that I was too straightlaced. So, I had been cleaning up my act and my reputation, and I have been celibate for years at this point, and I had been working very hard to become the kind of human being I could be proud of again, and now here is a member of my extended family doing something so horrendously horrible, and I felt like it was damaging to my reputation.

MR. DOLAN: How were you used to help cover up something?

MR. BURESH: Other than what she has already testified to?

MR. DOLAN: I didn't hear anything about that.

MR. BURESH: Well, in your opinion, I'm sure.

MR. DOLAN: How were you used to help cover up something other than what you have testified to already?

ELISABETH WATERS: Other than that, I wasn't.

MR. DOLAN: How does that, in your mind, constitute a cover-up?

ELISABETH WATERS: At the time I wrote this I was obviously very upset. I was feeling sick, horrified, disgusted, homicidal. I wanted to kill Walter, and I felt that he had used our association, tenuous as it was, as a cloak for his activities. I was overreacting.

MR. DOLAN: You indicate here, and earlier in that paragraph, that Marion said he has been impotent since Moira was two-years old?

ELISABETH WATERS: Uh-hum.

MR. DOLAN: "I didn't think he was gay; I thought he was celibate. Why shouldn't I think that?" And then several lines down you say that you feel you have been used to help cover up something. Did you believe that Marion had deliberately deceived you as to Walter being impotent?

ELISABETH WATERS: Absolutely not. She believed that, no question.

MR. DOLAN: Did you believe that Marion ever withheld any information from you regarding Walter's sexual activity with children?

ELISABETH WATERS: Well, I don't believe she described to me every accusation that was ever made because I don't imagine she considered most of them relevant.

MR. DOLAN: The question was–

ELISABETH WATERS: Marion and I generally did not discuss Walter's sex life. Why should we have?

MR. BURESH: Listen to the question.

MR. DOLAN: The question is, do you think that Marion withheld information from you regarding accusations that Walter had molested children?

MR. BURESH: I have got to object on the basis that it's uncertain as to what the word "withheld" means, as opposed– it's a failure to disclose or withholding of information.

MR. DOLAN: Do you think Marion knew about other accusations of child molestation about Walter that she hadn't shared with you as of 10/8/89?

ELISABETH WATERS: Yes.

MR. DOLAN: Do you have any understanding, as you sit here today, about how many episodes or accusations against Walter Marion had known about that she had not shared with you as of 10/8/89?

ELISABETH WATERS: No, I don't know for sure that she did not tell me about some. I simply assumed that in the– let's see, 15 years that she knew him before I knew him, she probably heard a few.

MR. DOLAN: Okay. Let's go to 10/9/89. It says, "Marion always said she'd divorce Walter if he did this again." Did you write that?

ELISABETH WATERS: Yes.

MR. DOLAN: Had Marion told you that she would divorce Walter if he did this again?

ELISABETH WATERS: When she was sitting in the car she said, "That does it. I always said I would divorce him if he did this again."

MR. DOLAN: Now, this was a statement made verbatim to you from Marion Zimmer Bradley, correct?

ELISABETH WATERS: To the best of my recollection, yes.

MR. DOLAN: Do you know who she had always made that statement to before, as she described it?

ELISABETH WATERS: I assumed either to herself or to Walter.

MR. DOLAN: Did you ask her anything like, "Wait, you mean you had told him if he did this again you would divorce him?"

ELISABETH WATERS: No, I did not ask her. She was in the middle of a rant, I mean, he had– we had just told her her husband was a child molester. She was furious. She was shouting.

MR. DOLAN: And you indicated in 10/8/89 that she seemed to think that he had molested both [Glenn] and [other name]; is that correct?

ELISABETH WATERS: I'm sorry, where are we?

MR. DOLAN: 10/9/89, next sentence?

ELISABETH WATERS: Yes.

MR. DOLAN: You indicate in the next part of that sentence that she was rather startled when you told her about the letter to Dr. Morin about Sterling; hadn't you already discussed this with her at the time that you read the letter?

ELISABETH WATERS: Yes.

MR. DOLAN: Do you have any understanding as to why she appeared to be "rather startled"?

ELISABETH WATERS: Probably because ten years had intervened between the two incidents. Not everybody remembers things accurately for 10 years.

MR. DOLAN: We are going to come back to some of these things. I just want to cover some of them before we break today. Let's turn to 10/14/89. The last paragraph you say, "Still, when I think of the things for the past 10 years we simply accepted as parts of Walter's normal behavior, I want to kill myself." What "things" were you referring to?

ELISABETH WATERS: His habit of sitting around with children on his lap at conventions; his hanging around with his kids and their friends; his having friends who were teenage boys. A lot of his friends were like in the 15- to 22-year-old range.

MR. DOLAN: Any other things?

ELISABETH WATERS: No, I think that's about it.

MR. DOLAN: How about any activity of drugs, were those included in those things that you were thinking of that he had done in the past ten years that you accepted as part of his normal behavior?

ELISABETH WATERS: I wasn't thinking about drugs at the time I wrote this.

MR. DOLAN: Did you think it was awkward that most of Walter's friends were between the ages of 15 and 22?

MR. BURESH: Objection, vague. I don't know what you mean by the word "awkward."

MR. DOLAN: Do you think it was unusual, different, strange, bizarre, any of those?

ELISABETH WATERS: Well, it would be unusual for a normal man, but Walter had the emotional maturity of the average 15 year old, so it seemed to me that he was seeking friends of his emotional age.

MR. DOLAN: Were you ever concerned that Walter was sexually attracted to any of these boys between the ages of 15 and 22?

ELISABETH WATERS: No, I thought he was impotent.

MR. DOLAN: Well, I'm not asking whether he was sexually involved, but whether he was sexually attracted to them?

ELISABETH WATERS: If you're impotent, aren't you not sexually attracted?

MR. DOLAN: It doesn't appear to be in Walter's case, but, I mean, you're asking my opinion now, and I don't think you want that. It appears that he was very active.

ELISABETH WATERS: It was my belief that if you are impotent, you're not sexually attracted.

MR. BURESH: Off the record. (Discussion off the record.)

MR. DOLAN: Back on, please.

MR. DOLAN: Did you write in here this next part about someone saying they wouldn't let Ian stay overnight unless you or Marion were there because they had heard Ian when he was sitting on Walter's lap on the stairs saying, "Stop it. That tickles. Don't touch me there"?

ELISABETH WATERS: Yes, I wrote that.

MR. DOLAN: What were you referring to about that?

ELISABETH WATERS: To the best of my recollection now, what I was doing was confusing together was Tracy saying that Walter wasn't adult enough to take care of children unsupervised and Moira's telling me that Tracy had said that she had heard Ian saying, "Don't touch me there. That tickles."

MR. DOLAN: So it's your testimony that you were confusing something Moira said to you about something that you had heard regarding Ian not being able to stay there overnight unless you were there because Walter was too immature; is that correct?

ELISABETH WATERS: My testimony is–

MR. BURESH: Before you testify, I want to hear the answer read back, please. (Whereupon, the record was read by the reporter.)

MR. DOLAN: Look to 10/16/89. Do you see where you say, "The divorce is going to make a lot of extra work, but it beats losing the house in a messy lawsuit." At the end of the first second full paragraph?

ELISABETH WATERS: Yes.

MR. DOLAN: Did someone tell you that there was a potential that you could lose the house in a messy lawsuit?

ELISABETH WATERS: No.

MR. DOLAN: Did you believe that if there was a lawsuit you might lose the house in a messy lawsuit?

ELISABETH WATERS: No. It's– we were sensitive about losing the house because of Walter's activity because Marion had already lost one house because of Walter's failure to pay bills. I would find them under the desk blotter and he would say he paid them, and they lost the house, and Marion never forgave him for that, so she was hypersensitive on the subject.

MR. DOLAN: So did you have any concerns when you wrote this that Walter's molestation of children might lead to losing the house in a messy lawsuit?

ELISABETH WATERS: I suppose I thought it was a possibility.

MR. DOLAN: I asked you earlier whether that was one of the reasons why– that prompted the divorce. Do you wish to at all change your testimony after reading this document?

ELISABETH WATERS: I don't know exactly why Marion divorced him. It was her decision and not mine. My impression was that she was just totally furious with him.

MR. DOLAN: Were you present when Marion talked to Camille about her divorce?

MS. DURRELL: I think that's been asked and answered.

MR. DOLAN: I don't think so.

MR. BURESH: It has. Go ahead. I'll object. Asked and answered. Go ahead and answer.

MR. DOLAN: Were you in the room when they were talking about it?

ELISABETH WATERS: Some of the time, yes.

MR. DOLAN: Was the issue of Marion's liability because of Walter's activities discussed during that time that they were talking about the divorce?

MR. BURESH: I'll object on the basis of the attorney-client privilege. I will instruct the witness not to answer.

MR. DOLAN: She wasn't getting a divorce. She was sitting there in the room with them. She wasn't the client. There's no– that's totally waived.

MR. BURESH: Camille was the lawyer for the Marion Zimmer Bradley Enterprises.

ELISABETH WATERS: Camille actually was my lawyer as well.

MR. BURESH: She's her lawyer as well.

MR. DOLAN: Were you getting divorced?

ELISABETH WATERS: No.

MR. DOLAN: Were you there seeking information about the divorce?

ELISABETH WATERS: No.

MR. DOLAN: With you there seeking information about Marion's divorce?

ELISABETH WATERS: I was there lending Marion moral support, I guess.

MR. DOLAN: So you weren't there seeking legal advice that day were you, personally?

ELISABETH WATERS: As Marion's secretary, I was.

MR. DOLAN: But you personally weren't sitting there looking for legal advice for your own person, Elisabeth Waters, that day when you were in Camille LeGrand's office, were you?

ELISABETH WATERS: No.

MR. DOLAN: What did Marion and Camille LeGrand talk about regarding Walter's behavior as it related to the divorce?

MR. BURESH: Same objection, same instruction. I will research this issue in the intervening days between this deposition and the next deposition. I still think it's attorney/client privilege.

MR. DOLAN: It's not.

MR. BURESH: I understand.

MR. DOLAN: She's sitting there just like you or somebody else sitting there. Mark it, please. (Whereupon, the previous question was marked for the record.)

MR. DOLAN: You state that your mother was surprised that Marion was going to divorce Walter. Do you recall having conversations with your mother about this?

ELISABETH WATERS: Uh-hum.

MR. DOLAN: Is your mother still alive?

ELISABETH WATERS: Yes.

MR. DOLAN: She lives now in Stamford?

ELISABETH WATERS: Yes.

MR. DOLAN: On Cascade Road?

ELISABETH WATERS: Yes, with my father.

MR. DOLAN: What is her name?

ELISABETH WATERS: Elaine.

MR. DOLAN: Elaine Waters?

ELISABETH WATERS: Yes.

MR. DOLAN: And what is their address on Cascade Road?

ELISABETH WATERS: 379.

MR. DOLAN: I may get a trip home out of this.

ELISABETH WATERS: Are you planning on going to question my parents?

MR. BURESH: We'll fly them out here.

MR. DOLAN: Not Connecticut.

MR. DOLAN: You indicate in the next sentence, "What did she expect—that Marion was going to say, 'You molested a 12 year old; that's nice dear. What would you like for dinner?'" You wrote that, correct?

ELISABETH WATERS: Yes.

MR. DOLAN: Did you tell your mother that Marion was divorcing Walter because he molested a 12-year-old boy?

ELISABETH WATERS: Yes.

MR. DOLAN: Who is the Beth that's referenced in this letter?

ELISABETH WATERS: Elizabeth Rousseau.

MR. DOLAN: There's some discussion in the last paragraph about, "And Beth said something about Ian today—and I can't remember exactly what it was. (I guess I'm still trying to block some of this), but it sounded like Officer Harris should talk to him. And she also now thinks it wasn't Kenny in the hot tub with Walter—it was little Sean." What episode are you talking about in the hot tub?

ELISABETH WATERS: Beth and her boyfriend were in the hot tub with Walter and some kid one night.

MR. DOLAN: Do you know approximately when?

ELISABETH WATERS: Nope.

MR. DOLAN: Was it before or after the report of the molestation of Ken Smith?

ELISABETH WATERS: Before.

MR. DOLAN: Did Beth ever tell you that prior to 10/16/89, this being in the hot tub with Walter and a young boy?

ELISABETH WATERS: It was prior to 10/16/89, but I think it was after– I think it was sometime in September or October when we were talking about Walter's behavior.

MR. DOLAN: What do you recall Beth telling you about this episode of a young boy being in the hot tub with Walter?

ELISABETH WATERS: That she and her boyfriend and Walter and some kid were in the hot tub and Walter was saying to the kid, "Feel how good the jets feel on your skin."

MR. DOLAN: Was he saying, "See how good the jets feel on your skin," or "Feel how good they feel on your legs"? Do you recall if that was the comment?

ELISABETH WATERS: Since I wasn't there and I don't remember exactly what Beth said.

MR. DOLAN: Do you recall anything else of Beth's description of what happened in the hot tub?

ELISABETH WATERS: No, just that she said it made her uneasy.

MR. DOLAN: Did Beth tell you that at any time prior to Walter's identification of– strike that. Did Beth tell you any of this prior to Moira reporting Walter to the police in 1989?

ELISABETH WATERS: No, it was after.

MR. DOLAN: Beth was a resident of the house on Prince Street; is that correct?

ELISABETH WATERS: Yes.

MR. DOLAN: This hot tub you're referring to is on Prince Street?

ELISABETH WATERS: Yes.

MR. DOLAN: Did you ever investigate any further to find out if anybody was molested in that hot tub by Walter? Please let the record reflect that the witness is laughing.

ELISABETH WATERS: I'm sorry, it's just that you haven't seen the property and the hot tub. The hot tub is fully visible right as you come in the back gate, from the porch of the office, from the kitchen, from the living room, from the room that, I think, was then Marion's office and is now Marion's bedroom. Philip and I were making out in the hot tub one day, and we got caught, I mean, there's no expectation of privacy in that hot tub. It's not a good place to molest anybody.

MR. DOLAN: Okay. My question was, did you ever undertake any investigation to find out whether or not Walter had ever molested either Sean or Kenny in that hot tub?

ELISABETH WATERS: No, because I thought the idea was totally silly.

MR. DOLAN: Did you think that Beth was lying to you?

ELISABETH WATERS: No.

MR. DOLAN: Then why did you think it was silly?

ELISABETH WATERS: There was a difference between sitting in a hot tub saying, "see how good the water feels" and sexually molesting somebody.

MR. DOLAN: Beth indicated it made her uncomfortable, correct?

ELISABETH WATERS: Yes.

MR. DOLAN: Did you think Beth was a prude?

ELISABETH WATERS: I don't know that I ever thought about it much one way or the other.

MR. DOLAN: Who was Beth's boyfriend?

ELISABETH WATERS: I don't remember.

MR. DOLAN: To your knowledge was Walter ever in the hot tub with any other young children other than this child identified by Beth?

MR. BURESH: Other than what she has already testified to.

MR. DOLAN: We went over that this morning.

MR. DOLAN: Well now, this morning she said she was unaware of him ever being in the hot tub with any young children. Now we've seen a document which shows he was in the hot tub.

MR. BURESH: Well, you're misstating her testimony.

ELISABETH WATERS: Yeah, I did so say that he was in the hot tub with young children.

MR. DOLAN: You said somebody's baby. Philip's baby?

ELISABETH WATERS: Alex, and Moira, and Patrick, and Fiona, and Eric. There's a whole bunch of people who came over and used the hot tub.

MR. DOLAN: Was it the policy to use the hot tub generally naked?

ELISABETH WATERS: Grown-ups were usually naked. A lot of the kids who were going through the self-conscious stage wore bathing suits. The rule was you had to be sure to wash the soap out of the bathing suit before you got in the hot tub so you didn't clog the filter.

MR. DOLAN: Did you ever hear Marion tell her children that nudity was an appropriate method of presentation around the house?

ELISABETH WATERS: No, by the time I moved out there, most people wore clothes most of the time.

MR. DOLAN: Do you ever talk to Jane Reynolds Conger, Ph.D. regarding Moira's condition?

ELISABETH WATERS: No.

MR. DOLAN: Did you ever talk to a psychiatrist regarding her condition?

ELISABETH WATERS: I spoke briefly to Joan Sandberg when I was visiting Moira at the mental hospital down in southern California, but I don't recall that we were really discussing Moira's condition much.

MR. DOLAN: Did you ultimately tell Walter if he didn't resign from his position in Marion Zimmer Bradley Enterprises that you were going to terminate him?

ELISABETH WATERS: Yes, for just cause, because at that point he was in jail and could no longer work for us.

MR. BURESH: It's after 5:00 now. I would like to adjourn.

MR. DOLAN: Okay. (Whereupon, the deposition concluded at 5:03 p.m.)

ELISABETH WATERS

(STATE OF CALIFORNIA)

(COUNTY OF SAN FRANCISCO)

I, Karla Shallenberger, do hereby certify: That I am a Certified Shorthand Reporter, License No. 10752 of the State of California; that I was duly licensed Shorthand Reporter; That on the 16th day of October, 1997 I fully, truly and correctly took down in shorthand writing all of the proceedings had and all of the testimony given in said matter; That I thereafter truly, fully and correctly transcribed the same into typewriting, and that the foregoing pages, 1 through 228 inclusive, are a full, true and correct transcript of my said notes taken at the time and place therein stated.

IN WITNESS WHEREOF, I have hereunto set my hand this 9th day of November 1997.

Karla Shallenberger

Certified Shorthand Reporter License No. 10752 SHALLENBERGER REPORTING SER-VICES - (415) 771-1988

Appendix D: Walter's Annotated Bibliography

**From "An Annotated Bibliography of
the Numismatic Writings of Walter H. Breen", by David Fanning**

By David Fanning, edited for length. Used by permission.

- "1795 S-80a: A New, Old Copper Cent," by Dan Demeo, followed by a comment by Walter Breen, *Penny-Wise*, Vol. 25, No. 6 (November 15, 1991; Serial 147), pp. 321–323.
- "1795 Silver Dollar Struck over a 1794 Dollar," *The Metropolitan Numismatic Journal*, Issue 1 (May-June 1961), pp. 2–6.
- "The 1797 NC-7—A New, Unlisted Variety," *Penny-Wise*, Vol. 2, No. 6 (November 15, 1968; Serial 9), pp. 218–219.
- "1797 S-121a: A Legitimate Subvariety," *Penny-Wise*, Vol. 24, No. 2 (March 15, 1990; Serial 137), pp. 61–62.
- "The 1848 Quarter Eagle with CAL," by Richard S. Yeoman, *The Numismatist*, Vol. 66, No. 7 (July 1953), pp. 674–686.
- "The 1856 Flying Eagle Cent," *Rare Coin Review*, No. 11 (June-July 1971), pp. 55–56. Reprinted in *The Numismatist's Bedside Companion*, edited by MR. DOLAN: David Bowers (Wolfeboro, NH: Bowers and Merena Galleries, 1987), pp. 117–121.
- "The 1880 Legal Tenders," *Paper Money*, Vol. 16, No. 3 (May-June 1977; Serial 69), pp. 133–141.
- "The 1922 Type of 1921 Peace Dollar," *The Numismatic Scrapbook Magazine*, Vol. 27, No. 7 (July 1961), pp. 1721–1729.
- "The 1943 Bronze Cents," *The Numismatic Scrapbook Magazine*, Vol. 26, No. 2 (February 1960), pp. 306–310.
- "Additional Comment on St. Patrick Farthings," *The Colonial Newsletter*, Vol. 7, No. 4 (December 1968; Serial 24), p. 233.
- "Additions and Corrections to Glossary," *Penny-Wise*, Vol. 2, No. 3 (May 15, 1968; Serial 6), pp. 75–76.
- "American Coin Symbols," *The Numismatist*, Vol. 67, No. 11 (November 1954), p. 1203.
- "American Coin Type Names: An Essay in Ancestor Worship—or Something," *The Whitman Numismatic Journal*, Vol. 5, No. 1 (January 1968), pp. 32–37; continued in Vol. 5, No. 2 (February 1968), pp. 71–75; Vol. 5, No. 3 (March 1968), pp. 157–161; Vol. 5, No. 4 (April 1968), pp. 217–221; Vol. 5, No. 6 (June 1968), pp. 343–347; Vol. 5, No. 7 (July 1968), pp. 393–398.
- "Anatomy of a Coin Census," *The Numismatic Scrapbook Magazine*, Vol. 29, No. 7 (July 1963), pp. 1921–1929; continued in Vol. 29, No. 8 (August 1963), pp. 2245–2255.
- "Another Postscript to 'Speculations on the New England Stiver,'" *The Colonial Newsletter*, Vol. 16, No. 3 (November 1977; Serial 50), TN-54B, p. 612.
- "An Appeal for Assistance," Letter to the Editor, *The Colonial Newsletter*, Vol. 8, No. 1 (March 1969; Serial 25), TN-13, p. 252.
- "Attribution Shortcuts for 1838 Cents," *Penny-Wise*, Vol. 4, No. 4 (July 15, 1970; Serial 19), pp. 145–147.

- "An Autobiography," *Penny-Wise*, Vol. 12, No. 1 (January 15, 1977; Serial 64), pp. 23–26.
- "The Billon Sous Marques of Canada," *The Whitman Numismatic Journal*, Vol. 2, No. 8 (August 1965), pp. 581–590; continued in Vol. 2, No. 9 (September 1965), pp. 644–653; Vol. 2, No. 10 (October 1965), pp. 752–761.
- "Blundered Dies," *The Whitman Numismatic Journal*, Vol. 2, No. 12 (December 1965), pp. 867–872; continued in Vol. 3, No. 1 (January 1966), pp. 25–29; Vol. 3, No. 4 (April 1966), pp. 259–263; Vol. 3, No. 5 (May 1966), pp. 325–329; Vol. 3, No. 6 (June 1966), pp. 433–438; Vol. 3, No. 7 (July 1966), pp. 483–487.
- Blundered Dies of Colonial and U.S. Coins," *Empire Topics*, No. 2 (July-September 1958), pp. 15–18.
- "Book Review: *A Guide Book of United States Coins*, 1951–2, by Richard S. Yeoman," *The Numismatist*, Vol. 64, No. 4 (April 1951).
- "Book Review: *A Guide Book of United States Coins*, 1952–3, by Richard S. Yeoman," *The Numismatist*, Vol. 65, No. 5 (May 1952), p. 506.
- "Brasher and Bailey: Pioneer New York Coiners, 1787–1792," *Centennial Publication of the American Numismatic Society*, edited by Harald Ingholt (New York: ANS, 1958), pp. 137–145; plate 12.
- "Bristles and Barbs," *Coins*, Vol. 13, No. 7 (July 1966), p. 38.
- "Bristles and Barbs," *Coins*, Vol. 13, No. 8 (August 1966), p. 21.
- "Bristles and Barbs," *Coins*, Vol. 13, No. 9 (September 1966), p. 22.
- "Bristles and Barbs," *Coins*, Vol. 13, No. 10 (October 1966), p. 44.
- "Bristles and Barbs," *Coins*, Vol. 13, No. 11 (November 1966), p. 37.
- "Bristles and Barbs," *Coins*, Vol. 13, No. 12 (December 1966), p. 53.
- "Bristles and Barbs," *Coins*, Vol. 14, No. 1 (January 1967), p. 26.
- "Bristles and Barbs," *Coins*, Vol. 14, No. 2 (February 1967), p. 31.
- "Bristles and Barbs," *Coins*, Vol. 14, No. 3 (March 1967), pp. 62–63.
- "Bristles and Barbs," *Coins*, Vol. 14, No. 4 (April 1967), p. 28.
- "Bristles and Barbs," *Coins*, Vol. 14, No. 5 (May 1967), p. 30.
- "Bristles and Barbs," *Coins*, Vol. 14, No. 6 (June 1967), p. 31.
- "Bristles and Barbs," *Coins*, Vol. 14, No. 7 (July 1967), p. 36.
- "Bristles and Barbs," *Coins*, Vol. 14, No. 8 (August 1967), p. 25.
- "Bristles and Barbs," *Coins*, Vol. 14, No. 9 (September 1967), p. 29.
- "Bristles and Barbs," *Coins*, Vol. 14, No. 10 (October 1967), p. 25.
- "Bristles and Barbs," *Coins*, Vol. 14, No. 11 (November 1967), p. 33.
- "Bristles and Barbs," *Coins*, Vol. 14, No. 12 (December 1967), p. 31.
- "Bristles and Barbs," *Coins*, Vol. 15, No. 1 (January 1968), p. 33.
- "Bristles and Barbs," *Coins*, Vol. 15, No. 2 (February 1968), p. 27.
- "Bristles and Barbs," *Coins*, Vol. 15, No. 3 (March 1968), p. 41.
- "Bristles and Barbs," *Coins*, Vol. 15, No. 4 (April 1968), p. 46.
- "Bristles and Barbs," *Coins*, Vol. 15, No. 5 (May 1968), p. 43.
- "Bristles and Barbs," *Coins*, Vol. 15, No. 6 (June 1968), p. 47.
- "Bristles and Barbs," *Coins*, Vol. 15, No. 7 (July 1968), p. 31.
- "Bristles and Barbs," *Coins*, Vol. 15, No. 8 (August 1968), p. 43.
- "Bristles and Barbs," *Coins*, Vol. 15, No. 9 (September 1968), p. 31.
- "Bristles and Barbs," *Coins*, Vol. 15, No. 10 (October 1968), p. 49.

- "Bristles and Barbs," *Coins*, Vol. 15, No. 11 (November 1968), p. 47.
- "Bristles and Barbs," *Coins*, Vol. 15, No. 12 (December 1968), p. 41.
- "Bristles and Barbs," *Coins*, Vol. 16, No. 1 (January 1969), p. 42.
- "Bristles and Barbs," *Coins*, Vol. 16, No. 2 (February 1969), p. 55.
- "Bristles and Barbs," *Coins*, Vol. 16, No. 3 (March 1969), p. 29.
- "Bristles and Barbs," *Coins*, Vol. 16, No. 4 (April 1969), p. 43.
- "Bristles and Barbs," *Coins*, Vol. 16, No. 5 (May 1969), p. 43.
- "Bristles and Barbs," *Coins*, Vol. 16, No. 6 (June 1969), p. 48.
- "Bristles and Barbs," *Coins*, Vol. 16, No. 8 (August 1969), p. 40.
- "Bristles and Barbs," *Coins*, Vol. 16, No. 9 (September 1969), p. 47.
- "Bristles and Barbs," *Coins*, Vol. 16, No. 11 (November 1969), p. 25.
- "Bristles and Barbs," *Coins*, Vol. 16, No. 12 (December 1969), p. 41.
- "Bristles and Barbs," *Coins*, Vol. 17, No. 1 (January 1970), p. 43.
- "Bristles and Barbs," *Coins*, Vol. 17, No. 2 (February 1970), p. 59.
- "Bristles and Barbs," *Coins*, Vol. 17, No. 8 (August 1970), p. 34.
- "Bristles and Barbs," *Coins*, Vol. 17, No. 9 (September 1970), p. 43.
- "Bristles and Barbs," *Coins*, Vol. 18, No. 3 (March 1971), p. 29.
- "Bristles and Barbs," *Coins*, Vol. 18, No. 4 (April 1971), p. 64.
- "Bristles and Barbs," *Coins*, Vol. 18, No. 5 (May 1971), p. 44.
- "Bristles and Barbs," *Coins*, Vol. 18, No. 6 (June 1971), p. 45.
- "Bristles and Barbs," *Coins*, Vol. 18, No. 7 (July 1971), p. 70.
- "Bristles and Barbs," *Coins*, Vol. 18, No. 8 (August 1971), p. 72.
- "Bristles and Barbs," *Coins*, Vol. 18, No. 9 (September 1971), p. 30.
- "Bristles and Barbs," *Coins*, Vol. 18, No. 10 (October 1971), p. 40.
- "Bristles and Barbs," *Coins*, Vol. 18, No. 11 (November 1971), p. 50.
- "Bristles and Barbs," *Coins*, Vol. 18, No. 12 (December 1971), p. 38.
- "Bristles and Barbs," *Coins*, Vol. 19, No. 1 (January 1972), p. 40.
- "Bristles and Barbs," *Coins*, Vol. 19, No. 2 (February 1972), p. 70.
- "Bristles and Barbs," *Coins*, Vol. 19, No. 3 (March 1972), p. 82.
- "Bristles and Barbs," *Coins*, Vol. 19, No. 4 (April 1972), p. 56.
- "Bristles and Barbs," *Coins*, Vol. 19, No. 5 (May 1972), p. 52.
- "Bristles and Barbs," *Coins*, Vol. 19, No. 6 (June 1972), p. 44.
- "Bristles and Barbs," *Coins*, Vol. 19, No. 7 (July 1972), p. 59.
- "Bristles and Barbs," *Coins*, Vol. 19, No. 8 (August 1972), p. 51.
- "Bristles and Barbs," *Coins*, Vol. 19, No. 9 (September 1972), p. 25.
- "Bristles and Barbs," *Coins*, Vol. 19, No. 10 (October 1972), p. 51.
- "Bristles and Barbs," *Coins*, Vol. 19, No. 11 (November 1972), p. 40.
- "Bristles and Barbs," *Coins*, Vol. 19, No. 12 (December 1972), p. 96.
- "Bristles and Barbs," *Coins*, Vol. 20, No. 1 (January 1973), p. 46.
- "Bristles and Barbs," *Coins*, Vol. 20, No. 2 (February 1973), p. 61.
- "Bristles and Barbs," *Coins*, Vol. 20, No. 3 (March 1973), p. 68.
- "Bristles and Barbs," *Coins*, Vol. 20, No. 4 (April 1973), p. 55.
- "Bristles and Barbs," *Coins*, Vol. 20, No. 5 (May 1973), p. 60.

- "Bristles and Barbs," *Coins*, Vol. 20, No. 6 (June 1973), p. 46.
- "Bristles and Barbs," *Coins*, Vol. 20, No. 7 (July 1973), p. 39.
- "Bristles and Barbs," *Coins*, Vol. 20, No. 8 (August 1973), p. 64.
- "Bristles and Barbs," *Coins*, Vol. 20, No. 9 (September 1973), p. 54.
- "Bristles and Barbs," *Coins*, Vol. 20, No. 10 (October 1973), p. 88.
- "Bristles and Barbs," *Coins*, Vol. 20, No. 11 (November 1973), p. 66.
- "Bristles and Barbs," *Coins*, Vol. 21, No. 1 (January 1974), p. 64.
- "Bristles and Barbs," *Coins*, Vol. 21, No. 2 (February 1974), p. 56.
- "Bristles and Barbs," *Coins*, Vol. 21, No. 3 (March 1974), p. 78.
- "Bristles and Barbs," *Coins*, Vol. 21, No. 4 (April 1974), p. 56.
- "Bristles and Barbs," *Coins*, Vol. 21, No. 5 (May 1974), p. 50.
- "Bristles and Barbs," *Coins*, Vol. 21, No. 6 (June 1974), p. 70.
- "Bristles and Barbs," *Coins*, Vol. 21, No. 7 (July 1974), p. 57.
- "Bristles and Barbs," *Coins*, Vol. 21, No. 8 (August 1974), p. 32.
- "Bristles and Barbs," *Coins*, Vol. 21, No. 9 (September 1974), p. 59.
- "Bristles and Barbs," *Coins*, Vol. 21, No. 10 (October 1974), p. 42.
- "Bristles and Barbs," *Coins*, Vol. 21, No. 11 (November 1974), p. 32.
- "Bristles and Barbs," *Coins*, Vol. 21, No. 12 (December 1974), p. 32.
- "Bristles and Barbs," *Coins*, Vol. 22, No. 1 (January 1975), p. 60.
- "Bristles and Barbs," *Coins*, Vol. 22, No. 2 (February 1975), p. 81.
- "Bristles and Barbs," *Coins*, Vol. 22, No. 3 (March 1975), p. 54.
- "Bristles and Barbs," *Coins*, Vol. 22, No. 4 (April 1975), p. 69.
- "Bristles and Barbs," *Coins*, Vol. 22, No. 5 (May 1975), p. 59.
- "Bristles and Barbs," *Coins*, Vol. 22, No. 6 (June 1975), p. 60.
- "Bristles and Barbs," *Coins*, Vol. 22, No. 7 (July 1975), p. 58.
- "Bristles and Barbs," *Coins*, Vol. 22, No. 8 (August 1975), p. 70.
- "Bristles and Barbs," *Coins*, Vol. 22, No. 9 (September 1975), p. 44.
- "Bristles and Barbs," *Coins*, Vol. 22, No. 10 (October 1975), p. 65.
- "Bristles and Barbs," *Coins*, Vol. 22, No. 11 (November 1975), p. 44.
- "Bristles and Barbs," *Coins*, Vol. 22, No. 12 (December 1975), p. 41.
- "Bristles and Barbs," *Coins*, Vol. 23, No. 1 (January 1976), p. 68.
- "Bristles and Barbs," *Coins*, Vol. 23, No. 2 (February 1976), p. 43.
- "Bristles and Barbs," *Coins*, Vol. 23, No. 3 (March 1976), p. 70.
- "Bristles and Barbs," *Coins*, Vol. 23, No. 4 (April 1976), p. 44.
- "Bristles and Barbs," *Coins*, Vol. 23, No. 5 (May 1976), p. 43.
- "Bristles and Barbs," *Coins*, Vol. 23, No. 6 (June 1976), p. 76.
- "Bristles and Barbs," *Coins*, Vol. 23, No. 7 (July 1976), p. 77.
- "Bristles and Barbs," *Coins*, Vol. 23, No. 8 (August 1976), p. 49.
- "Bristles and Barbs," *Coins*, Vol. 23, No. 9 (September 1976), p. 78.
- "Bristles and Barbs," *Coins*, Vol. 23, No. 10 (October 1976), p. 79.
- "Bristles and Barbs," *Coins*, Vol. 23, No. 11 (November 1976), p. 50.
- "Bristles and Barbs," *Coins*, Vol. 23, No. 12 (December 1976), p. 50.
- "Bristles and Barbs," *Coins*, Vol. 24, No. 1 (January 1977), p. 52.

- "Bristles and Barbs," *Coins*, Vol. 24, No. 2 (February 1977), p. 44.
- "Bristles and Barbs," *Coins*, Vol. 24, No. 3 (March 1977), p. 52.
- "Bristles and Barbs," *Coins*, Vol. 24, No. 4 (April 1977), p. 58.
- "Bristles and Barbs," *Coins*, Vol. 24, No. 5 (May 1977), p. 42.
- "Bristles and Barbs," *Coins*, Vol. 24, No. 6 (June 1977), p. 79.
- "Bristles and Barbs," *Coins*, Vol. 24, No. 7 (July 1977), p. 45.
- "Bristles and Barbs," *Coins*, Vol. 24, No. 8 (August 1977), p. 42.
- "Bristles and Barbs," *Coins*, Vol. 24, No. 9 (September 1977), p. 57.
- "Bristles and Barbs," *Coins*, Vol. 24, No. 10 (October 1977), p. 57.
- "Bristles and Barbs," *Coins*, Vol. 24, No. 11 (November 1977), p. 58.
- "Bristles and Barbs," *Coins*, Vol. 24, No. 12 (December 1977), p. 50.
- "Bristles and Barbs," *Coins*, Vol. 25, No. 1 (January 1978), p. 43.
- "Bristles and Barbs," *Coins*, Vol. 25, No. 2 (February 1978), p. 50.
- "Bristles and Barbs," *Coins*, Vol. 25, No. 3 (March 1978), p. 44.
- "Bristles and Barbs," *Coins*, Vol. 25, No. 4 (April 1978), p. 60.
- "Bristles and Barbs," *Coins*, Vol. 25, No. 5 (May 1978), p. 58.
- "Bristles and Barbs," *Coins*, Vol. 25, No. 6 (June 1978), p. 58.
- "Bristles and Barbs," *Coins*, Vol. 25, No. 7 (July 1978), p. 57.
- "Bristles and Barbs," *Coins*, Vol. 25, No. 8 (August 1978), p. 45.
- "Bristles and Barbs," *Coins*, Vol. 25, No. 9 (September 1978), p. 52.
- "Bristles and Barbs," *Coins*, Vol. 25, No. 10 (October 1978), p. 52.
- "Bristles and Barbs," *Coins*, Vol. 25, No. 12 (December 1978), p. 60.
- "Bristles and Barbs," *Coins*, Vol. 26, No. 1 (January 1979), p. 61.
- "Bristles and Barbs," *Coins*, Vol. 26, No. 2 (February 1979), p. 52.
- "Bristles and Barbs," *Coins*, Vol. 26, No. 4 (April 1979), p. 91.
- "Bristles and Barbs," *Coins*, Vol. 26, No. 5 (May 1979), p. 80.
- "Bristles and Barbs," *Coins*, Vol. 26, No. 6 (June 1979), p. 78.
- "Bristles and Barbs," *Coins*, Vol. 26, No. 7 (July 1979), p. 84.
- "Bristles and Barbs," *Coins*, Vol. 26, No. 8 (August 1979).
- "Bristles and Barbs," *Coins*, Vol. 26, No. 10 (October 1979), p. 53.
- "Bristles and Barbs," *Coins*, Vol. 26, No. 11 (November 1979), p. 72.
- "Bristles and Barbs," *Coins*, Vol. 26, No. 12 (December 1979), p. 58.
- "Bristles and Barbs," *Coins*, Vol. 27, No. 1 (January 1980), p. 81.
- "Bristles and Barbs," *Coins*, Vol. 27, No. 2 (February 1980), p. 86.
- "Bristles and Barbs," *Coins*, Vol. 27, No. 3 (March 1980), p. 66.
- "Bristles and Barbs," *Coins*, Vol. 27, No. 4 (April 1980), p. 79.
- "Bristles and Barbs," *Coins*, Vol. 27, No. 5 (May 1980), p. 78.
- "Bristles and Barbs," *Coins*, Vol. 27, No. 6 (June 1980), p. 58.
- "Bristles and Barbs," *Coins*, Vol. 27, No. 8 (August 1980), p. 80.
- "Bristles and Barbs," *Coins*, Vol. 27, No. 9 (September 1980), p. 79.
- "Bristles and Barbs," *Coins*, Vol. 27, No. 10 (October 1980), p. 43.
- "Bristles and Barbs," *Coins*, Vol. 28, No. 2 (February 1981), p. 68.
- "Bristles and Barbs: Trends for the '80s," *Coins*, Vol. 28, No. 3 (March 1981), p. 53.

- "Bristles and Barbs: Deja Vu Susie," *Coins*, Vol. 28, No. 4 (April 1981), p. 60.
- "Bristles and Barbs: Expecting the Apocalypse," *Coins*, Vol. 28, No. 5 (May 1981), p. 60.
- "Bristles and Barbs: Gold Standard's Cost," *Coins*, Vol. 28, No. 6 (June 1981), p. 60.
- "Bristles and Barbs: Where Confusion Reigns," *Coins*, Vol. 28, No. 7 (July 1981), p. 59.
- "Bristles and Barbs: Commemorative Questions," *Coins*, Vol. 28, No. 9 (September 1981), p. 42.
- "Bristles and Barbs: Dubious Awards," *Coins*, Vol. 28, No. 10 (October 1981), p. 42.
- "Bristles and Barbs: Mixed Bag Reopened," *Coins*, Vol. 28, No. 11 (November 1981), p. 87.
- "Bristles and Barbs: Zinc Cent Folly," *Coins*, Vol. 28, No. 12 (December 1981), p. 78.
- "Bristles and Barbs: End Harassment," *Coins*, Vol. 29, No. 1 (January 1982), p. 86.
- "Bristles and Barbs: Questions Coinage," *Coins*, Vol. 29, No. 2 (February 1982), p. 43.
- "Bristles and Barbs: Call of Cassandra," *Coins*, Vol. 29, No. 3 (March 1982), p. 52.
- "Bristles and Barbs: Survival Goals," *Coins*, Vol. 29, No. 4 (April 1982), p. 50.
- "Bristles and Barbs: Knocking ANACS," *Coins*, Vol. 29, No. 5 (May 1982), p. 78.
- "Bristles and Barbs: Mixed Bag," *Coins*, Vol. 29, No. 6 (June 1982), p. 78.
- "Bristles and Barbs: Bagging Turkeys," *Coins*, Vol. 29, No. 7 (July 1982), p. 81.
- "Bristles and Barbs: Try Eye Test," *Coins*, Vol. 29, No. 8 (August 1982), p. 50.
- "Bristles and Barbs: Review Exhibit Rules," *Coins*, Vol. 29, No. 9 (September 1982), p. 64.
- "Bristles and Barbs: Great Gold Grab," *Coins*, Vol. 29, No. 10 (October 1982), p. 78.
- "Bristles and Barbs: Bronx Cheer," *Coins*, Vol. 29, No. 11 (November 1982), p. 86.
- "Bristles and Barbs: Plutocrats' Gold," *Coins*, Vol. 29, No. 12 (December 1982), p. 79.
- "Bristles and Barbs: Stop It Now," *Coins*, Vol. 30, No. 1 (January 1983), p. 52.
- "Bristles and Barbs: Chocking Hobby," *Coins*, Vol. 30, No. 2 (February 1983), p. 87.
- "Bristles and Barbs: In the Bag," *Coins*, Vol. 30, No. 3 (March 1983), p. 69.
- "Bristles and Barbs: Radical Book," *Coins*, Vol. 30, No. 4 (April 1983), p. 78.
- "Bristles and Barbs: Supports Gold, but...," *Coins*, Vol. 30, No. 5 (May 1983), p. 91.
- "Bristles and Barbs: Hobby Truths," *Coins*, Vol. 30, No. 6 (June 1983), p. 43.
- "Bristles and Barbs: Need New Method," *Coins*, Vol. 30, No. 7 (July 1983), p. 61.
- "Bristles and Barbs: H.R. 1783: 'Anti-Hobby Act,'" *Coins*, Vol. 30, No. 9 (September 1983), p. 88.
- "Bristles and Barbs: Coin Photography," *Coins*, Vol. 30, No. 11 (November 1983), p. 80.
- "Bristles and Barbs: The Story behind the C-Note's Demise," *Coins*, Vol. 30, No. 12 (December 1983), p. 85.
- "Bristles and Barbs: Krugerrand Ban and Olympic Coins," *Coins*, Vol. 31, No. 3 (March 1984), p. 73.
- "Bristles and Barbs: The Stuff of Auction Catalogues," *Coins*, Vol. 32, No. 2 (February 1985), p. 37.
- "Bristles and Barbs: How to Get Rich—Maybe," *Coins*, Vol. 32, No. 3 (March 1985), p. 43.
- Breen's remarks at Scott Travers's Coin Collector's Survival Conference. The last "Bristles and Barbs."
- *California Pioneer Fractional Gold: Historic Gold Rush Small Change 1852–1856 and Suppressed Jewelers' Issues 1859–1882*, by Walter Breen with the collaboration of Ronald J. Gillio (Santa Barbara: Pacific Coast Auction Galleries, 1983). Issued in a limited edition hardcover bound in half morocco and regular edition paperback, 160 pages. Revised edition: *California Pioneer Fractional Gold: Historic Gold Rush Small Change 1852–1857 and Suppressed Jewelers' Issues*

1858–1882, by Walter Breen and Ronald J. Gillio; revision by Robert D. Leonard, Jr., Jay Roe, Jack Totheroh, Ronald J. Gillio, Robert B. Lecce and Richard A. Lecce (Wolfeboro, New Hampshire: Bowers and Merena Galleries, 2003). Released in both hardcover and paperback, 263, (1) pages.

- *The Care and Preservation of Rare Coins* (Albertson, New York: First Coinvestors [FCI Press], 1977). 7.5 inch plastic audio record in 4 page card stock booklet.
- "Cent Collectors' Forum," *The Numismatist*, Vol. 70, No. 1 (January 1957), pp. 25–26.
- "Cent Collectors' Forum," *The Numismatist*, Vol. 70, No. 2 (February 1957), p. 136.
- "Cent Collectors' Forum," *The Numismatist*, Vol. 70, No. 3 (March 1957), p. 280.
- "Cent Collector's Forum," *The Numismatist*, Vol. 70, No. 4 (April 1957), p. 419.
- "Cent Collector's Forum," *The Numismatist*, Vol. 70, No. 5 (May 1957), p. 514.
- "Cent Collectors' Forum," *The Numismatist*, Vol. 70, No. 6 (June 1957), pp. 658–660.
- "Cent Collectors' Forum," *The Numismatist*, Vol. 70, No. 7 (July 1957), p. 807.
- "Cent Collectors' Forum," *The Numismatist*, Vol. 70, No. 8 (August 1957), p. 922.
- "Cent Collectors' Forum," *The Numismatist*, Vol. 70, No. 11 (November 1957), p. 1322.
- "Cent Collectors' Forum," *The Numismatist*, Vol. 71, No. 2 (February 1958), p. 170.
- "Cent Collectors' Forum," *The Numismatist*, Vol. 71, No. 3 (March 1958), p. 293.
- "*Le Chameau* Treasure," historical commentaries, Parke-Bernet Galleries A auction catalogue of December 10–11, 1971.
- "Chasing Rainbows," *Paper Money*, Vol. 16, No. 2 (March–April 1977; Serial 68), pp. 69ff.
- "'Coin' Notes Nearly Bankrupted Treasury," *Numismatic News*, Vol. 25, No. 12 (March 19, 1977),
- "Coinage for Colonial Virginia," book review, *The Numismatist*, Vol. 70, No. 2 (February 1957), pp. 170–171.
- "Coinage of the New Orleans Mint in 1861," *The Numismatist*, Vol. 64, No. 4 (April 1951), pp. 387–394.
- "The Coinage Patterns and Proposals of 1791–1792 Featuring Washington's Portrait and Other Federal Types," *Numismatic News Weekly*, October 23, 1973; continued through December 3, 1973 [?]. Reprinted in adapted form in the Stack's catalogue of Part II of the John J. Ford, Jr. collection (May 11, 2004).
- "A Coiner's Caviar": *Walter Breen's Encyclopedia of U.S. and Colonial Proof Coins, 1722–1977* (Albertson, New York: FCI Press, 1977). Hardcover with dust-jacket, (8), 324 pages. Revised second edition published as *Walter Breen's Encyclopedia of United States and Colonial Proof Coins, 1722–1989: With Additions and Corrections to the 1977 Volume* (Wolfeboro, New Hampshire: Bowers and Merena Galleries, 1989). Paperback, (8), 338, (2) pages.
- "Coins, Currency and Economic History," Chapter 8 of the *American Numismatic Association's Intermediate Numismatic Correspondence Course*, Colorado Springs: 1978, 24 pages.
- "A Collection of Observations on TN-31, 'A Biennial Pairing Puzzle,'" letter to the editor, *The Colonial Newsletter*, Vol. 11, No. 3 (September 1972; Serial 35), pp. 372–373.
- "The Collector's Necessary Equipment," *The Numismatic Scrapbook Magazine*, Vol. 29, No. 3 (March 1963), pp. 653–659.
- *Colonial American Coin Club. A Service of First Coinvestors, Inc.* N.p.: First Coinvestors, n.d. [c. 1973]. Loose sheets in three ring binders.
- "Colonial Overstrikes," *The Colonial Newsletter*, Vol. 5, No. 2 (December 1963; Serial 10), p. 72.
- "Comment on First Paper Money Issued in Ohio," *The Colonial Newsletter*, Vol. 16, No. 3 (November 1977; Serial 50), G-4A, p. 609.

- "Comment on St. Patrick Halfpence and Farthings," *The Colonial Newsletter*, Vol. 7, No. 2 (April 1968; Serial 22), pp. 214–217.
- "Comments from the Members," *Penny-Wise*, Vol. 2, No. 6 (November 15, 1968; Serial 9), p. 221.
- "Comments from Walter Breen," *Penny-Wise*, Vol. 4, No. 4 (July 15, 1970; Serial 19), pp. 132–134.
- *A Complete Course in Numismatics* (Beverly Hills: American Institute of Professional Numismatics, n.d. [c. 1970]), 21.5 by 28 cm, (1), 70 pages. Blue heavy paper cover, staple bound.
- "Complete Description of the Recently Discovered, New, 1795 Large Cent," *Penny-Wise*, Vol. 3, No. 4 (July 15, 1969; Serial 13), p. 126.
- *The Comprehensive Catalogue and Encyclopedia of United States Coins.* 1971 edition. Edited by Don Taxay. Omaha: Scott Publishing Company, 1970.
- *The Comprehensive U.S. Silver Dollar Encyclopedia*, by John W. Highfill (Broken Arrow, Oklahoma: Highfill Press, 1992), xlv, 1233 pages.
- "Confederacy Operated the Charlotte Mint in 1861," *The Numismatist*, Vol. 64, No. 6 (June 1951), pp. 606–607.
- "Connecticut Shilling," RF-17, *The Colonial Newsletter*, Vol. 6, No. 2 (December 1965; Serial 16), p. 162.
- "Constellatio Nova," *The Colonial Newsletter*, Vol. 13, No. 3 (September 1974; Serial 41), TN-46, pp. 453–455.
- "Davy on Mint Processes in 1794," *The Numismatist*, Vol. 64, No. 8 (August 1951), pp. 870–872.
- "A Descriptive Essay of the Liberty Seated Half Dimes with Arrows of 1853–55," *Gobrecht Journal*, Vol. 1, No. 2 (April 1975), pp. 9–11.
- *Dies and Coinage* (New York: Robert Bashlow/QWERTYUIOPress, 1962). Self covered, 40 pages. Reprinted as part of Hewitt's Numismatic Information Series (Chicago, 1965).
- "Draped Bust 1795 Dollars," letter to the editor, *The Numismatic Scrapbook Magazine*, Vol. 30, No. 1 (January 1964), p. 34.
- "Early American Tokens from Birmingham: Who, Where, Why?," *Italiam fato profugi Hesperinaque venerunt litora: numismatic studies dedicated to Vladimir and Elvira Eliza Clain-Stefanelli*, edited by R.G. Doty and T. Hackens (Louvain-La-Neuve: Dép. d'archéologie et d'histoire de l'art, 1996), pp. 69–79.
- *The Early Quarter Dollars of the United States, 1796–1838*, by A.W. Browning. Completely updated by Walter Breen with the collaboration of Robert W. Miller, Sr. New commentary by MR. DOLAN: David Bowers. With notes on rarity, attribution, new varieties, pedigrees of finest known specimens, etc. Edited and compiled by Michael Hodder (Wolfeboro, New Hampshire: Bowers and Merena Galleries, 1992). 183 pages. Reprinted in 1998 by Sanford Durst.
- *Early United States Half Eagles, 1795–1838*, Hewitt's Numismatic Information Series (Chicago: Hewitt, n.d. [c. 1966–1967]). Card covers, 72 pages.
- *The Empire Guide to United States Half Cents, 1793–1857*, by MR. DOLAN: David Bowers and James F. Ruddy (Johnson City, New York: Creative Printing, 1962). Card covered, (2), 47, (3) pages. Reprinted as United States Half Cents, 1793–1857, by MR. DOLAN: David Bowers and James F. Ruddy and United States Half Cents by Ebenezer Gilbert to Which are Added Several Supplemental Chapters (New York: Sanford J. Durst, 1984).
- *The Encyclopedia of United States Silver and Gold Commemorative Coins, 1892–1954*, by Walter Breen and Anthony Swiatek (New York: FCI Press/Arco Publishing, 1981). Hardcover, xxii, 362 pages. Revised edition published as *The Encyclopedia of United States Silver and Gold Commemorative Coins, 1892–1989*, by Walter Breen and Anthony Swiatek (Wolfeboro, NH: Bowers and Merena Galleries, 1990). Paperback only, xxii, 386 pages.

- "The Evolution of American Numismatics," *Numismatic News*, Vol. 14, No. 11 (May 23, 1966), pp. 12–13.
- *The Fantastic 1804 Dollar*, by Eric P. Newman and Kenneth E. Bressett; associates in research: Walter H. Breen and Lynn Glaser (Racine, Wisconsin: Whitman Publishing, 1962).
- "Federal Shinplasters," *Numismatic News Weekly*, serial beginning July 18, 1972.
- "A Few Unpublished Major Varieties of U.S. Coins," *The Numismatist*, Vol. 66, No. 6 (June 1953), pp. 569–572.
- "Fifty-fourth New Netherlands Auction," *The Numismatist*, Vol. 73, No. 6 (June 1960), pp. 740–742.
- *First Coinvestors Presents the Walter Breen U.S. Rare Coin Portfolio.* N.p.: First Coinvestors, n.d. [1973]. Two volumes in three ring binders.
- "First Crowned Rose Pattern for the Rosa Americana Coinages," *The Colonial Newsletter*, Vol. 8, No. 3 (September 1969; Serial 27), TN-15, p. 267.
- "The First Perfectionist," *Penny-Wise*, Vol. 6, No. 4 (July 15, 1972; Serial 31), pp. 127–134.
- "Fiscal Year of the U.S. Mint," letter to the editor, *The Numismatist*, Vol. 67, No. 10 (October 1954), p. 1097.
- "Fish Scales to Forgotten Sleepers," *Coins*, Vol. 19, No. 8 (August 1972), pp. 55–61.
- "From Junk to Gems: Half Cents Then and Now," Rare Coin and Stamp Advisory, December 1979; reprinted in *Penny-Wise*, Vol. 14, No. 2 (March 15, 1980; Serial 77), pp. 81–84.
- "From Walter Breen," *The Colonial Newsletter*, Vol. 8, No. 2 (July 1969; Serial 26), pp. 255–256.
- *A Guide Book of United States Coins*, by R.S. Yeoman (Racine, Wisconsin: Whitman, various dates).
- "Half Cent Miscellany," *The Numismatic Scrapbook Magazine*, Vol. 19, No. 12 (December 1953), pp. 1170–1171.
- "Hancock's Revenge," *Numismatic News Weekly*, 1971, serial.
- "Head of Copper, Feet of Clay: Dr. Sheldon after 35 Years," *Penny-Wise*, Vol. 18, No. 6 (November 15, 1984; Serial 105), pp. 337–342.
- "The High Cost of Money," *The Whitman Numismatic Journal*, Vol. 3, No. 12 (December 1966), pp. 866–874; continued in Vol. 4, No. 1 (January 1967), pp. 50–58.
- *Highlights from the Kenneth Lee Collection*, by Walter Breen and Ron Gillio. 240 35 mm slides showing coins from the Lee collection of California gold, accompanied by a six-page text by Breen. 1983.
- *A Historic Sketch of the Coins of New Jersey*, by Edward Maris. Reprint (Lawrence, Massachusetts: Quarterman, 1974), vii, 21 pages, double page plate.
- "The Historic Wreath Cent," *Coins Magazine*, Vol. 14, No. 11 (November 1967), pp. 24–26.
- *The History and Future of American Numismatics* (Chicago, August 1991), produced by the American Numismatic Association. Moderated by Ken Hallenbeck, featuring Ken Bressett, MR. DOLAN: David Bowers, Elvira Clain-Stefanelli, Eric Newman and Walter Breen. Video tape, 120 minutes.
- "History of the Fractional Currency Specimen Sets," *The Numismatic Scrapbook Magazine*, Vol. 30, No. 1 (January 1964), pp. 22–29; continued in Vol. 30, No. 2 (February 1964), pp. 298–305.
- "The History of the Silver Dollar," by John W. Highfill and Walter H. Breen, *The Comprehensive U.S. Silver Dollar Encyclopedia*, by John W. Highfill (Broken Arrow, Oklahoma: Highfill Press, 1992), pp. 2–5.
- "How Coins Are Made," Beverley Hills: American Institute of Professional Numismatists, c. 1970. 14 by 21.5 cm.

- "How Our Coinage Became Mechanized," *The Numismatist*, Vol. 64, No. 3 (March 1951), pp. 284–287.

- "How to Stay Ahead of the Coin Forgers," *The Numismatic Scrapbook Magazine*, Vol. 29, No. 5 (May 1963), pp. 1329–1333; continued in Vol. 29, No. 6 (June 1963), pp. 1648–1655.

- "The Hundred Year Vendetta," *The Numismatic Scrapbook Magazine*, Vol. 28, No. 8 (August 1962), pp. 2177–2189.

- "I Remember Dr. Sheldon," *Penny-Wise*, Vol. 11, No. 6 (November 15, 1977; Serial 63), pp. 276–277.

- *The Indian Cent Numisma: 1856–1909*, edited by Bruce A. Vogel (Longmont, Colorado: 1998), 277 pages.

- "Just Walter," *John Reich Journal*, Vol. 2, No. 1 (January 1987), pp. 8, 34.

- Silver coinage of the United States is discussed. Title not Breen's .

- "A Key to 1837 Large Cents," *Penny-Wise*, Vol. 4, No. 6 (November 15, 1970; Serial 21), pp. 218–220.

- "Large Cents of the U.S. 1816–1857; New Varieties and Additions," book review, *The Numismatist*, Vol. 67, No. 11 (November 1954), pp. 1199–1200.

- "The Legacy of 'Silver Dick,'" *Numismatic News*, Vol. 23, No. 16 (April 19, 1975), pp. 6ff; continued in Vol. 23, No. 21 (May 24, 1975), pp. 22ff; Vol. 23, No. 26 (June 28, 1975), pp. 37–38; Vol. 23, No. 30 (July 26, 1975), pp. 14ff; Vol. 23, No. 34 (August 23, 1975), pp. 14ff; Vol. 23, No. 36 (September 6, 1975), pp. 18ff; Vol. 23, No. 42 (October 18, 1975), pp. 16ff; Vol. 23, No. 45 (November 8, 1975), pp. 18ff; Vol. 23, No. 48 (November 29, 1975), pp. 20ff; Vol. 23, No. 49 (December 6, 1975), pp. 14ff; Vol. 23, No. 51 (December 20, 1975), pp. 24ff; Vol. 23, No. 52 (December 27, 1975), pp. 14ff; Vol. 24, No. 1 (January 3, 1976), p. 12.

- "Legal and Illegal Connecticut Mints, 1785–1789," *Studies on Money in Early America*, edited by Eric P. Newman (New York: ANS, 1976), pp. 105–133.

- "Let's Visit an Auction," *The Whitman Numismatic Journal*, Vol. 5, No. 6 (June 1968), pp. 327–330.

- "A Letter from Walter Breen," *Penny-Wise*, Vol. 6, No. 3 (May 15, 1972; Serial 30), p. 88.

- "A Letter from Walter Breen," *Penny-Wise*, Vol. 8, No. 2 (March 15, 1974; Serial 41), pp. 91–92.

- "Letter from Walter Breen," *Penny-Wise*, Vol. 20, No. 1 (January 15, 1986; Serial 112), p. 11.

- "A Letter from Walter Breen—Finally," *Penny-Wise*, Vol. 9, No. 4 (July 15, 1975; Serial 49), pp. 173–175.

- "Letter to and from Walter Breen," *Penny-Wise*, Vol. 10, No. 6 (November 15, 1976; Serial 57), pp. 270–271.

- Letter to the Editor, *The Asylum*, Vol. 1, No. 4 (Summer 1981), pp. 57–58.

- Letter to the Editor, *The Colonial Newsletter*, Vol. 2, No. 1 (January 1961; Serial 2), p. 7.

- Letter to the Editor, *The Colonial Newsletter*, Vol. 2, No. 1 (January 1961; Serial 2), p. 7.

- Letter to the Editor, *The Colonial Newsletter*, Vol. 2, No. 3 (July 1961; Serial 4), p. 17.

- Letter to the Editor, *The Colonial Newsletter*, Vol. 5, No. 6 (March 1965; Serial 14), p. 131.

- Letter to the Editor, *The Colonial Newsletter*, Vol. 6, No. 5 (April-June 1967; Serial 19), pp. 187–188.

- Letter to the Editor, *The Colonial Newsletter*, Vol. 10, No. 3 (September 1971; Serial 32), TN-20A, p. 333.

- Letter to the Editor, *The Numismatic Scrapbook Magazine*, Vol. 24, No. 4 (April 20, 1958), p. 902.

- Letter to the Editor, *Penny-Wise*, Vol. 23, No. 1 (January 15, 1989; Serial 130), pp. 48–52.

- Letter to the Editor, *Penny-Wise*, Vol. 23, No. 1 (January 15, 1989; Serial 130), pp. 48–52.
- Letter to the Editor, by Charles Davis, *Penny-Wise*, Vol. 27, No. 4 (July 15, 1993; Serial 157), p. 297.
- "Letters from Members," *Penny-Wise*, Vol. 4, No. 3 (May 15, 1970; Serial 18), p. 125.
- "Letters from Walter Breen," *Penny-Wise*, Vol. 2, No. 3 (May 15, 1968; Serial 6), pp. 84–86.
- *The Lincoln Cent Numisma: 1909–1997*, edited by Bruce A. Vogel (Longmont, Colorado: 1998), 285 pages.
- "Location of Unique 1786 Connecticut 5.3-B.2," *The Colonial Newsletter*, Vol. 8, No. 4 (December 1969; Serial 28), Comments on RF-26, p. 283.
- "Major Varieties of the United States Three Dollar Gold Pieces," *The Numismatic Scrapbook Magazine*, Vol. 30, No. 12 (December 1964), pp. 3285–3290; continued in Vol. 31, No. 1 (January 1965), pp. 266–268; Vol. 31, No. 2 (February 1965), pp. 596–600; Vol. 31, No. 3 (March, 1965), pp. 903–906.
- *Major Varieties of the United States Three Dollar Gold Pieces*, Hewitt's Numismatic Information Series (Chicago: Hewitt, n.d.).
- "Major Varieties of U.S. Gold Dollars," *The Numismatic Scrapbook Magazine*, Vol. 29, No. 10 (October 1963), pp. 2813–2819; continued in Vol. 29, No. 11 (November 1963), pp. 3134–3140; Vol. 29, No. 12 (December 1963), pp. 3446–3453.
- *Major Varieties of U.S. Gold Dollars*, Hewitt's Numismatic Information Series (Chicago: Hewitt, 1964).
- "Making Half Cents: How the Early American Coiners Prepared Planchets," *COINage*, Vol. 21, No. 2 (February 1985), pp. 8ff.
- *MANA News*. (Later *MANA Journal*.) Various issues, 1953–1959.
- "Massachusetts Silver—A Tentative Checklist," *The Metropolitan Numismatic Journal*, Issue 1 (May-June 1961), pp. 6–9.
- "Massachusetts Silver—A Tentative Checklist," *Numismatic Journal*, No. 2 (November 1961), pp. 22–26.
- "Medals Challenge to Artisans for Centuries," *Coin World*, No. 101 (March 23, 1962), p. 10.
- "Members Comment on ANACS Sale," letter to the editor, *The Numismatist*, Vol. 103, No. 9 (September 1990), pp. 1389–1390.
- "The Metal Called 'Tutanaigne,'" *The Colonial Newsletter*, Vol. 19, No. 2 (July 1980; Serial 58), TN-93, p. 732.
- "Metallic Composition of the Continental Currency," *The Colonial Newsletter*, Vol. 6, No. 1 (September 1965; Serial 15), TN-1, p. 146.
- "Metallic Panaceas: Gold Bugs, Silver Crusaders, and the Wizard of Oz," *America's Gold Coinage*, Coinage of the Americas Conference Proceedings No. 6 (1989), ed. William E. Metcalf (New York: ANS, 1990), pp. 33–54.
- *The Metropolitan Numismatic Journal*, edited by Walter Breen and Lynn Glaser, No. 1 (May-June 1961), 16 pages, self-covered.
- "Mintage Figures for the New Jersey Coinage from the Receipt Books of James Mott, Treasurer to the State of New Jersey," *The Colonial Newsletter*, Vol. 9, No. 1 (March 1970; Serial 29), pp. 295–297.
- *The Minting Process: How Coins Are Made and Mismade* (Beverly Hills: American Institute of Professional Numismatists, 1970). (2), 162, (4) pages, one leaf (two page) final exam bound in. Orange card covers, staple bound. 21.6 by 14 cm.
- "Miss Liberty's American Debut," by Walter Breen and Lynn Glaser, *Numismatic Journal*, No. 2 (November 1961), pp. 3–17.
- "The Money Censors," *COINage*, Vol. 8, No. 8 (August 1972), pp. 70–72.

- "More about Longacre's Indian Cent Model," *The Numismatic Scrapbook Magazine*, Vol. 17, No. 4 (April 1951), pp. 297–299.

- "More on Early Usage of the Horse Head Design," *The Colonial Newsletter*, Vol. 17, No. 1 (April 1978; Serial 51), TN-68A, p. 627.

- "More on H.N. Rust Research," *The Colonial Newsletter*, Vol. 15, No. 3 (October 1976; Serial 47), RF-21I, p. 569.

- "More on the Importation of 1749 Halfpence and Farthings," *The Colonial Newsletter*, Vol. 16, No. 1 (March 1977; Serial 48), TN-57A, p. 585.

- "Mr. Breen Answers Mr. Slife," *The Numismatic Scrapbook Magazine*, Vol. 27, No. 10 (October 1961), p. 2590.

- "My Friend Walter," by John D. Wright, *Penny-Wise*, Vol. 27, No. 3 (May 15, 1993; Serial 156), p. 251.

- "The Mysterious Miss Liberty," by Walter Breen and Michael Turoff, *Coins*, Vol. 18, No. 10 (October 1971), pp. 62–65.

- "New Discoveries in the Early Cents," *Penny-Wise*, Vol. 2, No. 5 (September 15, 1968; Serial 8), pp. 163–165.

- "New Jersey Center Dots," *The Colonial Newsletter*, Vol. 15, No. 3 (October 1976; Serial 47), TN-56A, p. 566.

- "New Looks at Old Notes," *Numismatic News*, Vol. 20, No. 38 (September 19, 1972), pp. 16, 29; continued in Vol. 20, No. 39 (September 26, 1972), pp. 12, 30.

- "New Looks at Old Notes," *Paper Money*, Vol. 15, No. 4 (July-August 1976; Serial 64), pp. 207ff.

- "New Specimen of 1797 NC-1 Discovered," by Rob Retz and Walter Breen, *Penny-Wise*, Vol. 24, No. 2 (March 15, 1990; Serial 137), pp. 62–63.

- "A New Sub-variety of 1794 Cent," *The Metropolitan Numismatic Journal*, Issue 1 (May-June 1961), pp. 10–12.

- *New Varieties of $1, $2.50 and $5.00 United States Gold*, Hewitt's Numismatic Information Series (Chicago: Hewitt, n.d.). Card covers, 16 pages.

- *New Varieties of U. S. Gold Coins in 1968.* (Not listed in Fannin's book)

- "A New Variety of 1795 Silver Dollar," *The Numismatist*, Vol. 66, No. 7 (July 1953), p. 706.

- "The New York Immunis: A Mystery Unraveled," *The Colonial Newsletter*, Vol. 18, No. 1 (April 1979; Serial 54), pp. 668–676.

- "'New-merical' Grades?," letter to the editor, *The Numismatist*, Vol. 99, No. 9 (September 1986), p. 1787.

- "North American Colonial Coinages under the French Regime (1640–1763)," *Studies on Money in Early America*, edited by Eric P. Newman (New York: ANS, 1976), pp. 43–74.

- "Notes on Early Quarter Dollars," *The Numismatic Scrapbook Magazine*, Vol. 20, No. 2 (February 1954), pp. 137–146.

- "Notes on the Confederate Restrike," *The Numismatist*, Vol. 63, No. 12 (December 1950), p. 846.

- "Notes on U.S. Quarter Eagles," *The Numismatic Scrapbook Magazine*, Vol. 30, No. 4 (April, 1964), pp. 901–906; continued in Vol. 30, No. 5 (May, 1964), pp. 1235–1240; Vol. 30, No. 6 (June, 1964), pp. 1571–1574; Vol. 30, No. 7 (July, 1964), pp. 2071–2074; Vol. 30, No. 8 (August, 1964), pp. 2120–2123; Vol. 30, No. 9 (September 1964), pp. 2625–2628; Vol. 30, No. 10 (October 1964), pp. 2666–2669. Later published in monograph form as Varieties of United States Quarter Eagles.

- "Notes That Almost Weren't ," *Paper Money*, Vol. 16, No. 1 (January-February 1977; Serial 67), pp. 5–14.

- "Numbered Seats and 4-Year Terms Questioned," letter to the editor, *The Numismatist*, Vol. 93, No. 3 (March 1980), pp. 595–596.
- *Numisma*, edited by John J. Ford, Jr. and Walter Breen. New Netherlands Coin Company, 1954–1960.
- *Numismatic Directory for 1957*, compiled by D. Wayne Johnson and Walter H. Breen (St. Louis, 1957), (2), 101, (1) pages.
- "Observations on RF-27, the Danske Americansk," *The Colonial Newsletter*, Vol. 10, No. 3 (September 1971; Serial 32), p. 330.
- "Old Time Collectors and Dealers," written in collaboration with Warren A. Lapp, *Penny-Wise*, Vol. 3, No. 4 (July 15, 1969; Serial 13), pp. 136–141.
- "On Crosby's 'Missing Letter,'" *The Colonial Newsletter*, Vol. 16, No. 1 (March 1977; Serial 48), TN-58A, p. 586.
- "On Freeman's Two Cent Series," *The Numismatist*, Vol. 67, No. 8 (August 1954), pp. 837–838.
- "On the Eckfeldt Process at the First U.S. Mint," *The Colonial Newsletter*, Vol. 15, No. 3 (October 1976; Serial 47), G-1B, p. 571.
- "An Open Letter to U.S. Treasurer Angela M. Buchanan," letter to the editor, *The Numismatist*, Vol. 95, No. 8 (August 1982), pp. 1943–1945.
- "An Original Breen Attribution Guide for Cents of 1822, 1827, 1828," by Ed Janis, *Penny-Wise*, Vol. 27, No. 4 (July 15, 1993; Serial 157), pp. 283–287.
- "Our $3 Coin: Born to Placate the Gold Interests," *Coins Magazine*, Vol. 15, No. 8 (August 1968), pp. 27–30.
- "Our Warlike Heraldic Designs," letter to the editor, *The Numismatist*, Vol. 64, No. 2 (February 1951), pp. 167.
- "An Outstanding Collection of Connecticut Coppers," *The Colonial Newsletter*, Vol. 13, No. 2 (June 1974; Serial 40), TN-45, p. 446.
- "Paper Coins," *COINage*, Vol. 8, No. 9 (September 1972), pp. 42ff.
- "Penny Quiz," *Penny-Wise*, Vol. 3, No. 6 (November 15, 1969; Serial 15), p. 178.
- *Penny Whimsy: A Revision of Early American Cents, 1793–1814: An Exercise in Descriptive Classification with Tables of Rarity and Value*, by William H. Sheldon with the collaboration of Dorothy I. Paschal and Walter Breen (New York: Harper & Brothers for the John J. Ford, Jr. Numisco Series, 1958), xii, 340 pages, 51 halftone plates. Hardcover with dust-jacket. Reprint: (New York: Harper & Row for Krause Publishing Company, 1965), "exactly as printed in 1958 except for corrections of proofreaders' errors," xii, 340 pages, 51 plates. Hardcover with dust-jacket. Reprint: (Lawrence, Massachusetts: Quarterman, 1976), best plates and corrected text (reissued 1981), xii, 340 pages, 51 plates. Hardcover with dust-jacket. Reprint: (New York, Durst, 1990), xv, 340 pages; 51 plates, text is exactly as 1958 with proofreader's corrections, worst plates, new introduction and appendices by Denis Loring. Hard cover, no dust jacket.
- "Pennymanship to the Editors," *Penny-Wise*, Vol. 11, No. 4 (July 15, 1977; Serial 61), p. 181.
- "Pennymanship to the Editors," *Penny-Wise*, Vol. 18, No. 6 (November 15, 1984; Serial 105), p. 380.
- "The Peter Principle Meets the Mint: Scot, Barber and the 'Arabic' Dates," *New England Journal of Numismatics*, Vol. 1, No. 1 (Summer 1986), pp. 3–9.
- "Philadelphia Story: 1791–1794," *Coin World*, No. 105 (April 20, 1962), pp. 82, 84; continued in No. 106 (April 27, 1962), p. 42; No. 107 (May 4, 1962), p. 76.
- "Philadelphia's Original Flying Disks: Early American Coppers—Blanks, Sources, Identifying Marks," *The American Numismatic Association Centennial Anthology*, edited by Carl W.A. Carlson and Michael Hodder (Wolfeboro, New Hampshire: Bowers and Merena Galleries, 1991), pp. 35–50.

- "Pick Nits, Get Lice," *The Repository*, Vol. III, Nos. 1–2 (January-March 1985), pp. 1–2.

- "Pointers Regarding the 1838 Large Cents," *Penny-Wise*, Vol. 2, No. 4 (July 15, 1968; Serial 7), p. 123.

- "Preface," *Early United States Dimes, 1796–1837*, David J. Davis, Russell J. Logan, Allen F. Lovejoy, John W. McCloskey and William L. Subjack (Ypsilanti, Michigan: John Reich Collectors Society, 1984), p. vii.

- "'Processed' Coins," *The Numismatic Scrapbook Magazine*, Vol. 28, No. 5 (May 1962), pp. 1293–1295.

- "Profile — Walter Breen," *Penny-Wise*, Vol. 2, No. 3 (May 15, 1968; Serial 6), p. 80.

- *Proof Coins Struck by the United States Mint*, 1817–1921, *Coin Collector's Journal*, Vol. 20, Nos. 2–3 (March-June 1953; Serial 148–149), 48 pages. Reprinted by Sanford J. Durst (New York, 1983), with new supplement by Durst, 57 pages.

- "Proof Large Cents," *Penny-Wise*, Vol. 9, No. 3 (May 15, 1975; Serial 48), pp. 138.

- "Proof Large Cents—Preliminary Notes," *Penny-Wise*, Vol. 3, No. 3 (May 15, 1969; Serial 12), pp. 83–90.

- "The Proofing Process," *The Whitman Numismatic Journal*, Vol. 2, No. 1 (January 1965), pp. 37–41; continued in Vol. 2, No. 2 (February 1965), pp. 123–127; Vol. 2, No. 3 (March 1965), pp. 175–181; Vol. 2, No. 4 (April 1965), pp. 229–233; Vol. 2, No. 5 (May 1965), pp. 345–349; Vol. 2, No. 6 (June 1965), pp. 399–402; Vol. 2, No. 7 (July 1965), pp. 489–493.

- "Proper Care of Your Coin Collection," audio cassette tape, approximately 13 minutes, 40 seconds. Part of *Home Study Course in Fundamentals of Rare Coin Collecting and Investing* (New York: Institute of Numismatic and Philatelic Studies, Adelphi University, 1981), a collection of 20 cassettes with various numismatists speaking on different topics. Also includes 104 page booklet (loose sheets) describing the various lessons in varying detail and including an exam and course evaluation.

- "A Quintet of Problems Concerning Number of Silver Certificates Issued," *Paper Money*, Vol. 13, No. 4 (July-August 1974; Serial 52), pp. 155ff.

- *The Rare Gold Management Investment Portfolio of _____ with Special Monographs by Walter Breen*. N.p.: First Coinvestors, n.d. [1973]. Three ring binder.

- "The Rarest American Colonial and United States Gold Coins," *The Numismatic Scrapbook Magazine*, Vol. 23, No. 6 (June 1957), pp. 1065–1071.

- "Rarity and Value: A New Scientific Approach," *The Numismatic Scrapbook Magazine*, Vol. 23, No. 2 (February 1957), pp. 209–215.

- "Recut Dates and Overdates," *The Numismatic Scrapbook Magazine*, Vol. 21, No. 2 (February 1955), pp. 161–168.

- "Regarding RF-43 (CNL, April 1973, p. 398) Why Were the Early American Halfpence Called Coppers Rather Than Halfpence, and What Is the Origin of the Term 'Coppers?,'" *The Colonial Newsletter*, Vol. 12, No. 3 (October 1973; Serial 38), RF-43A, p. 416.

- "Regarding RF-44 (CNL, April 1973, p. 398) 'Counterfeit" pieces of brass and tin," *The Colonial Newsletter*, Vol. 12, No. 3 (October 1973; Serial 38), RF-44A, p. 417.

- "Regarding RF-46 (CNL, April 1973, p. 399), 'The Questionable Coinage of Machin's Mills,'" *The Colonial Newsletter*, Vol. 12, No. 3 (October 1973; Serial 38), RF-46A, p. 421.

- "Replies to Chuck Funk's Letter," *Penny-Wise*, Vol. 9, No. 2 (March 15, 1975; Serial 47), pp. 62.

- "Reply on Washington Half Dollar, 1792," *The Numismatist*, Vol. 67, No. 9 (September 1954), p. 974.

- "Research in the Archives: Gold Coinage Revisions by Dates — Philadelphia," *Coin Collector's Journal*, Vol. 18, No. 6 (November-December 1951), pp. 123–124.

- "Research in the Archives: Report in the Proofs, Essais, Restrikes and Related Material," *Coin*

Collector's Journal, Vol. 18, No. 2 (March-April 1951), pp. 30–34.

- "Research in the Archives: Revised Copper Coinage Figures, 1793–1857," *Coin Collector's Journal*, Vol. 18, No. 3 (May-June 1951), pp. 51–56.

- "Research in the Archives. Silver Coinage Figures Revised," *Coin Collector's Journal*, Vol. 18, No. 5 (September-October 1951), pp. 104–116.

- "Research in the Archives: Silver Coinage Figures Revised, Philadelphia Mint," *Coin Collector's Journal*, Vol. 18, No. 4 (July-August 1951), pp. 81–89.

- "Response to Comments," *Penny-Wise*, Vol. 19, No. 1 (January 15, 1985; Serial 106), pp. 12–15.

- "A Review of Half Cent Literature," *The Asylum*, Vol. 1, Nos. 2–3, (Fall-Winter 1980), pp. 33–38.

- "Robert Scot's Earliest Device Punches," Coinage of the Americas Conference Proceedings No. 1 (1984), *America's Copper Coinage 1783–1857* (New York: ANS, 1985), pp. 9–29.

- The Secret History of the Gobrecht Coinages, 1836–1840, *Coin Collector's Journal*, Vol. 21, Nos. 5–6 (September-December 1954; Serial 157–158), 28 pages.

- "Semiofficial Restrikes of the Philadelphia Mint," *The Numismatist*, Vol. 66, No. 10 (October 1953), pp. 1038–1039.

- "Several Questions Answered," *The Numismatist*, Vol. 70, No. 2 (February 1957), pp. 152–153.

- Silver Coinages of the Philadelphia Mint, 1794–1916, *Coin Collector's Journal*, No. 159 (1958), 28 pages.

- "A Silver Dollar's Story," *Gobrecht Journal*, Vol. 18, No. 54 (July 1992), p. 38.

- *Silver Dollars and Trade Dollars of the United States: A Complete Encyclopedia*, by MR. DOLAN: David Bowers (Wolfeboro, NH: Bowers and Merena Galleries, 1993).

- "Six Connecticut Mints?," *The Colonial Newsletter*, Vol. 13, No. 3 (September 1974; Serial 41), TN-48, p. 459.

- "Some Legendary Liberty Seated Rarities," *Gobrecht Journal*, Vol. 3, No. 7 (November 1976), pp. 3–5.

- "Some Neglected Colonials," *The Colonial Newsletter*, Vol. 6, No. 2 (December 1965; Serial 16), pp. 160–162.

- "Some Thoughts on the Quantities of Small Pine Tree Shillings," *The Colonial Newsletter*, Vol. 17, No. 1 (April 1978; Serial 51), TN-75, p. 624.

- "Some Unpublished Gobrecht Rarities," *The Numismatist*, Vol. 70, No. 5 (May 1957), pp. 531–532.

- "The S.S. Central America: Tragedy and Treasure," *The Numismatist*, Vol. 103, No. 7 (July 1990), pp. 1064–1072; 1126–1130; 1166–1167.

- *The Standard Catalogue of United States Coins from 1652 to the Present Day*, edited by Wayte Raymond (New York: Wayte Raymond, various dates).

- "The Stepney Hoard: Fact or Fantasy?," by Philip L. Mossman, with contributions from Eric P. Newman, John Kleeberg, Robert M. Martin, MR. DOLAN: David Bowers, Michael Hodder, Jeff Rock, Terry Lenz, Neil Rothschild and Thomas Kays, *The Colonial Newsletter*, Vol. 38, No. 2 (August 1998; Serial 108), pp. 1809–1851.

- "Stop the Presses! Bulletin!!!!," *Penny-Wise*, Vol. 11, No. 4 (July 15, 1977; Serial 61), p. 176.

- "The 'Strawberry' Leaf Cents of 1793," *Empire Topics*, No. 8 (November-December 1959); reprinted in *Penny-Wise*, Vol. 2, No. 6 (November 15, 1968; Serial 9), pp. 210–212; reprinted in *Penny-Wise*, Vol. 35, No. 3 (May 15, 2001; Serial 204), pp. 199–201.

- "A Suggested Classification of Mint Errors," *The Numismatic Scrapbook Magazine*, Vol. 23, No. 4 (April 1957), pp. 660–665.

- "Survey of American Coin Hoards," *The Numismatist*, Vol. 65, No. 1 (January 1952), pp. 7–24.
- "Survey of American Coin Hoards," *The Numismatist*, Vol. 65, No. 10 (October 1952), pp. 1005–1010.
- "Through Darkest Los Angeles with Glass and Notebook," *Rare Coin Advisory*, March 1973.
- "Tips for Convention Exhibitors," *The Numismatist*, Vol. 71, No. 5 (May 1958), pp. 526–527.
- "Trade Dollars of 1884 and 1885," *The Numismatist*, Vol. 65, No. 7 (July 1952), pp. 684–686.
- *Travers' Rare Coin Investment Strategy*, by Scott A. Travers. New York: Prentice Hall, 1986; second edition, 1990. 142 pages.
- "Trial Piece Designed for U.S. Cent 1792," *The Numismatist*, Vol. 64, No. 12 (December 1951), pp. 1310–1313.
- "The Twentieth Century U.S. Notes: Part IV," *Paper Money*, Vol. 16, No. 5 (September-October 1977; Serial 71), pp. 266ff.
- "A Unique Liberty Seated Dollar: 1851-O," *The Comprehensive U.S. Silver Dollar Encyclopedia*, by John W. Highfill (Broken Arrow, Oklahoma: Highfill Press, 1992), pp. 106–108.
- "United States Coins," *Encyclopædia Britannica* (Chicago, 1965); reprinted in the 1967 edition (Vol. 16, pp. 775–776)
- "United States Copper Cents 1816–1857," book review, *The Numismatist*, Vol. 70, No. 2 (February 1957), p. 169.
- "United States Eagles 1795–1933," *The Numismatic Scrapbook Magazine*, Vol. 33, No. 9 (September 1967), pp. 1723–1729; Vol. 33, No. 10 (October 1967), pp. 1760–1764; Vol. 33, No. 12 (December 1967), pp. 2247–2249; [and issues to] Vol. 34, No. 4 (April, 1968), pp. 673–677.
- *United States Eagles*, Hewitt's Numismatic Information Series (Chicago: Hewitt, n.d. [c. 1968]). Card covers, 59, (5) pages.
- "United States Half Cents: Addenda and Corrections to Gilbert," *The Numismatist*, Vol. 65, No. 5 (May 1952), pp. 461–462.
- United States Half Dimes: A Supplement, *Coin Collector's Journal*, No. 160 (1958), 16 pages. Reprinted in D.W. Valentine, The United States Half Dimes (Lawrence, Massachusetts: Quarterman, 1975).
- "United States Half Eagles 1795–1929," *The Numismatic Scrapbook Magazine*, Vol. 31, No. 4 (April 1965), pp. 978–981; continued in Vol. 31, No. 5 (May 1965), pp. 1277–1284; Vol. 31, No. 6 (June 1965), pp. 1852–1859; Vol. 31, No. 7 (July 1965), pp. 2157–2162; Vol. 31, No. 8 (August 1965), pp. 2413–2418; Vol. 31, No. 9 (September 1965), pp. 2680–2683; Vol. 31, No. 10 (October 1965), pp. 2964–2969; Vol. 31, No. 11 (November 1965), pp. 3257–3261; Vol. 31, No. 12 (December 1965), pp. 3515–3519; [and issues to] Vol. 33, No. 6 (June 1967), pp. 1201–1202. Reprinted in two parts in monograph form: Early United States Half Eagles, 1795–1838 and Varieties of United States Half Eagles, 1839–1929.
- The United States Minor Coinages, 1793–1916, *Coin Collector's Journal*, Vol. 21, No. 3 (May-June 1954; Serial 155), 16 pages.
- "Introduction," *The United States Nickel Five-Cent Piece: A History and Date-by-Date Analysis*, by Michael Wescott with Kendall Keck (Wolfeboro, New Hampshire: Bowers and Merena Galleries, 1991), p. 15.
- *United States Pattern, Experimental and Trial Pieces*, by J. Hewitt Judd, with the collaboration of Walter H. Breen and Abe Kosoff (Racine, Wisconsin: Whitman Publishing, 1959), 253 pages. Revised second edition (1962; 260 pages). Revised third edition (1965; 260 pages). Revised fourth edition (1970; 260 pages). Revised fifth edition (1974; 260 pages). Revised sixth edition (Racine, Wisconsin: Western Publishing, 1977; 276 pages). Revised seventh edition (Racine, Wisconsin: Western Publishing, 1982; 276 pages).

- The United States Patterns of 1792, *Coin Collector's Journal*, Vol. 21, No. 2 (March-April 1954; Serial 154), 16 pages.

- "The United States Peace Dollar: Its Roots in History," *The Whitman Numismatic Journal*, Vol. 1, No. 11 (November 1964), pp. 25–33; continued in Vol. 1, No. 12 (December 1964), pp. 41–48.

- "Unlisted Massachusetts Threepence," *The Numismatist*, Vol. 65, No. 1 (January 1952), p. 45.

- "U.S. Gold Coins: Some Unsolved Problems," *The Numismatic Scrapbook Magazine*, Vol. 30, No. 3 (March 1964), pp. 593–598.

- "Valentine's U. S. Half Dimes; A Supplement" for *Coin Collector's Journal* #160 in 1958. (Not in Fanning's account)

- *Varieties of United States Half Eagles, 1839–1929*, Hewitt's Numismatic Information Series (Chicago: Hewitt, n.d. [c. 1967]).

- *Varieties of United States Quarter Eagles*, Hewitt's Numismatic Information Series (Chicago: Hewitt, n.d.). Card covers, 32 pages.

- *Walter Breen Answers Your Numismatic Questions* (Seattle, 1990). Video tape, 1 hour, 22 minutes.

- *Walter Breen Answers Your Questions about Numismatics*, audio cassette (ANA, 1989), 1 audio cassette, 90 minutes.

- *Walter Breen Answers Your Questions about Numismatics*, video tape (Pittsburgh, 1989), 43 minutes.

- "Walter Breen Comments," *Penny-Wise*, Vol. 2, No. 4 (July 15, 1968; Serial 7), pp. 126–127.

- "Walter Breen Comments," *Penny-Wise*, Vol. 2, No. 5 (September 15, 1968; Serial 8), p. 172.

- "Walter Breen Comments," *Penny-Wise*, Vol. 3, No. 5 (September 15, 1969; Serial 14), pp. 155–156.

- "Walter Breen Comments on 'Penny-Wise' No. 11," *Penny-Wise*, Vol. 3, No. 3 (May 15, 1969; Serial 12), pp. 93–94.

- "Walter Breen Comments on the 1795 G-3, CMM #2a Half Cent," *Penny-Wise*, Vol. 8, No. 2 (March 15, 1974; Serial 41), p. 69.

- "Walter Breen Replies," *Penny-Wise*, Vol. 7, No. 6 (November 15, 1973; Serial 39), p. 260.

- "Walter Breen Replies," *Penny-Wise*, Vol. 24, No. 2 (March 15, 1990; Serial 137), p. 101.

- "Walter Breen Speaks," *Penny-Wise*, Vol. 3, No. 1 (January 15, 1969; Serial 10), pp. 11–12.

- "Walter Breen Speaks Out," *Penny-Wise*, Vol. 10, No. 5 (September 15, 1976; Serial 56), pp. 222–223.

- "Walter Breen to Dick Young," *Penny-Wise*, Vol. 29, No. 6 (November 15, 1995; Serial 171), p. 303.

- "Walter Breen Writes," *Penny-Wise*, Vol. 3, No. 2 (March 15, 1969; Serial 11), pp. 56–58.

- "Walter Breen Writes," *Penny-Wise*, Vol. 4, No. 2 (March 15, 1970; Serial 17), pp. 72–73.

- "Walter Breen Writes," *Penny-Wise*, Vol. 7, No. 1 (January 15, 1973; Serial 34), pp. 3–4.

- "Walter Breen Writes," *Penny-Wise*, Vol. 7, No. 3 (May 15, 1973; Serial 36), pp. 98–99.

- "Walter Breen Writes," *Penny-Wise*, Vol. 11, No. 2 (March 15, 1977; Serial 59), pp. 83–85.

- "Walter Breen Writes," *Penny-Wise*, Vol. 12, No. 1 (January 15, 1978; Serial 64), pp. 19–20.

- "Walter Breen Writes to David Hall," *Penny-Wise*, Vol. 25, No. 5 (September 15, 1991; Serial 146), p. 274.

- "Walter Breen Writes to Denis Loring," *Penny-Wise*, Vol. 26, No. 1 (January 15, 1992; Serial 148), p. 54.

- *Walter Breen's Complete Encyclopedia of U.S. and Colonial Coins* (New York: FCI/Doubleday, 1988). Hardcover with dust-jacket, xiv, 754 pages.

- *Walter Breen's Encyclopedia of Early United States Cents*, 1793–1814, written in collaboration with Del Bland; edited by Mark R. Borckardt (Wolfeboro, New Hampshire: Bowers and Merena Galleries, 2000). Hardcover, 857 pages, 34 plates

- *Walter Breen's Encyclopedia of United States and Colonial Proof Coins, 1722–1989*, see entry for "A Coiner's Caviar": *Walter Breen's Encyclopedia of U.S. and Colonial Proof Coins, 1722–1977*.

- *Walter Breen's Encyclopedia of United States Half Cents, 1793–1857* (South Gate, California: American Institute of Numismatic Research, 1983). Hardcover, x, 501, (2), [11 plates,] (4) pages.

- *Walter Breen's Encyclopedia of U.S. and Colonial Proof Coins, 1722–1977*, see "A Coiner's Caviar": *Walter Breen's Encyclopedia of U.S. and Colonial Proof Coins, 1722–1977*.

- *Walter Breen's Numisma: The United States Cent, 1793–1814*, edited by Bruce A. Vogel (Longmont, Colorado: 1998). Hardcover and paperback issued, 403 pages.

- *Walter Breen's Numisma: The United States Cent, 1816–1857*, edited by Bruce A. Vogel, (Longmont, Colorado: 1998). 365 pages.

- "Walter Mould and the Morristown Mint," *Penny-Wise*, Vol. 11, No. 4 (July 15, 1977; Serial 61), pp. 162–167.

- "Weights of Sommer Islands Coins," *The Colonial Newsletter*, Vol. 16, No. 3 (November 1977; Serial 50), TN-72, p. 612.

- "What Were the Coppers Brought over by the Quakers in 1682?," *The Colonial Newsletter*, Vol. 16, No. 3 (November 1977; Serial 50), G-3B, p. 610.

- "Who Are Portrayed on the Voce Populi Coppers?," *The Colonial Newsletter*, Vol. 16, No. 3 (November 1977; Serial 50), TN-71, p. 606.

Non-coin writings:

- *The Darkover Concordance: A Reader's Guide* Berkeley: Pennyfarthing Press, 1979.
- *The Gemini Problem: A Study in Darkover* (chapbook) Baltimore: T.K. Graphics, 1975
- *Lusty Limericks & Bawdy Ballads* (monograph self-published in 1956)

Walter Breen, writing as J.Z. Eglinton:

- *Greek Love*. New York: Oliver Layton Press, 1964; second printing 1965; British edition, London: Neville Spearmen, 1971; German edition, Grieschische Liebe, trans. Albert Y. Millrath. Hamburgh: Gala Verlag, 1967

- "Introducing a New Journal," *International Journal of Greek Love* 1:1 (January 1965), 3–4.

- "Shakespeare's Boyfriend and Sonnet XX," *International Journal of Greek Love* 1:1 (January 1965), 24–30

- "The Later Career of John Francis Bloxam," *International Journal of Greek Love* 1:2 (November 1966), 40–42

- "Responses to Letters to the Editor from Noel I. Garde," *International Journal of Greek Love* 1:2 (November 1966), 50–52.

- "Review of John Valentine's Puppies," *NAMBLA Journal* 2:3 (March 1980), 15

- "An Open Letter from J.Z. Eglinton," *NAMBLA Bulletin* 2:3 (April 1981), 4–5.

Appendix E: Mother's Bibliography

Awards:

- Sword of Aldones: Nominated for a Hugo in 1963
- The Forbidden Tower: Nominated for a Hugo in 1978
- The Heritage of Hastur Nominated for a Nebula Award in 1975
- World Fantasy Award for lifetime achievement (2000, awarded posthumously.)

Novels

In chronological order in categories by publication date. It should be noted her first written (The Forest House) was her last published. She wrote it when she was all of seventeen, in 1947, and it is, at heart, a retelling of Bellini's Norma: a story where an unfaithful husband drives his wife to thoughts of murdering their children. Instead, she decides to have him convicted for his crime of having unlawful relations with a high priestess, and then, in an act of heroic idiocy, joins him on the funeral pyre.

- Falcons of Narabedla (1957)
- The Door Through Space (1961)
- Seven from the Stars (1961) (1962?)
- The Colors Of Space (1963)
- Falcons of Narabedla (1964)
- Castle Terror (1965)
- Souvenir of Monique (1967)
- Bluebeard's Daughter (1968)
- The Brass Dragon (1970)
- In the Steps of the Master - The Sixth Sense #2 (1973) (based on television series The Sixth Sense, created by Anthony Lawrence)
- Hunters of the Red Moon (1973)
- The Jewel of Arwen (1974) (novelette)
- The Parting of Arwen (1974) (novelette)
- Can Ellen Be Saved? (1975) (adaptation of a teleplay by Emmett Roberts)
- The Endless Voyage (1975)
- Drums of Darkness (1976)
- The Ruins of Isis (1978) (1980?
- The Catch Trap (written in 1948: published in 1979)
- The Endless Universe (1979) (rewrite of The Endless Voyage)
- The House Between the Worlds (1980) (1981?)
- Survey Ship (1980)

- The Colors of Space (1983) (unabridged edition)
- Night's Daughter (1985) (A reworking of Mozart's The Magic Flute)
- Warrior Woman (1985)
- The Firebrand (1987)
- Black Trillium (1990) (with Julian May and Andre Norton)
- Lady of the Trillium (1995) (with Elisabeth Waters (initially uncredited))
- Tiger Burning Bright (1995) (with Mercedes Lackey and Andre Norton)
- The Gratitude of Kings (1997) (with Elisabeth Waters) (dedicated to my firstborn son RJ, Mother's first grandchild.)

Short story collections:

- The Dark Intruder and Other Stories (1964)
- The Best of Marion Zimmer Bradley (1985)
- Jamie and Other Stories (1988)
- Marion Zimmer Bradley's Darkover (1993)

Series:

Atlantean Series

- Web of Light (1983)
- Web of Darkness (1983)
- The Fall of Atlantis (1987) (omnibus edition of Web of Light and Web of Darkness)

Avalon Series

- The Mists of Avalon (1979)
- Mistress of Magic (audiobook edition of The Mists of Avalon, part 1) (1994)
- The High Queen (audiobook edition of The Mists of Avalon, part 2) (1994)
- The King Stag (audiobook edition of The Mists of Avalon, part 3) (1994)
- The Prisoner in the Oak (audiobook edition of The Mists of Avalon, part 4) (1994)
- The Forest House (1993) (with Diana L. Paxson) (also now known as The Forests of Avalon)
- Lady of Avalon (1997) (with Diana L. Paxson)
- Priestess of Avalon (2000) (with Diana L. Paxson)
- Ancestors of Avalon (2004) (written by Diana L. Paxson)
- Ravens of Avalon (2007) (written by Diana L. Paxson)
- Sword of Avalon (2009) (written by Diana L. Paxson)

Colin MacLaren Series:

- The Inheritor (1984)
- Dark Satanic (1988) (published already in 1972 by Berkley, NY)

- Witch Hill (1990) (published possibly already in 1972 by Greenleaf under the pseudonym ValerieGraves')
- Heartlight (1998)

Shadow's Gate Series (with Rosemary Edghill)

- Ghostlight (1995)
- Witchlight (1996)
- Gravelight (1997)
- Heartlight (1998)

Darkover Series:

- The Planet Savers (1958)
- The Sword of Aldones (1962)
- The Bloody Sun (1964)
- Star of Danger (1965)
- The Winds of Darkover (1970)
- The World Wreckers (1971)
- Darkover Landfall (1972)
- The Spell Sword (1974) (with Paul Edwin Zimmer, uncredited)
- The Heritage of Hastur (1975)
- The Shattered Chain (1976)
- The Forbidden Tower (1977)
- Stormqueen! (1978)
- Thunderlord! (sequel to Stormqueen!, not yet released)
- The Bloody Sun (1979) rewritten and expanded edition
- Two To Conquer (1980)
- Sharra's Exile (1981)
- Hawkmistress! (1982)
- Thendara House (1983—with Jacqueline Lichtenberg, uncredited)
- City of Sorcery (1984)
- The Heirs of Hammerfell (1989)
- Rediscovery (1993) (with Mercedes Lackey)
- Exile's Song (1996) (with Adrienne Martine-Barnes)
- The Shadow Matrix (1997) (with Adrienne Martine-Barnes)
- Traitor's Sun (1999) (with Adrienne Martine-Barnes)
- The Clingfire trilogy
- The Fall of Neskaya (2001) (with Deborah J. Ross)
- Zandru's Forge (2003) (with Deborah J. Ross)
- A Flame in Hali (2004) (with Deborah J. Ross)
- Modern Darkover (also known as The Children of Kings trilogy) (written principally by Deborah J. Ross)
- The Alton Gift (2007)

- Hastur Lord (2010) (written principally by Deborah J. Ross)
- The Children of Kings (2013) (written principally by Deborah J. Ross)

Omnibus editions

- The Children of Hastur (omnibus edition of The Heritage of Hastur and Sharra's Exile) (1982)
- The Oath of Renunciates (omnibus edition of The Shattered Chain and Thendara House) (1984)
- The Darkover Saga (a slipcase set containing Hawkmistress, Sharra's Exile; The Shattered Chain; Stormqueen!; Sword of Chaos) (1984)
- The Ages of Chaos (omnibus edition of Stormqueen! and Hawkmistress!) (2002)
- The Forbidden Circle (omnibus edition of The Spell Sword and The Forbidden Tower) (2002)
- Heritage And Exile (omnibus edition of The Heritage of Hastur and Sharra's Exile) (2002)
- The Saga of the Renunciates (omnibus edition of The Shattered Chain, Thendara House and City of Sorcery) (2002)
- A World Divided (omnibus edition of Star of Danger, Winds of Darkover and The Bloody Sun) (2003)
- First Contact (omnibus edition of Darkover Landfall and Two to Conquer) (2004)
- To Save a World (omnibus edition of The Planet Savers and World Wreckers) (2004)

Glenraven Series (with Holly Lisle)

- Glenraven (1996)
- In the Rift (1998)

Survivors Series (with Paul Edwin Zimmer)

- Hunters of the Red Moon (1973)
- The Survivors (1979)

Anthologies:

- The Best of Marion Zimmer Bradley's Fantasy Magazine (1994)
- The Best of Marion Zimmer Bradley's Fantasy Magazine—Vol. II (1995) (with Elisabeth Waters)
- Darkover anthologies (edited by Marion Zimmer Bradley, with some short stories by her, but mostly by other writers)
- The Keeper's Price (1980)
- Sword of Chaos (1982)
- Free Amazons of Darkover (1985)
- The Other Side of the Mirror (1987)
- Red Sun of Darkover (1987)
- Four Moons of Darkover (1988)
- Domains of Darkover (1990)

- Renunciates of Darkover (1991)
- Leroni of Darkover (1991)
- Towers of Darkover (1993)
- Snows of Darkover (1994)
- Greyhaven (1983) (with Paul Edwin Zimmer)
- Lythande (1986) (with Vonda N. McIntyre)

Marion Zimmer Bradley's Fantasy Magazine (1988–2000)

- Marion Zimmer Bradley's Fantasy Worlds (1998)
- Spells of Wonder (1989)
- Sword and Sorceress series (1984–2013) (edited by Marion Zimmer Bradley, after her death by Elisabeth Waters and Diana L. Paxson)

Novels under pen names:

Writing under the pseudonym Lee Chapman

- I am a Lesbian (1962)

Writing under the pseudonym John Dexter

- No Adam for Eve (1966)

Writing under the pseudonym Miriam Gardner

- My Sister, My Love (1963)
- Twilight Lovers (1964)
- The Strange Women (1967)

Writing under the pseudonym Morgan Ives

- Spare Her Heaven (1963)
- Anything Goes (1964)
- Knives of Desire (1966)

Other pseudonyms:

- Valerie Graves
- Elfrieda Rivers (also Alfrida Rivers and Elfrida Rivers)
- Astara Zimmer (also Astra Zimmer and Astra Zimmer Bradley)

Poems:

- The Maenads (1978)

Music:

- Songs from Rivendell (a.k.a. The Rivendell Suite) music and arrangements for several poems from the novels The Hobbit and The Lord of the Rings by
- J.R.R. Tolkien (1960) - included with other Tolkien songs on Broceliande's CD "The Starlit Jewel", available from Flowinglass Music. (Recorded earlier with many of the same musicians by the group Avalon Rising)

Editorial positions:

The Darkover Newsletter (1975 to 1993)

- Starstone a Darkover fanzine (5 issues 1978–1982)
- Marion Zimmer Bradley's Fantasy Magazine (50 issues 1988–2000)

Scholarly work:

- Bradley, Marion Zimmer. "Feminine equivalents of Greek Love in modern fiction" International Journal of Greek Love, Vol.1, No.1 (1965). Pages 48–58.
- Checklist: A complete, cumulative checklist of lesbian, variant, and homosexual fiction in English (1960) and addenda (1961, 1962, 1963).
- A Gay Bibliography (1975)
- The Necessity for Beauty: Robert W. Chambers & the Romantic Tradition (1974)

Other works:

- Contributions to The Ladder and The Mattachine Review.
- As Elfrieda or Elfrida Rivers, she contributed to the underground newspaper The East Village Other, the neo-Pagan periodical Green Egg and also Sybil Leek's Astrology Journal, where she wrote horoscopes and book reviews and had her own column as well as occasionally worked as editor with her husband Walter Breen.

Printed in the USA
CPSIA information can be obtained
at www.ICGtesting.com
LVHW091947051023
760300LV00023B/493